# Toward
# a Christian
# Theology of
# Religious
# Pluralism

# Toward
# a Christian
# Theology of
# Religious
# Pluralism

## JACQUES DUPUIS, S.J.

ORBIS BOOKS

**Maryknoll, New York 10545**

Sixth Printing, April 2005

**Library of Congress Cataloging-in-Publication Data**

Dupuis, Jacques, 1923–
    Toward a Christian theology of religious pluralism / Jacques Dupuis.
       p.    cm.
    Includes bibliographical references and index.
    ISBN 1-57075-264-8 (pbk.)
    1. Religious pluralism – Christianity.   2. Christianity and other religions.   3. Religious pluralism – Catholic Church.   4. Catholic Church – Relations.    I. Title.
BR127.D865   1999
261.2–dc21                        99–22418
                                         CIP

# Contents

# A Note on Orthography

The problem of rendering non-Western systems of writing into Roman letters for English and other modern European languages is notoriously difficult. With regrets, this book omits diacritical marks.

Scholars and others who know languages such as Sanskrit, Pali, Arabic, or Japanese do not need the diacritical marks to identify words in their original written form. And persons who do not know these languages gain little from having the marks reproduced. We recognize that languages employing different orthographic systems have a richness and distinctiveness that *are* partially conveyed by the orthographics of diacritical marks. And while we do not wish to be part of flattening out the contours of our linguistically plural globe, the high cost of ensuring accuracy in using the diacritical marks does not justify reproducing them here.

# Abbreviations of Key Documents, Reference Works, and Organizations

AAS     Acta Apostolicae Sedis

ACW     Ancient Christian Writers

AF     The Apostolic Fathers

AG     *Ad Gentes*

ANF     The Ante-Nicene Fathers

CBCI     Catholic Bishops' Conference of India

CCL     Corpus Christianorum, series latina

CSEL     Corpus Scriptorum Ecclesiasticorum Latinorum

DM     "Dialogue and Mission" (document published by the Secretariat for Non-Christians)

DP     "Dialogue and Proclamation" (document published by the Pontifical Council for Interreligious Dialogue and the Congregation for the Evangelization of Peoples)

DS     H. Denzinger and A. Schönmetzer, eds., *Enchiridion Symbolorum: Definitionum et Declarationum de Rebus Fidei et Morum*

DV     *Dei Verbum*

EN     *Evangelii Nuntiandi*

ES     *Ecclesiam Suam*

FABC     Federation of Asian Bishops' Conferences

GCS     Griechischen christlichen Schriftsteller

GS     *Gaudium et Spes*

LG     *Lumen Gentium*

NA     *Nostra Aetate*

ND     J. Neuner and J. Dupuis, eds., *The Christian Faith in the Doctrinal Documents of the Catholic Church*

OT     *Optatam Totius*

| PG | Patrologia Graeca |
| PL | Patrologia Latina |
| RH | *Redemptor Hominis* |
| RM | *Redemptoris Missio* |
| SC | Sources Chrétiennes |
| ST | *Summa Theologiae* (Thomas Aquinas) |
| UR | *Unitatis Redintegratio* |

# Introduction

IN THE INTRODUCTION to *Jesus Christ at the Encounter of World Religions* (Dupuis 1991b), we observed that the discussion of a Christian theology of the religious traditions of humanity, together with the debate on liberation theology, has gradually been taking center stage in recent theological endeavor. We added confidently that the same questions were assured of keeping their central position in the years to come. We attributed this dramatic entry into the scenario of theological debate to what has been called, correctly enough, the "irruption" of the third world and of the "third Church" (Bühlmann 1976, 1986; Fabella and Torres, eds., 1983). The pressing issues with which the "two-thirds world" churches are faced first and foremost have, in fact, gradually become concerns of prime importance on the theological agenda the world over. This situation is demonstrated by a double fact: on the one hand, versions of liberation theology have not only spread to the entire third world but also sprung up among various depressed sections of society in the first world; on the other hand, the encounter of cultures and religions, which is increasingly becoming a fact of life in the first world countries themselves, has turned the theological debate on other religions into a primary concern in the churches of the Western world as well.

The book to which I referred above was a monograph, with no claim to offer an overall treatment of the theological questions raised by the meeting of religions; much less did it intend to offer a historical survey of Christian attitudes and theological approaches to the other religious traditions through the centuries. Rather, it focused directly on the present debate about the theology of religions, to which it responded by developing what may be called a "theocentric Christocentrism." The aim was to open up a theological perspective which, while holding fast to faith in Jesus Christ as traditionally understood by mainstream Christianity and Church tradition, would at the same time integrate, in their difference, the religious experiences of the living religious traditions and assign to those traditions a positive role and significance in the overall plan of God for humankind, as it unfolds through salvation history. This appeared to be the narrow road which lay open for a theological discourse that would be simultaneously faithful to Christian identity and committed to conversation and dialogue with the "others."

To this debate we shall have to return in the present volume. However, the aim here is broader and the scope more comprehensive. What is intended, in effect, is to trace a path "toward a Christian theology of religious pluralism." While being aware of past liabilities and frankly exposing the negative attitudes toward other religious traditions which have marked nearly twenty centuries of Christian tradition, an account must be given of the dramatic change which has come upon us in recent years, and an organic presentation should be made of the present state of theological reflection on the main issues which are raised today in the context of religious pluralism. In sum, what is intended is an *introduction* to a theology of religions, at once historical and synthetic; genetic and up-to-date. The first task in introducing such a project is situating it in relation to similar attempts which have gone before it.

## A New General Introduction

Theology of religions is a recent theological subject. While discussing method below, we shall have to ask to what extent and in what sense it can be considered a distinct theological *subject*. Presently we need only observe its recent origin. Notwithstanding the theological writing on other religions which marked the period preceding Vatican II — still principally centered on the problematic of the possibility of salvation for the members of other religions and characterized by a guarded attitude toward the religions themselves (Daniélou 1957, 1958, 1962a, 1962b) — and limiting ourselves here to the Catholic tradition,[1] it may be said that the theology of religions came to be born around the time of Vatican II, that is, during the years which directly prepared for it and those that followed. A quick look at the literature produced around and during the 1960s shows that this was the time when the possibility of a positive role played by the other religions for the salvation of their members became an object of theological reflection in its own right. Witness the writing of H. U. von Balthasar, H. de Lubac, E. Cornelis, H. Fries, H. Maurier, H. Nys, K. Rahner, H. R. Schlette, G. Thils, R. C. Zaehner, among others. Yet the bulk of that writing consisted of monographs with a limited scope. They pointed to particular problems (Thils 1966), to Christian values contained in other religions (Cornelis 1965; Maurier 1965), to their salvific value or lack of the same (Lubac 1967c; Balthasar, 1963, 1964, 1968b, 1969), to their relationship to Christianity (Fries 1965a; Zaehner 1964), to salvation without the Gospel (Nys 1966). Few put forward a theological perspective upon which a theology of religions could be built, such as the comprehensive concept of "salvation history" elaborated by H. R. Schlette[2] or the "transcendental anthropology" project which K. Rahner developed into his theology of "anonymous Christianity."[3] Clearly, the time was not ripe for building a synthesis, much less for a general introduction or systematic studies.

The first extensive study which presented itself as a synthetic treatment was

---

1. For an analysis of different positions in the Protestant tradition, see Knitter 1974.
2. Schlette 1966. For a more elaborate statement, see Darlap 1965a, 3–156.
3. Rahner 1966a, 1969a. A more synthetic treatment is found later in Rahner 1978.

V. Boublik's *Teologia delle religioni,* published in 1973.[4] This has remained a standard work, and a new attempt at a general introduction to the theology of religions must perforce be situated in relation to it.

Boublik's comprehensive study includes not only a theology of religions but also — in the first place — a theology of religion. The two are distinct though dynamically interrelated. The theology of religion studies, in the light of the Christian faith, the religious experience common to all humanity as an "anonymous waiting" for the mystery of Christ: religious experience, with its double component of transcendence and immanence, represents, in the history of humankind, the highest manifestation of "human creatureliness" related to an Absolute which impinges upon it. The religions of the world are various "faces" or expressions of human religious experience, which is at once one and manifold. The theology of religion thus leads to a theology of religions. Boublik recognizes that an "organic solution to all the problems related to a systematic theology of religions" is not yet available (Boublik 1973, 37). His effort consists of "meeting the main problems in an organic manner," while being aware of not being able to "offer a definitive solution" (Boublik 1973, 38).

Such an organic treatment calls for a salvation-history theological perspective in which the mystery of Christ is seen as the climax of God's self-manifestation to humankind through history. A theology of religions cannot therefore but be Christocentric. However, Boublik disagrees with K. Rahner's way of understanding the relationship of the religious traditions of the world to the mystery of Christ: instead of "anonymous Christianity," according to which the mystery is there present and operative, though hidden and unperceived, Boublik proposes the concept of "anonymous catechumenate," which keeps people who belong to other religions oriented throughout their lives to an encounter with the mystery of Christ which will come only at the end. Human death will be for them "the hour of salvation." This solution will hereafter be submitted to a critical appraisal and will appear seriously inadequate in the light of more recent theological discussion and advances. Meanwhile, let it suffice to note that on this score already there is room for a new general introduction to the theology of religions, both more generous in its appraisal of the other traditions and better equipped for dialogue with their members.

It has been said earlier that the theology of religions was born during the period surrounding Vatican II and that the 1960s witnessed a strong wave of theological publications on the subject, even though more by way of groping than of providing definite answers. The 1970s marked the beginning of a new quest, arising worldwide from the situation created by the ever-increasing interaction between people of different religious faiths. Traditional Christocentrism, which had so far provided the backbone for a theology of religions, was now

---

4. Boublik 1973. A much briefer introduction to the theology of religions is Bürkle 1977. See also Damboriena 1973. For a recent introduction, see Waldenfels 1990.

being submitted to serious questioning in Christian circles; it has since then been under increasing pressure.

An account will have to be given hereafter of the debate on the theology of religions which has developed over the last twenty years and continues today unabated. An evaluation will moreover have to be made of such recent questioning, whose positive and negative results will have to be sorted out in terms of maintaining the Christian identity while being committed to interfaith dialogue and conversation. In this context a new introduction to the theology of religions appears all the more urgent; such an introduction will have to integrate the recent questioning in its organic and synthetic way of dealing with the reality of religious pluralism. The enterprise is as risky and challenging as it is important and urgent.

## Defining the Terms

The terms which provide the title of the book have been deliberately chosen to express as clearly as possible both its scope and intent: "Toward a Christian Theology of Religious Pluralism." Each of these terms needs to be clearly defined.

### Theology

We have already mentioned that, at least on the part of the Roman Catholic Church, a theology of religions is a recent venture; we have suggested that its birth may be traced to the years surrounding Vatican II.[5] Various sciences of religion and a philosophy of religion had developed and been operative long before their theological counterpart came to existence. As a matter of course, the development of the sciences and philosophy of religion served as a powerful incentive for, and were instrumental in calling upon, theologians to reflect on the meaning and value of the religious traditions of the world in the light of the Christian revelation.

There is no need here to document the various sciences of religion in any detail; it is enough to mention them and to take note of the invaluable service they render to the theology of religions, to which they furnish the indispensable data without which such a theology would run the risk of being an altogether a priori and abstract exercise, out of touch with the concrete reality of the religious traditions. Among sciences of religion the following may be distinguished: the history of religions, the phenomenology of religion, the psychology of religion, religious sociology, and philosophy of religion (see Cantone, ed., 1981; Latourelle and Fisichella, eds., 1994, s.v. "Religion," 819–86).

---

5. Schlette (1967) observes that there still exists no convincing theology of religions on the Catholic side, notwithstanding some valuable work that has gone before the council.

What is important for our purpose is to distinguish clearly the theology of religions from any human science of religion or religions, philosophy included. In scholastic terminology it may be said that, while all share the same "material object" — Christianity being one of the religious traditions of the world — they differ as to their "formal object." Boublik distinguishes them as follows: "hierography" studies religions under the historical aspect; "hierology" offers a hermeneutic of the religious fact and considers its psychological content; "hierosophy" asks what meaning religion has and what role it plays in the realization of the human person; "theology" attends to the storico-salvific aspect of religion and religions; it "offers an interpretation of religions in the light of the Word of God, with the help of the faith-experience and within the perspective of the history of salvation, of which Christ is the Beginning (Alpha) and the End (Omega)" (Boublik 1973, 41).

Each science of religion has its own method which distinguishes it from the others. Proper to theology is the formal reliance of its hermeneutic of religion and religions on the Christian revelation contained in the word of God and interpreted by the Church's living tradition. The theology of religions is an integral part of the Church's theological discourse, a part to which the Anselmian definition can and must be applied: *fides quaerens intellectum* (faith seeking understanding). This is its distinctive character, from which there immediately follow weighty consequences. While the sciences of religion observe, evaluate, and compare religious phenomena from without, with the objective detachment that is claimed for positive science, the theology of religions begins and remains at every step within a faith perspective, with the presuppositions which faith implies.

To pronounce value judgments on the religious data they handle lies beyond the scope and competence of positive sciences of religion; they can but offer relative evaluations based on a comparative study of the data. The theology of religions, on the other hand, interprets the data in the perspective of a personal commitment to a religious faith and claims the right to pronounce, within that perspective, value judgments. Terms such as "uniqueness," "universality," and others belong to distinct linguistic registers when handled by one discipline or the other. More, however, will have to be said below with regard to the various understandings of such terms (see Moran 1992), as well as to the method which a theology of religions may suitably follow.

### *A Christian Theology*

It may seem redundant to state explicitly that the theology of religions proposed here is specifically Christian. It is true that, until recently, "theology" often seemed, in Christian circles, to belong to Christianity as its exclusive property; worse still, in Western Christianity first world theology seemed to have the monopoly, as G. Gutiérrez, the father of South American liberation theology, has often pointedly remarked. However this may be, it is not unimportant, in view of recent discussions, to state clearly that theology is understood here as Christian theology. Nor is it inconsequential.

In recent years W. Cantwell Smith has advocated a "world theology" which he envisages to be the only adequate response for the future to the new global awareness of religious diversity and to the present interaction of the various traditions.[6] A world theology would be one "for which the 'religions' are the subject, not the object; a theology that emerges out of 'all the religions of the world,' or...all the religious communities of the world" (Smith 1981, 124). Such a theology would be one "of faith in its many forms," a "theology of the religious history of humankind" (Smith 1981, 125). It would give conceptual articulation to "the faith of all of us" — Christians and others; it would not, for that matter, dilute Christian faith, but transcend it; it would be theology "Christian, plus" (Smith 1981, 125), in the sense of being built and shared by people belonging to communities with distinct beliefs yet sharing a common faith. The theology called for in the future is, according to Smith, a "theology of comparative religion," constructed by all, "acceptable to, even cogent for all humankind" (Smith 1981, 126). This "theology of the faith of man" may well be a dream, a utopia; yet this is the direction in which we must move, even if the goal be eschatological rather than historical.

This is not the place to enter into a substantiated critique of W. Cantwell Smith's reductive view of the concept of faith and theology;[7] the occasion will offer itself later. Meanwhile, however, it needs to be pointed out that religious faiths are distinct in their essential content and that each demands by its nature a total commitment on the part of the person. This being so, just as the content of distinct faith-commitments differs, so also will the theologies built upon them from within, by way of reflexive articulation and elaboration. A theology cannot be at once Christian-Muslim-Hindu or whatever; it needs to be either one or the other. In other words, every theology is either "confessional" (in the best sense of the word) or does not exist. "Confessional" here refers to the faith-commitment of the person or religious community which is the subject of theologizing.

This being so, it must immediately be added that, while being necessarily "confessional," a Christian theology of religions need not, or for that matter, cannot, be insular or parochial. For the opposite is true: a Christian theology of religions must adopt a global perspective which embraces in its vision the entirety of the religious experience of humankind (Balasuriya 1984; Thils 1983). Its horizon must be truly universal. Moreover, even while the various religious traditions differ in their foundational experience of faith, they can nevertheless hold some truths in common. It belongs to interreligious dialogue in its various forms to discover whatever Christians and others can say and do in common,

---

6. Smith 1981; 1987, 51–72; Swidler 1987, 5–50. In the same direction, see C. G. Hospital, who envisages not a "super-religion" or a syncretic mixture but a "metatheology that arises out of...the wide-ranging history of human religiousness" (Hospital 1985, 167 and n. 76).

7. For a critique of Smith's universal theology, see Whaling 1986.

despite their irreducible differences, and it is part of ecumenical goodwill to provide the thrust for it.

Raimon Panikkar is therefore right in his disagreement with W. Cantwell Smith on the question of building a universal theology. He notes correctly that, as religious faiths differ substantially, so will theologies. What is called for is not a common theological enterprise which levels differences in a search for a common denominator, but the frank admission of the plurality and diversity of beliefs and the mutual acceptance of the others in their very otherness (see Panikkar 1978, 1984, 1987a, 1987b; see also Barnes 1989). The model that needs to be developed then is not that of mutual assimilation through a reduction of faith-content but that of interpenetration and cross-fertilization of the various traditions in their diversities; not a leveling of religious identities but a dialogical openness and mutual enrichment through conversation. Personal commitment to one's own faith and openness to the faith of others need not be mutually exclusive; rather they ought to grow in direct proportion.

It still needs to be added that, while a Christian theology of religions cannot but be Christian, it must leave room and indeed create space for other "confessional" theologies of religions, be they Muslim, Hindu, or otherwise. The term "theology," which is of Christian origin, will not be used by Jewish rabbis, Muslim mullahs, or Hindu pandits reflecting, in the light of their own faith, on the significance and value of the religious faith of others. They will nonetheless construct their own faith-interpretation of the pluralism of religious traditions in general and of specific elements of distinct traditions in particular. Examples of the latter in relation to Christianity are: the Qur'anic and Islamic understanding of Jesus Christ (see, e.g., Cragg 1985; Arnaldez 1980, 1988) or the various interpretations of his person among authors belonging to the Hindu Renaissance.[8] Notwithstanding the divergences or even contradictions existing between such interpretations of religious pluralism — and of Christology in particular — and those derived from the Christian faith, the various confessional theologies of religions should be viewed positively as likely springboards and useful points of departure for interreligious conversation and dialogue.

### A Christian Theology of Religious Pluralism

A distinction has been made earlier between a theology of religion and a theology of religions: they differ, though being organically related and indeed inseparable (see Boublik 1973; Artigas 1981, 233–306). The theology of religion asks what religion is and seeks, in the light of Christian faith, to interpret the universal religious experience of humankind; it further studies the relationship between revelation and faith, faith and religion, and faith and salvation. However, since, owing to the nature of the human being as spirit incarnate and a person in society, religious experience is naturally embodied in a religious tra-

---

8. See Thomas 1969; Samartha 1974; Staffner 1985; Dupuis 1991b, 15–45.

dition — made up of creed, cult, and moral code — the theology of religion becomes in turn a theology of religio*ns*. Christian theology of religions studies the various traditions in the context of the history of salvation and in their relationship to the mystery of Jesus Christ and the Christian Church.

In his *Teologia delle religioni,* V. Boublik offers a theology both of religion and of religions, taking care to show their organic relationship. However, the theology of religion often runs the risk of staying at the level of abstract thought, divested of concrete reality. The number of current definitions of religion and of religious experience offers a case in point. The present introduction does not intend to enter into such abstract discussions. It would rather ask concrete questions dealing with the reality — no matter how mysterious — of the religious experience actually lived by people in the context of their respective religious traditions; and it seeks to interpret this existential experience of the "others" in the light of the Christian faith and the mystery of Jesus Christ. Priority is thus laid upon reality over abstraction, upon existence over essence. What matters is not definitions but people's living experience in the concrete circumstances in whom God has placed them. The questions on hand then are: How do the circumstances in which people live their religious life fit into God's one plan of salvation for humankind? What meaning in God's own eyes — insofar as we may claim to penetrate God's secrets — has the reality of religious pluralism in the world, of which humankind (and Christianity within it) has acquired today a new consciousness?

However, the danger of abstraction may threaten us in another way; and the question has indeed been asked whether a Christian theology of religions, which claims to treat them all in bulk, is a viable project. To be concrete, should not the theology of religions address itself individually to each of the religious traditions in particular? It is being suggested, therefore, that what is required is a distinct Christian theology of Islam, of Hinduism, and so on. Nor should only the great "world religions" be considered; attention must also be paid to the "traditional religions" of Africa, the Americas, Asia, and Oceania.

The suggestion is not only valid but important. Moreover, such distinct Christian theologies of particular religious traditions are already becoming a reality. A case in point is the Christian theology of Judaism which has developed in recent years (see, e.g., Thoma 1980; Mussner 1984). In fact, as will be observed later, the case of Judaism may be viewed as paradigmatic for a Christian theology of the relationship between Christianity and other religious traditions. This is due to the special link which exists between the two biblical traditions and to their common heritage in God's revelation to Israel. A theology of other religious traditions will seek to apply — insofar as is possible and *mutatis mutandis* — what can be said concerning the relationship of the two biblical religions.

It is also important to keep in mind the traditional distinction between the monotheistic or prophetic religions and those usually referred to as oriental or mystical. This distinction — of which R. C. Zaehner has been one of the main exponents (see, e.g., Zaehner 1957, 1958, 1970) — must, however, be handled carefully. That the three "religions of the Book" — Judaism, Christianity, and Islam — are called "monotheistic" and "prophetic" must not be intended to imply that all the other religions are "polytheistic" (or nontheistic) or to deny them any prophetic significance; conversely, the Eastern religions — Hinduism and Buddhism in particular — are called "mystical" without prejudice to the "mystical" dimension of Christianity and the other prophetic religions. The merit of the distinction consists in, on the one hand, stressing the common foundation of the three religions of the Book in the faith of Abraham, while, on the other hand, recognizing the "wisdom" or "gnosis" characteristic of the Eastern traditions.[9] This goes to show that while the relationship between Judaism and Christianity has a unique character, Islam too has a special affinity to Christianity insofar as Islam also goes back to the faith of Abraham as to its last foundation. The three "monotheistic" faiths thus constitute between themselves one family of religions, while the Eastern religions share special ties of which account must also be taken.

The irreplaceable role of Christian theologies of distinct religions notwithstanding, there still remains room for a general theology of religions which embraces them all and asks how the other religious traditions — and their component parts — relate to the Christian mystery: to the event of Jesus Christ, which is at the heart of Christian faith, and, derivatively, to the Christian Church established by Jesus Christ as the "universal sacrament of salvation" (LG 48) in the world. Indeed, such a general theology of religions comes before the particular theologies dealing with the distinct relationship of one religious tradition to the Christian mystery. It asks the general questions which apply to all cases and need to be studied before specific questions can be considered which concern Christian conversation with one specific tradition.

From this it does not follow that a general theology of religions will consider all religious traditions "in bulk," without keeping in mind the necessary distinctions. For, as will be seen later, while all religions find their place within the overall plan of God for the salvation of humankind, not all have the same place or an identical significance within this plan's organic unfolding in history. This is the reason why, after the necessary distinctions have been made in a general way in the theology of religions, there remains room — and there is a pressing need — for theologies of Christian conversation with Judaism in particular, with Islam, and with the religious traditions of the East.

To mention only Buddhism: a theology of the encounter between Buddhism and Christianity has been developing in recent years and has produced an abundant literature. A parallel is often being drawn between the historical figure of Gautama-the-Buddha and Jesus-the-Christ, as well as between

---

9. Aloysius Pieris refers to Christianity as "agapeic gnosis," to Buddhism as "gnostic *agapè*." See Pieris 1988b, 110–19.

the interpretation the two founders receive in later developments in the two traditions.[10]

## Theology of Religious Pluralism

Our title is "Toward a Christian Theology of Religious Pluralism," not simply " . . . of Religions." Why? Reference has been made above to the new awareness that has been dawning upon theologians of the reality of "religious pluralism," characteristic of today's world. The term "religious pluralism," though coined only recently, is now widely used in the context of the "theology of religions";[11] today the new expression tends gradually to replace the former one.[12] The change in terminology indicates a change in theological perspective. The new perspective is no longer limited to the problem of "salvation" for members of the other religious traditions or even to the role of those traditions in the salvation of their members. It searches more deeply, in the light of Christian faith, for the meaning in God's design for humankind of the plurality of living faiths and religious traditions with which we are surrounded. Are all the religious traditions of the world destined, in God's plan, to converge? Where, when, and how?

"Pluralism" and "plurality" seem, as a matter of fact, to be used indifferently in this context. The renewed problematic is expressed as follows in the statement published by the Thirteenth Annual Meeting (December 1989) of the Indian Theological Association, entitled "Towards an Indian Christian Theology of Religious Pluralism: Our Ongoing Search":

> We want to express what the plurality of the religions we meet everyday of our lives in India means to us as believers, as people who experience themselves as touched and strengthened by the ineffable mystery of existence. As we perceive the signs of the Absolute Presence also in the lives of our sisters and brothers around us professing various religions, we ask in the light of the Divine Truth revealing itself, what we should affirm about these religions, and how we [should] understand the purpose and meaning of the wonderful religious variety around us and its role and function in the attainment of salvation. . . .

---

10. From the abundant literature see: Pieris 1988b, 1996; Cobb 1982; Waldenfels 1980; Cobb and Ives, eds., 1990; Panikkar 1989; Keenan 1989, 1995; Lefebure 1993; Corless and Knitter, eds., 1990; O'Leary 1994; Vallet 1996.

11. See, among others, the following titles: Pathil, ed., 1991; Barnes 1989; Rouner, ed., 1984; D'Costa 1986; Hillmann 1989; Race 1983; Coward 1985; Hick 1985; Dawe and Carman, eds., 1978; Anderson and Stransky, eds., 1981a; O'Leary 1994; Cobb 1975; Krieger 1991; Hamnett 1990; Schwager, ed., 1996.

12. Symptomatic in this regard are the titles of the statements of two consecutive annual meetings of the Indian Theological Association, held in 1988 and 1989, both of which were devoted to the theology of religions. The statement issued by the 1988 meeting is entitled "Towards a Theology of Religions: An Indian Christian Perspective"; the statement of the 1989 meeting bears the title "Towards an Indian Christian Theology of Religious Pluralism." Both are published conjointly in Pathil, ed., 1991, 324–49. For an analysis of the two statements, see Dupuis 1992c, 21–47.

As Christians, we approach these questions from our faith perspective. (8, 9) (Pathil, ed., 1991, 340–41)

This goes to show that the current theology of religions means to look at religious pluralism not merely as a matter of course and a fact of history (pluralism de facto) but as having a raison d'être in its own right (pluralism de jure or "in principle") (see Geffré 1993b; Schillebeeckx 1990, 171–82). The question no longer simply consists of asking what role Christianity can assign to the other historical religious traditions but in searching for the root-cause of pluralism itself, for its significance in God's own plan for humankind, for the possibility of a mutual convergence of the various traditions in full respect of their differences, and for their mutual enrichment and cross-fertilization (see Panikkar 1978). Expressions are being coined to describe this new perspective and the problematic it generates. "In a pluralistic society like [India's]," it is said, "genuine religion necessarily entails a relationship with the other religions.... In short, to be religious is to be interreligious" (Indian Theological Association 1991, no. 36, p. 348). By way of consequence, a theology of religions becomes "interreligious theology" with a "universal imperative" (see O'Leary 1994, 291).

### *Toward*

In the light of the above, the "Toward" in our title needs little explanation. The new perspective which is being opened for a Christian theology of religions makes it clear that an updated introduction to such a theology cannot, even less than did its predecessors, bring definitive solutions to all the questions which are being asked — many of which are new to no small extent. The present introduction will, perhaps, raise as many questions as it will propose solutions. It will hopefully, at least, sort out the issues clearly in the light of recent discussions and advances and indicate avenues for solutions to new questions, consonant with the profession of Christian faith.

This is not to say that the new problematic can afford to disregard or ignore the past. It must, no doubt, go beyond past solutions that no longer square with reality and leave behind the negative attitudes that have characterized centuries of Christian relations with other religions. Yet it must at the same time keep in touch with the living tradition of the Church — itself the outcome of past tradition — and build upon what the Christian centuries, first in the revealed word and later in the postbiblical tradition, offer that remains valuable by way of an open attitude likely to lead to a positive theological assessment. Disregard leads to contempt; acquaintance to critical evaluation.

This goes to show that the renewed theological vision which is called for will require a clear, if guarded, historical perspective. It needs to be made clear that Vatican II has marked a true break with the past and a new beginning where the Church's relations with the other religions and, consequently, the faith evaluation which it makes of them are concerned. Perhaps the importance of the new attitudes brought about by the council has not yet been fully appreciated; nor have its theological implications been yet adequately worked out. While a certain continuity with the past remains in order even here, it is no less true that a clear discontinuity, amounting to a true conversion, is equally called for.

Attitudes toward the other religions and the theological evaluation which is made of them have gone hand in hand through the centuries. The spectrum of attitudes has moved the whole way from the dialectical opposition inherited from a long past, through an attitude of tolerance, to the dialogical conversation of recent times. In a parallel fashion, the theological evaluation has gone all the way from the disregard and rejection which characterized much of the Christian tradition, through a guarded acceptance and openness, to a positive assessment and the recognition of positive values. No introduction to the theology of religions can afford to overlook these dramatic changes, even if it need not — as indeed it cannot afford — give a complete historical account of the relations of Christianity to other religions through the centuries.[13]

Looking back only to the different perspectives from which the other religions have been approached and studied during the century which is now coming to a close, we can observe the same spectacular changes. The first quarter of this century remained dominated by an apologetic attitude, mostly negative. In such a climate, the question which continued to retain the attention of theologians was the problem of the possibility of salvation for the members of other religions. Characteristic of this problematic are, among other writing, entries on the "salvation of infidels" in classical theological dictionaries.[14] The middle of the century and the years leading to and immediately following Vatican II witnessed a gradual change of climate, to which the council gave a powerful impetus. During this second period, the approach became less defensive and more positive: in the wake of the council, theology became more affirmative and optimistic with regard to the salvation of the members of other religions; the traditions themselves were progressively considered as containing positive values or even as playing a positive role in the salvation of their members. With this new approach, as we have noted earlier, the theology of religions was born.[15]

The third period is that which we have entered in recent years; it can be traced to the beginning of the 1980s. A broader perspective, as we have noted above, is now being advocated, which is giving birth to a "theology of religious pluralism."[16] Going beyond the problematic of people's salvation in and through their religious traditions, the new perspective seeks to penetrate more

---

13. G. H. Anderson has observed: "There is no book in any language that provides a comprehensive study of Christian attitudes and approaches to people of other faiths throughout the history of Christianity" (Anderson 1990, 172). One may, however, consult usefully Ries 1987.

14. See Harent 1927, cols. 1726–1930; d'Ales 1928, cols. 1157–82; Billot 1919–23; see also Lombardi 1956; Eminiyan 1960.

15. See the literature mentioned in the section above entitled "A New General Introduction."

16. See the literature mentioned in n. 11, above.

deeply into God's plan for humankind. It asks about the significance of the plurality of religious traditions in that plan — and consequently in the unfolding
of the history of God's dealings with humankind which we call the history of
salvation. This problematic will characterize the years ahead leading us into
the twenty-first century. An introduction to the theology of religions for today
cannot afford to ignore this.

This is not to say that the new perspective is, even today, universally accepted
and followed by theologians of religions. A broad spectrum of opinions can be
observed, even recently, oscillating from theological integralism to eclectic liberalism. This is not the place to describe the present theological scene and to
account for the ongoing debate on Christianity and world religions. We shall
return to it hereafter. Meanwhile, let it suffice to note that negative attitudes
flowing from a theological exclusivism die hard. Symptomatic in this regard is
the recent publication of a book by H. van Straelen, entitled — not without am-
bition — *L'Eglise et les religions non chrétiennes au seuil du XXIe siècle.*[17] A
long personal experience as a missionary in Japan notwithstanding, the author
of this volume continues to hold on to negative opinions hardly in keeping with
the official teaching authority of the Church. He does not hesitate to write that
"the Church has always taught that in order to be saved man must accept the
Gospel message" and turn to God "as revealed in Jesus Christ" (Straelen 1994,
281). No mention is made here of the long traditional distinction between explicit and implicit faith. Vatican II itself did more than merely recognize in the
other religions "good *natural* elements on the level of human culture" (Straelen 1994, 289). Without questioning the sincere intention of the author, one is
forced to observe that the book disappoints on more than one count. In contrast
to the professed attitude of openness of the Church's recent teaching authority,
the book offers a hardened position toward the other religions; it sets itself as
judge to condemn theological opinions in which nothing is objectively repre-
hensible from the point of view of Christian faith. In sum, the author lacks the
openness and sympathy toward the other religious traditions which alone make
it possible to recognize in them the action of God and the presence of God's
Spirit.[18] Such an attitude betrays on the part of a Catholic theologian a striking
affinity to a rigid "evangelical" standpoint.[19]

## Questions about Method

The Anselmian definition of theology as "faith seeking understanding" is still
valid, and not a few contemporary theologians make explicit reference to it.
However, the axiom is open to different interpretations and has given rise to
distinct, even contrasting, theological methods. To recall the methods that have

---

17. Straelen 1994. The same author had previously published Straelen 1982.
18. For a review of the book, see Dupuis 1995b.
19. A recent example of such a standpoint is Netland 1991.

succeeded each other in a limited lapse of time will help to situate the problem of a methodology suitable for the subject under consideration.

The time is not so far remote when the so-called *dogmatic* method prevailed in theology. It took as its point of departure the Church's dogmatic enunciations, the content of which, as by a process of retrojection, it sought to verify in scriptural citations chosen for the purpose. This verification being done, the method went on digging further into the meaning of the dogmatic data, hoping to derive from them further theological conclusions, ever more precise. The limits and dangers of such a method are well known today, and there is no need to press the point. The dogmatic method has mostly been blamed for its abstract character: the more deductions are drawn from abstract principles, the more real is the risk of being cut off from reality. Moreover, the method did not give to the revealed message contained in the scripture the place due to it in all theological endeavor.

This is why the dogmatic method has been replaced by a new method, called *genetic*; this method has been recommended by Vatican II in its decree *Optatam Totius* (OT 16). It starts from the revealed data and goes on to show the understanding and interpretation which it has received through history, in the tradition of the Fathers and of the councils, through the theological schools and recent authors. The method thus follows the development of theological reflection on a specific theme of faith, to finally reach the questions which these centuries-old data meet or raise today. The genetic method has the advantage of being inspired by a serious return to biblical and patristic sources; however, it runs the risk of assuming too linear a concept of doctrinal development within the biblical data, and even more so in the postbiblical tradition. A concept of continuous progress in a straight direction is a simplification of history, which often does not do justice to the complexity of the data.

Notwithstanding their different starting points — the dogmatic enunciations in the first case, the biblical data in the second — both the dogmatic and genetic methods shared a common feature in that both were principally *deductive*: they progressed from basic assertions to conclusions, from the better known to the less known. The process consisted of starting from general principles to reach their concrete applications to the problems of today. A methodological about-face took place with the progressive introduction of a reverse method which, in contradistinction from the earlier ones, can be qualified as *inductive*. It is no longer a question of going from principles to concrete applications but, in the opposite direction, of taking as point of departure the reality as experienced today with the problems it raises, to search for — in the light of the revealed message and through theological reflection — a Christian solution to those problems.

It has often been remarked that, compared to the other conciliar documents, the constitution *Gaudium et Spes* (GS) of Vatican II inaugurated a new method. The novelty consisted in passing from a deductive method to an inductive one: the constitution listens to the world of today and to its problems, learns to read the "signs of the times" in the aspirations of today's humanity; it then seeks to throw light on these problems and to respond to these aspirations in the light of the Gospel message. Appropriately called the Pastoral Constitution on the Church in the Modern World, *Gaudium et Spes* undoubtedly inaugurates a new genre in conciliar documents; it likewise represents an important landmark toward what in the postconciliar period would mark a new departure in theological method.

Much is being said today about *contextualization* of theology — a principle which goes beyond that of adaptation or even of inculturation (see Dupuis 1992d) — and about the theological model to which it gives rise, under the name of *hermeneutical theology.* To adopt an inductive method, as Vatican II has done in *Gaudium et Spes,* means starting from historical reality, allowing ourselves to be challenged by it, and seeking to throw upon it the light of the revealed word. In other words, it means starting from the concrete context in which the Church lives its faith and interpreting the surrounding reality with the help of the Gospel message. Fundamentally, it means *contextualization* and *hermeneutics.*

Claude Geffré has appropriately defined "hermeneutical theology" as "a new act of interpretation of the event of Jesus Christ on the basis of a critical correlation between the fundamental Christian experience to which tradition bears witness and contemporary human experience" (Geffré 1987, 50). The new interpretation of the Christian message is born "on the basis of the circle between reading in faith the founding texts that bear witness to the original Christian experience on the one hand and Christian existence today on the other" (Geffré 1987, 53). It follows that "theology of the hermeneutical type is of necessity pluriform" (Geffré 1987, 53; see also Bevans 1992).

Christian existence is everywhere conditioned by the historical context in which it is lived, with its cultural, economic, social, political, and religious components. Hermeneutical theology will therefore consist of a progressive and continuous going-and-coming between the present contextual experience and the witness of the foundational experience entrusted to the memory of Church tradition. This continuous going-and-coming between "context" and "text," between present and past, is what is called the "hermeneutical circle."

In reality, it is not a circularity between two members which is at work here but rather a triangularity and the mutual interaction of three angles: the "text" or the "given" of faith, the historical "context," and today's "interpreter."[20] The circular image would then advantageously be replaced by the graphic representation of a triangle. But each of the three poles in mutual interaction, each of the constitutive elements of the triangle, needs to be viewed in the integrity of its complex reality.

"Text" means not only the revealed data contained in the Bible, specifi-

---

20. See Dupuis 1994c, 8–9. See also Bevans 1992, 97–102, esp. 101, where he refers to the "transcendental model" of contextual theology.

cally in the New Testament. It covers all that goes under the term "Christian memory," the objective tradition. It extends to the various readings and interpretations the ecclesial tradition has made of the revealed message, including official conciliar formulations. The text therefore comprises scripture, tradition, and the Church's magisterium (in its objective aspect), between which Vatican II has shown the intimate connection (see DV 10).

Where "context" is concerned, the elements that constitute it will differ from place to place as well as between distinct periods of history. Yet the context also needs to be taken in its complex reality, including sociopolitical, economic, cultural, and religious reality.

As for the "interpreter," this is not, properly speaking, the individual theologian but the ecclesial community to which the theologian belongs and at whose service he or she is placed. This is the local church, a believing people living its faith-experience in diachronic communion with the Apostolic Church and in synchronic communion with all the local churches — a communion over which the bishop of Rome presides in charity.

The hermeneutical triangle consists of the mutual interaction among text, context, and interpreter, as these have just been described — that is, the interaction among the Christian memory, the surrounding cultural and religious reality, and the local church. The context acts upon the interpreter by raising specific questions; it influences the precomprehension of faith with which the interpreter reads the text. The text, in turn, acts on the interpreter, whose reading of it will provide a direction for Christian praxis. As can be seen, the interaction between text and context, or between memory and culture, takes place in the interpreter, that is, in the local church.

Applying these principles to a theology of religions, the following may be said. It must be acknowledged that Western theologians, even the most successful, who have concerned themselves with a theology of religions have most often adopted a purely deductive method.[21] They begin with certain statements in the New Testament that they judge to be clear and indisputable in their meaning; then they ask what Christian faith can grant to other religious traditions. Do the premises of revelation authorize the ascription to these traditions of a positive meaning and value in God's plan of salvation? Going a step further, do these premises permit Christians to look upon these traditions as actual ways of salvation — not parallel ways to that opened by God in Jesus Christ, surely, but genuine ways of salvation nonetheless, in virtue of some relationship they might enjoy with the Christian way?

The reaction to an exclusively deductive method, an aprioristic one, and as such necessarily inadequate, has arisen, as might be expected, in the churches in which coexistence with other religious traditions is an integral part of everyday life, where the great world religions mingle on a daily basis. Indeed, in recent times, even in the West — as there, too, religious pluralism has grad-

---

21. The deductive method is also being followed by Boublik 1973, 38–49.

ually become a daily reality — theologians have been found to champion a resolutely inductive method. One begins with the praxis of interreligious dialogue among the various traditions — lived, on either side, in one's own faith, as is fitting — and theological reflection concerning the relationship of these traditions follows as a "second act." Let us note, in passing, the analogy with the method underlying liberation theology, precisely as a new method for the *actus theologicus:* G. Gutiérrez insists on the priority of a liberative praxis over theological discourse, which of its nature follows in the second place (see Gutiérrez 1973). Similarly, where the relationship between the Christian mystery and the religious traditions of humanity is concerned, priority belongs to the praxis of interreligious dialogue as an obligatory foundation for a theological discourse. The a priori operation, it is said, must be replaced by an a posteriori procedure.

At issue is the hermeneutical problem. Obviously the datum of faith and the living context of religious pluralism must be brought together. There are two possible routes to this encounter: the deductive and the inductive. However, as has been observed above, though legitimate in itself, the deductive operation nevertheless has its inbuilt limits. It is based on principles and so is in danger of remaining abstract, of not really encountering the concrete reality of other religious traditions. Similarly, the inductive operation too, based as it is on the praxis of dialogue, has its own limits. Whether by ineffectuality or hesitancy, it may fail to attain its goal: a theological discourse that harmonizes with the Christian datum.

In a situation such as this, the preferable methodology would seem to be a combination of the deductive and inductive methods. Their reciprocal movement would ensure the indispensable encounter between the datum of faith and the living reality of religious pluralism. Paul F. Knitter labels this approach the "global theological method" and describes it as follows, applying it to the subject with which we are concerned:

> Any viable method of theology will have to make use of two sources — Christian tradition (scripture and its living interpretation through history) and human experience (which includes both thought and praxis). Both these sources must be listened to openly and honestly; both must be brought into a mutually clarifying and mutually criticizing correlation.
>
> Applying the two-source approach to a method for a theology of religions, we must recognize that a Christian understanding of and approach to other religions cannot be fashioned only from the fabric of Christian beliefs. We will want to start with what the Bible or the official statements of councils have to say about other religions. And what we find must be taken seriously. But no final conclusions as to the value of the truth of other traditions can be reached until our Christian "data" is brought into relationship with a concrete knowledge (theory) and experience (praxis) of other religions. (Knitter 1985, 91–92)

With a view to guaranteeing this obligatory encounter of Christian datum and praxis of dialogue, we must insist on the role of dialogue as the necessary foundation of a theology of religions because of its frequent omission in the past and the need to reestablish a balance between the two sources. From a point of departure in the praxis of dialogue, the inductive operation is immediately immersed in the concrete religious experience of others. This is its strength and its irreplaceable contribution. Here too, of course, limitations are immediately in evidence, and we must subject these limitations to an attentive examination. Faith itself, by definition, is a commitment of the whole person. To what extent is it possible, as dialogue seems to require, to enter into the religious experience of another and make it one's own? If it is true that the very authenticity of dialogue demands that one's own faith never be "bracketed," what reception is it possible to accord the religious faith of another? We shall return to this later, especially to ask whether it is theologically intelligible and justified to regard and style oneself a "hyphenated Christian," Hindu-Christian, Buddhist-Christian, or whatever: Can one person share two whole and entire religious faiths?

For the moment, we need only notice that the operation that seems indicated is the one that combines both the deductive method (one's own faith not being placed between brackets) and the inductive method (involving an encounter of the other believer, insofar as possible, in the concrete reality of his or her actual religious experience).

If the principle of contextualization and the hermeneutical model of theology are applied seriously to the religious reality of the world, it will readily be seen that theology of religions cannot be viewed simply as a new *topic* or *subject* on which to reflect theologically. Such new topics for theologizing have arisen in recent times, among them the "theology of earthly realities," of "politics," of "ecology," and so forth. However, where the "theology of religions," or of "religious pluralism," is concerned, the genitive must not be taken as objective, referring to an object on which to theologize. More than a new topic *for* theologizing, the theology of religions must be viewed as a new *way of doing theology,* in an interfaith context; a new *method* of theologizing in a situation of religious pluralism (see D'Costa 1986; Barnes 1989; Bevans 1992). Such an "interreligious" hermeneutical theology is an invitation to broaden the horizon of theological discourse; it should, as we hope to show hereafter, lead to discover at a new depth the cosmic dimensions of the mystery of God, of Jesus Christ, and of the divine Spirit.

Here the comparison with liberation theology suggests itself once more. In a context of human oppression and the cry of large masses of people for human liberation, theology starts with a liberating praxis in order to lead thereafter to a theological reflection in the light of revelation; this theology presents itself as a new method of theologizing (see Gutiérrez 1973). So too, in an interfaith context, does the theology of religious pluralism. Its point of departure is a praxis of interreligious dialogue, on the foundation of which it searches for a

Christian interpretation of the surrounding plural religious reality. It too figures as a new *way* of theologizing. Such a theology, in effect, does not look at the praxis of interreligious dialogue merely as a necessary condition, premise, or even a first step; it further maintains a dialogical attitude at every stage of the reflection; it is theological reflection *on* and *within* dialogue.

This being so, it should become clear that the lead for building up a theological hermeneutics of religious pluralism will belong primarily, though not exclusively, to the churches in the African, and even more so in the Asian, continents, where the encounter and conversation between people belonging to distinct religious traditions is an important dimension of everyday life.[22]

Special reference may be made in this context to the complex nature of the Asian scene. It has often been remarked that the Asian context consists of two massive realities: the dehumanizing poverty of immense masses of people, which is the common lot of the third world continents and has been referred to as "third worldness"; and the plurality of religious traditions, characteristic of "Asianness," in the midst of which the Christian communities most often represent but a tiny minority. From there it follows that Asian churches will need to engage both in a liberation praxis and the praxis of interreligious dialogue; Asian local theologies — and also the African ones — will likewise integrate both a liberative and an interfaith dimension in their reflection.

Yet there is a difference: on the one hand, in the context of the oppression of depressed classes of society, liberation praxis must denounce the causes of oppression and confront them; on the other hand, the praxis called for by the reality of religious pluralism must consist in dialogue and conversation. Aloysius Pieris has shown that the praxis of both liberation and interreligious dialogue need in fact to be combined and united.[23] Christians and the members of the other religious traditions must seek in dialogue how they can commit themselves together to a liberation praxis and contribute together to an Asian model of liberation theology. Such a program, however, implies a critique of the religious traditions themselves inasmuch as these may contain elements which militate against integral liberation for all or may be manipulated in favor of the maintenance of unjust structures. Religion cannot be severed from justice; and, as already noted, to be religious in the Asian context implies being "interreligious."[24]

---

22. What is being said here is not, however, meant exclusively. Writing in the Western context, David Tracy has stated: "We are fast approaching the day when it will not be possible to attempt a Christian systematic theology except in serious conversation with the other great ways" (Tracy 1990, xi).

23. See, e.g., Pieris 1980a; 1983, 113–39. Both essays are reprinted in Pieris 1988a, 69–110. In another essay, entitled "Asia's Non-Semitic Religions and the Mission of Local Churches," Pieris calls on churches *in* Asia to be "baptized in the Jordan of Asian religion and in the Calvary of Asian poverty," in order to become truly "local Churches *of* Asia" (Pieris 1988a, 50).

24. See Indian Theological Association 1991, no. 36, p. 348. The statement also declares: "A liberative hermeneutic of religions . . . opens up towards a liberative ecumenism of religions" (no. 15, p. 343).

## Outline and Sequence of the Work

We have stressed the need for a theology of religious pluralism to be contextual. This would mean that every particular context, and indeed every single religion, be addressed individually and separately. The present "general introduction," however, aims, by its very nature, at being, insofar as is possible, applicable to distinct situations. It will, therefore, not be possible to remain directly and distinctly in any particular context. What is thereby unavoidably lost by way of immediate relevance to a concrete situation will, it is hoped, be made good inasmuch as the concerns of vastly different contexts will be kept in mind. Thus, while being primarily concerned with general questions regarding the relationship between the Christian mystery and other religious traditions, we shall, nonetheless, keep in touch with particular situations which form part of the global reality. To this end, and in order not to fall into abstraction, we shall frequently make appeal to concrete elements of particular religious traditions with a view to verify and substantiate the theological views proposed. Moreover, wherever it seems important and necessary, we shall branch off from general considerations and make particular applications to distinct religious traditions.[25]

The book is divided into two parts: one historical or "positive"; the other synthetic and thematic. The twofold structure seemed to recommend itself for more than one reason. First, as has been stated earlier, the present awareness of the Christian Church regarding the significance of religious pluralism, however new, cannot be severed from the Christian memory which has developed over the centuries; it needs to remain in touch with the Christian roots and make constant reference to them. Second, the evaluation of the other religions has changed so dramatically in the course of the Christian tradition that it seemed advisable and, indeed, necessary to give in the first place a substantial account of this centuries-long evolution before proposing, in a second part, a synthetic view of the matter in keeping with the Church's present awareness. Third, the problematic itself has evolved remarkably over the centuries; to make these spectacular changes perceptible, it again seemed necessary to give a historical account of successive problematics before presenting the subject matter in an organic way.

The historical part does not, however, claim to be all-comprehensive; nor did it seem necessary that it be so. What is intended is not an encyclopedic knowledge but an understanding in historical perspective of distinct and largely

---

25. In order to show explicitly how an inductive method can be combined with a deductive one, we devoted the first part of *Jesus Christ at the Encounter with World Religions* (Dupuis 1991b) to the "stepping stones of a tradition." We described the reception which authors belonging to the Hindu Renaissance have given to the "unbound" Christ and gave an account of the living dialogue between the Christian mystery and Hindu mysticism (see 13–110). Immediate reference was thus made to a particular context. The same cannot be done here, due partly to the sheer vastness of the material. The concrete applications with which this present book is interspersed will, it is hoped, partly remedy this shortcoming.

different positions and perceptions. To this end, what was required was a survey of the various problematics which succeeded one another through the Church's tradition; we therefore proceed by examining whole slices of history rather than by following mere chronological succession.

Chapter 1 will analyze the main data of scripture, with regard to the religions of the other "nations" in the Old Testament and of the "gentiles" in the New. This will be done thematically rather than analytically; the aim will be to show which factors brought about the distinct attitudes which are perceptible in the Jewish and the Christian scriptures.

Chapter 2 will examine, in contrast with the prevalent negative attitude of the Church Fathers toward the religions they encountered, the noteworthy positive posture which some of the early apologists of the second and the early third century developed. This will enable us to discover the first foundations in the postbiblical tradition for a theology of "salvation history" destined to become later the backbone of a theology of religions.

The axiom "Outside the Church no salvation," which in its rigid form has its historical origin mostly in the successors of Saint Augustine, has been for centuries the symbol of the Church's negative stand on the possibility of salvation for members of other religions. Chapter 3 will study the historical origin of the axiom and its progressive narrow interpretation, down to later official pronouncements by the Church's teaching authority. By way of contrast it will also point to some glimpses of a more open outlook during the same protracted period.

With the discovery of the New World in the fifteenth century a dramatic change took place with regard to European views on the requirements for salvation on the part of the members of other religious traditions: a shift from insisting on explicit faith to recognizing implicit faith. Chapter 4 will review the various ways in which substitutions for the Gospel were devised through the centuries to account for the possibility of implicit faith down to the years preceding Vatican II.

Chapter 5 will study the preconciliar theological renewal in its bearing upon the question of the salvation of the "others" and the value of their religious traditions in salvation history. It will show how the change in attitude and the new openness characteristic of Vatican II had been progressively prepared for by the theological renewal that started before the council.

Chapter 6 will examine the doctrine of the council and assess it critically; it will further show how, and to what extent, the open attitude of the council has been confirmed and progressively further developed by the Church's teaching authority, down to the most recent official documents.

Chapter 7 will conclude the historical part with a detailed account of the debate on the theology of religions which has developed in the Christian churches in the period following the council, leading up to several new perspectives which are now emerging and need to be critically assessed. This assessment will lead to a theological perspective which will serve thereafter as the leading thread for an organic presentation of the main theological issues involved in a theology of religious pluralism.

Part II is called "synthetic," not "systematic"; for, while attempting to present a synthetic view of the complex questions involved, it does not claim — nor could it — to fit the mystery of God's plan for humankind and the unfolding of the divine plan in history, into a neat, human-made system. Rather than systematic, it is, therefore, thematic. What is intended is an organic overview of the various aspects of the mystery, thus allowing their unity to stand out.

Chapter 8 opens up the perspective of the history of salvation as the framework in which the plurality of religious traditions needs to be viewed in keeping with the divine plan. This already goes to show that the various religious traditions represent distinct divine manifestations through history — not, however, without unity and order, for the divine plan for humankind which unfolds through history is one.

Chapter 9 follows up the question of divine revelation and human faith, in their various forms and under distinct models, applying these to the sacred writings of the religious traditions and concluding with a differentiated or diversified word of God in history.

Chapter 10 takes up the problem of the Absolute or Divine Mystery as the transcendental horizon of humans' religious experience in the different traditions. It purports to show what light the mystery of the divine communication which obtains in God as revealed in Jesus Christ can throw on a theology of religious plurality.

Chapter 11 is crucial for our entire work. It shows the decisive role which the historical event of Jesus Christ plays in God's plan for humankind and the central place which it occupies in the historical unfolding of that plan. The chapter further illustrates the unity which obtains between the Christological and the pneumatological dimensions of the economy of salvation, as well as their interaction and complementarity as they bear upon the presence of the mystery of salvation in the religious traditions.

Building on this foundation, chapter 12 examines in what sense a Christian theology of religions can recognize in the other religious traditions a true mediation for their members of the mystery of salvation in Jesus Christ, viewing those traditions as channels through which the saving grace of God is met through the abiding presence of the Word of God and his Spirit. It asks how elements of "truth and grace" can be discovered in those traditions which give expression to such a mediation.

From God, Jesus Christ, and the economy of the Spirit, chapter 13 passes to the role of the Church, in relation to the Christ-event, in the economy of salvation. It asks about the role of the Church in relation to the Reign of God established by God in Jesus Christ and how in turn the members of the other religious traditions are related to the Reign of God. It shows that a regnocentric perspective, correctly understood, offers a broader horizon for a theology of religious pluralism than can be opened by an ecclesiocentric perspective, often narrowly conceived in the past.

Chapter 14 shows what place interreligious dialogue occupies in the evangelizing mission of the Church according to the recent teaching authority and how in a global vision of evangelization such dialogue relates to the proclamation of the Gospel of Jesus Christ. The chapter likewise illustrates the process of mutual enrichment which interreligious dialogue, mutual interaction, and common involvement in the problems of people and society can bring about between Christians and the members of other religious traditions.

A full round will thus have been made, starting with the discovery of an active presence of the Word of God throughout history (Jn 1:1–5, 9) and ending up with the recognition of the universal action of the Spirit of God in the world today, as Christians engage, together with the others, in promoting the Reign of God upon the earth. At the end of the journey, it will hopefully be possible to conclude that, far from placing the Christian faith in jeopardy, the more generous and broader perspective opened up by recent theological inquiry for a positive evaluation of the religious traditions of the world deepens that faith and helps to discover, with joy and thankfulness to God, the cosmic dimensions of the mystery of God's dealings with humankind. With Saint Paul we shall thus be able to confess with wonder "the breadth and the length and the height and depth" (Eph 3:18) of the mystery of God and of his Christ.

*Part I*

# An Overview
# of Christian Approaches
# to Religions

A CHRISTIAN THEOLOGY of religious pluralism cannot be construed a priori, or built on principles merely relying on present-day consciousness, without reference to the past twenty centuries of interaction between Christianity and the other religious traditions. The present, even if eventually in sharp contrast with the past, is never independent of it or entirely without link with it. Whatever discontinuity may exist between historical periods that succeed each other, there nevertheless always exists some organic continuity between them. The present is the outcome of the past, and whatever newness it may bring does not cancel its historical roots.

This goes to show that a historical overview of Christian attitudes toward the religious traditions which Christianity encountered through the centuries ought to serve as an indispensable background to the theological perception of these traditions and their relationship to Christianity that has emerged in recent years in the context of present religious pluralism. This first, historical part is devoted to such a historical account.

The historical overview is, however, intentionally limited in more than one way. To begin with, no study will be provided here of the historical events that have influenced the relationships of Christianity with other religions over the centuries: such as the official recognition of Christianity as the religion of the Roman Empire under Emperors Constantine and Theodosius; the movement for the Crusades in defense of the Holy Land, which during the Middle Ages so adversely influenced the relations between Christianity and Islam; the 1492 expulsion from Spain of Muslims and Jews who refused to be converted to Christianity; the colonization by European powers of the Americas, Asia, Oceania, and Africa; and the traumatic experience of the Shoah, or "Holocaust," designed this century by leaders from Christian nations as the "Final Solution" for the extermination of European Jews. All these events — and many others — constitute a contentious past history which has deeply affected the theological evaluation of other religions on the part of Christianity, and vice versa. In this study, however, this contentious past and the "dangerous memory" which it nourishes must be supposed rather than exposed. The theological evaluation of other religions on the part of the Christian Church must, no doubt, be viewed against the context of the concrete historical reality of each period; yet for an elaborate account of the historical context recourse will have to be had to works specifically dealing with the history of the interaction of Christianity and other religions over the centuries.[1] Our primary concern is the Christian theological evaluation of other religions rather than the concrete Church interaction with their members.

Another, no less consequential, limitation needs to be made clear from the outset. The present overview of Christian theological evaluations of world religions has no pretension — nor could it — to be in any way comprehensive. Comprehensiveness here would imply that all theological currents on the matter through twenty centuries of Christian theological thinking be reviewed and evaluated, including the theological presuppositions of the different schools as well as the personal thought of individual Fathers and theologians. Such an encyclopedic treatment of the subject, though not without interest in itself, is neither practicable nor desirable here. It seems more to the point and more useful to indicate the great currents of thought which have exercised a lasting influence on the Christian evaluation of other religions through the centuries; to show their historical origin, follow their genesis and development, and eventually trace their decline as other perspectives and new horizons opened up which rendered previous approaches obsolete. Our concern, therefore, is with the main models or paradigms which have developed through the Christian tradition and have served for a certain, more or less extended, period of time as the standard approach on the part of mainline Christianity — or a section thereof — to the question of a Christian evaluation of the other religions of the world.

The principal perspectives have already been noted rapidly in the general introduction to this study. These are often in sharp contrast with each other. Thus, after a precocious and short-lived second- and third-century "theology of history" there followed, by contrast, a negative stand founded on the adage "Outside the Church no salvation," which, though understood differently at different periods, will hold sway for centuries and become official teaching expressed in authoritative documents. The way in which models and paradigms succeed each other will have to be investigated as well as the reasons for which one takes over from another, henceforth considered obsolete. Various paradigms will thus stand out which over the centuries defined the Church's overall self-comprehension in relation to the other religious traditions which it encountered — often in contentious circumstances.

The models may be said to fall into four periods, not all of which covered the same length of time or met with the same widespread acceptance. However, "periods" are not understood here in the sense given to the term in history text-

---

1. For one such basic treatment, see Ries 1987.

books; it rather has a theological meaning. In a celebrated essay entitled "Basic Theological Interpretation of the Second Vatican Council," Karl Rahner has been able to identify — from a theological viewpoint — distinct periods in the Church's self-understanding which do not correspond to the classical periods of Church historians (Rahner 1981a). The formal object or point of view differs. Rahner's concern is to identify the main stages in the Church's growth toward a concrete awareness of being a "world Church." His contention is that Vatican II marks a breakthrough by way of a newly acquired and slowly developing consciousness of being such a "world Church." The council thus represents a "qualitative leap" in the Church's self-comprehension. In a similar way the "periods" which are distinguished here need not correspond to those dealt with by the history of theology; the intention is to point to the fundamental standpoints which Christian theology has adopted in its evaluation of the religious traditions it encountered through history.

Four fundamental attitudes can be distinguished. The first is a negative attitude, characterized by a disparaging evaluation of the other religions, symbolized by the adage "Outside the Church no salvation." The second is a guarded, partial acceptance and limited openness toward the other religions which, besides recognizing — with greater or lesser conviction — the possibility of salvation for their adherents, sees the religions themselves as the recipients of a "primordial" (natural) divine revelation which can be the source in their adherents of an innate desire for union with the Absolute. A third standpoint developed later and prevailed at the time of Vatican II. It recognized in the religious traditions themselves the existence of positive values which, however, are subject to different interpretations ranging from natural endowments to elements of truth and grace in some way conducive to the salvation of their members. A fourth perspective — that in which we find ourselves today — is characterized by a more positive approach to the religious traditions themselves. It asks what positive significance these traditions have in God's plan of salvation for humankind in the context of the universal value which Christian faith attributes to the Jesus Christ–event in the historical unfolding of that plan. Our historical part thus leads to a new problematic which part II, the synthetic and thematic part, will develop, hoping to contribute to what we have called a "Christian theology of religious pluralism."

To the four standpoints in dealing with the theological interpretation of religions, there correspond as many different problematics concerning their salvific significance. A first problematic is restricted to the question of the possibility of salvation for individual persons who lived outside the Christian dispensation, either before the Christ-event or outside the Christian fold after it. That stage questions the possibility that such persons may have had the faith in Jesus Christ without which there is no salvation.

A second problematic raises the question of possible substitutes for faith in Jesus Christ leading to salvation. The horizon remains that of the possibility of salvation for individual persons outside the Christian fold; but the concept of salvific faith is broadened to include a variety of substitutes — not all equally convincing — down to the "theology of death" of recent origin.

The third problematic recognizes that the religious traditions are not devoid of positive values, though the exact significance of these remains open to question. The problem then becomes the role which such values may or may not play in the salvation of the adherents of those traditions. The fundamental perspective still remains that of the modality in which salvation in Jesus Christ becomes available to persons outside the Christian fold.

Only the fourth model, which our own time has recently entered, goes beyond the question of individual salvation to resolutely inquire into the significance and value — in God's own design and in the unfolding of that design in history — of the religious traditions themselves. The problematic then becomes how to interpret the religious pluralism inscribed in the concrete reality of the present world. A theological hermeneutics must account for the plurality and variety of "ways" through which men and women of our own time seek — and find — a response to their aspirations for fuller life and integral liberation. On what foundation can it be maintained that the existence of a plurality of "ways" has in itself a positive significance? Is this to be assigned to the inexhaustible depth of the Divine Mystery and to the inherent limitations of every historical divine manifestation, or else to the ever-imperfect comprehension on the part of the human intellect of any divine manifestation? How, from the point of view of a Christian theology, does religious pluralism square, within God's plan for humankind, with the traditional Christian faith in the universal significance of God's self-manifestation and self-gift in Jesus Christ? The fourth problematic, as is clearly evident, puts the traditional understanding of the Christian faith in Jesus Christ under unprecedented strain and questioning. The second part of this work will have to meet this questioning and suggest avenues for a response.

# One

# The Religions of the Nations
# in the Bible

**A**T THE END of an elaborate survey entitled *The Biblical Foundations for Mission* (Senior and Stuhlmueller 1983, 345–47), Donald Senior and Carroll Stuhlmueller remark that "no comprehensive solution" is found in the Bible to the staggering question for the contemporary Church of Christianity's relationship to other religions. Among the "leads" that can be gathered in the Bible for a solution to the question, the authors mention the following elements: (1) The roots of biblical religion are deeply implanted in the religions and cultures surrounding Israel. (2) The sharp self-consciousness in Israel of its religious identity as God's chosen people resulted in negative judgments on other religious systems looked upon as worthless idolatry. (3) The same powerful sense of identity and authority often prompted in the New Testament equally negative evaluations of other religions, no validity being attributed to any religious "system" other than Judaism and Christianity. (4) The Bible's attitude to individual gentiles ran the whole spectrum from hostility to admiration, some biblical writers acknowledging a genuine religious experience in individual "pagans." (5) Some biblical writers, Paul among them, recognized the possibility of "natural religion," "whereby the true God could be detected in the order and beauty of his creation," but it remained inconceivable for a biblical writer to "express admiration for a full-blown cult or non-biblical religion."

The results are rather meager and reveal a prevalent negative attitude. However, taking note of the profound mutations which have come over our present world and of the consequent changes in problematic, the authors point to some biblical themes capable of orienting us toward a more positive evaluation of nonbiblical religions. To quote them:

> Many of the biblical themes we have discussed, such as the expansive nature of religious experience, the revelation of God in creation, the recognition of the gentiles' capacity to respond to the Gospel, and the awed awareness that God and his Spirit range far beyond the boundaries of human expectation, are some aspects of the biblical data that suggest positive links with non-Christian religions. (Senior and Stuhlmueller 1983, 346)

This goes to show that the biblical data on the religions of the gentiles are complex and need to be handled carefully. These data are often more implicit

29

than explicitly stated; they range over an extensive period of time with different situations leading to distinct evaluations and attitudes; they, moreover, are often ambivalent, not to say in apparent mutual contradiction among themselves. Special attention needs also to be given to the organic relationship between the Old and the New Testaments, to the continuity and discontinuity which obtain between them. The Christ-event, its interpretation by the Apostolic Church as witnessed to by the New Testament, and the ensuing self-understanding of the Apostolic Church itself notoriously influenced its evaluation of the religious traditions — first Jewish, and later Hellenistic — with which it found itself confronted.

In such a complex situation, our survey of biblical data concerning a theological evaluation of other religious traditions on the part of God's chosen people in the Old Testament, and of the Christian Church in the New, cannot claim to be in any way comprehensive. It must be satisfied to point to some specific elements — some of which have sometimes been inadequately attended to — capable of influencing, implicitly or explicitly, distinct theological evaluations of the religions of the "heathen" and of the "nations."

It must be squarely admitted that in the past the biblical data liable to found a negative evaluation, or even derogatory statements on nonbiblical religious traditions, have often been one-sidedly considered. Thus the Old Testament's unambiguous condemnation of idolatrous practices among the nations and the inanity, or even the inexistence, of the false gods they venerate have repeatedly been stressed, as they seemed to provide an unequivocal basis for a negative theological evaluation of the traditions concerned. The openly negative attitude which the Christian Church professed over many centuries toward the other religions, as well as the strongly guarded, though less intolerant, posture which it adopted in more recent times, naturally inclined theologians to lay heavy emphasis on the negative data.

In the new situation, however, which today's search for mutual comprehension and openness to dialogue have created, it seems fair for a theological account of the Bible's evaluation of the religions of the nations to allow such positive elements to stand out as are liable to provide in a new context a valid foundation for a more generous theological evaluation of the other religious traditions of the world. An attempt is made here to bring forward some of the biblical data capable of providing a valid basis for such a positive evaluation. The account does not claim to be exhaustive. It does not intend to draw a complete picture, much less to follow the stages of a historical development. It proceeds by slices of history, pointing to some currents of thought — often in tension with contrary tides — which remain open-ended, allowing for further positive developments.[1]

---

1. Works explicitly treating the Bible's evaluation of the surrounding religions remain few. Several articles by P. Rossano can be usefully consulted. Among these are: Rossano 1967a, 1967b, 1968, 1972, 1981. Several relevant essays are gathered in Rossano 1993. For the bibliography of Rossano, see Penna, ed., 1993, 12–18.

# I. Israel and the Nations

## A. God's "Cosmic Covenant" with Humankind

In regard to divine covenants with humankind, the Christian reader of the Bible is primarily struck by the personal interventions of God first in the story of Abraham and later of Moses. In both cases the Bible makes explicit use of "covenant" terminology, in the theological sense which the term *berith* has throughout the revealed book, referring to the free, gratuitous, personal, salvific intervention of God in the history of a people (see "Diathèkè" 1966). The story of Abraham, of his vocation on the part of God, of his unswerving faith in the fulfillment of God's promises, culminates with the striking of a covenant which God establishes with the patriarch (Gen 15:17–21; 17:1–14). In similar fashion, the striking of the covenant by God with his chosen people is the high point of the biblical account of Moses' story. Moses' vocation and mission, God's revelation of his name to his servant, and the long story of God's deliverance of his people from the slavery of Egypt through the Exodus-event — all culminate with the covenant struck by God through Moses with Israel which establishes Israel as God's chosen people (Ex 24:1–11).

The covenant struck by God with the patriarch Abraham was already oriented toward that of God with Moses which constitutes Israel as God's specially chosen people. Indeed, the covenant creates the identity of Israel as the people of God. There one finds the foundation of Israel's religious experience, the starting point of a dialogue with God in a history of salvation. "I will be your God and you shall be my people" (Lev 26:12): such is the theological meaning of the covenant. The religious awareness that a covenant has been struck between Yahweh and Israel is really the consciousness that God and his people now belong together in a community of life. Israel's theology views the covenant at the heart of its religious life. Yahweh stands before Israel as a partner in dialogue. The awareness of the personal irruption of God into the history of his people served in Israel as the point of departure for a reflection on the identity of Yahweh. He who had intervened so powerfully in their history, who vowed to be with them (Ex 3:13–15), who worked wonderful deeds (*mirabilia Dei*) for their liberation, leading them to the promised land, must also have been in the first place he who made the world and the things it contains. Thus, by way of retrojection, Israel, starting from its experience as the covenanted people of God, discovered the transcendence of God the Creator who made all things (Gen 1–2).[2]

Israel's history was a history of salvation; one might even think that it initiated salvation history. But it did not conclude it. Already the prophets, Jeremiah in particular, announced a new covenant which God was to make with Israel:

---

2. The vast subject of the rootedness of biblical religion in the surrounding religions and cultures cannot be touched upon here. For some indications, see besides the works of P. Rossano mentioned in n. 1, Cazelles 1981 and Commission Biblique Pontificale 1981. On "inculturation" in the New Testament, see Vanhoye 1984; Soares-Prabhu 1976.

"Behold, the days are coming, says the Lord, when I will make a new covenant with the house of Israel" (Jer 31:31–34). Whatever may have been the understanding in Israel of God's new covenant with his people — the return from exile and the rebuilding of the temple — the New Testament testifies to the initiation by God of the "new covenant" in Jesus Christ (see Lk 22:20; 1 Cor 11:25; 2 Cor 3:6; Heb 8:8; 9:15; etc.). The "new covenant," however, is broader than the first; henceforth the one "people of God" expands, extending as it does to the "gentiles" or "nations," indeed, to the whole of humankind (see Dupont 1989). One would be inclined to conclude that the two covenants, the "first" and the "new," make up the whole history of salvation brought about by God.

Yet it is not so, and the Old Testament testifies to the use of covenant terminology before God's covenant with Abraham and Moses. In the Book of Genesis, the Abraham cycle begins with chapter 12. It is preceded by two previous cycles: that of Adam (Gen 1–5) and that of Noah (Gen 6–9). The Genesis account of Adam's creation does not speak of a covenant relationship between God and the first human being he created, but it does testify to the intimate personal dealings of the Creator with Adam, the father of the human race. These relations — as the Fathers of the Church well understood — are symbolic of a first universal covenant with the human race. Such interpretation is not, moreover, without foundation in the Bible: Sir 17:12 speaks of the "eternal covenant" established by God with the first parents; Jer 33:20–26 and Ps 89 make reference to a "cosmic covenant" through creation.[3]

The first time that the Priestly writer uses covenant terminology is in the Noah cycle (Gen 9) (see Murray 1992, 32–39, 173). This covenant had already been announced before the flood (Gen 6:18) to Noah, "a righteous man, blameless in his generation, . . . [who] walked with God" (Gen 6:9). It is struck by God through Noah with all creation (Gen 9:1–17). The sign of this "everlasting covenant" (Gen 9:16) between God and the earth is the rainbow,[4] symbol of the persistence of the cosmic order, of a new world order that cancels out the destruction of the flood. How is the covenant with Noah to be understood, and what is its theological significance?

It is a question of a "cosmic covenant"; but the permanence which it promises is due not to natural laws but to the fidelity (*èmèt*) of the living God. It is part not of a natural history but of a history of salvation. For Israel the fidelity of God in the cosmic order is the guarantee of his fidelity in the historical order. So too will the cosmic covenant be understood by Paul when he will speak of a lasting revelation of God through the cosmos, directed to all people. Jean Daniélou comments:

---

3. See Murray 1992, 1–13. See esp. p. 16: "Covenant language has not been used in the context of creation. Outside Genesis, however, hints remain which suggest that there existed a covenantal idea of cosmic order, disturbance of which could be thought of as a break of covenant."

4. The sign of the covenant with Abraham will be circumcision; that of the covenant with Moses, the Law to be observed by the people.

Cosmic religion is not natural religion in the sense of being outside the concrete historical supernatural order....It is natural only in the sense that the unique God comes to be known through his action in the cosmos and his appeal to conscience. The cosmic covenant is already a covenant of grace. But it remains imperfect inasmuch as God reveals himself only through the cosmos. (Daniélou 1956, 28–29)

He adds: "The cosmic covenant is already a supernatural covenant. It does not belong to a different order than does the mosaic covenant or the Christic covenant" (Daniélou 1956, 33). In conclusion, Daniélou writes:

The living God has never ceased to manifest himself to human beings, his creatures....Before manifesting himself to Abraham and Moses, he had manifested himself to...Noah, that is to say to the nations. This revelation remained, no doubt, obscure. It pertained, however, to what constitutes the proper object of revelation, viz. the saving action of God in the world. (Daniélou 1956, 37; see also Dupuis 1991b, 131; Thils 1966, 67–79)

We in turn may conclude: the covenant with Noah is not to be understood as simply guaranteeing a knowledge of God through the elements of nature. It deals with a personal, universal intervention on the part of God in the history of the nations, previous to the subsequent covenant with the chosen people. The religious traditions of humanity are the chosen testimonials of this covenant with the nations.

One understands then how the Fathers of the Church spoke not of two covenants, through Abraham-Moses and Jesus Christ, but of four, beginning with the covenants with Adam and Noah. They perceived that the history of salvation is not limited to a chosen people but extends to all humankind and human history. Thus Irenaeus wrote:

Four covenants were given to the human race: one, prior to the deluge, under Adam; the second, that after the Deluge, under Noah; the third, the giving of the Law, under Moses; the fourth, that which renovates the human being, and sums up all things in itself by means of the Gospel, raising and bearing human beings upon its wings into the heavenly Kingdom.[5]

In a somewhat analogous manner the Fathers of the Church distinguished different "ages" of the world designed by the divine pedagogy. The different

---

5. Irenaeus, *Adversus Haereses*, III, 11, 8 (The Ante-Nicene Fathers [ANF], vol. 1, ed. A. Cleveland Coxe [Grand Rapids, Mich.: Eerdmans, 1977], 429). See *Demonstration of Aphraates*, 11, 11: "The Law and the covenant have been completely transformed. God transformed the first covenant, granted to Adam, and gave another to Noah; yet another to Abraham, which he transformed in order to give another to Moses. And as the Mosaic covenant was not observed, he gave another, in these latter days, which is not to be transformed....All of these covenants were different from one another." See *Patrologia Syriaca*, I, 1, pp. 498–502. On the relationship between the various covenants, see Dupuis 1991b, 119.

ages are the progressive phases, organically connected, of one and the same history of salvation.[6]

## B. *The Pagan Saints of the Old Testament*

A search in the Jewish Bible for data capable of lending support to a positive evaluation of the religiosity of the nations ought to distinguish clearly two different questions. The first concerns the personal life of individuals who lived outside the dispensation of God's chosen people; the other inquires about the intrinsic value of the religions of the nations to which these individuals belonged. The first is the question of the "pagan saints of the Old Testament"; the other, the Old Testament theology of the religions of the nations based on God's cosmic covenant. We are concerned here with the first question, leaving the other to be examined later.

A second distinction ought to be made. Among the pagan saints of the Old Testament, some are understood to have preceded in time the Israelite dispensation initiated by God's covenant with Abraham and Moses; others are contemporary to the Jewish dispensation, though finding themselves outside it. Among the first group are Abel, Enoch, and Noah, who characteristically are set forward — before Abraham — in a celebrated passage of the Letter to the Hebrews (Heb 11:4–7), as models of the faith "without [which] it is impossible to please [God]" (Heb 11:6).

In each case it is faith that made the "pagan saints" righteous before God. The Letter to the Hebrews thus testifies that saving faith was possible outside the Jewish dispensation, even before it. Before God manifested himself to Abraham and Moses, he had done so to the nations. However obscure this divine manifestation may have been, it concerned God's salvific action in the world. The Bible does not tell us how many pagan saints responded positively to the divine revelation. It is satisfied to tell us that some did and to set them as models of faith for the people in the Old and New Dispensation who would emulate their faith. That some of the pagan saints represent mythical rather than historical figures (Job, Melchizedek) does not stand up against the revealed message which is being conveyed: the faith of Israel — and of the Apostolic Church — held that pagan faith and holiness before God were possible and were indeed realities. How this faith was manifested and expressed must be examined for each case in particular.[7]

**1. Saints of the Nations before Israel.** "By faith *Abel* offered to God a more acceptable sacrifice than Cain, through which he received approval as righteous" (Heb 11:4). Abel inaugurates the line of the saints of the cosmic covenant; he is presented by the Bible as the first pagan saint (Daniélou 1956,

---

6. See Luneau 1964; for Irenaeus, see 96–102; see also Houssiau 1955.
7. The following analysis of the pagan saints relies much on Daniélou 1956.

9–54). His righteousness before God is a matter of election: "Abel is not chosen because he is just; he is just because he is chosen.... Abel is the first of the elect, chosen by God, at the beginning of history, in the midst of the pagan world, to be the first recipient of the liberality of love" (Daniélou 1956, 47–48). He is also the first martyr (see Mt 23:34–35), whose spilt blood prefigures the sacrifice of Christ (see Heb 12:24).

"By faith *Enoch* was taken up so that he should not see death.... Now before he was taken he was attested as having pleased God. And without faith it is impossible to please him" (Heb 11:5–6). The Old Testament witnesses to Enoch's familiarity with God: "Enoch walked with God" (Gen 5:22); "Enoch pleased the Lord...; he was an example of repentance to all generations" (Sir 44:16). The Letter to the Hebrews explains the content of the faith of Enoch that made him pleasing to God: "For whoever would draw near to God must believe that he exists and that he rewards those who seek him" (Heb 11:6) — a text, J. Daniélou comments, which "is perhaps the most important in the Scriptures on the religious situation of the pagan world" (Daniélou 1956, 59). The saving faith of pagans is faith in the covenant of the living God with the nations. This faith implies believing in a personal God who intervenes in human affairs through his providence and remunerates people for their righteousness. With such faith Enoch appears as the prototype of the salvation of the pagans; he is the prophet of cosmic religion (Jude 14).

"By faith *Noah*, being warned by God concerning events as yet unseen, took heed and constructed an ark for the saving of his household; by this he condemned the world and became an heir of the righteousness which comes from faith" (Heb 11:7). The Bible witnesses repeatedly to Noah's holiness: "Noah found favor in the eyes of the Lord" (Gen 6:8); he "walked with God" (Gen 6:9). Wisdom mentions his justice (Wis 10:3). For Ben Sirach "Noah was found perfect and righteous" (Sir 44:17). Ezekiel numbers him among the elect (Ez 14:14). The Letter to the Hebrews celebrates his fear of the Lord (Heb 11:7). But it is Noah's faith that the New Testament exalts above all. Heb 11:7 explains what characterizes Noah's faith: on God's testimony he believed events yet unseen (as Abraham did later, when "he went out, not knowing where he was to go" [Heb 11:8]). The deluge showed Noah's faith to be right. Jesus himself praises Noah for obeying God's word regarding God's impending judgment in the midst of the people's incredulity (see Mt 24:37–39); in the time of "God's patience," adds 1 Peter, which was designed to allow people the chance to repent (1 Pet 3:20). Noah is also "herald of righteousness" (2 Pet 2:5), a prophet who announces God's judgment to the nations and calls them to repentance. Noah escaped God's judgment of the nations through his righteousness and by his faith "condemned the world" (Heb 11:7). He typifies the person who is saved. Thus he became also the instrument of the world's salvation (Sir 44:16–17); the "remnant" which is saved from God's judgment is the principle of a new humanity. Thereby Noah prefigures Christ.

Against this background God's *covenant* with Noah — of which Genesis speaks — takes on its full significance. "The covenant with Noah corresponds to cosmic religion and bears essentially on God's fidelity in the world order" (Daniélou 1956, 100). It is a covenant with the whole of humankind and with the cosmos itself (Gen 9:10), an "everlasting" and irrevocable covenant (Gen 9:16) which manifests God's fidelity to his creation, of which the rainbow appears as the sacramental sign (Gen 9:12–15).

**2. Saints of the Nations Foreign to Israel.**   The Book of Job presents *Job* as a model of the justice and piety of cosmic religion: that is, in the order of the cosmic covenant. "That man was blameless and upright, one who feared God and turned away from evil" (Job 1:1); he is clothed with righteousness (see Job 29:14). He is filled with riches and honor, as a witness given by God to his virtue. But is he sincere in his virtue or complacent in his righteousness? It is on this that Job will be put to the test. The theme of the Book of Job is the test of righteousness. Having had blessings heaped upon him, Job finds himself destitute. The friends who had seen in his success the blessing of God now see in his downfall God's condemnation. But the trial does not shake Job's justice; he persists in his integrity. His faithfulness in the midst of misfortune proves his integrity in the abundance of God's blessings. Job's case shows that true righteousness is possible in the order of the cosmic covenant.

The Book of Job inquires into the meaning of suffering in a pre-Mosaic context, in the order of cosmic revelation. The suffering of the righteous is devoid of all rational explanation, but it frees his justice from all self-deception. Job does not accuse God of his suffering; God remains just, no matter how much the righteous may suffer. His destitution brings him to the realization that everything is on God's part a gratuitous gift, to which the human being can claim no right. God's freedom is sovereign. One can only confess the mystery of God's almighty power and his supreme freedom in creation, committing oneself in faith and adoration. Such is, in the cosmic order, the climax of holiness to which one may reach.

*Melchizedek* ranks among the most eminent non-Jewish figures of the Old Testament. Genesis describes him as "priest of God Most High," blessing Abram: "And Melchizedek king of Salem brought out bread and wine; he was priest of God Most High. And he blessed him and said: 'Blessed be Abram by God Most High, maker of heaven and earth; and blessed be God Most High, who has delivered your enemies into your hand' " (Gen 14:18–20). Psalm 109 (110) sees him as a model of the "eternal priest": "You are a priest forever after the order of Melchizedek" (Ps 110 [109]:4). The Letter to the Hebrews devotes much space to him: Christians exalt in him the type of Christ the Priest. "Melchizedek is the high priest of the cosmic religion. He gathers in himself all the religious wealth of sacrifices offered from the beginning of the world till Abraham and attests that they were acceptable to God" (Daniélou 1956, 130). He knows God the Creator (*El*). Of the first religion of humankind which extends to all people, he is the priest who offers the pure oblation of bread and wine, the thanksgiving sacrifice. He is sent by God to Abraham, from whom he received the tithe to serve for the divine cult (Gen 14:20). Abraham, the initiator of a new and higher covenant, pays homage to the lawfulness of the earlier covenant celebrated by its high priest. He is the perfect example of the basic need of humankind to express in sacrifice its dependence upon God; in this he is at the same time the type of him who will be the eternal High Priest. The Letter to the Hebrews will see realized in Christ, the eternal High Priest, what the Psalmist had foretold: "You are a priest forever after the order of Melchizedek" (Heb 7:17; see Ps 110 [109]:4). Melchizedek is thus in the cosmic religion the type of Christ (Heb 7:1–3), who will assume and bring to perfection all sacrifices in his eternal offering (Heb 9:11).

Other saintly figures outside Abraham's descent would have to be recalled, such as *Lot,* another model of the just according to the law inscribed by God in people's heart (see Rom 2:12); or again the *Queen of Saba,* another saint of the cosmic religion, who "came from the ends of the earth to hear the Wisdom of Solomon" (Mt 12:42; see 1 Kings 10:1–13). Having adored the true God revealed to her through conscience, she greeted in Solomon a more perfect revelation.[8]

Daniélou sums up as follows the cosmic religion typified in the pagan saints of the Old Testament:

> Holiness in the order of cosmic religion consists in responding to God's call through conscience. It is true holiness. For the Bible there exists no profane morality.... Only the will of a person who deserves absolute homage can make absolute claims. To obey the moral law is to recognize God's infinitely loving will; it is to love God. Moral life is already worship. This is why conscience is a revelation of God and there exists no a-religious morality. (Daniélou 1956, 166)

## C. The God of Israel and the Gods of the Nations

Old Testament monotheism is based not on rational considerations seeking an explanation of the world but on Israel's experience of Yahweh's saving deeds. Yahweh intervened in the history of his people by his own free choice. Karl Rahner writes:

> First comes the experience of God as a free person...; and it is only from this historical experience of *who* Yahweh is that it becomes progressively clear *what* he is; [Yahweh is not] *a* God, not just *a* powerful Lord in the history of perhaps this people alone, but the *Lord* of history of all peoples..., the transcendent spiritual cause of all reality.... The basic form of Old Testament monotheism is not: "One God exists" (there is

---

8. On Lot and the Queen of Saba, see Daniélou 1956, 139–57. On the pagan king Daniel whom Ez 14:12–20 associates with Noah and Job as a just man, see Daniélou 1956, 73–84.

a single primary cause of the world); but: "Yahweh is the unique God."
(Rahner 1961c, 93–94)

This thought process is well marked in Ps 114–115, which forms one unit:
from the consideration of Yahweh's marvelous deeds for the salvation of Israel
the Psalmist's mind ascends to the exaltation of him who wrought them.

The theological formulation of Israel's monotheistic faith is found in the
Shema Israel: "Hear, O Israel: The Lord our God is one Lord; and you shall
love the Lord your God with all your heart, and with all your soul, and with
all your might" (Deut 6:4; see Mt 12:29). This clear monotheistic faith is not,
however, the original form of Hebrew belief; rather it is the culmination of a
lengthy development, involving a protracted religious crisis. The monotheistic
faith of Israel has developed progressively and has known fluctuations.

From its initial stage Israel's monotheistic faith implies that *for Israel* there is
no other object of worship beside Yahweh: Yahweh alone is the God who made
a covenant with Israel, through which he has acquired over Israel an exclusive
right. "Monolatry" thus characterizes Israel's faith from the start; all "henothe-
ism" is excluded from it. "You shall have no other gods before me" (Ex 20:3);
for Yahweh is a "jealous God" (Ex 34:14). The exclusive right of Yahweh over
his people and his overwhelming superiority over other gods, in power as well
as in loving-kindness (*hèsèd*), do not, however, prevent the recognition of other
gods to whom other nations are committed. Only, these can in no way compete with Yahweh, and Israel can have no recourse to them: "Who is like thee,
O Lord, among the gods? Who is like thee, majestic in holiness, terrible in glo-
rious deeds, doing wonders?" (Ex 15:11); "For the Lord is a great God, and a
great King above all gods" (Ps 95:3).

However, Yahweh's universal power extending to the whole earth, though
affirmed by Moses (Ex 19:5), takes long to penetrate deeply into the consciousness of Israel; only after a period of temptation and struggle will strict
monotheism be strongly implanted in the faith of the people, in the post-
exilic period. Israel has been tempted to worship "foreign gods," especially
the Canaanite Baal. The period from the entry of Israel into Canaan until
the Exile has known several setbacks in the monotheistic faith of the people
and the danger of syncretism. Ezekiel 8 and 2 Kings 21–23 testify to the
fact that the temple of Jerusalem had become the abode of many idols. The
prophets' mission consisted, in part, in combating all idolatrous tendencies
as alien to the Hebrew tradition and ethos (see Isaiah, Jeremiah, Ezekiel).
The prophets call to mind the demands made on the people by the covenant
relationship entered into with them by Yahweh. The prophetic reaction includes disparaging statements concerning the alleged gods of other nations.
The nothingness of idols is stressed by the prophets (see Amos 5:26; Hos 8:4–
8; Jer 2:26–28; 3:6–13; 10:1–16; etc.). The prophets' critique will go a long
way in bringing about faith in the universality of Yahweh's power and its
exclusive claim.

The monotheistic faith will emerge from the trial of the Exile, strengthened and purified. Deuteronomy 6:4 represents that pure monotheistic faith. It no longer consists of mere "monolatry." Other gods are henceforth denied existence; they simply are not: "That you might know that the Lord is God; there is no other beside him" (Deut 4:35; see 4:39; 32:39; etc.). Faith stresses Yahweh's jealousy based on his covenantal love (Deut 5:9–10). According to the theologian of Deutero-Isaiah (40–55), Israel's monotheistic faith imposes upon it a missionary vocation: Israel must preach Yahweh's exclusive dominion, the nonexistence of other gods. Isaiah 41:21–23 challenges the other gods to prove their existence; Is 44:9–20 is a satire on idolatry. Characteristic in this regard is Ps 115:3–8 where dead idols are compared with the living God (see also Deut 4:28):

> Our God is in the heavens; he does whatever he pleases. Their idols are silver and gold, the work of human hands. They have mouths, but they do not speak; eyes but they do not see. They have ears, but they do not hear; noses, but they do not smell. They have hands, but they do not feel; feet, but they do not walk; and they do not make a sound in their throat. Those who make them, are like them; so are all who trust in them.

Gods made by human hands are naught. In Deutero-Isaiah monotheistic formulas recur as catchwords: Is 43:10–11; 44:6–9; 45:6, 14–15, 18–22, and so on. Never before in the Bible had monotheism been formulated so explicitly.

It is against this background that one must ask how Israel valued the divine cult of the nations. Condemnations abound, for the idols of which the Bible speaks — to whom Israel had been tempted to surrender itself — were those it encountered mostly during the Exile. Deutero-Isaiah and Wis 13–15 are here exemplary.[9] Yet Israel also knows that not all people among the nations are idolatrous. Some have recognized the living God who manifested himself through the cosmic covenant. The case of the pagan saints of the Old Testament is here emblematic. Yet, however exemplary those may be, they are not isolated cases. Cyrus, for example, the pagan conqueror who came from Persia, is the "shepherd," the "anointed" of God who will accomplish God's desires (Is 44:28–45:1). Remarkable too is the conversion of Nineveh, a pagan city accursed by the prophets, whose people, in response to Jonah's call, turned in repentance and worship to the God of Israel under the common name of Elohim (Jon 3:1–10). Jonah's short book develops a theology of God's pardon conditioned by a change of heart on the invitation of the prophet of Anathoth. It is a striking witness to the universality of God's love and pardon extending to other peoples (see Feuillet 1949b, cols. 1104–31; Magonet 1992, 936–42).

The Old Testament does not tell us how many among the nations have recognized the living God. What it says is that all are called to it. Israel's vocation is to announce the living God to all the nations. The "Psalms of the Reign"

---

9. For the critique of idols in Wisdom, see Gilbert 1973.

(47; 93; 97; 98; 99) praise God in his universal royalty and invite the nations to share in his praise (see Legrand 1988, 30–32). The Book of Consolation in Deutero-Isaiah goes beyond that: all the nations, from "the end of the earth," are invited to "sing to the Lord a new song" (Is 42:10–12); the history of the nations is seen as part of the universal dominion of the Creator. All peoples are called upon to acknowledge that the God of Israel is the only God and there is no other (Is 45:14). The perspective is that of the universality of salvation. All the nations will walk in the light of God's glory.

In particular, the Servant of Yahweh will be "a covenant to the people, a light to the nations" (Is 42:6; 49:8). But his mission is not to lead a campaign for the salvation of the pagans; it consists in the witness given "before the eyes of all the nations" by God's deeds to save his people (Is 52:10). Lucien Legrand writes:

> The "Light of the Nations" . . . is the power of God manifesting itself to the entire world through Israel. It has two specific characteristics. Firstly, it is directly a *divine action:* God manifests his glory under the eyes of the nations by saving his people. Secondly, this action is directed *in the first place to the people of Israel,* and to other peoples through it. . . . Reference to the election is as clear as the call to the nations. (Legrand 1988, 36)

This is also how the texts on the "eschatological gathering of the nations" around the Lord (Is 60:1–20; see 2:2–5) need to be understood.

The awareness of the election on which Israel's identity is based and its vocation toward the nations raises the question of the universalism versus the particularism of the Old Testament. Donald Senior and Carroll Stuhlmueller see this as a dialectic of "centripetal" and "centrifugal" elements competing with each other, with the doctrine of election prevailing over the call to the nations. The call to the nations keeps an ethnocentric perspective: gentiles could become Jews and thus share in Israel's privileged status. Distinct elements are present: the universal sovereignty of God over all peoples and all history and a projection of future history in which the nations would form one elect people with Israel in acclaiming God. Yet these elements did not coalesce; intuitions of a collegial role for the nations remained on the periphery (Senior and Stuhlmueller 1983, 315–18). It is "with the figure of Jesus [that] the centrifugal forces surging within the Scriptures break out into the non-Jewish world" (Senior and Stuhlmueller 1983, 321).

Legrand is more positive. The term "particularism," though often used, is totally inadequate to account for the thought of the Old Testament. The God of Israel does not limit his action to the one people of Israel; he is the Lord of universal history. The Old Testament manifests a universalism where everything is placed under God's providence.[10] Far from leading to particularism, the sense of election calls in Israel for a universal vision of God's plan; Israel's attitude to

---

10. Legrand 1988, 22–29. He refers to Westermann 1982, 41–44, 51–59.

the nations is characterized by a universal humanist interest. The election does not cut off Israel from the nations; it situates it in relation to them.

Legrand prefers therefore to distinguish a "centralized universalism" and a "decentralized universalism" (Legrand 1988, 36–44; see also Feuillet 1949a, cols. 706–10, 726–27). It is true that the first often prevails: conversion of the nations to Yahweh consists concretely of turning to Israel (Is 2:1–5). But a certain decentralized universalism appears in the oracle on Egypt of Is 19:19–22, in which the cult of Yahweh is decentralized: "And the Lord will make himself known to the Egyptians; and the Egyptians will know the Lord in that day and worship with sacrifice and burnt offering, and they will make vows to the Lord and perform them" (Is 19:21). Yet, while Egypt becomes "people of God," Israel remains "the Lord's heritage" (Is 19:25). What about the oracle of Mal 1:11: "From the rising of the sun to its setting my name is great among the nations, and in every place incense is offered to my name, and a pure offering, for my name is great among the nations, says the Lord of hosts"? It throws a new light on the religions of the surrounding world, though any openness toward them still remains focused on Jerusalem. However, the Wisdom tradition witnesses to a "decentralized universalism" in the case of Job, the pagan saint who has met God: "I had heard of thee by the hearing of the ear, but now my eye sees thee" (Job 42:5). And if "the problem of Job is a universal problem," "the divine answer has also universal value" (Legrand 1988, 41).

Legrand concludes that universalism is an "integral dimension" of the entire Old Testament, not opposed but complementary to the election. The double polarity of the election of a people and its openness to the nations reflects the plan of God for humankind: election and universalism call for each other (Legrand 1988, 43). We in turn may conclude as follows: throughout its history Israel is vividly aware of the danger that threatens every people of turning upon itself in adoring false gods of its own making — a danger which Israel has experienced in its own flesh; it also knows that all peoples are called by the living God to worship him who alone is. Israel's own vocation consists in witnessing to this universal call.

## D. A Universal Economy: Word, Wisdom, and Spirit

Against a long-standing theological tradition according to which God was revealed as one in the Old Testament and as triune in the New, it must be said that the Father was revealed in Yahweh's dealings with his people, the Son in Jesus Christ, and the Spirit in Pentecost, which begins the "time of the Church" — better called the time of the growth of the Reign of God unto its eschatological fullness (Rahner 1961c). Thus Gregory of Nazianzus wrote in the fourth century:

> The Old Testament proclaimed the Father quite clearly, and the Son only dimly. The New Testament revealed the Son and allowed us to glimpse the

divinity of the Spirit. Now the Spirit dwells among us and shows himself
more clearly. When the divinity of the Father was not yet recognized it
would not have been prudent openly to proclaim the Son; and when the
divinity of the Son was not yet admitted it would not have been fair to
impose — I dare to put it like that — a new burden on people by talking
to them about the Holy Spirit. Otherwise, like people . . . who have stared
at the sun's light with eyes still weak from illness, they would have run the
risk of losing the strength they had already gained. It was necessary therefore to work toward perfection by stages, by an "upward journey," to use
David's phrase; it was necessary to go forward by way of successive clarifi-
cation, by increasingly enlightening improvements and advances, in order
to see the light of the Trinity shine out at last. (Gregory of Nazianzus, *Fifth
Theological Discourse* 26; PG 36:161–64)

This is not to say that the Old Testament did not know about the "Word of
God" (who would become incarnate in Jesus Christ) or the "Spirit" (who in the
New Testament became a "person" distinct from the Father and the Son). However, neither the Word nor the Spirit — any more than the Wisdom of God —
represented divine persons distinct from Yahweh; they rather stood for dynamic
expressions of Yahweh's manifestation in human history. Nor do they cover
tightly distinct spheres of God's action. For God's speech and his deeds are intimately connected; the biblical categories unite them closely. Yahweh does not
only speak through his Word, but acts; the Word of God is essentially efficacious and creative. Similarly, the Spirit is the agent not merely of prophetic
inspiration but of divine action as well (G. E. Wright 1960). Not rarely the
Word overlaps with the Spirit, or Wisdom is associated with the Spirit (see Wis
7:6); as for God's Word and Wisdom, they often figure in parallel, showing a
tendency to identification (see Ps 111; Sir 24:1–3, 9, 23; Wis 9:1–2).

While none of the three dynamic attributes of God is conceived as a distinct
person, they are nonetheless, in virtue of their dynamic character, given a "literary personification" — not as intermediaries between God and the world but as
referring to God insofar as he manifests himself in the world and history. That
God does reveal himself in the history of Israel need not be shown. From the
standpoint of an Old Testament positive approach to the religions of the nations, the question is whether God, through the Word-Wisdom-Spirit, manifests
himself in deeds and words beyond the boundaries of Israel. While a universal
action of the Spirit is less apparent in the Old Testament, the Word of God, and
even more so the Wisdom of God, are clearly gratified with a universal efficacy.
This will be shown below.

   **1. The Word of God.** The Word of God (*Dabar*) (see "Logos" 1967) manifests the divine Law (Ex 20:1–17; Deut 5:6–22); it also interprets the meaning
of Yahweh's historical interventions (Ex 20:2). As a dynamic reality, the Word
of God is infallibly efficacious of God's designs. Whether these refer to histori-

cal interventions or to God's cosmic action, the Word once uttered necessarily accomplishes what is contained in it: "My Word that goes forth from my mouth...shall not return to me empty, but it shall accomplish that which I purpose, and prosper in the things for which I sent it" (Is 55:11). The Old Testament applies the efficacy of the Word of God primarily to God's intervention in the history of Israel: the saving events are the "confirmation of his Word" (see Deut 9:5). In retrospect, however, the efficacy of the Word is applied to God's creation: "God said... " (Gen 1:3ff.; see Ps 33:6–9; 107:20). It thus takes on a universal significance which will recur in the New Testament (Jn 1:1–3).

The Word is conceived as a distinct reality charged with power; it is not, however, distinct from Yahweh, except as the dynamic expression of God and God's self-manifestation throughout salvation history, in deeds and words. It is God turning to human beings to reveal himself, God calling human beings to a communion of life. This, as Genesis testifies, is the universal call of humankind.

**2. The Wisdom of God.** God who alone is wise communicates God's wisdom to people. Old Testament Wisdom literature dwells on divine Wisdom (*Hokmah*) (see "Sophia" 1971; *La Sagesse biblique* 1995) as the origin of all wisdom. We should especially note Prov 8, Sir 24, and Wis 6–13. Wisdom was "created" by Yahweh "before all things," "at the beginning of God's work, the first of God's acts of old..., before the beginning of the earth" (Prov 8:22–26; Sir 1:1–9). The Lord "poured her out upon all God's works" (Sir 1:9). She was present when God's purpose of creation first unfolded (Prov 8:27–29): "I was beside him, like a master workman; and I was daily his delight, rejoicing before him always, rejoicing in his inhabited world and delighting in the sons of men" (Prov 8:30–31), teaching them and instructing them to be wise (Prov 8:32–36). The Book of Wisdom describes her as "the breath of the power of God, and a pure emanation of the glory of the Almighty" (Wis 7:25).

Like the Word, Wisdom is an essentially dynamic reality, closely associated with all the works of God in the world. God has shaped in her the plan of his work; through her God brings it to realization. She was by God's side in the act of creation (Prov 8:27–31). Throughout the unfolding of salvation history she is sent by God on mission. "While remaining in herself, she renews all things; in every generation she passes into holy souls and makes them friends of God and prophets" (Wis 7:27). She is the dispenser of all goodness and of God's friendship (Wis 7:14; 8); the source of right and perfect conduct who teaches fear of God and justice (Prov 3:7; 8:13; Sir 17:14); the source of salvation for those who welcome her (Wis 6:19–20, 24). She is life for the person who finds her (Prov 8:35). She makes herself familiar with people to teach them (Prov 8:32–36). She presided over the destinies of humankind from the start: "Wisdom protected the first formed father of the world, when he alone had been created," being at work from Adam to Moses (Wis 10:1–24). Having "come forth from the mouth of the Most High" (Sir 24:3), she takes possession of every people and nation (Sir 24:6), seeking among them a resting place (Sir

24:7). She likewise presides over the destiny of the chosen people (Wis 10:15–11:3; Bar 3:9–4:3). She "pitches her tent" in Israel to exercise her ministry there (Sir 24:8–12), calling people who seek her (Sir 24:19) and filling them with wisdom (Sir 24:25).

Wisdom is thus spoken of as a person in the same manner as the Word of God. She is seen as a popular preacher standing at the crossroads, calling passersby, inviting them to enter her house, to sit at her table and profit by her lessons (Prov 9:1–12). She looks after her children like a mother, providing them with God's blessings (Sir 4:11–15). The personification of Wisdom stands out clearly in Proverbs (1–9) and Ben Sirach (1–6; 24); it is further accentuated in the Book of Wisdom (6–9): Wisdom is all-powerful as is God himself; she is God's associate in all God's works, and God's counselor; she sits on a throne by the side of Yahweh (Wis 9:4) and is presented as the spouse of Yahweh (Wis 8:3).

Yet the personification, as was the case with the Word, is a literary device. Wisdom emanates from Yahweh as Yahweh's radiance and Yahweh's image (Wis 7:25–26). She represents God's self-manifestation, standing for the beauty, order, and wisdom of the divine plan that unfolds in the history of salvation as a reflection of the harmony that exists in God's self. In the last analysis, the Wisdom of Yahweh is Yahweh relating to human beings, in works and self-manifestation, and directing the destinies of the chosen people. Her action in Israel is a privileged one, but by no means exclusive. She is universally present in humankind and history. The Word of the Old Testament, as we have observed, recurs in the New by way of a Word-Christology; not surprisingly, Wisdom too will develop, mostly in John and Paul, into a Wisdom-Christology.[11]

**3. The Spirit of God.** The *Ruah* of God (see "Pneuma" 1968) represents God's divine energy and power, already operative in God's creative act. The Spirit of God, hovering over the primordial waters (Gen 1:2), arouses life out of chaos. Life is entirely dependent upon God's Spirit: "When thou sendest forth thy Spirit, they are created; and thou renewest the face of the earth" (Ps 104:30). More deeply, however, than in creation itself, the *Ruah* of God is at work within human beings as a quickening energy. It is present in creation and re-creation. In the Day of Yahweh the Spirit will be poured out "upon all flesh" (Joel 2:28) — a prophecy which Peter's discourse in Acts 2:16–21 sees fulfilled in the miracle of Pentecost (Acts 2:17). The Spirit endows people with divine power to make them into instruments through which God intervenes in history. It is called "Holy Spirit" (Wis 1:5; 7:22; Is 63:10–11) because it belongs to the divine sphere.

The action of the Spirit of God stands out clearly in the history of Israel in distinct ways. On the one hand, the Spirit of God lays hold of human beings to

---

11. On John's Wisdom-Christology, see, e.g., Brown 1994, 205–10; Willet 1992. On Paul, see Feuillet 1966.

transform them into the instruments of God's action among his people. Such in particular is the case of the king of Israel, "seized upon" by the Spirit of God (1 Sam 16:13). Similarly, the Spirit will "rest upon" the Messiah foretold by Isaiah (Is 11:2; see 61:1); it will be "put" by God upon his Servant (Is 42:1; see 61:1). On the other hand, the Spirit of God also falls on the prophets to empower them to speak the Word of God. In late Judaism, the Spirit will be above all else he "who has spoken by the prophets."

The privileged action of the Spirit in Israel does not, however, prevent his universal influence. "The Spirit of the Lord has filled the world" (Wis 1:7): God's omnipresence (see Jer 23:24) is understood in terms of his Spirit (Ps 139 [138]:7), and the Spirit's universal, life-giving activity (Jdt 16:14; Job 34:14–15). "When thou sendest forth thy Spirit, they are created; and thou renewest the face of the earth" (Ps 104 [103]:30). A clear witness to the Spirit's universal, life-giving activity is Wis 11:24–12:1:

> Thou lovest all things that exist,
> and hast loathing for none of the things
> which thou hast made,
> for thou wouldst not have made anything
> if thou hadst hated it.
> How would anything have endured
> if thou hadst not willed it?
> Or how would anything not called forth by thee
> have been preserved?
> Thou sparest all things, for they are thine,
> O Lord who lovest the living.
> For thy immortal Spirit is in all things.

The conclusion seems to be the following: Word-Wisdom-Spirit witness in the Old Testament to God's dealings with humankind throughout salvation history. History is from beginning to end a history of salvation, that is, a dialogue initiated by God with humankind from the dawn of time which through distinct phases is leading humankind to God's appointed destiny. In the Old Testament, Word-Wisdom-Spirit already testify to such commitment on the part of God, pending its realization in the Word-Wisdom made flesh and in the Spirit poured out.

## II. The New Testament and the Nations

### A. *Jesus and the Pagans*

The historical mission of Jesus was principally, if not exclusively, directed toward Israel. In Mt 15:24, Jesus states explicitly that he was sent "only to the lost sheep of the house of Israel." When he sent the twelve out on mission, he charged them not to go "among the gentiles," not to enter any "town of the Samaritans," but to "go rather to the lost sheep of the house of Israel" (Mt 10:5–6). These data have every chance of being substantially authentic (see Legrand 1988, 68–92; see also Jeremias 1958).

Jesus, however, showed himself full of admiration for the faith of the centurion: "Truly I say to you, not even in Israel have I found such faith" (Mt 8:10). This faith found in a "pagan," in fact, provides Jesus with the occasion to announce that many, coming from East and West, will be admitted to the Kingdom of Heaven (Mt 8:11–12). The entry of "others" into the Kingdom is not purely eschatological; it is brought about first in history, as the parable of the banquet testifies (Mt 22:1–14; Lk 14:15–24) (see Song 1993, 3–38, esp. 24–38). Later, Mark's Gospel will place on the lips of the centurion under the cross an astonishing profession of faith: "Truly this man was the Son of God" (Mk 15:39).

Moreover, on the occasion of "excursions" through the Syro-Phoenician region, Jesus came into contact with persons who did not belong to the chosen people. Once more he is astonished at the faith of these "pagans," and at their request he performs for them miracles of healing. Tyre and Sidon are mentioned several times. According to Mt 15:21–28, Jesus heals there the possessed daughter of a Canaanite woman and marvels at her faith: "Woman, great is your faith! Be it done for you as you desire" (Mt 15:28).

There should be no misunderstanding here: the miracles worked by Jesus on behalf of "strangers" have the same meaning that Jesus gives to all his miracles. They signify that the Reign of God is already present and at work (see Mt 11:4–6; 12:25–28; Lk 4:16–22). The healing miracles and the exorcisms worked on behalf of "others" are thus an indication that the Reign of God is present and at work among them also; it extends to all those who enter it by means of faith and conversion (see Mk 1:15).

Returning from Judea — presumably after having celebrated the Pasch in Jerusalem — Jesus passed through Samaria and came to a city called Sychar (Jn 4:1–6). The Gospel of John shows him there conversing with a Samaritan woman. This by itself was wont to arouse wonder among the disciples, and the Gospel does not fail to note it: "for Jews have no dealings with Samaritans" (Jn 4:9), who were considered as foreigners. Jesus, however, wonders at the woman's disposition to believe and at her thirst for "living water" (Jn 4:7–15). Nor does he reject the Samaritan worship on Mount Gerizim as opposed to worship in Jerusalem; what he does is to announce to the woman that "the hour is coming when neither on this mountain nor in Jerusalem will you worship the Father..., when true worshippers will worship the Father in Spirit and truth, for such the Father seeks to worship him" (Jn 4:20–23). All worship, Jewish as well as foreign, must give way to true spiritual worship.

It is not by accident that, in the parable called by his name, the attitude of the "good Samaritan" is opposed by Jesus to that of a priest and a Levite (Lk 10:29–37). "A man was going down from Jerusalem to Jericho, and he fell among robbers, who stripped him and beat him, and departed leaving him half dead" (Lk 10:30). While the priest and the Levite "passed by on the other side" (Lk 10:31–32), "a Samaritan..., when he saw him, had compassion... and took care of him" (Lk 10:33–35). The Gospel goes into details explaining what taking care of the wounded man implied. The conclusion is that of the three it is the Samaritan who was "neighbor to the man who fell among the robbers" (Lk 10:36). Jesus proposed him as an example to the Jews: "Go and do likewise" (Lk 10:37).

It was not by chance either that the faithful leper cleansed by Jesus at Lk 17:11–16 was a Samaritan. This occurred while Jesus, on the way to Jerusalem, was passing along between Samaria and Galilee; on entering a village, he was met by ten lepers and cleansed them (Lk 17:11–14); the one who "turned back praising God with a loud voice and fell on his face at Jesus' feet, giving him thanks," was a Samaritan (Lk 17:15–16). Jesus asked: "Was no one found to return and give praise to God except this foreigner?" And he said to him: "Rise and go your way; your faith has made you well" (Lk 17:18–19).

Clearly, then, for Jesus, saving faith is not only remotely accessible to pagans and foreigners; it is actually operative among them. So too foreigners may already belong to the Kingdom of God, the call to which extends beyond the limits of Israel's chosen people. This attitude seems to contrast sharply with Jesus' professed admission — recorded earlier — of having been sent "only for the lost sheep of the house of Israel" (Mt 15:24).

In a study entitled *Jesus' Promise to the Nations,* Joachim Jeremias has tried to resolve the apparent contradiction: on the one hand, Jesus limited his activity to Israel and, when sending the disciples on mission during his life-time, charged them not to cross the boundaries of Israel; on the other hand, he consistently and firmly promised to pagans a share in the Kingdom of God. Jeremias thinks he can solve the contradiction as follows: "We have to do with two successive events, first the call to Israel, and subsequently the redemptive incorporation of the Gentiles in the Kingdom of God" (Jeremias 1958, 71).

After healing the centurion's son at Capernaum in response to his faith (Mt 8:5–10), Jesus declared: "I tell you, many will come from East and West and sit at table with Abraham, Isaac, and Jacob in the Kingdom of Heaven, while the sons of the Kingdom will be thrown into the outer darkness" (Mt 8:10–12; see Lk 13:28–29). There is question here of the eschatological gathering of the nations in the Kingdom of God, symbolized by the banquet with the patriarchs. The entry into it of the pagans is the eschatological action of God's power, the ultimate manifestation of God's gratuitous love.

However, the "eschatological Kingdom" which opens up to the gentiles is not to be understood as being delayed to the end of time. Announced by Jesus at the beginning of his ministry (Mk 1:15), already breaking in during his ministry (Mt 12:28; Lk 4:21), it is established by God on earth in Jesus' death and resurrection (see Lk 22:16), to be announced by the Church (see Mk 16:15; cf. Acts 28:30–31) until it grows unto its fullness (Mt 6:10; 25:31–32; Lk 11:2).

The Kingdom of God to which the nations have access is at one and the same time historical and eschatological.

## B. The Apostolic Church and the Nations

After Jesus' resurrection the Church announced the Good News (see Mk 16:15) that in him the Kingdom of God had come about. However, the Apostolic Church had to grow progressively in the awareness of the universality of its mission. First preached to the Jews, the Good News of the Kingdom would spread gradually to the Jewish-Hellenistic world and then to the Greeks. Paul, Barnabas, and the Church of Antioch would play leading roles in the spreading of the Gospel outside Jewish territory. We need not follow here the development of the Church's mission. What pertains to our subject is to show what attitude the Apostolic Church showed toward other "religions" as it began to spread into the wider world.

The data of the New Testament regarding the Apostolic Church's attitude toward the pagans are complex and ambivalent (see Dupont 1979). A first step toward the pagans is made by Peter in his preaching to the household of the centurion Cornelius at Caesarea (Acts 10:1–44). Luke notes that while Peter was announcing to them the Good News of Jesus, "the Holy Spirit fell on all who heard the word" (Acts 10:44). That "the gift of the Holy Spirit had been poured out even on the gentiles" (Acts 10:45) became for Peter a sign that they too were called. However, the gift of the Spirit to them followed upon Peter's kerygmatic announcing of Jesus. Nevertheless, the entire episode brought Peter to the realization that the gentiles too can be acceptable to God: "Truly I perceive that God shows no partiality, but in every nation anyone who fears him and does what is right is acceptable to him" (Acts 10:34–35).

A first element may be gathered from that sentence. Yet we are on safer ground with the theology and the ministry of Paul. But this is also where the data become complex. Paul's pessimism in the Letter to the Romans (Rom 1–3) is well known. Paul declares that the wrath of God will fall upon the pagans for not having recognized God's permanent revelation through the cosmos (Rom 1:18–32). However, the Jews fall under the same condemnation in spite of the superadded gifts they have received (Rom 2–3). Their special status as chosen people does not spare them. For Paul, in fact, while the gifts differ, the situation of the gentiles is parallel to that of the Jews; all will be judged according to their deeds: "When gentiles who have not the law do by nature (*phusikòs*) what the law requires, they are a law to themselves, even though they do not have the law. They show that what the law requires is written on their hearts" (Rom 2:14–15). Saving faith is proportional to the gifts received.

No doubt, for Paul, Christians are in a privileged position: in comparison with the new, the past — whether that of the nations or of Israel itself — is like a state of perdition, now a thing of the past. Faith, once offered to Christians, abolishes, by virtue of a divine decree, the value of all religions (Rom 6:6;

2 Cor 5:17; Eph 4:22; Col 3:9). Yet what we are dealing with in Paul here is a reflection on the privileged situation of whoever has found Jesus Christ and has shared in him in the new life of these last times (Rom 6:4; 7:6; 2 Cor 5:17; Gal 2:15; 4:8–11). It is no declaration of principle, no absolute denial of any value in other religious traditions.

However that may be, the preaching to the gentiles attributed to Paul in Acts, at Lystra first (Acts 14:8–18) and later before the Areopagus of Athens (Acts 17:22–31), witnesses to an open attitude of the "apostle of the gentiles" toward their "religiosity." At Lystra, Paul perceives that the crippled man who is listening to him "had faith to be made well," and he heals him (Acts 14:8–11). Commenting on the religion of the Greeks now superseded by faith in Jesus Christ, he notes: "In past generations [God] allowed all the nations to walk in their own ways; yet he did not leave himself without witness, for he did good and gave you from heaven rains and fruitful seasons, satisfying your hearts with food and gladness" (Acts 14:16–17). This corresponds to God's permanent revelation through the cosmos of which the Letter to the Romans speaks (Rom 1:18–32). God's manifestation through "nature" is already divine revelation.

Paul's speech at Athens (Acts 17:22–31) is more affirmative. Here Paul praises the religious spirit of the Greeks and announces to them the "unknown God" whom they worship without knowing. Whatever be the exegetical problems raised by this passage — among others, concerning the Pauline or Lukan authenticity of the discourse[12] — the message surely seems to be that the religions of the nations are not bereft of value but find in Jesus Christ the fulfillment of their aspirations. In comparison with what is offered in Jesus Christ, they seem very spare, but this does not prevent them from being a positive preparation for Christian faith.

"Men of Athens, I perceive that in every way you are very religious. For as I passed along, and observed the object of your worship, I found also an altar with this inscription: To an Unknown God. What therefore you worship as unknown, this I proclaim to you" (Acts 17:22–23). Paul goes on to refer to the one God who made the world and everything in it, who "gives to all human beings life and breath and everything," and who "from one made every nation to live on the face of the earth, having allotted periods and the boundaries of their habitation that they should seek God, in the hope that they might feel after him and find him" (Acts 17:25–27). This returns to the doctrine of Rom 1 on God's self-revelation to all peoples through the cosmos, by which God could be recognized by them.

But Paul proceeds one step further, affirming God's proximity to each people: "For indeed (*kai ge*) he is not far from each one of us" (Acts 17:27). In proof of this, Paul refers to an expression suggested by the Greek poet Epimenides (sixth century B.C.E.): "In him we live and move and have our being," and goes

---

12. See Dupont 1967, 1981, 1984. See also Legrand 1974, 1981, 1987, 1988, 144–53. Also Bossuyt and Radermakers 1995.

on to quote another Greek writer, the poet Aratus (third century B.C.E.) who had written: "For we are indeed God's offspring" (Acts 17:28). Apart from any rhetorical devices and appeal for goodwill, this amounts to recognizing in the Greek tradition (Platonic and Stoic) a genuine "feeling after God." That the conversation breaks down when Paul speaks of Jesus' resurrection (Acts 17:32) changes nothing; nor does it mean that Paul's approach ends up in failure, for Luke adds: "Some people joined him and believed, among them Dionysius the Areopagite and a woman named Damaris and others with them" (Acts 17:34). However limited Paul's success at Athens may have been, the Areopagus speech inaugurates a missionary strategy based on a positive approach to the religiosity of the Greeks.

Comparing Paul's attitude in Rom 1 and that in Acts 17, Legrand concludes to "two great axes...of continuity and discontinuity." Discontinuity places the stress on the radical newness of Christ and his resurrection and by contrast sees the ancient world as darkness and sin. That is the viewpoint of Rom 1. The continuity, on the contrary, underlines the homogeneity of salvation unfolding according to God's plan. It is the viewpoint of Acts 17, which, where the religion of gentiles is concerned, presents a Greek world waiting for the unknown God and prepared by its poet-theologians to meet him (see Legrand 1995, 75–76). And elsewhere Legrand writes:

> One could dramatize the difference of outlook between Luke and Paul. It must be kept in mind that their view-points correspond to different historical situations: Paul, a man of the first Christian generation, experienced the dazzling newness of Christ. Luke, a man who lived and wrote in the eighties, and possibly even later, made the experience of a protracted ongoing history. The history of Christian tradition continued to reflect those two tendencies. (Legrand 1981, 231)

One more step may still be taken and a broader view arrived at in searching for the New Testament approach to the religions of the gentiles. It consists in considering the entire breadth of salvation history. To this end it is necessary to sketch the whole range of the Johannine Gospel, of the Prologue in particular.[13] According to the Prologue, all salvation history, beginning with creation, is wrought by God through the Logos. This history, from the beginning (Jn 1:1), is ordered to the incarnation of the Word in humanity (Jn 1:14). But long before the incarnation, the Word was present in the world as the source of life (Jn 1:4), as "the true light that enlightens every human being by coming into the world. He was in the world, and the world was made through him" (Jn 1:9). Here we are surely dealing with the active presence of the divine Logos, not yet incarnate, throughout the whole of human history. For John, then, the Word's incarnation is the culmination of God's manifestation through his Word that

---

13. On the Christology of John's Gospel and of the Prologue, see, e.g.: Boismard 1953, 1958; Feuillet 1968; Potterie 1977; Dodd 1963; Brown 1960, 1966–70; Schnackenburg 1987.

encompasses the entire history of humankind: "And the Word became flesh and dwelt among us" (Jn 1:14).

The Johannine vision of the divine Logos links with the economy of the Word of God and of divine Wisdom in the Old Testament. We have seen that in the Old Testament theology, the Word of God (*Dabar*) and his Wisdom (*Hokmah*) stood for Yahweh's self-manifestation in deeds and words in human history. They were dynamic attributes of God to which a "literary" or poetic personification was attributed. John now sees in Jesus Christ the culmination of God's universal manifestation through the Logos — with the difference, however, that through his incarnation the Logos is now revealed as a person distinct from God, yet one who shared with God in the divine life "in the beginning" (Jn 1:1), later to enter human history as a human being.

This Johannine theology has at once Logos and Wisdom connotations. The Logos reference is explicit; the Wisdom connotations are also apparent. According to Wisdom literature, Wisdom, present with God before the world was made (Prov 8:22; Wis 7:22), and by whom all things were created (Prov 8:27–31; Wis 9:9), is sent to earth to reveal God's hidden designs (Prov 8:32–36; Wis 9:10–11), to deliver a message of salvation to the world and lead people to life (Prov 4:13; 8:32–35) and immortality (Wis 6:18–19). All this is transposed by John from Wisdom to God's incarnate Word. As Wisdom set up her tent in Israel (Sir 24:8–12), so for John the Word set up his tent among us (Jn 1:14). Remarking on this parallel, R. E. Brown observes pointedly:

> Personified Wisdom language appears in the synoptic tradition on a few occasions [see Mt 11:19, 25–30; 12:42; etc.]; but there is nothing to match the massive number of echoes in John; and there can be little doubt that this background supplied a major element in the vocabulary and imagery for the Johannine presentation of Jesus as a preexistent who came into this world from another, heavenly realm where he had been with the Father. (Brown 1994, 210; see also Feuillet 1966; Willet 1992)

Neither is there any doubt that the Logos-Wisdom theology of John, which embodies the universal self-manifestation of God throughout history, offers the widest New Testament perspective on God's universal involvement with humankind. It is this universal and continuous involvement of God in human history that allows for a positive approach to the religions of the world.

Such, then, are the data available in both the Old and New Testaments. It must be remembered that the Bible was not directly concerned with the questions which today's theology of religions is seeking to answer in the present context of religious pluralism. The revealed word was primarily concerned to stress in the Old Testament the privileged situation of Israel, and in the New that of Christians; the other religions faded away in comparison. Nevertheless, the ambiguity between negative and positive data notwithstanding, a lead is found in the sacred books for a positive approach to religions, firstly and principally in the biblical faith in God's universal involvement with humankind in a dialogue of salvation.

Summing up the data, Heinz R. Schlette writes pointedly:

> Obviously we have no right to exaggerate the theological implications of the account of Noah, or of the discourse in the Areopagus. But neither may we allow ourselves to underrate such declarations. They furnish a basis for judging religions from a frankly positive standpoint, since they are seen as constituting a real relationship with God. On the other hand, neither must we forget that, for scripture, one cannot adhere to the Christian faith without a "decision" in which we take our distance from the "past." (Schlette 1967, 64)

# Two

# The Cosmic Christ
# in the Early Fathers

THE PRECEDING CHAPTER ended by noting that the Prologue of the Gospel according to John lays the biblical foundation for a theology of the history of salvation: throughout history, starting from creation itself, God manifested himself through his Word; this self-revelation of God came to a climax in the incarnation of the Word (Jn 1:14). This vision, which remained unsurpassed in the New Testament, became in the postbiblical tradition the leading thread with which to further develop a first elaboration of what in today's terminology can be called a "theology of history." In the view of the Church Fathers, salvation history, as we shall see, extends beyond the Judeo-Christian dispensation to the surrounding cultures which they encountered — indeed, in some cases, to the ancient wisdom of the East of which they had but a scanty knowledge. The goal of this chapter is to show that there exists in the early tradition an awareness of the universal and active presence of God through his Word, which is not without bearing on a theological evaluation of the religious traditions of the world.

Caution is, however, required. For one thing, the context in which the early Fathers wrote was vastly different from the one in which today we reflect on the significance of the other religious traditions of the world; it would be a dangerous anachronism to transpose directly what was said in one context to the other. Second, opinions differed vastly, going from an open attitude toward the culture of the "nations" to downright condemnation. Third, where those early Fathers are concerned who discovered positive values in the cultures of the gentiles, precision is required as to where in their estimation such values were to be found and where not. Positive assessments of some elements of Greek culture more often than not coexist with negative statements about other elements of the same culture. In such a situation, hasty generalizations and conclusions must be carefully avoided. Distinctions are in order.

Some general assertions can, however, be made concerning the aspects of the surrounding Hellenistic culture which the early Fathers as well as their successors were unanimous in condemning. Special reference must be made here to all forms of polytheism and idolatry. The Fathers of the Church untiringly recall the precept of the Decalogue: "You shall have no other gods before me. You shall not make for yourself a graven image or any likeness of anything that is in heaven above, or that is on the earth beneath, or that is in the water under the earth; you shall not bow down to them or serve them" (Deut 5:7–9). Denunciation of polytheism and idolatry is as emphatic as it is unanimous in the context of the Greco-Roman world, imbued as this world was with religious mythology. The Fathers saw in the legends of pagan mythology false stories which the truth of Jesus Christ had mercifully debunked. They likewise condemned religious practices widespread during the Hellenistic period, such as magical incantations and soothsaying; in particular, they denounced astrology, in which they saw an ungodly manifestation of ancient fatalism.

Furthermore, the Fathers opposed vehemently the "mystery religions" which, at the time when more traditional beliefs were on the decline, were spreading everywhere around the Mediterranean Sea; they branded as impious the search for salvation through mysteric initiation and other rites prevalent in those mystery religions. Again they denounced the seduction of the East from which new cults had come to the West, such as that of Mithras. It is from the East too that the religion of Mani originated in the third century; the Fathers of the Church denounced its radical dualism, not only in Persia and Syria but in the West as well, where Manichaeism soon implanted itself. Augustine of Hippo, once a follower of the sect, later engaged in refuting its doctrines. Nor is it possible to forget the Fathers' opposition to some doctrines of middle- and mostly neo-Platonism which were incompatible with the doctrine of "creation" and in a bid to uphold the radical transcendence of the Absolute remained impervious to the Christian revelation of the Word of God made human (see Fédou 1992; Luneau 1967).

The vehement opposition of the early Fathers to many aspects of the cultural and religious scene of their time cannot be underestimated. But neither must it be thought to represent the entire picture. Many negative assessments notwithstanding, the fact remains that the early tradition witnesses to a remarkable opening toward other aspects of surrounding culture and religion. Which aspects, and how? The Logos-theology of some of the early Fathers is here of special significance.

At the beginning of the Christian era, both in Hellenistic philosophy and in Semitic thought, the concept of, respectively, Logos or *Dabar* occupied a prominent place in the minds of thinking people. To the former, the term "Logos" stood for reason, thought, intelligibility; it gave expression to a philosophical ideal and, not unlike "science" in the nineteenth-century West, served as a slogan to the intelligentsia. For the latter, and more precisely in Old Testament literature, *Dabar* meant a dynamic divine attribute by which the God of the covenant intervened in the history of his chosen people in deeds and words. In the mind of the Hellenistic philosopher, Logos represented a principle of intelligibility, immanent in the world; to the pious Jew, *Dabar* referred, by way of literary personification, to Yahweh's personal manifestation and revelation. Both, however, were at one in thinking of the Logos, or *Dabar*, as in itself impersonal (or not distinctly personal). Thus, when the Johannine Gospel and other writings spoke of the man Jesus as the incarnate Word of God, this must have seemed a rather revolutionary innovation. Why Christ was called the Logos in the Fourth Gospel remains disputed in New Testament exegesis even today; it is likely, however, that the Gospel according to John meant to emphasize the fact that in Christ's person the revelatory function of the Old Testament *Dabar* Yahweh had been fully realized.[1]

But that the Johannine Gospel did so call Christ was a factor of immense significance for Christianity, one which was to give a definite orientation to centuries of theological thinking on the Son of God. The Logos of the Christians is a person and is a divine person: this truth became the core of the Christian message, often challenged by outsiders, yet never denied by those who shared the faith of the Church. This is not to suggest that all the implications of Jn 1:14 were clearly perceived from the start. It took centuries to bring these out: beyond the economy of the manifestation of the Logos, there is — but this had to be unveiled progressively — the theology of his immanent origin in God; the eternal generation, if truly declared in the incarnation, must yet be clearly distinguished from it. Long struggles were involved in this process; that they have not been in vain is borne out by the clear formulation arrived at in the Council of Nicea: the Logos is "consubstantial" with the Father.[2]

But Christian thinking concerning the dispensation of the Logos could not be put off until decisive formulas were reached as regards his eternal reality. Christianity had to meet the challenge of other doctrines; or, as we prefer to put it today, a dialogue was opened with human wisdom outside the Church. This forced Christianity to define itself in relation to the partners it encountered. In the early centuries, much of this dialogue took the form of a Logos-theology. The Logos-idea was in the air; the Christian Logos had to be defined in relation to its counterparts. As a matter of fact, with all the originality of his personal character, the Logos in the mind of the early Fathers did nonetheless exercise the functions which Hellenism attributed to its impersonal Logos. Was he not God's immanent thought? And, as such, did he not sustain the comparison with the Platonic world of ideas, or, again, with the soul of the world? Other questions, too, were asked which were even more searching. Saint Paul had spoken of Christ's cosmic significance; he had conceived his influence as extending through concentric circles beyond the sphere of the Church even to the limits of the universe (Eph 1:22–23). His was a theology of the cosmic Christ. How, then, did the Logos exercise this universal cosmic function? And, if one passed from the consideration of the cosmos to the universe of humankind, did the eternal Logos manifest himself to all human beings, or was knowledge of him confined

---

1. See McKenzie (1963, 57), who writes: "Most Old Testament scholars...wonder why anyone has ever thought it necessary to appeal to any source beyond the Old Testament to explain John's application of Logos to Jesus Christ....Old Testament thought is a sufficient explanation for the appearance of the term....Logos is one of the great New Testament fulfillments....In Jesus Christ is fulfilled the Word as a distinct being, as a dynamic creative entity, as that which gives form and intelligibility to the reality which it signifies, as the self-revelation of God, as a point of personal encounter between God and man." See also "Logos" 1967.
2. See Dupuis 1994c, 57–110, where the continuity-in-discontinuity between the New Testament Christology and the Church's Christological dogma is studied. See also Grillmeier 1975.

to the Judeo-Christian tradition? Did people before and outside this tradition partake of him, or did only those who received him when he came into the world? The sages of old had meditated on *a* Logos: was *he, the* Logos, however hidden and unknown, the object of their contemplation?

These questions were mighty ones; they raised many problems, to which the Fathers turned their attention, even though often with a perspective and always with mental categories different from ours. Creation and history; revelation and incarnation; Christianity, religions, and philosophy; nature and the supernatural: all these important theological issues were in one way or another involved in Logos-theology. In short, as we shall show, Logos-theology seems to be the early version of a theology of history. And as such it keeps its significance for us today; indeed, it is taking on new significance today.

For two reasons. First, Christian theology today more universally than yesterday centers on the history of salvation and finds there its inner articulation (Feiner and Löhrer, eds., 1965–76). Second, Christianity has entered a new phase of dialogue with the world at large. The value of the early Logos-theology is not purely academic; it has practical significance. The questions which were asked then are those which even today we are asked to answer: What does Christ mean to the world? What newness, if any, does he bring to it?

Not all the Fathers shared the same approach to these questions, nor did they all give the same answers. There were those who condemned the world to obscurity until the light of the incarnate Word dawned upon it: for them, prior to and outside the Judeo-Christian fold, divine truth remained hidden from people. There were those who, while admitting that divine truth was found outside the fold, were yet unwilling to ascribe it to any agency other than the historical revelation. Fanciful chronological computations were, if the need arose, resorted to in order better to vindicate the thesis of pagan plagiarism from Christianity. Or else the wise from among the Greeks were supposed to have borrowed from Jewish tradition — so, for instance, Plato and Socrates. Or again, a primordial tradition was invoked, remnants of which, it was alleged, having been handed down through the ages, could be found among the nations.

But there were others who approached the problems with a broader mind and laid down the foundation for a theology of history. They distinguished successive ages of the universe; these they understood to be the successive stages in the self-manifestation of the divine Logos. From the beginning, the eternal Word had been at work in the cosmos, even though the mystery of his self-disclosure was to pass through various economies before culminating in the incarnation. It is with these theologians, who remain eminently actual, that we are concerned here.

We will concentrate primarily on the second century (and the beginning of the third) and on its greatest representatives: Saint Justin, the philosopher, the most important of the Greek apologists; Irenaeus, who, while very distrustful of futile gnostic speculation, became as it were the founder of the theology of history; and in Alexandria, where systematic theology was born, Clement, the first speculative theologian. All these shared a common outlook. Yet we shall treat them separately, so as better to point out their respective contributions.

The views of our three protagonists have, however, given rise to different interpretations which need to be discussed if a correct evaluation of their work is to be reached. The exposition will therefore be followed by a critical assessment. We shall further ask whether the same views were pursued by the successors of the early Fathers in later patristic thought. This will bring us to a rapid description of the "history of salvation" as understood by the Church Fathers and to an evaluation of its relevance today for a theology of religions.[3]

## I. Saint Justin and the Logos-Sower

Being confronted with the philosophers of his time, Justin was led to organize what may well be called the first Christian synthesis of the universe, in which he stresses the cosmological function of the Logos. In fact, in Justin's writings, the Logos designates the Son precisely in his cosmological function, namely, in his relation to the cosmos. The divine efficacy from which the world proceeds is concentrated in him. He is the *dunamis* of God, an energetic Word (*logikè dunamis*), the creator and organizer of the cosmos. Characteristically Justin refers the term *Christos* not to the mission of Christ the man but more fundamentally to the creative and organizing function of the Logos:

> The Son of God, the only one who may properly be called Son, the Word existing with him and begotten before all creatures, when in the beginning he created and ordered (*ekosmèse*) all things, was called Christ because he was anointed and because God ordered (*kosmèsai*) the universe through him. (*2 Apol.* VI, 3)[4]

One is made to think of the Platonic soul of the world. The difference, however, is clear: on the one hand, Justin speaks of the divine Word existing with God; yet, on the other hand, all the cosmological functions, all God's interventions in the world, are attributed precisely to the Logos.

The cosmological function of the Logos is, in effect, the foundation for Justin's theology of revelation. The Father acts through the Son; all divine manifestations in the world take place through him. This, which is true of the divine act of creation, remains true where God's personal manifestation is concerned. Such manifestation of God through his Word is not limited to the Christian dispensation. It took place before the incarnation of the Word, among the Jews and the Greeks; everywhere there have been people who lived by the Word and deserve to be called Christian:

---

3. For the theology of the three authors under consideration, one can consult, among other studies: Daniélou 1973; Saldanha 1984; Lubac 1969. See also Luneau 1967; Fédou 1992; Adinolfi 1991; Ries 1987, 11–193.

4. All quotations from Justin are from Daniélou 1973; here 347–48.

We have been taught that Christ is the first-begotten of God, and have previously testified that he is the Logos (*Logos*) of which every race of humans partakes (*metechein*). Those who have lived in accordance with the Logos (*meta logou*) are Christians, even though they were called godless, such as, among the Greeks, Socrates and Heraclitus and others like them; among the barbarians, Abraham, Ananias, Azarias, Misael, and Elijah, and many others, whose deeds and names I forbear to list, knowing that this would be lengthy. So also those who lived contrary to the Logos were ungracious and enemies to Christ, and murderers of those who lived by the Logos. But those who lived by the Logos, and those who live so now, are Christians, fearless and unperturbed. (*1 Apol.* XLVI, 1–4; Daniélou 1973, 40–41)

A text such as this brings us straight to the heart of the matter. It is not, however, an isolated occurrence in Justin's writings. We shall let Justin speak for himself by quoting from the *Second Apology:*

In moral philosophy the Stoics have established right principles, and the poets too have expounded such, because the seed of the Word (*sperma tou logou*) was implanted (*emphuton*) in the whole human race. (*2 Apol.* VIII, 1; Daniélou 1973, 41)

Our doctrine surpasses all human teaching, because we have the Word in his entirety in Christ, who has been manifested for us, body, reason and soul (*sòma, logos, psuchè*). All the right principles that philosophers and lawgivers have discovered and expressed they owe to whatever of the Word they have found and contemplated in part (*kata meros*). The reason why they have contradicted each other is that they have not known the entire Word, which is Christ. (*2 Apol.* X, 1–3; Daniélou 1973, 41)

It is not, therefore, that the teaching of Plato is alien to that of Christ, but it is not like it in all points, any more than is that of other men, Stoics, poets, or writers. Each of them, indeed, because he saw in part (*kata meros*) that which derived from the divine Word and was sown by him (*tou spermatikou theiou logou*), was able to speak well; but by contradicting each other on essential points they show that they do not possess the higher learning and the knowledge which is irrefutable. (*2 Apol.* XIII, 2–3; Daniélou 1973, 41)

The Christ whom Socrates knew in part (*apo merous*) — for he was and is the Logos present in all things (*ho en panti òn*), and it is he who by means of the prophets foretold the future, and by means of himself, being made like to us, gave us his teaching — has convinced not only the philosophers and the educated, but also craftsmen and utterly ignorant people, who have scorned public opinion, fear and death; for he was the power (*dunamis*) of the ineffable Father, and not a product of human reason (*logos*). (*2 Apol.* X, 8; Daniélou 1973, 42)

All that they have said well belongs to us, the Christians. For next to God we worship and love the Word, born of the unbegotten and ineffable God, because for our sakes he became man in order to heal us of our ills by himself sharing in them. These writers were able to perceive the Truth obscurely (*amudròs*) thanks to the sowing (*spora*) of the Word which had been implanted within them. But it is one thing to possess a seed (*sperma*), and a likeness proportioned to one's capacity, and quite another to possess the reality itself, both the partaking and the imitation of which are the results of the grace which comes from him. (*2 Apol.* XIII, 4–6; Daniélou 1973, 42)

If we try to put some order in the ideas, Justin's thought may be summarized in four points: (1) there exist three kinds of religious knowledge: that proper to the nations, the Jewish, and the Christian; (2) of all religious knowledge in its different kinds, the Logos is the unique source; (3) the difference between the various kinds of knowledge corresponds to various forms of participation in the Logos: extending to the whole cosmos and to all human beings, the intervention of the Logos in Israel becomes more decisive; it is complete only in Christ's advent in the flesh; and (4) all persons who have known the Truth and lived righteously are Christians, for, and insofar as, all have partaken of, and lived according to, the Logos who is all Truth.[5]

The key to the whole system is in differentiated participation of the Logos: all people share in him, but while others have received from him partially (*apo merous*), we to whom the Logos revealed himself in his incarnation have been blessed with his complete manifestation. In all persons a seed of the Logos (*sperma tou logou*) may be found, for the Logos-sower (*spermatikos logos*) sows in all; yet to us only the entirety of the Logos has been made manifest. The expressions of Justin must not be emptied of their true meaning. The Logos which he attributes to all people is not the "product of human reason," but a participation in the person of the Word, from whom all truth, however partial and uncertain, is derived: that of which we all have partaken is "the *dunamis* of the ineffable Father, not just a product of human reason" (*2 Apol.* X, 8). Daniélou writes pointedly: "He [Justin] is not in the least tempted by the idea of an order of natural truth which is the proper object of reason on the one hand, and of an order of supernatural truth, the object of revelation, on the

---

5. Referring to what I wrote earlier, Saldanha (1984, 179) observes that "Dupuis' statement . . . about the religious knowledge of the pagan, the Jew and the Christian being three different *degrees* of participation of the Word does not go far enough and tends to be somewhat misleading. Following the Fathers, we have to speak of different *kinds* of participation in the Word by the pagan, the Jew and the Christian, with each kind bearing a relationship to the others." For my previous text, see Dupuis 1966, 110. However, Saldanha himself writes in another place: "The Fathers saw the whole matter in terms of participation, a sharing in different *degrees,* and in different *ways* in the same central reality of Jesus Christ" (1984, 186).

other. There are only an obscure knowledge and a clear knowledge of the one Truth, which is the Word" (Daniélou 1973, 44).

The implications of the texts quoted are clear: all possession of religious truth as well as all righteous conduct come to all people through a personal manifestation of the eternal Word fully realized in Christ. Christianity exists beyond its visible boundaries and prior to its historical appearing, but up to the incarnation, it is fragmentary, hidden, even mixed with error, and ambiguous. It may be asked if this is not, but for the expression, the theology of "anonymous Christianity," even eighteen centuries before K. Rahner. We shall return to this hereafter. Meanwhile, it may already be observed that Justin is developing in his writings a "history of the Logos" which is a "history of salvation." As E. Osborn wrote: "Here the history of the Logos is a history of salvation. The climax of *Heilsgeschichte* is the coming of Christ who was known to all as reason and became present in fullness by his incarnation" (Osborn 1993, 153).

## II. Saint Irenaeus and the Revealing Word

"Down to the theologians of the 'redemptive history' school in the nineteenth century..." — so writes Oscar Cullmann in *Christ and Time* — "there has scarcely been one theologian who recognized so clearly as did Irenaeus that the Christian proclamation stands or falls with the redemptive history, that the historical work of Jesus Christ as Redeemer forms the mid-point of a line which leads from the Old Testament to the return of Christ" (Cullmann 1952, 56–57). Irenaeus may be said to be the founder of the theology of history. Not only did he bring out the historical significance of the Mosaic and Christian dispensations, but he also integrated the pre-Mosaic dispensation in the history of salvation, thus making room for a salvific value of prebiblical religions. For this theology, Justin had laid the foundation; Irenaeus would organize it systematically. This he did with his theology of the revealing Logos:

> Since it is God who works all things in all, he is, by virtue of his nature and his greatness, invisible and ineffable to all his creatures, but not therefore unknown; for, through his Word, all learn that there is one sole God and Father who contains all things, who gives being to all things, as it is said in the Gospel: "No one has seen God at any time; the only-begotten Son, who is in the bosom of the Father, he has made him known" [Jn 1:18]. Thus from the beginning the Son of the Father is the one who makes him known, since it is he, who from the beginning is with the Father, who has shown to the human race both the visions of the prophets and the various kinds of charismatic gifts and his own ministries and the glorification of his Father, all in their right order and arrangement and at the time most useful for them.... Moreover, the Word was made the dispenser of his Father's grace for the benefit of people, for whose sake he carried out such

great divine plans (*dispensationes=oikonomias*), showing God to people, presenting them to God and preserving the invisibility of his Father so that the human being should never come to despise God, and that he should always have a goal toward which to advance; on the other hand, showing God to people in many ways, lest they, wholly lacking God, should cease to exist. For the glory of God is the living human being; but the life of the human is the vision of God. For if that manifestation of God which comes through the creation gives life to all who live on the earth, how much more does the manifestation of the Father which is performed by the Word give life to those who see God. (*Adv. Haer.* IV, 20, 6–7)[6]

This is a truly admirable text, where the whole theology of Irenaeus is contained in compact form: the divine philanthropy which creates human beings, that they may live; the economy of the divine manifestations through the Logos who, present to creation from the beginning, reveals the Father progressively. The fundamental principle of this theology is *Visibile Patris Filius* (The Son is the visible of the Father). Not precisely the sacramental sign of the Father — for Irenaeus is not thinking only of the incarnate Logos — but more generally the manifestation, visible or invisible, the revelation, the knowability of the Father. In himself, the Father is and remains through all economies the unknown; but he is manifested in the Son: *Invisibile etenim Filii Pater, visibile autem Patris Filius* (The Father is the invisible of the Son, but the Son is the visible of the Father) (*Adv. Haer.* IV, 6, 6). Irenaeus, who never tired of commenting on Jn 1:18 and on the "Johannine" logion of Matthew (11:27) (see, e.g., *Adv. Haer.* IV, 6–7), explained that all divine manifestations take place through the Logos: "Through the Son who is in the Father and who has in him the Father, the God 'who is' [cf. Ex 3:8] manifested himself, the Father giving witness to the Son and the Son announcing the Father" (*Adv. Haer.* III, 6, 2; SC 211:71).

What are those divine manifestations? The first is creation itself. Justin had explained the cosmological function of the Logos; Irenaeus draws the conclusions. The knowledge of God which humans can reach through the cosmos is already on their part a response to a revelation of the Logos, for creation is itself a divine manifestation: *per conditionem ostensio Dei* (*Adv. Haer.* IV, 20, 7); and all divine manifestations are Logos-manifestations:

The Son, controlling all things for the Father, guides all things to their goal from beginning to end, and without him none can know God. For the knowledge of the Father is the Son (*agnitio enim Patris Filius*); and the knowledge of the Son in the Father is also revealed by the Son. That is why the Lord said: "No one knows the Father save the Son, and those to

---

6. Quotations from *Adv. Haer.* are from Daniélou 1973, wherever available. Otherwise, they are taken from The Ante-Nicene Fathers (ANF) vol. 1, ed. A. Cleveland Coxe (Grand Rapids, Mich.: Eerdmans, 1977) or translated from *Contre les hérésies* III, Sources Chrétiennes 211, ed. A. Rousseau and L. Doutreleau (Paris: Cerf, 1974). Here, Daniélou 1973, 359. Corrections are made to the translations where appropriate.

whom the Son has revealed him (*revelaverit*)." The word "has revealed" was not spoken referring only to the future, as though the Word began to make the Father manifest only when he was born of Mary; but he is present at every point in time. For from the beginning the Son, present to the creatures whom he has formed, reveals the Father to all those to whom the Father wills, and at the time and in the way he wills; and therefore in all things and through all things there is one God and Father, and one Word, his Son, and one Spirit, and one salvation to all who believe in him. (*Adv. Haer.* IV, 6, 7; Daniélou 1973, 361–62)

This doctrine seems to upset our theological categories; for where we insist on distinguishing two orders of divine manifestations, cosmic and historical, Irenaeus finds in the order of creation itself a historical and personal manifestation of the Logos. In his view, the human person's knowledge of God is already a response to a personal divine initiative. This means that for Irenaeus, to know God is to know him as a person on an existential level. The knowledge of God which he considers does not consist in showing, by a process of reason in which one is not personally involved, the existence of a first principle of being, but in acknowledging God as the infinite person who graciously addresses himself to us. In this sense knowledge of God always supposes a personal encounter with God. In Irenaeus's view, such an encounter, which in every event is an encounter with the Logos, is made possible through creation; for through it the Logos speaks to people. In other words, the order of creation itself is part of God's historical and personal manifestation.

At this first stage of the divine dispensation, the universality of the Word's revealing function is manifest: "Since the Father is invisible, it is his Son, who leans upon his breast, that reveals him to all. Therefore those know him who receive this revelation from the Son" (*Adv. Haer.* III, 11, 6; SC 211:157).

We, with our theological habits, might suppose that the knowledge of the Father which is intended here is to be distinguished from that which we call natural knowledge. Not so, it seems, for Irenaeus, for precisely the only knowledge he seems to know of is this knowledge of the Father through the Son:

> The Father therefore has revealed himself to all, by making his Word visible to all; and, conversely, the Word has declared to all the Father and the Son, since he has become visible to all. And therefore the righteous judgment of God [shall fall] upon all who, like others have seen, but have not, like others, believed.
>
> For by means of the creation itself, the Word reveals God the Creator; and by means of the world [does he declare] the Lord, the Maker of the world; and through that which is moulded, the artisan who moulded it; and by the Son the Father who begat the Son. And these things do indeed address all humans in the same manner, but all do not in the same way believe them. (*Adv. Haer.* IV, 6, 5–6; ANF 1:468–69)

On this issue a study of Irenaeus's theology of revelation concludes that "according to Irenaeus's thought the knowledge of God achieved through the contemplation of the universe cannot be dissociated from the personal revealing activity of the divine Word" (Ochagavía 1964, 77; Houssiau 1955). One text, in particular, if rightly understood, seems to support this interpretation. Speaking of the Master and Lord of creation, Irenaeus explains that knowledge of him has been granted to all; this knowledge, however, he identifies with the knowledge of the Father through the Son. He writes:

> As his dominion extended over all of them, it behove them to know their Ruler, and to be aware of this in particular, that he who created them is Lord of all. For since his invisible essence is mighty, it confers on all a profound mental intuition and perception of his most powerful, omnipotent greatness. Wherefore, although "no one knows the Father, except the Son, nor the Son except the Father and those to whom the Son will reveal him" [cf. Mat 11:27], yet all [beings] do know this one fact at least, because the Word, implanted in their minds (*ratio mentibus infixa* for *logos mentibus infixus*), moves them and reveals to them [the truth] that there is one God, the Lord of all. (*Adv. Haer.* II, 6, 1; ANF 1:365)[7]

The revelation of the Father by the Son constitutes a permanent dispensation. The order of creation was only the first stage of God's manifestation through the Logos. According to the scheme already developed by Saint Justin, the Jewish and Christian dispensations follow after. Thus, after considering creation, Irenaeus goes on to write:

> But by the law and the prophets did the Word preach both himself and the Father alike [to all]; and all the people heard him alike, but all did not alike believe. And through the Word himself who had been made visible and palpable, was the Father shown forth, although all did not equally believe in him; but all saw the Father in the Son: for the Father is the invisible of the Son, but the Son the visible of the Father. (*Adv. Haer.* IV, 6, 6; ANF 1:469)

Irenaeus is definite in attributing to the Logos God's self-disclosure in the old dispensation. He gives here a theological interpretation which, after him, will become common property of the Fathers. All the Old Testament theophanies

---

7. This text has been differently interpreted by various authors. Does the *Logos mentibus infixus* refer to "human reason" or to the Logos? See for various interpretations Saldanha 1984, 89–95. The majority of commentators opt for an active presence of the Word of God. Thus, among others: Houssiau 1953, according to whom the "Word implanted in the mind" refers to the Logos, not to reason; Ochagavía 1964, 70–80; A. Rousseau 1982, 220. The opposite opinion, according to which *ratio* refers to reason and a "natural" knowledge of God is meant, is defended, among others, by Orbe 1966. T. L. Tiessen (1993) has made a strong case in favor of the Logos representing natural reason. He rejects (5–6) the interpretation which I have proposed of this and other texts in Dupuis 1977, 3–19. He claims that "Irenaeus does not speak of an activity of the Logos through pagan philosophers, as Justin does. The 'seed of the Word' was not found in pagan philosophers, but in the Old Testament prophecies, whose fruit the Church reaped" (278). It remains, however, difficult to believe that Irenaeus, any more than Justin, would have distinguished between natural and supernatural knowledge.

are applied to the Word: they are theophanies insofar as they are Logophanies. In Irenaeus's own expressions, the Word, or even Jesus Christ, was "present in," "descended in," or "passed through" the Old Testament economies; in the theophanies, he was present rehearsing his future coming in the flesh. Again, the words of the prophets are not merely words about Christ, but the words of Christ, and in like manner their actions are "typological events," types of the things to come.

Here are a few examples. The Word manifested himself already to Adam in the garden: "And how beautiful and good that garden was: the Word of God would walk around it constantly and talk with the man, prefiguring the things to come, how he would become his dwelling companion and talk with him and would be with humankind, teaching them justice" (*Demonst.* 12).[8]

With Noah he inaugurated the second covenant with humankind. Let us recall in passing that Irenaeus distinguishes four covenants. *Quattuor data sunt testamenta humano generi:* one through Adam, one through Noah, one through Moses, one through Christ (*Adv. Haer.* III, 11, 8); but in each the Logos is operative. When Abraham received the divine calling and left everything behind, it was in order to follow the Word of God: *sequebatur Verbum Dei* (*Adv. Haer.* IV, 5, 3); at Mambre, he "saw what was to come to pass in the future, the Son of God in human form" (*Demonst.* 44). For Irenaeus, there is no doubt that at Mambre, Jesus Christ appeared to Abraham. Of Moses he writes that the Logos "talked to him, appearing in his presence, as one who talks to a friend" (*Adv. Haer.* IV, 20, 9); what in Num 12:8 and Ex 33:11 is said of the Lord is here applied to the Logos, who is "the one who spoke with Moses" (*Adv. Haer.* III, 15, 3; IV, 5, 2; etc.), the same who "came into Judaea, begotten by God through the Holy Spirit and born of the Virgin Mary" (*Demonst.* 40). Furthermore, not only did the Word speak to Moses, but in the salvific events of Exodus, he was actively present, descending upon us, rehearsing future events: "For in these things what concerns us [today] was being rehearsed, the Word of God prefiguring then what was to come" (*Demonst.* 46; SC 406:151).

In like manner, not only did Moses write about Christ (as Jn 5:46 states: "for he wrote of me"), but his words are the very words of Christ: *suos esse sermones, . . . sermones ipsius sunt* (*Adv. Haer.* IV, 2, 3). Uniting in one breath both prophetic word and typological events, Irenaeus sees in each one the action of Christ: "It was not by means of visions alone which were seen, and words which were proclaimed, but also in actual works, that he [the Word of God] was beheld by the prophets, in order that through them he might prefigure and show forth future events beforehand" (*Adv. Haer.* IV, 20, 12; ANF 1:492).

In both works and words, not only the Logos but Christ, the incarnate Word, was at work in anticipation: "By means of his patriarchs and prophets, Christ was prefiguring and declaring beforehand future things, fulfilling his part by

---

8. Quotations from *Irénée de Lyon, Démonstration de la prédication apostolique,* ed. A. Rousseau, Sources Chrétiennes 406 (Paris: Cerf, 1995), here SC 406:101.

anticipation in the dispensations of God, and accustoming his inheritance to obey God, to pass through the world in a state of pilgrimage, to follow his Word, and to indicate beforehand things to come. For with God there is nothing without purpose or due signification" (*Adv. Haer.* IV, 21, 3; ANF 1:493).

"He fulfilled his part by anticipation in the dispensations of God." This point raises an important problem: Does the theology of the universal revelation of the cosmic Christ, so brilliantly exposed by Irenaeus, show sufficient awareness of the unique and irreplaceable significance of his coming in the flesh? If the history of Israel is already full of the personal interventions of Christ, what becomes of the *ephapax*-character of the Christ-event? A theology of history must be judged on how felicitously it combines cosmic revelation with the singularity of the revealer, how it succeeds in harmonizing the universality of God's gracious initiative with the apparent scandal of the once-for-all historical happening. But if, in Irenaeus's view, Jesus Christ in some way anticipates — in the typological events of the Old Testament — his incarnation, then is not the newness of his coming in the flesh seriously impaired? No: for there remains the whole difference between Christ heralded and Christ given. Irenaeus writes:

> What then did the Lord bring when he came? Know this, that he brought something completely new, for he brought himself (*omnem novitatem attulit seipsum afferens*), who had been heralded....For the coming of a king is proclaimed to his servants by those who are to welcome their lord. But when the king has come, and those who are his subjects have been filled with the joy that before was but proclaimed, and have received that liberty which he gives, and share the sight of him, and have heard his words, and enjoyed his gifts, will they still ask what new things the king himself has brought in comparison with those who merely proclaimed his coming? (*Adv. Haer.* IV, 34, 1; Daniélou 1973, 172)

Irenaeus has no doubt that the universal revelatory function of the Logos makes him present to humankind from the beginning; again, the Old Testament Logophanies are for him authentic anticipations of the Christophany. Yet the human manifestation of Christ which took place once for all in space and time is in his mind ample guarantee of the newness of historical Christianity. For if in the old dispensation the Logos in a certain sense was already made visible — visible to the mind, in as far as he is the revelation, the manifestation, of the Father (*visibile Patris*) — then to the eyes of the flesh he became visible only by his advent in the flesh. Irenaeus distinguishes two ways of visibility of the Word. Of these, A. Orbe writes: "The Word's visibility according to the flesh corresponds to his essential visibility or cognoscibility according to the mind. Both generations, the one *ex Patre Deo* and the other *ex Maria Virgine*, correspond to each other in this respect" (Orbe 1958, 407).

They correspond to each other in the sense that he, to whose nature it belongs to manifest the Father to the minds of people, once incarnate, demonstrates him to their eyes. Yet they remain essentially distinct. For if the Logos from the beginning reveals the Father, he becomes — to use a recent idiom — the "sacrament of the encounter with God" by his incarnation. The historical Christ is a sacramental Logophany. The assumption of human flesh constitutes the decisive mission of the Son, the climax of the Father's manifestation through the visibility of the Logos.

## III. Clement of Alexandria and the Covenant of Philosophy

The first feature which distinguishes Clement's theology of the Word is the emphasis it lays on the term "Logos." Clement's predecessors called Christ primarily "Son," as he had been in the New Testament itself. In Clement's writings, the term "Logos" occupies the first place. The basic principle of his Christology remains that of Irenaeus. All personal manifestation of the Father takes place through the Logos: "We understand the Unknown by divine grace, and by the Word alone that proceeds from him" (*Strom.* V, 12).[9]

More exactly, Clement distinguishes in the Father that which is entirely unknowable, called by the Gnostics the abyss, and that which can be known once manifested in the Son (see *Excerpta* 23, 5). A significant difference must, however, be mentioned. While Justin and Irenaeus seemed to attribute all knowledge of God to the action of the divine Word, Clement distinguishes two distinct levels. A common, elementary knowledge of God can be acquired through the use of reason (*logos*, which means here human reason); it is accessible to all human beings and is called natural: "There was always a natural (*phusikès*) manifestation of the one Almighty God, among all right-thinking people" (*Strom.* V, 13; ANF 2:465).

At another level, the personal action of the Logos introduces people into God's secrets otherwise inaccessible. Clement thus makes distinctions, unknown to his predecessors, which bring him closer to our own theological categories.

How far does the influence of the Logos extend? Beyond the boundaries of the Judeo-Christian tradition, for the pagan world has had its own prophets. Some among the Greeks under the action of the Logos have truly prophesied: "By reflection and direct vision, those among the Greeks who have philosophized accurately see God" (*Strom.* I, 19; ANF 2:322).

Their philosophy — to be understood in Clement's rich meaning of the term, according to which Christian philosophy stands for Christian truth and practice — and therefore their achievements in human wisdom and religiosity witness to a special divine assistance granted them. Philosophers — in the sense just explained — have among the nations a divine mission: "The Shepherd cares for each of his sheep; and his closest inspection is given to those who are excellent in their natures, and are capable of being most useful. Such are those

---

9. Quotations are from The Ante-Nicene Fathers, vol. 2, ed. A. Roberts and J. Donalson (Grand Rapids, Mich.: Eerdmans, 1979) (ANF 2), here ANF 2:464.

fit to lead and teach, in whom the action of Providence is conspicuously seen; whenever either by instruction, or government, or administration, God wishes to benefit" (*Strom.* VI, 17; ANF 2:517).

Philosophy comes from God; it constitutes for the Greek world a divine economy, parallel, if not in all things equal, to the Jewish economy of the Law. Both were designed by God to lead people to Christ:

> To the ones he [the Lord] gave the commandments, to the others philosophy, that the unbeliever may have no excuse. For, by two different processes of advancement, both Greek and barbarian, he leads to perfection which is by faith. (*Strom.* VII, 2; ANF 2:526)

> To the Jews belonged the Law and to the Greeks philosophy, until the Advent; and after that came the universal calling to be a particular people of righteousness, through the teaching which flows from faith, brought together by one Lord, the only God of both Greeks and barbarians, or rather of the whole race of humans. (*Strom.* VI, 17; ANF 2:517–18)

And again: "As the proclamation [of the Gospel] has come now at the fit time, so also at the fit time were the Law and the Prophets given to the barbarians, and philosophy to the Greeks, to fit their ears for the Gospel" (*Strom.* VI, 6; ANF 2:490). More clearly still, philosophy has been to the Greeks a means of salvation given them by God:

> Before the advent (*parousia*) of the Lord, philosophy was necessary to the Greeks for righteousness. And now it becomes conducive to piety; being a kind of preparatory training to those who attain to faith through demonstration.... For God is the cause of all good things; but of some primarily, as of the Old and New Testament; and of others by consequence, as philosophy. Perchance too philosophy was given to the Greeks directly and primarily, until the Lord should call the Greeks. For this was a schoolmaster (*epaidagògei*) to bring the "Hellenic mind," as the Law of the Hebrews, to Christ. Philosophy, therefore, was a preparation, paving the way for him who is perfected in Christ.... The way of truth is therefore one. But into it, as into a perennial river, streams flow from all sides. (*Strom.* I, 5, 1–3; ANF 2:305)

Clement has no hesitation to call philosophy a covenant (*diathèkè*) made by God with people, a stepping-stone (*hupobathra*) to the philosophy of Christ: "All things necessary and profitable for life came to us from God, and philosophy more especially was given to the Greeks, as a covenant (*diathèkè*) peculiar to them — being, as it is, a stepping-stone (*hupobathra*) to the philosophy which is according to Christ" (*Strom.* VI, 8; ANF 2:495).

But, as is the case for the Jewish Law itself, the function of philosophy is a transitional one. Having prepared people for Christ's coming, it must finally make room for him: as a lamp loses its raison d'être once the sun is up, so, too, philosophy in Christ's advent (*Strom.* V, 5). Philosophy is a partial knowledge; Christ alone is the whole truth.

We have spoken of philosophy in the Greek world, and yet for Clement the Greek philosophers are not the truly great leaders whose God-given inspiration served to orient the nations to Christ. In fact, many among the Greek philosophers have borrowed from others. The authentic guides of humankind are the ancient philosophers who, truly inspired by God and acted upon by the Logos, have taught the nations divine truths. Clement mentions Indian sages along with others: "The Indian gymnosophists are also in the number, and the other non-Greek philosophers. And of these there are two classes, some of them called Sarmanae, and others Brahmins.... Some, too, of the Indians obey the precepts of Buddha; whom, on account of his extraordinary sanctity, they have raised to divine honour" (*Strom.* I, 15; ANF 2:316). This amounts to affirming, together with the presence of partial Christian truth in the Hindu and Buddhist traditions, a positive significance of these traditions in the history of salvation.

Before the *Stromata,* Clement had written the *Protreptikos* (Exhortation to the heathens), in which he developed a Logocentric theology, asserting that the Logos at work in Judaism, and in the best of what the Greek philosophers and poets had to offer, is that very Logos who became incarnate in Jesus Christ. As Irenaeus had done before him, so too Clement stresses the identity between the not-yet-incarnate Logos and the Logos-made-flesh, while at the same time asserting the entire newness which the Word's incarnation brings about, as compared to his earlier manifestations to humankind. The goal of the *Protreptikos* is to win the "pagans" to the Christian faith. With this end in view, Clement is not afraid to expose the dark side of paganism. Even among philosophers not all have reached a true knowledge of the truth; however, some have, thanks to the action upon them of the Word of God. Yet their perception of the truth through the Logos remains partial; it is in Jesus Christ, the Logos incarnate, that the truth about God is fully revealed to human beings, as well as true life in God, who through his Word-made-flesh shares with us his own incorruptibility and immortality. Some quotations will illustrate the doctrine:[10]

> Inasmuch as the Word was from the first, he was and is the divine source of all things; but inasmuch as he has now assumed the name Christ, consecrated of all, and worthy of power, he has been called by me the New Song. This Word, then, the Christ, the cause of both our being at first (for he was in God) and of our well-being, the very Word has now appeared as man, he alone being both, God and man — the author of all blessings for us; by whom we, being taught to live well, are sent on our way to life eternal....
>
> This is the New Song, the manifestation of the Word that was in the beginning, and before the beginning. The Saviour, who existed before, has in recent days appeared. He, who is in him that truly is, has appeared; for

---

10. Quotations are from ANF 2.

the Word who "was with God," and by whom all things were created, has appeared as our Teacher. (*Protrept.* I, 6–7; ANF 2:173)

From this first quotation it might seem that before the incarnation the Logos manifested himself only in creation. Not so, however; for whatever Greek philosophers have known of the truth, no matter how incomplete, has been communicated to them from the "scintillations of the divine Word" they have received:

If, at the most, the Greeks, having received certain scintillations of the divine Word, have given forth some utterances of truth, they bear indeed witness that the force of truth is not hidden, and at the same time expose their own weakness in not having arrived at the end. For I think it has now become evident to all, that those who do or speak aught without the Word of truth are like people compelled to walk without feet. (*Protrept.* VII, 74–75; ANF 2:193)

For Clement the "Word of the Father, the benign light, the Lord who brings light, faith to all, and salvation" (*Protrept.* VIII, 80), has been active everywhere, bringing light and truth. The Logos is "the light of humans" (*Protrept.* IX, 84); he "is not hidden to anyone; he is the common Light, that shines for all humans" (*Protrept.* IX, 88). Similarly, Clement writes:

For "The Lord who created the earth by his power," as Jeremiah says, "has raised up the world by his wisdom" [Jer 10, 12]; for wisdom, which is his Word, raises us up to the truth, who have fallen prostrate before idols, and is itself the first resurrection from our fall. (*Protrept.* VIII, 80; ANF 2:195)

Great is the grace of his promise, "if today we hear his voice" [Ps 95, 7]. And that today is lengthened out day by day, while it is called today. And to the end the today, the never ending day of God, extends over eternity. Let us then ever obey the voice of the divine Word. For the today signifies eternity. And day is the symbol of light; and the light of humans is the Word, by whom we behold God. (*Protrept.* IX, 84; ANF 2:196)

Hear, then, you who are far off, hear you who are near: the Word has not been hidden from any; light is common, it shines "on all human beings." (*Protrept.* IX, 88; ANF 2:197)

Whatever manifestation of the Word there may have been in the truth perceived by philosophers, the fact remains that the fullness of the manifestation of God in his Word is found in Jesus Christ, the Word made man. Indeed, "the Word of God became human, that [we might] learn from a man how human beings may become God" (*Protrept.* I, 8). From the knowledge of God we receive from him and the divine life we share through him, there ought to be no turning back to what was given before only in part:

Since the Word himself has come to us from heaven, we need not... go any more in search of human learning to Athens and the rest of Greece, and to Ionia. For if we have as our teacher him that fills the universe with his holy energies in creation, salvation, beneficence, legislation, prophecy, teaching, we have the Teacher from whom all instruction comes; and the whole world, with Athens and Greece, has already become the domain of the Word.... We who have become the disciples of God have received the only true wisdom; and that which the chief of philosophy only guessed at, the disciples of Christ have both apprehended and proclaimed. (*Protrept.* XI, 112; ANF 2:203)

It has been God's fixed and constant purpose to save the flock of humans: for this end the good God sent the good Shepherd. And the Word, having unfolded the truth, showed to humans the height of salvation, that either repenting they might be saved, or refusing to obey, they might be judged. (*Protrept.* XI, 116; ANF 2:204)

In chapter 12 of the *Protreptikos,* Clement invites both "barbarians and Greeks" to entrust themselves to Jesus Christ. If they do so, "the Word of God will be [their] pilot, and the Holy Spirit will bring [them] to anchor in the haven of heaven" (*Protrept.* XII, 118). The book ends with a double exhortation endowed with power and beauty: the first, addressed by the Word made man in Jesus to all humans, that coming to him they may find life in God; the other, by Clement himself, that in Jesus Christ they may become friends of God (*Protrept.* XII, 120–22).

## IV. Hermeneutics of the Early Logos-Theology

The Logos-theology of Justin, Irenaeus, and Clement is not lacking in similarity from one author to another. All three make reference to a manifestation of God in the Logos before the incarnation of the Word, indeed throughout human history and from creation itself; for all three the manifestation of God in the Logos culminates in his becoming human in Jesus Christ — an event which, while being prepared by previous manifestations, is nonetheless entirely new and unexpected. Various nuances differentiate the thought of the three authors; they too have recourse to different concepts to characterize the action of the Logos: Logos-sower in Justin, Logos-revealer in Irenaeus, covenantal Logos in Clement; or, equivalently, *Logos spermatikos* in Justin, *Logos emphutos* in Irenaeus, *Logos protreptikos* in Clement (Saldanha 1984, 185–87). Yet in the main lines the Logos-theology of the three authors shows a remarkable consistency.

It does not, however, fail to raise problems of interpretation; but the consistency between the three authors is such as to allow the questions to be put to all of them. Some questions of interpretation are the following: What does Clement of Alexandria intend by "philosophy" when he states that God has made with philosophy a covenant destined to lead the Greeks toward Christ? Does the Logos, everywhere present among humans in the works of the three authors, go back to the immanent *logos* (or "reason") of the Stoa and of Philo the Jew? Or is it to be identified with the Word of God of the Prologue of the Gospel according to John, everywhere present and active in human history and finally incarnate in Jesus Christ? Do the three authors consider that whatever truth Greek philosophers have attained has been borrowed by them from the religion of Israel? Or do they attribute such truth, in spite of its concordance with Israelite religion, to the influence of the Word of God upon them? Contrasting answers have been given to these questions, which need to be critically considered.

Clement has defined what he means by philosophy when he wrote: "Philosophy — I do not mean the Stoic, or the Platonic, or the Epicurean, or the Aristotelian, but whatever has been well said by each of these schools, which teach righteousness along with a science pervaded by piety (*euseboûs*) — this eclectic whole I call philosophy" (*Strom.* I, 7; ANF 2:308). "Righteousness pervaded by piety" indicates that the philosophy intended by Clement refers more to "wisdom" and "religiosity" than to mere knowledge through reason. Such a philosophy can be considered as leading to the "philosophy which is according to Christ" (*Strom.* VI, 8, quoted above). Commenting on Paul's discourse to the Areopagite, Clement writes: "The apostle . . . approves of what had been well spoken by the Greeks; and he intimates that, by the 'unknown God,' God the Creator was in a roundabout way worshipped by the Greeks; but that it was necessary by positive knowledge to apprehend and learn him by the Son" (*Strom.* I, 19; ANF 2:321). One may not forget what has been stated earlier: our three authors agree with the other Fathers of the Church in condemning the polytheism and idolatry of surrounding religions. Nevertheless, the philosophy of which they approve is not devoid of "religious" elements. M. Fédou is right in commenting: "It is true that there is no question of religions as such. Yet, the 'philosophy' of which Clement speaks must be understood in a relatively broader meaning, which covers not only the doctrines developed by different schools of thought but makes room for 'piety' and 'religiosity' (*eusebeia*)" (Fédou 1992, 178). And the same author adds: "The 'philosophy' as used by Justin or Clement of Alexandria evoked among other things the practice of an honest life, the pursuit of values, the aspiration to justice and wisdom — to which formal 'religiosity' can be added" (Fédou 1992, 184).

It is in philosophy as thus understood that our authors recognized, under the influence of the Word of God, a preparation for the message of Jesus Christ. The Wisdom of God present in the one and the other functioned as the meeting point between them. The patristic theme of the "seeds of the Word" offers, today, a valid foundation for a positive approach to the "religions" inasmuch as in them too, thanks to the active presence of the Word of God, justice and piety (*eusebeia*) are not wanting.

Does the Logos of whom our three authors speak refer to the Word of God which, in the Prologue of the Gospel according to John, was already present and active in human history previous to his incarnation in Jesus Christ? Or does it refer to the immanent "reason" (*logos*) of the Stoa and of Philo the Jew? The answer to these questions has great consequences for the theology put forward by the three authors. If the second interpretation turns out to be the correct one, all that can be read in the texts is the attainment of some "natural" truth through the philosophical use of reason. If the first interpretation is to be retained, what is being affirmed is a universal presence and action of God's immanent Logos in human history; reference would then be made, through the Prologue of the Fourth Gospel, to the "literary personification" of the Word of God (*Dabar*) which in the Old Testament stood for God inasmuch as he manifests himself through deeds and words in history.

These questions cannot be answered by an either-or statement. The Prologue of the Fourth Gospel already integrated features of the *logos* of Stoic philosophy into its concept of the Word of God acting in history; the early Fathers of the Church continued to do likewise. Interpreters do not fail to note the complex meaning which they give to the Logos, seeing the Word of God as the principle of intelligibility of creation, world, and history. Though being very critical of any attempt to attribute to the early Fathers an incipient theology of history and a positive value to the religious traditions, P. Hacker recognizes nonetheless that, according to Saint Justin, some individuals, Greek philosophers in particular, have allowed themselves to be "guided by the divine Logos in whom every human being has received participation and who at a definitive point of time became incarnate in Jesus" (Hacker 1980, 39–40). He writes:

> In some places Justin doubtless overstresses the Greek meaning of the Logos (reason) and he oversimplifies the problem of identifying Christ with Reason. Nevertheless his theory is a magnificent approach to a theological evaluation of paganism. Extending the line that had been traced out in New Testament texts, he felicitously adapts an element of Stoic philosophy, in teaching that there are "germinal *logoi*" or seeds of the one divine Logos, sparks of his Light, in every soul. (Hacker 1980, 40)

The same is true, according to Hacker, where Clement of Alexandria is concerned. In spite of Clement's vehement critique of "strictly religious elements of Hellenism," Clement recognizes that some philosophers have allowed themselves to be acted upon by the divine Logos universally present and active:

> Clement is following what St. John meant when speaking of the light of the Logos that illuminates every man, and what St. Paul said regarding man's faculty of knowing God....Clement speaks of a divine inspiration ...which enables philosophers and also poets at times to see the truth. Even though the Greeks have not attained to the goal..., still they have received some light which has proceeded from the divine Logos. (Hacker 1980, 46)

A more positive evaluation of the integration of the Stoic concept of *logos* with the Johannine Word of God in Justin and Clement is expressed by M. Fédou. With reference to the *Logos spermatikos* of Justin, this author writes:

> The allusion to the Stoics indicates one of the sources of the theme in question: that philosophical school held that Reason, principle of the world (*logos*), was universally disseminated (*spermatikos*) in the cosmos. But Logos also meant the Word, of which the Gospel according to John had said that it was with God from the beginning; and was not the parable of the sower to be understood as applying to the Word of God himself? Justin thus daringly combines the Stoic concept of Reason immanent to the universe and the biblical tradition of the Word spread on the earth. He thus invites us to affirm a presence of the Word of God to humans outside the Judeo-Christian tradition — a presence which, no doubt, they could refuse, but which they were also enabled to welcome. (Fédou 1992, 177–78; see also Saldanha 1984; Daniélou 1973)

We shall not enter into a discussion of the alleged dependence of the elements of truth and wisdom attained by ancient philosophers upon the Jewish tradition, with which they would have been in contact. That the hypothesis of historical dependence has sometimes been advanced by the Fathers in a bid to uphold the monopoly of truth of the Jewish-Christian tradition, even with the help of fanciful chronology, is certain. But it is no less certain that the three authors under consideration here did not have recourse to apologetic devices meant to disprove the active presence of the Logos outside the Judeo-Christian tradition; though within certain limits, they clearly affirmed the universally active presence of the divine Logos.

All theological questions are not solved thereby. It must still be asked what theological significance our authors attributed to the influence of the divine Logos, in Greek wisdom and elsewhere, outside the Christian dispensation. We must likewise ask whether such efficacy was understood by them to apply exclusively to pre-Christian times or could, on the contrary, be viewed as extending to the period following the Christ-event. And, if so, what value did the active presence of the Word of God among human persons have in terms of bestowal upon them of divine grace and justification by faith?

It is certain that the Fathers considered the pre-Christian active presence of the Logos as a divine "pedagogy" toward things to come, or — to use the expression which Eusebius of Caesarea would illustrate later — as a "preparation for the Gospel" (*praeparatio evangelica*). Clement of Alexandria is especially clear on this point when he writes: "Before the advent (*parousia*) of the Lord, philosophy was necessary to the Greeks for righteousness.... Philosophy was given to the Greeks directly and primarily, until the Lord should call the Greeks. For this was a schoolmaster (*epaidagogei*) to bring the 'Hellenic mind,' as the Law the Hebrews, to Christ" (*Strom.* I, 5, 3, quoted above).

How must, however, "till the Lord should call the Greeks" be understood? Has the value of Greek Wisdom as a "schoolmaster" to the Gospel come to an end with the historical event of Jesus Christ? Or does it abide thereafter until such time as individuals would be personally challenged by the Christian message? Saldanha is right in upholding the second position. He asks the question and answers it forthrightly:

> Did...the Fathers consid[er] the divine education of mankind to be now at an end? And that with the coming of the Lord Greek philosophy...had forfeited [its] role in the economy of salvation? By no means. The answer to this question lies in understanding what precisely the Fathers meant by "the coming of the Lord" (*parousia*). To be sure, the *parousia* referred to the coming of the Word in the flesh, but it did not remain confined to his earthly life. We find Clement...repeatedly exhorting the Greeks in the *Protreptikos* to accept the Savior who had *now* appeared and was *now* inviting men to salvation...[*Protrept.* IX, 84, quoted above]. Clement was not stating something new, but rather a belief that was widely held in the apostolic and sub-Apostolic Church, namely, that with the taking on of the flesh, the Incarnate Word became present to the subsequent history of humanity, the incarnation being the initial point of insertion of his new and permanent presence in history....To Clement's way of thinking, the role of Greek philosophy as a divine pedagogy before the Advent meant that role lasted *till the Lord should call the Greeks....*
>
> The call was still going out to men in Clement's time. The "promulgation of the Gospel" was still taking place. Until the call was "heard," in the fullest sense of the word, Greek philosophy, and likewise...the other religions, would continue their divine role of education among men. (Saldanha 1984, 169–70)

Greek philosophy and other similar wisdom bestowed upon humans by the Word of God did not, according to our authors, forfeit their role in the economy of salvation, even after the Lord's historical coming; their providential role endured until such time as individual persons would be directly challenged by the Christian message. This broad interpretation of the "promulgation of the Gospel," as will be observed hereafter, was destined to be abandoned later by the official teaching of the Church, to be recovered only by recent theology. It is all the more important to take note of it at this early stage of Christian reflection.

There still remains, however, the decisive question of the theological significance of the pre- and pro-Christian divine pedagogy operative through the Logos in terms of the bestowal upon persons of divine life and grace, whether before the Christ-event or after it, outside the boundaries of the Christian fold. Divergent interpretations must be taken note of, going from one end of the spectrum to the other.

According to Hacker, while Justin recognized that individual persons — as distinct from their pagan religious environment — could "allow themselves to be guided by the divine Logos," he yet remained "silent on the possibility for pious gentiles to reach final consummation in eternity" (Hacker 1980, 39–40). Hacker writes:

> Clement deems it possible that there is a kind of justification through philosophy.... But this justification is only relative and is not yet "total righteousness" (*katholou dikaiosunè*). Philosophy is not a substitute for faith, which alone leads to eternal life. Nor does philosophy cleanse a man from his sins.... There were men who in their life-time had no occasion to know the Gospel and yet strove after perfection under the guidance of philosophy. According to Clement, such men obtain a chance for conversion in Hades where Christ and the apostles preach the Gospel to them. To attain final salvation, it is indispensable that the souls of the righteous gentiles in Hades should do penance and accept faith in Christ. (Hacker 1980, 43–44)

Saldanha's interpretation, while being less negative than Hacker's, remains nonetheless restrictive. According to Saldanha,

> the Fathers — ... Justin, Irenaeus and Clement of Alexandria — ... suggest a kind of middle ground between two alternatives: they envisage a situation in which the "good pagan" would possess justification/faith/grace, but not — or better, not yet — *Christian* justification/faith/grace. (Saldanha 1984, 157)

According to Saldanha, in Justin's view "there was no question of [the pagans] being in possession of the grace Christians possessed" (Saldanha 1984, 161). Justin held a "*qualitative* difference between the good pagan and the Christian. The difference was not of partial versus full or implicit versus explicit" (Saldanha 1984, 162). It consisted in the fact that the good pagan did not "know God, the Maker of all things through Jesus Christ the crucified" (*Dial.* 34, 8). For Irenaeus, likewise, the coming of the incarnate Word into the world produced not just a "greater gift of paternal grace" (*Adv. Haer.* IV, 36, 4) but a "real difference in the gifts" (Saldanha 1984, 162). Saldanha continues:

> Notwithstanding the righteousness the just possessed before the incarnation, they still needed the Lord to proclaim the *Gospel* to them in Hades and to grant them the *remission of their sins* (cf. *Demonst.* 78; *Adv. Haer.* IV, 27, 2). Although the Spirit was poured out "even from the creation of the world to its end upon the human race simply as such, from whom those who believe in God and follow his Word receive that salvation which flows from him," Irenaeus spoke of an *outpouring of the same Spirit of God "after a new fashion* in these last times" (*Adv. Haer.* IV, 33, 15). (Saldanha 1984, 163)

Saldanha thinks, however, that among the three Fathers, Clement is the clear-est one about the difference between righteousness among Jews and gentiles and among Christians:

> The situation of the just men of Old Testament, be they Jews or Greeks, was not one of a total lack of faith and righteousness; but neither was it one of possessing the faith and righteousness of Christians. There was an *intermediate state of justification,* different from either pole and yet authentic enough to be a stepping-stone to the ultimate conversion to Christianity. (Saldanha 1984, 164; emphasis added)

Summing up what he views as the conviction of the Fathers, Saldanha again writes:

> In spite of the grace, faith and justification he possessed, the good pagan or Jew of the Old Testament stood in need of a new grace, a new faith, a new justification in order to attain salvation — and this could only come to him through the knowledge and acceptance of the Crucified One, be it in life (through conversion and baptism) or in death (by coming into contact with Christ's death in some mysterious way). (Saldanha 1984, 166)

That the difference between faith, justification, and grace in the good pa-gan or Jew and in the Christian was "not only in degree but in kind," "not just...quantitative but qualitative," the Fathers explained through their concept of "participation in salvation." Just as universal salvation history com-prised various stages and culminated in the incarnation, death, and resurrection of Jesus Christ, so too, "the Greeks and the Jews were able to participate in salvation through the providential arrangements God had made for them, but their participation in salvation remained different from, though oriented to, *the* salvation through Christ's Paschal Mystery" (Saldanha 1984, 167).

In the end, Saldanha applies his findings in the early Fathers to the situation of members of the other religions today, saying: "The condition of a man who participates in grace even before he has been evangelized occupies some kind of *middle ground* between 'non-justification' and 'Christian justification'; hence to call such a condition by the latter term is to jeopardise the transcendent newness of Christianity" (Saldanha 1984, 174; emphasis added).

With this last observation Saldanha means to reject the theory of "anony-mous Christianity" propounded by K. Rahner. This is not the place to enter into a complex discussion; we shall have to return to this topic later. Meanwhile, keeping to the evaluation of the early Fathers, it must be said that the *qualita-tive* difference between pre-Christian justification and Christian grace, as well as the *intermediate* state of pre-Christian justification without the remission of sins, besides lacking in precision, fails to convince. The interpretation of F.-X. Durrwell, otherwise very similar to that of Saldanha, has the merit of greater precision. He holds that "there must be a qualitative difference between the grace of the Old Testament and [the New Testament] gift of the Spirit" (Durr-well 1972, 116–17). According to Durrwell, the difference consists, in effect, in the abiding immanent presence of the Spirit, implied in New Testament grace, which is absent in the pre-Christian economy of grace. To deny this would be to obscure the newness of Christianity.

One must ask, however: If — as Durrwell is right to stress — grace consists in God's self-communication, does not such self-gift entail, necessarily and in all situations, the immanent abiding presence of the Spirit? What can be the mean-ing of the proposition that, while in the Old Testament the Spirit was present by its activity (for instance in the prophets), its presence is "personal" only in the New Testament dispensation, as it was in Jesus himself (Durrwell 1967; 1986)? Clearly a better explanation will have to be found to account for the distinction between the pre-Christian and the Christian regimes of grace.

Yves Congar, in contrast, is more reserved and limits himself to speaking of distinct moments or regimes of faith and grace: there is "faith before faith," as there is "grace before grace" (Congar 1961, 103ff.). Referring to the early Fathers, he writes:

> The thought of the ancient Fathers could, I believe, be expressed in the following terms in conformity with Pauline categories: between the faithful or the saints before Christ and ourselves, *grace is the same* — that is: there is one and the same project (*propos*) of grace, one and the same process of salvation gratuitously bestowed; but there is a difference in the spiritual gifts bestowed in keeping with that grace. (Congar 1952, 80–81; emphasis added)

Or again, says Congar, there is a difference "in the *regime* and quality of the spiritual gifts" (Congar 1952, 84). Even this way of speaking seems to be in need of refinement: as will be seen later, the distinction between the two "regimes" of God's self-communication in grace consists in the coming into play of the glorified humanity of Jesus Christ as the universal channel of grace through his resurrection from the dead and, therefore, of the communication through it of the indwelling Spirit.[11]

## V. Toward a Theology of History

The early Fathers were concerned to affirm the "entire newness" which the coming in the flesh of the Word of God brought about. Irenaeus expressed it in a lapidary formula: *omnem novitatem attulit seipsum afferens* (*Adv. Haer.* IV, 34, 1). This did not prevent them from asserting as well a universal active presence

---

11. We may already take note of the affirmation made by Vatican II in the decree *Ad Gentes* 4: "With-out doubt, the Holy Spirit was at work in the world before Christ was glorified." The council refers to Saint Leo the Great, *Sermo* 76 (PL 54:405–6). More clearly, Pope John Paul II states in the encyclical *Dominum et Vivificantem* (1986) that already before the Christian economy "grace bears within itself both a Christological aspect and a pneumatological one" (53) (AAS 78 [1986], 874).

of the Word of God previous to the incarnation; these Logophanies announced and prepared the Word's decisive manifestation in the flesh. They recognized his action in particular in Greek philosophy, which in their view contained not merely human reasoning but such wisdom, piety, and religiosity as needed to be assigned to the action of the Word of God. They proclaimed their conviction about the underlying continuity which existed between the Word's partial manifestation through human history and his decisive disclosure in the incarnation; at the same time they stressed the discontinuity by affirming the thorough newness of God's advent in human flesh. The relation between the old and the new was, as they saw it, one of continuity-in-discontinuity. As Saldanha puts it:

> If it was the Incarnate Word crucified who *set Christianity apart* in its novelty and transcendence, it was the same Incarnate Word crucified who *brought the religions and Christianity together* in a preparation-fulfillment relationship.... The new was intimately related to what the Word had been doing before.... [One] universal economy compris[es] both the Old and New Testaments, creation and redemption, the whole history from the beginning to the end; within this economy [there was] a progressive development in the revelation by the Word leading up to its culmination in the Incarnate Word:... a certain *continuity* between the religions and Christianity by way of preparation and a certain *discontinuity* in the form of Christianity's transcendence and novelty vis-à-vis those same religions. To eliminate, exaggerate or minimize either of these poles would amount to a distortion of Christianity or of non-Christian religions. (Saldanha 1984, 161)

In order to illustrate the continuity-in-discontinuity of God's manifestation in history through the Word, Irenaeus — in a text already quoted — distinguished four covenants as follows:

> Four covenants were given to the human race: one, prior to the deluge, under Adam; the second, that after the deluge, under Noah; the third, the giving of the Law, under Moses; the fourth, that which renovates the human being, and sums up all things in itself by means of the Gospel, raising and bearing human beings upon its wings into the heavenly kingdom. (*Adv. Haer.* III, 11, 8; ANF 1:429)

Among the four covenants the first two are universal and express God's manifestation to all human beings through history, from creation on. The theological significance of the Noah covenant as distinct from the Adam covenant, and its bearing upon the religious traditions of the world, will be further considered at a later stage. The third covenant concerns the chosen people of Israel and serves as direct historical preparation for God's decisive manifestation in Jesus Christ, in whom the entire process comes to a climax. The Word of God has thus been present to the human race throughout history; yet his presence to it culminates in Jesus Christ.

It seems legitimate to think that—even while the term "theology of history" is of recent origin and has a specific meaning in theological discussion — the early Fathers' global view of God's manifestation to humankind well deserves to be considered as an early version of that recently rediscovered dimension of theology which we call "theology of history" (Luneau 1964; Surgy 1969; Spanneut 1957). In the early Fathers' view, Christianity was destined to integrate, while purifying and transforming it, whatever good it found in the religious life of the nations. They looked upon Christianity "not as a limited confession, but as the total cosmic religion — precisely as *katholon* — in which partial elements fitted in after undergoing due purification" (Balthasar 1966, 132). Their evaluation of the religiosity of the nations was, in the words of Henri de Lubac, of "a dynamic order, inserted in a theology of history" (Lubac 1967c, 132).

There remains to ask whether the successors of the early Fathers entertained the same open attitude toward the Greek religiosity as did their forebears of the second century. Only a rapid glance at Origen, among the Greeks, and, among the Latins, at Saint Augustine, is possible here. The complex and ambivalent attitude of these two great protagonists can be viewed as exemplary; it is also symptomatic of the negative views which were to develop thereafter, of which the next chapter will have to give an account.

Though generally more severe toward philosophy than were Justin or Clement, Origen did nevertheless admit that what is best in the doctrine of philosophers can serve as a useful propaedeutic (*propaideuma*) for the study of Christian doctrine and be of use in the exposition of the word of God.[12] He saw only polytheism and idolatry in the pagan religions with which he was confronted; yet, at the same time, he recognized "seeds of the Word" in the wisdom of the nations, mostly in the best philosophical tradition. Like his predecessors, Origen professed a universal manifestation of the Word of God to humankind while affirming at the same time the singular and unique character of his incarnation in Jesus Christ: the same divine Logos had been and was universally present who took flesh in Jesus Christ. Against Celsus, who in his "True Discourse" (*alèthès logos*) understood the *logos* to refer to the power of human reason and challenged the identification between the divine Logos and the person of Jesus Christ, Origen insisted in his *Contra Celsum* that the same who is the divine Logos or Son of God had communicated himself to the nations before the coming of Jesus Christ and had become human in him (Fédou 1988, 515ff.). For Origen, as M. Fédou writes, "The essential values of humankind must be understood as diverse ways of sharing in the true Logos, who dwells in the universe in order that reasonable creatures might, in their diversity, share the nature of the one First-Born" (Fédou 1988, 569).

While such a vision is partly derived from the Stoic doctrine of the *logos spermatikos*, Origen borrows it more directly from the scriptures:

---

12. *In Levi hom.* 7, 6; *In Jesu Nave hom.* 7, 1; *Contra Celsum* VI, 4; etc. See Crouzel 1962.

The Logos does not merely refer to universal reason, but to the Word that expresses itself in the Bible, in the person of Christ, in the preaching of the apostles, in the eucharistic bread and the ecclesial body. That Word is God's revelation, unfolded through human history, which invites to faith; it is the true light that shines on Judaea and from there spreads its rays to the whole universe. (Fédou 1988, 569)

Thus God arouses in the wisdom of the nations the seeds of the Logos, leading them to true wisdom in Christ. Where Irenaeus had insisted on the discontinuity between God's previous manifestation through the Logos and the "thorough newness" of the incarnation, Origen seems more sensitive to the continuity of God's revelation in his Word. M. Harl writes the following:

Because of his philosophical formation so closely bound to middle Platonism, [Origen] insists much more on the eternal revelation of God than on the particular event of the incarnation of the Word. God reveals himself always, acts always. The Son reveals God always, revelation still lasts. God's revelation is spread in various moments (Irenaeus among others had stressed the *kairoi* of the history of revelation), but it would seem that for Origen the moments of revelation are sensibly equal, that there is no sudden leap by the fact of the incarnation. God reveals himself through time, *dia kronou*. Creation, the Law, the coming of Christ, the founding of the Church ensure the continuity of this revelation. It is always the Son that reveals, just as much, it would seem, through the world of which he is the law, through the Old Testament which he has inspired, through Jesus in whom he is present, through the Church that he loves. The incarnation of the Word in Jesus is not the only moment which once for all would have manifested the whole truth. Revelation does not pertain exclusively to Christ, nor was it given through him entirely, definitively: after him his Spirit and his power continue to be at work in the whole world, to the end of time. Origen is more interested in the fact that God acts always in all sorts of ways, rather than in the historical manifestation of the Word who took flesh.[13]

More than Origen, Saint Augustine liked to see in Greek philosophy a preparation for the Christian religion. However, while philosophers have been able to recognize the Word of God, which is truth, and to catch a glimpse of the aim of human life, which is the vision of God, they could not discover the way leading to it because they have not known the Word made flesh, Jesus in the

---

13. Harl 1958, 337–38. Crouzel (1960) rejects what he understands to be M. Harl's interpretation that Origen underestimated the newness of the incarnation. For clarifications and rectifications, see Fédou 1994, 126–41. Origen does not deny the newness of the incarnation but shows its continuity with all previous manifestations of the Logos. The newness of the incarnation "is not the irruption of a mystery never before unveiled in any way, nor only the gift of a Revelation which would accomplish anterior revelations, bringing them to fulfillment; it is, more radically, 'the manifestation of the Truth,' the unveiling of what was previously hidden but already present, the coming in the flesh of him who had already communicated himself to human beings and was from all eternity with the Father" (137).

humility of his flesh. If then human wisdom contains a preparation for Christ, this needs to be fulfilled by the Christian message, and passing from one to the other entails a true conversion.

Yet in his *De Civitate Dei* and elsewhere in his literary production, Augustine stresses the universal saving influence of Christ before the incarnation. He proceeds further to the affirmation that the Church itself existed before Christ's coming in the flesh, in fact, from the beginning: *Ecclesia ab Abel*. Abel, supposedly the first just man (*primus iustus*), and every just human person after him, whatever their historical situation, belonged to Christ and to his Church:

> Abel was the beginning of the City of God. (*Enar. in Ps.* 142, 3)

> The Church...was not absent on earth at the beginning of the human race. Abel the saint is the first-fruits of it. (*Enar. in Ps.* 118 = *Sermo* 29, 9)

Yves Congar has shown that a possible shortcoming of this, as of every theology of history, would be to reduce the truly historical, and therefore temporally conditioned and progressive, character of God's salvific dispensation (Congar 1952, 86). Two spiritual cities may well have coexisted from the start, yet it must not be forgotten that the city of God has passed through various economies. But, precisely, long before Augustine, Irenaeus had distinguished the Word's visibility to the mind from his visibility to the eyes; after him Origen would speak of a "spiritual descent" (*pneumatikè epidèmia*) of the Logos, prior to his coming in the flesh. These expressions and others seem to witness to the Fathers' awareness of the fact that Christ's universal influence had all along depended upon and presupposed the historical event of the incarnation. They knew that, even though from the beginning of time the Father, according to his dispensation, could be reached through the Son, never had the encounter of God with humans been so profound, so authentic, and finally so human as since it has passed through and taken place in the flesh of the incarnate Word. Yet in their mind — and in their terminology — it remained true that Christ, and in a sense Christianity itself, had existed from the beginning. A celebrated passage of Augustine's *Retractationes* affirms it:

> The very thing which is now called the Christian religion existed already among the ancients, nor was it absent at the beginning of the human race, until the coming of Christ in the flesh when the true religion which had already existed began to be called Christian.... Therefore, if I have written: "This is the religion which exists in our days, the Christian religion," the meaning is not that it had not existed previously, but that it took the name Christian only later. (*Retract.* I, 13, 3; CSEL 36:58–59)

That Christianity and the Church have existed from the beginning must be understood correctly, according to Augustine's mind. What is meant is not that the Church as a historical reality preexisted its foundation by Jesus Christ, but that salvation has been available to all people through history, and that is salvation in Jesus Christ (Congar 1952; Saldanha 1984, 180–83). "The ancient believed in the Christ to come; we believe in him as having come" (*Enar. in Ps.* 50, 17). A. D. Sertillanges has used in this connection the telling expression, "the Church before the Church."[14]

It must, however, be recognized that Augustine insists much more than did Irenaeus on the destructive effects of sin in the history of humankind. The leading theme of *De Civitate Dei* is the opposition between the city of God and the earthly city. The two cities represent two groups of people, "the one consisting of those who live according to humankind, the other of those who live according to God" (*De Civ. Dei* 15, 1). In other terms: "The two cities have been formed by two loves: the earthly by the love of self, even to the contempt of God; the heavenly by the love of God, even to the contempt of self" (*De Civ. Dei* 14, 28). Although the city of God has become manifest in the Church, the "two cities are entangled together in this world and intermixed until the last judgment effects their separation" (*De Civ. Dei* 1, 35).

To one part of the earthly city God granted that it become a foreshadowing symbol of the heavenly city, "which served to remind humans that such a city was to be rather than to make it present." This was the city or commonwealth of the old covenant (*De Civ. Dei* 15, 2). "There was no other people who were specially called the people of God;... but they [the Jews] cannot deny that there have been certain persons even of other nations who belonged, not by earthly but by heavenly fellowship, to the true Israelites, the citizens of the country that is above" (*De Civ. Dei* 18, 47). Augustine thought that Job was an example of a holy man from among the nations (*De Civ. Dei* 3, 1). Christ had given to all nations the possibility to turn toward the city of God. Present history remains, nevertheless, marked by the conflict between the two cities and will remain so to the end of times. In this struggle between the two cities, which began with Abel and Cain and will last to the end of times, the religious destiny of humankind is at stake. Such is Augustine's reading of history (Piret 1991).

The theme that salvation in Jesus Christ — and, therefore, in that sense, Christianity — has existed from the beginning received an ample development in a letter (*Epistola* 102; PL 33:370–86; CSEL 34:544–78), where Augustine answers a pagan philosopher's questions concerning the Christian religion. The opponent had challenged the Christian doctrine that salvation is given only to those who have faith in Christ, which implies the claim of universal and exclusive validity for the Christian religion. The doctrine seemed to entail that all nations that lived before Christ, except the Jews, were excluded from salvation (*Epistola* 102, 2, 8). Augustine's answer is that at all times salvation in Jesus Christ has been available, for the Christian religion has in some way been present from the beginning.[15] He writes:

> At all times and in all places from the origin of humankind those who believed in him, who came to know him in whatever manner, and who led

---

14. Sertillanges 1933. The expression is the title of chapter 1.
15. For a detailed analysis of Letter 102, see Hacker 1980, 53–56.

godly and righteous lives, have doubtless become saved through him.... Thus, it is one and the same true religion which was signified earlier by names and signs other than those we use now, and which was observed in a more hidden way previously and more manifest later, by a few previously and by a greater number later. (*Epistola* 102, 2, 12)

Commenting on Augustine's Letter, Hacker writes: "The Saint's reply [to the philosopher's questions] includes the most important and original contribution to a theological appraisal of the problem of religions" (Hacker 1980, 53, cf. 56).

We in turn may conclude this review of the early Fathers' theology of history and their sequel in Origen and Augustine by quoting Karl Rahner:

When the early Fathers kept a look-out on such an activity of the Logos, the beginnings of his incarnation, as it were, in saving history before Christ, ... they were better advised than we are, for whom God rules there simply from heaven.... The history of religions as a whole ... [must be] integrated ... in the single history of the dialogue between God and the world, a dialogue which flows into the Word made flesh.... Religions ... were an unconscious Yes or No to the Word of God who was to come in human flesh. (Rahner 1961a, 189)

# Three

# No Salvation outside the Church?

C HAPTER 2 ended up noting that some of the early Fathers designed an early version of a theology of salvation history that allowed them to attribute a positive significance to the other religions in God's plan for humankind. Their views remained partly alive among some of their successors. Origen and Augustine, for instance — the two pillars of patristic tradition, the Greek and the Latin — enunciate ideas which in some way prolong the broad perspective of Justin, Irenaeus, and Clement. Salvation in Christ had been possible for the people who lived before the Christ-event, whether Jews or gentiles. What happened to them after the Christ-event was, however, quite another question. What happened, moreover, to those, once members of the Church, who had separated themselves from it?

Soon after Clement of Alexandria (d. ca. 211), a current set in, destined to have a protracted history through the Christian tradition, which was characterized by the axiom: "Outside the Church no salvation" (*Extra ecclesiam nulla salus*). This axiom, as will be seen, gradually received an increasingly rigid interpretation.

The adage was not without a true foundation in the New Testament. We have shown in chapter 1 the ambiguity and ambivalence of the scriptural data on the significance of the surrounding religions. Next to some positive data regarding the religiosity of the Greeks, there are pessimistic views concerning their situation with regard to divine salvation. The New Testament, in fact, did not address the theological question for its own sake; it was satisfied to state what was wanting in the others, Jews and Greeks, in regard to faith in Jesus Christ, which the Church was committed to announce.

The New Testament is, to be sure, quite explicit regarding the need of faith for salvation. It affirms emphatically that salvation is in Jesus Christ alone (Acts 4:12). It likewise insists on the necessity of faith and baptism (Jn 3:5; see Mk 16:15–16; Acts 2:37–41). However, John's text, by contrasting the flesh and the spirit, puts the stress on the new life in the Spirit which is needed for salvation. As for the Markan text, it runs thus: "He who believes and is baptized will be saved; but he who does not believe will be condemned" (Mk 16:16). While it is clear that faith is in every case required for salvation, it cannot be said that the New Testament excludes from salvation those who through no fault of their own remain unbaptized. Nevertheless, the salvific role of the Church was clearly implied inasmuch as faith and baptism give access to it. Already in

1 Pet 3:18–22 a comparison is made between those who were saved by the ark of Noah and Christians passing through the waters of baptism. Later, Christian writers will base on this text their understanding of the Church as the "ark of salvation," of which Noah's ark was a type, and eventually will conclude that outside the ark of the Church there is no salvation.

However, while the Church's role in salvation is implied in many images of the New Testament, it would be unwarranted to affirm that these are meant to exclude from salvation those who do not belong to it. Jerome P. Theisen is correct when he writes: "It would be better to conclude that the scriptures do not consider our precise question, namely, that any salvation that there is in the world comes through the Church, that the Church is necessary for the salvation of every person who is in fact being saved" (Theisen 1976, 2). Yet this is just what the adage "Outside the Church no salvation," understood in its rigid form, will be asserting. Caution is nonetheless required in view of the many problems of interpretation which the axiom raises, a few of which must be stated from the outset.

First, there is the historical evolution of the axiom, from a form which, while stating the role of the Church, did not necessarily claim exclusivity for it, down to the rigid interpretation excluding all salvation outside the Church. There is, too, the long span of time through which the axiom runs, from the writings of some third-century writers down to the authoritative statement made by the Council of Florence (1442). Again, distinct applications are made of the axiom depending on different situations, or else on different dispositions of persons. Moreover, distinct concepts are at work regarding the Church itself.

In the previous chapter we have taken note of a trend in Augustine's theology where the "Church" is identified with all persons who de facto are saved in Jesus Christ, including those who lived before him: *Ecclesia ab Abel*, who is "the first just man." It is easy to see that with such a broad notion of the Church, the axiom under consideration would be self-evident and would raise no problem. What can, however, be discussed is the legitimacy of such a broad concept of the Church, more problematic, in fact, than any modern theory of "implicit" or "anonymous" Christianity by which a relationship of the redeemed with Christ, not with the Church, is directly affirmed.

An even broader understanding of the Church has sometimes been proposed according to which the Church is identified with the whole of humankind already saved *in principle* through the Christ-event. In other instances, on the contrary, the Church refers strictly to the ecclesial community, access to which is through the sacrament of baptism.

Such will be, it may be noted, the modern concept of the Church, proposed by the encyclical *Mystici Corporis* of Pius XII (1943) and taken up by the constitution *Lumen Gentium* of Vatican II, according to which the Church is made up of two inseparable elements, invisible and visible: it is at once spiritual communion and human institution (LG 8). It is, however, in the context of this precise understanding of the Church that the axiom under consideration, if taken in its rigid form, raises serious problems. This goes to show that, in every instance where the axiom is found, its interpretation requires that the notion of Church which is implied be clearly ascertained.

Our exposition will adopt the following sequence. A first part will trace the origin and development of the axiom, first among the Church Fathers and second in official documents of the Church. A second part will be devoted to the hermeneutical problems raised by the axiom in its historical context and to the reinterpretation which a different context seems to make imperative. A third part will give a rapid overview of opinions belonging to the historical period during which the axiom was officially proclaimed by the Church, but which nevertheless depart considerably from the received opinion to propose wider perspectives.[1]

## I. The Evolution of a Controverted Axiom

### A. *The Fathers of the Church before Augustine*

The axiom "Outside the Church no salvation" is usually linked with the name of Saint Cyprian; however, it had historical antecedents, though in different forms and with different understandings. Saint Ignatius of Antioch seems to be the first Church Father to whom reference can be made in this connection. Ignatius, as is well known, stresses the need for unity within the Church and union with the bishop as a requirement for union with God in Jesus Christ. Directing his attention to schismatics willfully breaking this union, he writes: "Be not deceived, my brethren: if anyone follows a maker of schism, he does not inherit the Kingdom of God" (*Letter to the Philadelphians* 3, 3; The Apostolic Fathers [AF] [Cambridge, 1965], 2:242–43). In this first instance, willful and guilty separation from the Church is clearly the reason for exclusion from salvation.

Though the immediate context is different, Irenaeus too supposes guilt on the part of those deprived of salvation for separating from the Church. The context in Irenaeus is that of the Gnostics claiming for themselves a superior knowledge to which ordinary Christian communities have no access. Irenaeus warns those separatists that only in the true Church is it possible to share in the life of grace of which, by separating themselves from the Church, the Gnostics are depriving themselves: "Where the Church is, there is the Spirit of God, and where the Spirit of God is, there is the Church" (*Adv. Haer.* III, 24; PG 7:966–67). Once again, guilty separation from the Church is here the reason for exclusion from salvation.

The situation becomes more complex with Origen. On the one hand, he

---

1. On this entire question, the following literature can be consulted: Sullivan 1992; Theisen 1976; Eminyan 1960; Kern 1979; Ratzinger 1970; Canobbio 1994. Our exposé of the evolution of the axiom is based in part on the works of Francis A. Sullivan and Jerome P. Theisen.

continues the Logos-theology of Saint Justin, as a passage in *The First Prin-ciples* shows, in which the Logos is said to be at work in all "rational beings" (*logikoi*), while the Spirit dwells only in the saints (*peumatikoi*): the action of the Logos is more extensive than that of the Spirit.[2] On the other hand, Ori-gen is very explicit about salvation in the Church only. In the *Homilies on Josuah* 3:5, commenting on the episode of Jos 2:19, he understands the house containing the family as representing the Church, and comments:

> If anyone wishes to be saved, let that one come into this house of her who once was a prostitute. Even if someone belonging to that people [Hebrew] wishes to be saved, let such a one come into this house, so as to find sal-vation. Let one come into this house, in which the blood of Christ is the sign of redemption.... So, let no one persuade oneself, let no one deceive oneself: outside this house, that is, outside the Church no one is saved (*ex-tra hanc domum, id est extra ecclesiam, nemo salvatur*); for, if one goes outside, one is responsible for one's own death. (*Homilies on Josuah* 3, 5; PG 12:841–42)

And he adds: "By that sign [of the blood of Christ] let all those find salvation who are found in the house of her who was once a harlot, after their cleansing in water and the Holy Spirit and in the blood of our Lord and Savior Jesus Christ" (*Homilies on Josuah* 3, 5; PG 12:841–42). Salvation is ensured only for those within the Church. The Church is compared here with the ark of salvation, of which the ark of Noah is seen as a type. Origen makes reference to the Jews who have not accepted the Christian message and, more clearly, to Christians who, having once been in the Church, have separated themselves from it willfully; all have only themselves to blame for their loss.

However, in some passages Origen widens considerably the notion of the Church. Thus, commenting on 1 Cor 15:28, he writes: "The body of Christ...is the whole of humankind, nay rather perhaps the whole of cre-ation, and each one of us is a member and part" (*Homily 2 on Ps.* 36; PG 12:1330). Here Origen envisages a time when the sick members of the body will be restored to health and all will be saved. According to J. P. Theisen, such universalism regarding the Church and the presumed restoration of its sick members "tones down considerably the ultimate seriousness of the stand taken in his *Homilies on Josuah*" (Theisen 1976, 7). This passage leads, in effect, to Origen's eschatological perspective of universal restoration in the *apokatas-tasis* which, however, Origen propounded only as a "working hypothesis," a provisional opinion (Crouzel 1985, 331–42; Dupuis 1967, 210–18).

The thought of Origen remains, thus, somewhat ambiguous. Saint Cyprian, in contrast, his contemporary and bishop of Carthage, is much more straight-forward, and it is not without good reason that the axiom "Outside the Church

---

2. *On the First Principles* I, 3, 5 (New York: Harper and Row, 1966), 34. On the meaning of the Logos as distinct from the Spirit (*Pneuma*) in the trichotomous anthropology of Origen, see Dupuis 1967; also Crouzel 1956, 1985, 123–37.

no salvation" is traced back principally to him. The axiom recurs repeatedly in his writings. It must, however, be noted that in each instance Cyprian addressed his warnings to people in danger of being separated from the Church or already separated from it, always supposing personal guilt on their part. Here are some examples.

Addressing Christians threatened with excommunication for defiance of their bishop, Cyprian writes:

> Let them not think that the way of salvation exists for them, if they have refused to obey the bishops or priests.... The proud and insolent are killed with the sword of the Spirit, when they are cast out from the Church. For they cannot live outside, since there is only one house of God, and there can be no salvation for anyone except in the Church. (*Epist.* 4, 4; CSEL 3, 2:476–77)

Referring to heretics, Cyprian notes that not even martyrdom can avail them salvation, "because there is no salvation outside the Church" (*Epist. ad Iubaianum* 73:21; CSEL 3, 2:795). Nor can martyrdom purge away the guilt of schism: "Even though they should suffer death for the confession of the Name, the guilt of such people is not removed even by their blood; the grievous irremissible sin of schism is not purged even by martyrdom" (*The Unity of the Catholic Church* 14; ACW 25:56). More clearly still, and again with heretics and schismatics in mind, Cyprian writes:

> The spouse of Christ cannot be defiled, she is inviolate and chaste.... Whoever breaks with the Church and enters on an adulterous union, cuts oneself off from the promises made to the Church; and one who has turned one's back on the Church of Christ shall not come to the rewards of Christ: such a one is an alien, a worldling, an enemy. You cannot have God for your Father if you have not the Church for your mother. (*The Unity of the Catholic Church* 6; ACW 25:48–49)

The case of heretics and schismatics is, therefore, clear in Cyprian's mind: guilty as they are for separating from the Church, there is for them no salvation. For Cyprian, moreover, the baptism conferred outside the Church is invalid — an opinion which will be contradicted later but which testifies to the rigid notion of the Church on which the axiom is based (Theisen 1976, 11). Did Cyprian, however, pass a negative judgment also on the pagans who have remained outside the Church? Were they too considered guilty and therefore excluded from salvation? On this point, Francis A. Sullivan writes as follows:

> There is no instance in his writings in which Cyprian explicitly applied his saying: No salvation outside the Church, to the majority of people who were still pagans in his day. We know that he judged Christian heretics and schismatics guilty of their separation from the Church. Did he also judge all pagans guilty of their failure to accept the Christian Gospel and enter the Church? We do not know. (Sullivan 1992, 22–23)

And, looking back to the thought of Ignatius, Irenaeus, Origen, and Cyprian, he adds:

> We see that when these early Christian writers spoke of people being ex-
> cluded from salvation for reason of being outside the Church, they were
> consistently directing this as a warning to Christians whom they judged to
> be guilty of the grave sin of heresy and schism. It is quite possible that, if
> asked, they would have answered that there was no salvation outside the
> Church for Jews and pagans either. But it is significant for the history of
> this axiom that we do not find them applying it to others than Christians
> at this time when Christians were still a persecuted minority.... The case
> was different when Christianity had become the official religion of the Ro-
> man empire and most people had accepted the Christian faith. (Sullivan
> 1992, 23–24)

It is after the Christian religion had become the official religion of the empire that we find the Church Fathers applying the axiom "Outside the Church no salvation" to the situation of Jews and pagans. As guilt had previously been supposed on the part of heretics and schismatics who had separated themselves from the Church, it is now equally presumed in the case of Jews and pagans who have failed to become Christians. The reason behind this judgment was the assumption that the Gospel had by then been promulgated everywhere and everyone had had the opportunity to accept it.

Thus Saint Ambrose wrote:

> If someone does not believe in Christ one defrauds oneself of this universal
> benefit, just as if someone were to shut out the rays of the sun by closing
> one's window.... For the mercy of the Lord has been spread by the Church
> to all nations; the faith has been spread to all peoples. (*In Ps* 118 *Sermo*
> 8:57; PL 15:1318)

Likewise, Saint Gregory of Nyssa, in his *Catechetical Oration,* insisted that all had now heard the call to faith, to the effect that those outside the Church were guilty for it (*Oratio catechetica* 30; PG 45:76–77). Similarly, Saint John Chrysostom wrote:

> Do not say: "How is it that God has neglected that sincere and honest pa-
> gan?" You will find that such a one has not really been diligent in seeking
> the truth, since what concerns the truth is now clearer than the sun. How
> shall they obtain pardon who, when they see the doctrine of truth spread
> before them, make no effort to come to know it? For now the name of
> God is proclaimed to all, what the prophets predicted has come true, and
> the religion of the pagans has been proved false.... It is impossible that
> anyone who is vigilant in seeking the truth should be condemned by God.[3]

---

3. *In Epist. ad Rom. hom.* 26:3–4; PG 60:641–42; see also *In 1 Tim. 2 Hom.* 7:2; PG 62:537.

It was undoubtedly Saint John Chrysostom's judgment that there is no salvation for pagans outside the Church and that they are guilty for being outside it. His judgment about the guilt of the Jews was even harsher. Thus, while before Christianity spread considerably in the empire the axiom was applied to those who willfully had separated themselves from the Church, with the spread of Christianity through the empire it was extended to Jews and pagans under the presumption that they were equally guilty for not having joined the Church.

## B. Saint Augustine and After

In his controversy with the Donatists, Saint Augustine disagreed with Cyprian's view regarding the nonvalidity of baptism conferred by heretics and schismatics; such baptism was valid. But he joined with Cyprian in considering such baptism as inoperative with regard to salvation. The reason was that baptism conferred in a sect separated from the Church did not and could not confer the Holy Spirit and hence the gift of salvation. Those separated from the Church, though baptized and practicing the sacraments, were excluded from salvation. Thus, referring to a Donatist bishop, Augustine wrote:

> Outside the Church he can have everything except salvation. He can have honor, he can have sacraments, he can sing Alleluiah, he can resound with Amen, he can have the Gospel, he can hold and preach the faith in the name of the Father, and the Son and the Holy Spirit: but nowhere else than in the Catholic Church can he find salvation. (*Sermo ad Caesarensis ecclesiae plebem* 6; CSEL 53:174–75)

Augustine, it is true, spoke of some being "inside" the Church who seem to be "outside," and vice versa, which — as some thought — seems to indicate that people separated from the Church might nevertheless be on the way to salvation. However, as Francis A. Sullivan explains, "this distinction is based on the foreknowledge of God"; that is to say: God in his foreknowledge knows who among the heretics will be reintegrated into the Church, thereby recovering salvation. Augustine writes:

> There are some of that number [of those who will be saved] who at present are living sinful lives, or are even wallowing in heresies or in pagan superstitions, and yet even there "the Lord knows who are his own," for, in that ineffable foreknowledge of God, many who seem to be outside are really inside, and many who seem to be inside are outside. (*De baptismo* 5:27, 38; CSEL 53:174–75)

And, elsewhere he explains: "If it be the case that some of these people [presently separated] belong to us in the hidden foreknowledge of God, it is necessary that they should return to us" (*Enar. in Ps.* 106:14; CCL 40:1581).

On the one hand, as for the Jews and pagans after the Christ-event, Augustine was convinced that, unless they believed in Jesus Christ and were baptized, there was no salvation for them. Now that the Gospel had been preached and the Church established, they were held guilty for not having joined the Church in which salvation is found:

> God wants all to be saved and come to the knowledge of the truth [1 Tim 2:4], but not in such a way that he takes away their free will, whose good or bad use brings upon them a just judgment. Hence, unbelievers act against the will of God, when they do not believe in the Gospel message. They do not triumph over it, but rather they defraud themselves of a great, indeed, of the greatest good, and involve themselves in great evils. They have to experience in suffering the power of him whose mercy and gifts they have contemned. (*De Spiritu et littera* 33:58; PL 44:238)

On the other hand, Augustine did know that there were tribes in Africa to which the Gospel had not been preached. These too he considered to be outside salvation. A first explanation for this consisted in saying that, if God refused to anyone the opportunity for becoming Christian, it was because they were unworthy: God foresaw that they would refuse the gift. A second explanation is given by Augustine in the context of the anti-Pelagian controversy: the universality of original sin and its consequences were enough reason for God to condemn infants dying without baptism as well as adults dying in ignorance of the Christian faith. Augustine thus arrived at the idea of the descendants of Adam as a *massa damnata* that could be spared only through God's mercy by receiving the Christian faith and baptism. According to Augustine, God's salvific will, then, was not universal; it applied to those freely destined by God to be saved (Sullivan 1992, 36–37).

J. P. Theisen concludes as follows:

> In short, Augustine transmits to the Middle Ages a rather exclusivist understanding of the adage *Extra ecclesiam nulla salus*. While he refuses Cyprian's position with regard to the validity of baptism outside the Church, he still insists on the necessity of the Church for salvation. Union with the Church is conceived rather rigidly; it is required for the reception of the Holy Spirit and eternal life. (Theisen 1976, 16)

Prosper of Aquitaine, a faithful follower of Augustine, while holding the doctrine of the absolute primacy of grace and God's freedom in bestowing it, insisted against his master that God willed in some fashion the salvation of all people. His solution to the dilemma consisted in saying that, while God made a universal offer of "general" grace, he reserved "special" graces to those he chose to favor with such gifts. In the work entitled *The Call of All Nations*, Prosper departs from Augustine's idea in stressing that Christ died not only for believers but for all people, including nonbelievers and sinners (*De vocatione omnium gentium* 2:16; PL 51:702–3; ACW 14:118–19). For those who, as he was aware, had not had the opportunity to hear that Good News, his solution was that, while they had not received the "special" grace of hearing the Gospel which God freely bestows on those he chooses, they nevertheless had benefited by the "general" help as has always been bestowed to all people, even before Christ, by which seemingly they could be saved: "We have no doubt that in God's hidden judgment, for them also a time of calling has been appointed, when they will hear and accept the Gospel which now remains unknown to them. Even now they receive the measure of general help which heaven has always bestowed on all people" (*De vocatione omnium gentium* 2:17; PL 51:704; ACW 14:125). Thus, Prosper seriously toned down Augustine's rigorism which excluded from salvation all those living after Christ who had not heard and received the Gospel message.

On the contrary, Fulgentius of Ruspe (468–533), another follower of Augustine, and like him a North African bishop, followed Augustine's anti-Pelagian teaching to the letter. In his work *On the Truth of Predestination,* he wrote as follows:

> If it were true that God universally willed that all should be saved and come to the knowledge of the truth, how is it that Truth itself has hidden from some people the mystery of his knowledge? Surely, to those whom he denied such knowledge, he also denies salvation. . . . Therefore, he willed to save those to whom he gave knowledge of the mystery of salvation, and he did not wish to save those to whom he denied the knowledge of the saving mystery. If he had intended the salvation of both, he would have given the knowledge of the truth to both. (*De veritate praedestinationis* 3:16–18; PL 65:660–61)

Not surprisingly, then, we find in Fulgentius, applied to pagans and Jews, as well as to heretics and schismatics, the axiom "Outside the Church no salvation," formulated in its most rigid form. It is with clear reference to Fulgentius, as we shall see hereafter, that the axiom would be taken over nine centuries later by the Council of Florence (1442). Of heretics and schismatics, Fulgentius wrote:

> Hold most firmly and do not doubt that anyone baptized outside the Catholic Church cannot come to eternal life if before the end of his life one does not return and become incorporated into the Catholic Church. For the apostle says: "If I have all faith and know all mysteries, but do not have charity, I am nothing" [see 1 Cor 13:2]. And we read that also in the days of the flood no one could be saved outside the ark. (*De fide ad Petrum* 37; PL 65:703)

And, including pagans and Jews, he adds:

> Most firmly hold and by no means doubt, that not only all pagans, but also all Jews, and all heretics and schismatics who die outside the Catholic Church, will go to the eternal fire that was prepared for the devil and his angels [Mt 25:41]. (*De fide ad Petrum* 38 (79); PL 65:704)

## C. The Church's Magisterium: Popes and Councils

Saint Cyprian and Fulgentius of Ruspe had been the two main artisans of the axiom "Outside the Church no salvation." They also served as the main reference when, much later, the axiom found its way into the official documents issued by the Church's teaching authority. Four documents must be considered here: two are papal pronouncements; the other two belong to the Church councils.

The first is a letter of Pope Innocent III to the archbishop of Tarragona (18 December 1208). It includes a profession of faith demanded of Durandus de Osca on his return from the Waldensians to the Roman Church. The profession of faith contained the various disputed issues that separated the Waldensians from the Church. Among these is found the need to belong to the Church for obtaining salvation: "We heartily believe and orally confess the one Church, not of heretics, but the Holy, Roman, Catholic, apostolic [Church], outside which we believe no one can be saved."[4] The axiom was well known. Noteworthy is, however, the explicit reference to the *Roman* Church, which did not figure in the ancient documents referring to the axiom. The stress is now placed on the Roman character of the one Catholic Church in which salvation is found.

The second document belongs to the Fourth Lateran Council (1215). This general council was directed primarily against spiritualist and antiecclesial movements which, reducing the Church to a *congregatio fidelium*, denied its incarnational and mediatory nature and consequently its visible and sacramental structure. Thus, in its definition against the Albigensians and Cathars, the council included a profession of faith in the visible, sacramental, and eucharistic community, "outside which no one at all is saved." The relevant part of the text reads as follows:

> There is indeed one universal Church of the faithful outside which no one at all is saved, and in which the priest himself, Jesus Christ, is also the sacrifice (*idem ipse sacerdos est sacrificium Jesus Christus*). His body and blood are truly contained in the sacrament of the altar under the appearances of bread and wine, the bread being transubstantiated into the body by the divine power and the wine into the blood, to the effect that we receive from what is his in what he has received from what is ours (*ut...accipiamus ipsi de suo, quod accepit ipse de nostro*) in order that the mystery of unity may be accomplished.[5]

The text goes on to explain the sacramental structure of the Church. As for the insistence on the need of belonging to the Church for salvation, it probably stems directly from Cyprian of Carthage's *Letter to Jubaianus* (Cyprian of Carthage, *Letter 73 to Iubaianus* 21; CSEL 3, 2:795), to which reference

4. H. Denzinger and A. Schönmetzer, eds., *Enchiridion Symbolorum, Definitionum et Declarationum de Rebus Fidei et Morum*, ed. 36 (Freiburg: Herder, 1976), 792; hereafter DS.

5. DS 802; J. Neuner and J. Dupuis, *The Christian Faith in the Doctrinal Documents of the Catholic Church* (New York: Alba House, 1996), 21; hereafter ND.

has been made earlier in this chapter. It may be noted that the main burden of the text is the mystery of unity of the sacramental Church realized by the Eucharist, while the reference to there being no salvation outside the Church appears in a dependent clause. In the opinion of J. P. Theisen, it is possible to conclude that "although the axiom is included here in a decree of a general council of the Church and even in a profession of faith, it does not form the subject of specific conciliar consideration. The council merely records the traditional (assuredly accepted) axiom and does not make it the subject of a definition" (Theisen 1976, 19).

The third document, and the weightiest in the long history of the axiom, is Pope Boniface VIII's bull *Unam Sanctam* (18 November 1302). The bull was issued at the time when the question of the two powers, spiritual and temporal, and of their interrelationship, dominated ecclesiastical thought. It admits that there are "two swords" (the temporal and the spiritual powers) but, dominated as it is by the idea and ideal of unity, affirms that the temporal is under the control of the spiritual, concretely under the control of the pope. Boniface seems, in effect, to propose the hierocratic theory in an extreme form. It is in this context that the need of belonging to the Church is stated here. The main part of the text runs as follows:

> That there is only one, holy, catholic and apostolic Church we are compelled by faith to believe and hold, and we firmly believe in her and sincerely confess her, outside of whom there is no salvation, nor remission of sins.... She represents one mystical body; the head of this body is Christ, but the head of Christ is God. In her there is "one Lord, one faith, one baptism" [Eph 4:5]. To be sure, at the time of the flood there was one ark of Noah, a type of the one Church; and this ark finished to one cubit from the top and one pilot and captain, that is, Noah. We read that outside the ark all living creatures were destroyed....
>
> This one and unique Church, therefore, has no two heads, like a monster, but one body and one head, viz., Christ and his vicar, Peter's successor, for the Lord said to Peter personally: "Feed my sheep" [Jn 21:17]. "My," he said in general, not individually, meaning these or those; whereby it is understood that he confided all his sheep to him. If therefore Greeks or others say that they were not confided to Peter and his successors, they must necessarily confess that they are not among Christ's sheep, for the Lord said in John: "There shall be one fold and one shepherd" [Jn 10:16]....
>
> Furthermore we declare, state and define that it is absolutely necessary for the salvation of all people that they submit to the Roman Pontiff. (DS 870, 872, 875; ND 804)

The conclusion of the bull is a doctrinal declaration: submission to the Roman pontiff is necessary for salvation. This sentence, as it stands, has commonly been regarded as dogmatic and binding. But it must be distinguished from the body of the document, which develops an ideology bound to the concepts of the time and a prevalently juridical and corporate notion of the Church, exalting in the process the role of the pope as head of the Church. Positively, the bull affirms clearly the unity of the Church, its necessity for salvation, its divine origin, and the foundation of the authority of the Roman pontiff. Nevertheless, the extent of the dogmatic value of its conclusion remains open to various interpretations.[6] In view of this, Francis A. Sullivan concludes as follows: "We can conclude by noting that no Catholic theologian now holds that Boniface's theory about the supremacy of the spiritual over the temporal power is a dogma of Catholic faith. It is safe to say that if the bull defined anything, it was simply the traditional doctrine that there is no salvation outside the Catholic Church" (Sullivan 1992, 66).

The fourth document to be considered is the Decree for the Copts of the General Council of Florence (4 February 1442). Florence represents an attempt under the leadership of Pope Eugene IV to bring about reunion between the eastern churches and Rome. After a sinuous and eventful history, which there is no need to trace here, this "council of union," now sitting in Florence, approved decrees of union with the Armenian, Greek, and Coptic (Jacobite) churches. It is the Decree for the Copts (or Jacobites) from Egypt which interests us here. The decree, actually a bull prepared by Eugene IV, offers a summary of Christian belief, in which the traditional doctrine on the necessity of the Church for salvation is expressed in a rigid formula taken almost verbatim from Fulgentius of Ruspe's *Treatise on Faith,* which has been examined earlier in this chapter. It exposes the order of salvation as follows: Jesus Christ is the final revelation of God; his mission is entrusted to the Church; thus, separation from the Church means separation from Christ, and hence loss of salvation. This is the first official document in which, besides heretics and schismatics, mention is made of Jews and "pagans" in connection with the axiom "Outside the Church no salvation." In view of the historical context, the reaffirmation of the axiom seems to be the council's main intention. The relevant text reads as follows:

> [The Holy Roman Church]...firmly believes, professes and preaches that "no one remaining outside the Catholic Church, not only pagans," but also Jews, heretics and schismatics, can become partakers of eternal life; but they will go to the "eternal fire prepared for the devil and its angels" [Mt 25:41], unless before the end of their life they are joined (*aggregati*) to it. For union with the body of the Church is of so great importance that the sacraments of the Church are helpful to salvation only to those remaining in it; and fasts, almsgiving, other works of piety, and the exercises of a militant Christian life bear eternal reward for them alone. "And no one can be saved, no matter how much alms one has given, even if shedding

---

6. Sullivan (1992, 65–66) refers to the different opinions proposed by A. Schönmetzer and G. Tavard.

one's blood for the name of Christ, unless one remains in the bosom of the Catholic Church." (DS 1351; ND 1005)[7]

It is significant that the pope and the council chose to enunciate the traditional doctrine in its most rigid formulation. What dogmatic value must be ascribed to the decree? The solemnity with which the decree is designed to formulate the faith of the Catholic Church is certain. The question, however, remains of knowing whether the direct intention of the council consisted in stating the relationship between the Church and salvation and the precise situation with regard to salvation of those finding themselves outside the Church. To the question put in this fashion, J. P. Theisen answers: "It would seem not. No one at the time questioned the traditional doctrine; thus it did not become the direct object of consideration and definition" (Theisen 1976, 27).

But how to account for the harshness of the doctrine and the rigid form in which it is formulated here? Francis A. Sullivan recalls pointedly:

> We have good reason to understand this decree in the light of what was then the common belief that all pagans, Jews, heretics and schismatics were guilty of the sin of infidelity, on the ground that they had culpably refused either to accept the true faith or to remain in it. . . . Their [the bishops of Florence] decree cannot be understood except in the light of their judgment concerning the culpability of all those who they declared would be condemned to hell.
>
> . . . The bishops of the Council of Florence certainly believed that God is good, that being good he is just and that a just God does not condemn innocent people to the fires of hell. The conclusion is inescapable that they must have believed all pagans, Jews, heretics and schismatics to be guilty, and deserving of eternal punishment. (Sullivan 1992, 67–68)

## II. The Hermeneutics of the Axiom

The interpretation of the axiom "Outside the Church no salvation" has raised and continues to raise many problems. Two different questions need to be clearly distinguished. The first consists of asking how, historically, the Church Fathers could reach the rigid position on the necessity of the Church for salvation which they expressed with such assurance, and how authoritative documents of the Church — no matter what doubt may remain on their precise dogmatic value — could include those judgments into the official doctrine of the Church. The second question to be asked is what significance the doctrine may still have for us today as we look back upon it with hindsight and in retrospect. For soon after the Council of Florence, as will be seen in the next chapter, the concrete situation came to be dramatically altered by historical events which

---

7. The quotations are from Fulgentius of Ruspe's *De fide ad Petrum* 38 (79) and 39 (80); PL 65:704.

resulted in a drastic change in the heretofore traditional worldview — a new situation which has only taken larger proportions down to the recent times.

## A. Interpreting the Axiom in the Historical Context

The historical question is, in itself, quite complex and comprises different aspects. One regards the universal condemnation which the traditional doctrine applied not only to heretics and schismatics but to Jews and "pagans" as well. Another concerns the grave culpability which the doctrine presupposed in all persons, belonging to any of the aforementioned categories, who had separated themselves from the Church or had failed to join it. Where those were concerned who had separated from the Church, through either schism or heresy, severe guilt precluding them from salvation was simply taken for granted. The state of separation from the Church was in every case an offense without remedy. The symbol of the Church as the "ark of salvation," of which the ark of Noah was a type, went a long way in accrediting this persuasion. The case of the Jews and pagans required further explanations.

The New Testament makes ample reference to the failure of the majority of the Jewish people of the time to accept the Gospel message. The historical fact is, moreover, often interpreted as a judgment of God. Suffice it to recall how in the Letter to the Romans, Paul wrestled with the problem of the refusal of his own people, only "a remnant" (Rom 11:5) embracing the faith in Jesus Christ which he preached. Paul was sure that "the gifts and the call of God are irrevocable" (Rom 11:29), that Israel remained that people to whom "belong the sonship, the glory, the covenants, the giving of the Law, the worship and the promises" (Rom 9:4). To the question: "Has God rejected his people?" he answered emphatically: "By no means" (Rom 11:1). Nevertheless, Paul was faced with the widespread unbelief of Israel. He proposed the solution that, while the time of the gentiles had now started (Rom 11:13–24) during the "rejection" of the people of Israel (Rom 11:15), the unbelieving people could still turn from their unbelief and be grafted again on the olive tree (Rom 11:23). In any event, Israel's hardening would not last forever, and all Israel would eventually be saved (Rom 11:25–33).

Paul's somewhat desperate solution, if confirmed by Israel's continued refusal, could easily develop in later times into a hardened position on the part of the Christian Church. Moreover, as exegesis has pointed out in recent times, clear traces of anti-Judaism are already noticeable in the Gospels, for instance in Matthew and John.[8] Such traces of anti-Judaism would later take general proportions, degenerating into the theory of the "deicide people," a theory which survived through the centuries, to be officially rejected only by Vatican II.

Apart from the Jewish religion, from which the early Church gradually distanced itself as it grew into a distinct religious faith, early Christianity

---

8. See, among others, Mussner 1984; Thoma 1980. On the covenant with Israel never revoked, see Lohfink 1991.

encountered the Greek world and the religion of the Roman Empire. The historical circumstances in which this encounter took place are well known. On one side, we have witnessed earlier an open attitude on the part of the early Church Fathers toward the "seeds of the Word" or God's "covenant" with Greek philosophy, which served as a "preparation for the Gospel." However, little was said on the permanent value after Christ of these gifts; the understanding of the Fathers was that, once the full light had come, to embrace it remained the only way to salvation: *omnem novitatem attulit seipsum afferens* (Saint Irenaeus). And to embrace the Christian faith necessarily meant to enter the Church.

On the Roman front, account must be taken of the ferocious clash which took place between the religion of the empire and the Christian Church, resulting in bloody persecutions of Christians. This situation, as is well known, endured until the conversion of Emperor Constantine and the recognition of Christianity as the state religion under Emperor Theodosius I. These circumstances offer some explanation, from a historical point of view, for the rigid attitude which prevailed down to the end of the fourth century.

The situation came to be reversed with the recognition of Christianity by the empire. This event marked the beginning of a rapid extension of Christianity to what in the worldview of the time represented more or less the horizon of the known world. Thus the persuasion grew that the Gospel had henceforth been "promulgated" everywhere. It may not be forgotten that such a conviction had some root in the New Testament itself. In Rom 10:18, Paul, quoting Ps 19:5, affirms implicitly that people have heard the message everywhere: "But I ask, have they not heard? Indeed, they have; for 'Their voice has gone out to all the earth and their words to the end of the world' [Ps 19:5]."[9] And when at the end of the Acts, Luke shows Paul in Rome, "preaching the Kingdom of God and teaching about the Lord Jesus Christ quite openly and unhindered" (Acts 28:31), he sees in this a symbol that the Gospel has reached to the whole world. Against this background it is more easily understood that, later, with the spreading of Christianity in the then-known world, the same persuasion could grow stronger.

We have taken note earlier of the problem that arose in the mind of Prosper of Aquitaine, a follower of Saint Augustine, from his awareness that there still were nations which had not had the opportunity to hear the Good News. This realization forced him to tone down the intransigence of his master with regard to the possibility of salvation. Nevertheless, the later rigid opinion of Fulgentius of Ruspe prevailed.

In the seventh century, Christianity encountered Islam. We need not enter here into the history of the tense relations which, from the start, obtained between the two religions. Islam presented itself as a new faith whose ardor — and fanaticism — sent it to conquer the whole world. While having its roots in the

---

9. It is to be noted that Paul is interpreting the text. In the psalm the verb is in the present: "their voice *goes out*"; Paul characteristically puts it in the past: "has gone" (*exèlthen*).

faith of Abraham, to Christian eyes it also presented itself as a Christian heresy for, while Jesus Christ was recognized in the Qur'an as a prophet of God greater even than Moses, he was second to Muhammad; moreover, the Christian mysteries of the Trinity and the incarnation were denied, at least in the mistaken sense in which Muhammad had come to know them. Historical events did the rest. Islam began to invade and dominate eastern Christianity, and from that base threatened the rest of Christendom. From the end of the eleventh century, the Crusades sent Christians to the Holy Land to free it from Islamic domination. In such a context it is easy to explain historically how Muslims fell under the same condemnation as the Jews with regard to exclusion from salvation. Though not all the documents referred to above make explicit mention of them, certainly they were included among the heretics.

## B. The Meaning of the Axiom for Today

There remains to ask what meaning the axiom "Outside the Church no salvation" can retain for the Church today, in vastly changed circumstances. Does its universal exclusion from salvation of entire groups of people, who find themselves outside the Church, either by leaving it or by failing to join it, still have any value for the Christian faith today? And what is there to say about the often fallacious reasons on which such persuasion is based, such as the conviction that the Gospel had been promulgated throughout the world?

Account must be taken, on the one hand, of the weight with which the official Church engaged its doctrinal authority in the axiom; but also, on the other hand, of the dramatically changed situation which was to overtake the world fifty years after the Council of Florence (1442), with the discovery of the New World (1492). From then on, it became impossible to continue to believe in any guilt on the part of entire masses of people who had failed to join the Christian faith. The axiom would, henceforth, have to be reconsidered. It will be the burden of the next chapter to account for the various "substitutes" which were proposed by theologians to make up for the lack of explicit faith and belonging to the Church. What meaning, then, does the axiom keep for today's Church? Opinions of theologians are divided on this point.

In defense of the axiom it must be stressed that in all cases and circumstances, whether heretics, schismatics, Jews, or pagans were concerned, the axiom supposed grievous guilt on the part of those not belonging to the Church. This presupposition, however, is totally unacceptable today. Indeed, the condemnation pronounced under Pius XII against the Jesuit Father Leonard Feeney (1949) for holding onto the axiom in its rigid form[10] suffices to show that in that rigid form the axiom is untenable today and, therefore, in need of being reinterpreted. We shall have to return to this document in our next chapter

---

10. See a letter of the Holy Office to the Archbishop of Boston (8 August 1949), in DS 3866–72; ND 854–57.

in connection with the "substitutes" which the Church's official doctrine has put forward ever since the Council of Trent. The Church has now long been holding the possibility of salvation in Jesus Christ for all people, whatever the circumstances of their life and the religious tradition to which they belong.

Furthermore, we shall at a later stage account for the affirmation made in recent years — in the years surrounding Vatican II — of elements of "truth and grace" (AG 9) in the other religious traditions, conducive to the salvation in Jesus Christ of their members. In such a renewed context, what does the axiom "Outside the Church no salvation" still teach us today? The question is all the more pressing because the document under Pius XII just mentioned restates clearly the axiom's dogmatic value: "The *infallible* dictum which teaches us that outside the Church there is no salvation, is among the truths that the Church has always taught and will always teach. But this *dogma* is to be understood as the Church itself understands it" (DS 3866; ND 854). What, then, is its present practical significance and value?

There are those who would see in the axiom a case of "development of doctrine," in the sense that the same affirmation of faith in the necessary role of the Church for the salvation of all people is everywhere present, though it is expressed differently and takes on distinct nuances in various contexts. At all events, the core of the doctrine remains unchanged, implying condemnation wherever guilt is involved for being outside the Church (as seemed at first to be the universal case), while allowing for the possibility of invincible ignorance (as came to be discovered later).

In his book *The Church*, Hans Küng expresses a different opinion:

Does not the negative and exclusive axiom lead to immeasurable misunderstandings which continue to recur in spite of all explanations both inside and outside the Church? Even if it were previously of help to the Church in her mission, it is certainly a hindrance to her today. And not only because the Church no longer forces anyone to believe in Christ out of fear of hell. The words are interpreted more often as either intolerance or duplicity: as intolerance when they are understood literally and exclusively in accordance with the old tradition; as duplicity when it means on the one hand that one will be saved outside the Catholic Church and on the other hand does not exclude the fact that people outside the Catholic Church are saved, in fact millions and billions of them, the greater part of humankind. (Küng 1968, 316; see also Küng 1967, 25–37)

And he concludes:

In its negative and exclusive formulation [the axiom] was highly dubious right from the beginning, has resulted in more or less serious errors, and has proved open to misunderstanding in its application to non-Christians and impossible to understand at all in its application to non-Catholic Christians.... As far as others [than Catholic Christians] are concerned, we do better to use a positive formulation: "Salvation inside the Church!," and so emphasize the positive truth at the heart of the easily misunderstood axiom. (Küng 1968, 318)

L. M. Bermejo is even more severe on the axiom. He sees in it, in effect, a case of reception by the Church over an extended period of time, later followed by "non-reception":

> The history of the *extra ecclesiam* shows conclusively that ecclesial reception is not always irreversible. The Magisterium of the Church...upheld the axiom in the rigorist sense of Cyprian from 1208 to 1854 [see Pius IX, *Singulari Quadam* (8 December 1854), in Pius IX, *Acta* I, 1:626; ND 813]....A position which was clearly untenable...sooner or later was bound to be changed....The change, the transition from reception to non-reception did come, but it was certainly slow in coming. (Bermejo 1990, 242–43)

This is tantamount to considering the axiom as henceforth null and void. Yves Congar is more nuanced in his judgment. He does not reject the axiom as meaningless, for he finds in it a biblical truth: "The Church is the only institution created and commanded by God to obtain for people the salvation which is in Jesus Christ; the Church has received from her founder and Lord all that is necessary to obtain the salvation of the whole of humankind."[11]

However, since in its formulation the axiom can no longer be taken *literally* and a correct understanding of it requires long explanations, Congar suggests that it be abandoned: "There is no longer a question of applying the formula to any concrete person....[The axiom] is no longer regarded as answering the question '*Who* will be saved?,' but...the question: '*What* is it that is commissioned to discharge the mystery of salvation?'"[12]

We in turn may conclude that the abiding value of the axiom consists in the affirmation made by Vatican II — which, this time, is formulated positively — according to which the Church is "necessary for salvation" (LG 14); or is constituted as the "general instrument of salvation" (UR 3); or, again, is the "instrument of salvation for all" (LG 9). The council equivalently defines the Church as "universal sacrament of salvation" (LG 48), "a sign and instrument, that is, of communion with God and unity among all human beings" (LG 1).

However, not all the questions are settled thereby; for there still remain theological questions as to how the universal "necessity" of the Church in the order

---

11. See Congar 1965, 354. Congar writes likewise: "The Church of Christ is commissioned and qualified to carry salvation, brought by Jesus Christ, to all people; and...she alone, as Christ's Church, is so commissioned and qualified" (Congar 1961, 98). With regard to the permanent value of the axiom correctly understood, D. Costa (1990d) writes in the same vein: "The axiom's basic theological *raison d'être* was to maintain the Christian conviction that God is the source of all salvific grace, and that Christ, through his mystical Body, the Church, is the prime mediator of that grace....It stipulates that when a Christian speaks of salvation he or she cannot do so without at the same time speaking of Christ and his Church" (141).

12. See Congar 1961, 98; cf. 112; see also Congar 1963, 417–32. In the same direction, Ratzinger 1970, 339–61.

of salvation needs to be understood, in relation to the "one mediation" which the New Testament attributes to Jesus Christ himself (see 1 Tim 2:5); and, similarly, how to understand the "promulgation of the Gospel" which creates a moral obligation to embrace it through Church membership. To such questions we shall have to return in the second part of this work.

### III. Positive Attitudes toward Religions

Before passing on to the "substitutes" designed by theologians to make up for the lack of explicit faith in Jesus Christ and of formal belonging to the Church, it seems useful to take stock of some positive attitudes to the other religions which belong to the period during which the axiom had found its way into the official doctrine of the Church. The data recorded here are given by way of examples and without a claim to be exhaustive; they only aim to show that the dark picture which has been drawn so far of a lengthy period does not represent the whole truth. There were other voices. It must, however, be said that the positive attitudes recorded hereafter vis-à-vis other religions hail from very diverse authorities and belong to different literary genres, ranging from papal documents, through theological treatises, down to dreams by visionaries. In their historical context, the texts deal primarily with Jews and Muslims.

A first document worth recording is a letter of Pope Gregory VII (1076) to the Muslim King Anzir of Mauritania. The pope thanks the king for gifts received from him and for freeing some prisoners as well as promising to free others. He also sends him a delegation as a token of Christian friendship and a proof of his desire to be of service to him "in all things agreeable to our Fathers." The most significant passage of the letter is the following, in which the pope explains that Christians and Muslims worship the same God:

> God, the Creator of all, without whom we cannot do or even think anything that is good, has inspired to your heart this act of kindness. He who enlightens all people coming into the world [Jn 1:9] has enlightened your mind for this purpose. Almighty God, who desires all people to be saved [1 Tim 2:4] and none to perish, is well pleased to approve in us most of all that besides loving God people love others, and do not do to others anything they do not want to be done unto themselves [Mt 7:12]. We and you must show in a special way to the other nations an example of this charity, for we believe and confess one God, although in different ways, and praise and worship him daily as the creator of all ages and the ruler of this world. For as the apostle says: "He is our peace who has made us but one" [Eph 2:14]. Many among the Roman nobility, informed by us of this grace granted to you by God, greatly admire and praise your goodness and virtues. . . . God knows that we love you purely for his honour and that we desire your salvation and glory, both in the present and in the future

life. And we pray in our hearts and with our lips that God may lead you to the abode of happiness, to the bosom of the holy patriarch Abraham, after long years of life here on earth. (*Epistolae* III, 21; PL 148:450–52; ND 1002)

Among the many works Peter Abelard (1079–1142) wrote is a short dialogue entitled *A Dialogue of a Philosopher with a Jew and a Christian*.[13] In this work, Abelard, acting as the author-narrator, recounts a dream he had in which a philosopher, a Jew, and a Christian came to him for help in adjudicating the values of their respective positions. The first dialogue takes place between the philosopher and the Jew; the second between the philosopher and the Christian. The work, however, ends before the promised judgment is rendered.

The philosopher speaks for Abelard himself in the discussion with the Jew. However, the book departs from the traditional anti-Jewish literature. The conversation of the philosopher with the Jew is inspired by rational, not by specifically Christian, considerations. The book contains no confrontation between the Jew and the Christian.

Some features of the discussion are the following. The philosopher notes that according to the Bible, God hears the prayers of foreigners not belonging to Israel's chosen people. He knows of the Bible's "pagan saints," such as Job, Noah, and Enoch. He then inquires: "If these two [faith and love] were sufficient for the salvation of some people before the Law or even now, why was it necessary to add the yoke of the Law and to increase transgressions through the multiplication of precepts?" (*Dialogue*, 44). As spokesman for Abelard, the philosopher thus refutes on the ground of natural reasoning the foundation of the Church's trite axiom: Outside the Church no salvation.

In his discussion with the Christian, the philosopher argues that the philosophers' intention of living justly is not different from that of Christians. What Epicurus calls pleasure, Christ calls the Kingdom of Heaven:

> However, what does it matter by what name it is called as long as the reality remains the same and the beatitude is not diverse, and the intention of living justly for the philosophers is not different from that of the Christians? For both you and we arrange to live here in justice in order to be glorified there; and we struggle here against vices in order to be crowned there with the merit for virtues, that is, we obtain that supreme good as reward. (*Dialogue*, 97)

Abelard's Christian begs here to disagree, saying that the intention as well as the merits of the philosopher and of the Christian "are considerably different." "We are also not a little in disagreement concerning the supreme good" (*Dialogue*, 97). The Christian then goes on to spell out the superiority of the Christian beliefs. Nevertheless, the main message of the entire *Dialogue*

---

13. Peter Abelard, *A Dialogue of a Philosopher with a Jew and a Christian*, trans. P. J. Payer (Toronto: Pontifical Institute of Mediaeval Studies), 1979; cited hereafter as *Dialogue*.

is that the philosopher, the Jew, and the Christian, though in different ways and in different measures, seek the same good and recognize the same God, the Absolute.

In the context of a Church tormented with fear of the Muslim world, Saint Francis of Assisi (1182–1226) was committed from the start to a peaceful approach to the Muslims. He wished to enter into friendship with them and to show that he considered them not enemies but friends. This attitude to the Muslims seems to go back to the time of Francis's conversion and to have been well present in his mind before the Fourth Lateran Council (1215). For the first time in the history of the Church a method of approach to the Muslim world, fully inspired by the Gospel spirit, was being clearly formulated; never before had the Christian, anti-Muslim apologetics taken a similar attitude. For the first time, too, in the "rule" of a religious order, a special chapter was included which dealt with the evangelization of Muslims and the way of approaching them. Francis's voice was truly prophetic in calling for mutual understanding and reconciliation between Christians and their "Muslim brothers," which would bear fruit later, not least in Vatican II (NA 3). Chapter 16 of the "Early Rule" (*Regula non bullata*) (1221) — considered by critics as written before the council (Sani 1975, 92–100) — reads as follows:

Chapter XVI
Those who are going among the Saracens
and other non-believers

1. The Lord says: "Behold, I am sending you as lambs in the midst of wolves." 2. Therefore, be "prudent as serpents and simple as doves" [Mt 10:16]. 3. Therefore, any brother who, by divine inspiration, desires to go among the Saracens and other non-believers should go with the permission of his minister and servant. 4. And the minister should give [the brothers] permission and not oppose them, if he shall see that they are fit to be sent; for he shall be bound to give an account to the Lord [cf. Lk 16:2] if he has proceeded without discretion in this or in other matters. 5. As for the brothers who go, they can live spiritually among [the Saracens and non-believers] in two ways. 6. One way is not to engage in arguments or disputes, but to be subject "to every human creature for God's sake" [1 Pet 2:13] and to acknowledge that they are Christians. 7. Another way is to proclaim the word of God when they see that it pleases the Lord, so that they believe in the all-powerful God — Father, and Son, and Holy Spirit — the Creator of all, in the Son who is the Redeemer and Savior, and that they be baptized and become Christians; because "whoever has not been born again of water and the Holy Spirit cannot enter the Kingdom of God" [cf. Jn 3:5].

...10. And all the brothers, wherever they may be, should remember that they gave themselves and abandoned their bodies to the Lord Jesus Christ. 11. And for love of him, they must make themselves vulnerable to their enemies, both visible and invisible, because the Lord says: "Whoever loses his life for my sake will save it" [cf. Lk 9:24] in eternal life [Mt 25:46]. (Quoted from *Francis and Clare* 1982, 121–22)

The text shows clearly the position of Francis. Muslims and other "infidels" are to be considered not as "enemies of the Cross of Christ" but as brothers and friends. In chapter 22 — added after the council — Francis adds:

1. Let us pay attention, all [my] brothers, to what the Lord says: "Love your enemies" and "do good to those who hate you" [cf. Mt 26:50]. 2. For Our Lord Jesus Christ, whose footprints we must follow [cf. 1 Pet 2:21], called his betrayer "friend" [cf. Mt 26:5] and gave himself willingly to those who crucified him. 3. Our friends, then, are all those who unjustly afflict upon us trials and ordeals, shame and injuries, sorrows and torments, martyrdom and death. 4. We must love them greatly for we will possess eternal life because of what they bring upon us....

41. Let us, therefore, hold on to the words, the life, and the teaching and the Holy Gospel of him who humbled himself to ask his Father for us and to make his name known to us. (*Francis and Clare* 1982, 127, 129)

The Gospel spirit of Francis in approaching the Saracens appeared a great innovation; for his contemporaries the Muslims were the wolves that tore to pieces the flock of Christ. This explains how the text from the "Early Rule" quoted above came to be substantially altered in the "Later Rule" (*Regula bollata*), composed under the direction of Cardinal Ugolini and approved by Honorius III (1223) (see text in *Francis and Clare* 1982, 144–45). To Francis's great dismay, the new text eliminated entirely the irenic program which he had devised for treating the Saracens. The author of the new text did not share the saint's ideas concerning the evangelization of Muslims, which he viewed as utopic, and decided to leave them out (see Sani 1975, 208–9).

The *Book of the Gentile and the Three Wise Men*, the most important apologetic and polemical work by Ramon Llull (1232–1316), needs also to be mentioned. Ramon wrote other works defending the articles of faith against Jews, Muslims, and Christian heretics, but this is the only work in which the three major religions, Jewish, Christian, and Muslim, are presented together and treated in detail. The book is a discussion between a gentile and three wise men, each representing one of the three monotheistic religions. The gentile, an agnostic, inquires from each of them which arguments they have to propose in defense of their own beliefs. The humanity of the four disputants and their exquisite courtesy toward each other are striking features of the work. It has been suggested that Llull wished to offer a model of how such discussions should be conducted. Perhaps, too, he hoped through the literary device of the gentile's inquiry to make his Christian convictions more acceptable to his Muslim and Jewish partners. However this may be, the arguments put forward by the three wise men convince the pagan about God's existence and infinite goodness, a thing for which he thanks his three interlocutors profusely. But before he declares in which religion he wants to be and work for the rest of his life, the three wise men depart together from him, leaving him to his choice. As for them they pledge themselves to continue their conversation and discussion.

One remarkable feature of the work, besides the courtesy and irenic spirit of the participants, is the desire expressed by the three wise men that between them there should exist but one common religion and faith in God. The idea is stressed especially in the last section when, after taking leave of the gentile, they continue for a while devising among themselves. One of the three men expresses himself as follows:

> If the gentile, who was so long in error, has conceived such great devotion, and such great fervor in praising God, that he now states that in order to do so he would not hesitate to suffer any hardship or death, no matter how harsh it were, then how much greater should be our devotion and fervor in praising the name of God, considering how long we have known about him, and all the more so since he has placed us under such obligation by the many blessings and honors he has given us and gives us every day. We should debate and see which of us is in truth and which in error. For just as we have one God, one Creator, one Lord, we should also have one faith, one religion, one sect, one manner of loving and honoring God, and we should love and help one another, and make it so that between us there be no difference or contrariety of faith or customs, which difference and contrariety cause us to be enemies with one another and be at war, killing one another and falling captive to one another. And this war, death, and servitude prevent us from giving the praise, reverence, and honor we owe God every day of our life. (Bonner, ed., 1985, 1:301–2)

This, it has been noticed, is "one of Llull's clearest statements of his ideal of unity for the sake of peace, of a human unity that would reflect divine unity, doing away with 'difference and contrariety' and leaving only 'concordance'" (Bonner, ed., 1985, 1:302, n. 5). This aspect of Llull's teaching will be further developed later by Nicholas of Cusa. Llull's text goes on:

> And, as they depart, one of the wise men asks the others: Would you like to meet once a day, and . . . discuss according to the manner the Lady of Intelligence showed us, and have our discussions last until all three of us have only one faith, one religion, and until we can find some way to honor and serve one another, so that we can be in agreement? For war, turmoil, ill will, injury, and shame prevent people from agreeing on one belief. (Bonner, ed., 1985, 1:303)

And the author closes the book with these words:

Each of the three wise men approved of what the wise man had said, and they decided on a time and place for their discussions, as well as how they should honor and serve one another, and how they should dispute; and that when they had agreed on and chosen one faith, they would go forth into the world giving glory and praise to the name of our Lord God. Each of the three wise men went home and remained faithful to his promise. (Bonner, ed., 1985, 1:303)

Probably the most important, but also the most controverted, among the works under consideration here is "The Peace of Faith" (*De pace fidei*) of Nicholas of Cusa (1401–61), published in 1454, that is, only twelve years after the Council of Florence published the Decree for the Copts (Jacobites) (1442), in which, as has been observed earlier, the axiom "Outside the Church no salvation" had been reproduced in its most rigid form.

The treatise was published one year after the fall of Constantinople into the hands of the Turks, which shook the whole Western world, not least Nicholas of Cusa, bishop of Bressanone and cardinal of the Roman Church, who in 1437 had been sent by Pope Nicholas V to Constantinople to invite the Orientals to the Council of Union of Ferrara-Florence. However, in contrast with the spirit of the Crusades, Nicholas's reaction to the event consists of writing a treatise in which he advocates peace between the different faiths (see Gaia 1993, 233–61; also Castellanelli 1994, 50–60; Santinello 1987).

The brief dialogue takes the form of a dream (*visio*).[14] The dreamer (Cusano himself) is convinced that the religious differences which are the cause of mutual hatreds can only be dispelled by calling a conference in which experts will seek an agreement between the religions and thus ensure peace. He imagines himself taken up to heaven, where the angels plead with God that people who on earth invoke him under various names and with different rites may find reconciliation in one universal religion with a variety of rites: *Una religio in rituum varietate*. Christ, the Word of God made flesh, intervenes to suggest a discussion destined to overcome errors and establish a true unique faith (*una fides orthodoxa*). The representatives of the different religions are convoked to discuss their differences in the presence of Christ and of Peter and Paul.

Each of the participants represents either a different religion or a point of doctrine on which there is no agreement. At the end of the discussion, Saint Paul communicates the decision that the different peoples are allowed to preserve "their own devotions and ceremonies, provided faith and peace are preserved." The dialogue concludes while God admonishes the representatives of the various nations to return to earth and to lead their peoples to the true cult of God, after which they would meet again in Jerusalem to formally profess the unique faith and build upon its foundation a lasting peace.

There is no need to enter into the detail of the argumentation; what matters is to point out the essential presuppositions upon which the universal

---

14. Text in Gaia, ed., 1971, 617–73.

religion must be based. These are: monotheistic, Trinitarian, and Christological (see Gaia 1993, 237–46). In these, as Nicholas attempts to show, all are agreed, if not explicitly, at least implicitly. If beliefs differ, the ultimate reason is that in himself God remains unknown and is ineffable. All historical religions, then, Christianity included, reflect the transcendent reality only imperfectly; none possesses the absolute truth, even if Christianity approaches it most closely with its explicit Trinitarian and Christological faith. From the one common faith Nicholas distinguishes the multiplicity of rites (*varietas rituum*), which can be retained by each group in a spirit of tolerance, while safeguarding the unity of the faith and peace. The discussion ends in reaffirming that "all divergences concern the rites rather than the cult of the one God," whom all religions presuppose and venerate under different cultural forms. It is on this one faith that the wise men meeting at Jerusalem will have to base permanent peace (*pax perpetua*) to the glory of the Creator (see Gaia, ed., 1971, 672–73).

As would be expected, Nicholas's treatise has been controversial and even recently has been differently interpreted and evaluated. Some have admired its tolerance of all religions; others, like Etienne Gilson, believe that Christianity pays the whole price in Nicholas's attempt at reconciliation among the different religions (Gilson 1952, 154–81). Others still look at Nicholas as trying to persuade his interlocutors of the claims of Christianity to absoluteness. Henri de Lubac considers the author of *The Peace of Faith* a utopist and reckless dreamer, without a true program of action (Lubac 1974, 299–302). Hans Urs von Balthasar sees in the work "a rash enterprise (*ein abenteuerliches Wagnis*) about which one wonders how it is that it was never placed on the Index" (Balthasar 1963, 187).

G. Castellanelli believes that "The *De pace fidei* has had the merit to face, perhaps for the first time, the other religions with a positive outlook, even if it has had to share the temerity, the courage and the inevitable limitations common to all pioneering work" (Castellanelli 1994, 59–60). P. Gaia, in his turn, thinks that the negative assessments of Nicholas of Cusa's work are based on the pre–Vatican II common theological opinion (exemplified by J. Daniélou), according to which the Christian revelation has rendered obsolete the other religions, even while these may have served as a preparation for the Gospel. He adds: "The opening brought about by Vatican II as well as studies in the theology of religions in which these are seen as paths traced by God in the course of history that salvation may be offered through practicing them faithfully, have made a new hermeneutics of *orthodox faith* possible" (Gaia 1993, 253–54). He goes on to explain that, thus, an "intrinsic finality" can be discovered, leading from the many religions to the transcendent Truth which is reflected more or less in them and sums them all up. Nicholas had gone beyond the theology of "fulfillment" according to which the historical religions find their fulfillment in Christianity; for him the complement is eschatological (Gaia 1993, 253–54).

The question must remain open at this stage, to be taken up later in this study. We shall have to ask later what kind of complementarity there may exist between the religions of the world and Christianity, what kind of mutual convergence, historical or eschatological. While Nicholas's theological position, as it stands, seems untenable, he may be thought to have opened the way to such sort of questioning in adverse circumstances. His theological view was, perhaps, at the least likely time, an unfinished attempt at proposing a universal convergence of religions in Christ, the omega-point.

_Four_

# The Substitutes for the Gospel

T HE PRECEDING CHAPTER examined the historical origin of the axiom "Outside the Church no salvation" and explained under what suppositions it was introduced by some of the Church Fathers, upheld by others, and later integrated into official Church teaching. It further proposed a hermeneutics of the axiom in order to show its precise significance in the historical context of the times and asked what abiding significance it may retain even today. This amounts to the necessity of the Church for salvation, which, however, will have to be examined more closely later.

Meanwhile, we may observe that some of the presuppositions on which the ancient axiom was built were already raising problems in the minds of some Fathers who nevertheless held or maintained the axiom. Among those shaky roots figured in the first place the alleged culpability of all individual persons, especially the "pagans," who found themselves outside the ark of salvation which is the Church, notwithstanding the fact that, as the general belief had it, the Gospel had been adequately "promulgated" to the "entire world" as it was explicitly known, that is, within the limits of what was then "Christendom."

On this point some of the Fathers, in view of the circumstances in which they found themselves, already expressed some hesitation. Among these were some successors of Saint Augustine who, nevertheless, still maintained the axiom by having recourse to the subterfuge of limiting God's universal saving will: God could not but deny salvation to those to whom he had not granted the knowledge necessary for it, even while imparting to them the "general" helps received by all, which in themselves are insufficient for leading to salvation. For this lack of divine help the unsaved were made accountable in some way or another. This desperate solution considerably weakened the universality of God's saving will, which, however, pertained to the core of the Christian belief. Clearly, other solutions would have to be devised.

After the axiom "Outside the Church no salvation" had found its way into the Church's official doctrine, indeed in its rigid form, at the Council of Florence, the historical context underwent a dramatic change. This was, fifty years after Florence's Decree for the Copts (1442), the discovery of the "New World" (1492). This amounted to a showdown which would shake irreversibly the ancient persuasion of an adequate promulgation of the Gospel throughout the whole world as it had been hitherto understood. The event confirmed in a dramatic way what some authors had vaguely perceived. It called on theologians to reconsider the entire case of the requisites for salvation. No longer would it be possible to hold, without qualification, that faith in Jesus Christ and belonging to the Church were absolutely required for salvation. Prominent in the reconsideration of the conditions for salvation were Dominican scholars at the University of Salamanca and the Jesuit professors of the Roman College. The new solution, as will be seen, would enter for the first time into the Church's official doctrine at the Council of Trent in 1547.

To attribute to the discovery of the New World a catalytic role in fostering new approaches to salvation is not equivalent to turning the geographical discovery of the Americas into an absolute beginning. Attempts at broader perspectives had in fact been made well before the Council of Trent by scholastic theologians, not least by Saint Thomas Aquinas who devised more than one alternative solution; these would be later developed and elaborated.

Thus it is that a number of "substitutes" for faith in Jesus Christ and Church membership for salvation came to be proposed in the course of time through the Middle Ages and after, some of which endured down to the period which shortly preceded Vatican II. It is those "substitutes" which are the object of this chapter's inquiry.

Their history must not be seen as a linear process, from timid suggestions to more elaborate theories. Negative solutions destined to be abandoned later sometimes coincided with others, more promising, which would abide for centuries. Some were explicitly disavowed by the Church because of either their rigorism or their tendency to laxity. Some have long been abandoned as unhelpful constructs or as offensive to the Christian sense, while others remain valid, even though still enshrined in a problematic which today is largely considered dated and inadequate.

Given the considerable amount of material to be taken into consideration, we shall not bind ourselves to follow strictly the chronological development of substitutes for the Gospel through the scholastic period down to present times. The approach will rather be synthetic. It will proceed by categories, following each model of substitution through its various forms with a view to decide how far each was — or was not — conducive to a solution of the problem of salvation outside the Church; whether too it still contributes — or not — today to the solution of the question.

The parameters of the problem are in themselves clear. The universal salvific will of God, sometimes doubted or weakened, must clearly be upheld because it belongs to the substance of the Christian message contained in the New Testament: "God our Savior...desires all human beings to be saved" (1 Tim 2:4). Equally to be retained is the need of faith for salvation, also unambiguously stated by the Christian revelation: "Without faith it is impossible to please God" (Heb 11:6). How, then, can that faith which is salvific be accounted for in the case of those who have not known Jesus Christ, the universal Savior (see 1 Tim 2:5), because they lived either before him or after him without having heard his message? If we prescind from those proposals which were to prove unacceptable because they do not fit within the parameters of faith, it may be said that the models conducive to a solution are the different ways of conceiving the possibility of an *implicit* faith in Jesus Christ, implying in its turn a *votum ecclesiae.*

The exposition will fall into two parts. The first will follow the various substitutes proposed by the theological tradition. The second will survey the Church's official teaching, taking note at the same time of its disavowal of doctrines opposed to it. In the process, some hermeneutical reflections will be proposed regarding the significance of implicit faith and the *votum ecclesiae.*[1]

## I. The Substitutes in the Theological Tradition

### A. *Evangelization beyond Death*

This solution shifts the problem of the possibility of coming to saving faith beyond the present life. It appears to find some New Testament foundation in 1 Pet 3:18–20, which speaks of Christ who "made alive in the spirit" after his death, "went and preached to the spirits in prison, who formerly did not obey." Some early Christian writers, Origen included, understood the passage as referring to conversion and baptism beyond the tomb. Thus, against Celsus, who ridiculed the idea of such coming to faith in the hereafter, Origen confirms the opinion. He writes in the *Contra Celsum:*

> After this, he [Celsus] says to us: You will not say of him, I presume, that having failed to convince people on earth he travelled to Hades to convince them there. — Even if he dislikes it, we maintain this, that when he was in the body he convinced not merely a few, but so many that the multitude of those persuaded by him led to the conspiracy against him; and that when he became a soul (*psuchè*) unclothed by a body he conversed with souls (*psuchai*) unclothed by bodies, converting also those of them who were willing to accept him, or those who, for reasons which he himself knew, he saw to be ready to do so.[2]

The risen Christ's descent to Hades has in fact been understood in various ways through the patristic tradition.[3] One explanation has it that the risen Christ *preached* there to people who had lived before him, or even to fallen angels, offering them another opportunity for conversion. Under that form the theory would contradict the Christian doctrine according to which the eternal

---

1. The literature on the subject is very abundant. Particularly important are some classical works: Capéran 1934; d'Alès 1928, cols. 1156–82; Harent 1927, cols. 1726–1930. More recently see, among others: Eminyan 1960; Lombardi 1956; Nys 1966, 17–161; Theisen 1976; Ries 1987; Sullivan 1992. The exposition is much indebted to this last work.

2. See *Contra Celsum* II, 43; GCS 1 (Koetschau), 166, 8–11; translation in H. Chadwick, *Origen: Contra Celsum* (Cambridge: Cambridge University Press, 1965), 99–100.

3. For more texts, see Capéran 1934, *Essai historique,* 63–67, 84–103, 106–69; *Essai théologique,* 3–4.

fate of souls is fixed in death. According to another interpretation, the risen Christ went to Hades (*limbo patrum*) to *announce* to the just of the Old Testament, who had believed in his future coming, his triumph over death, by virtue of which they could now enter heaven after him.

Even under this moderate form, Christ's descent into Hades does not seem to lend itself to such interpretation. The mythical nature of the narrative in 1 Peter must be kept in mind. William J. Dalton has brought out this mythical character. What the text really affirms in mythical Hebrew parlance is, on the one hand, the reality of the human death undergone by Christ on the cross and, on the other, his victory through death over the powers of evil. There is question here not of preaching to the people of the Old Testament with a view to their conversion but of the proclamation to the evil spirits of Christ's triumph over them in his death (Dalton 1989). Dalton writes:

> The point of the proclamation is not the conversion of the fallen angels, nor, for that matter, their punishment.... The author is thinking of the salvation of human beings. What is important is that the forces of evil are now powerless to harm the Christian believer. If you like, you can call this the proclamation of the Gospel, the proclamation of the definitive rescue of human beings from evil and evil powers. The "proclamation to the spirits" of 1 Pet 3:19 is the equivalent of the subjection of the principalities (1 Pet 3:22; Eph 1:21–22). (Dalton 1989, 186)

## B. Destination to Limbo

The limbo solution to the problem of salvation without faith in Jesus Christ has been proposed under different forms. An extreme version of it is held by Pelagius, who denied the raising of human nature to the supernatural order, as well as original sin and the fall. It followed that "infidels" before Christ who had practiced virtue were confined to an intermediary condition between that of sinners and of virtuous Christians — a natural beatitude in limbo. A more nuanced conception of the same theory, while accepting the doctrine of grace, held a natural beatitude as reward for the good actions of infidels devoid of supernatural motives. In his anti-Pelagian controversy, Saint Augustine, without denying the natural virtues of infidels, was inclined to underestimate them, believing the infidels labored under many constraints; consequently, he limited the scope for a natural beatitude. His successors, however, opened the natural beatitude of limbo to virtuous unbelievers more generously than Augustine had done.

At the beginning of the twentieth century the limbo theory was revived by Cardinal Billot and applied by him to vast numbers of infidels living after Christ, whom in the concrete circumstances of their life he thought to be deprived of the conditions required for reaching a true moral decision and, therefore, were to be assimilated to infants (*limbo puerorum*). They were adults by age, not by conscience and morality (see Billot 1919–23).

Its theological rigor notwithstanding, Cardinal Billot's theory contradicted Wis 13:1 and Rom 1:18, which both suppose that a valid knowledge of God is largely accessible to pagan adults. The theory, moreover, shockingly hurts the common human and Christian sense by its thoroughly negative view and radical depreciation of all human civilization outside Christianity. Its desperately negative solution must be laid to rest.

### C. Toward Implicit Faith in Jesus Christ

Long before the new worldview brought about by the discovery of the New World forced theologians to adopt a different approach to the problem of the salvation of the gentiles, the way had been opened by Saint Thomas Aquinas for a theory of faith that would account for the salvation in Christ not only of those who lived before the incarnation but also for those who came after. However, Saint Thomas's view needs to be clearly distinguished in both cases.

Saint Thomas never departed from the need for explicit faith for salvation. For him the true question concerned the content and object of such explicit faith. Following Heb 11:6, Thomas held that "whoever would draw near to God must believe that he exists and that he rewards those who seek him." He commented: "It must be said that in every age and for everyone it has always been necessary to believe explicitly in these two things" (ST II–II, q. 2, a. 8, ad 1). This could suffice for those who lived before Christ; in their case such faith could be considered as anticipating or implicitly containing faith in Christ, the mediator of salvation for all people. Thomas wrote, concerning those who had lived before Christ: "If some gentiles were saved, without receiving any revelation [about Christ], they were not saved without faith in the Mediator. Because even though they did not have explicit faith, they did have a faith that was implicit in divine providence, believing that God is the Liberator of humankind in ways that he himself chooses" (ST II–II, q. 2, art. 7, ad 3).

In the mind of Thomas, the same applied after Christ in the case of the centurion Cornelius, whose works, according to Acts, were pleasing to God, even before Peter announced Christ to him (Acts 10:1–2): "At the time, Cornelius was not an unbeliever, else his works would not have been acceptable to God, whom none can please without faith. However, he then had implicit faith [in Christ], when the truth of the Gospel had not yet been manifested to him. Hence Peter was sent to him, to give him full instruction in the faith" (ST II–II, q. 10, a. 4, ad 3).

The case of Cornelius was, however, an exception. For, while allowing for the sufficiency of implicit faith in Christ before the Gospel had been promulgated, Thomas firmly upheld the necessity of explicit faith thereafter: "After grace had been revealed, all, both the learned and the simple, are bound to have explicit faith in the mysteries of Christ, especially with respect to those mysteries which are publicly and solemnly celebrated in the Church, as those which refer to the mystery of the incarnation" (ST II–II, q. 2, a. 7).

How then could such explicit faith be verified in the case of people after Christ who had not had the Gospel preached to them? Saint Thomas upheld, as others had done before him, the principle, based on the universality of God's salvific will, that "to anyone who does what lies in his power, God does not deny grace" (*facienti quod in se est Deus non denegat gratiam*). He devised various expedients to make explicit faith available to those people in whatever circumstances, through either an "explicit revelation" or an "interior inspiration": "The exposition of what must be believed for salvation would be provided to the person by God, either by a preacher of the faith, as in the case of Cornelius, or by a revelation, so that it would then be within the power of the free will to make an act of faith" (In III Sent., dist. XXV, q. 2, a. 1, sol. 1, ad 1um.).

Thomas went so far as to imagine the case of a person brought up in the wilderness to whom God would reveal through inspiration or through a messenger what he must believe for salvation:

> If anyone were brought up in the wilderness or among brute animals, provided that he followed his natural reason in seeking the good and avoiding evil, we must most certainly hold that God would either reveal to him, by an inner inspiration, what must be believed, or would send a preacher to him, as he sent Peter to Cornelius. (Quaest disp. *De Veritate*, q. XIV, a. 11, ad 1um)

> If anyone born among barbarian nations were doing *quod in se est,* God would reveal to him what is necessary for salvation either by a God-given inspiration or through a teacher he would send to him. (In II Sent., dist. XXVIII, q. 1, a. 4, ad 4um)

These examples go to show how deep was Saint Thomas's conviction that explicit faith was in all cases necessary for salvation. The solution was indeed an extraordinary one; but, while it seems clear that Saint Thomas knew about people living in circumstances in which they had had no opportunity to hear the Gospel message, he still considered such cases as isolated ones. He continued to share the traditional persuasion according to which the message of the Gospel had actually penetrated to all the nations of his day. Nevertheless, in the *Summa Theologiae,* Thomas also developed a theory of *baptism of desire,* either explicit or implicit, conducive to justification. The first case was that of someone who, having heard about Christ, wished to be baptized but was overtaken by death before receiving the sacrament:

> The sacrament of baptism may be wanting to someone in reality but not in desire: For instance, when someone wishes to be baptized, but by some ill-chance is overtaken by death before receiving baptism. Such a person can obtain salvation without being actually baptized, on account of the person's desire for baptism, which desire is the outcome of faith that

works through charity, whereby God, whose power is not tied to visible sacraments, sanctifies a person inwardly. (ST III, q. 68, a. 2)

The second case was that of those who had not heard Christ announced to them but whose desire to conform to the will of God afforded them the faith and charity which justify. Such disposition implicitly included faith in Christ and the desire to be united with him in baptism.

A person receives the forgiveness of sins before baptism in so far as one has baptism of desire, explicitly or implicitly; and yet when actually receiving baptism, that person receives a fuller remission of the entire punishment. So also Cornelius and others like him receive grace and virtues through their faith in Christ and their desire for baptism, implicit or explicit; but afterwards when baptized, they receive a yet greater fullness of grace and virtues. (ST III, q. 69, a. 4, ad 2)

It is this doctrine of implicit *votum baptismi* that, in the new circumstances created by the discovery of the New World, later theologians would develop on a broad scale. As will be seen hereafter, it would also be followed by the Council of Trent, and through it would become received doctrine.

### D. The Fundamental Option in Reaching the Age of Reason

Saint Thomas contributed a further positive element to the possibility of salvation for grown persons who had not heard the message of Christ. According to him, it would be impossible for a person to commit a venial sin while still in the state of original sin. This was so because coming to the age of reason implied in all cases a firm moral decision before God, aided by grace. If the fundamental option were negative, to the person's original sin a grievous personal sin would be added; if it were positive, the grace of justification would be given which removed the state of original sin. Thomas wrote:

When a person reaches the age of reason, one is not at all excused from the guilt of venial or mortal sin. But the first thing that occurs to one to think about, is to make a decision about oneself. If one orders oneself towards the proper end, through grace one will obtain the remission of original sin. But if one does not order oneself toward the proper end, to the extent that at that age one is capable of this decision, one will sin mortally, through failing to do what lies in one's power to do. (ST I–II, q. 89, a. 6)

In Saint Thomas's view, the right ordering of self before God in reaching the age of reason included implicit faith in Jesus Christ as well as an implicit desire of baptism, both necessary for attaining justification. This Thomist theory was destined to play thereafter an important role in explaining the possibility of salvation for adults who had not heard the Christian message and did not belong to the Church. It came to be known as the theory of the "fundamental option."

However, against Thomas's theory of a free decision before God on reaching the age of reason, a decision from which there would result either justification and grace or grievous sin added to the original state of sinfulness, several objections have been raised. Among these are the following: Is a child incapable of venial sin before such time as it makes a fundamental option? Is one, as early as one reaches the age of reason, bound to such a fundamental option as would either justify or lead to grievous sin?[4] All things being considered, S. Harent notes: "With regard to its *intrinsic value*, [Saint Thomas's theory] does not seem to have been proved with certitude. Among the most celebrated Dominican theologians, several have considered as *only probable* either the entire system or at least some part of it" (Harent 1927, col. 1893).

As for A. d'Alès, he considers the theory of Saint Thomas as applicable only to children whose first awakening to moral responsibility coincides with the time of death. He adds: "Outside that extreme case, great objections arise concerning either the gravity of such an option applied to all, or the conditions required for a positive or negative outcome of it" (d'Alès 1928, col. 165).

## E. The Theology of the Act of Dying

The objections raised by S. Harent and A. d'Alès afford the opportunity to mention a further "substitute" for the Gospel, suggested by the theology of death as it has developed in recent years (see, e.g., Rahner 1958; Boros 1973; Troisfontaines 1960). Whatever be the merit or demerit of the fundamental option implied in a person's coming to the age of reason as conceived by St. Thomas, such an option by definition could not be attributed to children dying before reaching that moment of decision. On the contrary, the theology of death which has developed in recent years would make such a moment of decision possible not only for individuals when reaching the age of reason but before as well — indeed even for the unborn — since death by its nature and in all cases involves a "moment of truth," or of final decision. It would therefore be applicable to children, even unborn.

The theology of death is, however, proposed under two different forms. According to the first, death is, undoubtedly, the breaking apart, the disintegration, of human nature and, as such, a fate imposed on the human being which one undergoes passively. Nevertheless, concomitant with the passivity imposed by death — not following *after* it — a special illumination is possible, in the light of which the person is capable of a last and decisive choice. In the case of an adult, this choice ratifies and seals the direction which the person's religious life and moral conduct have taken during life.

According to the second and more complete form of this theology, the passivity imposed upon nature notwithstanding, death is, by its very nature, the

---

4. For an elaborate treatment of the discussion Saint Thomas's theory raised among later theologians, see Harent 1927, cols. 1864–94.

passing from this world to the other through an act of supreme awareness. It is not only passivity but fulfillment. The breaking apart of nature through the separation of body and soul frees the soul from the earthly condition which in this life irremediably hinders full consciousness and decision. Moral choices during life always remain open to change. Death, on the contrary, is the "moment of truth" in which in complete awareness the person makes a fully enlightened and decisive choice which decides one's eternal fate. Death, that is to say, sums up an entire human life; in that sense, it can and must be said that the human person is born in order to die. That is to say: to put a crown, by an act of wholesome awareness and decisive choice, from which there is no return, on the direction taken in life by one's conscious and moral life.

In the case of an infant or of the unborn, there also takes place, *in* the act of dying, the same blossoming of full awareness. In this passing over to unbound consciousness, the person is capable of a free and irrevocable decision in favor of the end proposed by God to human beings and, thereby, of opening oneself for the reception of divine grace and of salvation in Jesus Christ. Death is thus at once the absolute passivity imposed on nature and the supreme action of the person: disintegration and integration, determinism and self-determination, break and union. Paradoxically, death is the synthesis of fate imposed and of free action; at once the supreme trial inflicted on the person and one's full coming to self; a vacuum and a fullness.

Of all substitutes devised through the theological tradition, the theory of the "act of dying" is best capable of showing that salvation is possible not only for adults who, though not having heard the Gospel message, have made a moral decision during their earthly life but also for children and for the unborn who in this life have never reached the age of reason and of moral decision.

### F. The Flowering of Implicit Faith

But let us come back to earlier times. Saint Thomas, as has been seen, had laid the foundation for a theory of implicit faith conducive to salvation. The discovery of the New World (1492) — which, it may be recalled, came fifty years after the Decree for the Copts (1442) of the Council of Florence, in which were confined to perdition for sinful "infidelity" not only heretics, schismatics, and Jews but all "pagans" as well — forced the theological tradition to rethink substantially the conditions for salvation on the part of people living without the knowledge of the Gospel. It had now become evident that there existed vast masses of people who found themselves in this condition through no fault of their own. As Francis A. Sullivan puts it, the problem became "how to reconcile our belief in the universality of God's salvific will with the fact that he apparently has left all those people without any possibility of becoming members of the Church, outside of which they could not be saved" (Sullivan 1992, 69). This is where the theory of implicit faith and of baptism of desire began to develop well beyond what Saint Thomas had explicitly stated. The protagonists of such development were the theologians of the University of Salamanca, on the one side, and of the Roman College, on the other. For our purpose it will be enough to mention some more developed forms of this theory.[5]

Against those who, following the received tradition of sinful infidelity, considered people who had lived in the New World previous to the coming of missionaries culpable for their lack of faith, the Dominican D. Soto, writing in 1549, held that God would provide those people with the light necessary for an implicit faith (*fides confusa*) in Christ — and for salvation in him — which, according to Saint Thomas, had sufficed for people who lived before the coming of Christ (see Sullivan 1992, 75–76). Robert Bellarmine, teaching at the Roman College (1576–92), held a similar opinion: people who would not have heard the Gospel would be enlightened so as to arrive at faith in God and, with this, at an implicit desire for Christian faith and baptism. J. De Lugo, also teaching at the Roman College (1621–43), went much further by applying this solution not only to those who had never heard the Gospel but also to people who knew about Christ, though lacking orthodox faith. Not only pagans but even heretics, Jews, and Muslims, he thought, could be saved through their sincere faith in God. He wrote:

> A Jew or other non-Christian could be saved; for he could have supernatural faith in the one God and be invincibly ignorant about Christ. But such a person would not be Christian, because one is called a Christian by reason of one's knowledge of Christ. . . . The possibility of salvation for such a person is not ruled out by the nature of the case; moreover, such a person should not be called a non-Christian, because, even though he has not been visibly joined to the Church, still, interiorly he has the virtue of habitual and actual faith in common with the Church, and in the sight of God he will be reckoned with Christians.[6]

Francis A. Sullivan remarks on the "revolutionary" character of De Lugo's opinion, writing:

> After all, the Council of Florence had declared it to be a matter of faith to hold that all pagans, Jews, heretics and schismatics who died outside the Catholic Church would inevitably be damned to hell. Saint Thomas and the whole medieval tradition had taught that there was no salvation for any one in the Christian era without explicit faith in Christ. They were convinced that anyone who had heard about Christ and did not believe in him must be guilty of the sin of unbelief, for which he would be justly damned. Medieval popes and councils had declared again and again that

---

5. For a more elaborate treatment, see Sullivan 1992, 69–102. Included in this treatment are Melchior Cano, Domingo Soto, Alberto Pigge, Robert Bellarmine, Francesco Suárez, Juan De Lugo, and others.

6. *De virtute fidei divinae*, disp.12, n. 104, Lyon, 1646, vol. 3, p. 300; ed. Vivès, Paris, 1868, vol. 1, p. 425.

there was no salvation outside the Church. And yet here we have a Catholic theologian, teaching in Rome, who dared to suggest not only that people who had never heard of Christ might be saved, but that some Jews, Moslems and heretics might not be guilty of the sin of unbelief and, in that case, might find salvation through their sincere faith in God and contrition for their sins. (Sullivan 1992, 97–98)

And, summing up the theological current that led to De Lugo's "revolutionary" stand, the same author writes:

What we find in these Catholic theologians of the sixteenth and seventeenth centuries is an openness to truth from whatever source it came to them, and a readiness to reexamine traditional ideas and conceptions in the light of newly acquired knowledge. One has to admire not only their honesty in facing the problems which the discoveries of the age presented to them, but also their courage in proposing solutions that not only ran counter to the previous theological tradition, but seemed also to contradict the teaching of mediaeval councils and popes that there was no salvation outside the Church. (Sullivan 1992, 98)

Thus, with De Lugo's opinion we have reached the theory of salvific implicit faith in its more comprehensive form. Our survey of substitutes for the Gospel in the theological tradition may end here.[7] There remains to see how the theory of implicit faith and a concomitant *votum ecclesiae* entered into official Church doctrine.

## II. Implicit Faith and Desire for Baptism in the Church's Magisterium

### A. *The Council of Trent*

The Decree on Justification (1547) of the Council of Trent explained which are the "causes of justification." Among these it affirmed that the "instrumental cause is the sacrament of baptism, which is the 'sacrament of faith' without which [faith] none has ever been justified" (DS 1529; ND 1932). The council further explained:

When the apostle says that one is justified through faith and gratuitously [Rom 3:22, 24], those words are to be understood in the sense in which

---

7. To be historically complete, account would have to be given of still other "providential substitutes" for the preaching of the Gospel leading to supernatural faith through a direct influence either of the Church or of persons outside the Church, including heretics, schismatics, and even Jews. As for a "primordial revelation," passed over and preserved through history, suffice it to say that, while such revelation is witnessed to by God's familiarity with Adam according to the creation narrative in Genesis, its transmission through history defies historical proof. On those "providential substitutes," see Harent 1927, cols. 1912–27.

the Catholic Church has held and declared them with uninterrupted unanimity, namely, that we are said to be justified through faith because "faith is the beginning of human salvation" [see Fulgentius of Ruspe, *De fide liber ad Petrum*, Prologue, 1], the foundation and root of all justification, "without which it is impossible to please God" [Heb 11:6] and to come into the fellowship of his children. (DS 1532; ND 1935)

But the council explained:

After the promulgation of the Gospel, the transition [from the state in which one is born a child of the first Adam to the state of grace and adoption as God's children] cannot take place without the bath of regeneration or the desire for it (*eius voto*). As it is written: "Unless one is born of water and the Spirit, one cannot enter the Kingdom of God" [Jn 3:5]. (DS 1524; ND 1928)

Thus, without entering into current speculation by Catholic theologians on implicit faith, the council clearly affirmed the possibility of justification through "baptism of desire." This can be understood in the sense in which Saint Thomas had held that "desire of baptism" need not always have been explicit desire (see ST III, q. 69, a. 4, ad 2, quoted above).

## B. Baianism and Jansenism Condemned

The heresies of Baianism and Jansenism have their origin in an exacerbated reading of Augustine's pessimism. They may be treated rapidly. The first condemnation is by Pius V in the bull *Ex Omnibus Afflictionibus* (1567). It condemns the excessive reaction of "traditionalist" Michael de Bay (Baius) (1513–80) against the broad opinion of the Jesuits of the Roman College, especially De Lugo. Among de Bay's seventy-nine condemned propositions the following are relevant to our subject:

25. All the works of infidels are sins, and the virtues of the [pagan] philosophers are vices.

68. The purely negative infidelity of those to whom Christ has not been preached, is a sin. (DS 1925, 1968)

Equally condemned, though posthumously, is Cornelius Jansen (Jansenius) (1585–1638), who led the most important reactionary movement against the optimistic position of the Jesuits concerning the possibility of salvation without explicit faith in Jesus Christ. Innocent X condemned five propositions of Jansenius, the fifth among which reads as follows:

It is Semipelagian to say that Christ died or shed his blood for all human beings without exception. (DS 2005; ND 1989/5)

The condemnation meant that it is heretical to say that Christ died only for those predestined to be saved. The same condemnation was repeated against later Jansenist theologians by a decree of the Holy Office (1690) under Alexander VIII, which among thirty-one propositions included the following ones:

5. Pagans, Jews, heretics, and others of this kind receive no influence at all from Jesus Christ; hence one rightly concludes that their wills are naked and defenseless, totally lacking sufficient grace.

8. An infidel necessarily sins in every work.

11. Everything that does not proceed from supernatural Christian faith working through love is sinful. (DS 2305, 2308, 2311)

There followed, in the same line, the condemnation of Pasquier Quesnel (1634–1719) by the constitution *Unigenitus Dei Filius* (1713) of Clement XI. This document was the most thorough rebuttal of Jansenism. Among a hundred and one propositions, taken from Quesnel's works, the following is found: "No grace is granted outside the Church" (DS 2429).

Francis A. Sullivan makes the following comment:

> With the condemnation of this Jansenist proposition, Catholic theologians were assured that it was the doctrine of their Church that grace is granted to people who are "outside" it. However, during the eighteenth century there was far from unanimity among Catholic theologians about the possibility of salvation of those "outside." The strength of Jansenism had made many theologians wary of embracing any of the more optimistic solutions that had been proposed by such earlier theologians as Pigge, Soto, Suárez and De Lugo. Many felt obliged to uphold the teaching of Saint Thomas and the medieval theologians about the necessity of explicit Christian faith for salvation. In any case, there was no doubt about the fact that "No salvation outside the Church" was still the official doctrine. The decrees of the medieval popes and councils to that effect had never been repealed. (Sullivan 1992, 101–2)

## C. Nineteenth-Century Popes

The intellectual climate of Europe in the nineteenth century was largely derived from Descartes, Kant, and others. It was a strange combination of rationalism and fideism. The rationalist tenets led to the doctrine of religious indifferentism, which ascribed equal value to all religions. The philosophical roots of this movement were clearly incompatible with the Christian faith; they tended to deny all divine revelation or at least to refuse any finality to God's revelation in Christ. No word of God was recognized as demanding from human beings a religious assent. This doctrine was vigorously opposed by the official teaching of the Church. A first document is Leo XII's encyclical letter *Ubi Primum*

(1824), in which the pope explains what is the indifferentism which the Church condemns:

> [A certain sect], putting on airs of piety and liberality, professes what they call "tolerantism" or indifferentism, and extols it not only in matters of politics, about which we are not speaking, but also in matters of religion. It teaches that God has given to every human being a great freedom, so that one can embrace and adopt without any danger to one's salvation any sect that attracts one according to one's private judgment and opinion. (DS 2720; ND 1006)

A second document against religious indifferentism is the encyclical letter *Mirari Nos Arbitramur* (1832) of Gregory XVI. The pope condemns the liberal doctrines spread by the French writer F. de Lamennais (1782–1854):

> We now come to another important cause of the evils with which we regret to see the Church afflicted, namely indifferentism, or that wrong opinion according to which...one can attain the eternal salvation of one's soul by any profession of faith, provided one's moral conduct conforms to the norms of right and good.... From this foulest source of indifferentism there flows the absurd and wrong view, or rather insanity, according to which freedom of conscience must be asserted and vindicated for everybody. (DS 2730; ND 1007)

The condemnation of rationalist indifferentism culminated in a series of documents by Pius IX. The first among these documents is the pope's encyclical letter *Qui Pluribus* (1846). It will be followed by an allocution of the pope which bears the title *Singulari Quadam* (1854), then by another encyclical, *Quanto Conficiamur Moerore* (1863), and finally by the Syllabus of Condemned Errors (1864). We quote only the more relevant passages.

The first encyclical, *Qui Pluribus* (1846), condemns indifferentism in the following terms:

> [Among errors against the Catholic faith] must be included the horrible system, repugnant even to the natural light of reason, according to which there is no difference between religions [indifferentism]. These crafty people, doing away with all distinction between virtue and vice, truth and error, honesty and dishonesty, feign that people can attain to eternal salvation by the practice of any religion whatsoever. (DS 2785; ND 1008)

The allocution *Singulari Quadam* (1854), while reaffirming the necessity of the Church for salvation, is the first document which speaks of *invincible ignorance,* by which people are subjectively excused from embracing Christianity. As Francis A. Sullivan explains: "For the first time in the history of the Catholic Church, we have papal authority for explaining that the axiom [No salvation outside the Church] means: No salvation for those who are *culpably* outside the

Church" (Sullivan 1992, 114). This admission considerably tempers the harshness of the doctrine stated by the Council of Florence in the Decree for the Copts on the absolute exclusion from salvation of those outside the Church (DS 1351; ND 1005; see pp. 95–96, above), as well as the same document's negative stand on the obsolete character of the Jewish religion.[8] The pope says:

> It must, of course, be held as of faith that no one can be saved outside the Apostolic Roman Church, that the Church is the only ark of salvation, and that whoever does not enter it will perish in the flood. Yet, on the other hand, it must likewise be held as certain that those who are in ignorance of the true religion, if this ignorance is invincible, are not subject to any guilt in this matter before the eyes of the Lord. Now, who could presume for oneself the ability to set the boundaries of such ignorance, taking into consideration the natural differences of peoples, lands, talents and so many other factors? Only when we have been released from the bonds of this body and "shall see God as he is" [1 Jn 3:2] shall we understand how closely and wonderfully the divine mercy and justice are linked. But, as long as we dwell on earth, encumbered by the mortal body that dulls our soul, let us tenaciously hold the Catholic doctrine that there is "one God, one faith, one baptism" [cf. Eph 4:5]. To push our inquiry further is not right. (ND 1010; see 1009–11)

The same doctrine on the necessity of the Church and on "invincible ignorance" is repeated in the encyclical letter *Quanto Conficiamur Moerore* (1863), where it becomes evident that the "invincible ignorance" would apply not only to non-Catholic Christians but also to people belonging to other religions; moreover, the pope goes on to stress the duty on the part of the Church to enter into friendly relations with people of all religions:

> We all know that those who suffer from invincible ignorance with regard to our holy religion, if they carefully keep the precepts of the natural law which have been written by God in the hearts of human beings, if they are prepared to obey God, and if they lead a virtuous and dutiful life, can, by the power of divine light and grace, attain eternal life. For God, who knows completely the minds and souls, the thoughts and habits of all people, will not permit, in accord with his infinite goodness and mercy, anyone who is not guilty of a voluntary fault to suffer eternal punishment.
>   However, also well known is the Catholic dogma that no one can be saved outside the Catholic Church, and that those who obstinately oppose the authority of the definitions of the Church, and who stubbornly remain separate from the unity of the Church and from the successor of Peter, the Roman Pontiff, to whom the Savior has entrusted the care of his vineyard, cannot obtain salvation. (DS 2866–67; ND 814)

---

8. Decree for the Copts, DS 1348; ND 1003. We shall return to this document later.

But let it never happen that the children of the Catholic Church be in any way at enmity with those who are not joined to them by the bonds of the same faith and love. On the contrary, if they are poor or sick or afflicted by any other evils, let the children of the Church endeavour to succour and help them with all the services of Christian love. First and foremost, let them try to lead them from the shadows of error in which they lie to the Catholic truth and the most loving mother the Church. She never ceases to extend lovingly her maternal arms toward them and to call them to her bosom, so that, grounded in faith, hope and love, and "bearing fruit in every good work" [Col 1:10], they may find eternal salvation.[9]

The Syllabus of Condemned Errors (1864) lists and condemns the principal errors of the time. It is the final outcome of the pope's protracted effort to comply with a request made to him by a council held at Spoleto in 1851. The full title of the document is: "A Syllabus Containing the Most Important Errors of Our Time Which Have Been Condemned by Our Holy Father Pius IX in Allocutions, at Consistories, in Encyclical and Other Apostolic Letters." The document lists eighty errors divided into ten sections, drawing from previous statements of the pope in the light of which the propositions condemned need to be interpreted. We quote here from those directly relevant to our subject. They belong to the document's sections dealing with indifferentism and the rights of the Church:

15. Every one is free to embrace and profess the religion which by the light of reason one judges to be true.

16. Human beings can find the way of eternal salvation and attain eternal salvation by the practice of any religion whatever.

17. We should at least have good hopes for the eternal salvation of all those who are in no way in the true Church of Christ. (DS 2915–17; ND 1013/15–17)

21. The Church has no power to define dogmatically that the religion of the Catholic Church is the only true religion. (DS 2921; ND 1013/21)

It will be noted that the doctrine implied in the condemnation of these propositions upholds a rigid stand which in some way contrasts with the more open attitude expressed in *Singulari Quadam* and the encyclical *Quanto Conficiamur Moerore*. The Syllabus of Condemned Errors must, however, be interpreted in the light of those previous documents.

---

9. ND 1012. The doctrine of Pius IX on the Church's necessity of means for salvation and on the possibility of salvation for those outside the Church in "invincible ignorance" is reflected in the *Schema de Ecclesia* (7), which was prepared for Vatican I (1869–70). This part of the schema could not, however, be fully discussed and voted by the council before it adjourned in July 1870. See Sullivan 1992, 119–22; text of the schema in Mansi, *Sacrorum Conciliorum Nova et Amplissima Collectio* 51:570–71.

The last pope of the nineteenth century to be considered is Leo XIII. Besides condemning indifferentism, the syllabus had also condemned the liberalism according to which it was "no longer advisable that the Catholic religion be the State religion, excluding all other cult" (DS 2977; ND 1013/77). Thus, from his opposition to indifferentism, Pius IX had drawn the conclusion that the secularism of the state was also wrong, since it seemed intimately linked with religious indifferentism (see encyclical letter *Quanta Cura* [1864], in DS 2890). In his encyclical *Immortale Dei* (1885), Leo XIII softened the unnecessary conclusion:

> Although the Church does not consider it licit that various forms of worship of God should have the same rights as the true religion, yet she does not thereby condemn the authorities of the nations who, for the sake of attaining a great good or of avoiding to cause evil, tolerate in practice and by custom that they all have the same place in the city.[10]

### D. The Twentieth-Century Magisterium before Vatican II

Two important documents need to be considered here. The first is Pius XII's encyclical letter *Mystici Corporis* (1943). The encyclical letter identified the Roman Catholic Church with the Mystical Body of Christ, of which only Catholics are members in reality (*reapse*):

> If we would define and describe this true Church of Jesus Christ — which is the holy, catholic, apostolic, Roman Church — we shall find no expression more noble, more sublime or more divine than the phrase which calls it "the mystical Body of Jesus Christ." This title is derived from and is, as it were, the fair flower of the repeated teaching of Sacred Scripture and the holy Fathers. (ND 847)

> Only those are to be accounted as members of the Church in reality (*reapse*) who have been baptized and profess the true faith and who have not had the misfortune of withdrawing from the body or for grave faults been cut off by legitimate authority.... And so, if a person refuses to listen to the Church, that person should be considered, so the Lord commands, as a heathen and publican [cf. Mt 18:17]. It follows that those who are divided in faith and government cannot be living in one body such as this, and cannot be living of its one divine Spirit. (DS 3802; ND 849)

However, the pope recalled that from the beginning of his pontificate he had "committed to the protection and guidance of heaven those who do not belong to the visible structure of the Catholic Church" and that he ardently desired "that they may have life and have it abundantly." And he added:

---

10. DS 3176; ND 1014. The condemnation of the secularism of the state will be completely superseded by the doctrine of Vatican II in its declaration *Dignitatis Humanae* on religious freedom.

From a heart overflowing with love we ask each and everyone of them to be quick and ready to follow the interior movements of grace, and to seek earnestly to rescue themselves from a state in which they cannot be secure about their salvation. For even though, by a certain unconscious desire and longing, they are ordained to the mystical Body of the Redeemer (*inscio quodam desiderio ac voto ad mysticum Redemptoris Corpus ordinentur*), they lack so many great gifts and helps from God, which they can enjoy only in the Catholic Church. (DS 3821)

Let us observe that according to the encyclical, non-Catholics can be saved, even though they find themselves "in a state in which they cannot be secure about their salvation." Moreover, while they are not *reapse* members of the Catholic Church, they are nevertheless ordained (*ordinantur*) to it by a "certain unconscious desire and longing" (*inscio quodam desiderio ac voto*). Presumably, the "unconscious desire" of which the pope spoke would be implied in a person's sincere wish to do God's will. We shall come back later to the exact meaning, in Pius XII's mind, of the "orientation" (*ordinantur*) to the Church which such a desire implies. The pope did not distinguish the case of non-Catholic Christians from that of the members of other religions, as Vatican II would do later. In both cases he spoke of an "orientation" to the Catholic Church. Vatican II will speak differently, stating that non-Catholic Christians are "joined" (*coniuncti*) in many ways to the Church (LG 15) and applying the term "orientation" (*ordinantur*) specifically and exclusively to the members of other religions (LG 16).

The second document is a letter of the Holy Office to the archbishop of Boston, in which the position of Leonard Feeney is condemned (1949). Feeney had returned to a rigid interpretation of the axiom *Extra ecclesiam nulla salus*. The letter is important because it offers an explanation of the doctrine of the encyclical *Mystici Corporis*. It explains that the necessity of belonging to the Church for salvation is one of means, not only of precept. It goes on to clarify what this must mean for persons in different situations. All, in order to be saved, must be related in some way to the Church, but actual membership is not absolutely required. Provided one is related to the Church in desire or longing, even implicitly, and such a desire is informed by supernatural faith and love, one can be saved. Thus, this document officially states the Church's understanding of the axiom *Extra ecclesiam nulla salus*. It needs to be quoted extensively:

The infallible dictum which teaches us that outside the Church there is no salvation, is among the truths that the Church has always taught and will always teach. But this dogma is to be understood as the Church itself understands it. For the Savior did not leave it to private judgment to explain what is contained in the deposit of faith, but to the doctrinal authority of the Church.

The Church teaches, first of all, that there is question here of a very strict command of Jesus Christ. In unmistakable words he gave his apostles the command to teach all nations to keep whatever he had commanded [cf. Mt 28:19–20]. Not least among Christ's commands is the one which orders us to be incorporated by baptism into the mystical Body of Christ, which is the Church, and to be united to Christ and to his vicar, through whom he himself governs the Church on earth in a visible way. Therefore, no one who knows that the Church has been divinely established by Christ and, nevertheless, refuses to be a subject of the Church or refuses to obey the Roman Pontiff, the vicar of Christ on earth, will be saved.

The Savior did not make it merely a necessity of precept for all nations to enter the Church. He also established the Church as a means of salvation without which no one can enter the kingdom of heavenly glory.

As regards the helps to salvation which are ordered to the last end only by divine decree, not by intrinsic necessity, God, in his infinite mercy, willed that their effects which are necessary to salvation can, in some circumstances, be obtained when the helps are used only in desire and longing. We see this clearly stated in the Council of Trent about the sacrament of regeneration and about the sacrament of penance. (DS 1524, 1543; ND 1928, 1944)

The same, in due proportion, should be said of the Church in so far as it is a general help to salvation. To gain eternal salvation it is not always required that a person be incorporated in reality (*reapse*) as a member of the Church, but it is required that one belong to it at least in desire and longing (*voto et desiderio*). It is not always necessary that this desire be explicit, as it is with catechumens. When one is invincibly ignorant, God also accepts an implicit desire, so called because it is contained in the good disposition of soul by which one wants one's will to be conformed to God's will.

This is clearly taught by the Sovereign Pontiff Pope Pius XII, in his doctrinal letter on the mystical Body of Christ.... Towards the end of [the] encyclical, when with all his heart he invites to union those who do not pertain to the body of the Catholic Church, the pope mentions those "who are ordained to the mystical Body of the Redeemer by some kind of unconscious desire and longing." He by no means excludes these persons from eternal salvation; but, on the other hand, he does point out that they are in a condition "in which they cannot be secure about their salvation...since they lack the many great gifts and helps from God which they can enjoy only in the Catholic Church." ...

With these prudent words the pope censures those who exclude from eternal salvation all those who adhere to the Church only with an implicit desire; and he also censures those who falsely maintain that people can be saved equally well in any religion.

It must not be imagined that any desire whatsoever of entering the Church is sufficient for a person to be saved. It is necessary that the desire by which one is related to the Church be informed with perfect charity. And an implicit desire cannot have its effect unless a person has supernatural faith. (DS 3866–3872; ND 854–57)

Our survey of "substitutes" for the Gospel proposed by the theological tradition and the Church's progressive understanding of salvific faith outside the Church and the *votum ecclesiae* can end here. All through this development, the problematic remains that of the possibility of salvation in Jesus Christ without belonging to the Church. In later years this problematic will appear too narrow, and its ability to provide an adequate foundation for a theology of religions will be questioned; but this must be left for later treatment. Meanwhile, the next two chapters must be dedicated to further developments of the theology of salvation which marked the years closely preceding Vatican II (chapter 5) and to the new approach to the other religions initiated by the council itself (chapter 6).

*Five*

# Theological Perspectives
# Surrounding Vatican II

THE PREVIOUS CHAPTER has shown how Middle Ages and later theology solved the problem of the "salvation of the infidels" who found themselves outside the Church without imputable guilt. The theory of implicit faith in Jesus Christ, implied by faith in a provident God and the sincere following of one's partially enlightened conscience, became progressively refined. It received even more impetus as the world came to acquire proportions never suspected before and it became obvious that there existed immense territories where the Gospel had not been preached or heard. Throughout this protracted period the problematic remained strictly that of the "salvation of the infidels."

The problematic was, however, destined to open up to new horizons. This happened gradually, as the following chapters will show. A first step toward a broader horizon was taken with the theological renewal that characterized the pre–Vatican II period and grew even stronger in the wake of the council. No longer would the perspective be restricted to asking what kind of saving faith is necessary and sufficient for the salvation of people to whom the Gospel has not been "promulgated." It would further be asked how the religious traditions to which those people belonged stood in relation to the Gospel message and Christianity. What could a Christian theological discourse affirm concerning those religions? Were they to be attributed to the power of the devil, being made up, as previous ages had often thought, of polytheism, idolatry, and immoral practices? Did religion as such represent, as Karl Barth was convinced, the human person's demonic attempt at self-justification, while only faith in Jesus Christ was able to save? As is well known, what Barth affirmed regarding religion in general (Christianity included), as distinct from saving faith, was largely applied by his disciples to the other religions, as they came in contact with them in missionary situations.[1] As the only valid knowledge about God was that which human beings receive in Jesus Christ, it followed that the gods of the "pagans" were idols, their devotees idolaters, and the religions to which they belonged devil's work and vain human attempts at self-righteousness.

Barth's negative verdict on religion — and, implicitly, on religions — was mercifully not the only possible attitude. Others, in a more generous fashion,

---

1. On the negative position of K. Barth, see Barth 1970, 280–361. Barth, however, softened his position in Barth 1976, 86–104. On the evolution of Barth's position, see Braaten 1992, 53–59. See Kraemer 1947. Kraemer is, however, more nuanced in Kraemer 1957. See also Kraemer 1960, 1962.

recognized a positive relationship between the other religions and Christianity. They asked, as the early tradition had suggested, whether these religions could, even today, be considered a "preparation to the Gospel" (*praeparatio evangelica*), to use Eusebius's expression. And, if so, in what sense? Far from being an obstacle to faith, could they be viewed as opening people up toward God's revelation in Jesus Christ? Did they embody, in themselves, the expression of the human person's innate desire for union with God and function, as it were, as "stepping-stones" for Christian revelation: *anima naturaliter christiana*, according to Tertullian's expression? In short, did they relate to Christianity as nature does to the supernatural, by which nature is not destroyed but perfected (*gratia non destruit sed perficit naturam*)? Or, as "potency" to "act"? As aspiration to fulfillment? As shadow to reality?

Others further asked whether the religions themselves contributed something — but what? — to the mystery of the salvation in Jesus Christ of their members. Were the others saved in Jesus Christ, outside or inside their own religion, in spite of it, or, in some mysterious way, by virtue of it? What positive role, then, did the other religions play, if any, in the mystery of the salvation in Jesus Christ of their followers? Could they, in the last analysis, be called "means" or "ways" of salvation? And, if so, in what sense? Was there, then, "salvation without the Gospel"?

These were mighty questions which already occupied the theologians' attention during the preconciliar period and would continue to be of concern to them even thereafter, until such time as an even broader perspective would open up to them in more recent years, as will be shown at a later stage.

The new questions regarding the possibility of a positive relationship of the other religions to Christianity, and the role which eventually they played in the mystery of the salvation of their followers, were, to no small extent, dictated by the new situation which obtained during the period now under review. For one thing, knowledge of the other religious traditions available to theologians had been considerably increased and deepened. Scholarly work was not wanting which examined the doctrines of the great religious traditions of the world, such as Hinduism, Buddhism, and Islam. Specialized studies inquired into the response which the various traditions gave to the perennial questions of humankind about the Absolute, the human person, the world, and history. Entire systems of thought thus came to the fore, each of which constituted a specific worldview, irreducible to the others. Nor were the various religious traditions mere carriers of religious systems: each had a mystical dimension; each possessed its seers and its prophets, its saints and saving figures, its ascetics and its mystics.

To scientific and academic study was added, moreover, a deeper experiential knowledge obtained through increased interaction between Christians and the members of other religious traditions. Barriers had begun to crumble, and communication was gradually developing, which brought home a new awareness of what the other traditions proposed to their adherents by way of salvation and liberation. Nor were those traditions on the decline, as earlier ages had anticipated they would be. They were in fact very much alive and continued to respond to and fulfill the aspirations of their adherents. Indeed, with the means of communication very much on the increase, they made their presence in the Western world felt ever more deeply. The irreversible process had begun by which the world would progressively shrink into a "global village," bringing with it a new awareness that Christianity was one of many traditions which claim and enjoy the allegiance of millions of adherents and disciples. In such a context the question could not but arise as to how the other traditions stood in relation to Christianity and, from the vantage point of Christian faith, what role they might be playing in relation to the salvation of their followers. Solutions were, however, varied.

We are concerned here with the main positions held on this subject by theologians in the Roman Catholic tradition during the years preceding and surrounding Vatican II, leaving the entire range of opinions that characterize the postconciliar period for consideration in a later chapter. At the risk of simplifying, the positions may be grouped under two headings which, in fact, represent two contrasting standpoints, mutually exclusive.

There were those according to whom the various religions of humanity represent the human being's innate desire for union with the Divine, of which there exist various expressions in diverse cultures and in the different geographical areas of the world. Jesus Christ and Christianity, however, denote God's personal response to this universal human aspiration. Thus, while all other religions are varied expressions of *homo naturaliter religiosus,* and so of "natural religion," only Christianity, as the divine response to the human quest for God, is "supernatural religion." This first position has often been referred to as the "fulfillment theory." According to this theory, salvation in Jesus Christ reaches the members of other religions as the divine response to the human religious aspiration expressed through their own tradition, but these religious traditions themselves play no role in this mystery of salvation.

According to the second — and opposite — position, humanity's various religions represent in themselves distinct interventions of God in salvation history. However, these divine interventions in history are ordained to the decisive salvific event in Jesus Christ. As such, they played a positive role before the Christ-event as *praeparatio evangelica;* indeed, they keep, even today, a positive value in the order of salvation by virtue of the operative presence in them, and in some way through them, of the saving mystery of Jesus Christ. This other theory may be called, for lack of a more adequate term, the "theory of the presence of Christ in the religions" or of "Christ's inclusive presence." Admittedly, the saving mystery of Christ is unique. But all other religious traditions, in virtue of the divine plan of salvation of which they are part, are set in relation to this mystery, in whose respect they represent, each in its own way, an ordering of mediation. Thus, no religion is purely natural. In every religion, historically, a divine intervention in the history of the nations is to be found and an existential mediation of the mystery of salvation in Jesus Christ acknowledged. All religions, then, for more than one reason, are supernatural.

Obviously, these categories represent a simplification of a reality which is in itself more complex. It seems, nevertheless, legitimate to view them as a workable general framework within which, during the period considered here, mainstream theologians of religions — at least in the Catholic tradition[2] — may be said to fall in and find their place.

This chapter, however, does not aim at giving a full picture of the complex reality. It is satisfied to provide working categories for a general grasp of the problematic at work during this period in the theological reflection on religions and to provide concrete examples by examining succinctly the opinions of some of the protagonists of the mainline positions. These protagonists, as will be seen, have, more often than not, had their followers or have even been the initiators of a school of thought.

As the labels appended to the two mainline positions mentioned above indicate, the debate has now shifted from the prominently ecclesiological question of salvation in or outside the Church to that of salvation in Jesus Christ knowingly or unknowingly; that is, from a primarily ecclesiocentric viewpoint to a more Christocentric perspective. What is now asked directly no longer is what happens outside the "ark" of salvation which is the Church, but how Jesus Christ and his mystery reach out to those who do not know him.

The chapter is divided into two parts, labeled after the two mainstream theories. Subtitles indicate what seem to be the leading threads that served as guiding principles for the theological positions of some of their protagonists.[3]

## I. The Fulfillment Theory

The opinion that became the fulfillment theory had been propounded in missionary situations in the first half of the twentieth century, well before it was developed as a theory, mostly by Western theologians. Examples, in the Indian context, are such works as J. N. Farquhar's *The Crown of Hinduism* (Farquhar 1915) and, even more so, P. Johanns's *Vers le Christ par le Vedanta*.[4] As the titles indicate, these works viewed other religions, especially Hinduism, as "stepping-stones" to Christianity, the religion in which the deepest human as-

---

2. For an elaborate survey of positions in the Protestant tradition one may consult Knitter 1974. During the period considered, some Protestant authors fall under either of the two mainstream categories mentioned here. Thus, for the main part, the theology of religions cuts across confessional boundaries. It must, however, be observed that the full spectrum of Protestant theology in this regard extends beyond the two main streams mentioned here. On one side of the spectrum, the Barthian pessimism remains rampant among evangelicals, while, on the other hand, liberal Protestantism generates positions departing from mainstream Christian tradition.

3. For a survey of opinions, Catholic and Protestant, during the period considered and after, see, among others, Knitter 1985; also Drummond 1985.

4. See Johanns 1932–33, 1938, 1946, 1952, 1996. In the same line and the same context, Lacombe 1937, 1956. For a study of these, see Mattam 1975.

pirations which they embodied found their fulfillment, in a way neither foreseen nor hoped for. It may be said that the "fulfillment theory" derived its name from such pioneering missionary work. Nevertheless, it became an object of elaborate theological discourse primarily among Western theologians who, however, did not always show the same openness and empathy toward other religions as did those with direct field experience of them.

### A. Jean Daniélou on Cosmic Religion and Christian Revelation

Jean Daniélou may be considered the first Western exponent of the fulfillment theory. From the early 1940s down to the 1970s he wrote abundantly on the subject.[5] The standpoint from which he looks at the religious traditions of the world is resolutely that of God's plan for the salvation of humankind in Jesus Christ as understood by Christian faith. In this context, Daniélou asks what Christianity may have to say with regard to the religions it has encountered in the past and continues increasingly to encounter in modern times. A leading thread of his thought is a theology of history as a progressive divine manifestation to humankind. However, salvation history proper is for Daniélou limited to the Judeo-Christian tradition: it starts with God's personal revelation to Israel through Abraham and Moses, runs through the history of the chosen people, and culminates in Jesus Christ, whose message of salvation has been entrusted to the Church. Whatever came before God's personal manifestation in history, even though already inscribed in God's unique plan for humankind, can at best be called "prehistory" of salvation. The same term would apply to whatever religious experience may be found today, outside the Judeo-Christian tradition, within the religions of the world. What then is the precise significance and value of the religions of the world? In what sense do they represent a "preparation for the Gospel"?

Daniélou draws a sharp distinction between nature and the supernatural, or equivalently between religion and revelation. "Non-Christian" religions belong to the order of natural reason, the Judeo-Christian revelation to the order of supernatural faith. Both constitute different orders. To this distinction of two orders corresponds that between two God-given covenants: the cosmic and the historical. The cosmic covenant is equivalent to God's manifestation through nature, even while in the concrete (supernatural) order of reality it is already oriented toward God's personal manifestation in history. It manifests God's abiding presence in creation and is symbolized, in Noah's episode in Genesis, by the rainbow, the sign of the "everlasting covenant between God and every living creature of all flesh that is upon the earth" (Gen 9:8–17; cf. v. 16).

It is this faithfulness of God in the course of nature which Paul had in mind when in the Letter to the Romans he wrote that through nature God had manifested himself to all human beings, as the maker of all things: "For what can

---

5. See principally, Daniélou 1957, 1958, 1962a, 1962b, 1966a, 1966b, 1970. For a study of Daniélou's approach to religions, see Veliath 1988.

be known about God is plain to them, because God has shown it to them. Ever since the creation of the world his invisible nature, namely his eternal power and deity, have been clearly perceived in the things that have been made" (Rom 1:19–20). Paul adds, in a sweeping statement, that people are guilty for not having recognized God in the things he made: "So they are without excuse; for although they knew God they did not honor him as God or give thanks to him, but they became futile in their thinking, and their senseless minds were darkened" (Rom 1:20–21). They fell victims to polytheism and idolatry.

Daniélou sees here the description of the situation of people finding themselves in non-Christian religions. The knowledge of God available to them is that corresponding to the order of nature, be it through the created world or through the voice of the personal conscience. Insofar as people have recognized God as Creator, they have acquired of him a valid, natural knowledge; insofar, however, as they failed to recognize their Creator, their minds were darkened and became Godless. In the first case, they have known God, though their knowledge was confined to the order of nature; in the opposite case, they "exchanged the glory of the immortal God for images resembling mortal humans or birds or animals or reptiles" (Rom 1:23).

The religions of the world, as we historically know them, are thus made up of a mixture of truth and falsehood, of light and darkness, or of right conduct and evil ways. They belong to the order of "cosmic religion," corresponding as they do to the "cosmic covenant." This covenant, while it is part of God's plan for humankind and the world, serves only as a substratum for God's personal revelation in history. It represents the prehistory of salvation. Between the cosmic and the historical covenant, there is a certain continuity inasmuch as the first serves as necessary foundation for the other; but God's gratuitous intervention in history initiates a new order which commands an even greater discontinuity.

No doubt, some people living under the regime of the cosmic covenant have been "pleasing to God"; witness the "pagan saints" recorded by the Old Testament (see Daniélou 1957; see also chap. 1, pp. 34–37, above) and celebrated for their faith by the Letter to the Hebrews (Heb 11). The Bible does not tell us how many these were, but the Old Testament and Paul in Romans speak eloquently of the evil ways into which the nations fell. However this may be, if there is to be found in the religions of the world a "preparation for the Gospel," this is at best by way of a substratum in nature for God's personal commitment to humankind in the history of Israel and finally in the event of Jesus Christ, the summit of salvation history.

In every event, the "cosmic religions" — by which term are meant all world religions except the three "monotheistic" religions, Judaism, Christianity, and Islam — are but human elaborations of a knowledge of God obtained through the order of nature. As such they were unable in the past, and remain unable today, to lead to the saving faith which can only come from God's gracious intervention in the lives of people. They have in themselves no saving power; they represent at best various expressions in different cultures of the aspiration of the human person toward an absolute being. As a matter of course, within the purview of salvation history, they have become "doubly anachronistic," superseded as they have been first by Judaism and, even more definitively, by the Christ-event and Christianity. They are "outmoded survivals" of a bygone period of history. "Theirs is a sin of persistence" (see Veliath 1988, 76). They are "natural religion" as opposed to Christianity, the only "supernatural religion," which even today retains (unlike Judaism) and enjoys salvific validity. Christianity is the universal means of salvation; it is also the normative way. If salvation is possible for non-Christians outside the Church, this represents in each instance a "limit-situation," from which nothing can be derived by way of a positive role of non-Christian religions in the order of salvation.

A quotation from Daniélou may aptly sum up the entire matter. He writes, concerning the singular character of Christianity:

> Christianity does not consist in the strivings of men after God, but in the power of God, accomplishing in man that which is beyond the power of man; human efforts are merely the response called forth by the divine initiative. This, then, is the second mark of the transcendence of Christianity.

And he explains further:

> This is the heart and core of the irreducible originality of Christianity, that the Son of God came among us to reveal these two intimately related truths: that there is within God himself a mysterious living love, called the Trinity of Persons; and that in and through the Son we men are called to share this life of love. The mystery of the Trinity known to us through the Word made flesh, and the mystery of the deification of man in him — that is the whole of our religion, summed up in one person, the person of Jesus Christ, God made man, in whom is everything we need to know. Here we put our finger on the essential distinction, the specific element of Christianity, the ultimate reason of its unique transcendence: it is Jesus Christ, Son of God, our Saviour. The religions of nature bear witness (and this is the measure of their real worth) to the natural tendency of man towards God: Christianity is God's approach towards man in Jesus Christ, taking possession of man to bring him to himself. (Daniélou 1958, 115–16, 118–19)

The essential distinction between the Judeo-Christian religion and all other religions is expressed even more forcefully in another passage. Christianity is God's descent toward humankind in self-communication, answering the aspirations of the entire universe toward God; God's grace reversing the movement of humanity's cry:

> The essential difference between Catholicism and all other religions is that the others start from man. They are touching and often very beautiful attempts, rising very high in their search for God. But in Catholicism there

is a contrary movement, the descent of God towards the world, in order to communicate his life to it. The answer to the aspirations of the entire universe lies in the Judeo-Christian religion. The true religion, the Catholic religion, is composed of these two elements. It is the religion in which God's grace has made answer to man's cry. In other religions grace is not present, nor is Christ, nor is the gift of God. The vanity and illusion of syncretism lies in its belief that universality is a common denominator of all religions. (Daniélou 1962b, 8)

The fulfillment theory as propounded by Daniélou exercised a deep influence, and it has been possible to speak of a *tendance Daniélou* (see Verastegui 1970), representatives of which — to name only two — would be J. Dournes and H. Maurier.[6] As will be seen later, the fulfillment theory in the Daniélou tendency has had an important impact on the Church's magisterium and can still be found in some post–Vatican II documents.

## B. Henri de Lubac on Christianity as the Axis of God's Plan

Henri de Lubac came to the theology of religions through comparative studies between some "aspects of Buddhism" and Christianity in which, not without sympathy but with great lucidity and without complacency, he pointed to two apparently irreconcilable visions of the human person's path to liberation in different worldviews (Lubac 1951–55, 1952b). Early in his career, he published work on the mystery of the supernatural, first a historical study of tradition (Lubac 1946b) and, thereafter, a systematic monograph (Lubac 1967b). These studies had prepared him to confront Christianity and the other religions and to point to what made the singularity and uniqueness of the first in relation to the others, be it on the level of doctrine or of mysticism.

As early as his classical study on "Catholicism," de Lubac had written, after Irenaeus's fashion, on the "thorough newness" which Christianity represents in the religious history of humankind:

Christianity brought into the world something absolutely new. Its concept of salvation is not only original in relation to that of the religions that surrounded its birth; it constitutes a unique event in the religious history of humankind.... In this universal symphony (*concert*) [of religions] Christianity alone affirms, at once and indissolubly, a transcendent destiny of the human person and for the whole of humankind a common destiny. For this destiny the entire history of the world is a preparation. From the first creation down to the final consummation... a unique divine project is being fulfilled. (Lubac 1952a, 107–10; see also the entire chapter, entitled "Le Christianisme et l'histoire," 107–132)

---

6. Dournes 1963, 1967; Maurier 1968. However, Maurier defends a much more open attitude in Maurier 1976; see also Maurier 1993.

As was the case with Daniélou, so too for de Lubac the relation between the world religions and Christianity follows the structure that distinguishes — without separating them — nature and the supernatural. The supernatural, while it is absolutely gratuitous on the part of God, fulfills the natural desire of the human person for union with the Divine. Both have been intimately united in Jesus Christ. In him and through him the supernatural does not substitute for nature but informs and transforms it: "Christ does not compete with human nature, for Christ and his grace do not originate from nature" (see Eterovic 1981, 283). The same is true where the relationship between world religions and Christianity is concerned. Neither here is there competition between the one and the others. As the embodiment of God's grace in Jesus Christ, Christianity is *the* supernatural religion. It does not follow that the other religions lack everything that is true and good; for "grace does not destroy nature." Yet as human nature is both created and sinful, the religions of the world contain at once "seeds of the Word" and spurious elements, traces of God and traces of sin. Without competing with them, Christianity unveils their positive values; by assuming them, it purifies and transforms them (Eterovic 1981, 283–84).

The relationship between Christianity and the world religions, and singularly the way in which salvation in Jesus Christ reaches out to non-Christians, is expressed in a brief chapter of the book *Church: Paradox and Mystery.*[7] According to the fulfillment theory which de Lubac makes his own, the mystery of Christ reaches the members of other religious traditions as the divine response to the human aspiration for union with the Divine, but the religious traditions themselves play no role in this mystery of salvation. Henri de Lubac explains that to attribute positive salvific value to them would be tantamount to setting them in competition with Christianity, thus obscuring the latter's uniqueness. He observes, citing Pierre Teilhard de Chardin, that the divine plan will surely be an orderly one: it must have a single axis, a single point of convergence. That point is Christianity, the sole way of salvation. To regard other traditions as playing a positive role in the mystery of the salvation of their members would be, in effect, to establish them as parallel routes to salvation, and thus to destroy the unity of the divine plan (Lubac 1967c, 148–49). He writes:

> If there exist objectively several ways of salvation, which run as it were parallel, we are faced with a scattering, no longer with a spiritual conver-

---

7. Lubac 1967c. See the chapter entitled "Les religions humaines d'après les Pères," 120–63. Already in Lubac 1946a, H. de Lubac wrote: "In the many diverse religions . . . a similar trend emerges, a similar yearning is expressed which, under the divine light, we are able to discern. Borrowing the language of the Bible and the Fathers of the Church, we may say that every soul is naturally Christian. Not in the sense that it would already possess an equivalent or, as it were, a first 'stage' of Christianity, but because in the depth of that soul the image of God is shining, or rather, because the soul itself is that image; and, longing as it is to be reunited with its Model, it can be so united only through Christ. If Christianity is destined to be the religion of the world, if, being truly supernatural, it transcends all human endeavor, it must also gather in itself the human longing of the whole world" (71–72). And he added in a note: "Christianity does not come to add something to the human religions, except as the solution adds to the problem, or the goal to the race. . . . It comes to straighten out [the human religious endeavor], to purify it, to transform it so that it may reach its goal. Christianity is the religion that effectively unites man to God" (n. 1).

gence. What is then unduly called a "divine plan" lacks unity. There ought to be a single axis. . . . If in accordance with the design of God, we care for the salvation of humankind, if we believe in the reality of its history and aspire to unity, we cannot escape looking for an axis and a drawing and unifying force which is the Spirit of the Lord that animates the Church. (Lubac 1967c, 149)

Here, however, in answer to de Lubac, we may observe that, while the unity of the divine plan does indeed require a single point of convergence, that point — according to Teilhard de Chardin himself — is not primarily Christianity as such, or the Church, but Jesus Christ. The Teilhardian outlook is unmistakably Christocentric: the Church is the "reflexively Christified" portion of the world,[8] while the eschatological fulfillment of the Reign of God is to consist in universal Christification of all things (see U. King 1980). A single citation will suffice to establish that, for Teilhard, a Christified universe represents the end point of cosmic evolution. Teilhard writes:

Christ . . . is the alpha and omega, the principle and the end, the foundation stone and the keystone, the Plenitude and the Plenifier. He is the one who consummates all things and gives them their consistence. It is towards him and through him, the inner life and light of the world, that the universal convergence of all created spirit is effected in sweat and tears. He is the single center, precious and consistent, who glitters at the summit that is to crown the world. (Teilhard de Chardin 1965, 34–35)

It can be doubted whether ascribing to other religious traditions a positive role in the salvation of their followers necessarily places them in competition with Christ and the religion founded by him. Can there not be various — nonparallel — modalities of the mediation of the mystery of salvation, all in relationship with the mystery of Jesus Christ? At all events, according to the fulfillment theory, there is no salvation without the Gospel or any such thing as "anonymous Christianity." But, of this later.

One word must be added regarding de Lubac's view of non-Christian mysticism, as compared with the Christian mystery. Here too the governing principle is the structure natural-supernatural. Thus, his view on this matter remains consistent with that on Christianity and other religions in general. Quoting Dom A. Stolz, de Lubac writes: "Hors de l'Eglise, point de mystique" (Outside the Church no mysticism) (Stolz 1937, 255), and explains: "Whatever can be observed elsewhere which offers an analogy [with Christian mysticism] will, in the best hypothesis, *normally* belong only to 'natural mysticism' — a rough sketch or a 'natural dawn' of Christian mysticism — of which it is difficult to determine precisely the end towards which it is leading, though it seems certain that this end is not God" (see Lubac 1965b, 16).

---

8. See Pierre Teilhard de Chardin, "Comment je vois" (1948), n. 24, quoted in Lubac 1967c, 145.

This is not to say that all mysticism outside Christianity must be condemned as being led astray. For de Lubac explains:

> We may not reduce all spiritual striving — even if aborted — which is found where the light of Christ has not yet shone, to a refusal of that light by the human person who thus is guilty of relying only on one-self in an attitude of self-complacency. It must never be forgotten that the Word incarnate is no other than the One who enlightens all human beings.... Neither must it be thought that all [non-Christian mysticism] can be reduced to some ultimate experience the content of which cannot be grasped.... Outside the divine revelation and its zones of influence, the mystical impulse tends to run past the "prime given" (*le donné initial*) that served it as a springboard. (Lubac 1965b, 34)

The verdict is nuanced; while it maintains the specificity of Christian mysticism based on faith in the mystery of Jesus Christ, it nevertheless recognizes that a certain *élan mystique,* if well oriented, can constitute a stepping-stone toward Christian faith and mysticism.

This is not the place to advance further in the debate on natural versus supernatural, non-Christian versus Christian mysticism, which will be touched upon in some way in the synthetic part of this work. Let it suffice, for the time being, to note that, not unlike Jean Daniélou's, Henri de Lubac's version of the fulfillment theory has had a profound echo among friends and disciples. Some prominent names may be rapidly mentioned: J. Monchanin, J.-A. Cuttat, P. Teilhard de Chardin, to whom can be added R. C. Zaehner and E. Cornelis, all of whom were familiar with Eastern religions and mysticism.[9]

## C. Hans Urs von Balthasar on Christ the "Concrete Universal"

In the abundant literary production of Hans Urs von Balthasar nowhere is there to be found an elaborate theology of religions. This, however, is not to say that the theme does not surface in many of his writings, though admittedly less so in his great trilogy *Herrlichkeit, Theodramatik, Theologik.* Balthasar has indeed repeatedly compared Christianity with the other religions of the world, to show the contrast, the reversal in perspective, which exists between the one and the others and the absoluteness of Christianity. To give an account of the main lines of Balthasar's thinking on the subject it is necessary to glean items from his various writings.[10] It will then appear that his view rightly falls under the label of the "fulfillment theory," being akin to that of Daniélou and de Lubac,

---

9. See Monchanin 1955, 1974, 1985. On Monchanin, see *L'abbé Jules Monchanin* 1960; Duperray 1965; Lubac 1967a; Mattam 1975, 144–73; Jacquin 1996. J.-A. Cuttat 1960, 1964, 1965. On Cuttat, see Mattam 1975, 74–110. For a study of Teilhard de Chardin, see U. King 1980; also Lubac 1965a, 1967d. R. C. Zaehner 1957, 1958, 1964, 1970. On Zaehner, see Mattam 1975, 11–143; Newell 1981. E. Cornelis 1965, 39–79.

10. The principal works to be consulted are the following: Balthasar 1963, 1964, 1967b, 1969, 1978, 1979a, 1979b, 1983, 1986, 1995.

with some nuances.[11] The Balthasarian expression "Concrete Universal," which he uses with regard to the mystery of Jesus Christ, indicates well the absolute character of his person in the order of the relationship between God and humankind: in Christ alone is the antinomy between the concrete-particular and the universal-abstract overcome.[12]

In the short booklet *Das Christentum und die Weltreligionen*, Balthasar asks the question whether and in what sense it is legitimate to speak of a "convergence" and "integration" of religions. Certainly, there can be no question of speaking of all "universal religions" as of equal value. A first fundamental distinction must be made between the religions of revelation — Judaism, Christianity, and Islam — which share the faith in a personal Creator God, and the Eastern religions for which an impersonal Divine Reality lies hidden beyond transitory worldly phenomena. Both groups are characterized by contrasting and opposite approaches: from God to the human person in the monotheistic religions, from the person to the Divine Absolute in the others.

This is not to say that there is no common feature between the two groups. For a common foundation or substratum exists in all religions; it consists of the human person's search for self-transcendence and liberation. However, the attainment of this aim follows opposite lines: God's search for and turning to humankind in word and history, in love and self-gift, on the one side; and, on the other, the human's striving for self-liberation through merging into an impersonal Absolute. Between these two attitudes there is no possibility of convergence, but rather a complete turnover. They commend mutually contradictory worldviews (*Weltanschauungen*); one "universal religion" is an impossible utopia. In fact, in their mutual contradictions, both models of religion claim universalism and absoluteness.

Yet the fact is that the claim of Eastern religions to lead to self-liberation through human endeavor — be it through concentration, ascetic practices, or techniques — is vain. Self-transcendence can only be received as a gift from a God of love who communicates personally with human beings. Coming then to the three religions of revelation: the refusal of the Jews to pursue to the end the path of faith leading to God's unsurpassable self-gift in Jesus Christ has introduced a breach in the history of salvation which can only be healed at the end of time. As for Islam, while it partly depends on the Judeo-Christian tradition, it really is an aborted project inasmuch as it has forfeited the eschatological dynamism embodied in that tradition, either as waiting for the Messiah to come or as waiting for his return. There remains Christianity — and specifically Catholic Christianity — as the one universal religion destined for all people.

Christianity, in fact, assumes and fulfills all the positive elements involved in

---

11. For a study of von Balthasar's position, see Gawronski 1995.

12. The expression, which goes back to Nicholas of Cusa, is used by J.-A. Cuttat in his preface to Zaehner 1965, 35. It is found repeatedly in von Balthasar. See, for instance, Balthasar 1964, 89: *Universale concretum et personale*. On this concept in von Balthasar's Christology, see Marchesi 1977, 33–48.

the fundamental religious attitude of the human being, while at the same time transcending them. It fulfills the aspirations of the Eastern religions toward the "One" but without loss of the self to the person. The mystery of Jesus Christ is that of the total self-gift of the God of love to humankind in his Son made man, in whom through a "marvelous exchange" God calls all human beings to a personal communion with God as an I to a Thou. What is specific to Christianity and makes its absolute character is the "Trinitarian Christ." Jesus Christ is the "Concrete Universal" (*universale concretum et personale*). In him the factual and the normative coincide, beyond the dialectic of the unique and the historical. He is personally the "whole present in the fragment" (*das Ganze im Fragment*), for in him all things are integrated in the Word of God who is love (Balthasar 1963, 243–350).

In *Spirit and Institution* (*Pneuma und Institution*), von Balthasar develops at length what he calls "the Christian form" (*die Christliche Gestalt*) (Balthasar 1995, 41–64). It consists of the "once-for-all" character of God's decisive "action-word" in the world, with its transcendent and universal character. Jesus Christ is personally the Christian "form," exclusive and personal; he is the unconditional "yes" of God to the world—in the cross and resurrection—which gives absolute value to an ever present "today." While "paganism" seeks the redemption of the world in a flight from suffering, according to the Christian "form" Jesus Christ takes on himself the suffering of the world to unite it to God. The Christian project is the only *Weltanschauung* which assents to the world in its entire and concrete reality.

Comparing Christian and non-Christian mysticism, von Balthasar recognized between them a certain "analogy" and likeness, inasmuch as in both a sense of absolute dependence finds expression as well as an aspiration to overcome an unbridgeable distance. But the difference is even more manifest. For, while in non-Christian mysticism the human being seeks on his or her own a way toward the Absolute, in Christian mysticism it is God who, spontaneously and unexpectedly, goes out of himself to search for us in his incarnate Word. To God's initiative in "action-word" the human response can only consist of listening and following. In the last analysis, non-Christian mysticism — and in particular the Eastern methods — is the ultimate expression of the person's natural desire and attempt to free the self from the finite in a bid to reach out to the Infinite. Christian mysticism represents a complete turnaround: here the living God goes out in search of the person; God's outgoing attitude toward us culminates in the incarnation of the Word (see Balthasar et al. 1983, 154–63).

In an early work von Balthasar had written:

Natural mysticism and religion is an expression that proceeds from man and sets out in the direction of God. It does this out of a most profound necessity and without anyone being able to complain that this movement is an eros which struggles to leave earth, to ascend (*aufsteigen*) and to fly above (*überfliegen*). But in its drive to push past everything that could point the way to God in order to see in that thing the one truth that is not God, this eros is always in danger of losing both, the world as well as God. The world, because it is not God, and God, because he is not the world and because without the help of worldly things in which he is reflected he can only be experienced as the absolute emptiness (*Leere*), the primordial ground, Nirvana. (Balthasar 1959, 46, quoted by Gawronski 1995, 37–38)

This rapid analysis suffices to show that von Balthasar's approach to the theology of religions consists of setting in sharp opposition "non-Christian" religions and Christian revelation. The common substratum of both in human nature notwithstanding, both represent opposite attitudes and directions: from the human being to the One Absolute, on the one hand; from the living God to the human person, on the other. "Non-Christian" and the Christian religion stand to each other as nature and the supernatural. One assumes and fulfills what is good in the other; it purifies it in order to transform it.

## II. The Mystery of Christ in the Religious Traditions

From the fulfillment theories to those of the presence of the mystery of Christ in the other religious traditions the distance is indeed considerable. The first were built upon allegedly insuperable dichotomies, such as between the human and the Divine, the personal and the impersonal, the claim to self-liberation and God-given salvation. The others, while distinguishing these contrasting elements, refuse to separate nature from grace. They mean to transcend the dichotomies between the human search for self-transcendence and God's stooping down to meet us. As the first theories developed during the years that preceded and surrounded Vatican II, so did the others. Our task consists now in giving an account of some of those theological views which were able to look upon the other religious traditions with greater openness because they saw in them the operative presence of the mystery of Jesus Christ, the universal Savior. For those views, the members of those traditions are saved by Christ not in spite of their religious allegiance and sincere practice of their tradition but through that allegiance and practice. There is, then, salvation without the Gospel, although none without Christ or apart from him. To be sure, the operative presence of the mystery of Jesus Christ in other religious traditions is concealed and remains unknown to their members, but it is no less real for all that.

### A. Karl Rahner on "Anonymous Christianity"

It is the hidden, unknown operative presence of the mystery of Christ in other religious traditions that Karl Rahner has designated by the controverted term

"anonymous Christianity."[13] Rahner's theory is founded on his theological anthropology, that is, on a philosophico-theological analysis of humankind in the
concrete historical condition in which it is created by God and destined to
union with God. The "supernatural existential" inherent in the concrete historical human person is not to be identified with an "obediential potency" or
"natural desire" for the vision of God inherent in human nature as such, meta-
physically considered. In the concrete, supernatural order of reality, we carry in
us more than a passive potency for self-transcendence in God. We are concretely
and actively oriented toward the realization of such a self-transcendence. The
"supernatural existential" is the fundamental structure, built into us by God's
free initiative of grace, that spurs our intentional activity toward him. It is the
"transcendental experience" of God inherent in every activity of the human person, destined to become historically concrete in the "categorical" or "thematic"
order. It achieves a certain concreteness in the religious traditions of humankind in which is embodied an inchoate categorical mediation of supernaturally
elevated transcendentality.

This is where the Christian mystery finds at once its roots in the human person and its specific role. The human person is both the event and the locus of
God's self-communication in Jesus Christ. In him God has accomplished historically and definitively his self-gift to humankind, in grace and pardon. The
human person does not have the initiative of searching for God; God's self-gift
in Jesus Christ is the source of our search for him. One could say, partly ad-
justing Pascal's celebrated phrase: You would not seek me, *unless I had first
found you.* From the vantage point of Christian revelation, salvation history,
which culminates in Jesus Christ, is coextensive with world history (see Rahner 1966d). Throughout human history, each person experiences God's offer of
grace to which one must open oneself in free acceptance. Whether this is thematically apprehended by the person's awareness or not, the offer and gift of
grace always take place concretely and existentially in Jesus Christ.

Thus, existentially, human beings are awaiting in anticipation the mystery of
the incarnation. The supernatural existential inherent in them in their concrete
historical reality constitutes the a priori condition for the possibility of the incarnation. Or, to put it the other way round, the mystery of Christ is what happens
when God freely brings to realization in the deepest possible way the capacity
for union that in the concrete order of reality inheres in humankind through the
supernatural existential. Historical humanity is on the lookout for the mystery
of the incarnation; immanent in it is a "searching Christology." Thus, Christology becomes the perfect realization, the absolute fulfillment, of anthropology.
Jesus Christ, in whom the absolute mode of divine-human union is actualized,
is the "absolute Savior" of humankind, the center of salvation history, because

---

13. The theme is treated by Karl Rahner in several essays contained in *Theological Investigations*,
23 vols. (London: Darton, Longman and Todd, 1961–92). It has been restated in more synthetic form in
Rahner 1978. For studies of Rahner's thought on this point, see, among others, D'Costa 1986, 80–116;
Hillmann 1968; Sesboüé 1984.

in him the openness to God inscribed in transcendental human experience finds its total realization.

Here a first observation is in order. It would be wrong to attribute to Rahner the claim that the mystery of the incarnation can be deduced from our nature open to transcendence, or even from our historical condition as called to union with God. The incarnation can only become reality through God's free choice and gratuitous initiative. Only the Christian revelation can, and does, tell us that in Jesus of Nazareth our openness to God has come to a climax in what is its highest possible realization and that he is indeed God's Son made human. Outside the Christian revelation the experience of God's offer of grace in Jesus Christ remains veiled. While its thematization may in various forms already be partial in the concrete reality of the religious traditions of humankind, it remains there unfinished and ambiguous. Its "anonymity" can only be lifted by the Christian message communicating the explicit knowledge of Jesus Christ. Rahner writes:

> There is an implicit and anonymous Christianity.... There is and has to be an anonymous and yet real relationship between the individual person and the concrete history of salvation, including Jesus Christ, in someone who has not yet had the whole, concrete, historical, explicit and reflexive experience in word and sacrament of this reality of salvation history. Such a person has this real and existentiell [*sic*] relationship merely implicitly in obedience to his orientation in grace towards the God of absolute, historical presence and self-communication. He exercises this obedience by accepting his own existence without reservation.... Alongside this there is the fullness of Christianity which has become conscious of itself explicitly in faith and in hearing the word of the Gospel, in the Church's profession of faith, in sacrament, and in living an explicit Christian life which knows that it is related to Jesus of Nazareth. (Rahner 1978, 306)

Anonymous Christianity, Rahner explains, is lived by the members of other religious traditions in the sincere practice of their own traditions. Christian salvation reaches out to them, anonymously, through these traditions. This affirmation is based on the social character of a person's religious life, inseparable from the religious tradition and community in which it is lived (Rahner 1966a, 128–29). Thus we must acknowledge in these traditions "supernatural elements" arising out of grace.[14] As long as the obligation to adhere to Christ as Savior is not imposed on the personal conscience of a given individual by God's offer of faith, in Jesus Christ, the mediation of the saving mystery through the individual's religious tradition, and in its sincere practice, remains effective. To such a person the Gospel has not been "promulgated." One can, however, open oneself to God's self-gift in Jesus Christ, unknowingly, within one's religious

---

14. Rahner 1966a, 121, 130. Rahner leaves it to the historians of religions to identify concretely which elements in the historical religious traditions may represent such moments of grace for their members.

tradition. The anonymous Christian is a Christian unawares. The difference between such a one and the explicit Christian is partly one of subjective awareness (absent in the one, present in the other) of "being a Christian." What occurs when an anonymous Christian is confronted with the message of Christ and embraces it in faith? Rahner writes:

> The revelation which comes to him from without is not in such a case the proclamation of something as yet absolutely unknown.... [It is] the expression in objective concepts of something which this person has already attained or could already have attained in the depth of his rational existence.... In the last analysis, the proclamation of the Gospel does not simply turn someone absolutely abandoned by God and Christ into a Christian, but turns an anonymous Christian into someone who now also knows about his Christian belief in the depths of his grace-endowed being by objective reflection and in the profession of faith which is given a social form in the Church. (Rahner 1966a, 131–32)

A question has, however, been asked on this score. Is the difference between the anonymous Christian and the explicit Christian only a matter of the reflexive awareness, absent in the one case and present in the other, of being a Christian? And if the passage from anonymous to explicit Christianity transpires, does it consist solely in coming to a formal consciousness of being what one has always been without knowing it? Is there no difference as to the manner in which the salvific mystery of Jesus Christ is mediated — no new regime of mediation of this mystery? To be sure, an awareness of being a Christian is part of the mediation of the mystery of salvation proper to Christianity. However, that mediation is not reducible to this awareness. It entails an acceptance of the word of the Gospel; it involves the liturgical and sacramental life of the Church; it implies a profession of faith in the ecclesial communion.

If the essay cited immediately above should seem to allow any lingering doubts on this score, the *Foundations of Christian Faith,* cited earlier, erases all ambiguity. Between anonymous Christianity and explicit Christianity there are indeed, Rahner teaches, distinct regimes of salvation and distinct modalities of mediation of the mystery of Jesus Christ. Thus anonymous Christianity remains a fragmentary, incomplete, radically crippled reality. It harbors dynamics that impel it to join with explicit Christianity (see Rahner 1969a). Nevertheless, the same mystery of salvation is present on both sides, through distinct mediations. It is the mystery of Jesus Christ, whose operative presence is concealed and unconscious on the one side, reflexive and conscious on the other.

What, then, is meant by "anonymous Christianity"? The expression bears direct reference to the universal presence of the mystery of Jesus Christ, not of "Christianity" as meaning the Christian community in which the Christian faith is explicitly professed. "Anonymous Christianity" means that salvation in Jesus Christ is available to human persons, in whatever historical situation they may find themselves, inasmuch as in a hidden way they open themselves to God's self-communication which culminates in the Christ-event. It further means that that mystery of salvation reaches out to them not by a mere invisible action of the risen Lord but, in a mysterious manner, through the go-between action of the religious tradition to which they belong. There is an anonymous, or implicit, Christianity, then, and there is an explicit Christianity. Both are "Christian," despite the breadth of the gap that keeps them apart.

Rahner's theory has, however, met with several objections.[15] Some of these have to do with the terminology and can be disposed of rapidly. It is said that the term is offensive to "non-Christians" because it defines them by what they disclaim to be, instead of expressing their own identity as they themselves perceive it (see Küng 1977, 97–98). To this, Rahner's answer is that the term is intended for use in the context of Christian theological discourse, where it has the merit of evincing the relationship of other religions to the mystery of Christ, not in interreligious dialogue (Rahner 1976). He adds that the reality, not the term, is what matters; the term itself may be replaced by any other that may seem more suitable. If, on the other hand, it is said that the expression defines others in negative terms, rather than positively through what is specific to them, the answer is that to affirm in others and in their religious traditions the active presence of the mystery of Christ is to give them — from the Christian viewpoint — an eminently positive definition. Again, to those who object that the theory of anonymous Christianity is a subtle form of Christian religious and cultural imperialism, Rahner's answer is that the universality of Christ, the obligatory Savior of all men and women, belongs to the center of Christian faith.

Other objections appear more serious. We have already met the one according to which the difference between the anonymous and the explicit Christian would seem to consist merely in the awareness which the explicit Christian possesses of being Christian, while the anonymous Christian is a Christian unawares. While the early essays contain formulas which in this regard may seem ambiguous, *Foundations of Christian Faith,* as shown above, makes the difference between both situations very clear: they constitute various regimes of Christian salvation.

According to Henri de Lubac, while it is legitimate to speak of "anonymous Christians," the expression "anonymous Christianity" is, on the contrary, seriously misleading, for it fails to do justice to the newness of Christianity and its singular character as the way to salvation (Lubac 1967c, 152–56). Hans Urs

---

15. In a brilliant article entitled "Karl Rahner's Anonymous Christian — A Reappraisal" (D'Costa 1985), G. D'Costa exposes and answers the various objections which have been formulated against Rahner's theory of "anonymous Christianity" from opposite theological directions and in different Church traditions. Y. Congar rejects the term "anonymous Christians" because the term "Christian" refers only to those who are members of the Church through baptism. With regard to the theological question, Congar does not accept a salvific value or mediation of salvation in the religious traditions *as such,* objectively considered, while admitting that these may exercise a de facto mediation for persons who in good faith seek God in and through them. He thus distinguishes between religions in themselves and as they are lived by concrete persons. The foundation of this distinction is, however, questionable. See Congar 1972, 133–45; also Congar 1984a, 271–96.

von Balthasar considers the distinction proposed here by de Lubac as "enlightening" and accounting for both sides of the question: the possibility of salvation of non-Christians, on the one hand, and the uniqueness of Christianity as the way to salvation, on the other (Balthasar 1968a, 121–22).

However, the way in which the distinction proposed is understood by both authors is clear. We have shown earlier that, while reaffirming the traditional doctrine of the possibility of salvation for "non-Christians," both deny all salvific value to the religious traditions themselves. This presumably is what the distinction now being proposed would be meant to convey. As for Rahner, he uses both expressions indifferently and sees no difference in meaning between them, for one expression implies the other (Rahner 1969a). It is clear that "anonymous Christianity" exists concretely only in "anonymous Christians" — as does explicit Christianity in explicit Christians! But, while maintaining the difference between anonymous and explicit Christianity, it must be affirmed that the mystery of salvation in Jesus Christ reaches out to anonymous Christians through an act of faith posed by them in the concrete situation in which they live their religious life.

Another objection to "anonymous Christianity" is formulated by V. Boublik in his *Teologia delle religioni* (Boublik 1973, 254–81). Boublik rightly points out that between "anonymous Christianity" and explicit Christianity the difference cannot be reduced to one of awareness or lack of the same; it implies a true transformation (Boublik 1973, 254–66). But in the process he refuses all positive roles to the religions in the mystery of salvation of their members; all there is is a preparation through an "anonymous faith" for salvation to be obtained later through explicit faith in Jesus Christ (Boublik 1973, 249–54). This preparation for salvation Boublik calls "anonymous catechumenate." Actual salvation is held up until such time as the "non-Christian" will meet Jesus Christ personally and thus be able to receive salvation in him through an act of explicit faith. Unless the "non-Christian" hears and receives the Christian message in this life, such personal encounter with Christ will take place only at the time of death (Boublik 1973, 269–82). In the process, according to Boublik, the actual salvation of "non-Christians" is deferred to the time of death. Even the "substitutes" devised by theologians of previous ages for the "salvation of infidels" seem thereby to be forgotten. However this may be, with Boublik we have come a long way from Rahner.

The most incisive objections remain those formulated by von Balthasar (Balthasar 1968a, 79–90, 96–124; see Balthasar 1976, 378–84). According to him, the Christology underlying Rahner's theory of "anonymous Christianity" is akin to the "evolutionist" Christology of Soloviev, among others, for whom Jesus Christ represents "the law of evolution come into its own" (Balthasar 1968a, 83–84). It implies a "devaluing" of the theology of the cross (Balthasar 1968a, 84–86), which in turn reduces the importance of sin and the need for redemption (Balthasar 1968a, 89–90). In sum, the theory turns the supernatural into a "function of nature" (Balthasar 1968a, 111).

What transpires through these last objections is a deep divergence between von Balthasar and Rahner as regards the relationship between nature and the supernatural, human transcendence and God's gratuitous grace. Balthasar considers the "dynamism of ontological affirmation" proposed by J. Maréchal as a "mistaken path" in the interpretation of Saint Thomas. Rahner's "supernatural existential" becomes all the more suspect (Balthasar 1968a, 118–19). Two divergent ways of conceiving the newness of the mystery of Jesus Christ and Christianity are here face-to-face. At the limit it could be said that, while for von Balthasar the newness of the event of Jesus Christ would be undermined by any claim to a concrete orientation toward it in the reality of humankind, for Rahner, on the contrary, without such an orientation the event, when encountered in history through revelation, can be neither recognized nor understood. For Rahner, concrete humanity is "in search" of the mystery of Christ; this is why it is possible to encounter the mystery even before it is recognized "categorically" or "thematically" in the historical event.[16]

As was the case for Daniélou and de Lubac, so too Karl Rahner has had his followers and sympathizers, some of whom went beyond his own position while others followed him with some caution. Let it suffice to take note of the following names: H. R. Schlette, A. Röper, J. Neuner, H. Nys, J. Feiner, H. Fries, W. Kasper, J. Ratzinger, H. Waldenfels. In the same direction mention can also be made — to name one Lutheran theologian — of W. Pannenberg.[17]

## B. Raimon Panikkar on the "Unknown Christ"

The first book of Raimon[18] Panikkar on the subject under consideration was entitled *The Unknown Christ of Hinduism*.[19] It is from that book, it may be said, that the theory of the "presence of Christ" in the religious traditions, derives its name. Speaking not of religious traditions in general but specifically of Hinduism, Panikkar wrote: "There is a living presence of Christ in Hinduism" (Panikkar 1964, ix). This presence resides not only in the private and subjective life of religiously minded and sincere Hindus but in Hinduism as an objective and social religious phenomenon. With this affirmation, Panikkar expressed from the outset his firm stand in favor of a theory which would go beyond any form of "fulfillment theory," as the term has been understood here above. He writes: "Christ is not only at the end but also at the beginning. Christ

16. On the contrast between von Balthasar's and Rahner's theology, see Tourenne 1995, 395–99; Holzer 1995; Williams 1986. Objections against Rahner's "anonymous Christianity" have been formulated by other Catholic authors, not all of whom need to be considered here. See, among others, Hacker 1980, 61–77; Straelen 1965, 1982, 1994. From the opposite direction, see also Barnes 1989, 45–65.

17. See Schlette 1966. Schlette distinguishes between a general history of salvation, to which the world religions belong, and a special history of salvation in the Judeo-Christian tradition. See Röper 1966; Neuner 1964, 397–426; Nys 1966, 163–82; Feiner 1968; Fries et al. 1982, 212–42; Kasper 1972; Ratzinger 1968; Waldenfels 1985a, 1985b, 1990, 1994; Pannenberg 1971, 65–118; 1990; 1991; 1991–94, 1:119–87; 1992.

18. Professor Panikkar's Christian name has been written as both "Raimundo" and "Raimon." The latter is the version Panikkar personally uses today (1997).

19. Panikkar 1964. For an exposition of Panikkar's theology of religions, see Veliath 1988.

is not only the ontological goal of Hinduism but also its true inspirer, and his grace is the leading, though hidden, force pushing it towards its full disclosure" (Panikkar 1964, x). Christ, the only source of every authentic religious experience, is the "ontological meeting-point" between Hinduism and Christianity. For "Christ does not belong to Christianity, he only belongs to God. It is Christianity and Hinduism as well that belong to Christ, though in two different levels" (Panikkar 1964, 20–21).

Hinduism, then, has a place in the Christian economy of salvation. In order to determine this place, Panikkar develops a "peculiar dialectic" of Hinduism and Christianity: "Hinduism is the starting-point of a religion that culminates in Christianity"; it is "Christianity in potency"; it already contains "the symbolism of the Christian reality" (Panikkar 1964, 58–60). This, however, does not mean that a mere "natural prolongation" will eventually lead from one to the other or that the dialectic involved is similar to the relationship between the old and the new covenants. For although Hinduism and Christianity both move in the same direction, the transition from one *to* the other implies a conversion, "a pascha," a mystery of death and life. Hinduism must descend "into the living waters of baptism in order to rise again transformed." At the same time, what will emerge will not be "another thing, another religion"; rather it will be "a better form of Hinduism," for "the Christian mystery of resurrection is not an alienation" (Panikkar 1964, 60–61). Since Christ has been at work in anticipation in Hinduism, the task of Christian revelation consists, partly at least, of "the un-veiling of reality." "The Christian attitude is not ultimately one of bringing Christ *in,* but of bringing him *forth,* of discovering Christ" (Panikkar 1964, 45).

Thus, for Panikkar the mystery of Jesus Christ is present in a hidden way, perceptible to Christian faith alone, in the religious traditions and in Hinduism in particular. The two modes of active presence of the mystery in Christianity and elsewhere are not, perhaps, as clearly distinguished as would be desired. For Panikkar writes: "We are not self-sufficient monads, but fragments of the same, unique religion, though the level of the waters may be, and is, different"; we must "dis-cover" our unity and, "because we are the same," "discard [the] veil of *maya*" that separates us (Panikkar 1964, 21–22). This way of speaking seems to lend itself to the main criticism that was formulated — unduly — against Rahner's "anonymous Christianity." Can the distinction between Christianity and Hinduism be reduced to a veil of *maya* (nescience) or to mere awareness or lack of the same?

However this may be, in the volume so far considered, the Christ discovered hiddenly present in Hinduism seems clearly to be the Christ of faith understood by the Christian tradition as personally identical to the pre-Easter Jesus, transformed in his human existence by the mystery of his resurrection. However, the situation seems to change with some of Panikkar's more recent writings.[20]

---

20. Especially in the 1981 revised and enlarged edition of *The Unknown Christ of Hinduism: Towards an Ecumenical Christophany* (Panikkar 1981); see also Panikkar 1972, 1978. On some of the

*The Unknown Christ of Hinduism* appeared in a new English edition in 1981, revised and enlarged. Even the title of the work was expanded, to become: *The Unknown Christ of Hinduism: Towards an Ecumenical Christophany*. In a lengthy introduction, the author explains that, while he still regards the basic intuition of the book in its first edition as valid, he now sees it in a new light. He now describes his general theme as follows: "I speak neither of a principle unknown to Hinduism, nor of a dimension of the Divine unknown to Christianity, but of the unknown *reality,* which Christians call Christ, discovered in the heart of Hinduism, not as a stranger to it, but as its principle of life" (Panikkar 1981, 19–20). He continues: "The Christ of whom this book speaks is the living and loving reality of the truly believing Christian in whatever form the person may formulate or conceptualize this reality" (Panikkar 1981, 22).

What, then, does Christ represent? Panikkar explains that, for him, Christ is the most powerful symbol — but not one limited to the historical Jesus — of the full human, divine, and cosmic reality which he calls the mystery (Panikkar 1981, 23, 26–27). The symbol can have other names: for example, Rama, Krishna, Ishvara, or Purusha (Panikkar 1981, 27). Christians call him "Christ" because it is in and through Jesus that they themselves have arrived at faith in the decisive reality. Each name, however, expresses the indivisible mystery (Panikkar 1981, 29), each being an unknown dimension of Christ (Panikkar 1981, 30).

A new question arises here: How are we to conceive the relation of the "reality" or "mystery," the Christ symbol, to the historical Jesus? It is on this point that Panikkar's thinking seems to have evolved, not without consequences: a distinction is now introduced between the Christ mystery and the historical Jesus that no longer seems to give adequate account of the Christian assertion that Jesus *is* the Christ. It would seem, in fact, that Panikkar's actual thought on the subject appears more clearly in *The Intrareligious Dialogue* (1978), published before the new edition of *The Unknown Christ of Hinduism* (1981).

Panikkar introduces here a distinction between faith and belief. Faith, he explains, is the person's basic religious experience; it is a constitutive element of the human person. Belief, in contrast, is the particular expression adopted by this fundamental human attitude in any given tradition. The content of faith, which he calls "the mystery," is the lived relationship to a transcendence which seizes the human being. It is common to all religions. Panikkar calls this mystery "cosmotheandric reality," to denote a transcendence experienced by the human being in the cosmos. The content of beliefs, on the other hand, consists of the various religious myths in which faith takes concrete expression. In Christianity we have the "Jesus-myth"; other traditions offer other myths. All of these myths have equal value. Christianity gives the mystery the name of Christ, but the mystery can assume other names. While the various religious

problems raised by those later writings, see Smet 1981, 1983. On the Christology of Panikkar, see Menacherry 1996.

traditions differ on the level of belief, they are all seen to coincide on that of faith. Intrareligious dialogue cannot require a bracketing (*epochè*) of faith, but it can demand a bracketing of beliefs — indeed, their transcending. Panikkar hopes for a cross-fertilization of the beliefs of the various traditions.

If this rapid description gives a faithful account of Panikkar's thought, which is complex, the place held in Christian faith by the Jesus of history becomes problematic. For the first Christians, as the apostolic kerygma testifies (Acts 2:36), the historical Jesus was personally identical to the Christ of faith. He had become the Christ in his being raised by the Father. He was also the very mystery (Rom 16:25; Eph 3:4; Col 2:2; 4:3; 1 Tim 3:16) preached by Paul. Thus Jesus himself belongs to the actual object of faith. He is inseparable from Christ, on whom he bestows historical concretion.

Panikkar, on the contrary, makes a distinction between the mystery and the Jesus-myth — that is, the Christ of faith and the Jesus of history — whom he distinguishes as objects of faith and belief, respectively. Is a reduction of the Jesus-myth to an object of belief as distinct from faith compatible with the Christian profession of faith in the person from Nazareth? And as if by backlash, is not the content of faith reduced in turn to a neutral relationship to a transcendence, without a concrete object?

Though the terminology differs, the same question arises when, in the new edition of *The Unknown Christ of Hinduism*, Panikkar writes:

> The goal cannot be identified with any of the ways or means to it. Though Christ is the Mystery in the sense that to see Christ is to reach the Mystery, still the Mystery cannot be totally identified with Christ. Christ is only one aspect of the Mystery as a whole, even though he is *the* Way when we are on that way.... Only for the Christians is the Mystery indissolubly connected with Christ. (Panikkar 1981, 24–25)

Only the Christian is *aware* that Jesus is the way — this is perfectly clear. But must it not be added that Jesus-the-Christ is in reality the way for all, even for those who remain unaware of the fact? This is what seemed implied in Panikkar's original book but appears now to have become obscured. But is it not necessary that we maintain that it is the indissoluble mystery of Jesus-the-Christ that is present both in Christianity and in the other religions? That in and through that mystery not only Christians but others too encounter and receive the mystery of salvation? Such is, in every event, the way in which the theory of the "presence of Christ" in other religious traditions is commonly understood.[21]

Let us note finally that to Panikkar's fundamental dialogical approach to religions in general, and to Hinduism and Buddhism in particular, we may associate other names — in spite of vast differences existing between the various authors — such as, on the side of Hinduism, Henri Le Saux and Bede Grif-

---

21. Further precisions on the later developments of Panikkar's theology of religions must be left for treatment in a later chapter.

fiths,[22] and, on the side of Buddhism, H. Dumoulin, J. J. Spae, W. Johnston, and Y. Raguin.[23]

## C. *Hans Küng on "Ways of Salvation"*

Hans Küng touched upon the theology of religions for the first time in a communication he made at a conference entitled "Christian Revelation and Non-Christian Religions," held in Bombay in 1964 (25–28 November).[24] Küng affirms from the outset that the errors contained in the other religions notwithstanding, they nevertheless also proclaim God's truth in some way; he further states that their followers, when they convert to the Gospel, should not renounce whatever is good in those religions and comes from God. From the vantage point of Christian faith he makes an important statement on the value of those religions in the plan of God and for the salvation of their followers. This statement needs to be quoted at length:

> As against the "extraordinary" way of salvation which is the Church, the world religions can be called — if this is rightly understood — the "ordinary" way of salvation for non-Christian humanity. God is the Lord not only of the special salvation history of the Church, but also of the universal salvation history of all mankind; this universal salvation history is bound up with the special salvation history in having a common origin, meaning and goal and being subject to the same grace of God. *Every* historical situation, outside the Church as well as inside it, is thus included in advance within his grace. Since God seriously and effectively wills that *all* men should be saved and that none should be lost unless by his own fault, every man is intended to find his salvation within his own historical condition. "Within his own historical condition" here means: within his particular individual and social environment, from which he cannot simply escape, and, finally, within the religion imposed on him by society. Man's religion, being the religion of a social being, is never merely an individualist, subjectivist activity in a purely private interior zone, but always an activity in a particular social embodiment, i.e., in the form of a particular religion, a concrete religious community. But since God seriously and effectively wills the universal salvation history of the whole of humankind, whilst he does not, indeed, legitimize every element (some being erroneous and depraved) in these religions (even the old covenant was not perfect!), yet he *does* sanction the *religions as such* — as social structures. These, though in different senses and degrees, are "legitimate

22. Among the principal works of Henri Le Saux, see Le Saux 1976, 1984b, 1986. For studies on his theology of religions, see, among others, Davy 1981; Gozier 1982; Stuart 1989; Dupuis, introduction to Le Saux 1982, 11–34; Kalliath, 1996. Among the main works of Bede Griffiths, see B. Griffiths 1976, 1982. For studies of his theology of religions, see principally Spink 1989; Teasdale 1987.

23. Dumoulin 1974; Spae 1980; Johnston 1978, 1981, 1995; Raguin 1973, 1975, 1989.

24. H. Küng's communication is published in Neuner, ed., 1967, 25–66.

religions" [see Rahner 1966a, 121–31]. A man is to be saved within the religion that is made available to him in his historical situation. Hence it is his right and his duty to seek God within that religion in which the hidden God has already found him. All this until such time as he is confronted in an existential way with the revelation of Jesus Christ. The religions with their forms of belief and cult, their categories and values, their symbols and ordinances, their religious and ethical experience, thus have a "relative validity" [Neuner 1964], a "relative providential right to existence" [Schlette 1964, 39]. They are the *way of salvation* in universal salvation history; the general way of salvation, we can even say, for the people of the world religions: the more common, the *"ordinary"* way of salvation, as against which the way of salvation in the Church appears as something very special and extraordinary. The way of the Church can be considered as the great, the *"extraordinary" way of salvation!* ... The way of salvation for humankind, outside the Church appears as the "ordinary" way, that within the Church as the great "extraordinary" way [Schlette 1964, 85]. (Küng 1967, 51–53)

Küng writes here clearly under a double influence: of Karl Rahner, on the one hand, and of H. R. Schlette, on the other. Considering the social aspect of every religious life of the human person in which God's grace is at work, Rahner affirmed that the religious traditions themselves "contain quite certainly certain elements of a supernatural influence by grace which must make itself felt even in these objectifications" (Rahner 1966a, 131). The religions are thus in some manner "means" or "ways" of salvation.[25] Küng goes further, seeing them as the ordinary ways for their followers. Schlette, for his part, states clearly after Rahner that the religions remain valid ways of salvation for people as long as these continue to assent to them in faith and good faith (Schlette 1964, 100–103). From Schlette, Küng borrows the distinction between the general history of salvation, comprising the whole of human history, and special salvation history in the Judeo-Christian tradition (Schlette 1964, 66–87); similarly he follows Schlette in affirming that the other religions are ordinary ways of salvation while Christianity is the extraordinary way (Schlette 1964, 85–87).

This manner of speaking is known to have raised many objections. However, Küng explains how the distinction can be correctly understood. Apart from the fact that the vast majority of humankind as a matter of course reaches salvation outside the Church, the distinction has the advantage of connoting the excellence of membership in the Church as a means of salvation and the consequent orientation toward this membership of all those whose salvation in Jesus Christ passes through another route. For this very reason, however, the more traditional way of speaking (reaffirmed by Paul VI in the apostolic exhortation

---

25. H. Waldenfels refuses to follow here the position of Rahner. While it may be said that the others are saved "in" their tradition, "Christians should avoid the formula 'through' their religion." See Waldenfels 1985a.

*Evangelii Nuntiandi* [no. 80]) inverts the terms: according to the divine plan, salvation through explicit faith in Jesus Christ in the Church is understood to be the norm; therefore, the "ordinary paths of salvation" are those revealed by the word and the life of Jesus Christ, even though God can work salvation by "extraordinary ways" known to him. We shall return later to the significance in God's plan of the plurality of religions in the world.

Hans Küng has come back to the theology of religions in *On Being a Christian* (Küng 1977). He repeats here his thesis on general salvation history and on the other religions as "ordinary" ways of salvation enjoying "relative validity" (Küng 1977, 91). But while he is disposed to find in other religions elements of divine truth, his overall evaluation of them remains on the whole negative. In a section entitled "The Challenge of the World Religions," Küng summarizes as follows the concrete questions which Christianity has a right to pose to those religions: "Unhistoricity, circular thinking, fatalism, unworldliness, pessimism, passivity, caste spirit, social disinterestedness: the concrete questions to be put to the world religions in order to provide a diagnosis...may be summed up under these headings" (Küng 1977, 110).

To suppose on all these points a complete negative balance would be to make it too easy a task to establish, as the author purports to do, the credibility and superiority of Christianity.[26] Nevertheless, Küng recommends to Christians, with regard to other religions, an attitude of openness to mutual critique and, on both sides, an honest confrontation from the point of view of faith. He rejects an "exclusive particularism" as well as "syncretistic indifferentism." As for the way in which Küng means to establish the specificity and originality of Christianity upon the person of Jesus Christ, I have shown elsewhere (see Dupuis 1991b, 193–96) that it remains deficient, based as it is on the "project" or "program" of Jesus, on his "representative character" as God's "deputy" to humankind — in short, on a "functional" Christology which fights shy of an ontological Christology that affirms the personal identity of Jesus Christ as *the* Son of God.

Queried more recently about his position on the "uniqueness" of Jesus Christ and his "normative" character in the salvific order, Küng responded with a list of criteria for the truth of the various religions. These criteria are: the *humanum,* as a general ethical criterion; authenticity and canonicity; and, finally, a specifically Christian criterion, according to which a religion is true and good insofar as, in theory and in practice, it radiates the spirit of Jesus. Küng ends on a personal note:

> I am a Christian because I...with confidence and in practice trust that the God of Abraham, Isaac,...and Jacob...has...bestowed self-revelation in

---

26. A more adequate and positive evaluation of the main world religions — Islam, Hinduism, and Buddhism — is found in Küng's dialogue with exponents of those religions in Küng et al. 1993. Küng has published in collaboration with P. Lapide a volume on dialogue between Christianity and Judaism: see Küng and Lapide 1976. More recently, on Christianity and Chinese religions: see Küng and Ching 1989.

an incomparable, and for me decisive manner in the life and work, suffering and death, of the Jew Jesus of Nazareth....He is...for us, *the* way, *the* truth, and *the* life!...Jesus Christ is for Christians the *decisively regulative* norm. (see Küng 1987, 246–47; see also Küng 1988)

### D. Gustave Thils on "Mediations of Salvation"

Another protagonist of a positive role of the religious traditions in the mystery of salvation is Gustave Thils in his book *Propos et problèmes de la théologie des religions non chrétiennes,* written in 1966 (Thils 1966). Thils affirms a "universal revelation" of God to humankind. Natural knowledge of God must, admittedly, be distinguished from supernatural knowledge; but this does not mean that God's manifestation through nature does not yet contain in itself a personal divine revelation. Creation is able not only to disclose to human reason the existence of a Creator God but also to manifest to the eyes of faith the loving providence of God (Thils 1966, 113–17). To "cosmic revelation" already conceived as God's personal revelation through nature, the human being responds with an "authentic religion of awaiting" (*une authentique religion de l'attente*) (Thils 1966, 125–26).

God's plan for humankind implies that human beings have a religion in which and through which God may accomplish God's progressive revelation and saving work. Are people then saved by God *through* their religion? Thils answers by recognizing in the religions an "analogical" salvific value. The salvation of their members is not *in spite* of their religion, but *in* it, and in a certain sense *through* it: "*inasmuch* as they embody [God's] universal saving design and correspond to universal revelation, religions [have] a true salvific efficacy" (Thils 1966, 131–33). They thus have in God's eyes a certain "legitimacy" (Thils 1966, 133–34). They may be called "ways" of salvation insofar as they express and embody a "providential order" of God for their members; in that sense they can be said to be for them "ordinary ways of salvation" (Thils 1966, 135).

This, however, is not to say that all the religions have the same value. For while the "way of non-Christian religions" contains the means implied in the general economy of salvation corresponding to God's universal revelation, the "way of Christianity" is rich with all the means offered through the "special economy of salvation" realized in Jesus Christ. The different ways are neither equivalent nor parallel (Thils 1966, 136). Christianity is the "extraordinary" way in virtue of its specificity and the fullness of the means of salvation it has received through institution by Jesus Christ. Without being exclusive, it represents "the fullness of the way of salvation." Compared to it, the other religions are a "duplicate in a low key" (Thils 1966, 178, 187).

The relationship between Christianity and the other religions may, then, be formulated in terms of the "principal analogue" as against the "secondary analogue." The other religions represent a "sketch" (*ébauche*), a "veiled duplicate" of what Christianity offers. They too have a "signifying function" in the order of salvation — not, however, in the eminent way in which God's salvation is signified in Christianity (Thils 1966, 173–90). In the last analysis, there exists between Christianity and the other religions an "organic unity" in God's design for humankind: "All religions find their place within the one only design of God, even though some express this design more perfectly." In the hypothesis of a religious plurality destined to endure to the end of time, there is, from the eschatological standpoint, "a final and decisive unity towards which the various 'ways' of salvation converge, bound as they are to God's diverse covenants with humankind" (Thils 1966, 161).

In two subsequent works, Thils has further elaborated his views, without, however, any notable change or further development (Thils 1983, 1987).

Our study of the new perspectives and advances in the theology of religions that, mostly in Catholic theological circles, surrounded Vatican II comes to a close here. It was intended not to be exhaustive but to elaborate two main lines of thought which, being alive at the time of the council, would influence its deliberations on the subject and gather even more momentum after it. Both views have in common that they see the other religions as oriented to the Christ-event in the history of salvation: in this sense both could be called "fulfillment theories." But with a difference, which amounts to a sharp contrast. For while the first holds on to the dialectic of nature-supernatural, human search–divine gift, the other overcomes such dichotomies to visualize the unfolding of God's saving history as a process implying diverse modalities of God's revelation and personal involvement in human history. While for the first, the "pre-Christian religions" lose their propaedeutic value with the coming of the Christ-event, for the other, their positive role in the order of salvation continues to abide by virtue of their organic link to the all-embracing mystery of Christ.

It needs to be added straightforwardly that the spectrum of opinions is in fact broader than has been accounted for here. But that must be left for later treatment, when reviewing the debate on the theology of religions as it stands today (chapter 7). Meanwhile, the task of the next chapter consists in examining what influence the main opinions current among Catholic theologians at the time of Vatican II exercised on the council's discussion of the topic and what impact the council itself was in turn capable of making on the ongoing debate.

*Six*

---

# Vatican II and the Postconciliar Magisterium on Religions

THE CONCLUSION of the last chapter summed up the debate on the theology of religions that marked the years surrounding Vatican II as consisting of two contrasting visions; these were called the "fulfillment theory" and the theory regarding the "presence of the mystery of Christ." Both affirmed without qualification the possibility for people outside the Church to be saved in Jesus Christ; they differed where the evaluation of the religions themselves was concerned. For the first, while these could be seen as "preparation for the Gospel" before the Christ-event, they had become obsolete with the event and were henceforth deprived of any positive role in the salvation of their members. For the other, they retained their value for their followers until such time as the Gospel would be existentially "promulgated" to each individual person; they served in some way as the channels through which God's offer of grace in Jesus Christ reached out to the followers of those religions.

With such questions being debated among Catholic theologians — both sides claiming the patronage of prestigious authors — the theology of religions was being born. In the theology of religions, P. Rossano explains,

> the problem is not precisely that of the non-Christians as such, of the possibility of their justification and salvation, of the action of grace upon them, not even of the modality of their belonging to the Church of Christ. ... Here the question is different, even though it is linked with those under various aspects. It has to do with the value that belongs to the non-Christian religions as such. May the complex socio-doctrinal realities of the religions be considered as legitimate means of relating to God? Are they, then, providentially devised (*disposti*) by him as efficaciously promoting the salvation of their members? (Rossano 1965, 131)

Would Vatican II, which held its sessions in the midst of this theological debate, declare itself in favor of one of the two opinions mentioned above? This would, a priori, be unlikely for more than one reason. First, the council's standpoint was pastoral, not doctrinal. Where the other religions were concerned, the council's intention consisted of fostering between them and Christianity new attitudes of mutual understanding, esteem, dialogue, and cooperation. To foster such attitudes it did not seem necessary to opt for one particular position in the present debate on the theology of religions. The council quite deliberately

158

had no intention of doing so. To which must be added the fact that the Council Fathers, hailing from vastly distinct theological backgrounds, would have been strongly divided on the theological issues proper. The intention, on the contrary, was to rally the highest possible majority on the council floor in favor of a change of attitude of Christians and the Church toward the members of other religions. Such an aim could not be put in jeopardy by entering into intricate theological discussions.

It is, moreover, important to situate Vatican II in the conciliar history of the Church. A previous chapter has shown the rigid attitude taken by the Council of Florence (1442) concerning the salvation of all people — the "infidels" included — finding themselves outside the Church. The limited context of the council's pronouncement on this matter has been duly explained. It has, moreover, been noted that, one century later (1547), the Council of Trent, through its doctrine on "baptism of desire," solemnly stated the possibility of salvation for people finding themselves outside the Church. Later Church documents reaffirmed — though not without a marked caution — the same *possibility*. But hardly ever did the Church documents through the centuries — whether conciliar or otherwise — pronounce on religions as such; much less did they do so in any positive manner.[1] Would Vatican II depart from this guarded silence?

To understand the limits of Vatican II's treatment of the other religions, the genesis of the conciliar main document on the subject must also be kept in mind. The title of the declaration *Nostra Aetate,* Declaration on the Church's Relations to Non-Christian Religions, was a latecomer in the council's work and so was the document itself. It appeared only during the third session of the council (1964), in the third draft of a document to be appended to the Schema on the Church.[2] Initially the council — under the lead of Pope John XXIII — had only intended to append to the Decree on Ecumenism a statement which would help create a new climate in the tense relations between Christians and Jews. To this end, long-standing defamatory prejudices against the Jews on the part of Christians and the Church would have to be destroyed and deep wounds inflicted on them over the centuries — down to the Shoah experience of the Jews during the last world war — to be healed. Because of the request made by some bishops from predominantly non-Christian countries, the scope of the document was broadened to include other religions beside Judaism.[3] The creation by Pope Paul VI in 1964 of the Secretariat for Non-Christians,[4] the publication in

---

1. A notable exception is the altogether negative statement made by the Decree for the Copts of the Council of Florence (1442), regarding the abrogation of Jewish religious practices with the promulgation of the Gospel. Though tolerated at the beginning of the Church's existence, the Jewish religion no longer had any place in the Christian economy of salvation and was called to disappear. As for Christians, though they could licitly observe Jewish practices in the earliest period, this concession had long been abrogated. We shall return to this document later. Text in DS 1348; ND 1003.

2. For the history of the document, see Cottier 1966; Oesterreicher 1969, 1–136.

3. A request that salvation of non-Christians be treated not on a purely individual basis but with reference to the religious groups to which they belonged had already been made during the second session (1963), à propos of the schema on the Church, no. 10, destined to become LG 16.

4. Relations with the Jews were entrusted to the Secretariat for Christian Unity, already previously constituted.

the same year of the encyclical *Ecclesiam Suam* on dialogue (including dialogue with non-Christians); the pope's visit to India, again in the same year, and his meeting there with leaders of non-Christian religions whom he addressed with great humanity and warmth[5] — all these gestures served the council with a positive incentive to look beyond the narrow confines of the Western world and to think of the Church's relations to religions in terms not only of the Jewish question but also of religions the world over.

So it was that the scope of the declaration *Nostra Aetate* was broadened to include other religions beside Judaism, even though the largest section of the document is still dedicated to the Church's relations with the Jews. It is not out of place to note the inverse order in which the relations of the Church to other religions are proposed in *Lumen Gentium* 16 and in *Nostra Aetate* 2–4. The constitution *Lumen Gentium* speaks directly of the different ways in which members of non-Christian religions are "oriented to" (*ordinantur*) the Church: first come the Jews, with whom the Church entertains the closest ties; then the Muslims, who "profess to hold the faith of Abraham"; there follow those who "in shadows and images seek the unknown God," who is not remote from them "since he gives to all human beings life and breath and all things" (LG 16). *Nostra Aetate* follows the reversed order: human religiosity in general; the "religions which are found in more advanced civilizations," such as Hinduism, Buddhism, and others (NA 2); Islam (NA 3); and finally the Jewish religion (NA 4). At each level the declaration shows the closer links and the deeper ties that exist between the Church with each group. These differ vastly. While the three religions which trace their roots to the faith of Abraham have a common family origin, it is with Israel that the Church has the closest ties and entertains the deepest relations, having received the Old Testament revelation "by way of that people" with whom God established a special covenant. In *Nostra Aetate,* however, the council's intention is not to show a graded "orientation" of members of other religions toward the Church; it rather consists in exhorting all to overcome divisions and to foster friendly relations (NA 5). Such should be based on what all people, their specific allegiances notwithstanding, "have in common, [which] tends to promote fellowship among them" (NA 1). The nondoctrinal, concrete, and pastoral intent of the document is thus clear.

This is not to say that the council's thinking on religions is purely pragmatic and devoid of any doctrinal significance. For the council was bound to establish its open pastoral approach on some doctrinal foundation. The ancient prejudices and negative assessments had to be destroyed; this could be done only by pointing to positive values and divine endowments contained in the other religions. The council, therefore, could not be — nor was it — satisfied to talk about the orientation of non-Christian *individuals* to the Church; it had to speak — and did so in a positive manner for the first time in conciliar history — about a relationship of the Church to non-Christian *religions* as such. How far did

---

5. See text in AAS 57 (1965) 132–33; ND 1031–32.

the council go in the recognition of positive values in the religious traditions themselves? What significance — if any — did it assign to them in God's design for the salvation of humankind? How did it conceive the relationship of Christianity to other religions: as one-sidedly benefiting the others, or as mutual interaction and reciprocal advantage? To answer these and other similar questions will be the burden of this chapter.

Nor can we stop at the council itself, which, like every other council, must be viewed not as an end product but as a project for a new beginning and has, in any event, to undergo the test of reception and implementation. It is, therefore, necessary to examine the postconciliar magisterium of the Church to see whether and to what extent the intuitions of the council have been consistently pursued thereafter, whether they have been further deepened and promoted, whether the Church's doctrine on the other religions has made any significant step forward over the years that separate us from the council.

## I. Vatican II, a Watershed?

In assessing the council's teaching on the question of non-Christians and their religions, two questions must be clearly distinguished. One has to do with the individual salvation of persons belonging to the other religious traditions; the other, with the significance which these traditions may have in God's design for humankind and the role they eventually play in the salvation of their members.

The first question is not new. The possibility of salvation outside the Church had been recognized by the Church tradition long before Vatican II, as has been recalled earlier. If Vatican II innovates in any way on this account, the newness must be seen in the optimistic way in which the council looks at the world at large, as is best exemplified by the pastoral constitution *Gaudium et Spes*. The same optimistic approach is reflected in the council's way of speaking of salvation outside the Church, *Heilsoptimismus*. What in previous Church documents was affirmed — firmly but cautiously — as a *possibility* based on God's infinite mercy and in any event to be left to his counsel is being taught by the council with unprecedented assurance: in ways known to him, God can lead those who, through no fault of their own, are ignorant of the Gospel to that faith without which it is impossible to please him (Heb 11:6) (AG 7).

Nor is the council satisfied with stating the fact. It proceeds further to explain how this concretely happens, that is, through the universal working of the Spirit of God. The clearest text in this regard is that in *Gaudium et Spes* where, having explained how Christians come in contact with the paschal mystery of Christ's death and resurrection, the council goes on to affirm:

All this holds true not only for Christians but also for all individuals of good will in whose hearts grace is active invisibly [cf. LG 16]. For since Christ died for all [cf. Rom 8:32], and since all human beings are in fact called to one and the same destiny, which is divine, we must hold (*tenere debemus*) that the Holy Spirit offers to all the possibility of being associated, in a way known to God, with the Paschal Mystery. (GS 22)[6]

The second question is the more important; it is also the more complex. To decide whether the council's outlook goes beyond the "fulfillment theory" to the affirmation of an abiding role of the religious traditions in the order of salvation, the more relevant texts need to be reviewed and examined closely. In particular, attention needs to be paid to what in the texts concerns not merely the salvation of individual non-Christians but positive values enshrined in the religious traditions to which they belong and in which they live their religious life.

## A. Positive Values Enshrined in the Religious Traditions

The main texts under consideration belong — in the order of publication by the council — to the constitution *Lumen Gentium* (16–17), the declaration *Nostra Aetate* (2), and the decree *Ad Gentes* (3, 9, 11). In each of these the council develops three themes: (1) the salvation of people outside the Church; (2) the authentic values found in non-Christians and in their religious traditions; and (3) the Church's appreciation of these values and the consequent attitude which it takes toward the religious traditions and their members.

*Lumen Gentium* 16 affirms that God's assistance for salvation is available not only to people in different religious situations but also to those who, "without any fault of theirs, have not yet arrived at an explicit knowledge of God and who, not without grace, strive to lead a good life." The text goes on to say: "Whatever goodness or truth is found among them is considered by the Church as a preparation for the Gospel [cf. Eusebius of Caesarea, *Praeparatio evangelica* I, 1], a gift from him who enlightens all human beings that they may finally have life" (LG 16; ND 1018).

Positive value is attributed here to individual people's dispositions, not to any religious or other group to which they belong. The text goes on to state that, such positive endowments notwithstanding, people have often "exchanged the truth about God for a lie, serving a creature rather than the Creator (cf. Rom 1:21)." The Church's mission consists of announcing the Gospel of salvation for all in Jesus Christ: "By her activity whatever good is found sown in the minds and hearts of human beings, or *in the rites and customs proper to various peoples,* is not only saved from destruction, but is also healed, ennobled, and brought to perfection, for the glory of God, the confusion of the devil, and the happiness of human persons" (LG 17; ND 1136; emphasis added).

It will be noted how easily the council passes from the affirmation of rightful dispositions in people to that of positive values enshrined in their religious tradition and culture. The Church looks kindly on such rightful dispositions and

---

6. ND 1027a. For a critical study of the genesis of this text, see Tononi 1994.

positive endowments, while being aware that it belongs to its mission to bring them to fulfillment through the Gospel message.

The same combination of subjective dispositions and objective values is found in *Ad Gentes:*

> [The] universal design of God to save the human race is not achieved only in secret, as it were, in the hearts of people; nor merely through the undertakings, including religious ones (*incepta, etiam religiosa*), by which they seek God in many ways, in the hope that they may feel after him and find him, though indeed he is not far from each one of us [cf. Acts 17:27]. (AG 3; ND 1023)

Here too the "religious undertakings" seem to refer to objective elements belonging to the religious traditions, as distinct from the subjective dispositions informing people's personal religious life. Such "undertakings" (*incepta*), however, "need to be enlightened and healed, even though, in the merciful design of the provident God, they may sometimes be taken as leading the way (*paedagogia*) to the true God and as a preparation for the Gospel [cf. LG 16]" (AG 3).

The same doctrine recurs once more in *Ad Gentes* 9, where the council explains the function of the Church's missionary activity in relation to the non-Christian world. The Church's missionary activity purifies, raises, and brings to perfection in Christ whatever goodness there is found in people and the traditions to which they belong:

> Whatever truth and grace (*quidquid veritatis et gratiae*) is already found among the nations as a sort of secret presence of God [the missionary activity] frees from evil influences and restores to Christ, their author.... So whatever good is found sown in the hearts and minds of human beings, or *in the rites and cultures proper to various peoples,* is not only saved from destruction but is also healed, ennobled and brought to perfection, for the glory of God, the confusion of the devil and the happiness of the human person [cf. LG 17]. (AG 9; ND 1024; emphasis added)

From the recognition of goodness in the non-Christian world, *Ad Gentes* 11 draws conclusions with regard to the way in which the Christian mission must operate:

> In order to be able to witness to Christ fruitfully, Christians must be united to those [other] people in esteem and love. They must regard themselves as real members of the groups in which they live. They must take part in the cultural and social life through the various dealings and occupations of human life. They must be familiar with their national and religious traditions; with joy and reverence they must discover the seeds of the Word hidden in these traditions.... Just as Christ searched the hearts of people and led them to the divine by truly human contacts, so his disciples, deeply

imbued with the Spirit of Christ, should know the human persons among whom they live and associate with them. In this way, through sincere and patient dialogue they will learn what treasures the bountiful God has distributed among the nations. At the same time they should strive to illumine those riches with the light of the Gospel, to liberate them and bring them under the dominion of God the Saviour. (AG 11; ND 1025)

The declaration *Nostra Aetate* places the meeting of the Church with the world religions in the broad context of the common origin and destiny of all people in God and the search, common to all religious traditions, to answer the ultimate questions that beset the human spirit: "riddles which today as in olden times stir the hearts of people.... What, finally, is the ultimate and ineffable mystery which enfolds our existence, from which we come and to which we are going?" (NA 1). The declaration's general assessment of religions and the Church's consequent attitude toward them is expressed as follows:

The Catholic Church rejects nothing of what is true and holy in these religions. With sincere respect she looks on *those ways of conduct and life, those precepts and teachings* which, though differing on many points from what she herself holds and teaches, yet not rarely reflect a ray of that Truth (*radium illius Veritatis*) which enlightens all human beings. But she proclaims and must ever proclaim, "the way, the truth and the life" [Jn 14:6], in whom human beings find the fullness of religious life, and in whom God has reconciled all things to himself [cf. 2 Cor 5:18f].

And so the Church has this exhortation for her children: prudently and lovingly, through dialogue (*colloquia*) and collaboration with the followers of other religions, and in witness to the Christian faith and life, acknowledge, preserve and promote the spiritual and moral good, as well as the socio-cultural values found among them (NA 2). (ND 1021–22; emphasis added)

It will be noted that the existence of authentic values in the religious traditions themselves is expressed here more forcefully than in the previous texts: there is question explicitly of "ways of conduct and life,... precepts and teachings which ... not rarely reflect a ray of that Truth which enlightens all human beings." Though no explicit reference is made in the official text to Jn 1:9, the allusion is unmistakable. It is the incomplete but real presence of "that Truth" in the other religions which guides the Church's attitude of respect toward them and its wish to promote their spiritual and cultural values, while its mission also requires of it that it proclaim the "fullness of religious life" in Jesus Christ.

The council's doctrinal assessment of religions consists primarily of descriptive statements, in which various expressions are taken from the early tradition, without, however, their exact meaning in the council's mind being clearly defined. While the evaluation has a positive ring about it, it also suffers from a certain vagueness. A document published in 1984 (Secretariat for Non-

Christians 1984) by the Secretariat for Non-Christians has felicitously summed up the conciliar affirmation of positive values enshrined in the religious traditions by collecting the various expressions used by the council in their regard. The text reads as follows:

> This vision induced the Fathers of the Second Vatican Council to affirm that in the religious traditions of non-Christians there exist "elements which are true and good" [LG 16], "precious things, both religious and human" [GS 92], "seeds of contemplation" [AG 18], "elements of truth and grace" [AG 9], "seeds of the Word" [AG 11, 15], and "rays of that Truth which illumines all humankind" [NA 2]. According to explicit conciliar indications, these values are found preserved in the great religious traditions of humanity. Therefore, they merit the attention and the esteem of Christians, and their spiritual patrimony is a genuine invitation to dialogue [cf. NA 2, 3; AG 11], not only in those things which unite us, but also in our differences. (26; see Secretariat for Non-Christians 1984, 135–36)

### B. Contrasting Interpretations

The council's doctrine on other religions has met with divergent interpretations, ranging from resolutely reductionist, on the one hand, to frankly maximalist, on the other. Some clearly reductionist opinions, as will soon be seen, betray the negative theological outlook of their authors; other appraisals, resolutely positive, may call for critical refinement. A quick look at the spectrum of divergent interpretations which have been proposed may help toward a balanced evaluation of the council's achievement.

A minimalist appraisal of the council's doctrine on religions is proposed by P. Hacker (Hacker 1980, 61–77). Distinguishing two aspects of religion, one human or anthropological, the other theological and dogmatic, the author concludes that, as was the case with Paul's discourse at Athens (Acts 17), so too the texts of the council, if carefully analyzed, are found to refer positively only to the "anthropological aspect of religion": "They describe religious efforts undertaken by men of various religions and they approve of the fact that men thus seek God; but they remain silent regarding the possibility of reaching the goal through these efforts, nor do they say anything about whether the myths contain truth or whether the rites and practices are in conformity with the will of God" (Hacker 1980, 73–75). The council's insistence on the negative features of non-Christian religions makes it impossible to attribute to it the thesis according to which "pagans are saved through their religions or that their religions as such have a salvific significance. The thesis of the 'legitimacy' of pagan religions has received no sanction or support by the Council" (Hacker 1980, 72).

Equally negative regarding the council's appraisal of religions is a recent study by a Finnish Lutheran theologian (Ruokanen 1992). According to Mikka

Ruokanen's interpretation, in the council "a continuity seems to exist between non-Christian religions and the Christian truth. A possibility of the presence of God's saving grace in other religions thus seems not to be totally excluded." However, non-Christian religions "have no independent status as to revelation of the Divine Mystery; their religious truth must be related to the truth of Christianity" (Ruokanen 1992, 61). The author comments that the council's interpretation is in line with the "perfection or fulfillment theory so usual in postconciliar Catholic analysis of non-Christian religions" (Ruokanen 1992, 61).

How much, then, and what kind of truth does the council see in the other religions? The author notes that the council never speaks of "revelation" with reference to these religions. "In spite of nice positive formulations which seem to express respect towards various religious elements of non-Christian religions," what is valued in them by the council is "their natural aspects, i.e., natural knowledge of the one personal Creator and natural law given by him" (Ruokanen 1992, 68). Much less, then, are non-Christian religions viewed by the council as "ways of salvation": "The Council fully acknowledges the moral good which can be found in the doctrinal concepts and moral practices of religions. But in regard to *mysterium divinum,* non-Christian religions are still seekers of the truth" (Ruokanen 1992, 93). *Lumen Gentium* 16, as well as *Nostra Aetate* 2, "omits any mention of the possible contribution of the proper religious truth of non-Christians' own religion to salvation. Non-Christians reflect the truth only insofar as their life is in accordance with natural knowledge of the one God and of natural moral law" (Ruokanen 1992, 99). In other words, "non-Christian religions do not add any supernatural dimension of revelation or grace to the natural condition of man" (Ruokanen 1992, 100).

Ruokanen's interpretation of the council is, however, marred by a biased understanding of the working of divine grace. He distinguishes between a "way of grace inherent in creation and in providence" and "the way of universal supernatural grace, i.e., the specifically revealed Christological grace" (Ruokanen 1992, 96); or, equivalently, between "created common grace" (*gratia creata sive communis*) and Christian grace (Ruokanen 1992, 99):

> Every human being, every culture and every religion is graced because man, the rational being and the image of God, capable of knowing and worshipping his Creator, is graced in the meaning of creative and providential universal grace, *gratia creata sive communis.* But grace inherent in nature, including non-Christian religions, lacks the supernatural quality of grace needed for the re-establishment of the *similitudo Dei* lost in the Fall. (Ruokanen 1992, 116; see also 115–20)

It follows that the "religious substance of non-Christian religions has no specific role as a medium of supernatural revelation and grace." Religions are "manifestations of man's sincere search for God, and they contain moral truths common to all human beings.... A religion is good only because and insofar as it may contain elements of natural cognition of God and of natural moral law" (Ruokanen 1992, 117).

The author recognizes that, "being taken into the realm of the salvific *gratia praeveniens,*" non-Christians may receive "the hidden grace of the Triune God in proleptic manner"; but "in order fully to participate in the creative, redemptive, and sanctifying grace of the Triune God, all men need to receive the gift of *gratia increata sive supernaturalis* through the explicit means of grace entrusted to the Church of Christ" (Ruokanen 1992, 120). The conclusion is: "The important novelty of the Second Vatican Council in relation to non-Christians was the implementation of sympathetic language concerning them and the recognition of non-Christian religions as naturally good entities of human culture" (Ruokanen 1992, 117).

The council's doctrine of non-Christian religions, says the author, is "rather conservative and faithful to the accepted Catholic dogma" (Ruokanen 1992, 120). This is not the place to discuss the problems raised by the author's distinction regarding "common grace" and "supernatural grace"; or again, between supernatural grace received "proleptically" by non-Christians and full participation in sanctifying grace in Christianity.[7] For the moment let it suffice to say that for Ruokanen, even more than for Hacker, the council's doctrine on religions reaches nowhere beyond the traditional "fulfillment theory."

On the other side of the spectrum, having in mind the elements of "truth and grace" contained in the other religions, P. Rossano does not hesitate to write: "As for the salvific function of these religions, namely, whether they are or not paths of salvation, there is no doubt that 'grace and truth' do reach or may reach the hearts of men and women through the visible, experiential signs of the various religions. Vatican II is explicit on this point."[8]

An elaborate study of the council's documents by K. Kunnumpuram goes in the same direction (see Kunnumpuram 1971). Admittedly, the author points out, in view of its pastoral intent, the council did not mean to pronounce on the debated question of the theological status of religions. Nevertheless, it does stress the existence of positive values in the traditions themselves: in their doctrines, their rites, their rule of life (Kunnumpuram 1971, 66–68). Such endowments of "truth and grace" are supernatural gifts of God, "a sort of secret presence of God" (AG 9), the work of Christ who is the "true light that enlightens all human beings" (Jn 1:9; see NA 2), the "seeds of the Word" (AG 11).

---

7. The second question has been touched upon in chapter 2, above, in connection with C. Saldanha's and F.-X. Durrwell's opinions. See pp. 75–77, above.

8. See Rossano 1981a, 102–3. The same author is more circumspect in Rossano 1982b. There he writes: "It [is] improbable that an unqualified affirmative or negative answer can be given to the question asked [of religions as means of salvation]. It may be cautiously asserted that concrete elements of various religions or even, in the better cases, whole religious systems can be providential means and ways of salvation, to the extent that they reflect and give objective form to the light of the Word that enlightens every human being. It is clear, of course, that for a Christian Christ is the only way to salvation. The religions can be such a way to the extent that they receive and express the influence and enlightenment that come from Christ. This is the direction taken by the council in its statements on the matter (cf. AG 3, 11; NA 2; LG 16)" (p. 305).

The "preparation for the Gospel" contained in religions is not to be reduced to a natural substratum or passive recipient of God's gift. "Their deepest meaning lies in the fact that they are pointers to Christ. . . . They have an inner dynamism, an inherent dialectic towards him" (Kunnumpuram 1971, 87).

The council never asks directly whether God makes use of the rites and doctrines of non-Christian religions for the salvation of their members and whether, consequently, they are "providential means of salvation" for them. Nevertheless, for the council, God's salvation of people is not a purely internal affair. As the council says: "The universal design of God for the salvation of the human race is not carried out exclusively in the soul of people with a kind of secrecy" (AG 3). Nor is salvation of people a purely private matter: it always takes on a social form. That "seems to imply," the author writes, that the members of other religious traditions "are, or can be, saved in and through their non-Christian religions. For them these religions are ways of salvation" (Kunnumpuram 1971, 88–91).

Kunnumpuram sums up as follows:

> The Second Vatican Council recognizes that non-Christian religions possess many positive values such as truth and goodness, grace and holiness. It regards these values as a sort of secret presence of God, as the seeds of the Word and the fruits of the Spirit. The council realises that these religions cannot be considered merely as natural religions, since they contain supernatural elements, even saving faith. Despite error, sin and human depravity, non-Christian religions are a preparation for the Gospel, as they have an innate tendency, an inner dynamism towards Christ and his Church. For those who have not yet been existentially confronted with Christianity, non-Christian religions can serve as ways of salvation, in the sense that God saves these men in and through the doctrines and practices of these religions. (Kunnumpuram 1971, 91)

### C. A Balanced Critical Appraisal

The question was asked earlier whether the council simply followed the "fulfillment theory" in its classical form or, on the contrary, made its own the theory of the "presence of Christ's saving mystery" in the religious traditions. Asked in this manner, the question cannot be answered one way or the other. On the one hand, it is true that much of the terminology describing the Church's attitude toward other religions repeats terms familiar to the fulfillment theory: to assume and to save, to heal and to restore, to ennoble and to bring to perfection. On the other hand, the elements of "truth and grace" found "as a sort of secret presence of God" (AG 9) in the traditions themselves — in their teachings, their rites, their ways of life; or, else, their *c*reed, their *c*ult, and their *c*ode of conduct — strongly incline in the opposite direction.

For Paul F. Knitter, while "Vatican II forms a watershed in Roman Catholic attitudes toward other faiths," there remains "a residual ambiguity in its understanding of just how effective the truth and grace within the religions are" (Knitter 1985, 124). According to him, the ambiguity "stems from the tension between God's salvific will and the necessity of the Church that is evident throughout the history of Catholic thought" (Knitter 1985, 124). This dilemma must be examined later while discussing the manner in which the "necessity" of the Church affirmed by the council is to be understood. Meanwhile, it may suffice to answer that for many Catholic theologians the "necessity" of the Church need not a priori exclude all salvific value of other religions.

A balanced appraisal of the council's doctrine on religions has to be at once positive and critical. In Karl Rahner's view, the council's achievement consists of looking beyond the question of salvation of individual non-Christians to a positive relationship of the Church to the religions as such. However, while supernatural salvation in the actual self-gift of God for all people is looked upon with great optimism by the council, the same optimism is not explicitly professed where religions are concerned. Here "the essential problem for the theologian has been left open"; "the theological quality of non-Christian religions remains undefined." Is salvation achieved by non-Christians outside the life of their religions as such, or within? Are the religions salvific in themselves or not — the question is not explicitly answered (Rahner 1984b; see esp. 290). Even while much of what the council affirms inclines toward the positive statement, the conclusions are not firmly drawn.

Other limitations of the council's doctrine on religions have been pointed out, one of which seems especially pertinent here. H. Maurier remarks on the strongly "ecclesiocentric" perspective of the doctrine in general and of *Nostra Aetate* in particular. The Church seems to recognize as positive and good in the other religions only such elements as are found in it superabundantly. Are the "rays" of truth present in them necessarily to be related to the fullness of it possessed by the Church? Or would the declaration be prepared to acknowledge in the other religions the presence of rays of truth not found in the Church? The Church's way of thinking remains "egocentric" (Maurier 1966, 133–34). Such a perspective easily leads to the "fulfillment theory," according to which, inasmuch as they represent the search of the human person for God, the other religions become obsolete by the very fact of reaching their fulfillment (Maurier 1966, 135). The question must, however, be asked whether the dialogue with the other religions which the council meant to foster does not presuppose the recognition in them of authentic human values which Christianity does not possess. Only then is dialogue viable and meaningful. For, by definition, dialogue is a two-way street in which there is give-and-take. Does the Church of Vatican II show itself inclined to receive from other religions (Maurier 1966, 139–43)?

We have remarked elsewhere on the "ecclesiocentric" perspective of the council's theology of the other religious traditions, as the probable reason for its limitations and silences. We wrote:

The very title of the Declaration *Nostra Aetate* — "On the Relations of the Church with non-Christian Religions" — demonstrates this [ecclesio-centric perspective]. The question posed here is not directly that of the vertical relationship of humanity's religious traditions with the mystery of Jesus Christ. It is the question of the horizontal relationship of these same traditions with Christianity or the Church. The first question could have borne on the acknowledgment of a hidden presence of the mystery of Christ in these same traditions, and of a certain mediation of this same mystery through them. The second question, of course, did not naturally lead in this direction. Is not this the reason why, despite the council's assertion of the presence of values and positive elements in these religious traditions, it does not explicitly venture in the direction of an acknowledgment of these same traditions as legitimate paths of salvation for their members, although necessarily in relation to the mystery of Christ? (see Dupuis 1991b, 98).

The verdict still seems to be valid.

## II. The Postconciliar Magisterium

A certain ambiguity remained in the conciliar doctrine. Our task now consists in asking whether the Church's postconciliar teaching authority has thrown any more light on the council's teaching. In particular, has any further step been taken in the direction of a positive appraisal of the religions themselves? Has a too narrowly Church-centered perspective given way to a broader outlook, allowing for a clearer recognition of the role of religions in God's salvific design for humankind? These and other connected questions must be kept in mind while reviewing official Church teaching on religions during the years that separate us from the council. Only key texts with significant doctrinal import will be considered here.

### A. *The Pontificate of Paul VI*

The encyclical *Ecclesiam Suam* was published by Paul VI between the second and third sessions of Vatican II (6 August 1964).[9] It marks the appearance of "dialogue" (here called *colloquium*) on the program of the Church renewal intended by the council. The pope explains that the history of salvation is that of a continuous dialogue of God with humankind; the Church's role is to prolong that dialogue. The Church, then, finds itself in a privileged situation to enter into dialogue with the entire world — and this at a fourfold level. Drawing concentric circles and starting from the most remote, the pope distinguishes in

---

9. The text is found in AAS 56 (1964) 609–59; hereafter referred to as ES, with page numbers from AAS.

order: the Church's dialogue with the entire world; with the members of other religions; with the other Christian Churches; to end up, at the inner circle, with dialogue within the Church.[10] The second circle is "composed essentially of those who worship the one sovereign God whom we, too, adore" and includes not only Jews and Muslims but the faithful of the great Afro-Asian religions (ES 654–55). The pope is cautious in establishing the foundation and conditions of such interreligious dialogue on doctrinal considerations. He writes:

> It is obvious that we cannot agree with various aspects of these religions, and that we cannot overlook differences or be unconcerned with them, as if all religions had, each in its own way, the same value, which would dispense those who follow them from the need of inquiring whether God has revealed a way free from all error and certain, by which he desires to make himself known, loved and served. Indeed, honesty compels us to declare openly what we believe, namely that there is one true religion, the Christian religion, and that we hope that all who seek God and adore him, will come to acknowledge this. (ES 655; ND 1029)

Nevertheless, the pope states:

> We do acknowledge with respect the spiritual and moral values of various non-Christian religions, for we desire to join with them in promoting and defending common ideals. . . . On these great ideals that we share with them we can have dialogue, and we shall not fail to offer opportunities for it whenever, in genuine mutual respect, our offer would be received with good will. (ES 655; ND 1030)

Respect for the moral and spiritual values of other religions notwithstanding, the exclusiveness of Christianity as the "one true religion" is unequivocal. Nor will the refinements and nuances made by the council soften Paul VI's affirmation of Christianity's exclusive claims.

An important occasion offered itself to reaffirm those claims with the apostolic exhortation *Evangelii Nuntiandi*, following upon the 1974 synod of bishops on the evangelization of the modern world. The synod had been inconclusive for reasons which need not be explained here.[11] Among other themes bearing on evangelization, the synod had touched on interreligious dialogue and, in view of this, on a Christian evaluation of non-Christian religions which would serve as its necessary foundation. Far-sighted views on this subject had been heard on the synod floor, coming mostly from bishop-participants from Asia.[12] Unable to produce a substantial document in its own name, the synod

---

10. The same four concentric circles of dialogue will be taken up — in reverse order — by the council in the conclusion of the pastoral constitution *Gaudium et Spes* (GS 92). This text can be viewed as the council's Magna Carta on dialogue.

11. For an analysis of the synod, see Dupuis 1975. For the documentation of the synod, see Caprile 1975.

12. One theological statement, especially positive and well articulated, deserves to be mentioned here. Archbishop Angelo Fernandes of Delhi (India) expressed himself as follows: "A theology of world reli-

was satisfied to publish a brief "declaration" which, however, remained silent on the subject of world religions. In this situation, it was left to Pope Paul VI to return to the subject in the apostolic exhortation *Evangelii Nuntiandi*, published one year later (8 December 1975).

It must be said squarely that the pope did so in a clearly negative fashion which did not correspond to many opinions expressed on the synod floor. After duly recalling the Church's esteem for non-Christian religions professed by the documents of the council, the pope expressed himself as follows:

> Neither respect and high esteem for these religions nor the complexity of the theological questions raised is an invitation to the Church to withhold from these non-Christians the proclamation of Jesus Christ....
>
> Therefore, even in the face of the highest forms of natural religions, the Church thinks that she has a unique function: the religion of Jesus which she proclaims through evangelization truly puts human beings in contact with the plan of God, with his living presence and his action. It does enable them to meet the mystery of the Fatherhood of God that bends over towards humanity. In other words, through our religion an authentic and living relationship with God is truly established, such as other religions cannot bring about even though they have, as it were, their arms stretched out towards heaven. (53)[13]

The image of the "arms stretched out towards heaven," as against God's bending over towards humanity in Jesus Christ in response to human aspirations; the distinction between the "highest forms of natural religions" and the religion of Jesus through which alone an "authentic and living relationship with God is truly established" — all make it plain that the pope is resuming here the "fulfillment theory" in its classical form.[14] The more insightful elements of the

---

gions requires of us...full recognition of the fact that God has in the past dealt with diverse peoples in diverse ways, and that he continues to do so today. It is an urgent beckoning to us to frame a theology of the living religious traditions of the world and of their significance today in God's universal plan of salvation. It will be the task of this theology to show that the Risen Lord, who is the only mediator between God and human beings, and in whose name alone they can find salvation is, through his Spirit, present and operative, not only in the minds and hearts of those who may never have heard his name, but also in the concrete manifestations through which, within the framework of their religious tradition and in the midst of their religious communities, their religious life finds expression. To affirm that the religious practices of others, their sacred books and their sacramental practices, provide a channel through which the Risen Christ reaches out to them, in no way threatens the uniqueness of Christ and his message. Rather, our theology will make clear that the uniqueness of Christianity lies in this: It excludes no religion; it embraces them all. These other religions, in which Christ is present but hidden, his Spirit secretly at work within them, are destined to find their fulfillment in the explicit recognition of him who is the Lord of history. It is from within, not from without, that the members of these religious traditions are being challenged by the mystery of Jesus Christ." See Amalorpavadass, ed., 1975a, 130–31.

13. Text in AAS 68 (1976) 41–42; ND 1036.

14. In contrast with the pope's statement, the "communication" of the Federation of Asian Bishops' Conferences (FABC) in preparation for the synod (1974) adopted the opposite perspective. Speaking of the Asian religious traditions, it said: "We [Asian bishops] accept them as significant and positive elements in the economy of God's design of salvation" (14); and they asked: "How can we not give them reverence and honour? And how can we not acknowledge that God has drawn our peoples to himself through them?" (15). See "Evangelization in Modern Day Asia" 1992, 14. And they added: "[The Lord of history] has been present in our history, in our traditions, in hidden ways he has led us — the people of Asia — enlightening our ancient worship, guiding our traditional beliefs, appearing in strange forms

council are being lost view of here. Paul VI, who with the programmatic encyclical *Ecclesiam Suam* had become the "pope of dialogue," remains silent in *Evangelii Nuntiandi* on the subject of interreligious dialogue.[15]

## B. The Pontificate of John Paul II

*Nostra Aetate* had laid as the foundation for a Christian understanding of the Church's relationship to world religions a double commonality existing between all persons and peoples: their common origin from God, on the one hand; their common destiny in God according to God's design of salvation for humankind, on the other (NA 1). Such a design, as the council implied, was accomplished by God in Jesus Christ. No mention, however, was made in this connection of the universal presence and action of the Spirit of God among human beings through the ages. It is well known that Vatican II rediscovered gradually — and put progressive emphasis through its documents on — the universal economy of the Spirit of God.[16] While the pneumatology of the constitution *Lumen Gentium* remained somewhat underdeveloped even in its last redaction, the Spirit of God made a big entry in the pastoral constitution *Gaudium et Spes*. Characteristically, *Gaudium et Spes* sees the Spirit of God universally at work in the world, not only nor primarily in the religious aspirations of human beings, but in the human values they unanimously pursue, such as justice and kinship, peace and harmony (GS 32, 38, 39; etc.). His influence on people's religious life is touched upon more incidentally (GS 15, 37, 41; etc.). As for Pope Paul VI, the apostolic exhortation *Evangelii Nuntiandi* made no reference to the Holy Spirit with regard to the religious life of non-Christians; the Spirit was only mentioned in the document as the "principal agent of evangelization," who impels the Church and empowers it for the fulfillment of its mission (EN 75).

It may be said that the singular contribution of Pope John Paul II to a "theology of religions" consists in the emphasis with which he affirms the operative presence of the Spirit of God in the religious life of non-Christians and the religious traditions to which they belong. Reference to some key texts will make the point clear.

Already in his first encyclical letter, *Redemptor Hominis* (4 March 1979),

---

in our folklore, speaking to us in our oriental philosophies. Through the quiet centuries, patiently, he has drawn us to himself" (Briefer Statement, 31; "Evangelization in Modern Day Asia," 1992, 1.2:24–25).

15. For an assessment of *Evangelii Nuntiandi* in the Asian context, see Dupuis 1976, where I concluded: "The 'fulfillment theory' is thus exposed in its rigid form, without the refinements by which it has been softened in recent years thanks to much theological rethinking. Members of non-Christian religions are mere 'beneficiaries of evangelization'" (EN 49ff.), with nothing to communicate to Christians beyond the sincerity of their hearts. Such a stand is not without drawback; for in the present context of religious pluralism it makes dialogue rest on shaky ground and — more importantly still — establishes the Christian mission to non-Christians on a theological foundation which is no longer fully convincing. Thus is left undone the pressing task of explaining the mission, its need and urgency, in the context of a theology of non-Christian religions which for being more open would stand better the test of the encounter of religions and thereby gain more acceptance in mission lands" (230).

16. I have traced the progress of the rediscovery of the Holy Spirit through the council sessions in Dupuis 1991b, 157–65.

the pope saw in the "firm belief" of non-Christians an "effect of the Spirit of truth," and he asked:

> Does it not sometimes happen that the firm belief of the followers of the non-Christian religions — a belief that is also an effect of the Spirit of truth operating outside the visible confines of the Mystical Body — can make Christians ashamed at often being themselves so disposed to doubt concerning the truths revealed by God and proclaimed by the Church? (RH 6)[17]

Given the universal action of the Spirit in and outside the Church, the pope is able to show what unites all religions together: they are "so many reflections of the one truth," distinct paths to a single goal:

> The Fathers of the council rightly saw in the various religions as it were so many reflections of the one truth, "seeds of the Word" [cf. AG 11; LG 17], attesting that, though the routes taken may be different, there is but one single goal to which is directed the deepest aspiration of the human spirit as expressed in its quest for God, and also in its quest, through its tending towards God, for the full dimension of its humanity, or, in other words, for the full meaning of human life. (RH 11; ND 1038)

The missionary attitude, therefore,

> always begins with a feeling of deep esteem for "what is in the human being" (Jn 2:25), for what one has worked out in the depths of one's spirit concerning the most profound and important problems. It is a question of respecting everything that has been brought about in one by the Spirit, which "blows where he wills" (Jn 3:8). (RH 12; ND 1039)

John 3:8 is a quotation which recurs often from the pope's pen. Another is Rom 8:26, where Paul speaks of the Holy Spirit who prays in us. The pope applies Paul's words to every authentic prayer, whether of Christians or otherwise:

> What seems to bring together and unite, in a particular way, Christians and believers of other religions is an acknowledgment of the need for prayer as an expression of human spirituality directed towards the Absolute. Even when, for some, he is the great Unknown, he nevertheless remains always in reality the same living God. We trust that wherever the human spirit opens itself in prayer to this Unknown God, an echo will be heard of the same Spirit who, knowing the limits and weakness of the human person, himself prays in us and on our behalf, "expressing our plea in a way that could never be put into words" [Rom 8:26]. The intercession of the Spirit of God who prays in us and for us is the fruit of the mystery

---

17. Text in AAS 71 (1979) 257–347; ND 1037.

of the redemption of Christ, in which the all-embracing love of the Father has been shown to the world.[18]

Through these texts the same teaching is gradually emerging: the Holy Spirit is present and active in the world, in the members of other religions, and in the religious traditions themselves. Authentic prayer (even to an as-yet Unknown God), human values and virtues, the treasures of wisdom hidden in the religious traditions, and true dialogue and authentic encounter among their members — these are so many fruits of the active presence of the Spirit.

We must not omit a reference to the important discourse pronounced by Pope John Paul II to the members of the Roman curia on 22 December 1986. The allocution was entirely devoted to the event of the World Day of Prayer for Peace, which had been held at Assisi two months earlier (27 October 1986).[19] The pope explained the meaning of this event, showed that it was a prolongation and concrete application of the teachings of Vatican II, and indicated its theological foundation (see Dupuis 1987b). The overall fabric of the discourse — the oneness of the human race in creation and redemption and its consequent unity in origin and destination — was taken from the documents of Vatican II (see NA 1), although the address developed these elements further. It spoke of a "mystery of unity" which unites all people, however distinct may be the circumstances of their lives: "[T]he differences are a less important element, when confronted with the unity which is radical, fundamental and decisive" (3).

On one point, however, just as in the documents recalled above, the pope spoke more clearly than any of the council documents: on the active presence of the Holy Spirit in the religious life of the members of other religious traditions. Having observed that at Assisi all the participants had prayed for peace in accordance with their own respective religious identities, and in the quest for truth, the pope remarked that, nevertheless, there had been a "wonderful manifestation of that unity which binds us together beyond the differences and divisions which are known to all." He gave the reason for this as follows:

> Every authentic prayer is under the influence of the Spirit "who intercedes insistently for us..., because we do not even know how to pray as we ought," but he prays in us "with unutterable groanings" and "the One who searches the hearts knows what are the desires of the Spirit" [cf. Rom 8:26–27]. We can indeed maintain that every authentic prayer is called forth by the Holy Spirit, who is mysteriously present in the heart of every person. (11)[20]

---

18. John Paul II's "Message to the People of Asia" (Manila, 21 February 1981), no. 4; text in AAS 73 (1981) 391–98; ND 1040.

19. The texts from the World Day of Prayer for Peace have been published by Commission Pontificale "Justitia et Pax" 1987. The text of the pope's address is found on pp. 147–55. It is also found in *Bulletin* (Secretariat for Non-Christians) 64/22/1 (1987) 54–62.

20. The text recalls — but states more clearly — what the pope had already said in his "Message to the People of Asia" (21 February 1981), referred to above.

The most explicit text on the economy of the Spirit is, however, to be found in the encyclical on the Holy Spirit, *Dominum et Vivificantem* (18 May 1986). There the pope explicitly mentioned the universal activity of the Holy Spirit before the time of the Christian dispensation and today outside the Church.[21] Before the time of the Christian dispensation, the activity of the Spirit, in virtue of the divine plan of salvation, was ordered to Christ. Outside the Church today, it results from the saving event accomplished in him. Thus the pope explains the Christological content and pneumatological dimension of salvific grace:

> We cannot limit ourselves to the two thousand years which have passed since the birth of Christ. We need to go further back, to embrace the whole of the action of the Holy Spirit even before Christ — from the beginning, throughout the world, and especially in the economy of the Old Covenant. For this action has been exercised, in every place and at every time, indeed in every individual, according to the eternal plan of salvation, whereby this action was to be closely linked with the mystery of the incarnation and redemption, which in its turn exercised its influence on those who believed in the future coming of Christ.... Grace, therefore, bears within itself both a Christological aspect and a pneumatological one, which becomes evident above all in those who expressly accept Christ....
>
> But ... we need to look further and go further afield, knowing that "the wind blows where it will" ... [cf. Jn 3:8]. The Second Vatican Council, centred primarily on the theme of the Church, reminds us of the Holy Spirit's activity also "outside the visible Body of the Church." The council speaks precisely of "all people of good will in whose hearts grace is active invisibly [cf. LG 16]. For, since Christ died for all [cf. Rom 8:32], and since all human beings are in fact called to one and the same destiny, which is divine, we must hold that the Holy Spirit offers to all the possibility of being associated, in a way known to God, with the Paschal Mystery [GS 22]." (53)[22]

The theme of the universal presence and activity of the Spirit recurs once more in the encyclical letter *Redemptoris Missio* (7 December 1990).[23] The text states with great clarity that the presence of the Spirit affects not only individual persons but the religious traditions themselves. It says:

> The Spirit manifests himself in a special way in the Church and her members. Nevertheless, his presence and activity are universal, limited neither

---

21. The decree *Ad Gentes* of Vatican II had already noted the activity of the Spirit in the world before the Christ-event. It said: "Without doubt, the Holy Spirit was at work in the world before Christ was glorified" (AG 4); among other references it mentioned (in a note) Leo the Great, who wrote: "When the Holy Spirit filled the Lord's disciples on the day of Pentecost, this was not the first exercise of his role but an extension of his bounty, because the patriarchs, prophets, priests, and all the holy people of the previous ages were nourished by the same sanctifying Spirit ..., although the measure of the gifts was not the same" (*Sermo* 76; PL 54:405–6).

22. Text in AAS 78 (1986) 809–900; ND 1048.

23. Text in AAS 83 (1991) 249–340.

by space nor time.... The Spirit... is at the very source of the human person's existential and religious questioning which is occasioned not only by contingent situations but by the very structure of its being. The Spirit's presence and activity affect not only individuals but also society and history, peoples, cultures and religions. (28)

But if the question is asked whether the recognition of the active presence of the Spirit of God not only in the members of other religious traditions but in the traditions themselves influences positively the encyclical's approach to the significance and saving value of those traditions, the answer is altogether inconclusive. All the encyclical ventures to say on this count comes in two sentences. On the one hand, it affirms that salvation in Christ is accessible to people outside the Church "by virtue of a grace which, while having a mysterious relationship to the Church, does not make them formally part of the Church but enlightens them in a way which is accommodated to their spiritual and material situation" (RM 10). On the other hand, while stressing "Christ's one, universal mediation," the document recognizes the possibility in the order of salvation of "participated forms of mediation," saying: "Although participated forms of mediation of different kinds and degrees are not excluded, they acquire meaning and value *only* from Christ's own mediation, and they cannot be understood as parallel or complementary to his" (RM 5). It is not clear whether among the "participated mediations" contemplated in this text are included, for the benefit of members of the other religions, the traditions to which they belong.

Indeed, the repeated affirmation of the presence of the Holy Spirit of God in the religious traditions notwithstanding, in some recent pronouncements Pope John Paul II resumes the "fulfillment theory" in a way which is reminiscent of Paul VI's assessment of non-Christian religions in *Evangelii Nuntiandi* (53), recalled above. Thus, in the apostolic letter *Tertio Millennio Adveniente* (10 November 1994), the pope writes:

Jesus does not... merely speak "in the name of God" like the prophets, but he is God himself speaking in his eternal Word made flesh. Here we touch upon *the essential point by which Christianity differs from all the other religions,* by which *the human search for God* has been expressed from earliest times. Christianity has its starting-point in the incarnation of the Word. Here, it is not simply a case of a human search for God, but of God who comes in person to speak to human beings of himself and to show them the path by which he may be reached.... *The Incarnate Word is thus the fulfillment of the yearning present in all the religions of humankind:* this fulfillment is brought about by God himself and transcends all human expectations. It is the mystery of grace.

In Christ, religion is no longer a "blind search for God" [cf. Acts 17:27] but the *response of faith* to God who reveals himself.... *Christ is thus the*

*fulfillment of the yearning of all the world's religions and, as such, he is*
*their sole and definitive completion.* (6)[24]

Such a text visualizes the fulfillment of the other religions in Jesus Christ
and Christianity in terms of God's self-communication in his Son incarnate in
response to the universal human search for God expressed in the religious traditions — in other words, in terms of divine revelation and grace meeting the
natural religious aspiration of humankind. This seems to leave no room for
recognizing in the other religious traditions themselves a first divine initiative
toward human beings, no matter how incomplete, and for attributing to the
religious traditions a positive role in the mystery of salvation of their followers.

We come closest to such an affirmation in a document, jointly published by
the Pontifical Council for Interreligious Dialogue and the Congregation for the
Evangelization of Peoples, entitled "Dialogue and Proclamation: Reflections and
Orientations on Interreligious Dialogue and the Proclamation of the Gospel of
Jesus Christ" (19 May 1991).[25] This document has an elaborate section on "a
Christian approach to religious traditions" (14–32) — a first among documents
of the Church's magisterium on the subject of members of other religions and
their traditions. Toward the end of this section, the document contains an im-
portant paragraph which goes beyond whatever Church documents have stated
before regarding the role played by religious traditions in the salvation in Jesus
Christ of their followers:

> From this mystery of unity[26] it follows that all men and women who are
> saved, share, though differently, in the same mystery of salvation in Jesus
> Christ through his Spirit. Christians know this through their faith, while
> others remain unaware that Jesus Christ is the source of their salvation.
> The mystery of salvation reaches out to them, in a way known to God,
> through the invisible action of the Spirit of Christ. Concretely, it will be
> *in the sincere practice of what is good in their own religious tradition* and
> by following the dictates of their conscience that the members of other
> religions respond positively to God's invitation and receive salvation in
> Jesus Christ, even while they do not recognize or acknowledge him as their
> Saviour (cf. AG 3, 9, 11). (29; ND 1059; emphasis added)

Undoubtedly, the statement is a guarded one — not without reason, considering the circumstances and the context in which it was written.[27] Nevertheless,
a door seems to be timidly opened here, for the first time, for the recognition
on the part of the Church authority of a "participated mediation" of religious
traditions in the salvation of their members. With such a statement we seem to

---

24. Text in AAS 87 (1995) 8–9.

25. The text is found in Pontifical Council for Interreligious Dialogue 1991, 210–50.

26. Reference in nos. 27–28 is to the "mystery of unity" of which John Paul II spoke in the 1986
address to the Roman curia (see above).

27. For a critical study and the genesis of this document as well as a comparison between the encyclical
*Redemptoris Missio* and "Dialogue and Proclamation," see Dupuis 1993b, 119–58; see also Dupuis
1993a.

be definitely moving from the "fulfillment theory" to that of an active presence of the mystery of Jesus Christ in the traditions themselves.[28]

The present review of Vatican II and of the postconciliar magisterium will have shown that the Church doctrine is neither monolithic nor of one piece. Distinct overtones and shades of meaning can be found from one document to another. Neither is it always easy to decide the precise meaning or bearing of a particular statement or affirmation. However this may be, it seems possible to draw from the above survey the following conclusions.

The relevant texts of the council, without wishing to take sides on disputed doctrinal issues, display an openness toward the other religious traditions unprecedented in previous official Church documents. While never formally recognizing in the other religious traditions channels of salvation for their members in accordance with God's providence in Jesus Christ, the council nevertheless seems to incline in that direction by implication where it acknowledges the existence in those traditions not merely of positive human values but also of elements of "truth and grace" as a hidden presence in them of God's action.

As for the postconciliar magisterium, it is marked by a certain ambiguity. While Paul VI seems clearly to hold on to the fulfillment theory as traditionally understood before the council, John Paul II, principally with his emphasis on the universal active presence of the Spirit of God and of Christ in the religious traditions themselves, is more positive and shows a greater disposition toward a broader perspective, without, however, clearly going beyond the preconciliar understanding of fulfillment. Only a recent official document from the Vatican allows it to be prudently affirmed that God's grace and salvation in Jesus Christ reach out to the others in and through the "sincere practice" of their religious traditions.

Here is where the official doctrine allows us to arrive, but not go beyond. The last task of our historical part will consist of showing that the theological debate which has been going on among Christians at large, principally since the time of the council, is in effect much broader and variegated than has been accounted for so far, including as it does some extreme positions. The entire spectrum of opinions in the ongoing debate must be examined before a clear perspective can be devised for a synthetic treatment of a "theology of religious pluralism."

---

28. The recent document of the International Theological Commission entitled "Christianity and the Religions" (1996) is not considered in this chapter as it does not belong to the Church's magisterium. Occasional reference will be made to it in the second part of this work. The text of the document is published in Italian in *Civiltà Cattolica* 3518/148/1:146–83.

# Seven

# The Debate over
# Theology of Religions

THE PARAMETERS within which Vatican II considered "the relations of the Church with non-Christian religions" were limited in scope. The Church did wish to foster mutual esteem and cooperation, but within the limits imposed by its self-identity and its understanding of its mission. Many unnegotiable elements were presupposed in the discussion: the "uniqueness" of Jesus Christ in whom alone humankind could find salvation; the irreplaceable role of the Church as the universal sacrament of salvation in Christ. Within the limits imposed by these basic elements of traditional Christian faith, the space for negotiating different theological evaluations of religions appeared somewhat narrow. The rigid interpretation of the ancient adage "Outside the Church no salvation" being clearly excluded (as Pius XII had reminded in 1949), two streets seemed to be open — those in effect which current Catholic theology suggested at the time of the council and which have been reviewed in chapter 5. The council committed itself formally neither to one nor to the other. While it seemed to incline to the more positive vision, it left the theological debate open.

The theological debate had, in fact, long before the council taken much broader dimensions than the council could or would ever consider. This is evident if, looking beyond the positions widespread at the time among Catholic theologians, we visualize the whole range of opinions held earlier by theologians of various Christian traditions, from one end of the spectrum to the other: Karl Barth's "dialectical theology," on the one hand, and the liberal views with which he found himself in conflict, on the other. Nor has the breadth of the spectrum narrowed down in more recent times; rather it has been broadened, even as the debate itself has gained momentum. Today the debate on the theology of religions has pride of place on the theological agenda. The constant flow of literature on the subject is sufficient warrant for the assertion.

It is this debate, as it stands today, that the present chapter intends to review. A few preliminary remarks are called for regarding procedure. First, the account does not aim at being exhaustive; it does not intend to examine the opinion of every author. It aims at being synthetic rather than analytical.[1] Second, it is

---

1. The literature on the topic is very abundant. One can consult especially on the position of various authors: Knitter 1985; Richards 1989; Race 1983; Drummond 1985; Coward 1985.

not structured in such a way as to distinguish opinions characteristic of distinct Christian denominations; on the contrary, it takes note of the fact that the main theological positions, on either side of the spectrum, cut across the confessional barriers.[2] Third, it intends to identify the main paradigms according to which attempts have been made and are being made to construct a theology of religions and of religious pluralism — in other words, to determine the fundamental perspective, the principle of intelligibility, according to which theories are being proposed as to how the various religious traditions — Christianity included — relate to each other.

Before entering into the matter some precisions are in order with regard to terminology. The term "paradigm" is being used intentionally as opposed to "model," of which use is also being made. The distinction between the two terms is an important one. Succinctly, the following may be said. "Models" are descriptive; they call attention to aspects of some reality without claiming to define the reality in any adequate and distinctive manner. Consequently, models do not exclude each other; on the contrary, they must be viewed as complementing each other and need to be combined in order to yield a comprehensive view of the reality concerned (see Dulles 1987, 1992). The opposite is the case where "paradigms" are concerned. Here it is a question of principles of understanding, of overall keys of interpretation of reality which, being mutually opposed, exclude each other. One cannot hold at once — the comparison is in order, as will be seen hereafter — a Ptolemaic and a Copernican worldview! Hence the need, if one paradigm is thought inoperative, to abandon it and to "shift" to another. In the matter at hand, it will be important to keep in mind the contradiction intended between each of the two paradigms and the disavowal which every "paradigm shift" implies of that which went before it.

Some terms frequently used by theologians to express what distinguishes Jesus Christ from other "saving figures" or Christianity from other religious traditions also call for clarifications. There is talk of "singularity" and "unicity," of "centrality" and "finality," of "universality" and "normativity," of "transcendence" and "absoluteness." All these terms, however, are open to different significations; their ambiguity often leads to misunderstandings, either by excess or by default.

"Singularity" and "unicity" have two distinct meanings: in one sense, the terms convey the specific or original character which makes one reality different from every other. In this sense, every religious tradition, like every person, is "singular" and "unique," in its very difference from the others. The "unicity" conveyed is a "relative" unicity. In the second meaning, the terms take on a more restricted sense, referring now to a "unique uniqueness" or "singular uniqueness." As will be seen later, while the Christian tradition is known to

---

2. Knitter (1985) distinguishes among "Christian attitudes toward religious pluralism": the conservative evangelical model; the mainline Protestant model; the Catholic model. He must, however, remark — correctly — that each of those is shared by theologians of another tradition. As for the theocentric model, which he advocates, it is equally shared by some Protestant and Catholic theologians.

hold to the "unique uniqueness" of Jesus Christ as universal Savior of human-kind, there is no dearth of theologians today who understand his "uniqueness" relatively.[3] However, while such an understanding may seem reductionist, the other may be exposed to a narrow exclusivism.

A similar situation obtains with the terms "normativity" and "universality." Both may convey more or less. "Normativity" may be predicated of Jesus Christ as representing a privileged, even the ideal, model or symbol — among others — of God's relationships with humankind.[4] The term may also be used to convey more; Jesus Christ is not only an ideal model for humans' relationships with God but — for whatever reason — God's "representative" among them, cho-sen and attested by him, indeed "ultimately decisive" and "archetypal" (Küng 1977, passim; Dupuis 1991b, 193–96). In the first case does not the meaning fall short of the traditional understanding of Jesus Christ? In the other, does it not lean again toward exclusivism?

As for the term "universality," it too can be understood in a relative sense or, on the contrary, in a singular sense. It may refer to the universal appeal which the various religious traditions can possibly make on people insofar as each in its own way proposes a path for the religious quest of individual persons and brings fulfillment to their aspirations, without any particular tradition having for that matter the monopoly of such a universal appeal. It can also imply a claim to "unique universality," evoking once more an injurious exclusivism.

The terms "centrality" and "finality" would call for similar observations, on which there is no need to insist further. Christianity, as these last terms seem to imply, situates itself a priori at the center of the debate. Likewise, it claims for itself the last word on the matter of religions, the final verdict on the ques-tion of their mutual relationships. Questions arise, however, as to whether the Christian faith needs to be arrogantly exclusive. Is it possible to understand it and to formulate it in a way which would be neither reductionist nor intransi-gent? In brief, all concepts and words are full of ambiguities and so are prone to be misunderstood.

If from the terminology we pass on to the theological debate itself, we may note that the spectrum of opinions has been differently laid out by different au-thors. Summing up the debate as it stood in 1976, J. P. Schineller distributed the theological opinions under four major categories as follows: (1) ecclesiocentric universe, exclusive Christology; (2) Christocentric universe, inclusive Chris-tology; (3) theocentric universe, normative Christology; and (4) theocentric universe, non-normative Christology (see Schineller 1976). In these categories,

---

3. On the ambiguity of the term "uniqueness" in the context of the relationship between Christianity and Judaism, one may consult Moran 1992. The author writes: "The prominent use of the term [uniqueness] in Christian theology may seem to make its meaning a Christian rather than a Jewish question....The Christian assertion of uniqueness is often an anti-Jewish question....But...Christianity's legitimate use of uniqueness has to be directly related to the Hebrew Bible and the Jewish people. As soon as Jesus of Nazareth is lifted out of his Jewish context, Christianity will find itself defending an indefensible claim to uniqueness" (3).

4. Examples are: Troeltsch 1971; Tillich 1957–63; 1963. On the position of Troeltsch, see Coak-ley 1988.

ecclesiocentrism, Christocentrism, and theocentrism represent as many distinct paradigms or worldviews. However, the theocentric worldview comprises two alternative positions according to whether a "normative" function is or is not attributed to Jesus Christ in the order of relationships between God and humankind.

J. P. Schineller's classification, though incomplete today, retains some validity. It has the merit of putting in sharp relief a double paradigm shift as opinions change from an ecclesiocentric worldview to a Christocentric one, and again from a Christocentric to a theocentric. Both paradigm shifts carry weighty consequences. The shift from an ecclesiocentric to a Christocentric worldview refers to the abandonment of the untenable ecclesiological perspective according to which salvation was deemed available to people only through faith in Jesus Christ explicitly professed in the Church community. This paradigm shift is not new. The other, however, though not altogether new either, is widespread in the present debate and has consequential implications. For many authors today, not only the ecclesiocentric perspective but the Christocentric one as well appears untenable; it must be replaced by a theocentric worldview. The underlying implication is that it is no longer possible to refer universal salvation to Jesus Christ, whether or not faith in him be explicitly professed in the Church. Jesus Christ is no longer to be seen as the constitutive Savior for all humankind whose saving power is operative beyond the boundaries of the Christian Church. Rejected here is not only the notion of obligatory belonging to the Church for salvation but the universal mediatorship of Jesus Christ in the order of salvation.

While it rightly places the emphasis on a double paradigm shift, the categorization proposed by Schineller also has its shortcomings. The main one, and the more weighty, lies in the fact that the Christocentric paradigm, as described by him, fails to distinguish the two contrasting ways in which inclusive Christology has been understood by Catholic theologians before Vatican II and between which the council deliberately chose not to take sides (see chapters 5 and 6). Admittedly, both theories belonged to the same Christocentric worldview without a paradigm shift being involved between them; they nevertheless represented vastly diverse opinions.

In reverse fashion, a certain anomaly may also be seen in the fact that, though models 3 and 4 of Schineller's classification both belong to the same theocentric paradigm, the role which they respectively assign to Jesus Christ in the order of God's relationships with humankind differs considerably, from normative to non-normative. The difference between both opinions is more consequential than appears at first sight. It is a question of deciding what role may or may not continue to be assigned to Jesus Christ in a theocentric paradigm. Is it simply a matter of acknowledging that God's self-manifestation has taken different forms in the different religious traditions, without having to prioritize the manifestation in Jesus Christ as in any way "normative" (model 4)? Or, rather, while acknowledging that it is no longer tenable to regard universal salvation as dependent on the person and work of Jesus Christ — as the Christocentric paradigm would have it — are we to continue to prioritize Jesus Christ in some way as the most perfect symbol, or even as the ideal model, and in this sense as "normative" in the order of divine-human relationships for salvation (model 3)?

Despite the admitted merits of a fourfold grouping,[5] many recent authors prefer a tripartite division of opinions. They distinguish three fundamental perspectives: ecclesiocentric, Christocentric, and theocentric, and in parallel with these, three basic positions, respectively designated exclusivism, inclusivism, and "pluralism."[6] These distinctions correspond to the twofold paradigm shift mentioned above. It needs to be added that further discussions on the subject have caused more recent categories to arise. These, however, as will be seen later, do not represent new paradigm shifts in the sense defined above, but only suggest new models for assessing the respective value of different religions. Account will have to be taken of these more recent developments and of the new categories of opinions they have brought about.[7]

The burden of this chapter consists in accounting for the pressure under which the theology of religions has undergone a double paradigm shift, from ecclesiocentrism through Christocentrism to theocentrism. It will likewise have to show how more recent debates have resulted in the addition of new models for evaluating the truth of different religions. In the process, it will become apparent that the Christological question, which originally was found at the center of the entire discussion of the theology of religions, rightly or wrongly, tends in the minds of many to be progressively marginalized. This tendency itself needs to be discussed, and the models newly proposed need to be assessed. A workable model must be sought for a synthetic theology of religions at once Christian and universal.

---

5. A fourfold division of opinions, partly overlapping with that of J. P. Schineller, is found in other authors as well. Thus, for example, in *No Other Name?* (1985), Knitter distinguishes: (1) the conservative evangelical model (one true religion); (2) the most widespread Protestant model today (all salvation comes from Christ); (3) the open Catholic model (various paths, Christ the sole norm); and (4) the theocentric model (various paths, with God as center). In an article entitled "Catholic Theology of Religions at the Crossroads" (Knitter 1986), Knitter partly adopts the categories proposed by H. R. Niebuhr (in Niebuhr 1951) for the relationship between Christ and culture and distinguishes: a Christ against the religions, in the religions, above the religions, and together with the religions. Previously, in his "Roman Catholic Approaches to Other Religions: Development and Tensions" (Knitter 1984), he had distinguished: exclusive ecclesiocentrism; inclusive ecclesiocentrism or constitutive Christocentrism; normative Christocentrism or Christ above the religions; dialogical theocentrism or different religions as partners in God. The last categories coincide best with Schineller's four divisions. H. Küng, for his part, distinguishes four fundamental positions as follows: no religion is true; only one religion is true; every religion is true; one religion is the true one in whose truth all religions participate. See Küng 1987, 231–50.

6. The following, among others, adopt this nomenclature: Race 1983; Coward 1985. Pieris (1982) makes an equivalent distinction: Christ against the religions; the Christ of the religions; Christ among the religions.

7. See Amato 1992. The author expounds the four categories borrowed by Knitter from Niebuhr: Christ against religions: the exclusivist model; Christ in religions: the inclusivist model; Christ above religions: the normative model; Christ with other religions: the pluralistic or relativistic model. In view of the more recent developments (to be considered hereafter), he adds, somewhat polemically, a fifth model: religions without Christ: the liberation model (65–69). See also Amato 1994, 23–28.

# I. Shifting Paradigms

## A. From Ecclesiocentrism to Christocentrism

The first paradigm shift can be treated rapidly. We have recalled earlier Karl Barth's negative verdict on religion in general, and implicitly on religions, as well as the application of his "dialectical theology," which disciples such as H. Kraemer made to the religions they encountered in missionary situations. Non-Christian religions were at best futile human attempts at self-justification, salvation being attainable only through faith in Jesus Christ professed in the Church.[8] Karl Barth was not, however, alone in reacting vehemently against the liberal views that had been put forward by historians of religion, such as Ernst Troeltsch and Arnold Toynbee (see Troeltsch 1971; Coakley 1988; see also Toynbee 1957). Others did likewise — for instance, Emil Brunner, who, notwithstanding differences, is in this regard closely associated with Barth (Brunner 1947; see Richards 1989, 14–24).

Nor must it be thought that the exclusivist stand of Protestant neoorthodoxy has become altogether a thing of the past. It survives to some extent in evangelical circles, even today. Witness such recent works as those of H. A. Netland (Netland 1991); A. D. Clarke and B. M. Winter (Clarke and Winter, eds., 1992); and, on a more institutional level, the "Lausanne Covenant," issued by the International Congress on World Evangelism (1974), and the "Manila Manifesto," published by the same organization in 1989. The "Manila Manifesto" states that there is "no warrant for saying that salvation can be found outside Christ or apart from an explicit acceptance of his work through faith" (Stockwell n.d., 3). Positions closely approaching those can likewise be found even today among Catholic authors.[9] Such data recall the exclusivist paradigm, explicitly repudiated by the Church's teaching office, as per the 1949 letter of the Holy Office (see pp. 127–129, above).

The paradigm shift from ecclesiocentrism to Christocentrism represents, in fact, an important turnover with weighty consequences, not merely for a theology of religions (inclusivism versus exclusivism) but for theology in general. It implies a radical "decentering" of the Church, which now finds itself "recentered" on the mystery of Jesus Christ. He, indeed, not the Church, stands at the center of the Christian mystery; the Church, by contrast, is a derived, related mystery, which finds in him its raison d'être. Such a decentering of the Church and its consequent recentering on the person of Jesus Christ are required if theology would eschew maximalist ecclesiological tendencies, of which the axiom "Outside the Church no salvation" is an extreme example. A broad

---

8. See p. 130, above, and Kraemer 1947, 1957, 1960, 1962.
9. One example is Straelen 1982. More recently, Straelen 1994. The author writes: "The Church has always taught that, in order to be saved, one must accept the gospel message, reject the false gods, and turn toward the living God of Abraham, Isaac, and Jacob as he revealed himself in Jesus Christ" (281). For a review of this work, see Dupuis 1995b.

Christocentric perspective must be substituted for a narrow ecclesiocentric approach.

Where the theology of religions is concerned, the paradigm shift from exclusivism to inclusivism implies a clear-cut distinction between the role of Jesus Christ in the order of salvation and that of the Church. Both are not, and can never be, placed on one and the same level. Jesus Christ alone is, according to the New Testament, the mediator between God and human beings (see 1 Tim 2:5; Heb 8:6; 9:15; 12:24). Whatever role may have to be attributed to the Church in the order of salvation, it can never be placed on a par with that of Jesus Christ; nor can the same necessity ever be attributed to it. This goes to show that an ecclesiocentric outlook needs to be transcended. A theology of religions cannot be built on an ecclesiological inflation that would falsify perspectives. The Church, as a derived mystery and utterly relative to the mystery of Christ, cannot be the yardstick by which the salvation of others is measured. What role is to be assigned to it in relation to the religions and their members, in a decentered perspective, is a question to which we need to return later.

### B. From Christocentrism to Theocentrism

However, in the recent discussion on the theology of religions a second, even more radical, paradigm shift is being advocated by a growing number of authors. To inclusivist Christocentrism is being opposed a theocentric perspective, also called "pluralism." The significance of the term and the paradigm shift involved must be clearly perceived. They imply the disavowal of the preceding paradigm — in this case, of the centrality of Jesus Christ in the order of salvation, as traditionally understood by Christian faith. These authors wish to abandon not only the view which placed the Church at the center of the theological outlook but also the one according to which at the center is the mystery of Jesus Christ. In the theocentric perspective, God and God alone stands at the center. "Pluralism" refers to the substitution of many "ways" or saving figures leading to God-the-Center, in place of the one, universal, constitutive mediation of Jesus Christ. The various religions, Christianity included, represent as many ways leading to God, all of which, differences notwithstanding, have the same validity and equal value. Broadly speaking, the reasoning is as follows.

If Christianity sincerely seeks a dialogue with the other religious traditions — which it can only seek on a footing of equality — it must first of all renounce any claim to uniqueness for the person and work of Jesus Christ as a universal constitutive element of salvation. To be sure, this position is open to various understandings in terms of radicality. We have already observed, with J. P. Schineller, two divergent interpretations according to which the person of Jesus Christ, understood as nonconstitutive of salvation, is nonetheless normative for some, while for others it is neither constitutive nor normative. Examples for the normative Jesus would be, besides Troeltsch and Tillich already mentioned,[10] process theologians such as John B. Cobb and Schubert M. Ogden[11] For the non-normative Jesus, the main protagonist is undoubtedly John Hick, to whom we shall return presently.

The authors who advocate a theocentric pluralism, however, differ from one another in various respects, which we need not detail here. Let us simply note that, while for some of these authors, such as Alan Race, Christianity's renunciation of its Christological claims must be irrevocable (Race 1983, 106–48), others propound it as a working hypothesis along the lines of a methodical doubt or as an at least temporary "bracketing" necessary in order for the dialogue with others to be established honestly and authentically. The very practice of dialogue may well reestablish the validity of Christian claims regarding the mystery of Christ. These claims would then rest ultimately on the sole foundation that can establish them with solidity: the test of encounter (Knitter 1985, 163–231).

Hick's position is so representative of a theological pluralism understood in the radical sense that it is worthwhile to pause a moment to consider it.[12] Hick advocates a "Copernican revolution" in Christology, a revolution that must specifically consist of a shift in paradigm, a movement from the traditional Christocentric perspective to a new theocentric perspective. "Copernican revolution," an expression we frequently meet in other areas of theological discussion today, is indeed an appropriate term for what is under way here. Originally it designated the passage from one system for explaining the cosmos, now passé and overthrown, to another system that actually corresponds to reality. The Ptolemaic system was replaced by the Copernican. Having believed for centuries that the sun revolves around the earth, we finally discovered, with Galileo and Copernicus, that the earth actually revolves around the sun. Likewise, having believed for centuries that the other religious traditions revolved around Christianity as their center,[13] today we must acknowledge that the center around which all religious traditions revolve (including Christianity) is actually God. Such a paradigm shift necessarily entails the abandonment of any claim to a unique meaning not only for Christianity but for Jesus Christ himself.

---

10. For the relevant works of E. Troeltsch and P. Tillich, see note 4. For an interpretation of Tillich's normative Christology we can add Lai 1994. The author claims that in *Systematic Theology*, vol. 3, Tillich tones down his previous Christology in favor of a Spirit-Christology allowing for a Trinitarian approach to the theology of religions. However, the shift in emphasis seems to be overly emphasized by Pan-Chiu Lai. For Tillich, Christ remains even here the norm or criterion, as was the case in the previous volume. For a review of Pan-Chiu Lai's work, see T. S. M. Williams 1995. For a Spirit-Christology and Trinitarian approach to the theology of religions, see part II of this work.

11. See Cobb 1975, 1982; see also Ogden 1961, 1963, 1992.

12. See esp. Hick 1973, 1977, 1980, 1983, 1985. For critical studies of Hick's position, see D'Costa 1987; Carruthers 1990.

13. In his youth, Hick published a book entitled *Christianity at the Centre* (1968), before he himself underwent the Copernican Christological revolution. This was transformed, in a second edition, into *The Centre of Christianity* (1977), to become, in a third edition, *The Second Christianity* (1983).

To use Schineller's categories for the sake of clarity, we must say that the basic dilemma, as Hick conceives it, is between ecclesiocentric exclusivism and a theocentric pluralism — that is, between a fundamentalist interpretation of the axiom "Outside the Church no salvation" and a radical liberalism that regards all the various divine manifestations in various cultures, including that which took place in Jesus Christ, as enjoying the same basic equality in their differences.

This is not to say that Hick simply ignores theological writings representing the middle position, that of inclusivism, or, in Schineller's terminology, an inclusive Christology in a Christocentric universe, in the manner of Karl Rahner, for example.[14] Still, for Hick, all the efforts of an impressive number of recent theologians (especially Catholic theologians) to endow the theology of religions with an inclusive, open Christocentrism that would combine the "constitutive" sense of the Jesus Christ–event for the salvation of humanity, on the one hand, and, on the other, the value of other religious traditions as representing interventions of God in the history of human cultures, and comprising "elements of grace" for the salvation of their members — all of these efforts may be left out of account as unworthy of serious consideration. Indeed, they are comparable to the "epicycles" concocted by ancient science in its vain attempt to force certain recalcitrant phenomena into the Ptolemaic system, until the latter finally blew up in our faces, taking its epicycles with it and making room for the Copernican revolution. In analogous fashion, the Copernican revolution in Christology, which Hick not only enthusiastically approves but is determined to foster, rejects all inclusive Christologies as if they were useless, abandoned epicycles. The only remaining valid theology of religions will now be that of a theocentric pluralism, which accounts for all the phenomena, transcends any Christian claim to a prioritized, universal role for Jesus Christ, and at last establishes the interreligious dialogue on a genuinely equal footing.

Let us further observe that Hick's thinking has encouraged a veritable school of thought that vaunts a somewhat militant attitude, as its slogans attest. Besides the paradigm shift of the Copernican revolution, we have heard as well of "crossing the Rubicon." "Crossing the Rubicon," of course, will designate an irrevocable acknowledgment of the equal meaning and value of the various religions and the renunciation of any claim not only to exclusivity but also to normativity for Christianity or Jesus Christ.[15] If there is any universalism in Jesus Christ, it can only be that of the appeal his message might have in terms of the aspirations of all men and women. Of course, other salvific figures might have the same appeal.

---

14. See K. Rahner, various essays in *Theological Investigations*, 23 vols. (London: Darton, Longman and Todd, 1961–92); see also Rahner 1978. See pp. 143–149, above.

15. See Swidler, ed., 1987; in that volume, see especially Paul F. Knitter, "Hans Küng's Theological Rubicon," 224–30. See also Hick and Knitter, eds., 1987.

We have referred to Alan Race and Paul F. Knitter as joining with Hick in advocating and promoting the theocentric paradigm. Others, who previously appeared more moderate, have recently gotten on the same bandwagon. A case in point is S. J. Samartha, whose earlier work seemed to find its congenial place in the normative "model" of Christology (see, among other works, Samartha 1982) but whose latest work advocates a revisionist Christology which clearly falls into the radical theocentric perspective.[16]

Some authors belie any clear-cut categorization; among these is, for instance, Raimon Panikkar. Panikkar's early work, as we have observed earlier, seemed to fall in line with the inclusivist paradigm of Christology, while later developments raised questions with regard to the "unknown Christ" being personally identical with the historical man Jesus of Nazareth, raised from the dead (see pp. 149–153, above). In spite of Panikkar's claim to the contrary,[17] his more recent work does not entirely dispel the impression that the "cosmotheandric" reality present in and common to every religious experience in whatever tradition — a reality Christians call "the Christ" — remains loosely connected with the historical person Jesus of Nazareth. Such an object of faith runs the risk of becoming an abstraction, little in keeping with the inclusivist Christocentric paradigm.[18]

---

16. See Samartha 1991. A study of Samartha's position is Klootwijk 1992. More critical is Choy 1993. S. J. Samartha himself has written recently a brief account of the evolution of his thought through the various ecumenical ministries which he held during his career; see Samartha 1996.

17. See Panikkar 1992. Panikkar rejects the accusation leveled at him by some theologians that he disjoins a universal Christ from the Jesus of history. However, in spite of the clarifications made here, there still remain ambiguous formulations. For example: "Christ is the Christian symbol of all reality" (6); "the Christian knows Christ in and through Jesus" (7); "Jesus...became for Christians the revelation of the Christ" (8); "the mystery which Christians call Christ manifests itself in the other religions" (12); "Jesus Christ...[is] the harmonious blending of [the] three dimensions of the real," of the cosmotheandric mystery (21).

18. See, for instance, Panikkar 1987b. Explaining what he believes to be the Christ, Panikkar writes: "The mystery that is at the beginning and will be at the end, the alpha and omega by and through which all has to come into being, the light that enlightens every creature, the word that is in every authentic word, the reality that is totally material, completely human, and simply divine, which is at work everywhere and elusively present wherever there is reality, the meeting place at the crossroads of reality where all realms meet, that which does not come with fanfare and about which one should not believe that it is here or there, that which we do not know when we perform a good or an evil action and yet is 'there,' that which we are — and shall be — and which we were, that symbol of all reality not only as it was or is, but as it still shall freely be, also through our synergy, is what I believe to be the Christ" (113–14). See also Panikkar 1993. The present work was completed before I was able to read in manuscript form "The Mysticism of Jesus Christ" by Raimon Panikkar, to be published in Italian by Edizioni Dehoniane of Bologna, together with "A Christophany for Our Times" (Panikkar 1992), in *E' bene che me ne vada: L'esperienza di Cristo*. As the subtitle indicates, Panikkar attempts to give here an account of the religious experience of the man Jesus, which he calls a "Christology from within," or a "Christophany from the centre." The historical experience of being Son of God seems distinct from our own, according to Panikkar, only in degree. His is the prototype of our experience; ours a pale imitation of his. Nevertheless, all human beings are destined to experience the same self-awareness as Jesus had of himself as Son. The man Jesus realized fully what we truly are; his was the pure human experience. In the Indic context, Panikkar sees the mystical experience of Jesus as that of *ahambrahmasmi*; the Hindu experience of *advaita* is its homeomorphic equivalent. In conclusion, Panikkar writes, Jesus was "just a Being...living the fullness of humanness, which includes a share of the Divine — revealing thus what we are called to become." The danger here is that, while our share in the sonship of Jesus is correctly affirmed, the distinction between his unique Sonship experienced humanly and our share in his sonship by grace may not be adequately preserved.

## C. The Christological Question

From the above it will be seen that at the heart of the paradigm shifts analyzed so far is the Christological question. Involved in the first paradigm shift
is the centrality which Christian faith attributes to Jesus Christ in relation to
the Church; at stake in the second is the universal constitutive mediation which
traditionally Christian faith has assigned to him in God's plan of salvation for
humankind.

It must be made clear that the theocentric pluralists have no intention of un-
dermining the faith-commitment of Christians, nor the integral demands which
such a commitment makes on the person. At stake, however, is the universal
significance and constitutive role which Christianity attributes to it. The contention is that a person's faith in Jesus Christ implies that one has encountered
God's self-gift and communication of life in the human person Jesus of Nazareth — not, however, that this historical person is the obligatory way for all
human beings in whatever circumstances of place and time. In other words, to
believe in Jesus Christ is to believe that I am saved through him, not that he is
the Savior of the world. Jesus is the way for Christians, but other ways make
him unnecessary for others.

Viewed in this fashion, the theocentric paradigm shift revolves entirely
around the Christological problem. Its adoption or disavowal principally depends on the acceptance or refusal of a revisionist Christology substantially
departing from that of mainstream Christianity. It is not by coincidence that the
protagonists of the theocentric perspective base their advocacy of a paradigm
shift on a Christology "revised" or "reinterpreted" in the context of religious
pluralism.[19] Such a revisionist Christology seems required for several reasons,
among which figure the following: (1) a newly acquired historical consciousness; (2) the inseparability in every human experience between content and
context; (3) the relativity of every experience of the Divine Mystery, which in
itself remains beyond all telling and is inexhaustible; (4) the particularity and
contingency of the historical event Jesus of Nazareth; (5) the "theocentric" outlook of Jesus himself as against the Christocentric approach of the Apostolic
Church; (6) the total discontinuity between Jesus' own self-understanding and
the kerygmatic proclamation of him; (7) the "mythical" or "metaphorical" language of the late New Testament Christology and its sequels in postbiblical
tradition; and so forth.[20]

Fundamentally, the question which is being asked is whether in the present
context of dialogue the unequivocal witness of the New Testament — which
is not being denied — to the universal significance of Jesus Christ need not be
reexamined and reinterpreted. Does it belong to the substance of the revealed

---

19. See Hick, ed., 1977; 1993b. On this later book, see the critique in O'Collins (1995b). In Knitter
1985, see chap. 9: "How Is Jesus Unique?" (171–204). See Samartha 1991.

20. I have endeavored to answer some of these questions by showing the continuity-in-discontinuity
which exists between different levels of development of the Church's Christological faith. See Dupuis
1994c.

message, or is it due to the cultural idiom in which the experience of the early
Christians has been expressed and to the circumstances in which the experience itself was made? In the light of what we know today about the other
religious traditions and their followers, is it still possible to make the salvation of all depend on the particular, historical Jesus of Nazareth, about whom
often they have not heard or whom otherwise they have not been in a position
to recognize? More radically, what authority as a "norm of faith" does the New
Testament witness still retain, once it is confronted with our present experience
of dialogue? Some of these questions will claim our attention later.

Meanwhile, two observations are in order regarding the Christological debate in the theology of religions. The first is that the assumption made by a
growing number of theologians that a Christocentric perspective is no longer
tenable calls for some clarifications. Are Christocentrism and theocentrism mutually opposed, as is being claimed, as two contradictory paradigms? To affirm
this position constitutes by itself a theological and Christological option. The
Christocentrism of Christian tradition is not, in fact, opposed to theocentrism.
It never places Jesus Christ in the place of God; it merely affirms that God has
placed him at the center of his saving plan for humankind, not as the end but
as the way, not as the goal of every human quest for God but as the universal
mediator of God's saving action toward people. Christian theology is not faced
with the dilemma of being either Christocentric or theocentric; it is theocentric
by being Christocentric and vice versa. This amounts to saying that Jesus Christ
is the medium of God's encounter with human beings. The man Jesus belongs,
no doubt, to the order of signs and symbols; but in him who has been constituted the Christ by God, who raised him from the dead (Acts 2:36), God's
saving action reaches out to people in various ways, knowingly to some and to
others unknowingly.

The second observation has to do with the kind of Christology that underlies the Christocentric and the theocentric paradigms. In terms of the distinction
often made between a high and a low Christology, it is clear that the inclusivist or Christocentric model of a theology of religions is consonant with a high
Christology in which the personal identity of Jesus Christ as the Son of God is
unambiguously recognized; on the contrary, the pluralist or theocentric model
postulates a low Christology which questions and ultimately denies such ontological affirmations about Jesus Christ. Both paradigms are in this regard fully
coherent with themselves. The implication is, as the Christian tradition amply
testifies, that the only adequate foundation on which the singular uniqueness of
Jesus Christ can be based is his personal identity as the Son of God made man,
as God's incarnate Word. No other Christology can, in the last analysis, account
persuasively for Christ's universal mediatorship in the order of salvation.

Concretely, then, the choice between a Christocentric and a theocentric paradigm in the theology of religions depends on the option which is made between
a high, ontological Christology and a low Christology which remains deliberately at the functional level. Such a choice has weighty consequences. The price

involved for the traditional Christian faith in terms of the mystery of the person and work of Jesus Christ is considerable. It comes as no surprise to observe that some recent authors not only have rejected Hick's dilemma between two paradigms but have shown his position to be in fact untenable.[21] This happens in different ways. Some have accused the theocentric paradigm of naive relativism and ahistorical idealism (see Lipner 1981). Others have denounced the assumptions of the biblical interpretation on which it is based. Others still have shown the proposed model to be self-contradictory: while championing "pluralism," it ends up postulating homogeneity of means and uniformity of ends between the various religious traditions (see Heim 1995).

A book by Gavin D'Costa, entitled *Theology and Religious Pluralism,* deserves special mention in this regard (D'Costa 1986). The author recalls two basic axioms of traditional Christian faith: the universal salvific will of God and the necessary mediation of Jesus Christ. He shows that contrasting attitudes toward these two axioms account for the three basic positions of exclusivism, inclusivism, and pluralism. While exclusivism relies on the second axiom, neglecting the first, and pluralism on the first, to the detriment of the second, inclusivism alone succeeds in accounting for and holding both at once.

Expounding first the pluralistic theory, D'Costa shows that despite its seeming liberalism, Hick's either-or dilemma between exclusivism and pluralism actually represents a rigid, self-contradictory position. Its theocentric view imposes on the encounter of religions a divine model that corresponds exclusively to the God of the so-called monotheistic religions. It is not universal.

Exclusivism stands in the diametrically opposite corner but is equally rigid, it too being based on a dialectic of either-or. It is untenable from a biblical and theological point of view and actually involves intrinsic contradictions. An exclusive emphasis on merely one of the pair of crucial axioms that ought to govern a Christian theology of religions leads to insoluble theological problems.

There remains the inclusive model. Does this model, however, solve the problems left unsolved by the other two, while preserving whatever measure of validity may reside in the two extreme positions? D'Costa is of the opinion that this is indeed the case and that the inclusivistic position alone is capable of holding together and harmonizing the two traditional axioms of Christian faith that remain obligatory for any Christian theology of religions. On the one side, Jesus Christ is clearly asserted to be God's decisive revelation and constitutive Savior. On the other side, the door is open to a sincere acknowledgment of divine manifestations in the history of humanity in various cultures and of efficacious "elements of grace" to be found in other religious traditions: elements that are salvific for their members. Revealed in a decisive manner in Jesus Christ, God (and the mystery of salvation) is nonetheless present and at work in other religious traditions. How this is, bears further elucidation below, as well as further

---

21. Besides D'Costa 1987 and Carruthers 1990, see D'Costa, ed., 1990.

refinements. Meanwhile, D'Costa's conclusion reaffirms the abiding validity of the inclusivist model of Christology and indicates the task ahead as follows:

> The form of inclusivism I have argued for tries to do full justice to [the] two most important Christian axioms: that salvation comes through God in Christ alone, and that God's salvific will is truly universal. By maintaining these two axioms in fruitful tension, the inclusivist paradigm can be characterized by an openness and commitment: an openness that seeks to explore the many and various ways in which God has spoken to all his children in the non-Christian religions and an openness that will lead to the positive fruits of this exploration transforming, enriching and fulfilling Christianity, so much so that its future shape may be very different from the Church we know today. (D'Costa 1986, 136)

## II. Further Models and Beyond

### A. Regnocentrism and Soteriocentrism

One of the main objections raised against the theocentric paradigm was its uncritical assumption of a concept of the Absolute Reality akin to the monotheistic and prophetic religions of the Western Hemisphere, one totally alien to the mystical traditions of the East. How could a preconceived idea of God be imposed upon all in a bid to show how in their differences they do converge in the same Divine Center? This situation forced the protagonists of theocentric pluralism to propose further models which, however, amount to little more than new variations on the same theme. John Hick accordingly put forward the model of "Reality-Centeredness."[22] This means that all religions are oriented in different ways toward that which they view as the Central Reality or Divine Absolute. In Paul Tillich's words one could say that all traditions are intent on that which constitutes for humankind the "Ultimate Concern"; or, equivalently, that all search for the "Ground of Being." Sharing as they do in this universal search, all religious traditions have, in their differences, equal value: none has precedence over the others or is privileged with a special divine revelation. "Ultimate Reality" refers to the fact that, in the last analysis, the Divine can neither be considered personal (as in theistic traditions) nor impersonal (as in nontheistic traditions). The notion of "myth," used earlier with reference to Christology, must also be applied to the idea of the Divine Ultimate, whichever be the form under which it comes to be known in the different religions: the Hindu Brahman, the Allah of Islam, the Yahweh of Judaism, the *Abba* of Christianity (Hick 1989, 343–61). To speak of "Our Father in heaven" is to refer in the Christian mythical key to that which is "the Real."

---

22. See Hick 1989. For a more popular exposition of the same theory, see Hick 1995.

Hick, in effect, now denies any real equivalence between human knowledge and the Divine Reality; religious language has but a perfunctory function to play. What, on the contrary, matters is that all religions — whichever be their proper idiom — have the potential to spur on people to go out of themselves in search of the Divine Reality that breeds love and compassion. Applied to God, the notion of "myth" puts the theocentric model off-center, leading the way to the "centrality of the Real." In the soteriological key, all religions have the power to transform people from their self-centeredness to "Reality-centeredness." But all religious traditions, theistic or otherwise, must be subjected to a process of "demythization"; it will then be seen that none has or can claim a privileged access to Reality.[23]

Faced with the objections leveled at the theocentric paradigm, Paul F. Knitter has reacted in a more practical and concrete way. For the theocentric model he proposes now to substitute what he calls "regnocentrism" or "soteriocentrism" (see Knitter 1986, 1987, 1990a, with responses, 124–33, 1990b). Knitter observes that all religions propose a message of salvation or human liberation. However different be the way in which such attainment is conceived and pursued, all religions share the same potential of becoming ways of salvation for their followers. The criterion according to which they need to be evaluated is the measure in which, rather than being sources of enslavement and oppression, they actually contribute to the liberation of people. In specifically Christian parlance this means that all religions are destined to be visible signs of the presence in the world of the Reign of God; all can and ought to contribute on different counts to the growth of God's Reign among persons and peoples.

More recently still, Knitter has further developed the liberation model. In a work entitled *One Earth Many Religions*, following in the footsteps of Aloysius Pieris, he unites even more closely the double concern of a liberation praxis and interreligious dialogue. The *sotèria* he advocates calls for the global responsibility and shared commitment of the different religious traditions for "eco-human well-being" (see Knitter 1995a; see also 1995b). We shall have to return to this work later, as well as to the companion volume in which Knitter exposes his present underlying Christological position (Knitter 1996).

With the regnocentric model, an eschatological perspective is being substituted for the traditional Christocentrism. The theology of religions is no longer centered on the Christ-event but on the Reign of God, which builds itself up through history and is destined to reach its fulfillment in the eschatological time. The focus is no longer on the past but on the future; God and his Reign are the goal of history toward which all religions, Christianity included, tend together as to their common destiny.

The Reign of God model is intended by Knitter as a new version of the theocentric model. It has the merit of affirming that the followers of other religious

---

23. For a critique of this new version of the pluralistic model proposed by Hick, see D'Costa 1990c. D'Costa shows that Hick's new model leads to agnosticism, all religious traditions being reduced to the same impotence in relation to truth. See also D'Costa, ed., 1990.

traditions are already members of the Reign of God in history and that together with Christians they are destined to meet in God at the end of time. However, quite apart from the fact that it continues to refer to a concept of God proper to the monotheistic religions, it does not, nor can it for traditional Christian faith, represent a paradigm shift from the Christological. To affirm that it does would be to forget that the Reign of God has broken through to history in Jesus Christ and the Christ-event; that it is through the action of the risen Christ that the members of the various religious traditions share in the Reign of God historically present; finally, that the eschatological Reign to which the members of all religious traditions are summoned together is that Reign which the Lord Jesus Christ will hand over to his Father at the end (see 1 Cor 15:28). As theocentrism and Christocentrism go hand in hand, so too seem regnocentrism and Christocentrism, as two aspects of the same reality; they do not constitute distinct paradigms. Nevertheless, in the context of dialogue the Reign of God model has the advantage of showing how Christians and the members of other religious traditions are co-pilgrims in history, heading as they do together toward God's eschatological fullness. We shall return later to this important point.

## B. Logocentrism and Pneumatocentrism

Among models which are being proposed as possible substitutes for the Christocentric model, reference must also be made to the universal active presence in the world and history of the Word of God, on the one hand, and of the Spirit of God, on the other. In these models, the Logos and the Pneuma, "the Word and the Breath" of God (see Congar 1984b), whom Saint Irenaeus saw as the "two hands of God" (Saint Irenaeus, *Contra Haereses,* IV, 7, 4; SC 100:462– 65; see Mambrino 1957) conjointly doing his work, tend to be severed from the Christ-event, to be viewed as autonomous and independent agents, transcending the historical and the particular, whose distinct action constitutes alternative economies of divine salvation.

Where the Word of God (Logos) is concerned, it is remarked that the revealed message itself witnesses to his universal action through world history; the postbiblical tradition of the early apologists does likewise, as we have had the opportunity to observe previously. The conclusion is being drawn that in every event and in all circumstances it is the Word of God who saves, not precisely the Word-of-God-made-flesh, that is, Jesus Christ.[24] "He who reveals, who saves and transforms is the Word himself" (Pieris 1994a, 60). "The Christ" is a title; a title does not save. As for Jesus, he is "he in whom Christians recognize the Word, as seen, heard and touched by human senses" (Pieris 1994a, 60). The singularity of Jesus the man consists in that "Jesus is the contradiction between

---

24. Such a tendency is found in Pieris 1993a; see also Pieris 1993b; 1994a; 1994b. In the same direction, see Duquoc 1988; also Molari 1989. See on this, Canobbio 1994b. See also Molari 1994a, 1994b.

Mammon and Yahweh..., the defense pact between the oppressed and Yahweh" (Pieris 1993b, 595). In him is revealed and embodied the contradiction which exists between God and the poor who are oppressed at the hands of the rich. Jesus thus seals God's covenant with the poor. Such "singularity" is accessible to members of other religious traditions, while the "ontological oneness" of the Word incarnate is not. In every event, the Word as such is he who saves — Jesus Christ, he in whom the Word is recognized by Christians.

We must, no doubt, affirm after John's Prologue a universal presence of the Logos before his incarnation in Jesus Christ (Jn 1:1–4). He is the "true Light that enlightens every human being" (Jn 1:9). This anticipated presence and action of the Logos do not, however, prevent the New Testament from seeing in the Word incarnate, of whom the Prologue of the Johannine Gospel also speaks (1:14), the universal Savior of humankind. Christianity has traditionally understood this to mean that the anticipated action of the Word of God is related to the event of Jesus Christ in which God's plan for humankind comes to a climax. The Word-to-be-incarnate and the Word incarnate are one indivisible reality. Jesus Christ, the incarnate Word, remains at the center of God's plan of salvation and of its unfolding in history. Logocentrism and Christocentrism are not mutually opposed; they call to each other in a unique dispensation (see Dupuis 1991b, 188–90; Gibbs 1996, 184–95, 216–28).

Similar remarks may be made where the universal economy of the Spirit of God tends to be viewed as prescinding from the historical event Jesus Christ. This time, the suggestion is made that, in order to avoid the blind alley a narrow Christocentric perspective necessarily leads to, there is need for a new theology of religions built on a pneumatocentric model.[25] Unlike the economy of the Christ-event, unavoidably limited by the particularity of history, the economy of the Spirit knows no bounds of space and time. Free of all constraints, the Spirit "blows where it wills" (see Jn 3:8). The Spirit of God has been universally present throughout human history and remains active today outside the boundaries of the Christian fold. He it is who "inspires" in people belonging to other religious traditions the obedience of saving faith, and in the traditions themselves a word spoken by God to their adherents. Could it not, in effect, be thought that, while Christians secure salvation through the economy of God's Son incarnate in Jesus Christ, others receive it through the immediate autonomous action of the Spirit of God? The "hypostatic independence," or personal distinction between God's "two hands," is warrant for the two distinct channels through which God's saving presence reaches out to people in distinct economies of salvation.[26] In short, the Holy Spirit being God's necessary "point

---

25. See, in this direction, Knitter 1991a. Knitter writes: "A pneumatological theology of religions could dislodge the Christian debate from its confining categories of 'inclusivism or exclusivism' or pluralism" (35). See also Khodr 1991.

26. Thus, commenting on Khodr 1991, Knitter writes: "The Reign of God, as it may be taking shape under the breath of the Spirit, can be seen as 'an all-comprehensive phenomenon of grace'; that is, an economy of grace genuinely different from the one made known through the Word incarnate in Jesus" (1996, 113).

of entry" into the life of human beings and of peoples, his immediate action — which bypasses the punctual event of Jesus Christ — opens up the way for a distinct model of a Christian theology of religions, one no longer Christocentric but pneumatocentric.

That the Holy Spirit is God's "point of entry" wherever and whenever God reveals and communicates himself to people is certain. Indeed, it is so in virtue of the necessary correspondence which exists between the mystery of the Triune God in itself and that of God's manifestation in the world. In all circumstances the immanent presence of the Holy Spirit is the reality of God's saving grace. However, can a model centered on the Spirit be separated from the Christological model? It does not seem to be so. One needs to affirm clearly the universal action of the Spirit throughout human history, either before or after the historical event Jesus Christ. But Christian faith has it that the action of the Spirit and that of Jesus Christ, though distinct, are nevertheless complementary and inseparable. Pneumatocentrism and Christocentrism cannot, therefore, be construed as two distinct economies of salvation, one parallel to the other. They constitute two inseparable aspects, or complementary elements, within a unique economy of salvation (Congar 1986).

The Spirit is the "point of entry" of God's self-communication to human beings; but the Spirit of God is, at one and the same time, the Spirit of Christ, communicated by him in virtue of his resurrection from the dead. The cosmic influence of the Spirit cannot be severed from the universal action of the risen Christ. His saving function consists in "centering" people, through the medium of his immanent presence, on the Christ whom God has established as the mediator and the way leading to him (see Dupuis 1991b, 152–54, and 1977, 21–31). Christ, not the Spirit, is at the center as the way to God. To say it once more: Christocentrism and pneumatology must not be set in mutual opposition as two distinct economies of salvation; they are two inseparable aspects of one and the same economy.

If, then, the Spirit is present and active in history before the event Jesus Christ, he is so in view of, and in relation to, the historical event which stands at the center of the history of salvation. The specific function of the Spirit consists in allowing persons to become sharers, whether before or after the event, of the paschal mystery of Jesus Christ's death and resurrection (see GS 22). Thus, through the power of the Spirit, the Jesus Christ–event is being actuated through all times; it is present and active in every generation. In all cases the immediate influence of the Spirit gives expression to the operative presence of God's saving action which has come to a climax in Jesus Christ.

Much is being written today — and rightly — on "Spirit-Christology."[27] Walter Kasper has judiciously noted that a "pneumatologically oriented Christology" can best show how the mystery of Jesus Christ is at once unique and universal. He writes: "A Christology in a pneumatological perspective

---

27. See references in Dupuis 1994c, 170–71. To be added: Colle 1994; Bordoni 1995.

is...what best enables us to combine the uniqueness and the universality of Jesus Christ. It can show how the Spirit who is operative in Christ in his fullness is at work in varying degrees everywhere in the history of humankind, and also how Jesus Christ is the goal and head of all humanity" (Kasper 1976, 267–68).

It must, however, be made clear that a Spirit-Christology cannot stand without a Logos-Christology. Were this to be the case, Jesus Christ would be reduced to a man *in whom* and *through whom* God is present and active (see Haight 1992; J. H. Wright 1992; Weinandy 1995). He would not be the Son of God in whom God stands revealed and communicated. To be complete, a pneumatic Christology must stress, on the one hand, the active presence of the Spirit throughout the human story of the man Jesus and, on the other, the sending of the Spirit to the world by the risen Christ. It must, likewise, show that Christocentrism and pneumatology belong together in the same economy of salvation.

## C. Beyond Western Categories

What precedes will have shown that for the most part the recent debate on the theology of religions has been dominated by three perspectives incompatible among themselves. The argument evolved around the possibility or the need for changing paradigms from ecclesiocentrism to Christocentrism, and beyond to theocentrism. Other models, as has been seen, were but substitutes for the theocentric or pluralistic paradigm. However, it is being asserted today by a sizable number of theologians that the categories within which the debate is thus being framed betray a Western way of thinking which can yield no satisfactory answer to the problem. The main misgiving is that the problematic of shifting paradigms around which the discussion revolves implies an either-or (*aut-aut*) mode of contradiction, little congenial to the Eastern frame of mind, which thinks in terms of and-and (*et-et*). The Western problematic must be abandoned if we should hope to build a theology of religions founded not on mutual contradictions and confrontation but on harmony, convergence, and unity.

The implication seems to be that the theocentric paradigm itself, in its opposition to the Christocentric, has become incongruous — in sum, that talk about uniqueness must be abandoned. Only then shall we be able to discover the specificity and singularity of each religious tradition, as well as the positive significance of the plurality of those traditions. Religious pluralism, it is being suggested, has its roots in the depth of the Divine Mystery itself and in the manifold way in which human cultures have responded to the mystery. Far from being a hindrance that must be overcome, or else a fact of life to be tolerated, religious pluralism needs to be welcomed, with thankfulness, as a sign of the superabundant riches of the Divine Mystery which overflows to humankind and as an outstanding opportunity for mutual enrichment, "cross-fertilization," and "transformation" between the traditions themselves (Panikkar 1978; Cobb 1982).

A considerable number of authors, belonging especially to the Asian continent, have denounced recently the inadequacies of the problematic at work in the Christocentric, or even in the so-called pluralistic, paradigm. Some examples may be mentioned.

Aloysius Pieris writes: "I have found myself gradually appropriating a trend in Asia, which adopts a paradigm wherein the three categories mentioned above [of exclusivism, inclusivism, and pluralism] do not make sense" (see Pieris 1993a, 130). He goes on to say that a new paradigm is required which will recognize the "magisterium of the poor" and will teach a theology of liberation that is located in the basic human community and that affirms Jesus as God's "defense pact with the oppressed" (see also Pieris 1988a, 69–86).

For Felix Wilfred, the issue of "uniqueness" betrays a Western problematic:

> The debate around the issue is mainly a debate of Western factions — the dogmatics, and the reactionary liberals who try to relativize the claim of uniqueness. This language . . . has its presuppositions and epistemological background, and it is not clear that [it] could be extrapolated to other cultural areas. . . . Seen from the Indian perspective, tradition and frame of reference, the need to use the language of uniqueness does not arise. (Wilfred 1994, 57; see also Wilfred 1991, 1993, 224–37)

A view of religious pluralism which seeks to transcend conflicting claims to uniqueness on the part of Christianity and other religious traditions finds a favorable echo in recent Asian assemblies on the theology of religions. An example is the statement issued by the Thirteenth Annual Meeting of the Indian Theological Association (28–31 December 1989), under the title "Towards an Indian Christian Theology of Religious Pluralism."[28] The statement points to the limitations of the categories currently used in the debate on the theology of religions; these betray "theoretical approaches to the faith of other people," issuing "from a monoreligiocultural society and a mere academic and speculative point of view" (4). "We would rather approach the issue from a different perspective," that, namely, of a live encounter and dialogue. In such an approach, Christ remains for us "constitutionally the Way to the Father" (28). However, while we continue to approach the problem "from our own faith perspective" (9), we also "understand the purpose and meaning of the wonderful religious variety around us and its role and function in the attainment of salvation" (8). There follows an important statement:

> The religions of the world are expressions of the human openness to God. They are signs of God's presence in the world. Every religion is unique and through this uniqueness, religions enrich one another. In their specificity, they manifest different faces of the supreme Mystery which is never exhausted. In their diversity, they enable us to experience the richness of the

---

28. See Pathil, ed., 1991, 338–49. For a critical study of the statement, see Dupuis 1992c. Some works that take the same direction are: Puthiadam 1980, 1981; Amaladoss 1990, 1992, 1994; Rayan 1990.

One more profoundly. When religions encounter one another in dialogue, they build up a community in which differences become complementarities and divergences are changed into pointers to communion. (32; Pathil, ed., 1991, 347–48)

An ecumenical consultation held at Baar, Switzerland, in January 1990 speaks a similar language. Its final statement has the following to say on the plurality of religious traditions:

> We see the plurality of religious traditions as both a result of the manifold ways in which God has related to peoples and nations as well as a manifestation of the richness and diversity of humankind. We affirm that God has been present in their seeking and finding, that where there is truth and wisdom in their teachings, and love and holiness in their living, this like any wisdom, insight, knowledge, understanding, love and holiness that is found among us is the gift of the Holy Spirit. We also affirm that God is with them as they struggle, along with us, for justice and liberation.
>
> This conviction that God as Creator of all is present and active in the plurality of religions makes it inconceivable to us that God's saving activity could be confined to any continent, culture, type, or groups of peoples. A refusal to take seriously the many and diverse religious testimonies to be found among the nations and peoples of the whole world amounts to disowning the biblical testimony to God as Creator of all things and Father of humankind.[29]

Several voices in the Western world have responded positively to the new perspective advocated by Eastern theologians. M. Barnes argues that an escape must be negotiated from the rigid patterning of the threefold paradigm. The answer is not to be found in shifting from a Christocentric to a theocentric position. It lies beyond pluralism. Under the influence of interfaith encounter, the theology of religions is in fact shifting "from a pluralist to a post-modern mode" (Barnes 1994; see also Barnes 1989). This requires that theologians learn to be "systematic without being systemic." While holding on to their religious identity, they must engage in a "theology *of* dialogue," not merely build a "theology *for* dialogue" (Tracy 1990; see also Swidler et al. 1990). "The first demand of such a theology is to accept that all dialogue is established precisely in asymmetry, that is to say by the difference between the partners. Community or communality has yet to be established: this is the phenomenon which governs all faith encounter" (Barnes 1994, 273).

Other authors concur in saying that the dilemma between inclusivism and pluralism, or, equivalently, between Christocentrism and theocentrism, must be transcended. J. A. DiNoia notes that both inclusivists and pluralists minimize the differences of the others and hence the import of the interreligious conversation (DiNoia 1992, 127). The order of the day is not a "theology

---

29. See text in *Current Dialogue* 19 (January 1991) 48.

*for* dialogue" but a "theology *in* dialogue"(DiNoia 1992, 111). On the one hand, interreligious conversations must not "serve the purpose of disclosing Christian-like virtualities" in the doctrines of other religious communities, as the inclusivist thesis is prone to do, but should "entertain such doctrines as self-consistent alternative teachings about that upon which human life should be focused" (DiNoia 1992, 138). On the other hand, the pluralistic accounts of religious predications also appear to "attenuate the significance of religious differences in the course of trying to account for them" (DiNoia 1992, 152). The way out of the "current impasse" in the theology of religions consists in recognizing squarely that distinct religious communities actually propose distinct aims for human life, as well as the legitimacy of such claims from the point of view of their faith (DiNoia 1992, 163–65). That Christian theology interprets other aims in terms of its own understanding is normal and legitimate; but so too is the reverse. Nor must one interpretation become exclusivist of the other at any time.

Other voices could be heard in addition to these, not all of which are concordant among themselves. However, before concluding, let us note that in spite of diverse views regarding the way ahead beyond the contradictory inclusivist and pluralistic claims,[30] a certain consensus seems to be emerging as to the need to avoid on all sides absolutism as well as relativism. Plurality needs to be taken seriously and to be welcomed, not merely as a matter of fact but in principle. Its place in God's plan of salvation for humankind must be stressed. It must also be shown that commitment to one's faith is compatible with openness to that of others; that the affirmation of one's religious identity does not build on confrontation with other identities. A theology of religions must in the last analysis be a theology of religious pluralism. What model offers itself for such a theology to follow in order that it be truly Christian — this remains to be shown.

---

30. Transcending the dilemma between inclusivism and pluralism, or equivalently between Christocentrism and theocentrism, is visualized differently by different authors. S. M. Heim refutes the pluralist thesis on its own ground, exposing the covert "religious particularity" which it unwittingly betrays. Another kind of pluralism is needed which would recognize — as acceptable, even from the point of view of Christian faith — the different ultimate destinies proposed by the various religious traditions to their adherents. See Heim 1995. This thesis will be discussed hereafter. See also Heim 1985. S. M. Ogden (1992) holds that no one historical event can be considered as constitutive of salvation. The way beyond inclusivism and pluralism consists in recognizing the "love of God" as the Ultimate Reality constitutive of salvation, response to which is possible in different ways. See the discussion in Heim 1995, 237–42.

# Part II

# One God—One Christ—Convergent Paths

THE FIRST PART of this work ended up stressing the need, with a view to building up a Christian theology of religious pluralism, for a living interaction between the Christian and other interpretations of religious faith: a theology *of* dialogue or *in* dialogue. While Christian theology has the right and duty of interpreting reality—including the religious aims proposed by other traditions—from the vantage point of Christian faith, other religious communities enjoy the same right and have the same duty. None of these interpretations can ever claim to exclude the others; any attempt to become exclusive at any time would mean the refusal of true plurality and, consequently, of a genuine theology of pluralism. A theology of religious pluralism finds its place beyond the inclusivist and the "pluralist" paradigms conceived as mutually contradictory and excluding each other.

To recognize the legitimacy, on the part of other religious traditions, of proposing aims for human existence which differ even substantially from those proposed by Christian faith does not, however, prejudge the possibility of integrating such aims into the Christian view of a destiny appointed for human beings by God. It is one thing to recognize the legitimacy for distinct traditions of proposing different aims to human liberation;[1] it is another to assert that these different aims are compatible with the Christian view of the human destiny.[2] Such God-willed diversity of human destinies cannot be affirmed a priori; it requires close examination and a confrontation of the divergent claims, to which attention will have to be given later. Let it suffice to say here that openness does not gain from syncretism any more than commitment to faith does from isolation.

However this may be, a Christian theology of religious pluralism must be one based on the interaction of the Christian faith with the other living faiths, and in that sense it must be an interfaith theology. The general introduction to this work has stressed the need for a Christian theology to be "confessional" in the best sense of the term: that is, truly committed to one faith while at the same

---

1. As is stressed by Barnes 1989.
2. Heim (1995) suggests that a diversity of ultimate destinies is in fact in keeping with the Christian understanding of God's design for human beings.

time holding a global vision and being open to all human experiences of the Divine. It rejected as representing a theological contradiction every attempt at building a "world theology" or a "universal theology" in the sense of a super-theology of the religious history of humankind, as a common venture engaged in by the various religious traditions and binding on all of them.[3] More acceptable would be the idea of a "comparative theology," correctly understood.[4] The term would not betoken a falling back, from a theological elaboration founded in a faith-commitment, to the alleged neutrality of a comparative science of religions; it would on the contrary place in full relief the interfaith interaction that a Christian theology of religious pluralism postulates and on which it ought to be built, from within the distinctiveness of the Christian faith-commitment.

Some light may, perhaps, be thrown on the case of a Christian perspective for a theology of religious pluralism by considering the dialogical situation which in the field of Christian ecumenism exists in the mutual relationships between the various Christian churches and ecclesial communities. The recognition of the ecclesiality of non-Catholic Christian churches has opened the way for a new problematic in the search for Christian unity: unity through the "return" to the one true Church of Christ of all individual Christians and Christian bodies who had gone astray or found themselves separated from that true Church has given way to a "global ecumenism" in search of the "recomposition" of organic unity between churches and ecclesial communities in which the mystery of the one Church willed by Christ is present and operative in different ways and degrees. In a somewhat similar manner, though *mutatis mutandis,* the "ecumenical ecumenism" of the relationship between Christianity and the other religions can no longer be viewed in terms of contradiction and opposition between realization here and stepping-stones there, much less between absoluteness on one side and only potentialities on the other. It must henceforth be thought of in terms of the relational interdependence, within the organic whole of universal reality, between diverse modalities of encounter of the human existence with the Divine Mystery. The Catholic Church will, no doubt, continue to hold that the mystery of the Church willed by Jesus Christ "subsists" (*subsistit*) in it while it "exists" to a lesser extent in other churches. Similarly, the Christian faith will continue to imply a "fullness" of divine manifestation and revelation in Jesus Christ not realized elsewhere with the same fullness of sacramentality. Nevertheless, in both cases, the realities involved will have to be viewed as mutually related and interdependent, constituting together the complete whole of human-divine relationships. It is in this direction that a Christian theology of religious pluralism must seek to overcome the dilemma between Christocentric inclusivism and theocentric pluralism, understood as contradictory paradigms.

As we search for a model that would overcome this dilemma, we need to remember, as has been pointed out earlier, that the dichotomy referred to has

---

3. See the introduction, pp. 5–6, above, on Smith 1981.
4. The idea of a "comparative theology" is put forward in Ward 1994. See also Clooney 1995.

been gratuitously and wrongly construed. Models which in themselves ought to have been seen as mutually complementary have in effect been made into contradictory paradigms. We have noted above that in Christian theology, Christocentrism, if correctly understood, must not be viewed as contradicting theocentrism; on the contrary, it presupposes it and calls for it. The same is true where the various binaries discussed above are concerned: Christocentrism and soteriocentrism, Christocentrism and regnocentrism, Christology and Jesuology, Christology and Logology, Christology and pneumatology — all are and ought to be viewed as interrelated aspects and complementary elements of the indivisible, whole, and entire reality; they can only wrongly be set in opposition to one another.

The integral model we are searching for in view of a Christian interpretation of religious pluralism can best be expressed in terms of a *Trinitarian Christology*.[5] Such a Christology will place in full relief the interpersonal relationships between Jesus and the God whom he calls Father, on the one side, and the Spirit whom he will send, on the other. These relationships are intrinsic to the mystery of Jesus' person and of his work. Christology ought to be imbued with these intra-Trinitarian relationships in any situation; but this requirement obtains all the more in the context of a theology of religious pluralism. Indeed, it may be thought that the mistaken development of Christocentrism into a closed and restrictive paradigm, incompatible with theocentrism, when it occurred, was due to a past failure to pay adequate attention to the interpersonal dimension of Christology. As I have written elsewhere:

> Christology has often sinned by impersonalism. To remedy such a shortcoming, the personal and trinitarian dimension of the mystery must be present everywhere. A Christology of the God-man is an abstraction; the only Christology that is real is that of the Son-of-God-made-man-in-history. The personal intra-trinitarian relations must, therefore, be shown to inform every aspect of the Christological mystery. (Dupuis 1994c, 36)

What, then, would be the implications of a Trinitarian Christology for a theology of religious pluralism? On the side of God, it will have to be shown clearly that Jesus Christ must never be thought to substitute for the Father. As Jesus himself was entirely "God-centered," so must the faith-interpretation of Jesus-the-Christ proposed by the Christian kerygma remain at all times. The Gospel according to John called Jesus "the way, and the truth, and the life" (Jn 14:6) — never the goal or the end; the same Gospel made it clear that the goal of human existence — and of history — is the unfathomable mystery of God, whom no human being has ever seen but who has been "made known" to us by his incarnate Son (Jn 1:18). The unique closeness that exists between God and Jesus by virtue of the mystery of the incarnation may never be forgotten, but neither can the unbridgeable distance that remains between the Father

---

5. Several authors have written recently in the same direction. See, in particular, D'Costa 1990a, 1992; Schwöbel 1990; Williams 1990; Wong 1994; Lai 1994.

and Jesus in his human existence. In this sense, the theocentric paradigm advocated by pluralists in the present debate on the theology of religions points to an essential aspect of the mystery, which, however, it conceives one-sidedly and which should be stated more accurately: God, and God alone, is the absolute mystery and as such is at the source, at the heart and at the center, of all reality. While it is true that Jesus the man is uniquely the Son of God, it is equally true that God stands beyond Jesus. When he is said to be at the center of the Christian mystery, this is not to be understood in an absolute sense but in the order of the economy of God's freely entertained dealings with humankind in history.

The pneumatic aspect of the mystery of Jesus Christ is in need of being stressed, even more than the Godward orientation of his person and work. A Trinitarian Christology will have to express clearly Jesus' relatedness to the Spirit. This too is a requirement to which Christology ought to be attentive in every circumstance, and I have pointed out elsewhere the urgent need — in the Western tradition — of building a *Spirit-Christology* that would show the influence of the Holy Spirit throughout the earthly life of Jesus, from his conception through the power of the Spirit (see Lk 1:35) to his resurrection at the hands of God by the power of the same Spirit (see Rom 8:11) (Dupuis 1994c, 169). Such a Christology would, furthermore, "extend beyond the resurrection to illustrate the relationship between the action of the risen Lord and the economy of the Holy Spirit" (Dupuis 1994c, 169). While an "integral Christology" requires this Spirit-component in all situations, the same requirement appears once again especially binding in view of building up a Christian theology of religious pluralism. In such a theology the universal presence and action of the Spirit in human history and in the world will not only need to be affirmed; they will also have to serve as guiding threads and principles.

We have recalled earlier that Christology and pneumatology cannot be construed into two distinct and separate economies of God's personal dealings with humankind; nevertheless, the "hypostatic distinction" between the Word and the Spirit as well as the specific influence of each in the Trinitarian rhythm of all divine-human relationships, individual and collective, serve as a hermeneutical key for the real differentiation and plurality obtaining in the concrete realization of the divine-human relationships in diverse situations and circumstances. The Christian message and tradition imply such a differentiation when they hold together two affirmations which at first sight would appear contradictory: that, namely, on the one hand, before the resurrection "the Spirit had not been given as yet, because Jesus was not yet glorified" (Jn 7:39), and, on the other, "[w]ithout doubt, the Holy Spirit was at work in the world before Christ was glorified" (AG 4). While it is true that "[t]he Spirit is the Spirit of Christ and where the Spirit of Christ is, there is Christ" (see Cobb 1995,560), the reverse is also true: Christology does not exist without pneumatology; it cannot be allowed to develop into a "Christomonism."

The distinct stress laid by the Eastern and the Western traditions on the role of the Spirit, on the one side, and on the centrality of the Christ-event, on the other, is well known and need not be elaborated here.[6] The reproach of "Christomonism" — which has often been brought by Eastern Christianity against the Western tradition — has had the happy result of developing in recent Western theology a new insistence on the role of the Spirit in the divine economy of salvation (see, e.g., Congar 1983, 1986), not least in Christology proper. This is the origin of the Spirit-Christology which today is developing fast in the West.[7] A well-poised theological account of the relationship between Christology and pneumatology must combine various elements: on the one hand, the roles of both the Son and the Spirit may not be confused but must remain distinct, even as their hypostatic identities are distinct; on the other hand, there exists between both a "relationship of order" which, without implying any subordinationism of one to the other, translates into the divine economy the order of eternal relations of hypostatic origination in the intrinsic mystery of the Godhead.

Thus, while the functions of the Son and the Spirit need to be kept clearly distinct, there is between them no dichotomy but total complementarity in one divine economy of salvation: only the Son became man, but the fruit of his redemptive incarnation is the outpouring of the Spirit symbolized at Pentecost. The Christ-event is at the center of the historical unfolding of the divine economy, but the punctual event of Jesus Christ is actuated and becomes operative throughout time and space in the work of the Spirit. Several Eastern theologians have laid stress recently on the interrelatedness and complementarity of the "missions" of the Son and of the Spirit in the one divine economy. Thus, N. A. Nissiotis wrote:

> The salvific event of Christ and Pentecost can neither be confused nor separated. They imply one another; they are as it were the two hands of the Father's love. Their respective roles are equally essential and necessary, and, on this very account distinct.... Pentecost does not inaugurate a religion of the Spirit; it initiates the dispensation throughout space and time of the fruits of the incarnation.[8]

It follows that a theology of religious pluralism elaborated on the foundation of the Trinitarian economy will have to combine and to hold in constructive tension the central character of the punctual historical event of Jesus Christ and the universal action and dynamic influence of the Spirit of God. It will thus be able to account for God's self-manifestation and self-gift in human cultures and religious traditions outside the orbit of influence of the Christian message without, for that matter, construing Christology and pneumatology into two distinct economies of divine-human relationships for Christians and for the members of other traditions, respectively.

---

6. For a brief account, see Dupuis 1977. See also Colle 1994, 8–33.
7. See the works mentioned in Dupuis 1994c, 170–71, n. 1. To be added: Colle 1994; Bordoni 1995.
8. Nissiotis 1963, quote on 93; 1967. In the same direction: Zizioulas 1985, 123–42.

What terminology will best be adapted to refer to a Christian theology of religious pluralism built upon the hermeneutical key of Trinitarian Christology and Spirit-Christology? In the bid, referred to above, to transcend the dilemma between Christocentrism and theocentrism conceived as contradictory paradigms, M. Barnes views a Trinity-centered theology and, in particular, a Spirit-Christology as the way open, beyond a particularist exclusivism, toward a pluralistic inclusivism capable of accounting within the Christian faith-perspective for a plurality of religions not only in fact but also de jure. He writes, for instance:

> A Spirit-centered theory of the interpenetration of traditions can help us to solve the loyalty–openness dilemma. Instead of asking how other religions are related to Christ, and raising the inevitable conundrum of his "latent," "unknown" or "hidden" presence, we look to the way the Spirit of Christ is active, in all religions, in *revealing* the mystery of Christ — the mystery of what Christ is doing in the world.[9]

Whatever terminology may be used to refer to the Trinitarian pneumato-Christological model, what matters is that it be capable of leading the Christian faith-commitment beyond the suspicion of claiming for itself, if not exclusivity, at least the obligatory reference binding on all people vis-à-vis the divine-human relationships. The historical centrality of the Christ-event cannot be allowed to obscure the Trinitarian rhythm of the divine economy, with its distinct and correlated functions.

What has been said so far will help to clarify the meaning of the terms in which the general title of the second part of this work has been stated: "One God — One Christ — Convergent Paths."

*One God* refers to the Absolute Mystery of the Divine as it has been made known to us in Jesus Christ: Father, Son, and Holy Spirit, in the interpersonal communion of the Godhead. The mystery of the Trinity implies at once unity and plurality, personal identity in interpersonal relationships. It discloses to us the immanent life of the Godhead as consisting of total mutual exchange and sharing — in sum, that God is absolute communion of love. The diversity and communion of persons in the Godhead offer the proper key — to be explored hereafter — for understanding the multiplicity of interrelated divine self-manifestations in the world and in history.

*One Christ* refers to Jesus-the-Christ of the Christian kerygma, clearly witnessed to in the Acts of the Apostles (Acts 2:36), not to a mythical Christ divested of the earthly Jesus, nor to a pre-Easter Jesus apart from the Christhood of his risen state. The Christ-event is being taken in its integrity, without any reductionism in either of two directions, toward a mere Logology, on the

---

9. See Barnes 1989, 135–59; quote on 143. Also DiNoia 1993, 109–54. D'Costa (1990a) writes similarly: "The doctrine of the Holy Spirit allows us theologically to relate the particularity of the Christ event to the entire history of humankind" (19); and again: "The Trinitarian Christology proposed has the virtue . . . of reconciling both the exclusivist emphasis on the particularity of Christ and the pluralist emphasis on God's universal activity in history" (26).

one hand, or toward a mere Jesuology, on the other. In the Jesus Christ–event, God's self-communication to humankind and history is decisively disclosed and manifested. This basic factor of Christian self-understanding is the foundation for the centrality of the Christ-event in the history of the divine-human relations.

But far from reducing the orbit of God's dealings with humankind, the Christocentricity of Christian faith causes believers to expand their vision to the full dimensions of human history and the cosmos. For while the Christ-event plays an irreplaceable function in God's design for humankind, it can never be taken in isolation but must always be viewed within the manifold modality of the divine self-disclosure and manifestation through the Word and the Spirit. The expansiveness of God's inner life overflowing outside the Godhead is, in the last analysis, the root-cause for the existence in human history of *convergent paths,* leading to a unique common goal: the absolute mystery of the Godhead which draws all paths to itself, even as in the first place it launches them into existence. How such a convergence may be conceived and how it may be realized will have to be asked later.

The title of the second part of the work is therefore designed to express as clearly as possible the model which seems to recommend itself for a Christian theology of religious pluralism. It will be helpful to show how the model visualized here distinguishes itself from those which, as the foregoing account of the recent debate has shown, need to be transcended in one or another direction. On the one hand, the simpler expression "One God — Convergent Paths" would recall the theocentric or pluralistic paradigm advocated by John Hick and others likeminded, according to which the various traditions revolve around the one Divine Absolute, of which they constitute diverse manifestations and equivalent human approaches — with no singular, specific role to be assigned to the person and event of Jesus Christ. On the other hand, the equally simple title "One God — One Christ" would easily lean toward the opposite side of the spectrum, to evoke the exclusivistic paradigm which recognizes the possibility of salvation only in the explicit Christian faith in Jesus Christ.[10] The first paradigm, as we have observed, led to a pluralism without order or unity; the other, to a monolithic exclusivism. "One God — One Christ — Convergent Paths," on the contrary, evokes at once the foundational character of the Christ-event as the guarantee of God's manifold way of self-manifestation, self-revelation, and self-gift to humankind in a multifaceted yet organically structured economy of salvation through which the diverse paths tend toward a mutual convergence in the absolute Divine Mystery which constitutes the common final end of them all.[11]

---

10. See, for instance, Clarke and Winter, eds., 1992, where the title (*One God, One Lord*) corresponds exactly to the position described here.

11. The title of S. J. Samartha's book *One Christ — Many Religions: Toward a Revised Christology* (1991) seems misleading, for it hardly corresponds to the new stance proposed by the author in this work. Samartha develops here a revisionist Christology along the lines of J. Hick's "demythologized" or "demetaphorized" Christ. "One God — Many Religions" would seem to correspond better to the new position of the author. See in this connection Knitter 1991b, and the critical studies on Samartha's work mentioned in chapter 7, n. 16, above.

The task ahead consists in showing how the affirmation of Christian identity is compatible with a genuine recognition of the identity of other faith-communities as representing in their own right distinct facets of the self-disclosure of the Absolute Mystery in a single, unitary, but complex and articulated divine economy.

## Eight

# History and Covenants: One and Many

CENTRAL TO THE CHRISTIAN VIEW of God's dealings with humankind is a historical perspective capable of accounting at once for a variety of divine self-manifestations and the unity of a divinely preordained plan. God's design for humankind is neither monolithic nor piecemeal, but singular and complex at the same time. It is one and universal, in view of God's will to communicate with the entire human race, irrespective of historical situations and circumstances in which men and women find themselves; and it is manifold and variegated in the concrete forms which the divine unitary design takes on in historical unfolding.

While the concept of salvation history is of relatively recent coinage, a salvation-history perspective is deeply rooted in biblical revelation, ancient as well as new. It is no exaggeration to state that salvation history operates as an important hermeneutical key for Christianity's self-understanding as well as the way in which it situates itself in relation to world history in general and to the history of religion in particular.

This is not to say that the concept of salvation history is exempt of theological problems. However, the intention of this chapter is not to propose a full-fledged theology of history. Its limited intent is to show that the Christian view of salvation history allows for a more positive appraisal of other religious traditions than has often been held.

Often enough these traditions have at best been considered as provisional "stepping-stones" for "things to come," useful, no doubt, yet transitory by nature and in any event rendered obsolete and abrogated by the advent of the reality to which they pointed or of which they were "partial anticipations." What is being asked here is whether the salvation-history theological framework makes it possible to attribute to the religious traditions of the world more than a transient character — with whatever saving significance for their members — in God's design for humankind: that is, whether it allows us to assign to them a lasting role and a specific meaning in the overall mystery of the divine-human relationships.

More clearly still: Is the relationship between God's dealings with the "gentiles" through history, on the one side, and his self-manifestation in biblical history, on the other, one of mere substitution of reality for shadow? Or, on the contrary, is there, in the divine plan, a mutual interaction between distinct elements which, while not representing the reality in the same way, belong nevertheless inseparably together? Can salvation history not only accommodate the idea of a propaedeutic value for world religions — granting them merely, and hypothetically, some saving significance under clearly set conditions — but also make allowance for an abiding meaning of the plurality of world religious traditions in accordance with God's universal saving design for humankind?

These and other questions will be answered by having recourse to Trinitarian Christology, which we have suggested constitutes a possible integral model for a Christian theology of religious pluralism. Where the dimensions of salvation history are concerned, the Trinitarian model will make it possible to lay stress on the universal presence and activity of the Word of God and of the Spirit of God throughout human history as the mediums of God's personal dealings with human beings independently of their concrete situation in history. The relatedness of the action of the Word and of the Spirit to the punctual historical event of Jesus Christ will not thereby be overlooked or forgotten. The Trinitarian Christological model will likewise throw light on the meaning of the various covenants which according to the Christian tradition God has struck with humankind at various times; these need to be viewed as distinct but — equally importantly — as interrelated and inseparable. In the light of the model proposed here, a positive answer will be suggested to the vexing question of the abiding efficacy of "pre-Christian" covenants. Such lasting efficacy, as will be seen, is due to the interrelatedness in the overall history of God's dealings with humankind between the distinct modalities of God's self-communication to persons and peoples.

Admittedly, the salvation-history framework, which in a Christian self-understanding constitutes an important hermeneutical key, is not shared by other religious traditions. We should note from the outset the role it plays in the Judeo-Christian interpretation of the world and reality.

It is customary to distinguish three models of history, called "cyclic" or "circular," "linear," and "spiral."[1] Mircea Eliade has shown that the cyclic model is characteristic of "primitive cultures" (Eliade 1959). The concept is based on the recurring rhythm of the cosmos and of living things. For archaic human beings, Eliade writes: "Everything begins over again at its commencement every instant. The past is but a prefiguration of the future. No event is irreversible and no transformation is final. In a certain sense, it is even possible that nothing new happens in the world, for everything is but the repetition of the same primordial archetype" (Eliade 1959, 88–89).

For all its sophistication, the Greek philosophy and culture encountered by the Judeo-Christian tradition continued to preserve, as I have indicated (Dupuis 1991b, 114–15), many features of the cyclic model of history. Here we find the root of the pessimistic view of Greek philosophy with regard to all that is bodily and temporal. Where the individual is concerned, life is doomed to

---

1. I have accounted briefly for these three models in Dupuis 1991b, 114–16.

death; salvation can only consist in escaping from the prison of the body. As for collective history, it repeats itself in such wise that there is really nothing new under the sun. For all its distinctive characteristics, the "spiral" model of Hindu and other Eastern philosophies shares in the aimless return of its cyclic counterpart (Samartha 1959). Though composed of various periods, cycles follow each other without a definite direction. As each cycle yields to the next in indefinite succession — hence the so-called spiral movement — history does not seem ever to have a definite aim, a final goal.

The linear model of history contrasts sharply with both the cyclic and the spiral. Here history is conceived as creative advance toward a goal. It is moving toward fulfillment; it has a destiny. Here time is structured, dynamic, and forward-moving; events have meaning and value in themselves, in relation to each other, and, above all, in relation to the final goal of the totality of history. Eliade observes that the Hebrews were the first in the history of humanity to conceive and develop a linear model of history. The stories of Abraham and Moses are symptomatic in this regard. It is faith in God's personal intervention in the human affairs of a people that invests events with historical content and meaning, henceforth impressing on them purpose and direction. Faith in divine intervention meant freedom from the natural law of cyclic movement; it called for response and commitment to a divine call. As Israel's history unfolded, the Hebrew prophets perceived the will and the action of God in the vicissitudes of the nation: its victories and defeats, its joys and sufferings. Yahweh chastised the people for not keeping faith with him, but he also promised and worked deliverance, thus orienting the people toward the future and placing them in a trajectory of hope. As Eliade notes: "Under the 'pressure of history' and supported by the prophetic and messianic experience, a new interpretation of historical events dawns among the children of Israel" (Eliade 1959, 106). A more recent author further explains the significance of linear history as follows:

> Historical events began to be regarded as Yahweh's active presence. History appeared as a series of theophanies. Each theophany, each event, had its intrinsic value because it was Yahweh's intervention with a view to the people's final salvation. It was also a place of personal encounter between Yahweh and the people. In this way Israel came to face history instead of escaping from it and abolishing it through the possibility of repetitions without end. They accepted history "as the terrifying dialogue with Yahweh" (M. Eliade), and regarded every moment as decisive. (Rayan 1983, 10)

Eliade further shows how the Hebrew discovery of time as a one-way reality and of history as the theophany of God was taken up and further developed by early and traditional Christianity, even if, as we have observed earlier, the theological term "salvation history" is of recent coinage. The early Christian writers opposed the cyclic concept of history and traced a straight line for humanity's course from its inception to its final destiny. As Eliade sums up: "Christianity is the 'religion' of modern man and historical man, of the man who simultaneously discovered personal freedom and continuous time (in place of cyclic time)" (Eliade 1959, 161).

The central place which the discovery of linear time, made up of divine interventions and human freedom, occupied in the worldview of Judaism and Christianity can easily be substantiated. It served as a hermeneutical key for events, aspects of life, and celebration. History was made up of past, present, and future, all with a direction assigned by a provident God. The past lived on in the present, which it had brought forth; in the present the future already existed in hope. Worship has a threefold dimension: the celebration of God's being-with-his-people today, as "memorial" of an enduring prototypical event of salvation, and as the proleptic anticipation of the end-time of final fulfillment. In both cases, a prototypical event of salvation stood at the midpoint of the linear trajectory, impressing on the entire process, in both past and future, direction and movement. With a difference, however.

For the Hebrew people, the prototype standing at the midpoint of history was the Exodus-event in its complex reality, comprising God's revelation to Moses, the liberation from Egypt, the crossing of the desert, the covenant and the Law on Mount Sinai; for the Apostolic Church and the Christian movement, the Christ-event, with Jesus' tragic human career culminating in the showdown of his death and the vindication of his resurrection, became the focusing point, informing the entire trajectory in both directions, past and present, with new meaning and direction. History came to be seen as possessed of unique meaningfulness because at its heart stood the incomparable, prototypical event of Jesus Christ.

I have drawn attention elsewhere to the midpoint position which the Christ-event occupied in the early Christian worldview and to the vast difference this change introduced in the Hebrew historical perspective and religious psychology (see Dupuis 1991b, 116–18). Oscar Cullmann has shown admirably the newness of the Christian worldview, the unique place which the Christ-event occupied in it as the key to history, and the relation to it of all stages of salvation history, past, present, and future (see Cullmann 1952, 1967). There is no need to repeat except to point out once more the originality of the Judeo-Christian concept in contrast with the Greek and the Eastern and to reassert, in disagreement with suggestions made to the contrary,[2] the apparently indispensable role

---

2. See S. Rayan, who writes: "It...remains yet to be shown conclusively in the West or in the East, in ancient traditions or in more modern positions, that the Christian faith and its (theological) interpretation are necessarily bound up with any one conception of history, which is to say with any particular culture and experience of reality" (Rayan, 1983, 21). In an article entitled "A Matter of Theological Education: Some Critical Reflections on the Suitability of 'Salvation History' as a Theological Model for India," F. Wilfred doubts the validity for theology done in a pluralistic context of the concept of salvation history and of the linear concept of time which it entails. He writes: "By its inner logic, presuppositions and approach [salvation history as theological model] has rendered us incapable of integrating in a holistic vision the religious experiences of humanity.... The theological model of salvation history has created a chasm between the history of Israel and the history of the rest of humanity on the assumption that the operations of God are confined within the parameters of a particular history" (Wilfred 1984, 554).

which the linear concept of history plays in Christian self-understanding, especially in bestowing on the Christ-event the density of meaning which the Christian faith attributes to it as God's personal breaking into human history (Dupuis 1991b, 115).

Theologians writing in recent years on salvation history are substantially agreed on the exemplary meaning of the historical event of Jesus Christ, even while they hold distinct views regarding the articulation between what has already happened through the paschal mystery of Christ's death and resurrection and what remains to be accomplished in his second coming by way of fulfillment. The abiding tension between the "already" and the "not-yet" is visualized differently by various authors. While Cullmann quite clearly places the focal point in what has already been achieved through the death/resurrection of Jesus Christ, others, like Jürgen Moltmann, definitely lay the stress on the "eschatological remainder": the paschal mystery of Jesus Christ is the proleptic model for what remains in store until the eschatological fulfillment (Moltmann 1990). In a somewhat similar fashion, Wolfhart Pannenberg looks at the resurrection of Jesus Christ as the proleptic presence and anticipation in the glorified humanity of the eschatological transformation of world and history which is to take place at the eschaton (see Pannenberg 1969, 1991–94, vol. 2).

Such divergences will bear on questions under discussion in this chapter, in particular where the question of the abiding value of the Mosaic covenant will be raised and the context of the Jewish-Christian dialogue evoked. The case of the Mosaic covenant will stand out as exemplary, and the question will be asked whether lasting, theological value should not be affirmed as well of other covenants struck by God with peoples throughout the historical unfolding of his saving design for humankind. The chapter falls therefore into two main parts, dealing respectively with the extent in human history of God's saving plan and of the various covenants of which it is made up.

## I. God and Peoples in History

### A. Salvation History, Particular or Universal?

The first question to be asked is that of the extension of salvation history in the overall history of the world. Does salvation history coincide with profane history? And if they differ, must it nevertheless be said that salvation history is coextensive with the history of the world: that is, beginning with creation itself and extending to the end of the world?

Every attempt to situate the beginning of salvation history in the vocation of Abraham, and thereby to reduce its extension to "sacred history" (*histoire sainte*) initiated there, must be firmly resisted. Such an attempt, wherever it is made, always betrays an a priori tendency to discount any personal engagement of God with humankind prior to and outside the tradition that issued from the call of the biblical patriarch. It calls to mind Karl Barth's professed a priori certitude that "other religions are just unbelief" (quoted by D'Costa 1992, 141). Religion and religions being but vain human attempts at self-justification, it seemed logically to follow that salvation history could only start with the story of Abraham, the "father of all who believe" (Rom 4:11), and had to be confined to the spiritual descent originated from his faith.[3]

More recent theologians have proposed answers to the question of the extent of salvation history which, while being less negative, remain nevertheless unduly restrictive. Jean Daniélou is a case in point. We have heard him earlier affirming that the "cosmic religion" that precedes the Abrahamic covenant already belongs to the "concrete historical supernatural order" — not, however, in the sense that God would have manifested himself personally through it, for under the cosmic covenant God's self-revelation is only through the cosmos. Rather than being part, therefore, of salvation history, "cosmic religion" constitutes a "prehistory" of salvation based upon a natural knowledge which God gives through the order of creation (see above, pp. 31–34, above). Daniélou concluded logically that the religious traditions of humankind outside the Abrahamic-Mosaic stream of tradition could only represent natural human aspirations toward God, without involving any personal engagement of God toward peoples (see above, pp. 134–137; see Daniélou 1962b). By contrast with cosmic revelation,

> the substance of the Christian revelation is not in a knowledge of God's existence (which other religions have as well), but in the perception of his activity on the scene of time, his effective interventions in the world of human history. From the creation to the resurrection, by way of the choosing of our father Abraham, the Christian revelation is a sacred history, the chronicle of the wonderful works of God, a documentary narrative: alone among sacred books, the Christian's Bible is not a collection of doctrine but a story. (Daniélou 1958, 111)

The opinion of Hans Urs von Balthasar approaches very closely that of Daniélou. Only the Hebrew and the Christian religions, originated from the faith of Abraham, qualify for being called "religions of revelation" and, hence, belong to salvation history proper; for only they represent God's search for and turning to humankind in word and history, in love and self-gift (see pp. 140–143, above, and Balthasar 1964). Other religions are natural. Of natural religions Balthasar writes:

> Undoubtedly, the inherent dynamics of natural religion is to thrust from the bounds of the finite and the relativities of this world toward the absolute, and therefore one could say that religion is an escape from the world. Moreover, these forms of religion, all conceivable manifestations of the absolute in the finite, all approaches of the divine towards us, are merely

---

3. For the position of K. Barth on the extent of salvation history, see Barth 1970, 280–361.

temporary and symbolic. They point beyond themselves, because they are ultimately contradictory embodiments, *avatars,* of the infinite in the finite; all the more so when, through reflection, a religion has advanced from primitive mythical polytheism to a philosophical-mystical phase.

...[On] the other hand, [in] the Old Testament...it is no longer the man Abraham who starts out in search of God. It is God himself who speaks to man, who leads him, not to religious meditation on the absolute but to a way of simple obedience to the divine will. (Balthasar 1978, 7–8)

Against all reduction of the history of salvation-revelation to the Hebrew-Christian tradition it must be affirmed that salvation history coincides and is coextensive with the history of the world. It consists of human and world history itself, seen with the eyes of faith as a "dialogue of salvation" freely initiated by God with humankind from creation itself and pursued through the centuries until the fulfillment of God's Reign in the eschaton.[4]

Likewise to be rejected is the idea of a "prehistory" in which salvation and revelation would be disjoined from each other. Such a concept has given rise to two different views of salvation history, both unduly truncated. According to the first, prehistory implied some (natural) "revelation" of God through created reality but remained impervious to salvation; for the other, divine "salvation" was possible for individual persons during the prehistory of salvation, but divine self-manifestation or (supernatural) "revelation" remained hidden in the future until God's revelation to Abraham.

The difference in "formal object" notwithstanding, it must be affirmed that world history and salvation history coincide and are coextensive; moreover, since human history is, from the start and throughout, the story of God-with-humankind, it must likewise be said to imply from the outset and at all times both divine self-revelation and salvation (see Rahner 1966d, 1988b). The New Testament's unambiguous assertion that God "wills (*thelei*) all human beings to be saved" (1 Tim 2:4) supposes no less. Nor can God's universal saving will be reduced to some kind of conditional and ineffective wish or velleity; this divine will is subject to no condition other than each human person's free acceptance of God's gratuitous self-manifestation and self-bestowal. It is part of Christian tradition to assert that humankind has been at once and from the outset created and called by God to share in the divine life. The only concrete order in which humankind ever found itself in history is the "supernatural order" implying God's offer of self-communication through grace. Such an order of world and history always brings with it — in one way or another — a divine self-manifestation and the offer of salvation.

With good reason, therefore, Karl Rahner bases his affirmation of the universality of divine revelation and salvation on a philosophico-theological

---

4. This is the theme of the encyclical letter *Ecclesiam Suam* (1964) of Pope Paul VI. Text in AAS 56 (1964) 609–59.

analysis of the existential condition of historical humanity, which he calls the
"supernatural existential." He writes:

> Every man exists not only in an existential situation to which belongs the
> obligation of striving towards a supernatural goal of direct union with the
> absolute God in a direct vision, but he exists also in a situation which
> presents the genuine subjective possibility of reaching this goal by ac-
> cepting God's self-communication in grace and in glory. Because of God's
> universal saving purpose, the offer and possibility of salvation extend as
> far as extends the history of human freedom.... Furthermore, this offer
> of the supernatural reality of the person enabling one to move by one's
> spiritual and personal dynamism towards the God of the supernatural be-
> atifying life ... must be thought of as a change in the structure of human
> consciousness.... The horizon within which the normal, empirically expe-
> rienced realities of consciousness are grasped, and the ultimate orientation
> of consciousness are changed by grace.[5]

The "supernatural existential" consists, therefore, of a transformation of the
concrete "horizon of consciousness" by which, in the present grace-filled order
of creation, every human person is oriented toward a self-revelation and self-
gift of God to be freely and gratefully received. From the universality of this
concrete human condition it follows that there is one history of salvation, revelation, and offer of faith which coexists with world history. Rahner calls this
universal or general history of salvation-revelation "transcendental," as distinct
from the special history of salvation-revelation which he calls "categorical."[6]

The "transcendental" history of salvation, universally present, needs to take
concrete form in the history of people. It does so in the history of religion in
general and in particular in the historical religions of humankind. These may
serve as historical mediations for the transcendental, supernatural experience of
God as divine revelation and thus "stir up" salvation in a positive manner. They
may, therefore, be considered as willed by God insofar as they give concrete
shape to the divine offer of grace universally present and operative throughout
human history. In the religious traditions of the world, God's offer to people in
revelation-salvation takes on an initial concrete shape.

From general salvation history, special history of salvation needs, therefore,
to be distinguished. Here God's revelation-salvation becomes "thematized" and
categorical. An explicit awareness and recognition of historical happenings as
constituting divine interventions come here into play; this is guaranteed by a
"word of God" which narrates and interprets such happenings as representing
salvific events.

---

5. See Rahner 1966d, 103. More systematically, on "the history of salvation and revelation," see
Rahner 1978, pt. 5, pp. 138–75.

6. Karl Rahner's distinction between a general and a special history of salvation has been elaborated
upon in Darlap 1965a, 3–156, esp. 91–156. See also Darlap 1965b, 219–25; 1970.

The concept of special salvation history is, of course, clearly realized in the Jewish and the Christian traditions through the prophetic interpretation of historical events; it need not, however, a priori be reduced to those traditions. For other religious traditions too may contain prophetic words interpreting historical happenings as divine interventions in the history of peoples. In fact, the Judeo-Christian revelation itself testifies to saving acts performed by God on behalf of other peoples. Such historically tangible saving deeds of God are analogous to those performed by God in favor of Israel according to the Old Testament record — notwithstanding the fact that the Christian tradition ascribes to the history of Israel the singular distinctive character of being the immediate historical prologue to God's decisive saving intervention in the Christ-event. God's *mirabilia* on behalf of peoples are not limited to Israel; they may even extend to Israel's foes.

## B. General and Special

The last observation suggests caution against drawing too neat a line of demarcation between what theology is wont to consider as belonging to general salvation history, on the one hand, and to special salvation history, on the other. After having placed the Christ-event at the midpoint of the linear unfolding of the history of salvation, thereby distinguishing between a "pre-Christian" and a "post-Christian" regime of salvation, theologians usually introduce in addition a second caesura, to the effect that whatever lies before and outside the "sacred history" of Israel belongs to general salvation while the immediate and express historical preparation for the Christ-event in Israel inaugurates special salvation history, leading into the Christ-event and, after it, into what has been called — perhaps inappropriately — the "time of the Church."

According to this double schema, "pre-Christian" and "post-Christian" do not coincide entirely with "general" and "special." The reason is that, in Christian self-understanding, there exists between Israel's history and the Christ-event a unique, indissoluble bond, by virtue of which both the "First" and the "Second" Testaments must be interpreted in function of each other. No similar bond exists between the history of other peoples and the event Jesus Christ. In such a scheme, then, Israel is historically pre-Christian but belongs to special salvation history, while other peoples' history is pre-Christian and belongs to salvation history only generally.[7] Such a scheme readily leads to the idea that in the advent of special salvation history and, specifically, of the Christ-event, pre-Christian religions belonging to the "general" history of salvation are run past and ousted, having become obsolete or even "illegitimate" (see Darlap 1965a, 143–47).

The question must, however, be asked whether the history of other peoples cannot play for them, in the order of salvation, a role "analogous" to that

---

7. See, among others, Cullmann 1952; Schlette 1966; Küng 1967; Thils 1966.

played for the Hebrew people by the history of Israel, as comprising historical events whose divine salvific significance is guaranteed by a prophetic word. Does not "special" salvation history extend beyond the boundaries of the Hebrew-Christian tradition? Does not, perhaps, the story of each people contain traces of God's loving deeds on its behalf, constituting it as one of God's peoples and enlivening it with God's own life?

The Asian bishops were thinking along those lines when they saw the great religious traditions of their peoples as "significant and positive elements in the economy of God's design of salvation" and asked: "How then [could] we not acknowledge that God has drawn our peoples to himself through them?"[8] And the Theological Advisory Commission of the Federation of Asian Bishops' Conferences (FABC) commented on this statement, saying:

> Its experience of the other religions has led the Church in Asia to [a] positive appreciation of their role in the divine economy of salvation. This appreciation is based on the fruits of the Spirit perceived in the lives of the other religions' believers: a sense of the sacred, a commitment to the pursuit of fullness, a thirst for self-realization, a taste for prayer and commitment, a desire for renunciation, a struggle for justice, an urge to basic human goodness, an involvement in service, a total surrender of the self to God, and an attachment to the transcendent in their symbols, rituals and life itself, though human weakness and sin are not absent.
>
> The positive appreciation is further rooted in the conviction of faith that God's plan of salvation for humanity is one and reaches out to all peoples: it is the Kingdom of God through which he seeks to reconcile all things with himself in Jesus Christ... (2, 2–2, 3). (Theological Advisory Commission [FABC] 1987, no. 48, p. 7)

This would mean that the presence even today of the fruits of the Spirit of God in the religious traditions of peoples testifies to God's saving and revealing action among them through their history. The question will therefore have to be asked whether traces of a "word of God" spoken to peoples through their history are not found in the "sacred books" of their religious traditions and how these would relate, from a Christian standpoint, to the "Hebrew" Testament, on the one hand, and to the Christian, on the other. To this question we shall return in the next chapter.

## C. *Trinitarian and Christic*

Meanwhile, the proposed model of a Trinitarian Christology must be applied to God's saving self-manifestation in salvation-revelation in the history of the nations. In the Christian understanding of God's single but organic design of salvation for humankind and of its historical unfolding, the Christ-event is the

8. "Evangelization in Modern Day Asia," statement of the First Plenary Assembly of the FABC, Taipei (1974), nos. 14–15, in Rosales and Arévalo, eds., 1992, 14.

midpoint and the focal point (see Dupuis 1991b, 116–18). It is the pivot upon which the entire history of the dialogue between God and humanity turns, the principle of intelligibility of the divine plan concretized in the history of the world. It influences the entire process of history by way of a final cause, that is, as the end or the goal drawing to itself the entire evolutionary process: both pre-Christian and post-Christian history are being drawn by the Christ-Omega to himself (see Rahner 1966b).

Yet the Christocentrism of salvation history must not be construed into a Christomonism. The centrality of the Christ-event does not obscure but rather supposes, calls forth, and enhances the universal operative presence of the "Word of God" and of the "Spirit of God" through salvation history and, specifically, in the religious traditions of humankind. Not without reason did Pope John Paul II affirm in the encyclical letter *Dominum et Vivificantem* (1986) on the Holy Spirit that in every historical situation, before the Christ-event as well as after it and outside the Christian dispensation, "grace bears within itself both a Christological aspect and a pneumatological one" (no. 53).[9]

In the first part of this work we have drawn attention to the fact that, according to the Old Testament biblical tradition, the divine Wisdom-Word and the divine Spirit serve as "medium" for God's personal interventions in history, both in Israel and outside (see pp. 41–45, above). The "literary personification" of those divine "attributes" enhances the personal commitment of God to peoples which the revealed word intends to convey. The New Testament will later unfold the true personhood of the media of God's involvement in human history by progressively delving into the personal character of the Son (Logos-Wisdom) and of the Spirit. Henceforth, then, the Logos-Wisdom and the Spirit, who had already been operative in pre-Christian history, will be understood, by retrojection, as two distinct persons within the mystery of the Triune God: the Son who became incarnate in Jesus Christ, on the one hand, and the Spirit of Christ, on the other. The two divine persons had been present and operative in the pre-Christian dispensation without being formally recognized as persons.

The universal active presence of the divine Logos before the Christ-event is clearly affirmed by the Prologue of the Gospel according to Saint John: he was "the true light that enlightens every human being by coming into the world" (Jn 1:9). This Johannine affirmation has been dwelt upon and developed by Saint Irenaeus, for whom not only the Old Testament theophanies but all divine manifestations throughout salvation history, from creation onwards, were Logophanies (see pp. 60–66, above). The universal revelatory function of the Logos made him present to humankind throughout history from the beginning, even though that operative presence was to culminate in his coming in the flesh in Jesus Christ.

Where the Spirit is concerned, we have observed earlier that his universal presence and operation throughout human history in religious traditions as well

---

9. Text in AAS 78 (1986) 809–900.

as in individual persons have been stressed by the recent Church magisterium, notably in the teaching of Pope John Paul II (see pp. 173–177). The most explicit texts are found in the encyclical *Redemptoris Missio* (1990), from which one passage at least bears repeating, both for its clarity and insistence:

> The Spirit's ... presence and activity are universal, limited neither by space nor time. ... The Spirit ... is at the very source of the human person's existential and religious questioning which is occasioned not only by contingent situations but by the very structure of its being. The Spirit's presence and activity affect not only individuals but also society and history, peoples, cultures and religions. (no. 28)[10]

Thus, throughout human history, in the religious traditions as well as in individual persons, the Spirit has been present and active. The same conviction is echoed in the statement of the ecumenical consultation held at Baar (1990), also referred to above: "We affirm univocally that the Holy Spirit has been at work in the life and traditions of peoples of living faiths."[11]

What remains to be shown is how the universal action of the Word and the Spirit in the extrabiblical history of salvation combines theologically in one economy of salvation with the punctual historical event of Jesus Christ: that is, how, rather than being mutually exclusive, Christocentrism, on the one hand, and Logocentrism and pneumatology, on the other, call for each other. At this point, Rahner shows that the Christ-event is the goal or end of the anticipated action of the Logos-to-become-man and of the Spirit's universal working in the world. For this reason, the Logos's preincarnational action is oriented toward the Christ-event, even as the Spirit can rightly be called the "Spirit of Christ" from the beginning of salvation history. Thus, Rahner writes concerning the Spirit: "Since the universal efficacy of the Spirit is directed from the very beginning to the zenith of its historical mediation, which is the Christ-event (or in other words the final cause of the mediation of the Spirit to the world), it can be truly said that the Spirit is everywhere and from the very beginning the Spirit of Jesus Christ, the incarnate divine Logos" (Rahner 1981b, 46).

This amounts to saying that between the various components of the Trinitarian Christological salvation economy there exists a relationship of mutual conditioning by virtue of which no singular aspect can either be stressed to the detriment of the others or, on the contrary, played down in favor of them. The Christ-event never stands in isolation from the working of the Logos and the Spirit, any more than these ever operate without relation to it.

In the last analysis, we are here encountering the mystery of time and eternity as it affects God's dealings with humankind in history. While for our human discursive knowledge the historical unfolding of salvation is by necessity made up of beginning-center-end, or of past-present-future, in God's eternal awareness

---

10. Text in AAS 83 (1991) 249–340.
11. Text in *Current Dialogue* 19 (January 1991) 50.

and knowledge, all is continuous and coexisting, co-simultaneous, and interrelated (see Mouroux 1961; Jüngel 1983). Jesus Christ is the high point of God's personal involvement with humankind, eternally "preestablished," and, hence, in history the Christ-event is the punctual "moment" in which God "becomes" God-of-peoples-in-a-fully-human-way. But since the incarnation of the Logos is eternally present in God's intention, its realization in time informs the age-long story of God's dealings with humankind.[12]

The action of the Logos, the work of the Spirit, and the Christ-event are thus inseparable aspects of a unique economy of salvation. That according to the Pauline tradition human beings are "created in Jesus Christ" (Eph 2:10), to whom primacy belongs in the order of both creation and re-creation (Col 1:15–20), does not detract from, but postulates, the anticipated action of the Word-to-become-flesh (Jn 1:9) and the universal working of the Spirit: "Without doubt, the Holy Spirit was at work in the world before Christ was glorified," says Vatican II (AG 4). A theology of religious plurality ought to express clearly the universal presence of the Word and the Spirit in the extrabiblical traditions.[13]

## II. Covenanted Peoples of God

### A. One or Several Covenants?

Throughout the history of salvation the dealings of God with humankind are punctuated in the biblical account with covenants. The significance of the biblical term "covenant" (*berith*), when it refers to God's way of dealing with human beings, need not be explained here (see, e.g., Behm 1966; Mendenhall and Herion, eds., 1992). Let it suffice to recall that a covenant represents always a gratuitous initiative on the part of God, who freely enters into a personal relationship with human beings without any merit on their part. It is a pact of friendship unilaterally initiated by the divine partner which, however, calls on the human partner for commitment and fidelity in response to God's gracious love.

---

12. J. Mouroux writes the following: "In its radical newness the incarnation is the *foundation at once of what precedes and what follows*. The incarnation is indissolubly fulfillment, realization, and anticipation. But since this represents the irruption of the Eternal in time, and the rooting of the incarnate Word in the *Verbum incarnandum*, there is, in the midst of the new, of the irreducible, of the unique, in the very midst of the *ephapax, absolute continuity* of plan, of causality, of exemplarity, of finality between what precedes and what follows the incarnation. Because an eternal design is being realized which bears entirely on the mystery of Christ, there follows that, when the *Verbum incarnandum* is accomplished in the Word incarnate, eternity enfolds time more closely than ever into its own unity" (1962, 160).

13. AG 4 refers in a note to Saint Leo the Great, who wrote: "When the Holy Spirit filled the Lord's disciples on the day of Pentecost, this was not the first exercise of his role but an extension of his bounty because the patriarchs, prophets, priests, and *all the holy persons of the previous ages* were nourished by the same sanctifying Spirit..., although the measure of the gifts was not the same" (*Sermo* 76; PL 54:405–6; emphasis added). The reference to "all the holy persons of the previous ages" (*omnesque sancti qui prioribus fuere temporibus*) seems clearly intended to extend beyond the boundaries of the biblical religious tradition.

Regarding the use in the biblical tradition of the covenant terminology with reference to God's dealings with human beings, we note the following: the term "covenant" is not found in the Genesis narrative of creation (Gen 1–2); however, outside of Genesis there are hints that creation is viewed as a cosmic covenant (see Jer 33:20–26) (see Murray 1992). In Genesis the term "covenant" refers for the first time to the "everlasting covenant" struck by God with Noah (Gen 9:1–17); it recurs in the Abraham cycle (Gen 17:1–14). The covenant with Moses is dealt with at length in Ex 19–24. A "new covenant" is foretold by Jer 31:31–34, which the Christian New Testament will see realized in the Christ-event, more precisely in the paschal mystery of the death and resurrection of Jesus (Mt 26:28–29; Lk 22:20; 1 Cor 11:25).

Quite apart from the use of covenant terminology, interpreters are not agreed regarding the number of covenants that need to be distinguished in the biblical account and on the relationship existing between them. Are there distinct covenants, or do all those mentioned in the Bible refer to a unique cosmic covenant, established by God with humankind in creation?

According to some advocates of the one-covenant thesis, in creation God has struck one universal covenant with humankind in Adam.[14] The significance of the covenant with Abraham and Moses consists in that "the Hebrew religion is the sign of the universal covenant. It is not in itself the covenant, but brings the covenant to self-awareness.... The covenant with Moses is not new (*originario*). The original covenant is that with Adam, of which the covenant with Moses is the sign" (Rizzi 1992, 4).

As for Christianity, it radicalizes the Hebrew conviction regarding the universal covenant in Adam: "Jesus is not the founder of Christianity, but rather the 're-founder' of the universal covenant." He reconstitutes it and restores its actuality. Christianity has thus the role of a sign, analogous to that of Israel: it is "the sign that in Christ the universal covenant has been reestablished" (Rizzi 1992, 5). Judaism and Christianity are "two signs of one identical reality" (Rizzi 1992, 6).

This interpretation has the merit of showing the continuity which exists, in the history of salvation, from creation through Israel to Jesus Christ — though, in the process, it overlooks the covenant with Noah. However, the continuity is construed here as identity, whereby the true discontinuity between the various stages of salvation history and the thorough newness brought about by the Christ-event are overlooked and forgotten. The process of salvation history is reduced to the restoration of an original state, thereby being deprived of any dynamic movement. Israel and Christianity stand to each other as two "analogous" signs of God's universal covenant with humankind in Adam.

The question of the number of covenants — one or many — is asked principally in the context of the recent Jewish-Christian dialogue (see, among others, Pawlikowski 1980). It asks whether a mutual understanding is possible between

---

14. A case in point is Rizzi 1992.

Jews and Christians as regards the relationship between the Abrahamic-Mosaic covenant, on the one side, and the covenant in Jesus Christ, on the other. Are they one or two? And in what sense? We shall return to this question hereafter to ask whether Christian theology can attribute lasting validity, even today, to the Jewish covenant and, if this be the case, how to conceive theologically the relation between the "old" covenant and the "new" of which the Christian tradition speaks.

Meanwhile, we may recall the Christian tradition which distinguishes four covenants struck by God with humankind. Two celebrated texts, one from Saint Irenaeus's *Adversus Haereses* (III, 11, 8), the other from the *Demonstration of Aphraates* (11, 11), have already been referred to above and need not be quoted again (see p. 33, above, and the accompanying footnote). However, they do raise questions of interpretation with regard to the covenant with Noah, which need to be answered: What is the theological significance of that covenant? Is it understood to continue after the coming of the Christ-event?

To start with the second question: the context in which Irenaeus distinguishes four covenants gives us a clue for an answer. Irenaeus finds a symbolic meaning in the number four and enumerates accordingly distinct, fourfold realities as follows:

> Such as was the course followed by the Son of God, so was also the form of the living creatures; and such as was the form of the living creatures, so was also the character of the Gospel. For the living creatures are quatriform, and the Gospel is quatriform, as is also the course followed by the Lord. (*Adv. Haer.*, III, 11, 8; SC 211:169; ANF 1:429)

That is to say, the Word of God has spoken in four different ways: to the patriarchs before Moses through his divinity; under the Law through a priestly ministerial function; thereafter, in his incarnation through his humanity; finally, as risen Lord, through the gift of the Spirit. Similarly, the Gospel is fourfold: Matthew, Luke, Mark, and John. Four are likewise the covenants struck by God with humankind: in Adam, in Noah, in Abraham and Moses, and in Jesus Christ. Nothing in the succession of the four divine covenants suggests that one abolishes those preceding, anymore than one form of the fourfold Gospel substitutes for the other forms. All covenants hold together even as do the four Gospels.[15]

The covenants stand to each other as so many ways of divine engagement with humankind through the Logos. They are Logophanies through which the divine Logos "rehearses," as it were, his breaking into human history through

---

15. The abiding character of the four covenants is less clear in the text of the *Demonstration of Aphraates* (11, 11) (*Patrologia Syriaca* I, 1, pp. 498–502), referred to chap. 1, n. 5, above. Here the text speaks of transformation or "complete change" of one covenant to another. Thereafter, the text continues to say with regard to the covenant with Moses and that in Jesus Christ: "God gave the Law with its observances and commandments to Moses. When the Jews failed to keep it, he abolished this Law and its commandments and promised a new covenant, different from the old, although he himself is of course the same God who decreed them both. Here is the new covenant which he promised to give" (see *Patrologia Syriaca* I, 1).

the incarnation in Jesus Christ. As such, they relate to each other, not as the old that has become obsolete in the advent of the new that substitutes for it, but as the germ that already contains in promise the fullness of the plant which will issue from it.[16]

Let us turn to the significance of the covenant with Noah: there is no question here — as has too often been supposed — of a mere manifestation of God through the phenomena of nature and the constancy of their recurrence. In the case of the covenant in creation, the Genesis account testifies to God's familiarity with Adam and thus to a personal relationship between the Creator and humankind. Similarly, the intimate relationship between God and Noah is stressed in the inspired text (Gen 9:1–17),[17] as well as the universality of the "everlasting covenant" (Gen 9:16) struck by God with Noah and his descendants; these elements in the story symbolize a personal commitment of God toward the nations, that is, the universality of the divine intervention in the history of peoples, of which the religious traditions of humanity are the privileged testimonies. This true character of the Noah covenant has been well expressed by a recent author who wrote:

> The covenant with Noah constitutes the lasting foundation for the salvation of every human person. Its true significance is falsified if one sees in it — as a long tradition in Catholic theology has done — nothing beyond the setting up of a "natural" religion having nothing to do yet with a supernatural revelation. The particular characteristics recorded in the Scripture concerning the Noah covenant make it clear that there is question here of a true event of salvation, marked by grace.... The entirety of the covenant with Noah appears as an outline of the covenants with Abraham and Moses.... Israel and the nations have thus a common base: they are in a state of covenantship with the true God and under the same salvific will of that one God. (Stoeckle 1967, 1053–54)

The covenant with Noah thus takes on a far-reaching significance for a theology of the religious traditions of peoples belonging to the "extrabiblical" tradition.[18] They too are — and remain, as will be seen hereafter — in a state of covenantship with God. They too are covenant peoples and deserve to be called "peoples of God" (see Bühlmann 1982b). The one God is the God of all peoples. In this sense Deutero-Isaiah could rightly see in God's oath to Noah (and in him to all peoples) an image of his enduring love toward Israel:

> As I swore that the waters of Noah
> should no more go over the earth,

---

16. Irenaeus's theology of the "ages of the world" does not exactly correspond to that of the "four covenants." The "four ages" of the world are distinguished as follows: the first age in Adam and Noah; the second in Abraham and Moses; the third in Jesus Christ; the fourth in the return of the Lord. See Luneau 1964, 96–101.

17. See the description of Noah's righteousness before God, p. 35, above.

18. "Extrabiblical" is used rather than "prebiblical" to include the religious traditions outside the Jewish-Christian tradition, not only before but also after the Christ-event.

> so I have sworn that I will not be angry with you
> and will not rebuke you.
> For the mountains may depart
> and the hills be removed,
> but my steadfast love shall not depart from you
> and my covenant of peace shall not be removed.
>
> (Is 54:9–10)

## B. *The Trinitarian Rhythm of the Divine Covenants*

Earlier we quoted Gregory of Nazianzus stating the economy of the progressive revelation to humanity of the mystery of God's inner life.[19] This economy, it may be argued theologically, was in the order of things, insofar as between the order of origins in the divine communion of Father-Son-Spirit and that of their self-communication to humankind in history, there is a necessary correspondence and correlation: the "economic" Trinity prolongs the "immanent" Trinity, allowing it to overflow beyond itself (Rahner 1980). Or, conversely, the immanent Trinity is the a priori presupposition of a Trinitarian rhythm of divine self-communication: from the Father, through the Son, in the Spirit. Put more simply: God being a triune communion of persons cannot but communicate himself in this threefold way — God gives himself such as he is!

The Trinitarian rhythm of God's self-revelation described by Gregory of Nazianzus informs the stages of the unfolding of God's self-communication in salvation history. The same threefold feature is, moreover, present and operative at every stage of its development. This amounts to saying that every divine covenant with humankind necessarily involves the active presence of God, of his Word, and of his Spirit. The Bible already testifies to this threefold rhythm where creation is concerned: God created through his Word (Gen 1:3; Jdt 16:13–14; see Pss 33:9; 148:5; Jn 1:1–3) in the Spirit (Gen 1:2). The same threefold rhythm informs the history of Israel, based on God's covenant with Abraham and Moses. Suffice it to recall in general that God's interventions in favor of his people are accomplished through his Word; as for the Spirit of God, it takes possession of individual persons to make them the instruments of God's action and of the prophets to empower them to speak God's word (see pp. 41–45, above).

Such clear indications are not found in the Hebrew Bible where the covenant with Noah is concerned. Nevertheless, from the standpoint of Christian theology, the covenant with Noah too — and the extrabiblical religious traditions — cannot but bear an imprint of the economic Trinity. As the tradition has persistently sought and found "traces" of the Trinity (*vestigia Trinitatis*) in creation and, more especially, in the spiritual activity of the human being, so must we search for and discover similar traces, outside the biblical tradition,

---

19. See pp. 41–42, above, the quotation from the *Fifth Theological Discourse* 26; PG 36:161–64.

in the religious life of individual persons and the religious traditions to which they belong. They too in some way echo in history the Father's eternal uttering of the Word and issuing of the Spirit. If it is true that God conceives and wills all things that are in the act by which the Father utters the Word and breathes forth the Spirit, the same applies a fortiori and of necessity to God's covenantal relationship with peoples in history. That in the only existing world order God has freely chosen to communicate personally with human beings means that all — in whichever historical situation, including extrabiblical traditions — are included and, as it were, caught up into the Trinitarian rhythm of God's self-communication. From the vantage point of Christian theology, God's cosmic covenant with humankind in Noah cannot but be marked, as is the entire history of salvation, with a Trinitarian rhythm.

Salvation history is in its entirety the history of the origin of all things from God through his Word in the Spirit and of their return to God through the Word in the Spirit. It is "the *prosodos* and the *exodos* of divinized creation," by which the created world is assumed into the mystery of "the expansion and the concentration of the Trinity, from the *Deus absconditus* through the Word to the Spirit, and from the Spirit through the only-begotten to the Unborn" (Monchanin 1953, 76). Saint Paul affirmed no less when he wrote: "For us there is one God, the Father, from whom are all things and for whom we exist, and one Lord, Jesus Christ, through whom are all things and through whom we exist" (1 Cor 8:6) — a statement which the Letter to the Ephesians completes by adding that our journey from and to the Father through Jesus Christ is accomplished in the Spirit (see Eph 2:18).

Admittedly, the above considerations are significant only within a Christian perspective; indeed, they are based on a "high" Trinitarian theology, though not without foundation in the Christian scripture. But from the standpoint of Christian understanding, they have the merit of throwing light on the fact that, individually as well as collectively, extrabiblical religious humanity is assumed by God into fellowship with himself in grace and hope.

### C. "The Covenant Never Revoked"

The above subheading is borrowed from the title of a book by Norbert Lohfink (Lohfink 1991), itself inspired by Pope John Paul II, when in a speech delivered at Mainz, Germany (1980), he made reference to "the people of God of the Old Covenant, which has never been revoked (cf. Rom 11:29)."[20] The question under consideration here is whether with the coming of the Christ-event and of the "new covenant" established in him, the "old covenant" with Israel has become obsolete and been abrogated, as the Christian tradition has often affirmed. How is, then, the relationship between the Mosaic and the Christic covenants to be understood? What light does the Hebrew-Christian dialogue

---

20. Text in AAS 73 (1981) 80.

throw on the subject? More particularly: Is God's grace-filled relation today with persons belonging to the Jewish people to be assigned to an enduring efficacy of the Mosaic covenant *or* to the new covenant established in Jesus Christ? Does the latter simply substitute for the former, henceforth rendered inoperative? Israel and Christianity obviously represent a singular case, owing to the unique relationship existing between the two religions; however, as will be suggested below, it may furnish, *mutatis mutandis,* an emblematic model for the relationship between Christianity and the other religions.

The question of the perduring value of the Mosaic covenant is fraught with contentious historical evidence. The Council of Florence's Decree for the Copts (1442) has been quoted earlier, in connection with the axiom "Outside the Church no salvation" (see pp. 95–96, above), and passing reference has been made to the same council (see chap. 6, n. 1, above) regarding the abrogation of the Mosaic covenant by the Christ-event. This second text needs to be quoted here and correctly understood:

> [The Holy Roman Church] firmly believes, professes and teaches that the legal [statutes] of the Old Testament or Mosaic Law, divided into ceremonies, holy sacrifices and sacraments, were instituted to signify something to come, and therefore, although in that age they were fitting for divine worship, they have ceased with the advent of our Lord Jesus Christ, whom they signified. [With him] the sacraments of the New Testament have begun. Whoever puts one's hope in these legal [statutes] even after the passion [of Christ] and submits to them as though faith in Christ was unable to save without them, sins mortally. Yet [the Church] does not deny that between the passion of Christ and the promulgation of the Gospel (*usque ad promulgatum evangelium*) they could be observed, provided one in no way believed that they were necessary for salvation. But she asserts that after the promulgation of the Gospel (*post promulgatum evangelium*) they cannot be observed without the loss of eternal salvation. Therefore, she denounces as foreign to the faith of Christ all those who after that time observe circumcision, the Sabbath and other laws, and she asserts that they can in no way be sharers of eternal salvation, unless they sometime turn away from their errors. She therefore commands to all who glory themselves in the Christian name that they must, sometime or other, give up circumcision fully, either before or after baptism, because, whether one puts one's hope in it or not, it cannot in any way be observed without the loss of eternal salvation. (DS 1348; ND 1003)

The first part of the document states unambiguously that "with the advent of our Lord Jesus Christ" the institutions derived from the old covenant have lost their efficacy. As signifying things to come, they were by nature transitory and, with the coming of the things signified, have become ineffective. The second part deals with concrete attitudes to be observed by converts from Judaism with regard to Mosaic observances. After the event of salvation in Christ, faith can no longer be placed in such observances. However, until the "promulgation of the Gospel," though rendered ineffective for salvation, they could still be observed; on the contrary, after the Gospel has been promulgated, they may no longer be observed in any way.

The "promulgation of the Gospel" referred to in this text raises many questions: When can it be said that the Gospel has been promulgated, and where? How does this promulgation take place, and under what conditions does it become effective? Must the promulgation of the Gospel be viewed as having been realized for entire nations or groups of people at a certain point in time? Or must the case of each person be considered individually, regarding where one stands in relation to the Gospel? We have referred earlier — with approval — to Karl Rahner's opinion according to which the promulgation of the Gospel can only be said to have reached individual persons when through the offer of divine faith the question has been existentially raised for each one's personal conscience of having to respond positively to God's offer of salvation in Jesus Christ.[21]

What needs, however, to retain our attention here is the council's firm affirmation that the mystery of salvation accomplished in the death of Jesus Christ has abolished the Mosaic covenant and the divine institutions that accompanied it. Certainly, the rejection of Jesus by "a part" of the Jewish people did raise in Saint Paul's mind crucial problems with which he kept wrestling, especially in the Letter to the Romans (chaps. 9–11). Never did Paul seem to find a decisive answer to these questions. The solution he proposed, according to which, the time of its infidelity notwithstanding, Israel would be saved at the end (Rom 11:25–26), seems a somewhat resigned, if not desperate, suggestion. However, one conviction remained firmly engraved in Paul's mind: Israel was and continued to be God's people; the covenant with Moses endured unremittingly thanks to God's steadfast love and faithfulness. So, to the question, "Has God rejected his people?" he answered emphatically: "By no means" (Rom 11:1); and he explained: "The gifts and the call of God are irrevocable" (Rom 11:29). Israel did remain the people to whom "belong the sonship, the glory, the covenants, the giving of the Law, the worship, and the promises" (Rom 9:4).

Saint Paul's questions continue to beset Christian theologians and Jewish scholars even today, in the context of the Jewish-Christian theological dialogue.[22] In the book referred to above (Lohfink 1991), Lohfink has freshly

---

21. See p. 145, above. See Rahner 1966a, 115–34; 1973, 47–49. Rahner writes: "For [the individual] the non-Christian religion which one has inherited from past history, and which has been handed down to one in one's own sphere of life, is only abrogated as the authentic way of salvation at that point at which the message of Christ so penetrates into one's own conscience as an individual that it is only through a grave personal fault that one can any longer reject it as the way of salvation offered by God and as the fulfillment that goes beyond anything that one's former religion had to offer" (1973, 48).

22. See, among others, Pawlikowski 1980, 1982; Monti 1984; Mussner 1984; Remaud 1983; Thoma 1980; Kaufmann 1988; Braybrooke 1990; Christiansen 1995; Holwerla 1995; see also Gasperis 1993; Goedt 1992.

reconsidered the biblical evidence on the relationship between the old and the new covenants, especially in Jer 31:31–34, Rom 9–11, and 2 Cor 3:14. The author shows that the New Testament data are more refined and more subtle than has been supposed by the long-standing Christian tradition about "two covenants," of which the "new" in Jesus Christ has abolished the "old" in Moses. His main findings are as follows.

The "old covenant" which is spoken of in 2 Cor 3:14 (the only instance of the term in the New Testament) is not understood by Paul as abolished by the new but as "unveiled" by it. The apparent suppression of the "first" covenant by the "second" (in the Letter to the Hebrews) can "hyperbolically" be understood likewise. The new covenant is no other than the first; it unveils the first by spreading abroad the splendor of the Lord which the first contained without revealing it fully. The "new covenant" of Jer 31:31–34 contains no reference to two distinct covenants but to one, which God will reestablish in spite of the people's infidelity. Israel understood the restoration of the covenant to have happened with the people's return from the Exile and the rebuilding of the temple; on its side, the New Testament — for instance, Lk 22:20 — testifies to an eschatological, Christological interpretation of the same, by the Christian community. Similarly, for Paul in Rom 9–11, the "new covenant," sign of God's fidelity to his people of which Jeremiah spoke, takes on an eschatological and Christological form which, however, does not prevent its previous realization in Israel's return from the exile.

Toward the end of his analysis, Lohfink observes: "There is a definite sense ... in which the 'old covenant' of 2 Cor 3 is the 'new covenant' of the book of Jeremiah. We could say then that the contemporary Jewish people lives in the 'old covenant' though it is at the same time now a 'new covenant'" (Lohfink 1991, 77).

The fact is that in Jesus Christ the one covenant "has concentrated itself to eschatological radicalness" and so finds in him its "ultimate and most profound sense" (Lohfink 1991, 81). And this leads the author to conclude: "I lean therefore to a 'one covenant' theory which however embraces Jews and Christians, whatever their differences in the one covenant, and that means Jews and Christians of today" (Lohfink 1991, 84). But he adds: "From early Christian times Jews and Christians have been on two ways. Because the two ways run their course within the one covenant which makes God's salvation present in the world, I think that one must speak of a 'twofold way of salvation'" (Lohfink 1991, 84).

One will not speak, therefore, of one way which existed before Christ in Israel but which in the course of time bifurcated into two parallel ways, the one destined by God for the Jewish people, the other ordained by him for the gentiles in Jesus Christ, the "Messiah of pagans." Rather, one will speak, quite appositely, of "one covenant, and two ways of salvation for Jews and Christians." At stake in the choice of the second formulation is the dynamic of the history of salvation, as Paul conceived it in Romans. God has but one plan of salvation, which embraces the Jews and the nations alike, even though that one plan unfolds "dramatically" in two times; in spite of their present historical divergence, these two times will eventually converge — even if only in the eschaton (Lohfink 1991, 84–85).

To Lohfink's formula of "one covenant, two ways of salvation for Jews and Christians," D'Costa prefers that of "one normative covenant, within which there are many further legitimate covenants" (D'Costa 1990b, 452). The formula is partly designed with an eye to extending the question beyond the case of Jewish-Christian relations to that of other religions to which it also applies, though "analogically." D'Costa insists on holding distinct and complementary covenants, for fear that "one covenant" talk may seem to absorb all other ways into one considered as normative, as the Christian "fulfillment theory" has done to other religious traditions. However this may be, the continued legitimacy of God's covenantal relationship with Israel cannot be denied. Yet from a Christian standpoint, God's enduring covenant with the Jews can only be seen — as is the entire history of salvation — from a Christological and Trinitarian perspective and evaluated with related criteria. In conclusion, D'Costa proposes as the most coherent view that of "many possible covenants within a single revelatory history reaching its normative but proleptic fulfillment in Christ" (D'Costa 1990b, 452). He adds that "Christianity's relation to Judaism should act as a catalyst in reorienting Christianity's attitude toward the world religions" (D'Costa 1990b, 451).

Whatever formulation may be preferred, two extreme positions must be avoided in the present context of Jewish-Christian dialogue. These include, on the one hand, any "fulfillment theory" regarding Jesus Christ and the promises and the covenant with Israel, the fulfillment being conceived as mere substitution. Jesus' own claim to "have come not to abolish [the Law and the prophets] but to fulfill them" (Mt 5:17) prevents such interpretation. To be also avoided, on the other hand, is any semblance of dualism of parallel ways, which would destroy the unity of the divine plan of salvation for humankind which reaches in Jesus Christ its eschatological realization. The middle-way position, from a Christian standpoint, seems to be that of one covenant and two interrelated ways within one organic plan of salvation. The divine plan of salvation has an organic unity, of which history marks the dynamic process. This unfolding process contains various steps, mutually related and complementary. For Christian faith the Christ-event does not exist without Israel or making abstraction from it; conversely, Israel never was chosen by God otherwise than as that people from which Jesus of Nazareth would issue forth. Israel and Christianity belong together in salvation history under the compass of the covenant. The covenant through which the Hebrew people obtained salvation in the past and continues to be saved even today is the same covenant through which Christians are called to salvation in Jesus Christ. There is no substitution of a "new" people of God for another henceforward declared "ancient," but expansion to the boundaries of the world of one people of God, of which the election of Israel and the covenant with Moses were and remain "the root and the source, the foundation and the promise."[23]

Therefore, to the question whether the Jews are saved today through God's covenant with Israel *or* through Jesus Christ in whom a "new" covenant has been realized, the answer is that the dichotomy does not hold: salvation comes to the Jews through the covenant made by God with Israel *and* brought to perfection in Jesus Christ. The covenant remains even today a way of salvation, but not independently from the Christ-event.[24]

## D. *Enduring Value of the Cosmic Covenant*

The case of Judaism and Christianity can serve, as has been suggested, as a catalyst for a reorientation of the relationship between Christianity and the other religions. What applies in the first instance holds good, analogically, in the other. There remains, then, to be shown that the other religious traditions too, symbolized by the Noachic covenant, keep, *mutatis mutandis,* an enduring value. Even as the Mosaic covenant has not been suppressed by coming to its fullness in Jesus Christ, neither has the cosmic covenant in Noah with the nations been obliterated by reaching in the Christ-event the goal for which it was ordained by God.

The implication is that the distinction between the general and special history of salvation must not be taken too rigidly: extrabiblical religious traditions, as we have observed earlier, cannot be excluded a priori from belonging to special salvation history. To include them in it would presuppose, in Karl Rahner's view, events in the history of peoples which, in function of a prophetic charism, are interpreted as divine interventions. Only a positive study of the various traditions can show this. Suffice it to recall here that, according to the Bible itself, "Israel and the nations have ... a common base: they are in a state of covenant with the true God" (Stoeckle 1967, 1054).

To see this, it will be necessary to lay aside too rigid a distinction between myth and history, according to which the other religious traditions are made up exclusively of myth, while the historical is the exclusive preserve of the Jewish-Christian tradition. Myth is then considered as "story" without credentials to truth, only events traceable in history having a claim on truth. Such a negative concept of myth has, however, long been abandoned (see, e.g., Eliade 1959, 1963; Cassirer 1946, 1979). "Myth" is not historical untruth; it harks back to "primordial" time, of which historical events are considered concrete

---

23. See Dupuis 1994a, 166, 171. The last words just quoted are borrowed from the "Pastoral Orientations of the French Bishops' Commission for Relations with Judaism" (1973); text in *Documentation Catholique* 70 (1973) 419–22. The text reads: "The first covenant has not been invalidated by the new. It is its root and source, its foundation and promise" (421). On this and other documents of the recent magisterium on this question, see Dupuis 1991b, 121–24.

24. A. Vanhoye (1994) distinguishes the covenant as "prophetic revelation," which is irrevocable and whose value endures, from the legal covenant as provisional institution, which has become obsolete. For a response, see Main 1996.

exemplifications. Mircea Eliade defines it by saying: "Myth narrates a Sacred History; it relates events which have taken place in primordial time." Bede Griffiths, for his part, writes: "Myth is a symbolic story which expresses, in symbolic terms which rise from the depth of the unconscious, people's understanding of God and the mystery of existence. Myths are of infinite value and importance.... God revealed himself from the earliest times in the form of myth" (B. Griffiths 1985, 115). Nor can extrabiblical "stories" be tightly distinguished from the biblical as mythical versus historical. For such a dichotomy does not exactly correspond to reality.

That the extrabiblical religions are largely rooted in myth is certain; Hinduism is a case in point. But these foundational myths can carry a divine message. Nor is divine revelation through myth absent from the Hebrew-Christian tradition. The creation story in Genesis is a myth through which the mystery of creation of human beings and their communion with God is being revealed. Noah is himself a "mythical" figure or "legendary" character, and the story of God's covenant with him is mythical; yet it conveys the truth of a covenant relationship of all peoples with God. Further, the stories of Abraham and Moses are not devoid of a certain mythical background; nevertheless, they symbolize by excellence God's action in the history of the Israelite people and are the foundation-stone of the Hebrew concept of revelation as God's personal intervention in history. "Hebrew understanding emerged from the mythological background" (B. Griffiths 1985, 121, see 109–31). Through the charism of interpretation of the great prophets, Israel will resolutely move away from a mythological to a historical understanding. This movement will be further accentuated in the Christian view with the Christ-event standing at the midpoint of history.

The progressive evolution from a mythical understanding to a historical one as we move away from extrabiblical to the Hebrew-Christian tradition must not, however, obscure the fact that cosmic religion already conveys a covenant relationship of God with peoples, expressed through the medium of story and legend. Nor has the revelatory function of myth in extrabiblical religion come to an end with the advent of historical consciousness.

# Nine

# Word of God—
# Single and Universal

"IN MANY AND VARIOUS WAYS God spoke of old to our fathers through the prophets; but in these last days he has spoken to us by the Son, whom he appointed the heir of all things, through whom also he created the world" (Heb 1:1–2). When the author of the Letter to the Hebrews wrote these words in his prologue, he surely did not look beyond the prophets of Israel for a word spoken "of old" by God to humankind. What the writer intended was to show that the event of Jesus Christ outdid immeasurably whatever God had said and done for Israel through its prophets. Nevertheless, his explicit reference to the "many and various ways God spoke of old" and to the Son "through whom he created the world" strikingly evoke what the Prologue of the Gospel according to John affirms concerning the Word, through whom "all things were made" (Jn 1:3) and who was "the true light that enlightens every human being by coming into the world" (Jn 1:9). The similarity between the two texts leads beyond the explicit reference made by Hebrews to the word spoken by God to Israel and encourages us to inquire about a divine revelation not confined to biblical history but extending to the entire history of salvation.

The last chapter ended up noting that God's covenant with Israel may serve, analogically, as a catalyst for a deeper perception of God's covenantal relationship with the nations. This observation leads to the further question of God's self-revelation to them. Is divine revelation coextensive with the history of salvation, which — as has been said — extends to all world history? No matter how "many and various" the ways in which God may have spoken, can it be thought that he did not "leave himself without witness" (Acts 14:17) at any time in history, not merely "in the things that have been made" (Rom 1:20) but also in speech and self-disclosure? How does God's speech to the nations relate to the Word which "in these last days he has spoken to us by the Son" (see Heb 1:2)? And how is the "only Son" he who "made him known" (Jn 1:18) if it is true that he had spoken and disclosed himself earlier in varied ways? Stated more clearly: How are we to understand that Jesus Christ is the "fullness" of divine revelation if it is true that God revealed himself through prophetic figures in various other religious traditions, both before and after him? Do the "sacred books" or "oral traditions" of other religions offer but a human discourse about God or the Absolute; or do they, on the contrary, contain a "word spoken by God" to the people of those religions and even to all humankind?

235

If, moreover, Jesus Christ represents the "fullness" of divine revelation, has revelation come to a complete end with him? Or, on the contrary, can divine revelation in any way be conceived as an "ongoing process," both inside and outside Christianity?

The questions asked here are only partially distinct from those examined in the previous chapter. We stressed then that God's self-manifestation in history takes place inseparably under the double form of words and deeds; it consists at once, necessarily, of revelation and salvation: God tells himself by giving himself; he shares himself by uttering himself. To say, then, that the whole of history is salvation history implies by the same token the universality of revelation (see Fries 1965b). Deeds and words, events and prophecy: both go hand in hand. Such, in every case, is the biblical understanding of salvation-revelation, which has been felicitously expressed by the constitution *Dei Verbum* of Vatican II. It says: "[The] economy of revelation is realized by deeds and words, which are intrinsically bound up with each other. As a result, the works performed by God in the history of salvation show forth and bear out the doctrine and realities signified by the words; the words, for their part, proclaim the works, and bring to light the mystery they contain" (DV 2).

In virtue of the concomitance of the divine deeds and words, it seems theologically justified to search for divine speech in the nonbiblical religious traditions, even as it was thought necessary to include those traditions within the ambit of salvation history. "When interpreting anyone's situation before God," writes G. O'Collins, "we need to recall the two inseparable dimensions of the divine self-communication": revelation and salvation (see O'Collins 1993, 80–81). God has spoken to the whole of humankind, as he has offered his salvation to all its members. Revelation is universal, even as is the offer of salvation (see Thils 1966, 84–121).

To say this is not to forget that the understanding of concepts such as "revelation," "salvation," and other cognate concepts differs vastly from one religious tradition to another — some points of contact notwithstanding.[1] Nor is it to forget that, in its bid to transcend the dichotomy between inclusivism and pluralism, a "comparative theology" must build on the recognition of the differences, without giving in to the illusory presumption of a "common essence" (see p. 204, above), as recent authors have rightly pointed out.[2] But due attention and respect for the differences do not, as some among those authors equally point out, do away with the right and duty for the Christian believer to interpret the data of other traditions from the vantage point of his or her own faith.

An example is in order here. Joseph A. DiNoia rightly notes that "a Catholic theology of religions can affirm the distinctiveness of the aims fostered by other

---

1. As has been shown by Carpenter 1995, for the Christian and the Hindu traditions. See also Ward 1994; *Revelation in Christianity and Other Religions* 1971; *Salvation in Christianity and Other Religions* 1980; Swinburne 1992.

2. Carpenter (1995) refers especially to the following: P. J. Griffiths 1991; DiNoia 1992; Clooney 1993.

religions without prejudice to an affirmation of the unique valuation of the Christian community or of its doctrines about salvation" (DiNoia 1992, 91). Hence it is possible to assert that "God wills that the other religions perform functions in his plan for humankind that are now only dimly perceived and that will be fully disclosed in the consummation of history for which Christians long" (DiNoia 1992, 91).

But it still remains true that for the Christian believer "the existent with which all human beings are unconditionally engaged in all religious communities is the Triune God" (DiNoia 1992, 136). And "what else would a properly Christian theology of religions be competent to enunciate but appraisals of other religions framed in Christian terms?"[3]

What follows is, avowedly, a Christian evaluation, framed in Christian categories, of "divine revelation" in other religious traditions. According to such an evaluation, "an ineffable mystery, the center and ground of reality and human life, is in different forms and manners active among all peoples of the world and gives ultimate meaning to human existence and aspirations." But, it needs to be added, "this mystery, which is called by different names, but which no name can adequately represent, is definitely disclosed and communicated in Jesus of Nazareth."[4] The "ultimate mystery," universally present yet never adequately comprehended, is, for the Christian believer, the "God and Father of Our Lord Jesus Christ" (2 Cor 1:3). A Christian theology of the "Word of God" in history will, therefore, of necessity be Trinitarian and Christological. It will search for the signs of God's action, for the "seeds of his Word," for the imprint of his Spirit in the foundational experiences and events upon which religious traditions have been built, and for traces of the same in the sacred books and the oral traditions that constitute the official record and the living memory of those traditions.

# I. Revelation and World Religions

## A. Models of Divine Revelation

We have noted that the concept of revelation is understood in various ways in different religious traditions. It must further be observed that the Christian

---

3. DiNoia 1992, 160–61. The "orientational pluralism" of S. M. Heim (1995) differs from the "comparative theology" advocated by J. A. DiNoia and others, in that he holds between Christians and members of other religious traditions a real diversity of ultimate destinies in accord with their respective traditions. Such a perspective, even though it "does not fit easily into traditional Christian theological frameworks," the author thinks to be "fully consistent with biblical and Trinitarian convictions," while at the same time admitting that this consistency "can be more fully worked out" than he has done in his book (Heim 1995, 228). See chap. 12, below.

4. The quotation is from the declaration of the International Theological Conference on Evangelization and Dialogue in India (October 1971), no. 13, in Pathrapankal, ed., 1973, 4; also in Dhavamony, ed., 1972, 4.

theology of revelation has considerably evolved in recent decades.[5] In particular, a clear shift in emphasis has taken place, in the wake of Vatican II, from revelation as primarily doctrine or communication of divine truths to revelation as primarily event and divine self-disclosure (see O'Collins 1993). In his well-known *Models of Revelation,* Avery Dulles distinguishes five models of revelation — to be viewed not as mutually exclusive but rather as supportive of each other and complementary (Dulles 1992). His intention is to show how the different models have been applied by theologians to divine revelation in the Judeo-Christian tradition; nevertheless, he also asks which among those models can be found verified in other religious traditions and seen as more conducive to a recognition in them of a true divine revelation.

The five models are the following: (1) revelation as doctrine; (2) revelation as history; (3) revelation as inner experience; (4) revelation as dialectical presence; and (5) revelation as new awareness. There is no need here to analyze in detail the use of the five models made by various theologians. Suffice it to ask whether and to what extent they apply to religious traditions outside the Judeo-Christian. Comparing the models among themselves, Dulles asks what answer their protagonists are inclined to give to the question: "Is revelation given outside the biblical religion?" His answer is as follows:

> To this question the first and second model generally respond in the negative, though many proponents of those models speak of a "general" or "natural" revelation which is preparatory to the "special" or "supernatural" revelation of the Old and New Testaments. The third model holds that all peoples have access to revelation on the same basis as Jews and Christians. The fourth model rejects even the idea of general or natural revelation, insisting that Christ alone is God's revealing Word. The fifth theory holds that all humanity is affected by the offer of revelation, for God is everywhere at work, in various stages, in the history of creation.[6]

This summary of one-sided and often narrow theological positions on the subject goes to show — as has already been verified in the previous chapter — that too rigid a distinction between the natural and the supernatural (first model), too narrow a concept of salvation history (second model), as well as any unbridgeable gap between the subject and object of revelation (fourth model) inevitably result in limiting the extent of divine revelation to the ambit of biblical religions. On the contrary, concepts such as "inner experience" and "new awareness," while they do not by themselves imply divine origin, may connote the presence of a free transcendent element.

---

5. On the theology of revelation, see especially: Latourelle 1987; Moran 1966, 1972; Shorter 1983; Fries 1970; O'Collins 1968; Dulles 1970.

6. Dulles 1992, 121; see also 177, where Dulles writes: "The first, second, and fourth models, which tend to be reserved towards the category of symbol, are the least inclined to admit revelation in the world religions. Models three and five, which favor the symbolic approach, find it easy to acknowledge that revelation is present in all religions, but in so saying they frequently relativize the traditional claims of Christianity."

Speaking of revelation as "inner experience," Dulles appeals to Karl Rahner to the effect that revelation contains a transcendent movement or dimension, by which is meant "the self-communication of God in divinizing grace, insofar as that grace modifies the perspective in which we view the world" (Dulles 1992, 71–72). "Revelation," Rahner asserts, "is not possible... without the occurrence of what may be called 'mysticism as the expression of grace'" (Rahner 1975, 1010). Such illuminating grace can be called revelation even prior to the acceptance of any particular message divinely revealed; it will become "thematized" in doctrines, reflecting divine truths, conveyed by the religious traditions. Not only Christianity, then, but other religions too can, in different degrees, bear witness to a self-revelation of God.

Appeal to Rahner is likewise made by Dulles to show that revelation, seen as a new mode of human awareness, is also applicable to other religions. This is so inasmuch as divine grace — which is universally offered — "discloses God as communicating himself and the human subject as tending toward transcendent fulfilment in union with God" (Dulles 1992, 100). "To the extent that any individual or community, empowered by God's presence, experiences itself as grounded in the divine, God's revelation may be found in it" (Dulles 1992, 107).

Summing up his findings on "revelation and the religions," Dulles notes appropriately that

> in holding the salvific and revelatory character of the religions in general, Rahner does not relativize biblical revelation and Christianity.... Christ, the incarnate Word, is the absolute religious symbol in whom the aspirations of humanity for a definite and irrevocable self-communication of God are fulfilled. The religions can be interpreted as expressions of a "searching memory" which somehow anticipates God's culminating gift in Jesus Christ. (Dulles 1992, 182)

### B. God "Without" or the Absolute "Within": Ecstasy and "Instasy"

By applying Rahner's theological anthropology of the "supernatural existential" to the question of revelation, it seems therefore possible to conclude a priori to the universality of divine revelation in human history and further to affirm that "elements of truth" originating in divine revelation must be found in the various religious traditions of the world. This affirmation is, however, purely formal and would call for an a posteriori verification of traces of divine truth in the sacred writings and the living traditions of the world religions. Such a posteriori verification cannot be attempted here.[7]

It is, however, important to keep in mind some fundamental distinctions concerning the different religious traditions. We have recalled earlier the usual

---

7. We may refer in particular to the following anthologies: Novak, ed., 1994; Smart and Hecht, eds., 1992; Wilson, ed., 1991; also B. Griffiths, ed., 1994; Coward 1988; Kramer 1986; Panikkar 1979b; Zaehner 1966.

distinction between the "monotheistic" or "prophetic" religions (Judaism, Christianity, and Islam) and the "mystical" religions originating from the East. Though it needs to be handled carefully, the distinction has the merit of pointing to a common historical origin and consequently to a family resemblance between the prophetic religions. Similarly, the mystical religions of the East share — substantial differences notwithstanding — common traits, in particular a strong "wisdom" or "gnosis" characteristic which testifies to reciprocal ties between them (see p. 9, above). Between the one and the other group differences are so deep as to constitute distinct worldviews (*Weltanschauungen*).

Account must be taken of such differences in searching for divine revelation in the religious traditions outside the Judeo-Christian tradition. An existential approach to theology makes it incumbent upon the Christian interpreter to transcend the level of the imperfect ideas of God conveyed by the religions which, as they are outside the Jewish and Christian traditions, live in the dispensation of the "cosmic covenant," in order to attain, insofar as possible, to the living experience of the divine underlying these ideas and concepts.

We must acknowledge the certainty that many women and men living under the dispensation of the cosmic covenant have encountered the true God in an authentic religious experience. For example, prayer, of its very nature, entails a personal relationship between an "I" and an infinite "Thou." One does not pray to an impersonal God (Limet and Ries, eds., 1980). Authentic prayer is always a sign that God, in whatever secret, hidden way, has undertaken the initiative of a personal approach to human beings in self-revelation and has been welcomed by these human beings in faith. Those who entrust themselves to God in faith and charity are saved, however imperfect their conception of the God who has revealed himself to them. After all, salvation depends on the response made by sinful human beings, in faith, to a personal communication initiated by God.

There is a gap, however, between religious experience and its formulation. This is true even of the Christian experience; a fortiori, it will be true of the others. We never have access to the religious experience of another in its pure state, without the garment in which it is clothed by its enunciation in a discourse. Language, it is true, gives us access to this experience and communicates it to us; but it does so inadequately. Indeed, in transmitting it, it betrays it, inasmuch as religious experience, of its very nature, is beyond all expression. If we wish to reach to the religious experience of others and discover the hidden elements of truth and grace there, we shall be obliged to go beyond the concepts that enunciate that experience. Insofar as it is possible, we shall have to gather the very experience through the faulty concepts through which it is expressed.

As we know, in Eastern religious traditions religious experience is not always expressed in terms of a personal relationship with God. Hindu *advaita* mysticism conceives it as an awakening to one's identity with the Brahman. As for Buddhism, even while, despite its agnostic attitude and nontheistic appearance, it does imply an (impersonal) Absolute, no personal relationship with God is professed here, either. Buddhists speak of contemplation and meditation, not of prayer. By contrast, in Christianity and the other monotheistic and prophetic religions, religious experience takes the form of an interpersonal dialogue between God, who takes the initiative in manifesting himself, and the human being, who responds to that initiative. Thus while the mystical Asian religions cultivate "instasy" (the quest for an unknown Absolute "in the cave of the heart"), ecstasy (the encounter with the "utterly other" God) predominates with their prophetic counterparts; the former emphasize apophaticism (Nirvana, Sunyata), the latter place the emphasis on cataphaticism. It is easy to grasp the reasons for the limitations entailed in the concept of God in mystical Eastern religious traditions. They lack the benefit of the "special" revelation of God in the history of Israel and, a fortiori, the decisive self-revelation of God in Jesus Christ.

However, despite the limitations marking the enunciation of the experience of God in those traditions, still, wherever there is genuine religious experience, it is surely the God revealed in Jesus Christ who thus enters into the lives of men and women, in a hidden, secret fashion. While the concept of God remains incomplete, the interpersonal encounter between God and the human being — for which God takes the initiative, awaiting the response of faith on the part of the human being — is authentic.

This is not the place to pursue the question whether there is such a thing as a "purely natural" mysticism or whether, instead, all mysticism is, if not of its very nature, at least de facto "supernatural." What has been said earlier must suffice on the question of fact.[8] Theologically we must hold that wherever and whenever human beings turn toward an Absolute that addresses and bestows itself upon them, an attitude of supernatural faith is thereby on the scene, in response to a personal divine revelation. This attitude is directed toward, as well as originally aroused by, the God of Jesus Christ who communicates himself to them.

All differences notwithstanding, a Christian theology of religious experience cannot but interpret the experience as in all circumstances involving the self-disclosure and self-gift of the one God who fully manifested himself in Jesus Christ. The theological reason for affirming this is as simple as it is compelling. It holds to the Shema of Israel, as it is found in Deut 6:4: "Hear, O Israel: The Lord our God, the Lord is one" (see Mk 12:29). God is one, and there is no other! The same God it is who performs saving deeds in human history and speaks to human beings in the secret of their hearts. The same is at once the "utterly other" and the "ground of being" for all that is; the transcendent "without" and the immanent "within"; the Father of our Lord Jesus Christ and the Self at the center of the self. And while, in Jesus Christ, God has truly become our Father, that God remains the One "Who Is," while we are those who "are not." In ecstasy the same God is contemplated, awareness of whom may

---

8. On the nature of mysticism, the reader may consult among others: Gardet and O. Lacombe 1981; Zaehner 1957; Gardet 1953; Maréchal 1964; Ravier, ed., 1965.

gush forth in "instasy"; the same is affirmed through theological cataphaticism and inferred in mystical apophaticism.

This polarity and tension between distinct approaches to the reality of God are not new to the Christian tradition. God has been reached from both ends, as the "Father in heaven" and as "more deeply intimate to myself than I am" (*interior intimo meo*) (Saint Augustine, *Confessions* III, 6, 11; *CCL* 27:39). He has been known as the Unknowable: "If you have understood it is not God" (*Si enim comprehendisti non est Deus*) (Saint Augustine, *Sermo* 117, 3, 5; PL 38:663); "We can know neither God's being, nor God's essence" (*non possumus scire esse Dei, sicut nec eius essentiam*) (Saint Thomas Aquinas, ST I, q. 3, a. 4, ad 2um). The apophatic tradition should enable Christian interpreters to reconcile the two revelations, the cosmic and the historical, respectively exemplified by the prophetic and the mystical religious traditions, as ultimately springing from the same source. "We must try," B. Griffiths writes, "to see the values in each of these revelations, to distinguish their differences and to discover their harmony, going beyond the differences in an experience of 'non-duality,' of transcendence of all dualities." And he adds: "These two modes of experience, the cosmic and psychological on the one hand, and the personal and historical on the other, are not opposed but complementary. There is only one Reality, one Truth, whether it is known through the experience of the cosmos and the human soul or through encounter with a historic event" (B. Griffiths 1982, 177–80; see also B. Griffiths 1976; Robinson 1979). That one Truth is the God who revealed himself "in many and various ways" (Heb 1:1) through human history, until such time as his self-disclosure to the world culminated in Jesus Christ.

## C. The Trinitarian Structure of Revelation

Wherever there is a personal communication of God, it is always necessarily the God of Jesus Christ who engages in self-revelation and self-bestowal: that is, the Triune God, Father, Son, and Spirit. A Trinitarian structure is, from the standpoint of Christian faith, the a priori condition of possibility of every personal divine communication. It is so because, as has been shown earlier (see pp. 227–228, above, and Rahner 1980), the order of personal origins intrinsic to the communion of the divine life necessarily extends to the sphere of God's self-communication in history. The previous chapter has illustrated the Trinitarian rhythm of God's deeds in salvation history; the same Trinitarian structure must be said to apply to God's self-revelation: whenever God has spoken in human history, he has done so through his Word, in his Spirit.

That God's speech is always through his Word is clearly implied by the reference in the Johannine Prologue to the Word of God as "the true light that enlightens every human being by coming into the world" (Jn 1:1–3, 9). Vatican II refers to this passage when it speaks of the elements of truth in the doctrines of other religious traditions which "often reflect a ray of that Truth (*illius Veritatis*) which enlightens all human beings" (NA 2). The same reference seems implied in the council's repeated appeal to the "seeds of the Word" present in those traditions (AG 11, 15). Admittedly, the council did not explain in what precise sense it used the expression. Do the "seeds of the Word" refer to a human expectancy of a word spoken by God; or is the Word of God understood to be actually present and active in the elements of truth contained in the religious traditions? One thing is clear: the council borrows the expression from the early Fathers of the Church, specifically from Saint Justin, whose theology of the Logos *spermatikos*, as has been shown earlier, clearly intended differentiated participations by human beings with the divine Logos affirmed by the Johannine Prologue (see pp. 57–60, above). The encyclical letter *Redemptoris Missio* of Pope John Paul II concurs with this interpretation when it notes that the 'seeds of the Word' are sown in the various traditions by the Spirit of God: "It is the Spirit who sows the "seeds of the Word" present in various customs and cultures, preparing them for full maturity in Christ" (RM 28).

This goes to show that, before God's self-manifestation culminated in the incarnation of his Word (Jn 1:14), God had already "spoken" to humankind in the Word-to-become-incarnate. To the question, "Could a Christian affirm that the same divine Lord whom Christians worship in Jesus is worshipped, under other symbols, by the devotees of the Lord Krishna or of the Lord Buddha?" Avery Dulles answers in typically guarded fashion:

> It need not be denied that the eternal Logos could manifest itself to other peoples through other religious symbols.... In continuity with a long Christian tradition of the Logos-theology that goes back as far as Justin Martyr...it may be held that the divine person who appears in Jesus is not exhausted by that historical appearance. The symbols and myths of other religions may point to the one who Christians recognize as the Christ. (Dulles 1992, 190)

The universal significance of the incarnation of God's Word notwithstanding, room must be left for his anticipated action in history as well as his enduring influence under other symbols.

We have shown elsewhere that Vatican II and the postconciliar doctrinal statements of the Church have openly and increasingly acknowledged the activity of the Holy Spirit not only in the lives of persons belonging to the religious traditions of the world but in those traditions themselves (see Dupuis 1991b, 157–65). The active presence of the Spirit is universal. It anticipates the event of Jesus Christ and, after that event, extends beyond the confines of the Church. The Spirit spreads throughout the world, vivifying all things. The cosmic revelation itself is caught up in this transformation.

Is it true, then, that the activity of the Spirit reaches the members of other religious traditions precisely through their traditions? If so, what specific role might their sacred books play with respect to this activity? Do the nonbiblical scriptures mediate the activity of the Spirit in the religious life of others? How do these writings nourish and sustain their religious experience? How do they invite the members of these religions to the obedience of faith that saves? Can theology discover in the sacred scriptures of other religious traditions the harvest of an authentic divine revelation — a genuine word addressed by God to human beings?

To answer these and similar questions, we must continue to keep in mind the Trinitarian structure of every divine self-manifestation in history, by virtue of which the Holy Spirit is the necessary "point of entry" of divine truth and life into the human spirit. Every personal encounter of God with the human being and of the human being with God occurs in the Holy Spirit. God becomes God-for-the-human-being in the Spirit, and it is in the Spirit that we can respond to the divine advances. All "being together" of God and the human being is made possible in the Spirit, or — and this is the heart of the matter — all religious experience becomes truly personal in the Spirit. In the order of divine-human relationships, the Spirit, in the last analysis, is God rendered personally present to the human being — God felt by the human being in the depths of the human heart.

As this is an axiomatic truth in Trinitarian theology, we must say that all authentic experience of God is in the Spirit. Thus in all authentic experience of God, the Spirit is present and active, whatever be the manner in which human beings are situated in salvation history or the particular stage of this history to which they belong.

The Holy Spirit is at work at every stage of salvation history. In each of the progressive covenants struck by God with the human family, the Spirit is the immediate agent of the divine advance and of the commitment of God to human history. Thus we might say that the Holy Spirit presides over the divine destiny of humanity, in the sense that each divine covenant reaches humanity in the Spirit. In the various stages of the history of salvation, just as in the personal story of human beings' salvation, the same Spirit is at work, revealing and manifesting God. Such mediation of the Holy Spirit in God's self-disclosure is also operative in the sacred scriptures of the religious traditions.

## II. Revelation, Past and Present

### A. Word of God and Sacred Books

Can the "sacred scriptures" of other religions be acknowledged by theologians as the "word of God"? And, if so, to what extent and in what way?[9]

Here we must distinguish between divine revelation, propheticism, and sacred scripture, although the realities respectively denoted by these various terms are bound together by manifold relations. God has wrought a personal self-manifestation in the history of the nations in such wise that theology can speak

---

9. On this entire question the reader may consult Amalorpavadass, ed., 1975b; *Revelation in Christianity and Other Religions* 1971; Vempeny 1973; Rossano 1968; Aagaard 1974; Amaladoss 1985.

of a *divine revelation*, ordered though it may be to the Jewish and Christian revelation. To this effect we need only recall the "pagan" saints of the Old Testament and the divine covenants with humanity and the nations. At the same time, it is becoming more and more widely admitted today that the *prophetic charism* had antecedents outside Israel (see Neher 1972), both before Christ and after. Indeed, the prophetic charism itself must be correctly understood. It primarily consists not of a prediction of the future but rather of an interpretation, for a people, of the sacred history being lived by that people: an interpretation of the divine interventions in their history and of the divine will for them. The source of the prophetic charism is, in effect, a "mystical experience." This has been excellently formulated in the case of the prophets of Israel:

> [The prophet] has no doubt that the word of God has come to him and that he must pass it on to others. The source of this conviction is a mysterious, we may call it mystical, experience of a direct contact with God.... The divine seizure often provokes "abnormal" manifestations but, as with the great mystics, these are incidental. It is important to notice that the prophet, like the mystic, is raised to a "supranormal" psychological state by this divine intervention. To deny this would be to reduce the prophet to the rank of poet or to credit him with the illusions of misguided visionaries. ("Introduction to the Prophets" 1985, 1159)

The prophetic charism is not the exclusive privilege of Israel. Even the Old Testament acknowledged as genuine prophecy, having their origin in God, four oracles of Balaam (Num 22–24). As for Christian antiquity, it has sometimes regarded the Sibylline Oracles as prophetic.

The case of the prophet Muhammad is instructive here. On the basis of the description of the prophetic charism just cited, R. C. Zaehner observed that Muhammad (like Zoroaster) is a genuine prophet. And comparing the Old Testament with the Qur'an, he added: "It is impossible to read the two books together without concluding that it is the same God who speaks in both: the prophetical accents are unmistakable" (Zaehner 1970, 23–29). The acknowledgment of Muhammad as a genuine prophet of God is no longer unusual in Christian theology.[10]

Christian theologians who admit this, let us observe, are aware that the Qur'an in its entirety cannot be regarded as the authentic word of God. Error is not absent from it. But this does not prevent the divine truth it contains from being the word of God uttered through the prophet. Seen in its historical context, Muhammad's monotheistic message indeed appears as divine revelation mediated by the prophet. This revelation is not perfect or complete; but it is no less real for all that.

Actually, the real problem is not that of revelation, or even of prophetism, but of the *sacred scriptures* as containing the word uttered by God to human

---

10. See especially: Caspar 1987, 75–116; Cragg 1984, 92–93; Geffré 1983, 1985; Caspar 1983; Lelong 1984; GRIC 1989; Watt 1969.

beings over the course of salvation history. From the Christian standpoint, sacred scripture contains memories and interpretations of divine revelation; these have been recorded in writing under a special divine impulse in such a way that God can be called the author of this writing. This does not mean that the human authors of the sacred books, or the compilers who gathered the oral or written traditions contained therein, are bereft of the full exercise of their human faculties and cease to be the authors of their works. Rather, both to God and to the human being are to be ascribed, albeit on different levels, the status of author. Sacred scripture is "the word of God in the words of human beings." Because God is its author, it is not reducible to a human discourse about God; rather, it is a word addressed by God to human beings. But because a human being is the author as well, this word addressed by God to human beings is authentically a human word — the only word, after all, that would be intelligible to them.

To elucidate the mystery of God and the human being as coauthors, as realized in unique fashion in sacred scripture, Christian theology has recourse to the concept of *inspiration*. Traditionally, by divine inspiration we mean that God, while respecting the human author's activity, guides and assumes this activity in such wise that what is written is the word of God. However, it is doubtless a shortcoming of the traditional theology of sacred scripture that the proper role of the Holy Spirit therein is largely passed over in silence. That it constantly uses the term "in*spir*ation" changes nothing. The origin and deeper significance of the word seem most often to have fallen into oblivion or retain little attention. The theology of sacred scriptures should once more put in full relief the personal influence of the Spirit in the inspiration of these scriptures. Only then shall we be in possession of a theology of sacred scripture that will permit a more open attitude toward the scriptures of other religious traditions.

Karl Rahner has emphasized the communitarian character of the sacred scriptures. "The Bible is the book of the Church": it contains the word of God addressed to the ecclesial communion (Rahner 1961b; see also Rahner and J. Ratzinger 1966). In other words, in the books that compose it, especially in those of the New Testament, the Church has recognized the authentic expression of its own faith and the word of God that founds that faith. Sacred scripture is thus a constitutive element of the mystery of the Church, the community assembled and called into being by the word of God. But this does not require that the sacred author be aware of being moved by the Holy Spirit to write. As we know, the charism of scriptural inspiration extends well beyond the group of authors to whom various books are attributed. These authors often performed the function of the redactors, or editors, of oral or written traditions that they had received.

This being the case, the question is whether Christian theology may acknowledge in other sacred scriptures a word of God inspired by the Holy Spirit and addressed by God to other religious communities; and if so, how this word is the word of God. To put it another way: Are the writings recognized as sacred scriptures by other religious traditions, in which Christian theology is today accustomed to see the "seeds of the Word," sacred scripture in the theological sense of the word? Are we to acknowledge in them a word of God to human beings, inspired by the Holy Spirit? Or are we to see only a human word concerning God? Or, again, are we to see a human word addressed to God in the expectation of a divine response? If indeed it is a matter of a word of God, then we must further ask: What is the connection between this word, uttered by God to human beings, as contained in the sacred scriptures of various religious traditions, and the decisive word spoken by God to human beings in Jesus Christ, of which the New Testament constitutes the official record? To answer these questions we shall appeal, below, to the notion of a progressive, differentiated revelation and to an analogical concept of scriptural inspiration.[11]

Meanwhile, we must maintain that the religious experience of the sages and *rishis* (seers) of the nations is guided and directed by the Spirit. Their experience of God is an experience in God's Spirit. To be sure, we must simultaneously admit that this experience is not the good fortune of the *rishi* alone. In the divine providence, God, to whom alone belongs the initiative of any divine-human encounter, has willed to speak to the nations themselves, through the religious experience of their prophets. In addressing the prophets personally in the secret recesses of their hearts, God has willed to be manifested and revealed to the nations in the divine Spirit. Thus God has secretly entered the history of peoples, guiding them toward the accomplishment of the divine design. The social character of the sacred scriptures of the nations can thus be said to have been willed by God. These scriptures represent the sacred legacy of a tradition-in-becoming, not without the intervention of divine providence. They contain words of God to human beings in the words of the *rishis,* inasmuch as they report secret words uttered by the Spirit in hearts that are human, but words destined by divine providence to lead other human beings to the experience of the same Spirit. To say less would seem to underestimate the realism of God's self-manifestation to the nations.

What is suggested here is not tantamount to saying that the *whole* content of the sacred scriptures of the nations is the word of God in the words of human beings. In the compilation of the sacred books of other traditions, many elements may have been introduced that represent only human words concerning God. Still less are we suggesting that the words of God contained in the scriptures of the nations represent God's decisive word to humankind, as if God no longer had anything to say that he has not already uttered by the intermediary of the nations' prophets.

Our proposition comes down to this: the personal experience of the Spirit by the *rishis,* inasmuch as, by divine providence, it is a personal overture on the part of God to the nations, and inasmuch as it has been authentically recorded in their sacred scriptures, is a personal word addressed by God to them through

---

11. Parrinder (1971b) distinguishes the Qur'an as word of God from the scriptures of other non-biblical religious traditions; in Hinduism itself he distinguishes among the Vedas, the Upanishads, and the Bhagavad Gita.

intermediaries of divine choosing. In a true sense, this word may be called "a word inspired by God," provided we do not impose too strict a version of the concept and that we take sufficient account of the cosmic influence of the Holy Spirit.

This view is consonant with the findings of the Research Seminar on Non-Biblical Scriptures which was held in Bangalore, India (11–17 September 1974). The final statement of the seminar has the following to say:

> In the non-Christian communities of India Scriptures are considered as privileged and authoritative means of salvation. Through a living contact with these religions we are coming to realize in our Christian experience that the Holy Spirit is operative in them and that they are manifesting in diverse ways the one mystery of God. The working of the Holy Spirit which makes these texts reflect the experiences of these communities and thus makes them authoritative for their communities is expressed in such terms as vision, insight, divine speech, etc. This working of the Spirit does not entail complete adequacy of the distinct teachings and worldviews in these sacred texts, yet we Christians believe that this action of the Spirit brings to these scriptures an over-all religious authority for these communities as God-given means leading them to their ultimate destiny. (54) (Amalorpavadass, ed., 1975b, 684)

The same document further explains:

> The Ineffable Mystery of God has graciously given itself in various ways and modes to peoples of the world and . . . the experiences by religious persons of that contact with God are partially yet authentically recorded in their sacred books. . . . Ultimately . . . respect and openness given to those scriptures are a form of our openness to the Holy Spirit speaking in them. (56) (Amalorpavadass, ed., 1975b, 685)

### B. Fullness of Revelation in Jesus Christ

The Letter to the Hebrews states (Heb 1:1) that the word uttered by God in Jesus Christ — in the Son — is God's decisive word to the world. And Vatican II comments, saying that Jesus Christ "completes and perfects" revelation (*complendo perficit*) (DV 4). However, in what sense, and how, is Jesus Christ the fullness of revelation? Where precisely is this plenitude? To avoid any confusion, let us note that the fullness of revelation is not, properly speaking, the written word of the New Testament. The latter constitutes the official record and interpretation, the authentic memorial, of that revelation. This authentic memoir — which is part of constitutive tradition — is to be distinguished from the Jesus Christ–event itself, to which the accredited witnesses give testimony. It is the very person of Jesus Christ, his deeds and his words, his life, his death, and his resurrection — in a word, the total Jesus Christ–event itself — that constitutes the fullness of revelation. In him, God has uttered to the world his decisive word.

This is the understanding of Vatican II's constitution *Dei Verbum,* when it distinguishes the fullness of revelation in the Jesus Christ–event (DV 4) from its "transmission" in the New Testament, which belongs to apostolic tradition (DV 7). The authentic memorial transmitted by the New Testament is of course normative (*norma normans*) for the faith of the Church of all times. But this does not mean that it constitutes the fullness of the word of God to human beings. The New Testament itself bears witness that this memorial reports the event of Jesus Christ only incompletely (see Jn 21:25).

Thus Jesus Christ is personally the fullness of revelation. Furthermore, let us note, this fullness is a matter not of quantity but of quality. It is owing to his personal identity as Son of God that Jesus Christ is, properly speaking, the pinnacle and culmination of the revealed word. In order to understand this, we must begin with the human awareness that Jesus had of being the Son of God. Jesus lived his personal relationship to the Father in his human awareness. His human consciousness of being the Son entailed an immediate knowledge of his Father, whom he called *Abba.* Thus his revelation of God had its point of departure in a unique, unsurpassable human experience. This experience was actually none other than the transposition to the key of human awareness and cognition of the very life of God and of the Trinitarian relations among the persons. Thus Jesus prayed to the Father in whom he had his origin, while, according to the Fourth Gospel, he promised to send the Spirit that came through him (Jn 14:16–17, 26; 16:7).

If divine revelation attains its qualitative plenitude in Jesus, it is because no revelation of the mystery of God can match the depths of what occurred when the divine Son incarnate lived on a human key, in a human consciousness, his own identity as the Son of God. This is what took place in Jesus Christ, and it is this that is at the origin of the divine revelation that he delivers to us.

Nevertheless, this revelation is not absolute. It remains relative. On the one hand, Jesus' human consciousness, while it is that of the Son, is still a human consciousness and therefore a limited one. It could not have been otherwise. No human consciousness, even the human consciousness of the Son of God, can exhaust the Divine Mystery. On the other hand, it is precisely this human experience that Jesus had of being the Son, in relation to the Father, that enabled him to translate into human words the mystery of God that he revealed to us. We must go further and say that the Trinitarian mystery could be revealed to human beings only by the incarnate Son living as a human being his own mystery of being the Son and uttering that mystery to his brothers and sisters in human words. The Trinitarian mystery dawned on the awareness of the disciples of Jesus when at Pentecost the risen Lord poured upon them the Holy Spirit from the Father (Acts 2:33), as he had promised (Jn 16:7).

The qualitative fullness—let us say, the intensity—of the revelation in Jesus Christ is no obstacle, even after the historical event, to a continuing divine self-revelation through the prophets and sages of other religious traditions, as, for example, through the prophet Muhammad. That self-revelation has occurred, and continues to occur, in history. No revelation, however, either before or after Christ can either surpass or equal the one vouchsafed in Jesus Christ, the divine Son incarnate.

The Church, meanwhile, must continue to grow in a more profound understanding of the words uttered by God "once for all" in the divine Word incarnate. To this end, the Church is assured of the constant assistance of the Spirit that guides it "into all the truth" (see Jn 16:13).[12] The Church does this, furthermore, in reference to the authentic record of the event contained in the New Testament, which remains for all time the norm (*norma normans*) of an ecclesial comprehension of God and his Christ.

## C. Revelation, Differentiated and Complementary

But even given the singular character of the Jesus Christ–event and the unique place of the official record of this event by the eschatological community of the Church in the mystery of God's revelation to the world, there is yet room for an open theology of revelation and sacred scriptures. Such a theology will posit that, while uttering his decisive word in Jesus Christ, and besides speaking through the prophets of the Old Testament, God has uttered initial words to human beings through the prophets of the nations — a word whose traces can be found in the sacred scriptures of the world's religious traditions. The decisive word does not preclude other words: on the contrary, it supposes them. Nor may we say that God's initial word is the one reported in the Old Testament. No, the Old Testament itself bears witness that God spoke to the nations even before addressing Israel. Thus the sacred scriptures of the nations, along with the Old and New Testaments, represent various manners and forms in which God addresses human beings throughout the continuous process of the divine self-revelation to them.

Three stages can then be distinguished — which do not correspond to a chronological sequence. In the first stage, God grants to the hearts of seers the hearing of a secret word, of which the sacred scriptures of the religious traditions of the world contain, at the least, traces. In the second stage, God speaks officially to Israel by the mouth of its prophets, and the entire Old Testament is the record of this word and of human responses to it. In both of these two stages, the word of God is ordered, however differently in each, to the plenary revelation that will take place in Jesus Christ. At this third stage, God utters his decisive word in him who is "the Word," and it is to this word that the whole New Testament bears official witness.

The sacred scriptures of the nations contain initial, hidden words of God. These words do not have the official character that we must ascribe to the Old

---

12. See Potterie 1984. See also O'Collins 1993, 87–97, on revelation past and present, "foundational" and "dependent."

Testament, to say nothing of the decisive value of the New. We may call them divine words, however, inasmuch as God utters them by the divine Spirit. From the theological point of view, the sacred books containing them deserve the term "sacred scriptures." In the last analysis, the problem is a terminological one — a question of what we are to understand by "word of God," "sacred scripture," and "inspiration."

The traditional way of speaking has given to these terms a restrictive theological definition, limiting their application to the scriptures of the Jewish and Christian traditions alone.[13] But a broader definition can be assigned to them, not without valid theological foundation, according to which they will be applicable to the scriptures of other religious traditions. "Word of God," "sacred scripture," and "inspiration" will then not express precisely the same reality at different stages of the history of revelation and salvation. Important as it is to safeguard the special significance of the word of God reported by the Jewish and Christian revelation, it is no less important to recognize the true value and meaning of the words of God contained in the sacred books of other religious traditions. "Word of God," "sacred scripture," and "inspiration," then, are analogical concepts, applying differently to the various stages of progressive, differentiated revelation. Claude Geffré puts it well. Having acknowledged in the Qur'an "an authentic word of God, although in part formally different from the word revealed in Jesus Christ," he goes on to say: "A like acknowledgment leads us to a deeper theological appreciation of revelation as differentiated revelation. While the theology of the non-Christian religions has not yet emerged from the stumbling, searching stage, we must try to think how a single revelation can include different words of God."[14]

The history of salvation and revelation is one. In its various stages — cosmic, Israelite, and Christian — it bears, in different ways, the seal of the influence of the Holy Spirit. By this we mean that throughout the stages of the divine revelation, God, in the dispositions of divine providence, personally guides humanity toward the divinely set goal. The positive divine disposition of the cosmic revelation, as a personal revelation of God to the nations, includes the divine disposition of the sacred scriptures of those nations. The "seeds of the Word" contained in their scriptures are seminal words of God, from which the influence of the Spirit is not absent. The influence of the Spirit is universal. It extends to the words uttered by God to humanity in all stages of the self-revelation by that God upon that humanity.

Revelation is progressive and differentiated. It may even be said that between

---

13. The recent document of the International Theological Commission, entitled "Christianity and the Religions," keeps the traditional restrictive usage of the terms and applies them to the sacred scriptures of the Jewish and Christian traditions alone, while not excluding the possibility that "God may have enlightened in various ways the people" who are at the origin of the sacred books of other religious traditions (no. 91; cf. 88–92). See International Theological Commission 1997.

14. Geffré 1983. See also Geffré 1995, 28–29; Lelong 1984, esp. 274; GRIC 1989, 44–86; Dupuis 1992e.

revelation inside and outside the Judeo-Christian tradition there exists a true complementarity — without prejudice to the decisiveness of the Christ-event. And, equivalently, it may even be said that between the sacred books of the other religious traditions and the biblical corpus a similar complementarity may be found. "Truth is two-eyed," as has been recalled above; and the same God spoke in history through his prophets who also spoke to seers in the secret of their hearts. All truth comes from God who *is Truth* and needs to be honored as such, whatever the channel through which it comes to us.

Admittedly, a keen discernment needs to be observed to sift divine truth from untruth. For the Christian the normative criterion for such a discernment is unmistakably the mystery of the person and event of Jesus Christ, who *is* the Truth (Jn 14:6). Whatever is in contradiction with him who is "*the* Word" cannot come from the God who sent him. But, this being firmly asserted, there remains room for a complementarity of God's word, not only between the two testaments of the Christian Bible but also between the biblical and nonbiblical scriptures. The latter may contain aspects of the Divine Mystery which the Bible, the New Testament included, do not equally highlight. Examples are: in the Qur'an the sense of the divine majesty and transcendence and of the human being's submission to the holiness of God's eternal decrees (see GRIC 1989; see also GRIC 1993); and in the sacred books of Hinduism, the sense of God's immanent presence in the world and in the recesses of the human heart (see Le Saux [Abhishiktananda] 1976; 1984b).

To recognize the complementarity of the sacred scriptures is one of the elements which make an "open theology" possible without loss of Christian identity. K. Ward enumerates six main features of such a theology:

> It will seek a convergence of common core beliefs, clarifying the deep agreements which may underlie diverse cultural traditions. It will seek to learn from complementary beliefs in other traditions, expecting that there are forms of revelation one's own tradition does not express. It will be prepared to reinterpret its beliefs in the light of new, well-established factual and moral beliefs. It will accept the full right of diverse belief-systems to exist, as long as they do not cause avoidable injury or harm to innocent sentient beings. It will encourage a dialogue with conflicting and dissenting views, being prepared to confront its own tradition with critical questions arising out of such views. And it will try to develop a sensitivity to the historical and cultural contexts of the formulation of its own beliefs, with a preparedness to continue developing new insights in new cultural situations. (Ward 1994, 339–40)

Therefore, to the question: Has the word of God contained in other religious traditions the value of "word of God" only for the members of these traditions; or may we think that God speaks also to us Christians through the prophets and sages whose religious experience is the source of the sacred books of these traditions? a plain answer can be given: the fullness of revelation contained in Jesus Christ does not gainsay this possibility.[15]

Nor does it necessarily gainsay the use in Christian prayer, even in the Liturgy of the Word, of the words of God contained in the sacred books of other religious traditions.[16] Indeed, this ought to be done with prudence and with respect for the different stages of revelation history.[17] Also required will be the discernment necessary to avoid any ambiguities by a responsible selection of texts, in harmony with the mystery of Jesus Christ in which the Liturgy of the Word culminates.[18] Under these conditions, we shall discover, with joy and surprise, astonishing convergences between the words of God and the divine Word in Jesus Christ. Paradoxical as it may appear, a prolonged contact with the non-biblical scriptures — practiced within their own faith — can help Christians to a more in-depth discovery of certain aspects of the Divine Mystery that they behold unveiled to them in Jesus Christ.

---

15. Smith (1967) asserts it in the case of the Qur'an; see also Parrinder 1971b, 105–7; GRIC 1989, 44–86, esp. 68. More broadly, on the subject of nonbiblical scriptures in general, and those of Hinduism in particular, see Amaladoss 1985; Parrinder 1971b, 107–13.

16. See Abel 1969–70, 1974; Amaladoss 1970, 1975a; Le Saux (Abhishiktananda) 1973–74; Amalorpavadass, ed., 1975b.

17. The Research Seminar on Non-Biblical Scriptures, held in Bangalore in December 1974, shows how nonbiblical scriptures can be fitted into the Liturgy of the Word in such a way as to respect the various stages of revelation. It indicates the unique place that should be given to the revelation in Jesus Christ. See the "Statement of the Seminar," in Amalorpavadass, ed., 1975b, 681–95; esp. nos. 55–62 (pp. 685–89).

18. I have shown concrete applications in Dupuis 1974.

# Ten

# Faces of the Divine Mystery

"**B**EING IS ONE — sages name it variously."[1] In the context of the debate on the theology of religions, this Vedic verse is often quoted by upholders of the "pluralistic" thesis as a paradigmatic enunciation of their theological stand. "Being" (*sat*) is understood to stand for "God" or the Divine whom pluralistic theologians have substituted for Christ as the central point of reference for a viable theology of religious pluralism. Their understanding is that all religions represent diverse, historical manifestations of the one Divine Mystery and salvific ways tending toward the same mystery. The concept of God is, intentionally, kept sufficiently indeterminate to accommodate the various religious traditions in their manifold diversities; these are attributed to the distinct cultural areas in which the various traditions have originated. The point, then, is that, ultimately, all religious traditions have the same indeterminate God as ultimate point of reference, no matter how different the names with which they call it and the concept they may form of it.[2] In sum, the Christian Father/Mother-God, the Jewish Yahweh, the Muslim Allah, the Hindu Brahman, the Buddhist Nirvana, the Taoist Tao, and so on, are but different terms with which the various traditions articulate a human experience of Ultimate Reality; the reality is the same and the experiences of equal value, notwithstanding the divergences which characterize them. All religious ways are equally salvific because they all tend to the same Ultimate Reality.

We have shown earlier that the theocentric thesis in the theology of religions postulates a dilemma between theocentrism and Christocentrism which seems to contradict the faith in the mystery of God and of Jesus Christ as traditionally understood by the Christian Church (see pp. 191–193, above). In our next chapter we shall have to meet the arguments on which the "revisionist" Christology of the theocentric thesis is based. Meanwhile, the question of the Divine Mystery and of its many faces in the different religious traditions must be addressed (see Barnes 1991; *Many Faces of the Divine* 1995; Guerriero and Tarzia, eds., 1992). It poses many issues which need to be approached from the vantage point of a theology of religions, at once Christian and dialogical.

Is the God of other religions the same as the God of Christians? This is a question which was often asked in Christian circles in the past and has not disappeared even today; it is heard — surprisingly — even where Jews and

---

1. *Ekam sat vipra bahudha vadanti* (*Rig Veda* I, 164, 46).
2. See the title of J. Hick's book *God Has Many Names* (1980); also Hick 1973.

Muslims are concerned. Before we proceed to an answer, some terminological clarifications are in order: Which God? Which "sameness"? Which religion?

The words of Blaise Pascal are well known: "The God of Abraham, the God of Isaac, the God of Jacob, not of philosophers and the wise (*savants*)..., the God of Jesus Christ" (Pascal 1963, 618). Pascal was referring to God's revelation to Moses: "I am the God of your father, the God of Abraham, the God of Isaac, and the God of Jacob" (Ex 3:6). Pascal meant to distinguish the knowledge of God which we receive through the Judeo-Christian revelation from that limited knowledge which philosophy, even Christian philosophy, is able to reach; he did not mean to deny the personal identity of God in both cases. He deliberately stressed the limits of a philosophical apprehension of God as compared to the divine self-disclosure to Israel and in Jesus Christ. And rightly so: for there is a long way from the "Unmoved Mover" of Aristotle and the Pure Act of Being of the Schoolmen to the God of the Judeo-Christian revelation. Recent theology has in fact measured the distance between both better than had been done hitherto. It shows that traditional divine attributes, such as God's immutability and impassibility, need to be questioned anew and reinterpreted in the light of God's personal involvement with human beings in history, particularly in view of God's personally "becoming" flesh in the incarnation of his Word and the "death of God" on the cross. The divine identity must be clearly distinguished from the apprehension which human beings may have of it in different situations, through human reflection or divine revelation, in distinct religious traditions.

Equally to be kept in mind is the distinction made earlier between the monotheistic or prophetic religions, on the one hand, and the mystical religions of the East, on the other (see p. 9, above). Surely, the questions being asked here are as valid for one group as for the other, yet the answers are not got at with the same ease in both cases. Where the monotheistic religions are concerned, their common origin in the faith of Abraham guarantees the personal identity of the God worshiped by each. The continuity between the Yahweh of the Jewish religion and the "Father of Our Lord Jesus Christ" in Christianity can be historically substantiated, without prejudice to the differences between the Jewish scripture's concept of God and that of the Christian New Testament — as will be seen hereafter. The same is true, though less universally recognized, where the personal identity between the Judeo-Christian God and that of the Qur'an and of Islam is concerned. Surely, the divergences in the concept of God will prove to be, in this case, even greater. Nevertheless, the Muslim God is that God in whom Abraham, the "father of all who believe" (Rom 4:11), placed his faith, and, after him, Israel and Christianity (Heb 11–12). Islam traces its historical origins to the faith of Abraham as truly as do Israel and Christianity.[3]

The question is much more complex where the mystical religions of the East

---

3. This has been recognized with growing clarity by the magisterium of the Church, as I have shown in Dupuis 1991b, 123–24. See also Michel 1985.

are concerned; this for more than one reason—not least the luxuriant variety and enormous complexity of the data they offer and the distinct overall world-view (*Weltanschauung*) on which they build. Nevertheless, the question must be asked theologically how the Absolute Reality which they affirm relates to the God of the monotheistic religions who, according to Christian faith, has been disclosed in a decisive manner in Jesus Christ.

Is it legitimate to think, from a standpoint of Christian theology, that the Ultimate Reality to which those other religious traditions refer is, in spite of their vastly different mental constructs, the same which the monotheistic religions affirm as the God of Abraham, Isaac, and Jacob? Is there an Ultimate Reality common to all religious traditions, even if it is differently experienced and variously conceptualized by the various traditions? One Divine Mystery with many faces? And, if such is the case, can this Ultimate Reality be interpreted in terms of Christian Trinitarian theism, no matter how imperfectly apprehended? Or is it to be viewed as equally distant from all categories, theistic or otherwise?

The religious traditions offer a broad spectrum of contrasting positions, even of contradictory dichotomies: theism versus nontheism; monotheism versus polytheism; monism versus dualism; pantheism versus panentheism; personal God versus impersonal; and so forth. In this broad variety of standpoints can a *reductio ad unum* be practiced in favor of a Christian Trinitarian theism? Is it theologically justified and practicable? If we speak of a universal hidden presence of the God of Jesus Christ in the Ultimate Reality appealed to by the other traditions, do we not unduly absolutize a particular "referent" as the only possible hermeneutical key to whatever religious experience? And can any evidence be put forward to substantiate such a Christian interpretation?

"All have the same God," Walbert Bühlmann wrote;[4] and he understood it as the "God and Father of Our Lord Jesus Christ." We ourselves have written earlier that "wherever there is genuine religious experience, it is surely the God revealed in Jesus Christ who thus enters into the lives of men and women, in a hidden, secret fashion" (see p. 241, above). Admittedly, this is a Christian theological stand which members of other traditions will not be prepared to make their own. Nor must they be asked to. Hindu *advaita* theology will continue to interpret reality in terms of nonduality (*advaita*) between Brahman and the self; the Buddhist interpretation will be in terms of Sunyata. The Christian, for his part, who, in continuity with the Jewish revelation and the Christian tradition, adheres to a Trinitarian monotheism, cannot but think in terms of the universal presence and self-manifestation of the Triune God. For him, the Divine Mystery with many faces is, unequivocally, the God and Father who disclosed his face for us in Jesus Christ.

The chapter will be divided into two main parts. The first part will expound, in general terms, the Christian stand with regard to the Ultimate Reality. In doing this, recent developments in the ongoing debate on the theology of re-

---

4. This is the title of W. Bühlmann's book *All Have the Same God* (1982a).

ligious pluralism will be kept in mind, as well as the other religious traditions, monotheistic and otherwise, with which Christian Trinitarian monotheism must enter into dialogue. The second part will, by way of a case study, establish a dialogue between Hindu mysticism and the Christian experience, between the Brahman of Hindu theism and the Christian Trinity. On the foundation of such a study, we will ask whether some continuity or convergence may be affirmed between the Ultimate Reality of the mystical religions and the tripersonal God of Christian monotheism.

## I. The "Ultimate Reality": One and Three

### A. The "Real" beyond the "Personae" and the "Impersonae"?

The introduction to this chapter has recalled the fundamental standpoint of the pluralistic thesis on the theology of religions: not Jesus Christ but God is at the center of the new paradigm, even as he is the goal of the different religious ways. However, as has been reported in the first part of this work (see pp. 193–194, above), John Hick's theocentrism has further developed into a "reality-centeredness." The reason is that the concept of God of the theocentric paradigm, no matter how indeterminate it was in intention, was found to remain too dependent upon a Western and Christian concept of the Absolute to adequately express the pluralistic thesis. In Hick's later work, therefore, the theocentric model is replaced by that of "reality-centeredness."[5] The "central reality" toward which all religious ways are oriented transcends the dichotomies of the personal and the impersonal; as such it can serve as a common paradigm for both the theistic and the nontheistic traditions. It lies beyond the "personae" of the theistic traditions as well as beyond the "impersonae" of the nontheistic, providing a model for upholding the equality of the various traditions in their differences. This needs now to be further explained.

The Real "in itself" (*an sich*) always lies beyond human apprehension; it needs to be distinguished from the Real "as variously experienced-and-thought by different human communities." Hick argues that this fundamental distinction is present in all traditions, the Christian included (Hick 1989, 236–40). The distinction makes it possible to sustain the pluralistic hypothesis that "the great world faiths embody different perceptions and conceptions of, and correspondingly different responses to, the Real from within the major variant ways of being human"; "within each of them the transformation of human existence from self-centredness to reality-centredness is taking place" (Hick 1989, 239–40). "These traditions are accordingly to be regarded as alternative soteriological 'spaces' within which, or 'ways' along which, man and woman can find salvation/liberation/ultimate fulfilment" (Hick 1989, 239–40).

---

5. See mostly Hick 1989; see also Hick 1993a, 1995. See Swidler 1990.

Distinct from the Real *an sich*, the "divine personae" and the "metaphysical impersonae" represent, experientially, different manifestations of the Ultimate Reality (Hick 1989, 246–49). According to the theistic traditions the Ultimate Reality is conceived as personal and manifested alternatively by different figures. The gods are personae of the Real: such are, for example, the Hindu Krishna and the Yahweh of Israel. These represent, in effect, two independent facets of the human experience of the Real as personal. Krishna and Yahweh, reflected respectively in Hindu and Jewish faith, are two quite distinct personae who appear within different cycles of stories. They are divine figures, central to different streams of human existence. Other divine personae, each likewise describable only within the context of a particular strand of religious history, are "the heavenly Father of Christian faith, known through the distinctively Christian response to Jesus of Nazareth; the Allah of Islamic faith, known as self-revealed in the Qur'an through the prophet Muhammad; Shiva, known as intensely experienced with the Shaivite cults of India" (Hick 1989, 269).

Thus, the gods of the monotheistic traditions or divine personae — Vishnu or Shiva, Adonai, the heavenly Father, and Allah — are each the Real as thought-and-experienced from within a particular stream of religious life. Does the same apply to the nonpersonal ultimates, or the impersonae of the Real, upon which some Eastern traditions are focused: the Brahman of *advaita* Vedanta, the Nirvana, Dharmakaya, Sunyata, and Tathata of the Buddhist traditions, the Tao of the Chinese religions (Hick 1989, 278)? To this question Hick's answer is that what is experienced in the impersonae too is not the Real *an sich* but a manifestation of it. The universal structure of human consciousness also holds good here: what is directly experienced is not the Real *an sich* but the Real manifested as Sunyata, Brahman, and so forth. The Real *an sich* is neither the personal loving Lord of the theistic traditions, whether of the Jewish, Christian, Muslim or Hindu bhakti type; nor is it to be identified with the eternal, transcendent being-consciousness-bliss (*saccidananda*), spoken of as Brahman in the *advaitic* tradition, with which we are ultimately identical; or whatever other impersonal manifestation. In sum, the Real *in itself* remains in all events beyond all manifestations of it in human consciousness through the personae or the impersonae (Hick 1989, 293–95).

John Hick's general conclusion is as follows: the "primary affirmations" of the different religious traditions — the Hindu *tat tvam asi*, the Buddha's four Noble Truths, the Jewish Shema, the Christian recognition of Jesus as the Christ, the Islamic declaration that there is no god but God and that Muhammad is his prophet — reflect experiences that constitute different ways in which the Ultimate Reality has impinged upon human life. For

> these revelatory scriptures and persons point to Brahman, or to Nirvana
> or Sunyata or the Dharmakaya, or to Adonai, or to the Heavenly Father
> or the Holy Trinity, or to Allah or Vishnu or Shiva; and, according to [the
> pluralistic hypothesis] these are different manifestations, within different

streams of human life, of the Ultimate Reality.... The differences between the root-concepts and experiences of the different religions, their different and often conflicting historical and trans-historical beliefs, their incommensurable mythologies, and the diverse and ramifying belief-systems into which all these are built, are compatible with the pluralistic hypothesis that the great world traditions constitute different conceptions and perceptions of, and responses to, the Real from within the different cultural ways of being human. (Hick 1989, 373, 375–76)

It was necessary to expose at some length the radical stand taken by the "pluralistic" paradigm in the latest form in which it is proposed by Hick. According to this form of pluralism, the same Ultimate Reality is differently but equivalently manifested in the various strands, personalist or impersonalist, of human religiosity. The various forms of belief in a personal God, Christian Trinitarian monotheism included, are among diverse manifestations of the Real *an sich,* which otherwise remains totally inaccessible. The remainder of this chapter will substantiate disagreement with the Hickian "hypothesis." From the standpoint of the Christian faith, it seems necessary to hold not only that the Ultimate Reality differently manifested to humankind is a personal God; but, further, that the Christian Trinitarian God represents the Ultimate Reality *an sich.*

This is not to say that the Christian tradition claims to possess and provide a positive representation of God's inner Self; for it is well aware that God remains, even after his self-disclosure in Jesus Christ, beyond our intentional grasp (see Jn 1:18). But it does mean that the mystery of the Triune God — Father, Son, Spirit — corresponds objectively to the inner reality of God, even though only analogically. The Ultimate Real is personal; it is interpersonal. It consists in total interpersonal communion and sharing between three who are one-without-a-second (*ekam advitiyam*): Father/Mother; Son/Word/Wisdom; Spirit/Love (*saccidananda*). It needs, therefore, to be shown: (1) that the God of the three monotheistic religions is the same and only God, notwithstanding the vastly different apprehensions thereof in the various traditions; and (2) that the Ultimate Reality of the mystical Eastern traditions can, without violence being made to it, be interpreted, in a Trinitarian key, as potentially tending toward the unfolding of the Trinitarian God in Jesus Christ.

## B. "Our God and Your God, Is One"

The three monotheistic religions are equally emphatic on the uniqueness of the God they worship. Reference has been made earlier to the Shema of Israel: "Hear, O Israel: The Lord our God is one Lord" (Deut 6:4). The unicity of the God of Israel is further elaborated in Deutero-Isaiah: "I am the Lord, and there is no other; besides me there is no God" (Is 45:5); "I, I am the Lord, and besides me there is no Savior" (Is 43:11; see 43:8–13; 44:6–8, 24–28; 45:20–25; etc.). The same message is repeated in the Christian scripture: "Hear, O Israel: The Lord our God, the Lord is One; and you shall love the Lord your God with all your heart, and with all your soul, and with all your mind, and with all your strength" (Mk 12:29–30; see Mt 22:37–38); this is the first commandment. Christian monotheism claims to be in direct continuity with Israelite monotheism.

The doctrine of the Qur'an concurs: "Our God and your God, is One" (Surah 29:46). The context of the quotation clearly indicates that reference is being made to the "people of the Book," that is, to Israel and the Christians: "We believe in what has been revealed to us and to you; our God and your God, is One, and we are submissive (*muslimum*) to him" (Surah 29:46). And elsewhere in the Qur'an, Allah says: "There is no God but me (*illa ana*)" (Surah 16:2; 21:14).

Islam too traces its roots to the faith of Abraham, even though the Abrahamite covenant and the promise that goes with it are not found in the Qur'an. The Qur'an teaches the existence of a unique God, Creator, provident for his creation, almighty, all-knowing, living, and the lawgiver. It also evokes the mission of the prophets of whom the Bible speaks, and that of Jesus. While it does not narrate the history of Israel in detailed fashion as the Bible does, it does evoke the high moments of the lives of Abraham, Isaac, Moses, and Jesus. These high moments, reported in discontinuous fashion, mark the times when God reveals himself as the one God. However, more than the history of the people, what matters for the Qur'an is the intervention of God who, from his transcendence on high, "causes his Word to descend" on the prophets to reveal him.

All three traditions, then, unequivocally claim to have their roots in the God of Abraham. They share the same God (Kuschel 1995). This, however, does not mean to say that the concept of God is identical in the three monotheistic religions. For the opposite is true, at least at the level of doctrines. The Christian tradition claims to prolong Israel's monotheism, while developing it into Trinitarian doctrine; the monotheism of the Qur'an and the Islamic tradition also traces its origin to the God of Israel's faith, while claiming to complete it and purify it from the corruption of that faith by the Christian Trinitarian doctrine. As is pertinently shown by R. Arnaldez in a book entitled *Trois messagers pour un seul Dieu*,[6] the three founding religious communities point to largely different experiences of the same God.

For Israel, God is primarily the Almighty One who has delivered his people from Egyptian slavery and guided it through history; by a kind of retrojection the same God appears as the Creator of human beings and of the universe. Christianity interiorizes the monotheistic faith of Israel, while at the same time further stressing its universal import. But while for the Jews God is primarily Savior, for Muslims he is before all else the Lord, the Almighty Creator.

---

6. Arnaldez 1983; see 1993; Neudecker 1990; see also Masson 1976; Sibony 1992.

Summing up what distinguishes the experience of the one God in Israel and in Islam, R. Arnaldez writes:

> The biblical message was addressed to people in an existential situation different from that of the first Muslims. It oriented Jewish worship and reflection towards a concept of God as Savior, first, of his people, and thereafter as universal Lord and almighty Creator. Islam, on the contrary, leads the faithful in the opposite direction: God is at first the Lord in absolute transcendence, who speaks in his eternity and holds sway over human history from on high. Thereafter, he discloses himself as the Savior, clement and merciful, and the decrees of his unbending will (*mashî'a*) become for believers kindness and good-will (*irâda*). (Arnaldez 1983, 64)

Arnaldez further shows that, the identity of the same God notwithstanding, the concept of God differs vastly in the three monotheistic religions. On the level of doctrine, the three monotheisms are different:

> It is clear that the God of Islam who abrogates the Law of Moses and relativizes the covenant with Israel cannot be the God of the Jews. He cannot in any way either be the God of Christians since he unveils the error which belief in the Trinity and the incarnation — without which there is no Christianity — necessarily constitutes for every Muslim. On this level the three monotheisms cannot but exclude each other. But the Jew believes that God spoke through the Bible; the Christian believes that through his Word made flesh God speaks in the Gospels; the Muslim believes that God speaks in the Qur'an, or even that the Qur'an is his eternal Word. (Arnaldez 1983, 116)

For Israel, the Exodus is the paradigmatic event of salvation, wrought in the past by the God of the covenant in favor of his people; it is reenacted in history and celebrated in memorial as the promise of eschatological salvation. For Christianity, the Jesus Christ–event is the hinge on which the entire history of salvation revolves as it tends toward the second coming of the Lord. For Islam the salvific event is by priority the "eternal Word" spoken by God and consigned by him through Muhammad to the Qur'an; the Qur'an is God's last word to the world, the final disclosure of his transcendent mystery and of his gracious mercy. In rigorous terms, only Islam can be called a "religion of the Book"; Israel is the religion of a covenantal bond between God and his people; Christianity, that of a personal event, Jesus Christ. However, in spite of such irreducible divergences between the three "faiths," their common historical foundation — God's self-disclosure to Abraham at the beginning of biblical salvation history — still stands.

More than in their doctrine of God and their respective messages, it is at the level of faith as lived by the mystics that the three monotheistic religions can be said to converge truly. The mystics of all three religions are bent, with an unquenchable thirst, on a quest for union with the same one God, at once transcendent and immanent, the author of life who graciously communicates himself to unworthy creatures. Whether in the Kabbala tradition or in the Christian tradition or in Muslim Sufism, the mystics of the three monotheistic religions witness to the same values of communion and manifest a similar relentless search for union with the one God toward whom the whole of humankind is tending. At that level, the "three messengers" become the "bearers of a unique message," calling human beings to seek and to find the one God in the recesses of their hearts (Arnaldez 1983, 69).

Arnaldez concludes as follows:

> For the mystics of the three religions, [the] Word announces God's love for human beings, his mercy, his forgiveness of sins, his salvific will. The Word likewise guarantees God's assistance on the way it reveals, allowing the faithful to respond in love to the "prevenient" love of God.... Jewish, Christian, and Muslim mystics are essentially agreed in affirming the true reality of their experience of union with the will of God,... of their love for God made ablaze by the love of God for them. The specific trait of this experience in all monotheistic mystics consists in that it is felt as a gift received. (Arnaldez 1983, 116–17)

To sum up: the three monotheistic religions appeal to the God of Abraham, considered as the only God; their experience of that same God differs vastly, however, and so do by way of consequence their respective doctrines of God. Nevertheless, while divergence occurs on the level of doctrine, convergence obtains when faith becomes a quest for mystical union: in none of the monotheistic mystical traditions does ecstatic union with the "Absolute One" connote the fading away of the human ego into the "One." These monotheistic faiths uphold interpersonal communion between God and human persons, not the identity of the human with the Divine.

### C. The Triune God as Ultimately Real

The convergence between monotheistic mysticisms remains, however, partial, and the divergences in the doctrine of God in the three religions bear heavily on the mystical experience of their members. For Christians, the God of Abraham is inseparably the "God and Father of our Lord Jesus Christ." The doctrine of the Triune God does not merely stand at the center of the Christian message and doctrine; it also imprints a Trinitarian rhythm on the *exodos* of all things from God and their *eisodos* toward God: "For us there is one God, the Father, from whom are all things and for whom we exist, and one Lord, Jesus Christ, through whom are all things and through whom we exist" (1 Cor 8:6). Paul's schema is completed in Eph 2:18: "Through him [Christ Jesus] we both [Jews and gentiles] have access in one Spirit to the Father." According to Pauline and Christian mysticism, Christian and human existence consists of a twofold Trinitarian movement of issuing forth and turning back: from the Father through

Jesus Christ in the Spirit; and, conversely, in the Spirit through Jesus Christ to the Father.

The Christian faith further holds that the Ultimate Reality that has revealed itself to human beings through history and continues to do so even today is the Triune God, Father, Son, and Holy Spirit. Vatican II expresses this as follows:

> It pleased God, in his goodness and wisdom, to reveal himself and to make known the mystery of his will [cf. Eph 1:9]. His will was that human beings should have access to the Father, through Christ, the Word made flesh, in the Holy Spirit, and thus become sharers in the divine nature [cf. Eph 2:28; 2 Pet 1:4]. By this revelation, then, the invisible God [cf. Col 1:15; 1 Tim 1:17], from the fullness of his love, addresses human beings as his friends [cf. Ex 33:11; Jn 15:14–15], and moves among them [cf. Bar 3:38], in order to invite and receive them into his own company. (DV 2)

For Christian faith, then, the Triune God cannot be viewed as a manifestation or an appearance, among others, of an Ultimate Reality toward which men and women are tending in and through the various religious traditions of the world (John Hick). It is not a penultimate sign of the Real *an sich;* it is the Ultimate Reality itself. This is not to say that the Divine Reality is in itself within the purview of a direct human apprehension by mode of a positive representation; for the intrinsic mystery of God remains irremediably beyond our full grasp: *de Deo quid sit nescimus!* But it does mean that the divine Trinity, as revealed in Jesus Christ, objectively, though imperfectly and only analogically, corresponds to the reality of the Absolute. In God's Ultimate Reality there *is* parenthood/sonship/love; God *is* Father/Mother, Son/Word/Wisdom, Spirit/Love, even though we have no positive representation of the way in which these personal characteristics are realized in the Godhead.

Speaking of the content of Christian faith in the Divine Absolute, we should distinguish between primordial affirmations and derived assertions. The foundation of the Christian doctrine of God is the experience of the man Jesus during his earthly life, of living in his human awareness an intimate relationship as Son to the God whom he called his Father (*Abba*) and to the Spirit whom, according to the Fourth Gospel, he promised to communicate to his Church (Jn 14:16–17, 26; 16:7). Jesus' human awareness of the Divine Mystery of communion between Father-Son-Spirit is the source from which springs the axiom according to which the "economic Trinity" is the "immanent Trinity" *in self-communication*, and the locus where it is self-authenticating. It is also the foundation upon which the Apostolic Church — in the light of the Easter experience — and the later Christian tradition were able progressively to develop the doctrine of the Trinity. Between Jesus' human consciousness of the divine communion, the Apostolic Church's teaching, and the later Christian doctrine of the one-God-who-is-three, there is at once continuity and development. But while the primordial affirmation made by the Apostolic Church belongs to the foundational Christian revelation and as such to the *norma normans* of Christian

faith, the later elaborations do not have either the same authority or universality. The ecclesial enunciation of the faith in the divine Trinity remains open
to further elaborations and clarifications or even to other modes of expression.
The possibility of doctrinal pluralism, not only theological but dogmatic, must
be acknowledged (see Dupuis 1977, 59–82); nor is the recognition of the —
unavoidably — relative character of our knowledge of God to be construed as
"doctrinal relativism."[7]

However this may be, from a Christian viewpoint the doctrine of the divine
Trinity serves as the hermeneutical key for an interpretation of the experience
of the Absolute Reality to which other religious traditions testify (see D'Costa
1990a, 16–29; 1992, 139–54; also Schwöbel 1990, 31–46). This must be verified, at least summarily and in general terms, regarding the "personae" of
the other monotheistic religions and the "impersonae" of the mystical oriental
traditions.

For the Hebrew scripture, the God of Abraham, who revealed his name to
Moses as Yahweh, is the One-without-a-second. As has been recalled in the first
part of this work (see pp. 41–45, above), the First Testament speaks explicitly
of the dynamic attributes through which God intervenes in the history of Israel
and of other peoples. These do not represent "persons" distinct from Yahweh,
but Yahweh as he is manifesting himself in deeds and speech. They are, nevertheless, frequently given a "literary personification": Word (*Dabar*), Wisdom
(*Hokmah*), Spirit (*Ruah*). While it is true, then, that the mystery of the divine
Trinity is only revealed in Jesus Christ, it must be said that the First Testament
revelation contained in anticipation the main categories which God's revelation
of himself in Jesus Christ and its elaboration in the Christian tradition would
put to use later. No matter how great the distance may be that separates literary
personifications from the affirmation of distinct personhoods, the biblical revelation of God's mystery must be seen as a process that culminates in Jesus
Christ.

It is well known that the Christian concept of three distinct "persons" in God
has been and continues to be a stumbling block for both Judaism and Islam.
Both have accused the doctrine of the Trinity of contradicting the monotheism
of God's revelation to Abraham and Moses. There is no need to enlarge here on
the matter; a few observations must suffice which may help to dissipate some
misunderstandings. When Jesus spoke of God, his one point of reference was
Yahweh, the God who had declared his name to Moses, whom Jesus called "Father"; this is certain.[8] But it is equally certain that Jesus conceived and affirmed
his "oneness" with the Father as Son, in such a way as would provide a valid
foundation for the Church's — apostolic and postapostolic — doctrine of the

---

7. Congregation for the Doctrine of the Faith, *Mysterium Ecclesiae* (1973); text in AAS 65 (1973)
396–408; see ND 160–62; see comments in Rahner 1981c.

8. See Rahner 1961c. On the few disputed texts of the New Testament where *theos* may refer to Jesus
Christ himself, see the literature mentioned in Dupuis 1994c, 76, n. 13. The following may be added:
Brown 1994; Harris (1992) extends the use of the term *theos* to Jesus far beyond what is critically
warranted.

Trinity: the economic Trinity experienced by Jesus himself in his human awareness unmistakably led to the enunciation of the immanent Trinity of Father,
Son, and Spirit (see Dupuis 1994c, 39–76).

Admittedly, the terms — "person" and "nature" — used by the tradition to
convey the doctrine have but a relative value and need to be handled with caution. Saint Augustine — to mention but one Father of the Church — was aware
of the thinness of the concept of person when applied to the Trinity. He wrote:

> For, in truth, since the Father is not the Son, and the Son is not the Fa-
> ther, and the Holy Spirit, who is also called the Gift of God, is neither
> the Father nor the Son, then certainly there are three. Therefore, it was
> said in the plural number: "I and my Father are One" (Jn 10:30)....But
> when it is asked "Three what", then the great poverty from which our
> language suffers becomes apparent. But the formula "Three persons" has
> been coined, not in order to give a complete explanation by means of it,
> but in order that we might not be obliged to remain silent (*non ut illud
> diceretur sed ne taceretur*).[9]

The traditional concept of person has become even more problematic in
recent times in view of the distinct meaning it has acquired in reference to
consciousness. Because of this evolution of the concept, Karl Barth thought it
necessary to substitute the Cappadocian term of three "modes of being" (*tropoi
huparkseòs*) (*Seinweise*) for that of persons. Rahner, on his side, preferred to
speak of three distinct "manners of subsisting" (*Subsistenzweise*), as a better
rendering of the relational distinctions existing within the Godhead (Rahner
1970, 103–15). However, he added that the use of the term "three persons"
should not altogether be discontinued, for it has been consecrated by Christian
tradition, and, even today, "there is no other word which would be really better,
more generally understandable, and less exposed to misconceptions" (Rahner
1966f, 101).

The above observations make it easier to understand why the Christian doctrine of a threefoldness in the one God remains a stumbling block for both Jews
and Muslims. Is a formulation of Trinitarian doctrine possible which didacti-
cally would make the assimilation of the doctrine possible outside the sphere of
Christianity? With Muslims directly in mind, Karl Rahner suggests a preliminary step toward a dialogue in which Islamic and Christian theologians would
aim at the possibility of a joined profession of faith in the one God; the step
involves a way of speaking more closely in touch with the linguistic usage of
the New Testament. He writes:

> Without wanting to abolish the traditional modes of expression in the
> doctrine of the Trinity, the difficulty of finding appropriate terms must be
> kept in mind when we are talking about the mystery of the Trinity in the

---

9. Saint Augustine, *De Trinitate*, V, 9, 10; text in Saint Augustine, *The Trinity*, Fathers of the Church,
vol. 45 (Washington, D.C.: Catholic University of America Press, 1963), 187–88.

presence of strict monotheists. Even if we completely respect the linguistic usages of the classical theology of the Trinity, we might say that it is by no means absolutely necessary to speak of "three persons" even in regard to the Trinity (a usage which is not to be found anyway in the New Testament) in order to explain what Christianity really means by this doctrine. In religious language we could safely speak of the Father who is ineffably close as himself in his Logos in history and in his Spirit in ourselves; we could admit that this Logos and this Spirit, however much they are to be distinguished from him and from one another and cannot be reduced to a lifeless sameness, are God himself and not intermediate beings, which would have to be regarded as creatures or would introduce a subordinationist process of evolution into God. (Rahner 1984a, 120; see also Lapide and Moltmann, eds., 1979)

True as it may be that the mystery of the Trinity has been revealed in Jesus Christ, it is not without "stepping-stones" in Judaism. Where Islam is concerned, it has been noted that the ninety-nine names which the Qur'an attributes to Allah can, without violence being done to them, be grouped under three broad headings: God as omnipotent Creator and Ruler of the universe; God as gracious and forgiving; and God as intimately present to us (see Hick 1990, 98). Transposed into Christian Trinitarian doctrine, these categories are seen to correspond to the "appropriations" to the distinct persons of various divine activities: creation to the Father, salvation to the Son, indwelling to the Spirit.

Looking beyond the monotheistic religions, we have suggested above that the divine Trinity is for Christian theology the hermeneutical key for other experiences of the Divine Reality. There is, in fact, no dearth of comparative theologians who search for a Trinitarian structure in the experience of the Ultimate Reality to which various mystical Eastern traditions bear witness. We mention here some such attempts, which, however, are open to a critical evaluation.

In his *The Unknown Christ of Hinduism,* Raimon Panikkar establishes a parallel between Father-Son, on the one hand, and Brahman-Ishvara, on the other (see Panikkar 1981). He pursues the parallel between the Spirit and the Atman in *The Trinity and the Religious Experience of Man* (Panikkar 1973). Brahman, then, is the "Absolute," the *nirguna,* the Father; Ishvara, the *saguna,* represents the Son; Atman, the "immanent deity," the Spirit. Whatever the merits or the shortcomings of this parallel (see Dupuis 1971), Panikkar believes that the fundamental intuition of the nonduality (*advaita*) of God and the human being, conveyed by the Trinitarian experience, is found in most religious traditions, though expressed differently in each. God is the "boundary of man"; "man is more than man; he is a theandric mystery." For the human being is called upon to realize his or her oneness with the "ground of being," at once transcendent and immanent. Elsewhere Panikkar sees in the mystery of the Trinity the ultimate foundation for the plurality of world religious traditions.[10]

---

10. See Panikkar 1987b; see comments in Williams 1990, 3–15; see also Panikkar 1993.

In a somewhat similar fashion, Joseph A. Bracken considers the various views of the Divine, characteristic of different religious traditions, as "inseparable dimensions of one and the same august mystery," of which the doctrine of the Trinity is the model for Christian understanding (Bracken 1995, 128–40). As a process theologian, Bracken argues that the Infinite is not an entity but an activity which empowers all entities to exist in dynamic interrelation. The Infinite is the "divine Matrix," the nondual reality which is the transcendent source and goal of all beings. This idea, he believes, is consistent with the Western Christian tradition; it is also implicit in descriptions of the Ultimate Reality in the mystical traditions of the East. Bracken's hypothesis leads him, however, to distinguish between the divine nature as Ultimate Reality and the three divine persons of the Trinity through whom we come in vital contact with the Ultimate Reality of the mystery of being. He writes:

> Admittedly, in terms of the hypothesis of this book, only the underlying divine nature is infinite since it alone is absolutely formless and undifferentiated. The three divine persons as enduring subjects of the infinite activity and therefore as entities are "finite" in the sense of being fully determinate realities. But, insofar as they together constitute the limitless reality of God, they are qualitatively infinite with respect to all their creatures. (Bracken 1995, 138)

This way of speaking, akin to the distinction made by Meister Eckhart between the Godhead (*Gottheit, deitas*) beyond God and God himself (*Gott, Deus*), does not, however, seem fully to correspond to the Christian tradition, which professes a real identity between the Godhead (or divine nature) and the three "persons" of the Trinity; each of these *is* the Godhead while the three are mutually distinct through their interrelationships.

A similar conception is also found in Bede Griffiths's introduction to *Universal Wisdom* (B. Griffiths, ed., 1994). In his search for a Trinitarian structure of the religious experience to which the various religious traditions bear witness, Griffiths too is led to distinguish the hidden reality of the Godhead from its manifestation in a personal God and, in Christianity, from its manifestation in the three divine persons. He writes:

> We can thus discern a basic pattern in all the great religious traditions. There is first of all the supreme Principle, the ultimate Truth, beyond name and form, the Nirguna Brahman of Hinduism, the Nirvana and Sunyata of Buddhism, the Tao without a name of Chinese tradition, the Truth of Sikhism, the Reality — al Haqq — of Sufism, the Infinite En Sof of the Kabbala, the Godhead (as distinguished from God) in Christianity. There is then the manifestation of the hidden reality, the Saguna Brahman of Hinduism, the Buddha or Tathagata of Buddhism, the Chinese Sage, the Sikh Guru, the personal God, Yahweh or Allah, of Judaism and Islam, and the Christ of Christianity. Finally, there is the Spirit, the Atman of Hin-

duism, the "Compassion" of the Buddha, the Grace (*Nadar*) of Sikhism, the "Breath of the Merciful" in Islam, the Ruah, the Spirit, in Judaism, and the Pneuma of Christianity. (B. Griffiths, ed., 1994, 41–42)

Again, it may be asked whether this view is altogether consonant with the Christian tradition. The Christian tradition does see the person of the Father as the source of the entire Trinity, the "origin without an origin," while both the Son and the Spirit originate from him; nevertheless, the Son and the Spirit share with the Father one and the same Godhead. All "three" constitute, in their interrelationships, the Ultimate Reality and the source of all created beings.

Parallels such as are construed by the authors just mentioned seem, therefore, somewhat elusive and difficult to handle. However, differences notwithstanding and account being taken of the singularity of God's self-disclosure in Jesus Christ, it seems legitimate to find in the mystical traditions of the East foreshadowings of, and approximations to, the Ultimate mystery of Being such as will be decisively, though still incompletely, disclosed and manifested in Jesus Christ.

This affirmation, of course, would need to be verified and substantiated distinctly for the various mystical traditions of Eastern religions — a work which cannot be attempted here. Where Buddhism is concerned, we must be satisfied to refer to the various recent works in which a dialogue has been initiated between Buddhist "emptiness" (Sunyata) and the Christian Trinity (see Corless and Knitter, eds., 1990), or between Buddhist emptiness and the "emptying God" of Christianity.[11] The second part of the chapter will be a case study on the Hindu concept of Brahman in Hindu *advaita* mysticism in relation to the Christian mystery of the Trinity. It will ask whether insights into, or approaches to, the Trinitarian mystery of Christian revelation can be found there and how the two traditions can be said to relate with each other on this count and eventually to converge and to complete each other.

## II. Hindu Mysticism and Christian Mystery

### A. Advaita *Experience and Jesus' Consciousness*

Hinduism is a redoubtable interlocutor for Christianity in comparative theology as well as in interreligious dialogue. It poses searching questions (1) in the areas of the relationship between the Ultimate Reality and the finite and historical, between the nondual Absolute and the world, and, notably, (2) in the field of the significance and interpretation of the historical person of Jesus Christ (see Dupuis 1991b, 15–45; see also Brück 1991; Coward, ed., 1990).

Hinduism is, however, many-faceted and cannot be reduced to a monolithic entity. Various currents occur in it which view the Ultimate Reality either as nonpersonal or as personal and which conceive the relationship between the

---

11. See Cobb and Ives, eds., 1990. See also Panikkar 1989; Küng et al. 1993; Pieris 1988b. See other works mentioned in the introduction, above, n. 10.

Ultimate Reality and the world in terms either of monism, of nonduality (*advaita*), or of dualism (*dvaita*). All these currents cannot be reviewed here. We shall pause to consider what may be viewed not as the most widespread current of Hindu faith and theology, which, undoubtedly, must be found in bhakti theism, but as the most challenging view for Christian mysticism — that is, the *advaita* experience rooted in the Upanishads and elaborated by the Vedanta theologians. We shall have to show the specificity and the originality of Jesus' awareness of being one with God, as compared to *advaita* awakening, in order, thereafter, to compare the Hindu concept of Brahman as *saccidananda* with the Christian concept of the Trinity.

To begin with, let us note that the originality of Jesus' self-awareness cannot be defined or determined as easily as has often been supposed. For, just as the content of faith and the formulation expressing it cannot be relegated to two perfectly airtight compartments, so also it is impossible to extract Jesus' self-consciousness from the manifold elements of the idiom in which he himself expressed it as if we were dealing with some pure, incorporeal form. And yet, in the last analysis, the apostolic faith in Jesus Christ can be supported by the apostles' and disciples' paschal experience only if the latter is itself based on the testimony of the prepaschal Jesus. Thus, a penetration of Jesus' self-consciousness, or, equivalently, his experience of God, is an indispensable theological task. The originality of the state of "awakening to God" experienced by Jesus, and the singularity of his concomitant self-awareness, must become the object of explanations and elucidations.

The task is all the more necessary and urgent in our particular context, where our concern is to establish a dialogue between Jesus' and others' experiences of God. The genuine character of their difference has often been too casually glossed over. According to a widespread interpretation among representatives of neo-Hinduism, Jesus must be regarded as a *jivanmukta*: a self-realized spirit. Thus Jesus is imaged as one fully awake to his identity with the Brahman. His words in the Gospel according to John, "I and the Father are one" (Jn 10:30), are understood as expressing the equivalence, although in a different mental context, of Hindu mysticism's decisive experience of *advaita: Aham brahmasmi.* Certain Christian interpreters are inclined to think that the difference between the self-consciousness of Jesus and the experience of *advaita* would be mainly a question of context and language.[12] What, then, is the relationship between Jesus' self-awareness and the experience of *advaita?*

Do Jesus' self-consciousness and the experience of *advaita* coincide — although expressed differently, as we should expect, since they arose in philosophical views and conceptions of the world that issue from different cultures? Or must we maintain that there is a radical difference between what Jesus experienced and what was experienced by the sages of the Upanishads?

---

12. See Le Saux (Abhishiktananda) 1984a, 52: "This 'Son'/'Father' is the nearest equivalent in a semitic context to the *tattvamasi/aham brahmasmi.*"

Jesus' consciousness is essentially filial. Nothing is more central in Jesus' religious experience than his relation to God as his "Father." This God who is Parent is the Yahweh of the Jewish religious tradition, the God of the covenant, known and familiar to Jesus' hearers. The concept of Father as applied to Yahweh is not unknown to the Old Testament, which describes God's fatherly attitude toward the chosen people (see Ex 4:22). But in Jesus' consciousness, Yahweh's parenthood takes on an altogether new depth, a meaning bound up with the relationship to Yahweh that Jesus himself experienced. Its filial nature vis-à-vis God is unique in its kind and is of a distinct order: Jesus is *the* Son (Mk 3:11), the very Son of God (Mk 12:6), the Only-Begotten (Jn 1:14).

There is no better indication of the claim for the unique nature of Jesus' divine filiation, perhaps, than the familiar term of address "*Abba,*" preserved by the Gospel witness (Mk 14:36) in its original Aramaic form by which Jesus addressed God his Father. This word, which Jewish tradition used in family relationships, when addressed to God in prayer implies a familiarity and an intimacy with God never before so denoted. This term, then, functions to portray Jesus' lived experience and revelation of his unique divine filiation. The "hymn of jubilation" (Mt 11:25–27; Lk 10:21) is further testimony. It expresses the unique relationship that faith sees binding Jesus to God as Son to the Father. It shows that there is a mystery of the Son as there is a mystery of the Father, indeed that the Father and the Son share in one and the same mystery. The Gospel according to John sums this up, saying: "He [Jesus] called God his own Father, making himself God's equal" (Jn 5:18).

This claim of unique filiation implies that between Yahweh-Father and Jesus-Son there is at once a distinction and a unity. The distinction is evident and scarcely calls for explanation. Jesus refers to the Father as if he is addressing another, someone he praises, someone to whom he prays. But the other side of the coin (the unity side) bestows on Jesus' religious consciousness its specific character — *Jesus referring to the Father with a familiarity never before conceived or attested.* What Jesus reveals of the mystery of God could not be explained by an extraordinary knowledge of the scriptures. It was not something learned. It was something that flowed out of the living experience of a unique intimacy. If, as the Gospel testifies, no one had ever spoken as Jesus did (Jn 7:46), the reason is that no other human experience of God was comparable to his. The Gospel according to John offers us certain glimpses of this oneness between Father and Son: "I and the Father are one" (Jn 10:30). This unity implies reciprocal immanence (10:38; 14:11; 17:21), a mutual acquaintance (10:15), a mutual love (5:20; 15:10), a common action — what Jesus accomplishes, the Father accomplishes in him (5:17).

We may formulate the following conclusion: *Jesus' relation with God is an "I-Thou" relationship of Son with Father.* The two elements of this relationship — distinction (Son-Father) and unity ("are one") — together constitute the originality and specificity of the experience of God that Jesus lived. This is so eminently true that no other category seems even remotely capable of expressing this singular relationship. In Jesus' experience he is not the Father, but between him and his Father the communication of likeness and, indeed, the oneness are such that they call for expression in terms of a Father-Son relationship.

Jesus' consciousness of this unique relationship with God his Father is doubtless best manifested in his prayer. However, it finds expression in everything constituting his religious life — his obedience and his submission to the will of the Father, the self-offering he makes when he surrenders his spirit into his Father's hands. Jesus' entire religious life is centered on the person of the Father. When he prays and worships, when he supplicates or implores, the orientation of his entire human spirit to the Father is so profound that it is evidently rooted beyond the sphere of the human. His sense of total dependence vis-à-vis the Father surely seems a human echo of a deeper personal origin with regard to him. In the "economy" of Jesus' prayer, the "theology" of his person is transposed to the key of human awareness. The mystery of Jesus is the mystery of the Son as displayed in humanity, but without being exhausted there.

Thus, Jesus' human life and condition are a human expression of the mystery of the Son of God. In this way his human words are the human expression of the divine Word. Jesus not only addresses to human beings words received from God as the prophets did — he is himself the Word of God made flesh. The reason why God's self-revelation in Jesus is decisive and unsurpassed is that in his human consciousness Jesus experiences the mystery of the divine life which he personally shares. This transposition of the Divine Mystery into human consciousness permits its expression in human language. In Jesus, then, the revelation of this mystery is qualitatively different, since in the biblical record he is himself the Son of God, who expresses himself and elucidates his divine parentage in human terms. This revelation is central and normative for Christian faith, in the sense that no one is capable of communicating to human beings the mystery of God with greater depth than does the Son himself, who has become a human being. Jesus brings the word because he is the Word.

However, as has been noted above (see p. 249), even this revelation remains limited, incomplete, and imperfect. First of all, no human consciousness, not even that of the Son-of-God-become-a-human-being, can comprehend and contain the Divine Mystery. Human words, were they to be pronounced by God himself, must fail to exhaust God's reality. Furthermore, to this inescapable, intrinsic limitation affecting the revelation of God in Jesus Christ must be added a specific limit due to the particular idiom in which Jesus expressed himself — the Aramaic spoken in his time. This shows that the "fullness" attributed in Christian faith to the revelation in Jesus Christ must be qualified and correctly understood.

On the basis of what we have said, it is clear that Jesus' human awareness is crucial for the theological understanding of the mystery of Christ according to the Christian faith. Jesus' awareness as portrayed in diverse ways in scripture manifests the originality and unique character of his experience of God. It is also the human source of the divine revelation that takes place in and through him. In Hindu mysticism, the experience of *advaita* likewise occupies a central place, and it is this that authorizes its comparison, from a number of viewpoints, with the consciousness of Jesus.

Traditionally, two formulae serve to express the heart of the experience of *advaita*, both taken from the Upanishads: *Aham brahmasmi* (see Brihadaranyaka Upanishad 1, 4, 10) and *tattvamasi* (see Chandogya Upanishad 6, 8, 7). This experience, to which the tireless quest for the inner self leads, may be described, it would seem, as an entry, or better, assumption, into the knowledge that the Absolute has of itself, and thus as an insight into being literally from the viewpoint of the Absolute. From the special viewpoint of this absolute awareness, all duality (*dvaita*) vanishes, since the Absolute alone is absolutely, is One-without-a-second (*ekam advitiyam*). From this viewpoint, the universe and history have no absolute meaning (*paramartha*): their existence pertains to the domain of the relative (*vyavahara*), God's *lila* (God's play in creation). At the awakening of the experience of *advaita*, the ontological density of the finite seer itself vanishes. The awakening to absolute awareness leaves no room for a subjective awareness of self as finite subject of cognition: there remains only the *aham* ("I") awareness of the Absolute in the epiphenomenon of the body (*shariram*): *Aham brahmasmi* (see Le Saux [Abhishiktananda] 1984b, 31–41).

If this description is correct, then it is evident that the experience of *advaita* implies a radical fading away of all that is not the Absolute. When the consciousness of the absolute *Aham* emerges in the seer, the latter is submerged in it. "Who knows and who is known?" asks the Upanishad. Henceforth, there is no longer a finite "ego" who — regarding God and regarded by God — contemplates and addresses a prayer to God. What abides is the awakening of one to the subjective consciousness of the Absolute itself. And it is not an objective knowledge of the Absolute by a finite ego. In the process of illumination, the human "ego" gives way to the divine *Aham*. Such is the radical demand of *advaita*.

"I and the Father are one" — "You are that," "I am Brahman." These experiences seem at first glance to be entirely different. Jesus' words express the awareness of a distinction in unity, the experience of an interpersonal relationship whose two poles (distinction and oneness) are inseparable constituents: Jesus is not the Father, but he *is* one with him. The citations from the Upanishads, on the contrary, express an awareness of a real identity, in which all distinction has disappeared. At the awakening of self-realization, only the consciousness of the absolute *Aham*, the Atman-Brahman identity, abides. On the one side, Jesus is humanly conscious of being one with God his Father; on the other, the consciousness of the finite "ego" gives place to the consciousness of the infinite self, identical with the Brahman. On one side, the Word of God becomes humanly aware of itself in the human consciousness of Jesus; on the other, an awareness of the divine *Aham* invades and submerges the subjective consciousness of the finite self.

That the distinction between Jesus and the Father is an irreducible component of Jesus' experience is altogether certain in the scriptural record. But just as central to the experience in important New Testament strata is his oneness with the Father — a unity not solely due to his mission but founded, in the last analysis, on being: Jesus and the Father are one, nonduality (*advaita*). The "I" of Jesus' Gospel sayings, while it establishes the distinction from the "Thou" of the Father, also implies unity with him. Ultimately, this "I" does not mean, properly speaking, that a human person called Jesus is related to God as to a Father but rather that the Son-of-God-become-a-human-being is posited in relation with his Father.

As we see, the "I am Brahman," the *Aham brahmasmi* of the Upanishads, finds its truest application, paradoxically, precisely in Jesus. In him this proposition becomes literally true and acquires a new meaning: it proclaims Jesus' personal awareness of belonging, along with the Father, to the sphere of the divinity. Applied to Jesus, the *Aham brahmasmi* then seems to correspond to Jesus' "absolute" *ego eimi* in the Johannine Gospel (see Jn 8:24, 28, 58; 13:19). As we know, these words are taken from the Septuagint translation of Ex 3:14. In the original Hebrew of that text, the revelation of the name YHWH connotes God's "being with" Moses and his people, in fidelity to his promises. In the Greek version, by contrast, the connotation is more metaphysical — Yahweh is "the One who is." In the Gospel according to John, the absolute *ego eimi* can take on both nuances: in Jesus the Em-manu-el, God is "with us" in a decisive way, and at the same time Jesus is the one who, along with the Father, belongs to the sphere of the Divine; the one who is, and consequently is capable, in an acquired human consciousness, of declaring in all truth: "I am," *Aham brahmasmi.*

One can think, then, that Jesus' consciousness of his personal communion with the Father in the *advaita* of the divinity is the crown and fulfillment of the intuition of the seers of the Upanishads. After all, the intuition stretches the human mind to the limit — and beyond — of what it is capable of experiencing and of expressing in words. Perhaps we might say that Jesus' human consciousness resolves the insurmountable antinomy to which the experience of *advaita* leads — the antinomy between the values of absolute oneness, on the one hand, and of personal communion, on the other. At least we can assert that Jesus' awareness of his relationship with his Father is the supreme realization of *advaita* in the human condition — a realization, indeed, that even the seers of the Upanishads did not foresee or describe (see Le Saux [Abhishiktananda] 1976, 77–93; 1984b, 77–89).

Meanwhile, concerned as we may be to emphasize the notion that Jesus' awareness brings the experience of *advaita* to an unexpected fulfillment, we must likewise ascribe all due importance to the relentless quest for *advaita* which helps us purify our understanding of Jesus' communion with his Father: this communion is unique and simply irreducible to the measure of interpersonal relationships among human beings (Le Saux [Abhishiktananda] 1984b, 85–86). Jesus' awareness of his union with his Father is human, but it is a

human awareness of communion in divinity. While it finds its most perfect realization in the mystery of Christ, the experience of *advaita* also helps us discover
new depths in that same mystery.

## B. Saccidananda *and the Trinity*

Jesus' human awareness of his oneness-in-distinction with the Father is the
foundation of the Christian faith in the mystery of the divine Trinity: Father/
Mother — Son/Word/Wisdom — Spirit/Love. The question must now be asked
how this doctrine relates to the concept of God that underlies Hindu *advaita*
mysticism.[13]

The Nirguna Brahman, or the Absolute in itself, is conceived in terms of
*saccidananda* (being-consciousness-bliss). Being (*sat*), consciousness (*cit*), bliss
(*ananda*) stand for three intrinsic perfections of the Absolute Brahman. The
three terms are not found together in any single text of the Upanishads; in
the sacred texts they are only found separately: Brahman is "supreme being"
(*satyasya satyam*) (Brihadaranyaka Upanishad 2, 1, 20); "consciousness and
bliss" (*vijnanam anandam*) (Brihadaranyaka Upanishad 3, 9, 28); "being, consciousness, infinity" (*satyam jnanam anantam*) (Taittiriya Upanishad 2, 1); and
so on. It is the Vedanta theological tradition which on the foundation of the
scriptural assertions coined the compound expression *saccidananda*.

The term is designed to express the intrinsic nature of the Absolute, the
"One-without-a-second" (*ekam eva advitiyam*) (Chandogya Upanishad 6, 2,
2). A detailed analysis of the divine attributes would show that they correspond in a striking manner to the "transcendental perfections" which Christian
philosophy has traditionally affirmed of God, the Absolute Being (see Acharuparambil 1994, 201–6). This is not to say that they represent in the Hindu
tradition a mere philosophical understanding. For, as just mentioned, the *saccidananda* concept is derived from the Upanishads, that is, from the sacred
scriptures, and the Vedanta thinkers who elaborated on it were exegetes and
theologians — commenting and explaining the revealed word — not philosophers or metaphysicians. With good reason, then, Sri Aurobindo affirms that
the *saccidananda* intuition of Hindu mysticism represents an authentic spiritual
experience. He writes: "An absolute, eternal and infinite Self-existence, Self-
awareness, Self-delight of being that secretly supports and pervades the universe
even while it is also beyond it, is, then, the first truth of spiritual experience"
(Aurobindo 1970, 1:325, quoted in Acharuparambil 1994, 203).

It is all the more worthwhile, then, to inquire how the *saccidananda* concept
of Brahman relates to the Christian concept of the Trinity. The first observation
to be made is that the Christian tradition has made use of the same transcendental perfections of the Godhead to express the mystery of the three persons
of the Trinity: Father, Son, Spirit. The "psychological analogy" of the Trinity is

---

13. For the divine *Trimurti*, akin to a "personal" concept of God, see Acharuparambil 1994.

well known; it remains even today one of the deepest theological insights into the Divine Mystery. Saint Augustine developed the triads: *mens, notitia, amor,* and *memoria, intelligentia, voluntas,* the three members of which correspond respectively to the Father as being, the Son as consciousness, and the Spirit as love (see Saint Augustine, *De Trinitate* IX, X; see also *Confessiones* XIII, 11, 13). The same analogy was further evolved and more elaborately formulated by Thomas Aquinas.[14]

The analogy must, however, be correctly understood. It does not consist — nor could it — in identifying the divine act of knowing with the person of the Son, and, similarly, that of loving with the person of the Spirit. It rather affirms that the divine act of self-consciousness or understanding bears an immanent fruit (*verbum mentale*) which is the Son; in turn, the divine act of love also produces an immanent fruit (*impressio amati in amante*) which is the Holy Spirit. The transcendental perfections of knowledge and love are, therefore, put to use to express analogically the "origin" in God of the Son generated by the Father, and of the Spirit as the fruit of divine love. Clearly, some new and deeper meaning is implied in the process, which goes beyond what the transcendental perfections imply by themselves in God. Applied to the faith in the Triune God, these are made to signify three divine "persons" in their mutual relationships.

The tradition of the Upanishads insists that the Brahman — which is at once transpersonal (*nirguna*) and personal (*saguna*) — lies beyond human knowledge: it is *neti, neti,* "not this, not that" (see Brihadaranyaka Upanishad 2, 3, 6; 3, 9, 26; 4, 2, 4; 4, 4, 22; 4, 5, 15); it is "other than what is known, beyond the unknown."[15] Nevertheless, the notion of *saccidananda* conveys more than a description of it, an insight which truly corresponds to the reality of the Real. In a similar manner, the Christian tradition, as we have recalled above, does not tire of stressing that the Godhead remains beyond all human apprehension: *nada, nada.* Yet it also affirms that the Trinity of Father/Mother–

---

14. See mostly Thomas Aquinas, ST I, 27, 3, 4; 37, 1; *de Veritate* 4; *Contra Gentiles* IV, 11, 19. See also Paissac 1951; Lonergan 1967.

15. See Kena Upanishad I, 3–8, which reads as follows:

> 3. There no eye can penetrate,
>    No voice, no mind can penetrate:
>    We do not know, we do not understand
>    How one should teach it.
>
>    Other it is, for sure, than what is known,
>    Beyond [the scope of] the unknown too.
>    So have we heard from men of old
>    Who instructed us therein.
>
> 4. That which cannot be expressed by speech,
>    By which speech [itself] is uttered,
>    That is Brahman — know thou this....
>
> 5. That which cannot be thought by the mind,
>    By which, they say, the mind is thought,
>    That is Brahman — know thou [this].

Translation Zaehner 1966 (with corrections).

Son/Word/Wisdom–Spirit/Love objectively corresponds to the mystery of the Ultimate Reality.

From the standpoint of a Christian theology, how, then, can the *saccidananda* concept of Brahman be evaluated in relation to the divine Trinity of Christian faith? The evaluation will depend on the model which one entertains of the relationship between world religions and the Christian mystery.

While accounting for the different paradigms in the debate on the theology of religions, we have distinguished two different models of inclusivism, which we called respectively the "fulfillment theory" and the "theory of the presence of the mystery of Christ" (see chap. 5 above). We further suggested that a model of Trinitarian Christology would allow for a more positive evaluation of religious pluralism (see pp. 204–208, above). How do these distinct standpoints react to the *advaita* mysticism of *saccidananda*?

The fulfillment theory recognizes the presence in some Hindu doctrines of "stepping-stones" (*pierres d'attente*) toward the Christian mystery. The *saccidananda* doctrine of Brahman is a case in point.[16] According to this theory, the concept of *saccidananda* — among other Hindu doctrines — witnesses to the universal human search for the Divine which the Christian message brings to fulfillment. In itself, the Hindu concept merely conveys the transcendental perfections of the Divine, attainable to human reason independently from any personal manifestation on the part of God. These perfections are realized in the Brahman in the absolute degree: Brahman is by itself absolute being-consciousness-bliss. However, the Christian tradition has made use of the transcendental perfections of the Divine to give expression — analogically — to the mystery of the divine Trinity revealed in Jesus Christ. In virtue of this, the fulfillment theory is able to discover in the Hindu doctrine some (natural) "stepping-stones" to the mystery of the Trinity — no more.

By contrast, the "theory of the presence of the mystery of Christ" is prepared to recognize in the Hindu *saccidananda* concept more than a human waiting for the Divine; it recognizes traces, in the "spiritual experience" of Hindu mysticism, of a divine self-manifestation and, therefore, of a hidden, operative presence of the mystery of God and of Christ. For the "theory of the presence," there is more to be found in the Hindu tradition than a simple "natural" foundation for a divine self-communication; there are in it elements of "truth and grace" (AG 9) which witness to a self-manifestation of God in his Spirit. *Saccidananda* belongs to these; it represents an authentic presentiment of the Divine Mystery as revealed in Jesus Christ.

We can go a step further. It has been suggested above that a Trinitarian Christological model may serve as a useful hermeneutical key for an open Christian theology of religions. An effort has also been made to uncover a Trinitarian structure, no matter how inchoate and imperfect, in all human experience of the Divine. Following this cue, it may be said that the divine Trinity is experi-

---

16. Another is the *avatara* doctrine, on which there will be more in the next chapter.

enced, though hiddenly and "anonymously," wherever human beings allow the Divine Reality that impinges upon them to enter into their life. In every authentic religious experience the Triune God of Christian revelation is present and operative. It may further be said that contact with Hindu *advaita* mysticism may help Christians to purify and deepen their faith in the Divine Mystery. How?

In the light of the mysticism of the *advaita,* does not a tripersonal communion with God seem a propaedeutic to be transcended, that one may, at last, become one with the Divine Mystery beyond all distinctions? The question is a plausible one, even in the context of Christian tradition. If the Father is the unfathomable Trinitarian source beyond the Spirit and the Word, have we not the right to ask whether there is in turn a Beyond-the-Father? Is not the insurmountable Abyss beyond all personhood? Certain Christian mystics, Meister Eckhart in particular, have thought so and have spoken of the "Suressence" of the deity, beyond the three persons (see Barzel 1982).

Hinduism, for its part, regards all personal determination as imperfection: Brahman is impersonal, then, because it is transpersonal, or beyond personhood. For Hindu mysticism, all that the Christian mystery asserts of the "unknowable" Father is to be transcended, like any other propaedeutic — useful, surely, at its own level, but ultimately an encumbrance. One must not stop still at the threshold of the mystery. One must enter there, crossing "to the other shore": *neti, neti — nada, nada.*

The challenge is all the greater for the exaltation of its perspective. True, we have shown above that the Christian mystery of communion surpasses, by completing it, the Hindu mysticism of identification. Nonetheless, the challenge presented by the latter forces Christians to cast off simplistic conceptualizations; to rid themselves of certain gross anthropomorphisms; in sum, to purify their own faith. Indeed, the temptation is a real one to reduce interpersonal and pluripersonal relations with God to the level of relations among human persons. The intimacy characterizing our relations to God in Jesus Christ only renders the danger more real. But to reduce God to our own dimensions is to re-create God to our image and likeness — to make an idol of God, through forgetfulness of the inalienable transcendence of the deity.

It is here that the values of interiority cultivated by the Hindu tradition can come to the Christian's aid. God is the Utterly Other, but the divine otherness is not to be located outside ourselves, as on a horizontal plane. The relationship between the human being and God must be interiorized as it grows. This interiorization is the deed of the Spirit of God in the spirit of the human being. The Hindu tradition of the Atman can aid the Christian to interiorize the Christian experience of the God of history.

The Holy Spirit will then appear more as the mystery of the divine intimacy and interiority, of the being-together or nonduality (*advaita*) of the Father and the Son, and consequently, of the nonduality (*advaita*) of God and the human being. The experience of oneness of being may be necessary in order for the human being's invocation of the Absolute as the "Thou" of interpersonal communion not to risk being surreptitiously reduced to the dimension of an I-Thou relationship among human beings. God's being-together with human beings presupposes a radical mutual otherness; but the irruption of the Spirit of God into history, be it the personal history of the human being or the history of the world, overcomes all distances without suppressing distinctions.

The mystery of God is communion in nonduality. The mystery of the human being is that of our insertion, through Jesus Christ, into this divine communion. While the communion is the specific, inalienable contribution of God's revelation in Jesus Christ, the unity which necessarily underlies it can be strengthened by the experience of the nonduality (*advaita*) of Hindu mysticism.

### C. Complementarity or Convergence?

The question must, therefore, be asked whether between the concept of the Divine Mystery in Hindu mysticism and the Trinity of the Christian experience there exists a true complementarity or even — beyond complementarity — a certain convergence. The terms must be clearly defined.

"Complementarity" may, in this context, be viewed in terms of the fulfillment theory for which Hindu mysticism is one expression, among others, of the human aspiration toward the Divine Reality. As such it contains "stepping-stones" which the Christian revelation comes to fulfill. J.-A. Cuttat speaks, in this sense, of a Christian "assumptive synthesis," by integration and transcending, of all that Hinduism contains that is good and open to the Christian mystery (Cuttat 1967, 124; see 1960). Such complementarity, it will be noted — even if the term "convergence" is being used (Cuttat 1967, 126) — postulates a unilateral process from the other traditions to Christianity, a subordination which does not seem to do full justice to those traditions. It takes little notice of what they can positively contribute to the Christian perception of the mystery of God.

Others, on the contrary, understand "complementarity" as a reciprocal process in which the Eastern traditions on the Divine Reality can contribute positively to the Christian understanding of the mystery of God. The Judeo-Christian tradition and the Eastern traditions are seen as mutually complementary. *Advaita*, in particular, is a universal experience; *saccidananda*, a universal symbol of the Godhead which illustrates its nondual nature. It represents "a genuine penetration by the human consciousness into Divine Consciousness," "an intuitive insight into reality" (see Teasdale 1987, 108–12), which can contribute positively to a deepening of the Christian perception of the Divine Mystery. Here the names of Swami Abhishiktananda (Henri Le Saux)[17] and B. Griffiths[18] may be singled out as outstanding examples. Both advocate a Christian *advaita* which will articulate the unity-in-distinction of Jesus

---

17. See Le Saux (Abhishiktananda) 1984b. On Abhishiktananda, see Stuart 1989; Davy 1981; Dupuis 1991b, 67–90; Kalliath 1996.
18. See B. Griffiths 1976, 1982. On B. Griffiths, see Spink 1989; Teasdale 1987.

with the Father and, derivatively, of human beings with the divine *sacci-dananda*. Ultimate Reality is the inter-personal communion, in nonduality, of Father-Son-Spirit; human beings are called to share in this divine *koinònia*. In Christian *advaita*, the Hindu intuition of *saccidananda* and the Christian revelation really converge. *Saccidananda* and Trinity "share in a mystical continuum which makes an existential convergence possible" (Teasdale 1987, 127). Abhishiktananda writes:

> The experience of *saccidananda* carries the soul beyond all merely intellectual knowledge to the very centre, to the source of her being. Only there is she able to hear the Word which reveals within the undivided unity and *advaita* of *saccidananda* the mystery of the three persons: in *sat,* the Father, absolute Beginning and Source of being; in *cit,* the Son, the divine Word, the Father's Self-knowledge; in *ananda,* the Spirit of Love, Fullness and Bliss without end. (Le Saux [Abhishiktananda] 1984b, 178)

The conclusion seems to be as follows. The religious traditions of the world convey different insights into the mystery of Ultimate Reality. Incomplete as these may be, they nevertheless witness to a manifold self-manifestation of God to human beings in diverse faith-communities. They are incomplete "faces" of the Divine Mystery experienced in various ways, to be fulfilled in him who is "the human face of God."[19] For the Lord said to Moses: "You cannot see my face; for no one shall see my face and live" (Ex 33:2). And it is also written: "No one has ever seen God; the only Son, who is in the bosom of the Father, he has made him known" (Jn 1:18). To him who is the "human face of God" we now turn.

---

19. Title of the book by J. A. T. Robinson (1972).

## Eleven

# Jesus Christ — One and Universal

**W**HILE REVIEWING the current theological debate on the theology of religions, we noted the fact that the Christological question is at the center (see pp. 190–193, above; see also Dupuis 1991a). It could not be otherwise. What divides the different parties is their response to the question about the traditional understanding of Jesus Christ as the one universal Savior of humankind: Can and must this understanding be retained in the present context of religious pluralism and interreligious dialogue? The talk of "paradigm shifts" from Christocentrism to theocentrism — and other "isms" — is symptomatic of a renewed questioning in Christology. The protagonists of the theocentric paradigm — John Hick in particular — claim that the new Christological approach which they advocate is not primarily intended to meet the requirements of dialogue in a situation of religious plurality; it is required first of all for Christians themselves who, while being committed to faith in Jesus Christ, can no longer recognize their faith in the Church's traditional understanding of his person and work (see Hick 1985; 1993b; see also Swidler 1990, 109). They need a revised, intelligible Christology; such a revised Christology will have the added merit of removing the main impediment to a pluralistic theology of religions and, thereby, of fostering interreligious dialogue on a basis of equality between the partners.

Whatever may be the primary or secondary intention guiding the Christological position involved in the pluralistic paradigm, it is clear that the Christological question occupies central stage in a Christian theology of religions. The salvific role of other religious traditions, as well as the significance to be assigned (in God's overall plan for humankind) to other "paths" and other "saving figures," is intrinsically and inextricably linked — from a Christian standpoint — with the way in which the person and the event of Jesus Christ are understood and interpreted. We have noted above that what is at stake between the Christocentric and the theocentric paradigms is the choice between a "high," ontological Christology which unambiguously recognizes the personal identity of Jesus Christ as the Son of God and a "low" Christology which, remaining deliberately at the functional level, questions and ultimately denies such ontological affirmations about Jesus Christ (see p. 191, above). The choice is between a "difference-in-nature" Christology, dubbed by the pluralists as inflated, and a "degree" Christology considered by the inclusivists as revisionist. The question cannot be avoided.

The redimensioning of the person of Jesus Christ advocated by pluralists is based on various considerations which may be grouped under three headings: philosophical, historical-critical-exegetical, and theological. Some of these have been mentioned above in passing (see p. 190, above). They need to be examined here more closely.[1]

From the philosophical viewpoint, attention is drawn by pluralists to the new historical consciousness which sees truth no longer as static and eternal but as dynamic and historically conditioned. It is also noted that human knowledge, specially in religious matters, can never claim a disengaged objectivity but is always intrinsically affected by the presuppositions and "prejudices" of the knower. Moreover, in itself, the Divine Mystery remains irremediably and in all situations beyond human grasp; no religious tradition can, a priori, claim a privileged knowledge of the Divine Mystery, let alone a monopoly of knowledge. All human knowledge of the Absolute is relative.

In the field of biblical and New Testament exegesis, the claim is that a sound recourse to historical criticism leads unmistakably to a redimensioning of Jesus Christ, on more than one ground: the context of the New Testament affirmations about his person and work; the literary genre of these affirmations; the unbridgeable gap and total discontinuity between the claims of the historical Jesus and the interpretation made of him by the Church apostolic. Jesus, it is said, was entirely God-centered — he announced God and his Reign; the Apostolic Church's Christ-centered proclamation falsified Jesus' message. The Church apostolic was first responsible for the paradigm shift that took place from theocentrism to Christocentrism; it is time to reverse the situation by a new turn back to theocentrism.

Theologically, a dichotomy is being established between the particularity of the Jesus-event, localized in space and time and as such irremediably limited, and the Christian claim to a universal significance for the event. The contention is that no historical occurrence can claim the uniqueness and universality that Christianity attributes to the Jesus Christ–event. Nor does the history of religions sustain the Christian claim. It testifies rather to a variety of "paths" to salvation with similar credentials, all of equal value in their very differences; all — moreover — making contrasting claims to universality, if not to absolutism.

This list of misgivings is not complete (see Dupuis 1991b, 191–206). It will not be possible to examine here in detail each of those just mentioned. Our intention is somewhat different: it consists in showing that a well-poised claim to oneness and universality for Jesus Christ leaves room for an open theology of religions and of religious pluralism. In particular, a Trinitarian Christological

---

1. See the works of P. F. Knitter, J. Hick, and S. J. Samartha. Mostly: Knitter 1985; Hick 1973, 1989, 1993b; Samartha 1991. See also Hick and Knitter, eds., 1987. Recently published is Knitter 1996, which serves as companion volume to Knitter 1995a. See below.

perspective allows for the recognition of the ongoing presence and activity of the Word of God and of the Spirit of God. Such a perspective, as will be seen in the present and the following chapters, makes it possible to affirm a plurality of ways or paths to human liberation/salvation, in accordance with God's design for humankind in Jesus Christ; it also opens the way for recognizing other saving figures in human history.

Before proceeding further, some clarifications are, however, required which bear on the meaning of terms. First of all, there is talk here about the "uniqueness" of Jesus Christ, not of Christianity. Enough has been said previously to the effect that a Christocentric perspective must take the place of an ecclesiocentric perspective, too narrow to allow for a theology of religions (see pp. 185–186, above). This point need not be repeated, except to note that the wrong question about the "absoluteness of Christianity" has often been asked in the past. Hegel affirmed it in the framework of his idealistic philosophy; Ernst Troeltsch relativized it from the viewpoint of the history of religions (Troeltsch 1971; see Bernhardt 1994, 95–100; 1993, 144–208; see also Dupuis 1991b, 93–104); Karl Barth admitted it inasmuch as Christianity is the embodiment of saving faith in Jesus Christ, distinct from the Christian religion (see Bernhardt 1994, 83–85); Paul Tillich uttered prophetic protests against all self-absolutizing of religions (see Bernhardt 1994, 113–14). Karl Rahner used the expression "absoluteness of Christianity," perhaps unadvisedly, in the sense of its "uniqueness" (Rahner 1988a, 1973). Here, however, talk about "absoluteness" will be consistently avoided, with regard both to Jesus Christ and, a fortiori, to Christianity. The reason is that absoluteness is an attribute of the Ultimate Reality of Infinite Being which must not be predicated of any finite reality, even the human existence of the Son-of-God-made-man. That Jesus Christ is "universal" Savior does not make him the "Absolute Savior"[2] — who is God himself.[3]

This being said, many ambiguities remain over the terminology by which theologians express what distinguishes Jesus Christ from other saving figures, and Christianity from other traditions. We have noted earlier those ambiguities (see pp. 181–182, above; see also Dupuis 1995c, 128–31). Let it suffice to recall, where "oneness" (or "uniqueness") and "universality" are concerned, that both terms can be understood either in a "relative" or a "singular" sense (see Moran 1992). "Relative uniqueness" refers to the original character of every person or tradition, in its difference from others; "singular uniqueness" is said of Jesus Christ as the constitutive Savior of humankind. Similarly, "relative universality" indicates the universal appeal which various saving figures or religious tradi-

---

2. The expression is used repeatedly by Karl Rahner. See Rahner 1978, 193–95, 204–6, 279–80, 318–21.

3. See C. F. Braaten, who writes: "Absoluteness is rather a predicate of the God of the eschatological Kingdom proclaimed by Jesus as the power of the universal future in relation to the whole of God's creation, which includes the entire sweep of the history of religions. The presence of the eschatological Kingdom in Jesus and in the apostolic mission is the anticipation of the future of all religions as well as the entire religious life of humanity. These other religions are not striving after nothingness or false gods. They are looking toward union with the Divine Mystery that the Christian Gospel announces is ultimately the same divine reality as that revealed in the person of Jesus" (Braaten 1992, 47).

tions can possibly make on people as representing diverse paths to salvation; "singular universality" implies once again that Jesus Christ is the constitutive universal Savior. In both cases, the "relative" usage runs the risk of leading to a broad pluralism falling short of the Christian claim, while the restricted usage may be exposed to a narrow exclusivism. The first appears reductionist, while the other smacks of intransigence. How to avoid the pitfall on either side?

Elsewhere, I have suggested that uniqueness and universality need to be combined if we would wish to propound an open theology of religions. I wrote: "Oneness and universality: We must find a way of combining both and holding them together.... Without universality, uniqueness is exclusivism. Without uniqueness, universality would lead us down the pluralist path. In combination, however, the notes of uniqueness and universality accord with...inclusive Christology" (Dupuis 1991b, 192).

However this may be, the uniqueness and universality of Jesus Christ, as understood here, are neither "relative" nor "absolute." They are "constitutive," insofar as Jesus Christ holds saving significance for the whole of humankind and the Christ-event—in particular the Paschal Mystery of Christ's death and resurrection—is "cause" of salvation.[4] It is "relational," insofar as the person and the event insert themselves in an overall design of God for humankind which is multifaceted and whose realization in history is made up of diverse times and moments. Jesus Christ, it will be suggested, is, among different saving figures in whom God is hiddenly present and operative, the one "human face" in whom God, while remaining unseen, is fully disclosed and revealed. Throughout human history God has willed to be "in many various ways" (Heb 1:1) a God-of-people; in Jesus Christ he became God-of-people-in-a-fully-human-way (see Jn 1:14): the Em-manu-el (Mt 1:23) (see Dupuis 1991b, 101–2).

The chapter is divided into two main sections. The first section reasserts the constitutive uniqueness of Jesus Christ in the context of the present questioning on the part of pluralist theologians. This implies reassessing the evidence put forward by the Christian sources, encountering the contrasting claims made by other religious traditions for their respective saving figures, and a hermeneutics of Christological faith in the context of religious pluralism and dialogue. The second section aims to bring out the relational character of Jesus Christ's uniqueness and universality. To this end, it shows the distinction-in-identity of Jesus with the Christ, the coincidence in him of the particular and the universal. In a Trinitarian Christological perspective, it suggests how the one "human face" of God may be said to relate to other saving figures from which God has not withheld his saving presence and grace. Jesus Christ is thus seen as the "concrete universal," in whom all advances of God to human beings in history

---

4. Karl Rahner (1979) explains that the causality of Christ's death on the cross in the order of salvation must be conceived as quasi-sacramental rather than efficient. The cross does not cause salvation by determining God's salvific will; it is God's salvific will that results in Christ's death on the cross. He writes: "We must say: Because God wills salvation therefore Jesus died and rose again, and not: because the crucifixion occurred, therefore God wills our salvation" (207–8). See also Rahner 1978, 284.

are summed up and "re-headed" (see Eph 1:10). The philosophical and biblical questions raised by the revisionist Christology of pluralists are dealt with in the first part; those concerned with theology are deferred to the second part.

## I. One Saving Figure among Others?

### A. *The Christian Tradition Revisited*

That the theocentric paradigm in the theology of religions is based on a revisionist Christology which may be described as "degree" Christology is certain. It is plainly admitted by the protagonists of the pluralistic model themselves, John Hick[5] and Paul F. Knitter,[6] in particular. The nuances which the latter has introduced lately in his Christological position do not change the situation substantially.[7] A thorough critical study of the various considerations on which this revisionist Christology is based cannot be attempted here.[8] They must nevertheless be reviewed and evaluated rapidly; emphasis will be laid on the historical-critical-exegetical considerations.

Where the *philosophical* presuppositions are concerned, it is claimed that the newly acquired historical consciousness leads to a relativizing of truth. Static and eternal truth has given way to one which is dynamic and historical. There follows a "deabsolutizing" and a "deobjectifying" of truth, truth being always dependent on the knower's preconceptions and subject to change. "Objective" knowledge is a myth, in the face of which all claims to the "possession" of truth are rejected; all the more so any claim to "absolute" truth. Leonard Swidler (1990, 7–14) sums up the new situation in six points:

---

5. John Hick refers primarily to the following authors: Baillie 1963; Pittenger 1970; Knox 1967; Lampe 1977; Hick, ed., 1977. Also explicitly professing a "low" or "degree" Christology are, among other authors: Robinson 1973; Macquarrie 1992.

6. In *No Other Name?* Paul F. Knitter relied heavily, besides John Hick and S. J. Samartha, on the following: Cobb 1975; Ratschow 1982; Driver 1981; Tillich 1957, vol. 2; Ogden 1961.

7. In *Jesus and the Other Names*, Knitter's Christology has undergone some changes, also in terminology (see 171, n. 13). He now professes that Jesus is universal, decisive, indispensable, while denying that God's revelation in him is full, definitive, insurmountable (72–80). He holds a "relational uniqueness" (80) of Jesus, by which no distinctive uniqueness is meant (79). He writes: "To affirm Jesus as *truly* God's Word is to award him a distinctiveness that is his alone; to add that he is not *solely* God's Word is also to see that distinctiveness as one that has to be brought into relationship with other possible Words. Jesus is a Word that can be understood only in conversations with other Words" (80). Knitter suggests that "the title Spirit-filled Prophet be used as a hermeneutical flashlight to understand the many Christological titles given Jesus in the New Testament" (92; see 131). To profess him as "truly the Son of God and universal Savior" means to recognize him as "God's sacrament, as the embodiment, the historical reality, the symbol, the story that makes God real and effective *for me*" (105, emphasis added). It is difficult to see how this Christology corresponds — to mention only one name referred to by Knitter (see 105) — to that of Karl Rahner, for whom Jesus Christ is the "absolute Savior" of humankind. For Knitter, even in this latest work, Jesus Christ is not to be understood in terms of his unique personal identity as Son of God; accordingly, a "constitutive Christology according to which Jesus, especially in his death and resurrection, causes or constitutes the universal availability of God's salvific love" is untenable (133). See, however, Swidler and Mojzes, eds., 1996.

8. Such work has already been done where John Hick is concerned; see specially D'Costa 1987; Carruthers 1990. See also O'Collins 1995b. On S. J. Samartha, see Klootwijk 1992; Man 1993. No such critical work has yet been published on the Christology of Paul F. Knitter.

(1) All truth now holds only in relation to the historical context in which it was produced, i.e. it is historically conditioned and thus involved in constant change. (2) In addition to this historical conditioning there is the orientation of actions, i.e. the intention behind a practical action. (3) Truth is related to a standpoint; i.e. the cultural milieu in which the speaker and hearer of a communication of truth live, the class they belong to and their sex have an influence on the truth communicated. (4) Truth is bound up with language and thus limited to its frontiers; in other words, it always expresses a partial, selective, perspectivistic view of reality. (5) Truth is subject to interpretation, i.e. all experience relates back to a horizon of understanding, to the preunderstanding of the person experiencing it. The knower is involved in the knowledge since he or she knows in his or her way (as Thomas Aquinas recognized). There can be no such thing as purely objective, absolute knowledge, detached from the knowing subject. (6) Truth is dialogical, i.e. knowledge is achieved not in the mode of a one-sided acceptance of givens but reciprocally in dialogue with reality following the model of question and answer. (See Bernhardt 1994, 119)

And Bernhardt concludes:

If we take these six tendencies together — and it is certainly impossible to make a sharp distinction between them — we can say that "truth" no longer means absolute, i.e. detached, isolated, unconditional statements about reality. It is relational, and stands in relation to a network which is conditioned by many factors. But above all it is related to the one who receives it and expresses it; it is and remains tied to this person's point of view, perspective and language. There can no longer be any question of absoluteness in the sense of something that transcends time and culture, is independent of worldview and set apart from history. (Bernhardt 1994, 119)

What this conclusion shows clearly, however, is that Swidler and others are claiming to enjoy higher ground, above and beyond all the particular perspectives. This, in fact, looks very much like making an absolute objective judgment about the allegedly subjective and relative nature of any truth available to others with their limited worldviews.

Some clarifications are in order here. Truth, or reality, in itself needs to be distinguished from our human knowledge of it. That all human apprehension of Divine Reality is fragmentary and time-conditioned is certain; human knowledge of God — even after God's revelation in Jesus Christ — remains irremediably imperfect and provisional. This does not, however, invalidate it entirely, neither on the philosophical plane, much less on the theological, where it is founded on God's own word. Furthermore, while our apprehension of the Divine Mystery is "relative," God's mystery in itself (*an sich*) is "absolute": God *is* truth; he alone knows himself absolutely.

Applying these observations to the person of Jesus Christ, we can make the following points. We have remarked earlier about the "relative" character that necessarily affects the human consciousness of the Son-of-God-made-human; this does not, however, prevent it from being a privileged channel through which the Divine Mystery is truthfully disclosed to us (see p. 249, above). If the human awareness of the Son-of-God-made-man remains irremediably relative, this is a fortiori true of all knowledge which humans receive through him of the Divine Mystery. "Relative" does not, however, say invalid; and while the Divine Mystery will always lie beyond our grasp — *Deus semper maior* — the disclosure of it in "one who is Son" (Heb 1:1) offers special credentials to truthfulness. While, then, "God's truth, which is certainly one 'in itself' can only present itself in the plurality of particular views of the truth" (Bernhardt 1994, 126), it does not necessarily follow that all particular views of the truth have equivalent significance. Admittedly, in the Bible itself, the truth of God is historical and concrete; it concerns God's "truthfulness" and faithfulness but is never exhausted in history. The message of Jesus Christ too "stands under an 'eschatological proviso,'" inasmuch as final truth remains in store for full disclosure in the "not-yet" of the eschaton (Bernhardt 1994, 125). This notwithstanding, from the vantage point of Christian faith, the testimony of Jesus Christ and the witness borne to it by the foundational faith of the Apostolic Church as recorded in the New Testament have the privileged authority which attaches to the revealed word of God. The New Testament witness to the oneness and universality of Jesus Christ needs to be taken seriously.

Coming, then, to the *historical-critical-exegetical* considerations underlying the revisionist Christology of the pluralist paradigm, we may distinguish two basic attitudes. There are those who simply state in general terms that claims to uniqueness in the New Testament must be relativized, inasmuch as the context of the relevant passages either refers to the Jews or can at least be understood as bearing an exclusively Jewish reference.[9] Others readily acknowledge the New Testament's massive assertion of the uniqueness of Jesus Christ the Savior but ask whether this assertion still can or ought to be upheld today in the current context of religious pluralism.

The main texts directly concerned are Jn 14:6; Acts 4:12; and 1 Tim 2:5–6. To these can be added, among others, the Christological hymns of the Pauline and Deutero-Pauline letters, such as Eph 1:1–13 and Col 1:15–20. Elsewhere, I have observed that the uniqueness of Jesus Christ is in a true sense the message of the New Testament in its entirety, the deep faith that underlies the whole, which gives it its raison d'être, and without which it would not have been written (see Dupuis 1991b, 94). How must it be interpreted in our present context?

Various reasons are suggested for relativizing the statements of uniqueness.

---

9. See Rayan 1990, 133–38, where the author refers to Acts 4:12; Mt 28:18–20. As for 1 Tim 2:4–6, the text, according to the author, is to be interpreted in the present context of religious pluralism.

Recent hermeneutic investigations show that such claims actually result from a historically conditioned worldview and language modes dependent on a particular cultural context. We can no longer regard that uniqueness precisely as the "referent" of the Gospel message — the intangible kernel of the Christian kerygma (see Knitter 1985, 182–86; see also Tracy 1975, 72–79, 131–36).

It is also pointed out that in the context of the Jewish apocalyptic mentality, impregnated as it was with an eschatological expectancy, it was natural for the primitive Church to interpret the experience of God in Jesus Christ as final and unsurpassable. But this apocalyptic mentality was and is culturally limited. The finality it implies for the Jesus Christ–event, therefore, cannot be regarded as pertaining to the essence of Christianity; it belongs rather to the fortuitous cultural context in which it was first experienced and presented. If Jesus had been encountered and interpreted in some other cultural context, involving some other philosophy of history, he would have been considered neither final nor unique.[10]

Saint Paul is often held to bear the responsibility for the explicit assertion of the uniqueness of Jesus Christ. It is suggested that if the apostle had entered into contact with the rich mystical traditions of the oriental religions, he would have softened his sweeping, unnuanced assertions. Or again, this time with regard to Saint John, it is observed that the uniqueness of Jesus Christ is articulated in terms of "incarnation," but this is a mythical modality of thought, like the concept of preexistence with which it is bound up. But mythical language ought to be taken for what it is — "poetry, not prose" — and thus understood not "literally" but "metaphorically" (John Hick).[11] The incarnation must therefore be demythologized. The result would be the demythologization of Jesus Christ as universal Savior, a concept now recognized as belonging to a mythic mode of thought and hence not involving literal meaning (see Hick 1973, 148–79; 1993b; Hick, ed., 1977; McFadden 1974; Robinson 1973; Hick and Knitter, eds., 1987).

Finally, it is remarked that, in the historical context in which Christianity arose, and in the face of the opposition it encountered, it was natural for the disciples to present Jesus' "way" as unique. This absolute language is historically conditioned. It is survival language (see Baum 1974). Or, in Paul F. Knitter's interpretation, it is "action language" or "performative language" — that is, language designed to invite disciples to earnest following (see Knitter 1996, 68–69).

Apocalyptic, mythical-metaphorical, survival, performative — even "love language" has been mentioned.[12] R. Bernhardt sums it all up under the rubric of confession and doxology. He writes:

---

10. This is already suggested in Cupitt 1975; see also Hick 1973, 108–19.

11. This assessment of poetry is unfortunate: poetry no less than prose can refer truthfully to objective reality. Furthermore, the use of the term "metaphor" also seems inaccurate: metaphors extend ordinary linguistic usage and frequently, no less than literal language, make objectively true claims.

12. Knitter 1985, 184–86. We have already furnished, on biblical evidence, a short rebuttal of these ingenuous suggestions, in Dupuis 1991b, 198–99.

[The texts] are not decrees of eternal truths of God without a situation, revealed by Christ about himself, but confessions of him by his disciples and followers. They are not to be understood as metaphysical assertions about divine facts but as an existential expression of unconditional commitment and obligation, as an expression of trust and hope in situations which are desperate.

What stand out here as totalitarian claims to absoluteness are "statements in the witness box," personal or community testimony. Such statements first of all express the depth and seriousness of the person's own relationship to God in the face of external threats. The power of God is adduced against the powers from which the danger stems. One might almost say that this power is conjured up. So the Bible's supposed claims to absoluteness are simply public prayers of confession addressed to the oppressors and the oppressed alike and ultimately to God himself. In theological terms, they have the character of confession and doxology. Anyone who tears them from their historical foundation, generalizes them and uses them to condemn non-Christian religions is thus falsifying their original character.[13]

What we have here seems another case of confusion between personal motivation, on the one hand, and objective claims being made about reality, on the other hand. Motives should never be confused with meaning and truth. Moreover, it must be remarked that upholding — as the Christian tradition seems to require — the "constitutive" uniqueness of Jesus Christ does not necessarily result in "condemning" other religions and their "saving figures." A constant blemish of the pluralist paradigm consists in imagining that the only concretely possible alternative to its own standpoint is a dogmatic, exclusivist dismissal of other religions. Such a black-or-white dilemma is neither biblically nor theologically warranted. For the New Testament affirmation of Christ the man's uniqueness as "the way" (Jn 14:6), the "one mediator" (1 Tim 2:5), the "one name" (Acts 4:12) in whom human beings may find salvation does not cancel out faith in the Logos *asarkos* of which the Johannine Prologue speaks (see Foster 1990, esp. 31; also Parrinder 1990, esp. 51–52), through whom all people may be saved and in whom all ways may converge. He who was "the true light that enlightens every human being by coming into the world" (Jn 1:9) is the same who was to "become flesh" (Jn 1:14) in the "fullness of time" (Gal 4:4) in Jesus Christ.[14] Far from contradicting it, faith in Jesus Christ calls for a commitment and openness to plurality.

---

13. See Bernhardt 1994, 59–60. The same author sees defensive confessional language, arising out of threatening danger and tending to "absolute" statements, at work in the various situations referred to in Jn 14:6; Acts 4:12; Col 1:15–20. See Bernhardt 1994, 53–59.

14. In his *Readings in St. John's Gospel*, Archbishop William Temple wrote about this verse: "By the Word of God — that is to say by Jesus Christ — Isaiah and Plato, Zoroaster, Buddha and Confucius, uttered and wrote such truths as they declared. There is only one Divine Light, and every man in his own measure is enlightened by it" (quoted in Parrinder 1995, 78–79).

## B. Contrasting Claims to Uniqueness

I have shown elsewhere different ways in which neo-Hinduism tends to interpret Jesus Christ. I have distinguished six models of Hindu Christology: the Jesus of the beatitudes; the Christ of bhakti; the Christ of neo-Vedanta philosophy; Christ-*avatara*; Christ the *yogi*; the Christ of *advaita* mysticism (see Dupuis 1991b, 17–42; see also Thomas 1969; Samartha 1974). Similarly, one could show — leaving Judaism out of consideration here — how the Qur'an and Islam understand Jesus of Nazareth: as a prophet, one greater than Moses yet inferior to Muhammad, who is the "seal of the prophets" (see, among others, Arnaldez 1980, 1988). Again, the Buddhist view or views of Jesus Christ could be dwelt upon: Jesus, the "enlightened" one who, as such, is comparable to the Buddha; and, in later Mahayana developments, Jesus Christ the Bodhisattva (see, e.g., Keenan 1989, 1995; Lefebure 1993; Pieris 1988b; Vallet 1996).

Such is not, however, our intention here. Rather, it is to take note of the claims to uniqueness which other religions make either for their tradition or traditions or for their saving figures. These claims more often than not contrast sharply with those made by Christianity with regard to the person of Jesus Christ. To take cognizance of them is not without bearing on a Christian theology of religions that would claim to be open-ended; for such a theology will have to ask itself how it stands with regard to other claims that at first sight would seem to contradict its own (see Küng et al. 1993; Coward 1985).

R. Bernhardt observes pointedly that the prophetic religions are more prone to make "claims to absoluteness" than are the mystical religions of the East (see Bernhardt 1994, 101–2). Where *Islam* is concerned, he notes that "just as Christians worship Christ as the definitive Word of God made man, so for Muslims the Qur'an is the final word of God revealed through the prophet Muhammad" (Bernhardt 1994, 105). In fact, while for Christians the person of the Word-made-flesh is primarily important and, in relation to him, the word of God revealed through him, the situation in Islam is the reverse: the word of God contained in the Qur'an is what fundamentally matters; and Muhammad is important insofar as he is the channel through whom God's "eternal" word has been conveyed to us.[15] Claims to uniqueness are, therefore, concerned primarily with the Qur'an: "This book is not to be doubted. It is a guide to the righteous" (Surah 2:2); "the only true faith in God's sight is Islam" (Surah 3:19); "he that chooses a religion other than Islam, it will not be accepted from him, and in the world to come he will be one of the lost" (Surah 3:85). According to Islam's self-understanding, however: "This does not amount to an exclusive claim against [Islam's] predecessors, Judaism and Christianity, which denies these re-

---

15. M. Barnes writes pointedly: "If we restrict ourselves simply to Christianity and Islam, the correct parallel is not between the scriptures of the two traditions, nor between the central founder figures. The Word of God in Islam, the written word, is parallel to another Word, the *Logos* of John's Gospel. In the Qur'an the Word is made book; in Christianity the Word is made flesh. Jesus is the message; Muhammad the messenger of God's word, the mouthpiece through which God's will is made known to humanity" (1991, 52–53).

ligions their character as revelation and condemns them. Islam confronts these 'religions of the book' with the inclusive claim that it is the completion of their revelation" (Bernhardt 1994, 105).

Where Christianity finds the fullness of revelation in Jesus Christ, Islam finds it in the word of God embodied in the Qur'an—not in the sense that a new divine revelation came to the world with Muhammad (Surah 46, 10), but that the original "heavenly writing" given to humans in creation, proclaimed by the Jewish Torah and the Christian Gospel, but subsequently altered by their adherents, is restored to its pristine purity in the Qur'an (Bernhardt 1994, 106).

*Hinduism* often professes an attitude of tolerance and openness toward other religions, which may be characterized as "inclusive" in the sense that all religions are seen as striving toward the same divine primal ground. As all rivers lead through diverse meanders to the same ocean, similarly all religious "ways" are directed to the same Ultimate Reality—no matter how different the "paths" they traverse and the names by which the Real is called. This view, which has its roots in the Upanishads, may be considered as the one dogmatic truth of neo-Hinduism. Behind the differences of the various paths there lies the one dharma, or world order, as universal religious principle. As R. Bernhardt notes: "Unity and multiplicity belong together. In this perspective, claims to absoluteness advanced by one of the religious traditions against the others can only appear as a simple limitation of the horizon of consciousness" (Bernhardt 1994, 108–9).

However, the "inclusiveness" of Hinduism, paradoxically, often results in a claim to superiority, inasmuch as, in the view of its proponents, the prophetic religions are lacking the broad horizon of consciousness that grounds Hinduism's pluralistic outlook. Professed tolerance, when claimed unilaterally, may lead to intolerance.

Nor are claims to "inclusive universality" altogether absent in classical Hinduism. The Bhagavad Gita, undoubtedly the most widespread book of Hindu bhakti, is a case in point. The Bhagavad Gita surely seems to present Krishna as a universal savior. He saves not only those who have recourse to him (Bhagavad Gita 9:22, 25), but even those who, with faith, "adore other gods": "Even those who worship other gods with love (bhakti) and offer sacrifices to them, full of faith, really worship me, even though the rite departs from the norm" (Bhagavad Gita 9:23).[16]

Must we not see here the Hindu counterpart of "anonymous Christianity"—Krishna appearing as the Savior even of those who, by ignorance, but in the sincerity of their hearts, adore other gods and offer sacrifices to them? Let us observe, however, that the breadth of the outlook of the Bhagavad Gita does not seem to extend beyond that of the Hindu tradition of bhakti itself. The question whether Krishna's power to save is made to rest on a true "incarnation" of God among human beings is one to which we shall return hereafter.

Speaking of *Buddhism,* a striking parallel may first of all be established be-

---

16. Translation based on that of R. C. Zaehner (1966, 288). See also Parrinder 1971b, 109–13.

tween Jesus-the-Christ and Gautama-the-Buddha, on more than one count. As the Christian faith gave Jesus the title "the Anointed One" (*khristos*), so the Buddhist tradition has honored Gautama with that of "enlightened one" (*Buddha*). One tradition evolved from the Yeshua of history to the Christ of faith, the other from the Gautama of history (*Shakyamuni*) to the Buddha of faith (*Amida Buddha*). In both cases the religious traditions that ensued took their name from the titles bestowed on their founders: Christianity and Buddhism (see Swidler 1989, 119). But there is a difference. However exalted the rank of Gautama-the-Buddha in the Buddhist tradition, it is not equivalent to that which the Christian faith attributes to Jesus-the-Christ. Admittedly, Gautama preaches a message of liberation (dharma), as Jesus preached the Good News of God's Kingdom; Gautama did so with the authority which an outstanding religious experience (Nirvana) bestowed upon him, as Jesus' own authority flowed from his experience of God as *Abba* (see Pieris 1987). However, if the historical Gautama is savior, it is as the "enlightened one" whose example and teaching show others the way to liberation. According to Christian sources, in contrast, the historical Jesus *is* "the way" (Jn 14:6). From the apostolic age onward, Christian faith has professed him to be universal Savior.[17]

Yet it has been observed that in Mahayana Buddhism, the Buddhist faith underwent a development similar to that of primitive Christianity. Just as the first Christians came to recognize a divine presence in Jesus, so the Mahayanist Buddhist tradition registered a "deification" of the Buddha. Both traditions employ the same model of a divine descent to humanity (Knitter 1981, 1979). In the case of Gautama, the Buddha, however, a process of deification is avowedly what we have. By contrast, Jesus is not, for mainline Christianity, a deified human being but the Son of God humanized.[18] Progressive deification is an act of human beings; the incarnation is an act of God.

To the progressive "ontologization" of the Buddha there seems to correspond a gradual claim to uniqueness on the part of Buddhism. Bernhardt distinguishes different tendencies (Bernhardt 1994, 109–13). The first unequivocally professes the validity, in their differences, of different ways to salvation. Various parables are put to use to express their ultimate unity in plurality:

---

17. A. Pieris writes: "Quite unlike Jesus of the New Testament, Gautama of the *Tripataka* (early Buddhist scriptures) did not seem to have clearly claimed that the Saving Truth or the Liberating Path was identical with his own person. He was only the Path-Finder and Truth-Discoverer" (Pieris 1987, 164; 1988b, 124–31).

18. L. Swidler (1990) interprets the progressive "ontologization" of New Testament Christology in the sense of the pluralistic thesis: ontological language must be interpreted as "metaphorical." The case of Jesus is then seen as strictly parallel to that of Gautama-the-Buddha. He writes: "To use the Buddhist term enlightenment and to make the connection with both the biblical term *light* and the Christian understanding of the meaning of Yeshua's relation to God (*Light*), it might be said that Christians believed that Yeshua received en-Light-enment in the fullest possible manner; he was suffused with Light.... Hence he was a God(Light)-suffused man: He was 'the true light that enlightens every human being' (Jn 1:9)" (1990, 105). Again he writes: "The 'ontologization' of Yeshua into the divine Christ that occurred in Christianity as it moved from the Semitic cultural world into the Hellenistic was matched by a similar development with the 'ontologization' of Siddharta Gautama into the 'divine' Buddha ... as Buddhism moved from the Indian cultural world into the Chinese and Far Eastern" (1990, 111).

The religions are compared with the different reflections of the one moon
on the waters of the earth; with the different coloured refractions of the
one light in a prism; with the different fingers of a hand; different planes
of glass or windows through which the one sun shines; different rivers (or
canals) in which the same water flows from the same source or which issue
in the same ocean; with the colours of a rainbow, the branches of a tree
or the spokes of a wheel, which all end up at the hub. The motif in the
series of images is always the same: the religions are many, and they are
different; the gods called on by them are different and the faces of the gods
presented by them are different, but what inspires the religions, what the
names denote and what the faces point to, is one and the same. (Bernhardt
1994, 111)

Legitimate plurality does not, however, mean that all the religions are the
same. "The capacity of one's religion for integration, its tolerance and the
universality of its horizon are regarded as signs of religious maturity and in
this way form a claim to superiority" (Bernhardt 1994, 112). Buddhism, then,
makes a similar claim to inclusive superiority as does Hinduism — one which
"can even be intensified to become a claim to sole validity," as when the Buddha is made to say: "Of all the ways the Eightfold path is the best; of all the
truths the Four Noble Truths are the best. ... That is the only way, there is no
other way of reaching purity of insight" (Phra Khantipalo, *Tolerance: A Study
of Buddhist Sources* [n.p., 1964], 114, quoted in Bernhardt 1994, 112).

In conclusion, Bernhardt disagrees with the sweeping verdict that all religions — including the prophetic religions, in the exclusive form, and the
mystical ones from the East, in the inclusive form — understand themselves
as unique and universal. What is true is that each of the three monotheistic
religions "has its absolute basis of faith which it will not surrender" because
this foundation provides its identity (Bernhardt 1994, 113). In Christianity the
unnegotiable basis of faith is understood to be the doctrine of Jesus Christ as
the "only Son of God" in whom salvation is given to human beings. Is this
foundation still tenable in the face of other claims to uniqueness?

## C. Christological Hermeneutics

The first thing to say is that all talk of the absolute claims of Christianity about
Jesus Christ should be discontinued. Paul Tillich was right when he protested
about the self-absolutizing of religions, Christianity included.[19] The reason is
simple, and it has been mentioned earlier: "absolute" is an attribute of the Ultimately Real; only the Absolute is absolutely. However, once improper language
is set aside, the Christian claim for Jesus Christ, as traditionally understood,
still stands: faith in Jesus Christ does not merely consist in trusting that he is

---

19. See Geffré (1993a), who speaks of "the need to disabsolutize all historical religion as incarnation
of final revelation" (12).

"for me" the path to salvation; it means to believe that the world and human-kind find salvation in and through him. Nothing short of this does justice to the New Testament massive assertions.

But this is where a new hermeneutics of the New Testament seems required in the present context of pluralism and, not least, in view of interreligious dialogue. An inductive method of theologizing, it has been claimed in the introduction to the present work, leads to viewing theology as "interpretation in context" (see pp. 13–19). That in turn means that the first "act" consists in a "praxis," from which one turns to the "given" of the Christian revelation, for light and direction — and back again, following the hermeneutical circle. Whereas in a context of human oppression the first act involved is a praxis of liberation, in one of religious pluralism the praxis of interreligious dialogue takes over. The question, however, is asked which authority, doctrinal and moral, is attributed to the source of revelation if turning to it for direction follows as a "second" act upon a praxis of interreligious dialogue. Does the source of revelation continue to function as the *norma normans* for Christian thought and practice? Or is it, on the contrary, downgraded to a mere secondary norm, a sort of checking point?

To begin with, we can say in answer that the first act of praxis is itself inspired and informed by the Christian faith, as by its own point of departure. In the context of religious pluralism, this means that the praxis of interreligious dialogue never brackets out the faith of the practitioner by a sort of *epochè*; on the contrary, the authenticity of the dialogue requires that the partners, Christians or otherwise, enter into it with the integrity of their faith.[20] There is no interreligious dialogue in a vacuum of religious persuasion.

Not all is, however, settled thereby. For the question is urged as to whether the shock of the encounter between two living faiths may not be such as to force on Christian believers a "reinterpretation" of certitudes long possessed tranquilly, which have to do with the core of their faith.

In the context of liberation theology, biblical hermeneutics does not consider the sacred book as a mere memory of a past word. The word is being "reactualized" in present history, thus making present history part of the ongoing history of salvation. Some theologians speak, in this connection, not only of a "fuller sense" (*sensus plenior*) of scripture but of a "surplus meaning," insofar as God's original word is becoming actualized anew in the present.[21] The "paradigmatic" event of the Exodus is not merely a *kairos* of the past; it is being reactualized by God in the history of peoples even today; and while the Jesus Christ–event has happened once for all (*ephapax*) (Rom 6:10; Heb 7:27; 9:12; 10:10), it remains contemporary to all generations and operative in their ongoing history. The presence of the life-giving Word of God in history extends,

---

20. See Dupuis 1991b, 231–34. See also Panikkar 1978. This is said against P. F. Knitter (1985, 205–31), who suggests the opposite thesis.

21. See especially, Croatto 1981, 1984, 1983. See also Sugirtharajah, ed., 1991; "On Interpreting the Bible" 1987.

therefore, beyond the "foundational revelation" recorded in the sacred book; it makes divine revelation an ongoing reality.

As this scheme testifies, the word of God does remain, for a hermeneutical theology of liberation, the *norma normans;* but it is a dynamic norm, not a static one. The word is not confined to the dead letter; it abides with its creative power (see Is 55:11), spurring salvation history to forge ahead to fulfillment. The same is true in the context of religious pluralism. Here too the word of God stands as the *norma normans,* for the first act of dialogic praxis as well as the second act of theologizing. But an inductive theology of religions ought to see the word of God as a dynamic reality, calling for interpretation in the specific context of interfaith encounter.

This requires that the revealed message not be treated as a monolithic statement of truth. The "constitutive" uniqueness of Jesus Christ will stand as an affirmation of Christian faith, but it will not be absolutized by relying merely on the unilateral foundation of a few isolated texts: Acts 4:12; 1 Tim 2:5; Jn 14:6. The word of God will be seen as a complex whole, with the tensions involved between apparently contradictory, yet complementary, elements of truth. The Word "pitched its tent among human beings" (Jn 1:14) in Jesus Christ; but Wisdom had previously taken possession of every people and nation, seeking among them a resting place (Sir 24:6–7), and "pitched her tent" in Israel (Sir 24:8–12). Likewise, Jesus Christ is "the way, the truth, and the life" (Jn 14:6); but the Word who is before him was "the true light that enlightens every human being by coming into the world" (Jn 1:9). Again, "in these last days" God "has spoken to us by a Son"; but he had previously spoken "in many and various ways" (Heb 1:1). The Spirit "had not been given" before Jesus was glorified (Jn 7:39); but he had been present in "all things" that exist, well before (Wis 11:24–12:1). Jesus Christ is "the faithful witness" (Rev 1:5; 3:14); but God did not "leave himself without a witness" at any time (Acts 14:17). Interfaith encounter must help Christians to discover new dimensions to the witness which God gave to himself in other faith-communities. As Wesley Ariarajah writes:

> If Christians . . . believe that the Christ-event has a salvific significance for the whole of humanity, it has to be witnessed to as a claim of faith. We cannot use this faith-claim as a basis to deny other claims of faith. However true our own experience, however convinced we are about a faith-claim, it has to be given as a claim of faith and not as truth in the absolute sense. (Ariarajah 1985, 67)

## II. The Human Face of God

### A. *Jesus Is the Christ: Distinction and Identity*

What has been stated does not dispense us from showing, in response to the "revisionist" or "degree" Christologies on which the pluralistic paradigm of the theology of religions rests, that the Christian claim to a constitutive uniqueness of Jesus Christ rests on solid ground and has a valid foundation. Admittedly, a faith-conviction, by its very nature, lies beyond the purview of an empirical or scientific proof. Were it otherwise, it would cease to be a witness of faith and become merely the result of academic and historical research. What, however, can and needs to be done is to show the merits and the credibility of the Christian faith-claim for Jesus Christ.

The main historical-critical-exegetical argument put forward by the pluralistic Christologists returns to the trite contention that between the historical Jesus and the Christ of the Church apostolic and thereafter, there exists an unbridgeable gap. The allegation takes on different forms: Jesus was entirely centered on God, while the Church after him became Christ-centered; he announced the coming of God's Reign, while the Church proclaimed him; he affirmed God's universal fatherhood, while the Church asserted his unique sonship. In brief, while Jesus was "a man attested [to the Jews] by God with mighty works and wonders and signs which God did through him in [their] midst" (Acts 2:22) — as the early kerygma, ingenuously, acknowledged — the Church soon raised him, through a process of "deification," to the rank of a divine person. Or else, under the widespread impact of Hellenistic thought-patterns, the Church transposed into "ontological language" what was meant as purely "functional." What should have been taken as "mythical" or "metaphorical" language was interpreted "literally": "poetry" was construed as "prose" (John Hick).

In this context, the Christological task must consist in showing that the Christian faith in Jesus-the-Christ is firmly grounded in the historical person of Jesus of Nazareth — in other words, the Church's explicit Christology is grounded in the implicit Christology of Jesus himself. Continuity-in-discontinuity must be made to stand out at every stage: between the messianic expectation of the Jewish scripture and its coming to fulfillment in Jesus; between the prepaschal Jesus and the Christ of the apostolic kerygma; between the Christology of the early kerygma and later biblical enunciations; between New Testament Christology and that of the Church tradition; and so forth. This vast task has been attempted elsewhere and need not be repeated here (see Dupuis 1994c).

The expression "continuity-in-discontinuity" bears, however, some explanation, for it takes up different meanings at different stages of Christological development. Between Jesus and the Christ, there exists a real discontinuity inasmuch as the human existence of Jesus was transformed when he passed from the state of kenosis to the glorified state through the resurrection (see Phil 2:6–11); nevertheless, continuity endures insofar as the personal identity remains. The one who is glorified is he who has died: Jesus *is* the Christ (Acts 2:36). The historical Jesus *is* the Christ of faith.[22]

---

22. See Dupuis 1994c, 59–65; also Dupuis 1991b, 178–90, the discussion entitled "The Historical Jesus and the Christ of Faith in the Encounter of Religions."

"Continuity-in-discontinuity" takes on a different meaning where it concerns the relation between the "functional" Christology of the early kerygma and the later ontological Christology of the New Testament. The transition from the functional to the ontological level comes through the dynamism of the faith, inasmuch as the personal identity of the Son of God is presupposed, in the order of being, to the "divine condition" that shows forth in the glorified humanity of Jesus. The transition from the one to the other is a homogeneous development (Dupuis 1994c, 57–76).

The meaning of "continuity-in-discontinuity" differs where the relation between the ontological Christology of the New Testament and the Church's Christological dogma is concerned. Here the expression refers to a continuity of content in the discontinuity of idiom. The Christological dogma does not "Hellenize" the content of faith; rather, it represents a de-Hellenization of content in a Hellenization of terminology (Dupuis 1994c, 77–101). It is a question of "inculturation" — according to today's terminology.

Pluralists, John Hick in particular (Hick 1993b), dismiss the term "incarnation" as mythical and metaphorical language. If, however, the term is properly demythologized, it is seen to affirm — correctly — that God makes himself manifest and can be encountered through the man Jesus: understood as metaphorical parlance, the Word "becoming flesh" in Jesus Christ (see Jn 1:14) is then seen as equivalent to "Jesus of Nazareth, a man attested . . . by God" (see Acts 2:22). It is true that the concepts of preexistence and incarnation are both open to misunderstanding. Preexistence is not existence in a fictitious time before time. However, the fact remains that the incarnation of the Son of God involves, in a very real way, the becoming-human in history of the Word, who, independently of this becoming, exists eternally in the mystery of God (see Rahner 1966e). Such is the real sense conveyed through the symbolic language of incarnation.

Writing on the Christology of the Gospel according to John, Rudolph Schnackenburg indicates well the difference between any mythological speculation and the real language of preexistence, designed to substantiate the power to save of God's incarnate Son. He writes:

> Johannine Christology is not modelled on a set pattern of mythological speculation about a redeemer descending from heaven and returning there again. It is rather the desire to establish clearly the Christian redeemer's power to save that leads to the emphasis on his pre-existence, so that now his way is seen more clearly to begin from "above" and to return there once more. (Schnackenburg 1987, 555–56)

One witness will suffice. In a thoroughly documented and critical study, Karl-Josef Kuschel writes about Saint John's Christology:

> John's concern is the confession that the Word of God which is with God from eternity, God's Word and thus God himself, has become man in Jesus of Nazareth. Jesus *is* the eternal Word of God in person, not be-

cause people believe in him or because he asserts it of himself, but because this is what he is from God. Jesus *is* the eternal Son of God, not because human beings have understood this to be the case or because he has made it plausible, but because this is what he is, and always was from God. So what stands in the foreground is not the speculative question how the man Jesus could have had glory with God but the confession that the man Jesus of Nazareth is the Logos of God in person. And he is the Logos as a mortal man. However, he is the Logos only for those who are prepared to believe, trusting God's word in his word, God's actions in his actions, God's history in his career, and God's compassion in his cross. (Kuschel 1992, 389)

## B. Particular and Universal

I have suggested elsewhere that the constitutive uniqueness and universality of Jesus Christ must be made to rest on his personal identity as the Son of God (see Dupuis 1991b, 192–97). No other consideration seems to provide such an adequate theological foundation. The "Gospel" values which Jesus upholds, the Reign of God which he announces, the human project or "program" which he puts forward, his option for the poor and the marginalized, his denouncing of injustice, his message of universal love: all these, no doubt, contribute to the difference and specificity of Jesus' personality; none of them, however, would be decisive for making him or recognizing him as "constitutively unique."[23]

The universality of Jesus-the-Christ cannot, however, be allowed to overshadow the particularity of Jesus of Nazareth. It is true that Jesus' human existence, once transformed by his resurrection and glorification, has reached beyond time and space and become "transhistorical"; but it is the historical Jesus who has become that. The universality of the Christ who, "being made perfect," became "the source of eternal salvation" (Heb 5:9) does not cancel out the particularity of Jesus, "made like his brothers and sisters in every respect" (Heb 2:17). A universal Christ, severed from the particular Jesus, would no longer be the Christ of Christian revelation (see Reid 1990; see also Perkinson 1994). To stress the historical particularity of Jesus is not, in fact, without bearing on an open theology of religions. Nor is it indifferent in a context of interreligious dialogue. This, no doubt, is why, in such a context, the Indian Theological Association looks to the kenotic Christ as the model that provides both guidance and inspiration:

We look at Christ as one who, by emptying himself, takes us to the ineffable mystery of God. His *kenosis* signifies "not clinging to" his divine status (Phil 2:6). It was an act of unconditional surrender to the

---

23. The weakness of H. Küng's book *On Being a Christian* (1976) lies in his attempt to establish on these values Jesus' uniqueness, while failing to assert the ontological sonship. See discussion in Dupuis 1991b, 193–96.

Father. It was a presence in submission to his Father's universal salvific will. Christ accepted the human condition to the ultimate consequences. He gave himself totally to others; he did not hesitate to set aside even some of the religious convictions of his people in order to be faithful to his mission. This led him to the final expression of *kenosis,* namely, the death on the Cross, consecrated by the resurrection and symbolized in the Eucharist.

The kenotic Christ is present in every human vicissitude as servant and leaven. He belongs to the whole of humanity. Through this servanthood he gives himself incessantly to men and women of all cultures and leads them unobtrusively to their self-realization. His is a liberative action which makes the person whole, transforms the cultures it encounters by forming them into a community of love in which the other is respected and accepted in his or her self-understanding. (Indian Theological Association 1991, nos. 26–27, p. 346)

The historical particularity of Jesus imposes upon the Christ-event irremediable limitations. This is necessarily part of the incarnational economy willed by God. Just as the human consciousness of Jesus as Son could not, by nature, exhaust the mystery of God, and therefore left his revelation of God incomplete, in like manner neither does or can the Christ-event exhaust God's saving power. God remains beyond the man Jesus as the ultimate source of both revelation and salvation. Jesus' revelation of God is a human transposition of God's mystery; his salvific action is the channel, the efficacious sign or sacrament, of God's salvific will. The personal identity of Jesus as Son of God in his human existence notwithstanding, a distance continues to exist between God (the Father), the ultimate source, and he who is God's human icon. Jesus is no substitute for God (see Duquoc 1984).

If this is true, it will also be seen that, while the Christ-event is the universal sacrament of God's will to save humankind, it need not therefore be the only possible expression of that will. God's saving power is not exclusively bound by the universal sign God has designed for his saving action. In terms of a Trinitarian Christology, this means that the saving action of God through the nonincarnate Logos (Logos *asarkos*), of whom the Prologue of John's Gospel states that he "was the light that enlightens every human being by coming into the world" (Jn 1:9), endures after the incarnation of the Logos (Jn 1:14), even as God's saving action through the universal presence of the Spirit, both before and after the historical event of Jesus Christ, is real. The mystery of the incarnation is unique; only the individual human existence of Jesus is assumed by the Son of God. But while he alone is thus constituted the "image of God," other "saving figures" may be, as will be further explained in the next chapter, "enlightened" by the Word or "inspired" by the Spirit, to become pointers to salvation for their followers, in accordance with God's overall design for humankind.

Admittedly, in the mystery of Jesus-the-Christ, the Word cannot be separated from the flesh it has assumed. But, inseparable as the divine Word and Jesus' human existence may be, they nevertheless remain distinct. While, then, the human action of the Logos *ensarkos* is the universal sacrament of God's saving action, it does not exhaust the action of the Logos. A distinct action of the Logos *asarkos* endures — not, to be sure, as constituting a distinct economy of salvation, parallel to that realized in the flesh of Christ, but as the expression of God's superabundant graciousness and absolute freedom.

The particularity of the Jesus Christ–event in relation to the universality of God's plan of salvation opens to sensitive theologians new inroads for a theology of religious pluralism that would make room for diverse "paths" to salvation. Some outstanding examples may be referred to briefly.

Claude Geffré sees the paradox of the incarnation to lie in the simultaneity of the particular and the universal: Jesus Christ is, according to an expression of Nicholas of Cusa that has been taken over by Paul Tillich and Hans Urs von Balthasar, the "concrete universal." The particularity of the event, however, leaves room for holding together, within the one divine plan, the universal significance of Jesus Christ and the saving value of other traditions. Geffré writes:

> Jesus is the icon of the living God in a unique manner, and we need not wait for another "Mediator." But this does not lead to identifying the historical contingent aspect of Jesus with the "Christic" or divine aspect. The very law of God's incarnation through the mediation of history leads [us] to think that Jesus does not put an end to the story of God's manifestations.... In conformity with the traditional view of the Fathers of the Church, it is, therefore, possible to see the economy of the Son incarnate as the sacrament of a broader economy, that, namely, of the eternal Word of God which coincides with the religious history of humankind. (Geffré 1993b, 365–66; 1993a; 1995)

Edward Schillebeeckx asks how Christianity can maintain the uniqueness of Jesus Christ and at the same time attribute positive value to the different religions. He notes that "Jesus is indeed a 'unique,' but nevertheless 'contingent,' i.e., historical and thus limited, manifestation of the gift of salvation from God for all men and women." But Schillebeeckx goes on to say:

> The revelation of God in Jesus, as the Christian Gospel preaches this to us, in no way means that God absolutizes a historical particularity.... We learn from the revelation of God in Jesus that no individual particularity can be said to be absolute, and that therefore through the relativity present in Jesus anyone can encounter God even outside Jesus, specially in our worldly history and in the many religions which have arisen in it. The risen Jesus of Nazareth also continues to point to God beyond himself. One could say: God points via Jesus Christ in the Spirit to himself as creator

and redeemer, as a God of men and women, of *all* men and women. God is absolute, but no religion is absolute. (Schillebeeckx 1990, 165–66; 1994; see also Menard 1990, 55–78; 1994, 283–96)

Even before this, Schillebeeckx had written the following:

> Theology, talk about God, is more than Christology; in other words, while as Christians we can and may make Jesus the Christ the center of history for ourselves, we are not at the same time in a position to argue that the historical revelation of salvation from God in Jesus Christ exhausts the question of God, nor do we need to. Although we cannot attain Jesus in his fullness unless at the same time we also take into account his unique relationship with God which has a special nature of its own, this does not of itself mean that Jesus' unique way of life is the only way to God. For even Jesus not only reveals God but also conceals him, since he appeared among us in non-godlike, creaturely humanity. As man he is a historical, contingent being, who in no way can represent the full riches of God...unless one denies the reality of his real humanity....So the Gospel itself forbids us to speak of a Christian religious imperialism and exclusivism. (Schillebeeckx 1987, 2)

Christian Duquoc likewise warns about absolutizing the particularity of God's manifestation in Jesus Christ:

> By revealing himself in Jesus, God has not absolutized a particular event. He shows, on the contrary, that no particular historical event is absolute and that, in virtue of this relativity, God can be met in real history....The fundamental particularity of Christianity requires that differences be allowed to endure, not that they be abolished as if God's manifestation in Jesus had brought religious history to an end. (Duquoc 1977, 143)

The Trinitarian perspective on the theology of religious pluralism would call for similar remarks where the abiding universal presence of the Spirit is concerned. Trinitarian Christology shows that the particularity of the Christ-event leaves space for the action of the Logos *asarkos;* Spirit-Christology helps, likewise, to see that the Spirit of God is universally present and acting, before and after the event. The Christ-event is as much the goal of the working of the Spirit in the world as it is its origin; between one and the other there exists a "mutually conditioning relationship," by virtue of which the Spirit can rightly be called, throughout salvation history, the "Spirit of Christ" (Wong 1994, 627; cf. Rahner 1981b, 46). God's saving economy is one, of which the Christ-event is at once the culminating point and the universal sacrament; but the God who saves is "three," each being personally distinct and remaining distinctly active. God saves with "two hands."

## C. Searching Christology

That Jesus Christ is the "human face of God" means that in him God becomes God-for-human-beings-in-a-fully-human-way. In the light of this unveiling of the unseen God through the human face of Jesus, the Christian faith is able to appraise all the more positively the personal advances of God toward men and women to which, according to their own faith, their religious traditions bear witness. This requires substantiation with a concrete example.

We have remarked in the preceding chapter that the Hindu classical tradition probably offers, in the *saccidananda* doctrine, the concept of God closest to the Christian Trinity that the history of religions has to offer (see pp. 274–278, above). A striking parallel exists, likewise, between the *avatara* concept of the Hindu bhakti and the Christian concept of the incarnation. If this other parallel is verified, it will be legitimate to conclude that, in spite of the differences on either side, Hinduism has the singular distinction of offering elements of doctrine similar to, though not identical with, what constitutes the substance of Christian faith: the Trinity and the incarnation. This calls for some explanation.

According to the traditional understanding of Hindu theism, the *avatara* is a divine "descent" (from the root *tri*, "to come," with the prefix *ava*, "downward") to the world, a manifestation of the supreme Brahman in human form. The purpose of this descent is to establish or reestablish dharma (right, law, religion) in the world and to destroy *adharma* there. The basic text for the concept of the *avatara* in Hindu theism is to be found in the Bhagavad Gita (4, 5–10, esp. 6–8), where Krishna declares to Arjuna:

> Unborn though I am, though my Self is unchangeable,
> though I am Lord of Beings—
> in joining myself to the [material] nature (*prakriti*) that is mine,
> I come to be [in time] by my own creative energy (*sambhavamy atma-mayaya*). [v. 6]
> For, each time the law and the right (dharma) are in abeyance,
> and impiety (*adharma*) rears its head,
> I engender myself [on earth] (*atmanam srijamy aham*). [v.7]
> For the protection of the good and the destruction of malefactors,
> and to reestablish right (dharma),
> I come to be (*sambhavamy*), from age to age. [v. 8]

The Hindu theologians of the classic Vedanta, such as Shankara and Ramanuja, and after them, Chaitanya and Jiva Goswami, and modern authors, have interpreted the concept of the *avatara* and its principal source, just cited, in different ways. Without entering here into a detailed discussion, the following may be said. While Krishna surely represents the Absolute (conceived as personal God [*Vishnu*] along classic bhakti lines) (see Sheth 1984; Vempeny 1988), his earthly manifestation in human form has received different interpretations. Taking *maya* in the sense of "illusion," Shankara reduced the human existence of Krishna to a mere appearance. Against him, Ramanuja understands *maya* as God's "creative power" and concludes to an authentic human existence of Krishna. Modern commentators, among them S. Radhakrishnan and Sri Aurobindo, generally follow the realistic interpretation. Thus writes Radhakrishnan: "There is no suggestion here that the becoming of the one is a mere appearance. It is intended realistically."[24] The interpretation of Krishna's human existence as mere appearance represents, therefore, but one particular Hindu Krishnaite theological current. According to this interpretation — to put it in Christian terminology — the doctrine of *avatara* is both docetist and gnostic. The concept does not imply a real human existence as does that of incarnation.[25]

More problematic, however, is the historicity of the Bhagavad Gita's Krishna figure. Hindu interpreters do not attribute to the historicity or nonhistoricity of Krishna any special relevance as regards his soteriological significance. That the Krishna story is taken as historical event or legend or myth is inconsequential for his saving value (Vempeny 1988, 325–76). Sri Aurobindo writes:

> The life of Rama and Krishna belongs to the prehistoric past which has come down only in poetry and legend and may even be regarded as myths: but it is quite immaterial whether we regard them as myths or historical facts, because *their permanent truth and value* lie in their persistence as a spiritual form, presence, influence *in the inner consciousness* of the race and the life of the human soul.[26]

For Christian faith, on the contrary, the incarnation means the personal entry of the Son of God in the history of humankind and the world. The Word of God, made man, is truly and authentically a human being; having become a member of our human family in history, he has lived a human life, "in every respect tempted as we are" (Heb 4:15). He died for our salvation and was buried; raised from the dead, he was constituted Christ and Lord by God (Acts 2:36).

What positive significance can, then, the Christian faith attribute to the Hindu bhakti doctrine of *avatara*? When comparing *saccidananda* and the Christian Trinity, we noted two different ways of evaluating the respective beliefs of the two traditions (see pp. 276–78, above). For the "fulfillment theory," the *avatara* doctrine represents what may be called the best "stepping-stone" in Hinduism to the mystery of Jesus Christ, inasmuch as it embodies the universal human aspiration to enter into contact with the Ultimate Reality of the Divine

---

24. Quoted in Vempeny 1988, 254–67. S. Radhakrishnan, *The Bhagavadgita* (London: G. Allen, 1948), 154.

25. See, for that interpretation, Cuttat 1960; Parrinder 1971a; Neuner 1954.

26. See Aurobindo 1959, 230–31, quoted in Vempeny 1988, 349–50. We may recall a similar attitude of Mahatma Gandhi, regarding the historicity or nonhistoricity of Jesus in relation to his saving significance. He wrote: "I may say that I have never been interested in a historical Jesus. I should not care if it was proved by someone that the man called Jesus never lived, and that what was narrated in the Gospels was a figment of the writer's imagination. For the sermon on the Mount would still be true to me" (*Message of Jesus Christ* [Bombay: Bharatiya Vidya Bhavan, 1963], 37), quoted in Dupuis 1991b, 20.

on a human plane — a desire, however, that must remain forever unfulfilled unless God takes the initiative of stooping down to us in becoming human.

Can we go further? It seems that we can, especially if we consider the "worship" rendered in diverse Hindu traditions to the "sacred images." The worship of sacred images is distinct from idolatry insofar as the cult offered them by the devotees is directed not to the material image but to the symbolic and "sacramental" presence of God in the image. The Hindu ritual makes clear reference to a "consecration" ceremony (*prana pratistha*), an invocation, that is, pronounced by a priest by which God is begged graciously to come and dwell in the sacred image.[27] Before such time as the invocation has been pronounced, no act of worship is possible.

The sacred image is thus venerated as embodying, according to the faith of the devotees, a sacramental presence of the Godhead. This — to avoid misunderstandings — does not mean that idolatry does not exist. But idolatry is a corruption of image worship. Instead of being directed, through the sacramental sign, toward the God whose presence is ascertained by religious belief, the cultic act now stops at the image itself. Idolatry, then, consists in the human being's will to lay hold of God, to make God into one's own possession. Idolatry, therefore, is always cult of the self, while veneration of sacred images is divine worship.

Going beyond the fulfillment theory, the theory of the presence of Christ will hold that the worship of sacred images can be the sacramental sign in and through which the devotee responds to the offer of divine grace; it can mediate secretly the grace offered by God in Jesus Christ and express the human response to God's gratuitous gift in him. It can, then, truly be seen as a privileged instance of what Karl Rahner called "searching Christology" (Rahner 1979) — a search that starts from God.

These conclusions will be provisional, pending what must be left to be said in the next chapter on "paths to salvation." The uniqueness and the universality of Jesus Christ are neither absolute nor relative. We have called them "constitutive" insofar as the Christ-event has a universal impact: in it God has brought about universal salvation; Christ's risen humanity is the guarantee of God's indissoluble union with humankind.

Can such universality be called "relational"? Yes, in the sense that it is to be viewed in the framework of God's overall salvific design for humankind. In this plan of God, as will be further shown hereafter, the other religious traditions represent true interventions and authentic manifestations of God in the history of peoples; they form integral parts of one history of salvation that culminates in the Jesus Christ–event.

In this sense, one may speak of the "complementary uniqueness" of the mystery of Christ in relation to the religious traditions (Thompson 1985, 385);

---

27. See Fallon 1964. One such invocation has the following: "I invoke thee, calling thee to come into the image; come, Lord Shiva" (170).

but the expression risks stopping at the fulfillment theory. "Relational uniqueness" will be preferred (see Geffré 1993b, 1995) — not, however, in the sense
intended by Paul F. Knitter, for whom "relational uniqueness" refers, beyond
what he sees as an outdated Christocentrism, to the theocentric model.[28] For,
while it is true that "Christian singularity gains nothing by standing in absolute
isolation," but must on the contrary situate itself "within the totality of religious expressions" (see Breton 1981, 149–59), the Christian faith cannot stand
without claiming for Jesus Christ a constitutive uniqueness: in him historical
particularity coincides with universal significance.

---

28. Knitter 1985, 171. The term "relational uniqueness" recurs again in Knitter 1996, 80–83, in a
sense which excludes "the constitutive uniqueness" upheld here.

# Twelve

# Paths to Salvation

T HE UNIQUENESS of Jesus Christ is neither absolute nor relative, but, in precise terms, at once "constitutive" and "relational." "Constitutive" means that, for Christian faith, the paschal mystery of the death-resurrection of Jesus Christ has, according to God's saving design for humankind, a universal significance: it seals between the Godhead and the human race a bond of union that can never be broken; it constitutes the privileged channel through which God has chosen to share the divine life with human beings. "Relational" is intended to insert the universal significance of the Christ-event into the overall plan of God for humankind and the manner it unfolds in salvation history. In particular, the term is designed to assert the reciprocal relationship that exists between the path that is in Jesus Christ and the various paths to salvation proposed by the religious traditions to their members.

What has been said before should make clear that, when the phrase "paths to salvation" is applied here to the religious traditions, it refers not merely to a search for God, universally present in human beings even though never fulfilled through their own power, but, in the first place, to God's search for them and to God's gracious initiative in inviting them to share in the divine life. Paths to salvation are laid by God, not by human beings for themselves. The question to be asked, then, in the present chapter, is how, in God's own providence, the "one way" relates to the "many paths"; how, that is, Christian faith in the universal saving efficacy of the Christ-event does not gainsay the positive value and saving significance of paths opened in other religious traditions. As will be seen hereafter, far from precluding any saving value of other paths, the "way" which is in Christ implies it and postulates it.

To put it another way: the question is whether the Christian character of the economy of salvation leads to the conclusion that the members of other religious traditions are saved through him beside, or even in spite of, the religious tradition to which they adhere and which they practice with sincerity. Or are they, on the contrary, saved within this tradition and through it? And, if the second alternative is true, how does a Christian theology of religions account for the saving power of these other paths? Would such power so compete with the universal saving power of Jesus Christ that it must a priori be denied, as is done in fact by the exclusivist thesis? Or would it simply manifest the variety of ways along which, as the pluralists claim, God can be encountered in human cultures and traditions — a variety which belies every theological claim to a well-ordered and unified plan? Where, in a Christian perspective, might the saving power of the various "paths" fit into God's saving plan, and how does that plan become effective?

Before responding to these questions, some clarifications regarding the terminology are again in order. First, with regard to "paths" or "ways" of salvation, one point needs to be stressed from the outset. From a Christian viewpoint, God — and God alone — saves. This means that no human being is one's own savior; it also means that only the Absolute is the final agent of human salvation. In the Hebrew Bible, the title "Savior" belongs principally to God; in the New Testament, it is applied only to God and to Jesus Christ — in a derivative manner which does not prevent God being the root-cause and the source of salvation: God saves through Jesus Christ (see Jn 3:16–17). The principal cause of salvation remains the Father: "In Christ, God was reconciling the world to himself" (2 Cor 5:19).

It is an abuse of language, then, to say that religions save or even that Christianity saves. Quite remarkably, early Christian literature refers to what will later be termed "Christianity" as "the way" of Jesus (Acts 9:2; 19:9; 19:23; 22:4; 24:14; 24:22). Nor can it be the intention here to hold that "other religious traditions save," any more, in fact, than does Christianity. What is meant is that they too can be made use of by God as channels of his salvation; they can thus become ways or means conveying the power of the saving God — paths of salvation for the people who "walk the path." But this does not prejudge the kind of causality, instrumental or sacramental, final or otherwise, operative in them. Distinctions are called for.

Second, with regard to the concept of salvation, it is important to note that the concept differs vastly, as is well known, from one religion to another. It is neither necessary nor possible to enter here into lengthy discussions of such differences.[1] Suffice it to note that all religions present themselves to their followers as paths to salvation/liberation. The two concepts are being combined here for more than one reason. First, because the combined notion is easily applicable to diverse traditions, no matter how different their respective concepts. It is applicable to the Jewish concept of God's liberation of his people through his mighty deeds; to the Christian concept of freedom for love and of a share in the divine life. It is no less applicable to the Buddhist advocacy of liberation through concentration and detachment; to the realization of one's identity with Brahman advocated by Hindu *advaita* mysticism; and so forth. Furthermore, the double concept has the advantage of combining such complementary aspects, too often kept separate in Christianity itself, as: the spiritual and the temporal, the transcendent and the human, the personal and the social, the eschatological and the historical.

Without prejudice to the vast differences from one tradition to another, one may risk proposing a universal concept of salvation/liberation as follows: it

---

1. See Iammarrone 1995; Küng et al. 1993; *Salvation* 1980; *Ways of Salvation* 1981.

has to do with the search for, and attainment of, fullness of life, wholeness, self-realization, and integration. Whether, notwithstanding the many diverse concepts of salvation/liberation proposed by the various traditions, the reality of human salvation must, from a Christian theological viewpoint, be conceived after one common model for all human beings, is a question to which we must return in the light of recent discussion.

The term "mediation" also calls for clarifications. The New Testament uses the term *mesitès* with reference to Jesus (1 Tim 2:5; Heb 8:6; 9:15; 12:24) and to Moses (Gal 3:19–20); but the term does not have in both cases the same meaning. Jesus Christ, as the Christological faith of the Christian tradition will explain, is "mediator" between God and humankind, insofar as in him the Godhead and humankind have been joined together in a lasting bond: "By his incarnation the Son of God has united himself in some way to every person" (GS 22). Moses acted as the "intermediary" between God and his people in God's covenantal initiative toward them. In both cases, the same concept has a different theological content. The Christian tradition views the "mediation between God and human beings" realized in Jesus Christ as "unique." This, however, does not prevent speaking of "participated forms of mediation." To give an unlikely witness: after affirming clearly "Christ's one, universal mediation," the encyclical letter *Redemptoris Missio* goes on to say, "Although participated forms of mediation of different kinds are not excluded, they acquire meaning and value *only* from Christ's own mediation, and they cannot be understood as parallel or complementary to his" (5). It is not clear whether this text means to hint at the possibility of some participated mediation of salvation in the world's religious traditions. What, however, is clear is that any participated form of mediation must, according to the text, be seen as essentially related to, and deriving its power from, the unique mediation of Jesus Christ. In what sense, then, will a theology of religions apply the concept of "mediation" to the paths to salvation traced by the other traditions?

This chapter has two main parts. The first part discusses whether the salvation to which the various paths lead can, from a Christian theological viewpoint, be seen as distinct in every tradition. Or must the various paths be viewed as leading to a common goal? The second part asks in what sense the other paths and the saving figures they present can be understood to lead to divine salvation, as this has traditionally been perceived by Christian faith.

# I. Which Salvation? Which Liberation?

## A. Different Religious Ends?

The pluralistic theology of religions, as it has been exposed so far, looked at the various religious traditions as representing as many different paths leading to the same ultimate goal. It did not consider distinct ultimate ends as possible goals to which the different traditions would lead. The common goal of all traditions needed, of course, to be described in general terms that could — so it was thought — be applied to all religious paths. The theocentric paradigm considered God as constituting this common goal. However, "God" turned out to be too concrete and specific a term to represent the ultimate goal of all religious traditions. This is the reason John Hick, in his later writings, substituted "the Real" for "God" as the end toward which all religious paths are directed. The former term seemed sufficiently abstract to be applied to all religions, theistic or otherwise. "The Real" stood for the Ultimate Reality, unknowable in itself (*an sich*), of which the divine personae and the impersonae of the different religious traditions represented various expressions or manifestations. In soteriological perspective, the goal to which every religious path tends is the transformation from self-centeredness to "Reality-centeredness" (see pp. 193–194 and 257–259, above). The final end of all religions is one, though the paths differ vastly.

We have thought it necessary to observe that Hick's recent thesis about such an undifferentiated ultimate goal as "the Real" is not in agreement with the Christian tradition. For the Christian tradition the Triune God is the ultimate goal of human life, the Ultimate Reality which, though remaining beyond our human grasp, has nevertheless revealed himself in Jesus Christ (see pp. 262–266, above). It can be surmised that other religious traditions too, theistic or otherwise, would refuse to see their divine personae or impersonae reduced to manifestations of the Real *an sich*. This need not be elaborated where monotheistic religions are concerned (see pp. 259–262); but it seems equally true in the case of other theistic traditions, whether the Absolute be conceived as "personal" (personae) or "impersonal" or "transpersonal" (impersonae). Various currents of Hinduism to which reference has been made would be cases in point.[2] Where the Christian tradition is concerned, Hick rightly remarks that inclusivist models of the theology of religions naturally and of necessity hold that the God revealed in Jesus Christ is the Ultimate Reality itself, toward which the religious life of human beings is directed (Hick 1995, 112).

As for himself, Hick is satisfied to describe human salvation in general terms as consisting in the transformation of the human being from self-centeredness to Reality-centeredness; all traditions aim at this. In his most recent writing to date on the subject of religious pluralism, he describes the goal of human salvation, common to all traditions, as follows:

> Suppose, then, we define salvation in a very concrete way, as an actual change in human beings, a change which can be identified — when it *can* be identified — by its fruits. We then find that we are talking about something that is of central concern to each of the great world faiths. Each in its different way calls us to transcend the ego point of view, which is the

---

2. See pp. 274–276, above, on Brahman as *saccidananda*; pp. 301–303, above, on Krishna as the Absolute (*avatarin*) in human form.

source of all selfishness, greed, exploitation, cruelty, and injustice, and to become re-centred in that ultimate mystery for which we, in our Christian language, use the term God....

It is I think clear that the great post-axial traditions, including Christianity, are directed towards a transformation of human existence from self-centeredness to a re-centring in what in our inadequate human terms we speak of as God, or as Ultimate Reality, or the Transcendent, or the Real. Among these options I propose to use the term "the Real," not because it is adequate — there is no adequate term — but because it is customary in Christian language to think of God as that which is alone finally real.... And what is variously called salvation or liberation or enlightenment or awakening consists in this transformation from self-centeredness to reality-centeredness. For brevity's sake, I'll use the hibrid term "salvation/liberation." I suggest that this is the central concern of all the great world religions. They are not primarily philosophies or theologies but primarily ways of salvation/liberation. And it is clear that salvation, in this sense of an actual change in human beings from natural self-centeredness towards a recentring in the Divine, the Ultimate, the Real, is a long process — though there are often peak moments within it — and that this process is taking place not only within Christianity but also, and so far as we can tell to a more or less equal extent, within the other great traditions. (Hick 1995, 17–18)

For all their differences, the pluralists and the inclusivists hold together that the various religious traditions share a common ultimate goal; they differ, however, in identifying the common goal: for Hick it is the Real beyond the personae and impersonae; for Christian inclusivists it is God as revealed in Jesus Christ. This, however, is where the pluralistic thesis itself has been recently challenged.

In a book entitled *Salvations: Truth and Difference in Religion* (Heim 1995), S. Mark Heim questions the pluralistic thesis on its own ground: under cover of pluralism, the thesis which identifies the Ultimate Real as the common goal of all religious traditions falls into the trap of covert inclusivism. An authentic pluralism of religions ought, on the contrary, to recognize plainly the real plurality of religious ends that characterize the various traditions. "Orientational pluralism" becomes, then, the password. There seems to be no compelling reason why Christianity and Buddhism — to take two examples — should be thought to share in reality a common religious end. Nor does the affirmation of a plurality of religious ends — the argument goes on to say — appear contrary to God's providence for human beings or in contradiction with the Christian tradition; it seems in fact compatible with what in it is most fundamental.

Heim finds confirmation of his "orientational pluralism" in the way that Joseph A. DiNoia reproaches pluralists and inclusivists alike for failing to recognize a plurality of religious ends. Only by admitting a plurality of religious goals can space be created for recognizing plainly the role played by other religious traditions in God's plan for humankind (Heim 1995, 131, 160–63). DiNoia writes:

> Once it is clear that a Catholic theology of religions can affirm the distinctiveness of the aims fostered by other religions without prejudice to an affirmation of the unique valuation of the Christian community or of its doctrines about salvation, then it becomes possible to assert that God wills that other religions perform functions in his plan for humankind that are now only dimly perceived and that will be fully disclosed in the consummation of history for which Christians long. Accordingly, other religions are to be valued by Christians, not because they are channels of grace or means of salvation for their adherents, but because they play a real but as yet perhaps not fully specifiable role in the divine plan to which the Christian community bears witness. (DiNoia 1992, 91; see also 53–54, 64)

Heim's proposal is for Christians "to reflect on the possibility of the providential provision of a diversity of religious ends for human beings" (Heim 1995, 160); that is, "of a providential role for the religions in the divine plan other than or in addition to serving as channels for salvation as Christians understand it" (Heim 1995, 160). Nor should the distinct religious ends be viewed merely as "penultimate" states preparing and fitting the followers of other traditions for salvation to be received thereafter.[3] For such a view would reduce the other religious end, in typically inclusivist fashion, to a step towards the end of the "home" tradition, alone viewed as "ultimate."[4] Heim's "orientational pluralism," on the contrary, formally considers the possibility of ultimate ends, providentially ordained by God, to which the various religious traditions lead their followers. Only the acceptance of alternative ways for ultimate fulfillment of human beings allows for religious pluralism to be taken with all seriousness.

Heim is confident that his view on the diversity of religious ends "can be interpreted and defended on Christian grounds" (Heim 1995, 184). "Though it is a challenge for Christian thought to come to terms with this possibility, it is an approach with deep grounds in fundamental Christian sources and convictions" (Heim 1995, 213). While admitting that "it does not fit easily into

---

3. Heim (1995, 151) refers to K. Ward, according to whom the unselfish devotion to the truth to which the Buddhist way leads its followers, while not leading them "to that personal relationship with God which is salvation," fits them "to receive salvation from a personal God when his saving activity becomes clear to them."

4. This would seem to be DiNoia's intention. For he writes: "It by no means follows from the particular and unique role ascribed to Jesus Christ in central Christian doctrines that those who do not *now* acknowledge him will be permanently excluded from sharing in the salvation he both signifies and effects. Rather than attributing an implausible implicit faith in Christ to the members of other religious communities, theology of religions in a prospective vein contends that non-Christians will have the opportunity to acknowledge him in the future. This opportunity may come to them in the course of their lives here on earth or in the course of their entrance into the life to come. Certainly such a view accords well with specific doctrines about the nature and agency of Jesus Christ and with the distinctive doctrines of other communities" (DiNoia 1992, 107). As for John Hick, he considers the alternative ends suggested by S. M. Heim as representing but diverse "forms of a gradual transformation from self-centeredness to a new centring on the Real," which is the common aim of all religious paths (Hick 1995, 106–7).

traditional Christian theological frameworks," he remains, nevertheless, "convinced that the perspective [he suggests] is fully consistent with biblical and Trinitarian convictions, and that this consistency can be more fully worked out" (Heim 1995, 228).

This is an invitation to consider the Christian ground on which, in its present version, the possibility of "orientational pluralism" is based. Some distinctions must, however, be kept in mind for the clarity of the argument. That subjectively the members of the other religious traditions have in view the end proposed by the religious tradition to which they adhere is clear. Christian theology cannot, however, refrain from asking whether a "Christian end" does not objectively cover the subjective end. That the end proposed by the other tradition can be objectively realized by practitioners as a transitory, provisional or penultimate end is also certain. But this admission leaves open the question whether these practitioners are not ultimately destined to a common end intended by God for humankind and revealed by God in Jesus Christ. What is the Christian ground on which Heim builds his opinion that it need not be so?

He recalls the fact that Christian sources themselves, besides distinguishing between the saved and the lost, have made further distinctions regarding the destiny of persons belonging to both groups — as in the case of unbaptized children destined to limbo. That is, within the overall twofold pattern of the saved and the lost, further distinctions have been made in each category. Heim's conclusion runs as follows: "The possibility of alternative religious fulfilments can be viewed as a third division, a category that could be classed on one of the two sides or the other, depending on whether the emphasis is on the absence of the distinctive end Christians seek or on the intrinsic character of the alternative (Heim 1995, 163).

The argument is deceptive and hardly convincing. To put it briefly: the Christian tradition has always held that God wills the salvation of all human beings (1 Tim 2:4). By salvation it meant sharing in God's life here on earth and union with him in the other life. It did hold, of course, that God's grace is subject to acceptance by each individual person and that free acceptance implies the possibility of refusal. God respects the freedom of human beings who alone can be made responsible for not being saved. In all events, God's will to save endures even where it is frustrated by individual free choice. As for the intermediary state of the *limbo puerorum*, it has been devised as a desperate solution — long abandoned — for situations in which the conditions for the possibility of a free acceptance of God's offer of grace and salvation seemed to be irremediably inexistent. In no way did this solution, however, cancel God's universal saving will. This, in fact, is the reason why the Christian tradition has been impelled to devise solutions by which God's will to save could be realized in all situations.[5] This is also why the question is being asked anew today, even by theologians with a traditional bent, whether God could "suffer" the eternal damnation of

---

5. See chap. 4, pt. 1 ("The Substitutes for the Gospel"), above.

any human being. However possible eternal loss may be, would not hell as the actual, final fate of some persons seem to contradict God's universal will to save and to belie the efficacy of that will? God's ways, however mysterious, cannot contradict his own will (see Balthasar 1988).

It goes without saying that the salvation implied in the Christian sources is the "Christian salvation"; members of other religious traditions too are destined to it as their "ultimate" end, whether this end is actually realized or not and no matter when and how it is realized. In other words, salvation as revealed by God in Jesus Christ is the universal destiny devised by God for human beings, whichever situation they may find themselves in and whichever religious tradition they may belong to. The living Christian tradition implies no less. One witness will suffice. The constitution *Gaudium et Spes* of Vatican II has already been cited where it states: "Since Christ died for all, and since all human beings are in fact called to one and the same destiny, which is divine, we must hold that the Holy Spirit offers to all the possibility of being associated, in a way known to God, to the paschal mystery" (GS 22).

What is at stake here for Christian belief is not merely the efficacy of God's will to save. It is, even more profoundly, the unity of the human race both in its origin from God in creation and its destiny in him through salvation (see NA 1). Likewise, the unassailable rights of every human person are based on the equal dignity of all human beings before God: "God shows no partiality" (see Acts 10:34). To introduce distinctions between different ultimate ends, assigned by God to human beings according to the creed they profess, would run the risk of unwittingly fostering discrimination or a covert exclusivism.

To the considerations mentioned above, S. Mark Heim adds the following, based on the Christian vision of God: "The possibility of a more thorough-going diversity in the future of humanity is in some measure authorized by the Trinitarian vision of God and a notion of the divine plenitude. That is, it rests on the conviction that the most emphatic no of the human creature to the end of loving communion with God meets always some variation of God's merciful yes to creation" (Heim 1995, 163).

It is not clear, however, how the Christian view of the Triune God would lend support to the idea of an "orientational pluralism" of religious traditions. Surely, it is not enough to appeal to the divine communion of persons *in itself* to establish a de jure plurality of religious traditions. A more solid foundation will have to be looked for. Much less does the divine communion suffice to sustain the possibility of an "orientational pluralism" between the various traditions. To accredit the idea, Heim has recourse, among other authors, to Gavin D'Costa, according to whom "the Trinity provides the deep Christian grammar for relating particularity and universality" (Heim 1995, 167–68). D'Costa does see in the Trinity a safeguard against an exclusive particularism (Christomonism), on the one side, and a pluralistic universalism (theocentrism), on the other. He means thereby to establish a foundation for the validity of other religious traditions and their place in God's providential plan for humankind. But there is no hint of a plurality of ultimate ends which would accord with the divine plan. Thus he writes:

> Whenever and wherever God reveals herself, in a manner often unrecognized or misunderstood by Christians, this is the God who is disclosed in Jesus Christ. Christians therefore need to learn more deeply about God from God's self-revelation — wherever it has occurred.
>
> ...If we have good reasons to believe that the Spirit and Word are present and active in the religions of the world (in ways that cannot, a priori, be specified), then it is intrinsic to the vocation of the Church to be attentive to the world religions.
>
> ...It is only through this attentive listening that Christianity is itself fulfilled in its deepest understanding of Christ and the ways of the Holy Spirit. This is counter to the notion of fulfillment often employed whereby Christianity is seen to fulfill other religions, implying its complete self-sufficiency. (D'Costa 1990a, 19, 23, 26)

Below, we shall need to come back to the foundation opened up by the Christian vision of the Triune God for a positive evaluation of the religious traditions. Pending this, it must, however, be concluded that communion with the Triune God is the ultimate goal to which, in God's providence, human beings tend through the various religious paths to which they are devoted. The Ultimate Reality — and, therefore, the ultimate goal — is the God who revealed himself in Jesus Christ. How this is remains, however, to be specified.

### B. Various Paths to a Common Goal

"Various rivers flowing to the same ocean": this and other similar expressions have often served as catchwords for a pluralistic theology of religions, especially in the context of neo-Hinduism. As rivers flowing to the same ocean, so too the various religions tend to the same Divine Mystery. Paths differ, but the ultimate end is common to all. The pluralistic model of "Reality-centeredness" proposed by John Hick fits into the axiom; S. M. Heim's "orientational pluralism," on the contrary, contradicts it. As for us, the expression "various paths to a common goal" is used within the conviction that the last goal intended by God for all human life is personal union with God as revealed in Jesus Christ. Yet the various religious traditions represent various paths leading, though differently, to the common goal. This remains to be shown.

"It is possible to hold," K. Ward writes, "that, in an important sense, many faiths may offer different paths to a common goal, conceived in a number of rather different ways" (Ward 1994, 338, 310ff.). He goes on to explain that the specific Christian beliefs in the incarnation, atonement, and the Trinity can be interpreted in a number of distinctive ways, which already constitute diverse doctrines within the Christian spectrum; other religious traditions introduce further diversification in the way of conceiving the final goal of human beings. The goal, however, remains common, and this makes it possible to speak of a true "convergence" in a common quest (Ward 1994, 339). Differences in theological concepts do not necessarily prevent the real commonality of the end.

Mainline Christian thinking has often been reluctant, even in recent years, to see in the other religious traditions valid "paths," "ways," or "channels" through which the goal of union with the God of Jesus Christ may be reached; or, to put it the other way round — as is more appropriate — through which the God of Jesus Christ communicates personally and shares his own life with the followers of those traditions. Karl Rahner spoke, in this sense, of the other religions as "lawful" up to a point and to a time (Rahner 1966a, 121–31) — a weak expression which continues to suppose their provisional and transitory character. Vatican II, notwithstanding its openness to the positive values contained in those traditions, did not venture to call them "ways" of salvation, though it may be asked whether this is not — at least partly — implied in the council's recognition of elements of "truth and grace" contained in them "as a sort of secret presence of God" (AG 9).

The postconciliar central magisterium has been considered earlier and need not be reviewed again (see pp. 170–179). The text where it comes closest to the affirmation that other religions may constitute paths to salvation for their followers is the document "Dialogue and Proclamation" (1991), referred to above (see p. 178, above): "Concretely it will be in the sincere practice of what is good in their own religious traditions and by following the dictates of their conscience that the members of other religions respond positively to God's invitation and receive salvation in Jesus Christ, even while they do not recognize or acknowledge him as their Saviour" (29).

We have, however, also made reference to other documents which, though admittedly less authoritative, display a greater openness toward the other religious traditions. God is seen as present and active in them, drawing people to himself; their plurality itself witnesses to "the manifold ways in which God has related to peoples and nations."[6] Other witnesses belonging to the same period can easily be added. One is the "Guidelines for Inter-religious Dia-

---

6. See pp. 199–200, above, on the Thirteenth Annual Meeting of the Indian Theological Association (1989) and the Baar Ecumenical Consultation (1990). Recent Bishops' Institutes for Religious Affairs (BIRA), organized by the Office for Interreligious Affairs of the FABC, see even more clearly the root of religious pluralism in the self-manifestation of the Triune God in history, that is, in the "economic Trinity" which itself has its source in the "immanent Trinity." In this light they advocate a "receptive pluralism" in the sense that "the many ways of responding to the promptings of the Holy Spirit must be continually in conversation with one another" (16) (BIRA IV, 3; text in Rosales and Arévalo, eds., 1992, 261). BIRA V, 3 (New Delhi, October 1995) writes in this sense: "The Christian sages contemplated the Divine as Trinity: Father-Son-Spirit in eternal communion. The interpersonal polarity between Father and Son, and the transpersonal union in the Spirit are perceived as the ultimate foundation for interpersonal encounter and union among human persons created in the image of God.... Experience of this Triune Divine is a demand to accept the other as other and to respect differences and promote relationships, for one cannot exist without the other.... Beyond the extremes of inclusivism and exclusivism, pluralism is accepted in resonance with the constitutive plurality of reality. Religions, as they are manifested in history, are complementary perceptions of the ineffable divine mystery, the God-beyond-God. All religions are visions of the divine mystery" (5–6; text in *Weltkirche* 9 [1995] 276; also in *FABC Papers*, no. 76, Hong Kong, 32–33).

logue," published in 1989 by the CBCI (Catholic Bishops' Conference of India) Commission for Dialogue and Ecumenism. The text has the following:

> The plurality of religions is a consequence of the richness of creation itself and of the manifold grace of God. Though all coming from the same source, peoples have perceived the universe and articulated their awareness of the Divine Mystery in manifold ways, and God has surely been present in these historical undertakings of his children. Such pluralism therefore is in no way to be deplored but rather acknowledged as itself a divine gift. (25)[7]

Two years earlier, the Theological Advisory Commission of the Federation of Asian Bishops' Conferences (FABC) had published a document entitled "Theses on Interreligious Dialogue" (1987), in which a positive evaluation of the role of other religious traditions in the divine economy of salvation was clearly expressed (see text quoted, p. 220, above).

As compared to the foregoing witnesses, the 1996 document of the International Theological Commission on the theology of religions expresses extreme caution and apparent reluctance to recognize some "saving function" in the other religious traditions. The relevant sections read as follows:

> The presence of the Spirit in the religions being explicitly recognized, it *is not possible to exclude* that they may, as such, exercise a certain salvific function, that is, that they may help people to attain their final end, in spite of their ambiguity. The relation of the human being with the Absolute, its transcendent dimension, is stressed explicitly in the religions. *It would be difficult to think* that what the Holy Spirit does in the hearts of individual persons would have salvific value, while that which the same Spirit brings about in the religions and cultures would not. The recent magisterium does not seem to allow for such a difference. . . .
>
> The religions can then, within the terms specified, be a means (*mezzo*) which helps for the salvation of their adherents; but they cannot be made equivalent (*equiparare*) to the function which the Church exercises for the salvation of Christians and of those who are not. (84, 86 emphasis added; International Theological Commission 1997, 171–72)

What strikes the eye in comparing this last text with the Asian ones is the difference of perception which prolonged, everyday interaction with the members of other religious traditions provides, concerning their significance and value in God's plan for humankind. The Church's role of salvation in relation to the other religious traditions is a topic to which we must return in the next chapter. Meanwhile, the second part of the present chapter must show how the religious traditions mediate salvation for their followers; or, to put it in other words, how in and through them God communicates himself to their followers in various,

---

7. See Commission for Dialogue and Ecumenism 1989, 29; see also Kuttianimattathil 1995, 152–61.

differentiated ways. More specifically still, in which precise sense are the traditions "channels" of salvation? What causality is at work in them which justifies calling them — univocally or analogically — ways or paths to salvation?

## II. Mediations of Salvation

### A. *"Many and Various Ways"*

A Trinitarian Christology model opens the way for distinct considerations which, though closely interrelated, can nevertheless be clearly distinguished. Divine grace or salvation "bears within itself both a Christological aspect and a pneumatological one" (*Dominum et Vivificantem* 53). This is true in whatever historical situation or circumstances and whether before or after the Jesus Christ–event. As a recent author has written:

> It must...be emphasized that [the] understanding of the universality of God's presence to his creation and of the universality of God's reconciling and saving love for his creation is for Christian theology never independent of God's self-disclosure in the particularity of the Christ-event as the particular Trinitarian God — Father, Son, and Spirit. A Christian theology of religion loses its particular identity if it attempts to base its understanding of the religions not on the universality of God, who is disclosed in Christ, but on some supposedly universal anthropological constant such as an alleged "religious a priori." (Schwöbel 1990, 39)

This means that God's saving action, which always operates within the framework of a unified plan, is one and at the same time multifaceted. It never prescinds from the Christ-event, in which it finds its highest historical density. Yet the action of the Word of God is not constrained by its historically becoming human in Jesus Christ; nor is the Spirit's work in history limited to its outpouring upon the world by the risen and exalted Christ. The mediation of God's saving grace to humanity takes on different dimensions which need to be combined and integrated. We will consider in order: (1) the inclusive presence in history of the mystery of Jesus Christ; (2) the universal power of the Logos; and (3) the unbound action of the Spirit.

**1. The Inclusive Presence of the Mystery of Christ.**   That the historical event of Jesus Christ, which culminates in the paschal mystery of his death-resurrection, has universal saving significance need not be further elaborated. What, on the contrary, still requires to be accounted for is how its saving power reaches out to the members of other religious traditions. Is it merely through an invisible action of the glorified humanity which through its resurrection-glorification has become "transhistorical," beyond conditioning by time and space? Or does God's saving action in Jesus Christ reach them through a certain "mediation" of their own religious traditions? Are these, then, in a certain manner "channels" of Christ's saving power, and in what sense? Do the traditions lend a certain visibility and social character to the saving power of Christ as it reaches their members? Are they signs, however incomplete, of his saving activity?

To see that they are, it is of primary importance to stress the worldly and social character of the human being. Against the "fulfillment theory," which established a partition between the religious life of an individual person and the community of faith in which the person lives that life, the theory of the "presence of the mystery of Christ" shows — rightly — that such watertight partitioning is not theologically viable.

Human existence is essentially historical. This means two things. First, the human person, an incarnate spirit, is a becoming which expresses itself in time and space, in the history of the world. It exists only in thus expressing itself. What we call our body is, very precisely, this expression. This is the deep meaning of Saint Thomas's theory of a substantial union between soul and body. That the soul is the substantial form of the body means that soul and body do not compose two distinct, essentially independent elements in a merely accidental union and are therefore easily separable. Quite the contrary: human beings are persons only to the extent that they, as spirits, are incarnate. Modern existential philosophy has seen this and stated it better than Thomism. However, what is true of the life of a human being in general is also true of his or her religious life. The latter does not and cannot consist in purely spiritual states of soul. In order to exist, the religious life must express itself in religious symbols, rites, and practices. In view of the human being's essentially composite nature, such symbols, rites, and practices are necessary for the very existence of the religious life, as they serve both as expression and support of the aspirations of the human spirit. There is no religious life without religious practice. In this sense neither is there faith without religion.

Second, the anthropological principle here propounded also implies that the human being is not an isolated monad but a person living in human society. Every human being becomes a person in virtue of his or her interpersonal relationships with other human beings. While it is true that one must exist as a person in order to be able to maintain an interpersonal relationship with others, it is also true that the human being becomes and grows as a person through that relationship. One becomes what one is. This is what the philosophy of personalism has emphasized. It applies also to the human being's religious life. Religious human beings subsist not as separated individuals but as members of determinate religious communities with particular traditions. They grow and become by sharing the religious life of their respective communities, by entering personally into the respective historical religious tradition in which they are placed, and by taking up its social manifestations, ideas and teaching, moral code and ritual practices.

If all this is true, and if many members of the other religious traditions have an authentic experience of God, the inescapable conclusion is that these

traditions contain, in their institutions and social practices, traces of the encounter of human beings with grace; they contain "supernatural, grace-filled
elements" (Rahner 1966a, 121, 130). No dichotomy can be erected between
human beings' subjective religious life and the religion they profess, between
their personal religious experience and the historico-social religious phenomenon (or religious tradition composed of sacred books and practices of worship)
to which they adhere. Nor can it be said that, while the persons belonging to
these traditions can obtain salvation thanks to the sincerity of their subjective
religious life, their religion itself has no salvific value for them.

It is clear that the dichotomy upon which any such negative judgment rests
is gravely inadequate. Subjective and objective religion can and should be
distinguished; however, they cannot be separated. The religious traditions of humanity derive from the religious experience of the persons or groups that have
founded them. Their sacred books contain the memory of concrete religious
experiences with Truth. Their practices, in turn, result from the codification of
these experiences. Thus it seems both impracticable and theologically unrealistic
to maintain that, while the members of the various religious traditions can obtain salvation, their religion plays no role in the process. As there is no purely
natural concrete religious life, so neither is there any such thing as a purely
natural historical religion.

In order to show how the various religious traditions can serve their members as a mediation of the mystery of salvation, we must begin with the mystery
of Christ himself and then proceed to consider the presence of Christ to human
beings. In Christ, God enters into a personal relationship with human beings —
God becomes present to them.[8] Every authentic experience of God, among
Christians as among others, is an encounter of God in Jesus Christ with the
human being. God's presence to the human being, *qua* a "being with" of the
intentional order like any personal presence, sets God in relationship with the
human being in an interpersonal exchange of a "Thou" and an "I." The order
of faith or salvation consists precisely of this personal communication of God to
the human being, a communication whose concrete realization is in Jesus Christ
and whose efficacious sign is the humanity of Jesus.

God, however, is infinite Person, beyond all finitude, and the transcendence
of God profoundly stamps the nature of the personal divine presence to human
beings. Inasmuch as an infinite distance separates the Infinite from the finite,
the personal presence of God to the human being — and, a fortiori, to the
sinful human being — can only be gratuitous. The initiative of God's relationship to the human being comes necessarily from the side of the Divine. God's
condescension to human beings is at the center of the mystery of Christ.

In Christianity, God's personal presence to human beings in Christ reaches
its highest and most complete sacramental visibility. However, this perfect
mediation of the mystery of Christ reaches only Christians, members of the

---

8. On a Christology of presence, see O'Collins 1995a, 306–23.

sacrament-Church who receive its word and take part in its liturgical and sacramental life. Can other religions contain and signify, in some way, the presence of God to human beings in Jesus Christ? Does God become present to them in the very practice of their religion? It is necessary to admit this. Indeed, their own religious practice is the reality that gives expression to their experience of God and of the mystery of Christ. It is the visible element, the sign, the sacrament of that experience. This practice expresses, supports, bears, and contains, as it were, their encounter with God in Jesus Christ.

Accordingly — and in this particular sense — the religious tradition of others is indeed for them a way and means of salvation. To refuse that conclusion would be to commit the error of an undue separation of the personal, subjective religious life and objective religious tradition — made up of words, rites, and sacraments — in which the former is expressed. Such a separation is, as we have said, theologically inviable.

It is difficult, however, to determine in what precise sense the historical religions serve as a mediation for their members of the presence of the Christic mystery. However, we must distinguish various modalities of the sacramental presence of the mystery. The mystery of Christ knows different modalities of the mediation of its presence. The grace of God, while surely one, is visibly mediated in different modes — differing among them not only in degree but in kind. This means that the religious practices and sacramental rites of the other religions are not on the same footing as the Christian sacraments instituted by Jesus Christ; but it also means that we must ascribe to them a certain mediation of grace.[9] Thus the mystery of salvation remains one: it is the mystery of Christ. But this mystery is present to men and women beyond the boundaries of Christianity. In the Church, the eschatological community, it is present to them overtly and explicitly, in the full visibility of its complete mediation. In other religious traditions, it is present in an implicit, concealed manner, in virtue of an incomplete mode of mediation constituted by these traditions.

**2. The Universal Power of the Logos.**  But the Christ-event, however inclusively present, does not exhaust the power of the Word of God, who became flesh in Jesus Christ. The Prologue of the Gospel according to John makes explicit reference to the Word's universal action throughout history: "The Word was the true light that enlightens every human being by coming into the world" (Jn 1:9). Authoritative commentators show that, in spite of many difficulties the text raises, its meaning is quite clear: the Word of God — whose action is described after the model of Wisdom in Sir 24 — is the source of light for all human beings throughout history, including the period of history that preceded its coming into the flesh; its enlightening and saving power is universal, extending as it does to all times and all persons. Commenting on Jn 1:9, R. Schnackenburg writes:

---

9. On the subject of sacramental rites, see Abeyasingha 1984; Puthanangady, ed., 1988.

The power of the Logos to give light is universal, and indispensable to every person. In him, and in him alone, was the divine life for the true spiritual being of people, and he, and he alone, was the true divine life for all. In the original hymn this statement...certainly referred to the order of creation, that is, to the Logos before his incarnation. It transfers to the Logos the function ascribed in Jewish literature to Wisdom or the Torah, which took on later in Jewish thought the role of giver of light which Wisdom had played since creation....But the Christian hymn insists that Christ, the Logos, possessed this power before his earthly existence and merely exercises it anew in his mission of salvation, because it essentially belongs to him, and because he is the "true" light....Thus the Logos has a transcendent power of illumination, which comes from his Godhead and which can and must be displayed in all who desire to reach their goal. (Schnackenburg 1987, 253–54; trans. corrected; see also Feuillet 1968, 62–66, 166–67; Boismard 1953, 43–49)

The transcendent, illuminating power of the divine Logos, operative throughout human history, accounts for the salvation of human beings even before the manifestation of the Logos in the flesh. As the early apologists had already seen (see pt. 1, chap. 2, above), people could be "enlightened" by the Logos, who is the one source of divine light. Here too, however, the worldly and social character of the human being must be kept in mind. Not only could individual persons — Socrates, the Buddha, and so on — receive divine truth from the Logos; but human undertakings also — Greek philosophy and wisdom, as well as Asian wisdom — were the channels through which divine light reached to persons.

We have noted above that God's covenant with Noah is symbolic of the divine covenant with the nations in their respective cultures and religious institutions; the "covenant" with Greek philosophy, of which Clement of Alexandria spoke (see pp. 66–70, above), is one instance of this. We have further maintained that the cosmic covenant abides, even today, as truly as does the Mosaic covenant with God's chosen people (see pp. 233–234, above). This means that the religious traditions of humankind contain elements of "truth and grace" (AG 9), sown in them by the Logos, through which his enlightening and saving power is operative. The divine Logos continues, even today, to sow his seeds among peoples and in their traditions: revealed truth and saving grace are present in them through the agency of the Logos.

It is, of course, important to preserve the unity of the divine plan of salvation for humankind, which embraces the whole of human history. The becoming-human of the Word of God in Jesus Christ, his human life, death, and resurrection, is the culminating point of the process of divine self-communication, the hinge upon which the process holds together, its key of interpretation. The reason is that the Word's "humanization" marks the unsurpassed — and unsurpassable — depth of God's self-communication to human beings, the supreme mode of immanence of his being-with-them (see Dupuis 1991b, 99–104; 1994c, 144–50). However, the centrality of the incarnational dimension of God's economy of salvation must not be allowed to obscure the abiding presence and action of the divine Word. The enlightening and saving power of the Logos is not circumscribed by the particularity of the historical event. It transcends all boundaries of time and space. Through the transcendent power of the Logos, Trinitarian Christology is able to account for the mediatory function of religious traditions in the order of salvation, thus laying the foundation for the recognition of a pluralism in God's way of dealing with humankind.

**3. The Unbound Action of the Spirit.** Similar observations are called for where the Spirit of God is concerned. We have shown that the universal presence of the Spirit has been progressively stressed by the recent Church magisterium — without, however, the implications of such presence for the theology of religions being necessarily adequately brought out (see pp. 173–177, above). The Holy Spirit is seen as present not only in persons but in cultures and religions:

> The Spirit's presence and activity affect not only individuals but also society and history, peoples, cultures, and religions. Indeed, the Spirit is at the origin of the noble ideals and undertakings which benefit humanity on its journey through history.... Again, it is the Spirit who sows the "seeds of the Word" present in various customs and cultures, preparing them for full maturity in Christ. (RM 28)

Elements of "truth and grace" (AG 9) are thus present in the human cultures and religions, due to the combined action of God's Word and of his Spirit. From here it is only a short step to the recognition of a mediatory function of those religions in conveying to their adherents God's offer of grace and salvation and in giving expression to their positive response to God's gracious gift of self. The Word and the Spirit (see Congar 1986) — the "two hands" of God (Saint Irenaeus) — combine, through their universal action, in endowing the religious life of persons with truth and grace and in impressing "saving values" upon the religious traditions to which they belong. Can the "saving values" enshrined in the religious traditions be theologically discerned? Which criteria will such discernment follow?

## B. Discerning Saving Values

Hans Küng has formulated these questions and attempted to answer them (see Küng 1988, 228–56; 1987, 231–50; see also Küng 1991, 84–105). Wanting to propose an "ecumenical criteriology," not established exclusively on Christian ground, he distinguishes three successive criteria: (1) the *humanum* as general ethical criterion; (2) the "canonical" as universal religious criterion; and (3) a specifically Christian criterion.

1. The "common humanity" of human beings makes it possible to formulate a universal fundamental ethical criterion, based on the *humanum,* that is, on that which is authentically human — concretely, on human dignity and the fundamental values that go with it (Küng 1988, 240–45). Küng writes: "According to the basic norm of genuine humanity, *good* and *evil,* true and false, can be distinguished. We can also distinguish what is basically good and evil, what is true and what is false in *any individual religion*" (Küng 1988, 244).

2. The second is a general religious criterion, in virtue of which "a religion is measured by its *normative doctrine or practice* (Torah, New Testament, Qur'an, Vedas), and sometimes too by its normative *figure* (Christ, Muhammad, the Buddha)" (Küng 1988, 246). This criterion of "authenticity" or "canonicity" is concerned with the religious identity of a tradition; it asks what in it is "essential," "permanent," "obligatory," and what is not.

3. The third criterion is specifically Christian. According to it, "a religion is true and good if and insofar as it allows us to perceive the spirit of Jesus Christ in its theory and practice" (Küng 1988, 248). This criterion is directly applicable only to Christianity. It can, however, be applied indirectly to other religions as well; it consists of asking whether and to what extent something can be found in other religions of the "Christian spirit." "Jesus Christ is for Christians the *deciding regulative factor*" (Küng 1988, 251).

According to the Christian criterion, the truth of Christianity consists in its witness to the God of Jesus Christ. It does not possess the whole truth — God alone *is* Truth. Nor does it exclude the truth of other religions; it recognizes, on the contrary, their positive value: "So far as they do not contradict the Christian message on decisive points, [the other religions] can by all means complete, correct, and enrich the Christian religion" (Küng 1988, 254).

The mutual complementarity of Christian truth with that of other religions will be touched upon hereafter. Meanwhile, the "Christian" criterion for discerning truth and revelation, grace and salvation, in other religions can be proposed under a more concrete form. One thinks here spontaneously of the fruits of the Spirit mentioned by Saint Paul (Gal 5:16–24), on which Christians and the Christian tradition do not have the monopoly. The matter can be summed up in one word: love (*agapè*); for "God's central revelation, which is given in Jesus Christ, is *agapè*" (Starkey 1985, 433).

A distinction needs, however, to be made between the subjective faith-commitment of the individual person and the objective, historical religious tradition to which the person belongs and from which he or she derives religious life and inspiration. Christian theologians will agree that anyone who normally abides by what Christian revelation calls the law of love has heard God speaking in the secret of his or her heart and responded to that call within a faith-commitment. "Ubi caritas et amor, Deus ibi est" (Where there is charity and love, there God abides). The New Testament makes it clear that *agapè,* though made up of two dimensions, is one, and that the love of God necessarily passes through the love of neighbor (1 Jn 4:20). Recent theology expresses this mediation in terms of the "sacrament of the neighbor." The New Testament also insists that the empowering love of *agapè* is a gift of the Spirit, who has been poured into our hearts (Rom 5:5). *Agapè* is the overflow in us of the love by which God loved us first. That is why the practice of love is the sure criterion by which to recognize that a person has listened to the word of God and opened his or her heart to it. The practice of *agapè* is the reality of salvation, present and operative in human beings in response to God's self-disclosure and revelation.

But how far the habitual practice of *agapè* and the ensuing mystery of personal salvation are inspired by the religious tradition to which a person belongs is more difficult to ascertain. Nor is it easy to evaluate if, to what extent, and with what clarity saving charity is enjoined as a precept by the sacred books considered in other religious traditions as divine revelation. Do the scriptures of those traditions offer an equivalent to the Christian precept of love as it is disclosed in the New Testament? If not, do they nevertheless enjoin the love of God and of fellow human beings in such a way as to inspire saving *agapè?* How far, then, is the mystery of subjective salvation, present and operative in the lives of their adherents, a response to a divine revelation about love contained in those scriptures?

To begin with, what conditions must love of neighbor fulfill in order that it be saving *agapè?* The first is that it be disinterested and unconditional. Such an attitude involves a nonthematic recognition of the personal worth of the "other" and an implicit acknowledgment of a transcendent Absolute upon which this personal worth is based — whatever name may be given to this transcendent Absolute.

The Gospel further requires that love be universal. Jesus is clear about what has been called the "radicalism" of the Gospel. Love of God and of fellow humans go hand in hand (Mt 22:34–40; Lk 10:25–28); it is by that latter love that people shall be judged (Mt 25:31–46). *Agapè* extends not only to neighbors and friends ("Even the tax collectors do as much, do they not?...Even the gentiles do as much, do they not?") but to enemies as well (Mt 5:43–48). *Agapè* is universal, for "you must be perfect, as your heavenly Father is perfect" (Mt 5:48).

How do the sacred scriptures of other religious traditions stand in relation to the radical demands of *agapè* contained in the Gospel message? Do they provide such incentive for and invitation to outgoing love as can be recognized, from a Christian viewpoint, as divine revelation inspiring and sustaining in the followers of those traditions a commitment to saving *agapè?* In the article referred to above, P. Starkey reviews the evidence available in the various religious traditions in favor of a divine revelation inviting their followers to commit themselves to the practice of *agapè.* Her findings are being followed here, first with regard to the monotheistic religions (Judaism and Islam) and thereafter to some of the Asian traditions (Hinduism, Buddhism, and Confucianism).

The precept of the love of neighbor is very clearly taught in Jewish scriptures, where it is based on God's own attitude of covenantal love and faithfulness toward God's people. It is divine *agapè* extending as it were to human relationships. Is that love, however, universal? According to the Gospel tradition, Jesus sternly observed: "You have learned how it was said: You shall love your neighbor and hate your enemy. But I say to you: Love your enemies" (Mt 5:43–44). Exegetes note that the second part of the old command is not found in this abrupt form in the Law and that the brusque expression attributed to Jesus comes from the original Aramaic, which recognized few halftones. The equivalent meaning would be: there is less obligation to love one's enemies. Starkey observes: "The command to love one's neighbor is central to the Tanakh and to the Talmud" (see Lev 19:17–18). But she goes on to say: "Since antiquity the problem that has arisen among the rabbis is not the centrality of the command but the meaning of the word neighbor (*re'a*)" (Starkey 1985, 437). However, she remarks that "today the idea of neighbor is universalized by many Jewish writers" (Starkey 1985, 439). And she sums up: "A Christian can conclude from the examination of the Scriptures and traditions of Judaism, that Jews are called to live a life characterized by deeds of compassion, charity, loving kindness, respect, justice towards all.... According to the criterion of *agapè,* Judaism contains truth" (Starkey 1985, 441).

The Qur'an's message about love seems in many ways similar to that of the Jewish scriptures. It is based on the attitude of God — as merciful and compassionate — toward humankind. A certain universalism also characterizes that precept of charity: it extends at least to all Muslims and, according to some traditional interpretations, even to all people (Starkey 1985, 441–46).

Paradoxically, the universal demand of love seems to be more clearly formulated in the Asian traditions, Hinduism, Buddhism, and Confucianism, than in the two great monotheistic religions other than Christianity. Speaking of Hinduism, Starkey writes: "The Hindu Scriptures call for the action of *agapè* described as acts of compassion, justice, respect, generosity, uprightness, and selflessness towards *all*" (Starkey 1985, 451). Similarly, of Buddhism: "The Buddhist must not only treat friends and neighbors with *metta* (love), but also 'one's enemies should be treated with loving kindness'" (Starkey 1985, 454); and again, quoting E. A. Burtt (Burtt, ed., 1955, 46), *metta* is "an unlimited self-giving compassion flowing freely towards all creatures that live" (Starkey 1985, 455). Finally, having reviewed the evidence concerning Confucianism, the author concludes: "In the Confucianist tradition, *jen* is love that is universal and active in human relationships" (Starkey 1985, 461).

What, however, in those Asian traditions is the foundation for universal, compassionate love? Can it be said to be based on the prevenient love of God for humankind, the divine love being as it were reproduced in and extended to human relationships? Speaking of Hinduism, Starkey rightly points out: "The reason for [the] actions [of *agapè*]... is often different from the Western Christian view" (Starkey 1985, 451). Such is the case when altruist behavior is based, as in the Upanishadic tradition, on the identity of Brahman-Atman. On the contrary, in the bhakti tradition, altruistic love finds its foundation in the personal dignity of human beings in relation to a personal God. Of Buddhist compassion for all living creatures, the question has often been asked whether it can be equated with Christian charity. It must be admitted that the theological foundation for an altruistic attitude differs on both sides, as Buddhism's agnostic and neutral stand with regard to the existence of a "self" and a Divine Reality suffices to show. Similarly, in Confucianism, even though it may be correct to observe that *jen* (human heartedness) stands in "close resemblance to the Christian concept of *agapè*," this does not necessarily mean an equivalent theological foundation for the attitude of *agapè*. In Starkey's mind, however, the Christian use of the criterion of *agapè* must abstract from the theological foundation upon which the practice of *agapè* is based. In relation to Hinduism she writes: "The criterion used . . . makes no attempt to examine the reasons for or the motivations behind the action of *agapè*" (Starkey 1985, 451).

And not without reason. For, as has been pointed out earlier, acts of love or *agapè* in action are, from a Christian standpoint, the sign that God has entered into the life of a person in self-disclosure and manifestation — no matter how "anonymously" or secretly, no matter how imperfect the awareness of the God who has thus intervened may remain in the subject. They are also the sign that the person has responded positively to God's intervention in his or her life, no matter how unthematic may remain the knowledge of the self-revealing God. Nor is it to be thought that God's initiative in manifesting God's being to a person and the positive response the person gives to God's initiative are totally unrelated to the religious tradition to which he or she belongs and to what that tradition has taught him or her about the Absolute, no matter how limited this doctrine may be. Subjective faith-commitment expressed in *agapè* and the objective doctrine and practice of the faith-community to which one belongs cannot be severed without violence to both.

What, then, is the conclusion? That *agapè* is indeed the sign of the operative presence of the mystery of salvation in every man and woman who is saved. But there follows another conclusion: God has manifested and revealed God's own being throughout human history "in many and various ways" (Heb 1:1). The various religious traditions of the world are the many ways in which God has, in anticipation of the coming of his Son, disclosed the divine self to the nations and in which he continues to do so. They all form part of the history of salvation, which is one and manifold. They all contain elements of divine revelation and moments of divine grace, even though these remain incomplete and open to a fuller self-gift and disclosure on the part of God. The gracious moments enshrined in the religious traditions of humankind open their followers — through faith and *agapè* — to God's grace and salvation. They do so insofar as in God's providence they anticipate God's fuller disclosure and decisive self-gift in Jesus Christ. In Christ, who is God's Son made man, God has united with humankind in an irrevocable bond of love. This is why saving *agapè* finds in Christ its decisive theological foundation. If love is saving, the reason in the last analysis is that it imitates and reproduces in us that love with which God has loved us in the first place in the incarnate Son.

### C. Complementary Values and Convergent Paths

We have said that the various religious traditions of the world contain elements of "truth and grace" (AG 9) and that, the decisiveness of the Christ-event notwithstanding, it may not be thought that Christianity — or the Christian religion — possesses the whole truth or has a monopoly of grace. God is truth and God is love. He it is whose truth and love take possession of human beings in various ways "known to him" (see GS 22), often beyond our reckoning. The door is thereby open to the possibility of complementary values between the various religious traditions, Christianity included. "Complementarity" is not understood here in the sense of the fulfillment theory, according to which Christian truth "brings to completion" — in a one-sided process — the fragmentary truths it finds sown outside. There is question of a mutual complementarity, by which an exchange and a sharing of saving values take place between Christianity and the other traditions and from which a mutual enrichment and transformation may ensue between the traditions themselves.

Among "saving figures," a parallel suggests itself naturally between Jesus-the-Christ and Gautama-the-Buddha. We have already drawn the attention to some striking parallel aspects between the two historical "founders of religion" (see pp. 290–292). The question which is being asked now is that of a possible complementarity between the saving values which they represent and which are found enshrined in the traditions bearing their names. Aloysius Pieris has contributed much to bring out the complementarity between Buddhist *gnosis* and Christian *agapè,* or, more precisely — as he calls them — between the "agapeic gnosis" of Christians and the "gnostic agapè" of Buddhists (see Pieris 1988b, 1987, 1988a; see also Cobb 1982).

The mutual complementarity of the two traditions, in spite of their obvious differences, is based on the innate inadequacy of the basic medium proper to each, which leaves them open to completion. Pieris writes:

> In Buddhism the core-experience lends itself to be classed as gnosis or "liberative knowledge"; the corresponding Christian experience falls under the category of agapè or "redemptive love." Each is *salvific* in that each is a *self-transcending* event that radically transforms the human person affected by that experience. At the same time, there is an undefinable contrast between them, which largely determines the major differences between the two religions, differences quite obvious even to a casual observer. And yet, it must be recognized that both gnosis and agapè are *necessary* precisely because each in itself is *inadequate* as a medium not only for experiencing but also for expressing our intimate moments with the Ultimate Source of liberation. They are, in other words, com-

plementary idioms that need each other to mediate the self-transcending experience called "salvation." Any valid spirituality, Buddhist or Christian, as the history of each religion attests, does retain both poles of religious experience — namely, the gnostic and the agapeic. The movement of the spirit progresses through the dialectical interplay of wisdom and love. (Pieris 1987, 163; see 1988b, 110–35, esp. 111)

The first major obstacle to a core-to-core dialogue between Buddhism and Christianity, Pieris observes, is

> the failure on the part of Buddhists and Christians to acknowledge the reciprocity of these two idioms; their refusal to admit that gnosis and agapè are both legitimate languages of the *human* spirit or (as far as the Christian partner in dialogue is concerned) that they are languages that the same *divine* Spirit speaks alternately in each one of us.... The core experience of Christianity is not agapè pure and simple but agapè in dialogue with gnosis; conversely, the core experience of Buddhism is not mere gnosis, but a gnosis intrinsically in dialogue with agapè. (Pieris 1988b, 111, 119)

On the level of interpretation, Pieris observes, the focus of Buddhist-Christian dialogue is the historical figure of the founders of the two religions and the soteriological role attributed to them. In the Orthodox Theravada stream, the Buddha is never regarded as a Savior; his soteriological role is limited to being a pathfinder or truth-discoverer. However, in the Mahayanist schools, Buddha becomes the Savior who grants the grace of salvation to those who invoke him in faith (Pieris 1988b, 128). Pieris notes that, on both the Christian and the Buddhist sides, exclusivist and inclusivist theories of religion end up by asserting the supremacy of Christ over the Buddha and vice versa. "The crux of the problem is whether it is Jesus or Gautama who is *unique* in the sense of being *the exclusive medium of salvation for all.*" The way out of the dilemma lies in adopting another standpoint: "What saves is the *mediating reality* itself, in whatever way it may be recognized or named" (Pieris 1988b, 133). Liberation/ salvation comes through what both Christians and Buddhists can accept to be the "revelatory medium of salvation," with which neither Jesus nor Gautama is to be identified by means of titles attributed to them: the Christ, the Buddha (Pieris 1988b, 133). The uniqueness of Jesus "lies in that his claim to be the absolute medium of salvation is demonstrated on the cross by his double ascesis" — his *renunciation* (or his struggle *to be* poor) and his *denunciation* (or struggle *for* the poor). The double ascesis, Pieris writes,

> is the nucleus around which an Asian theology of liberation evolves into a Christology that does not compete with Buddhology but complements it by acknowledging the *one path* of liberation on which Christians join Buddhists in their *gnostic detachment* (or the practice of "voluntary pov-

erty") and Buddhists join the Christian *agapeic involvement* in the struggle against "forced poverty." (Pieris 1988b, 135)

Some ambiguity remains in what has just been quoted. What is the "mediating reality" that saves, which is to be distinguished from Jesus or the Buddha? In more recent writing, Pieris identifies it as the Word. "He who reveals, who saves and transforms," he writes, "is the Word himself" (Pieris 1994a, 60). We pointed out earlier that for the Christian tradition the transcendent action of the Word/Wisdom is related to the mystery of Jesus Christ in which God's plan for humankind comes to a climax (see pp. 195–196, above). This being made clear, it is legitimate to speak of distinct manifestations of the Word in history. The Word that "enlightens every human being" (Jn 1:9) is the source of the "enlight-enment" of Gautama-the-Buddha; the same became flesh in Jesus Christ (Jn 1:14). All manifestations of the Word do not have the same significance. Incarnation, as compared to enlightenment, has a historical density of its own.[10] This, however, does not prevent the reciprocal complementarity of the saving values of wisdom and love, conveyed by the two traditions: loving compassion and compassionate love.[11]

It seems legitimate, in concluding, to point to a convergence between the religious traditions and the mystery of Jesus Christ, as representing various, though not equal, paths along which, through history, God has sought and continues to seek human beings in his Word and his Spirit. Jesus Christ, it has been recently said, is the "integral figure (*figure intégrale*) of God's salvation"; the other religious traditions represent "particular realizations of a universal process, which has become preeminently concrete in Jesus Christ" (O'Leary 1994, 253). Salvation is at work everywhere; but in the concrete figure of the crucified Christ the work of salvation is seen to be accomplished. Jesus Christ, then, is the "unique Savior," not as the unique manifestation of the Word of God, who is God himself (O'Leary 1994, 261–65); not even in the sense that God's revelation in him

---

10. According to J. Macquarrie, in a recent book entitled *The Mediators* (1995), "the 'incarnation' of the divine Logos in Jesus Christ" was not "a solitary unrelated occurrence, totally unique." He sees it as "the culminating point of what God has been doing in all history" (148). He considers nine "mediators," not all of whom are known as "founders of religions." They are the following: Moses, Zoroaster, Lao-zu, Buddha, Confucius, Socrates, Krishna, Jesus, and Muhammad. Though professing to write "as a Christian theologian" (12), Macquarrie is — in his own words — "trying in these chapters to put forward as faithfully and impartially as I can accounts of nine great mediators of the spiritual life, and in order to do this, I try to confine myself to facts and hypotheses which are open to any of my readers and to suspend from consideration...judgments of faith" (112). The clear theological distinction which we are making here between the Word's "incarnation" in Jesus Christ and the "enlightenment" by the divine Logos of other saving figures disappears in the process. Macquarrie writes: "The incarnation [is] not a singularity or anomaly in world history but is a constant characteristic of God's relation to his creation. There are, one may say, degrees of incarnation" (149). On religious founders, see also Antes, ed., 1996; *Founders of Religion* 1984.

11. Another instance of a parallel between two "saving figures" and the complementary saving values they convey is between the historical Jesus and the Krishna myth in Vaisnavite Hindu bhakti. See esp. Vempeny 1988. That Krishna's saving figure, as known through the Bhagavad Gita, is largely mythical — with whatever doubtful historical background — does not prevent that a manifestation of God's Word be at the origin of the religious myth. The myth itself has, as such, a historical dimension the source of which is a divine manifestation in a religious tradition. On the complementary saving values of Krishna and Christ, see Vempeny 1988, 166–229, 325–53, 357–451.

be complete and exhaustive — which it is not and cannot be; but in relation to the universal process of divine revelation which occurs through concrete, limited manifestations:

> The contingency of the incarnation goes hand in hand with the universality of the manifestation of the Absolute. The incarnate Logos is searching for himself through history. Evangelization and dialogue are the encounter of the incarnate Logos, in the contingency of history, with the universal Logos sown in every human heart.... The fullness — to be realized only in the eschaton — of what we call revelation and incarnation can only be found in the accomplishment of this dialogue (O'Leary 1994, 280).

# Thirteen

# The Reign of God, the Religions, and the Church

**A** CERTAIN TRADITIONAL TYPE of theological vocabulary perpetuates expressions which no longer correspond to present theological understanding. If care is not taken, there is a risk of such expressions maintaining artificial barriers between Christians and "others," which more careful theological language would have helped to eliminate. This is why the term "non-Christians" is normally avoided throughout this book. For it has the disadvantage of defining the others by what they are not — namely, Christians; what is even more serious, it defines them with reference to what we are ourselves, thus placing the Christian community at the center of theological discourse as an obligatory point of reference.

It would be easy to make a list of the theological terms which can be criticized. A few examples will be sufficient. Some of these terms refer to the relationship between Christianity and Judaism, and thus the dialogue between Jews and Christians. The Church is said to be "the new people of God." This would imply that it takes the place of the former people of God, Israel. The dogmatic constitution *Lumen Gentium* does not itself escape from this danger when it speaks of the Church as the "new people of God" with which God has made a "new covenant" (LG 9). Similarly, the International Theological Commission, in its "Select Themes of Ecclesiology" (1985), gives to the second chapter the title "The Church as the 'New People of God.'" (International Theological Commission 1989, 271–73). After referring to LG 9, the document goes on to state: "The new people of God presents herself as a 'community of faith, hope and charity' (LG 8), whose source is the Eucharist (LG 3, 7)" (International Theological Commission 1989, 273). Now, whereas the term "new covenant" is biblical (Jer 31:31–34; 2 Cor 3:6; Heb 9:15; 12:14), even where the New Testament describes the Church as the "people of God" (1 Pet 2:9–10), it does not qualify it as the "new people." Recent exegesis, for its part, rightly reacts against an abuse of language according to which the coming of the Church would exclude Israel from being the people of God. This exegesis has shown that it is not here a question of the substitution of one people of God for another but rather of expanding the unique people of God beyond its own limitations by the extension to the nations of the Church which now belongs to it.[1]

---

1. See Dupont 1989, 209–22. The author takes account of "a widespread reaction making itself felt in recent times against an abuse of language which would speak of a 'new' people of God as opposed to

The distinction commonly made between the Old and the New Testament would call for similar remarks. It also runs the risk of leading one to think that the New is a substitute for the Old, just as the "new covenant" established by God in Jesus Christ would abolish that which he had earlier made with Israel under Moses, which is qualified as "old." Now it is obvious that the New Testament exists and can only be thought of in relation to the other. No one has expressed better than Saint Augustine the reciprocal bond uniting them: *Novum in Vetere latet, Vetus in Novo patet* (The New is hidden in the Old; the Old becomes manifest in the New). The New Testament neither replaces nor abolishes the one which precedes it. This is why exegetes today prefer to refer to them respectively as the "First" and the "Second." Moreover, Paul himself bears witness that the Mosaic covenant has not been abolished by that which God established in Jesus Christ. Paul, we have noted earlier, did not find a definitive answer to the question of the relationship between Israel and the Church. However, he expresses his firm conviction with regard to the permanent nature of God's election of the Israelites (see pp. 228–233, above, and Lohfink 1991). Accordingly, several recent documents of the magisterium state with a certain insistence that the Mosaic covenant remains valid and efficacious, even though God has established a "new covenant" in Jesus Christ, and in a parallel fashion the "First" Testament maintains its validity in relation to the New Testament.[2] Such clarifications are not without a profound effect on Jewish-Christian dialogue.

---

the 'old' " (221, n. 30). He refers to G. Betori, D. P. Moessner, X. Léon-Dufour. He explains that in the New Testament it is not a question "of the constitution of a new people of God, but of the fulfilment of the universal vocation to which Israel had been called by its God who, being unique, wished also to be the God of all human beings" (221); the one people of God henceforth extends by way of the Church to the nations. See also Menoud 1964, 390: "The people of God, after the coming of Christ, extends beyond . . . the limits of the Church, because it still includes the whole of Israel; the Jews, who cannot be part of the Church through belief in Jesus the Messiah, remain the people of God as sons of Abraham according to the flesh. Moreover, the Church, in virtue of the Christological faith which constitutes it, gathers together faithful 'of every race, nation, people and language,' and extends beyond the narrow limits of the Jewish people." See also N. T. Wright 1992.

2. A first document on this subject after Vatican II is "Orientations pastorales du comité épiscopal français pour les relations avec le Judaisme" 1973. This document states: "Contrary to what has been held by a very ancient but unreliable exegesis, it is not possible to deduce from the New Testament that the Jewish people has been deprived of its election. On the contrary, scripture as a whole encourages us to recognize in the concern of the Jewish people to remain faithful to the Law and the Covenant the sign of God's fidelity to his people" (240). "The first Covenant, in point of fact, has not been rendered null and void by the New one. It is its root and source, its foundation and promise" (240). Two pontifical documents also reflect a positive attitude with regard to the permanence of the "old" covenant. The first is "Orientations and Recommendations for the Application of the Conciliar Declaration *Nostra Aetate*, n. 4" 1974–75; the second is "Notes for a Correct Presentation of Jews and Judaism in the Preaching and Catechesis of the Catholic Church" 1985–86. Referring to the constitution *Dei Verbum* 14–15, the first document states: "An effort will be made to acquire a better understanding of whatever in the Old Testament retains its own perpetual value, since that has not been cancelled by the later interpretation of the New Testament. Rather, the New Testament brings out the full meaning of the Old, while both Old and New illumine and explain each other" (463). The second document takes up the expression used by John Paul II, when he spoke of "The People of God of the Covenant which has never been revoked." Then addressing the question of the relationship between the Old and New Testaments, the text explains that the expression "Old Testament" does not imply "invalid" or "out of date." The document underlines the "permanent value of the Old Testament as a source of Christian revelation": "Our aim should be to show the unity of biblical revelation (Old Testament and New Testament) and of the divine plan, before speaking of each historical event, so as to stress that particular events have meaning when seen in history as a whole — from creation to fulfilment" (104).

Now, in traditional theological vocabulary there exist expressions which have a negative effect on the relations between Christianity and other religious traditions even more harmful than their effect on the relationship between Christianity and Judaism. Such is the case with the term "people of God," already mentioned. Is it sufficient to include under the same term, though in different ways, the Jewish people and the Church, while continuing to exclude all others? Without denying the special choice God made of the people of Israel, which in Jesus Christ is extended and fulfilled in the Church, can the other peoples be considered as excluded from divine election? Or should one say rather that the divine choice extends, in one way or another, to all peoples and thus affirm that all are "chosen peoples" (see pp. 223–227, above, and Bühlmann 1982b)? It has often been observed — and with justification — that the introduction into the dogmatic constitution *Lumen Gentium* of chapter 2 on the people of God marked the transition point between the pyramidal preconciliar ecclesiology and the ecclesiology of the council, which is concentric or circular. There is less sensitivity to the exclusivism or triumphalism which the ecclesiology of the people of God may convey with regard to relations between Christianity and other religious traditions. Vatican II does not provide a remedy against this danger. Nowhere does the council state formally that the peoples of other religious traditions are the object of a divine election and that therefore they also are "chosen peoples," even though the Council Fathers recognized that the Spirit of God is present and at work in the persons constituting these peoples and in their traditions. "This impossible people of God!" said a theologian familiar with interreligious dialogue.[3]

In the context of the theology of religions and of dialogue, the term "Reign of God," in both traditional and recent theology, also raises problems. Is it limited to the hope of Israel and, in its historical realization in the world, to Christianity and to the Church? Are the "others" excluded from it? Or, on the contrary, are they full members, though remaining outside of the Church? Or again, do they belong to it in some way which could be qualified as implicit or invisible? In short, are Christianity and the Church to be identified with the Reign of God insofar as it is present in the world and in history? Or, on the contrary, is the Reign of God a universal reality which extends well beyond the boundaries of the Christian Church? If so, how do the Church and the religions relate respectively to God's universal Reign? And how do they relate to each other? What must, moreover, be said about the Reign of God in its eschatological fulfillment beyond history? How is it related to the Church and to the "others"? Do Christians and the others belong equally to the fulfilled Reign of God?

There are no unanimous answers to these different questions. Without any doubt, the theology of the Reign of God developed during the preconciliar period. Vatican II was able to draw benefit from this contribution. It did not, however, resolve all the questions; much less did it draw the consequences for

---

3. The remark comes from Henri Le Saux (Abhishiktananda).

a theology of religions. The intention here is to show the development of the theology of the Reign of God in postconciliar theology and, more importantly, to show its significance for a theology of religions in relation to the Church. This will be done in two parts. The first will show the slow rediscovery of the universality of the Reign of God, of which Christians and the "others" are co-members; the second will further specify the relationship of the Church and of the other religious traditions to the universal reality of the Reign of God.[4]

# I. The Universality of the Reign of God

## A. *A Survey of Recent Theology of God's Reign*

It was not so long ago that the theology of the Reign of God was characterized by a double identification. On the one hand, the Church was identified quite simply with the Reign of God; on the other hand, the Roman Catholic Church was well and truly thought to be identical with the Church itself. The encyclical *Mystici Corporis* (1943) of Pope Pius XII affirmed this second identification in no uncertain terms.[5] The Mystical Body of Christ, the mystery of the Church, was identified with the Roman Catholic Church. As for the identification of the Church with the Reign of God, this was commonly affirmed or presupposed by theologians at a time when theology was not overly concerned with distinctions which would be later called for by further studies in eschatology.[6] The result was a double identification between the Reign of God and the Church, on the one hand, and between the Church and the Roman Catholic Church, on the other hand. A single example will be sufficient. In his treatise *De Ecclesia Christi*, T. Zapelena wrote a few years before Vatican II: "The whole of ecclesiology could be summarized and put in the form of a rectangle: the Reign of God = the Church of Christ = the Roman Catholic Church = the Mystical Body of Christ on the earth."[7]

The "Schema on the Church" proposed at Vatican II by the preparatory commission referred to the encyclical *Mystici Corporis* in maintaining the strict

---

4. This chapter partly resumes two studies previously published: Dupuis 1994b and 1995c.

5. AAS 35 (1943) 199; see ND 1996, 847.

6. Examples can be given almost at random. Montcheuil (1949, 29–30) wrote: "The Reign of God exists in two states: on earth, in its inchoative realization, and in its heavenly fullness. But, in both states, it is always the Church. The Church on earth is already more than promise or preparation: she begins to realize the Kingdom.... The Church is not only a means, but an end; not only a way, but a goal.... She will not be abolished, but transfigured in the heavenly fulfilment.... Even in its life on earth, the Church is more than a means in view of an end, more than a way leading to a goal; she is the presence, already begun though still veiled, of what must become one day perfect and unveiled.... She is already the reality of the Kingdom present among us. We must not, therefore, simply reach the Kingdom in a beyond, but insert ourselves more and more here on earth into the Church." Cerfaux (1954, 386) wrote in the same vein: "The Church is already the heavenly Kingdom in progress (*en train de se constituer*). When the end of times will come, the external appearance of this world will only have to disappear, and the true reality covered under it will be fully unveiled. The Church is the Reign of God; all that is lacking is the light to illuminate what remains hidden." See also Snyder 1991.

7. "Integra ecclesiologia posset exhiberi et ordinari sequenti quadrilatero: regnum Dei = ecclesia Christi = ecclesia romana catholica = corpus Christi mysticum in terris" (Zapelena 1955, 41).

identification between the mystery of the Church and the Roman Catholic Church.[8] After it was rejected by the Council Fathers, the document went through several drafts on this particular point. It is not necessary to describe the process here (Schillebeeckx 1990, 189–95). The discussions during the council and the successive amendments to the document, however, led Vatican II to distance itself quite clearly from the identification of the mystery of the Church with the Roman Catholic Church. This nonidentification comes out very clearly in the formula: "*Haec Ecclesia . . . subsistit in Ecclesia catholica*" (This Church . . . subsists in the Catholic Church) (LG 8). In spite of the discussions which have arisen over the *subsistit in,* it appears from the "Acts of the Council" that it was chosen as a weakened version in order to break with the simple identification.[9] The new formula allowed for recognition in the other Christian churches of the existence of "many elements of sanctification and of truth" (LG 8) and so of real elements of the mystery of the Church. The mystery is present, without any doubt, in the Catholic Church, but it is also present elsewhere.[10]

What about the identification, made by traditional theology, of the Reign of God with the Church? Did Vatican II adopt this position, or did it, on account of a renewed eschatology, take a certain distance with regard to it? Care must be taken not to answer these questions in an oversimplified way. Various distinctions are called for.

**1. The Reign of God and the Church according to Vatican II.** Recent theology has rediscovered the Reign of God as an eschatological reality. As a result, it has now become essential to distinguish between the Reign of God in its eschatological fullness and the Reign of God as it is present in history, that is, between the "already" and the "not-yet." God has instituted his Kingdom in the world and in history through Jesus Christ. It could be said that he instituted it in two stages. For, in fact, the Reign of God is already instituted through the earthly life of Jesus, through his words and deeds; it has, however, been fully instituted through the paschal mystery of his death and resurrection. But the Reign of God instituted in history in Jesus Christ must develop to eschatological fullness at the end of time. So while Israel's eschatological expectation was entirely directed toward a definite but indeterminate future, in Christian faith this expectation follows henceforth a two-stage rhythm: the "already" of the Reign of God in history and the "not-yet" of its fulfillment at the end of time

---

8. See *Schemata Constitutionum et Decretorum,* 2d ser. (Vatican City, 1962), chap. 1, nn. 7, 12.

9. "Loco *est* dicitur *subsistit in,* ut expressio melius concordet cum affirmatione de elementis ecclesialibus quae alibi adsunt" (in *Relationes de singulis numeris,* Relation in nos. 8, 25, *Relatio super caput primum textus emendati Schematis Constitutionis de Ecclesia* (Vatican City, 1964).

10. Did the council restrict itself to recognizing the presence in other Christian communities of "elements" of the mystery of the Church, or, going further, did it admit the ecclesial character of these other communities, and not only of the Orthodox Church, even if the ecclesial character is not fully realized in them? Theologians are not fully agreed on this point. Basing himself not only on *Lumen Gentium* 8, but also on *Unitatis Redintegratio* 3, F. A. Sullivan is of the opinion that the council did recognize the ecclesial character of other Christian communities. See Sullivan 1989.

(see Cullmann 1952). This is a datum commonly accepted in recent eschatology, even if different theories accentuate either one or the other aspect.[11]

Vatican II, of course, took over this by now indispensable distinction. The dogmatic constitution *Lumen Gentium,* where it treats the establishment by God in Jesus Christ of the Reign of God in history, specifies that this Reign is progressing toward its fulfillment at the end of time (LG 5). It speaks clearly of "the Kingdom of God which has been begun by God himself on earth and which must be further extended until it is brought to perfection by him at the end of time" (LG 9). This does not, however, supply the answer to all the questions. It can still be asked whether Vatican II identified — or, on the contrary, distinguished between — the Reign of God and the Church. The question can be put first of all regarding the Reign of God in history: Is it to be identified with the pilgrim Church, or does it represent a larger reality which extends beyond the boundaries of the Church? The question further arises regarding the Reign of God in its final eschatological stage: Is this to be identified with the Church in its eschatological fulfillment, or does it, once again, extend to a larger reality which would include the Church?

In order to answer these questions, it is necessary to analyze closely the texts of the council and to inspect the affirmations contained in *Lumen Gentium.* The council recalls first of all that, to carry out the will of the Father, "Christ inaugurated the Kingdom of heaven on earth" (LG 3). More precisely, the birth of the Church coincides with the coming of the Reign of God in Jesus Christ. In fact, the council affirms: "The Lord Jesus inaugurated the Church by preaching the Good News, that is, the coming of the Kingdom of God" (LG 5). This Kingdom of God "shone out before people in the word, in the works and in the presence of Christ" (LG 5). It is made manifest in the word of Jesus: to listen to his word is to receive the Reign itself (LG 5). It is made manifest in his works: the miracles of Jesus "also demonstrate that the Kingdom has already come on earth" (LG 5). It is made manifest "principally" "in the person of Christ himself, Son of God and Son of Man" (LG 5).

What then, according to the council, is the relationship between the Reign of God instituted in Jesus Christ and the Church present in history? *Lumen Gentium* does indeed seem to identify the two. In fact, when it speaks of the mission which the Church has received to proclaim the Reign of Christ and of God, and of establishing it among all peoples, the council affirms that the Church "is, on earth, the seed and the beginning of the Kingdom" (*huiusque Regni in terris germen et initium constituit*) (LG 5). It then adds: "While she slowly grows to maturity, the Church longs for the completed Kingdom" (LG 5). This would seem to identify the "seed" or the "beginning" of the Reign of God with the pilgrim Church and to understand the progress of the Reign toward its final completion in terms of the passage of the Church on earth to the Church in

---

11. For example, the "realized" eschatology associated with the name of C. H. Dodd and the "consequent" eschatology associated with that of A. Schweitzer.

heaven. The constitution confirms this when, with regard to the destiny of the "messianic people," that is, the pilgrim Church, it affirms: "Its destiny is the Kingdom of God which has been begun by God himself on earth and which must be further extended until it is brought to perfection by him" (LG 9). Here also the "extension" of the Reign which tends toward its final completion seems to be identified with that of the Church in progress toward its perfection. It will be noted too that in chapter 7, entitled "The Eschatological Character of the Pilgrim Church and Its Union with the Church in Heaven," *Lumen Gentium* speaks of the "perfection" (LG 48) of the Church in heavenly glory without any reference to the theme of the fulfillment of the Reign of God. This would be a further indication that the completion of one coincides with the completion of the other.[12]

How is one then to understand the statement that "the Church — that is, the Kingdom of Christ already present in mystery (*Ecclesia, seu regnum Christi iam praesens in mysterio*) — grows visibly through the power of God in the world" (LG 3)? Here again the Church on earth seems to be identified with the Reign of God present in the world. If this presence is qualified as "mysterious," it is insofar as the Reign (or the Church which is identified with it), although present in the world, must still grow to its eschatological fullness. It would be forcing the intention of the council to interpret *in mysterio* to mean a "mysteric" or "sacramental" presence, in the Church on earth, of the reality of the Reign of God at work in the world and in history, but going beyond the boundaries of the Church, even if the latter is, in a privileged way, the sacrament of the Reign. Later on, we shall come back to this interpretation, which goes beyond the intention of the council. For the moment it would seem right to conclude that in *Lumen Gentium* the Church and the Reign of God are still identified, both in their historical realization and in their eschatological fulfillment.

**2. The Reign of God and the Church since Vatican II.** In 1985 the International Theological Commission published its document titled "Select Themes of Ecclesiology on the Occasion of the Twentieth Anniversary of the Closing of the Second Vatican Council." Chapter 10 is entitled "The Eschatological Character of the Church: Kingdom and Church" (1989, 300–304). It was to be expected that the document would take up again the distinction made by the council between the Church on earth and the Church in heaven. It does in fact insist on it, referring to the council: "To limit the Church to the purely earthly and visible dimension is unthinkable." The document then explains that the goal to which the Holy Spirit impels the Church on earth — that is, that heav-

---

12. It would seem that the pastoral constitution *Gaudium et Spes* has gone beyond the position of *Lumen Gentium*. For GS 39 speaks of the growth of the Reign of Christ and God in history (39, 2) and of its eschatological fulfillment (39, 3), without reference to the Church, but including the whole of humanity. The text concludes: "Here on earth the Kingdom is mysteriously (*in mysterio*) present; when the Lord comes it will enter into its perfection" (39, 3). Moreover, *Gaudium et Spes* affirms also that "the Church has but one sole purpose — that the Kingdom of God may come and the salvation of the human race may be accomplished" (45, 1).

enly Church united with its spouse, Christ — "determines at the deepest level the life of the pilgrim Church"; "it is part of the Church's mystery that this goal is already secretly present in the pilgrim Church." In fact, "in all her different stages of life the Church is essentially one: this is true whether we think of the Church's prefiguration in creation, her preparation in the Old Testament, her constitution in 'these, the last, times,' her manifestation by the Holy Spirit, or, lastly, her fulfilment in glory at the end of the ages (cf. LG 2)" (p. 301).

Having established the relationship — both of distinction and of unity — between the Church on earth and the Church in heaven, the document studies the relationship between the Church and the Reign. It notes that the council did not deal explicitly with this question, although it is possible, by comparing different texts of *Lumen Gentium,* to outline the council's teaching on this matter. It also warns against "accentuating somewhat unilaterally the eschatological aspect of the Kingdom and the historical aspect of the Church" (p. 302).

The International Theological Commission then observes that on examining the texts of the council, "one finds no difference between Church and Kingdom" with regard to the final consummation, despite the ambiguity of some of the expressions used: "It is clear that in the council's teaching there is no difference, so far as eschatological reality is concerned, between the final realization of the Church (as *consummata*) and of the Kingdom (as *consummatum*)" (p. 302). What about their relationship in the present time? The commission remarks that the relation is "subtle." According to *Lumen Gentium:* "In their beginnings, the destinies of the Church and the Kingdom seem inseparable.... The origins of the Church and the advent of the Kingdom of God are presented here in perfect synchronicity" (LG 5; p. 302). The same applies to their growth. For to receive the Kingdom through listening in faith to the word of Christ is equivalent to belonging to the Church. "And so one can use the same terms for describing the growth both of the Kingdom and of the Church. It is, in fact, in the growth of the Church that the Council discerns the growth of the Kingdom" (p. 302). The two in fact coincide. As the council has said, the pilgrim Church is "the Kingdom of God already mysteriously present" (LG 3); its growth is nothing other than the progressive growth, through its mission, of the Kingdom of Christ and of God of which the Church is "on earth, the seed and the beginning" (LG 5). According to the commission's document, "this evocation of the Church as 'seed' and 'beginning' of the Kingdom expresses their simultaneous unity and difference" (p. 303). So it concludes: "Belonging to the Kingdom cannot not be belonging — at least implicitly — to the Church" (p. 303).

Thus the unity and the difference of the Church and the Kingdom seem to be understood as the relation between the seed and the plant, between the beginning and the end, between the pilgrim Church which is the Kingdom in becoming and the Church in heaven which represents the Kingdom in its fulfillment. It is in this perspective that the International Theological Commission asks whether, and to what extent, one can describe the Church as the "sacrament of the Kingdom," according to a formula proposed by some theologians. The use of the expression is legitimate, it replies, but on certain conditions, of which the following are the main ones:

2. The expression's aim is to relate, on the one hand, the Kingdom, understood in the plenary sense of its final realization, with, on the other hand, the Church in its "wayfaring" aspect.

3. The term "sacrament" here is understood in its full sense of *iam praesens in mysterio* (cf. LG 3), where the reality present in the sacrament (the pilgrim Church) is the Kingdom itself.

4. The Church is not a mere sign (*sacramentum tantum*) but a sign in which the reality signified is present (*res et sacramentum*) as the reality of the Kingdom. (pp. 303–4)

It would seem that one must conclude that, in keeping to the teaching of *Lumen Gentium,* the theological commission, while distinguishing clearly between history and eschatology, affirms that at both levels Kingdom and Church coincide.[13]

The theme of the relationship between the Church and the Kingdom of God is, however, treated in a rather new fashion by the encyclical letter of Pope John Paul II, *Redemptoris Missio* (1990) (RM), on the permanent validity of the missionary mandate.[14] The second chapter of the encyclical is entitled "The Kingdom of God." The structure of the chapter is indicated clearly right from the beginning: it treats of the Reign of God, "prepared for in the Old Testament, brought about by Christ and in Christ, and proclaimed to all peoples by the Church, which works and prays for its perfect and definitive realization" (12).

The encyclical shows that in Jesus Christ the Kingdom is made present: "The proclamation and establishment of God's Kingdom are the purpose of his mission.... But that is not all. Jesus himself is the 'Good News.'... The secret of the effectiveness of his actions lies in his total identification with the message he announces: he proclaims the 'Good News' not just by what he says or does, but by what he is" (13). Thus the ministry of Jesus contains something new which is of primordial importance in relation to the Reign of God: "The eschatological reality is not relegated to a remote 'end of the world,' but is already close and at work in our midst. The Kingdom of God is at hand" (13). Jesus gradually reveals the "characteristics and demands" of this Kingdom. It is destined for all humankind: "To emphasize this fact, Jesus drew especially near to those on the margins of society, and showed them special favour.... The liberation and salvation brought by the Kingdom of God come to human persons both in their physical and spiritual dimensions. Two gestures are characteristic

---

13. The same identification between the Church and the Kingdom of God, both in history and eschatology, occurs again in the *Catechism of the Catholic Church.* See especially nos. 865, 541, 670–71, 732, 763, 768–69.

14. Text in *Origins* 20 (1990–91) 541–68; *Catholic International* 2 (15–31 March 1991) 252–92.

of Jesus' mission: healing and forgiving" (14). "The Kingdom aims at transforming human relationships; it grows gradually as people slowly learn to love, forgive and serve one another.... The Kingdom's nature, therefore, is one of communion among all human beings — with one another and with God" (15). There follows a description of the Kingdom of God, realized in Jesus Christ, which because of its importance is given here in full:

> The Kingdom is the concern of everyone: individuals, society, and the world. Working for the Kingdom means acknowledging and promoting God's activity, which is present in human history and transforms it. Building the Kingdom means working for liberation from evil in all its forms. In a word, the Kingdom of God is the manifestation and the realization of God's plan of salvation in all its fullness. (15)

Already present in the life and ministry of Jesus, the Kingdom of God is accomplished and proclaimed in the person of the Risen One: "By raising Jesus from the dead, God ... has definitively inaugurated the Kingdom.... The preaching of the early Church was centred on the proclamation of Jesus Christ, with whom the Kingdom was identified" (16).

The relationship between Christ and the Reign of God thus appears clearly. The encyclical insists on this, in opposition to a "Kingdom-centered" perspective conveyed by a certain type of theology of religions which passes over this relationship in silence, wishing to substitute a theocentric view of the Reign of God for the traditional Christocentric understanding. According to this view, Christians and others are called to build together the Reign of God in history by instilling into it the "Kingdom values" proclaimed by Jesus. Undoubtedly this perception is in part correct — and it will be necessary to come back to it later — but it is quite incomplete, says the encyclical, insofar as it disregards the relationship between Jesus Christ and the Reign of God. In so doing, it also weakens the relationship between the Church and the Reign of God. It "ends up either leaving very little room for the Church or undervaluing the Church in reaction to a presumed 'ecclesiocentrism' of the past" and perceives the Church only as a "sign, for that matter a sign not without ambiguity" (17).

"This is not the Kingdom as we know it from revelation. The Kingdom cannot be detached either from Christ or from the Church" (18). On the one hand, to detach it from Christ is to change its meaning and run the risk of transforming it into a purely human or ideological goal; it would also be to change Christ's identity. On the other hand, to disconnect it from the Church would be to lessen the importance of the Church and of the Church's mission. There follows an important passage on the relationship between the Kingdom and the Church:

> It is true that the Church is not an end unto herself, since she is ordered towards the Kingdom of God of which she is the seed, sign and instrument. Yet, while remaining distinct from Christ and the Kingdom, the Church

is indissolubly united to both. Christ endowed the Church, his Body, with the fullness of the benefits and means of salvation. The Holy Spirit dwells in her, enlivens her with his gifts and charisms, sanctifies, guides and constantly renews her (LG 4). The result is a unique and special relationship which, while not excluding the action of Christ and the Spirit outside the Church's visible boundaries, confers upon her a specific and necessary role; hence the Church's special connection with the Kingdom of God and of Christ, which she has "the mission of announcing and inaugurating among all peoples" (LG 5). (18)

The Church is, then, as the encyclical goes on to explain, "effectively and concretely at the service of the Kingdom." It fulfills this role "especially through her preaching which is a call to conversion"; it fulfills it also by establishing communities and founding particular churches; it fulfills it furthermore by spreading throughout the world " 'Gospel values' which are an expression of the Kingdom and which help people to accept God's plan" (20). Then the encyclical adds:

> It is true that the inchoate reality of the Kingdom can also be found beyond the confines of the Church among peoples everywhere, to the extent that they live "Gospel values" and are open to the working of the Spirit who breathes when and where it wills [cf. Jn 3:8]. But it must immediately be added that this temporal dimension of the Kingdom remains incomplete unless it is related to the Kingdom of Christ present in the Church and straining towards eschatological fullness. (20)

Finally, chapter 2 of the encyclical explains the function of the Church in relation to the eschatological Reign: "The Church is the sacrament of salvation for all humankind, and her activity is not limited only to those who accept her message. She is a dynamic force in humankind's journey toward the eschatological Kingdom, and is the sign and promoter of Kingdom values" (20).

These texts are decisive for our present concern. They contain an explicit recognition that the Reign of God in its historical reality extends beyond the Church to the whole of humankind (Why, however, insert the apparent restriction "can also be found"?), that it is present where Gospel values are at work and where people are open to the action of the Spirit. They affirm, moreover, that the Kingdom in its historical dimension (Why, though, insert "present in the Church," since it has just been said that it extends beyond the Church?) remains oriented toward its eschatological fullness and that the Church is in the world at the service of the Reign throughout history. Thus, while maintaining the unity, a distinction is made, on the one hand, between the Reign in time and its eschatological dimension and, on the other hand, between the Reign and the Church.[15]

---

15. With RM 20 we can compare a passage, very similar in content, from the document "Dialogue and Proclamation" (DP) (1991), already mentioned. The passage reads: "To the Church, as the sacra-

The recognition that the Reign of God in history is not restricted to the dimensions of the Church but extends beyond them to the world is not without interest and importance for a Christian theology of religions. Vatican II has recognized the presence and action of the Spirit in the world and among members of other religious traditions. It also spoke about the "seeds of the Word" among the nations (see pp. 162–165; Dupuis 1991b, 157–65). As regards the Reign of God, while distinguishing between the historical and eschatological aspects, it continued to identify the Reign in time with the Church. If our analysis is correct, the encyclical letter *Redemptoris Missio* is the first document of the Roman magisterium to distinguish clearly, while keeping them united, between the Church and the Reign of God in their pilgrimage through history: the Reign present in the world is a reality which is broader than the Church; it extends beyond its boundaries and includes — even if modalities may differ — not only the members of the Church but also the "others."

What the recent encyclical on the Church's missionary mandate has now recognized — with great caution and not without reservations — had already appeared in other expressions of the Church's magisterium, where it was presented simply as a fact to be affirmed without hesitation. By way of example reference can be made to a document of the Federation of Asian Bishops' Conferences (FABC), dated November 1985. It contains the following passage:

> The Reign of God is the very reason for the being of the Church. The Church exists in and for the Kingdom. The Kingdom, God's gift and initiative, is already begun and is constantly being realized, and made present through the Spirit. Where God is accepted, where the Gospel values are lived, where the human being is respected..., there is the Kingdom. It is far wider than the Church's boundaries. This already present reality is oriented towards the final manifestation and full perfection of the Reign of God. (II, 1)[16]

---

ment in which the Kingdom of God is present 'in mystery,' are related or oriented (*ordinantur*) the members of other religious traditions who, inasmuch as they respond to God's calling as perceived by their conscience, are saved in Jesus Christ and thus already share in some way the reality which is signified by the Kingdom. The Church's mission is to foster 'the Kingdom of our Lord and his Christ' (Rev 11:15), at whose service she is placed. Part of her role consists in recognizing that the inchoate reality of the Kingdom can be found also beyond the confines of the Church, for example in the hearts of the followers of other religious traditions, insofar as they live evangelical values and are open to the action of the Spirit. It must be remembered, nevertheless, that this is indeed an inchoate reality, which needs to find completion through being related to the Kingdom of Christ already present in the Church, yet realized fully only in the world to come" (Pontifical Council for Interreligious Dialogue 1991, no. 35). For a comparative study of the encyclical and this document, see Dupuis 1993b, 148–58.

16. Final statement of the Second Bishops' Institute for Interreligious Affairs on the Theology of Dialogue (Pattaya, Thailand, 17–22 November 1985), in Rosales and Arévalo 1992, 252. This text can be compared with another, published by the Theological Advisory Commission (TAC) of the FABC. "Theses on Interreligious Dialogue" (1987), produced by the commission, states: "The focus of the Church's mission of evangelization is building up the Kingdom of God and building up the Church to be at the service of the Kingdom. The Kingdom is therefore wider than the Church. The Church is the sacrament of the Kingdom, visibilizing it, ordained to it, promoting it, but not equating itself with it" (6, 3, p. 16). For a study of the growing emphasis on the Reign-of-God perspective in FABC documents over the last two decades, see Dupuis 1992b.

A more recent document produced by the Asian churches felicitously enhances further the perspective of the universality of the Reign of God. A theological consultation organized by the FABC's Office for Evangelization was held at Hua Hin (Thailand) in November 1991. In its final conclusions, entitled "Evangelization in Asia," it said, partly drawing on the documents previously mentioned:

> The Kingdom of God is therefore universally present and at work. Wherever men and women open themselves to the transcendent Divine Mystery which impinges upon them, and go out of themselves in love and service of fellow humans, there the Reign of God is at work.... "Where God is accepted, where the Gospel values are lived, where the human being is respected..., there is the Kingdom." In all such cases people respond to God's offer of grace through Christ in the Spirit and enter into the Kingdom through an act of faith....This goes to show that the Reign of God is a universal reality, extending far beyond the boundaries of the Church. It is the reality of salvation in Jesus Christ, in which Christians and others share together; it is the fundamental "mystery of unity" which unites us more deeply than differences in religious allegiance are able to keep us apart. Seen in this manner, a "Regnocentric" approach to mission theology does not in any way threaten the Christocentric perspective of our faith; on the contrary, "Regnocentrism" calls for Christocentrism, and vice versa, for it is in Jesus Christ and through the Christ-event that God has established his Kingdom upon the earth and in human history (cf. RM 17–18). (29, 30)[17]

## B. Jesus and the Reign of God

There can be no doubt that the Reign of God is at the center of the preaching and mission of Jesus, of his thought and life, of his words and actions. The Sermon on the Mount and the beatitudes are the charter of the Reign of God. Jesus' parables all refer to it; his miracles show it already present and operative.[18] That the Reign of God which God had begun to institute in the world through the earthly life of Jesus became really present through the mystery of his death and resurrection — this too is equally certain. There is therefore no break in continuity between the Kingdom-centered character of Jesus' proclamation and the Christocentrism of the kerygma of the apostolic times. Moreover, the Gospel bears witness that according to Jesus himself, the Reign he proclaims and which is already present must develop toward its fullness.

Now, did the historical Jesus connect the Reign of God with the Church? If he did refer to the relationship between the Reign and the Church, did he con-

---

17. Text in *FABC Papers*, n. 64 (Hong Kong, 1992), 31; Rosales and Arévalo 1992, 341–42.
18. See Dupuis 1994c, 42–46. Among the abundant literature the following can be consulted: Beasley-Murray 1986; Perrin 1963, 1967; Schnackenburg 1968; Fuellenbach 1993, 1995; Schlosser 1980; Fisher 1990; Willis, ed., 1987; Song 1993; Iammarrone 1996.

sider them to be identical, or, on the contrary, did he distinguish between them? Answering these questions is made more difficult by the fact that Jesus' references to the Church are only indirect. The term *ekklèsia* is found only twice in the Gospels, in Matthew. In Mt 16:18, "the foretelling of the Church" has been retouched editorially in the light of the Easter event; in Mt 18:18, *ekklèsia* refers to a local community without necessarily having any technical meaning. It remains a fact, nevertheless, that Jesus chose "the twelve" and entrusted to them in the first place responsibility for continuing his evangelizing mission in view of the Reign of God. "The twelve" will become (with others) the "apostles" through the event of Christ's resurrection and the gift of the Spirit at Pentecost (see Guillet 1985). Did Jesus conceive of this "movement," which he initiated — a movement which was destined to become the Church and in which he had established a competent authority — as being identical with the Reign of God which he was proclaiming? Or, on the contrary, was the Reign of God for Jesus a broader reality at the service of which he was, in anticipation, placing his Church-to-be?

It is recognized that the historical mission of Jesus was, principally, if not exclusively, directed toward Israel; we have noted this in the first part of our work. But we noted also that Jesus marveled at the promptness to believe of the centurion and, moreover, performed miracles on behalf and on request of "strangers" (see pp. 45–48). We added: "There should be no misunderstanding here: the miracles worked by Jesus on behalf of 'strangers' have the same meaning that Jesus gives to all his miracles. They signify that the Reign of God is already present and at work (see Mt 11:4–6; 12:25–28; Lk 4:16–22). The healing miracles and the exorcisms worked on behalf of 'others' are thus an indication that the Reign of God is present and at work among them also; it extends to all those who enter it by means of faith and conversion (see Mk 1:15)."

It cannot be said then that Jesus identified the Reign with the "movement" which he was creating and which was destined to become the Church.[19] Rather it must be recognized that already he was putting the Church at the service of the Reign when he commissioned the "twelve," charging them to proclaim the coming of the Kingdom (Mt 10:5–7). The Good News that the Church was to proclaim after the resurrection (see Mk 16:15) is the same as that which Jesus proclaimed during his life on earth, the coming of the Kingdom (Mk 1:15). The Church is destined to proclaim not itself, but the Reign of God.

Does the theology of the New Testament continue in this perspective, or, on the contrary, does one find that the Reign is identified with the Church? It is a well-known fact that the "Reign of God," an expression so often found on the lips of Jesus according to the Synoptic Gospels, largely disappears — though not

---

19. On the universality of the Reign of God in the thought of Jesus, see Song 1993, 3–38; 1994. In the second volume he writes: "The more Jesus is repelled from the center of power held by the religious authorities, the more he is drawn to the women, men, and children in his community excluded from that centre, and even to those outside his own religious community. The people whom the religious authorities considered to be beyond salvation have come to occupy the central place in his ministry of God's reign" (1994, 222).

entirely (see, e.g., the final verse of Acts, which refers to Paul's preaching of the Kingdom of God in Rome [Acts 28:30–31]) — in the rest of the New Testament. Yet it is present under a new form, that of the kingship of the risen Christ which continues it. Now this kingship extends not only to the Church but to the whole world. To give but one example: according to the Deutero-Pauline letters to the Ephesians and to the Colossians, the kingship of Christ extends to the Church and to the world; Christ is the head of the world (Col 2:10; Eph 1:10) as he is of the Church; but only the Church is his body (Col 1:18, 24; Eph 1:22; 4:15; 5:23). This has been brought out well by Oscar Cullmann. He explains that the Church and the world cannot be represented by two circles placed simply side by side, not even touching one another or intersecting; it is more a case of "concentric circles whose common centre is Christ" (Cullmann 1952, 187). In other words, the kingship of Christ, the presence of the Reign of God in history, extends to the whole world, both visible and invisible. Rudolph Schnackenburg states this very clearly:

> "Kingdom of Christ" is, therefore, a more comprehensive term than "Church." In the Christian's present existence on earth his share in Christ's Kingdom and his claim to the eschatological Kingdom [see also Phil 3:20] find their fulfilment in the Church, the domain in which the graces of the heavenly Christ are operative [Col 1:18, 24]. But Christ's rule extends beyond the Church, . . . and one day the Church will have completed her earthly task and will be absorbed in the eschatological Kingdom of Christ and of God. (Schnackenburg 1968, 301)

### C. Co-members and Co-builders of the Reign of God

The universality of the Reign of God consists in that Christians and the "others" share the same mystery of salvation in Jesus Christ, even if the mystery reaches to them through different ways. To recognize that the Reign of God in history is not confined to the boundaries of the Church but extends to those of the world is not without interest and bearing on a Christian theology of religions. Vatican II, we have recalled earlier, recognized the presence and action of the Spirit in the world and in the members of other religions; it likewise spoke of positive values contained in the traditions themselves. Its undeclared intention was to affirm a positive role of those traditions in the order of salvation, without explicitly declaring them to be "means" of salvation (see pp. 161–170, above).

It has been pointed out that the "others" have access to the Kingdom of God in history through obedience in faith and conversion to the God of the Kingdom. It has also been said that the Reign is present in the world wherever the "values of the Reign" are lived and promoted. According to the encyclical letter *Redemptoris Missio,* the inchoate reality of the Kingdom is present in the whole of humankind "to the extent that they live 'Gospel values' and are open to the working of the Spirit" (RM 20).

Liberation theology has laid stress on the role which the "Gospel values" — or "values of the Kingdom" — play in the coming of the Reign of God among people. The Kingdom of God, as Jon Sobrino has shown, was for Jesus "the truly ultimate objective," which gave meaning to his life, to his action, and to his destiny. Now this Ultimate Reality, to which all else is subordinated, is at work and comes close to human beings wherever, following Jesus himself, they share the values of the Kingdom — love and justice (Sobrino 1987, 81–97; 1993).

The theology of religions, for its part, must show how, through opening themselves up to the action of the Spirit, the "others" share in the reality of the Reign of God in the world and in history. For this purpose a Kingdom-centered model will be adopted. This does not mean — as was observed above following the encyclical *Redemptoris Missio* — that the Christocentric perspective can be dispensed with. In fact, one cannot separate the Reign of God in history from the Jesus of history, in whom it was instituted, nor from Christ, whose present kingship is its expression. Through sharing in the reality of salvation which the Reign of God is, the "others" are by this very fact subject to the saving action of God in Jesus Christ, in whom the Reign of God has been established. Far from being mutually exclusive, the Kingdom-centered and the Christocentric perspectives are necessarily interconnected.

The Reign of God to which the believers of other religious traditions belong in history is then indeed the Kingdom inaugurated by God in Jesus Christ. It is that Kingdom which God, in raising Jesus from the dead, has put into his hands; under the kingship of Christ, God has destined it to grow toward its final plenitude. While the believers of other religious faiths perceive God's call through their own traditions and respond to it in the sincere practice of these traditions, they become in all truth — even without being formally conscious of it — active members of the Kingdom. In the final analysis, then, a theology of religions following the Kingdom-centered model cannot bypass or avoid the Christocentric perspective.

Through sharing in the mystery of salvation, the followers of other religious traditions are thus members of the Kingdom of God already present as a historic reality. Does it follow from this that the religious traditions themselves contribute to the construction of the Reign of God in the world? To see that this is so, it must be recalled — as has been said earlier (see pp. 316–319, above; see also Dupuis 1991b, 143–51) — that the personal religious life of the followers of other traditions cannot in fact be separated from the religious tradition to which they belong and by means of which they give concrete expression to their religious life. If, as must be affirmed, their response to the divine invitation takes form in and is upheld by objective elements which are part of these religious traditions, such as their sacred scriptures and their "sacramental" practices, then it must also be admitted that these traditions themselves contain "supernatural, grace-filled elements" (Rahner 1966a, 121) for the benefit of the followers of these traditions. It is in responding to these elements of grace that they find salvation and become members of the Reign of God in history. It follows that the religious traditions contribute, in a mysterious way, to the building up of the Reign of God among their followers and in the world. They exercise, with regard to their own members, a certain mediation of the Kingdom — doubtless different from that which is operative in the Church — even if it is difficult to give a precise theological definition of this mediation.

There follow important consequences for interreligious dialogue. Dialogue takes place between persons who already belong together to the Reign of God, inaugurated in history in Jesus Christ. In spite of their different religious allegiance, such persons are already in communion in the reality of the mystery of salvation, even if there remains between them a distinction at the level of the "sacrament," that is, the order of mediation of the mystery. Communion in the reality is, however, more fundamental and is of more consequence than the differences at the level of the sign. This explains the deep communion in the Spirit which interreligious dialogue, if it is sincere and authentic, can establish between Christians and other believers (see Le Saux [Abhishiktananda] 1981). This shows also why interreligious dialogue is a form of sharing, both receiving and giving, in a word, that it is not a one-way process, not a monologue but a dialogue. The reason for this is that the reality of the Reign of God is already shared together in mutual exchange. Dialogue makes explicit this already existing communion in the reality of salvation, which is the Reign of God that has come for all in Jesus.

It also explains how Christians and "others" are called to build together the Reign of God in the world down the ages. This Reign, in which they already share, they can and must build together, through conversion to God and the promotion of Gospel values, until it achieves, beyond history, its eschatological fullness (see GS 39) (see Dupuis 1987a; 1992a).

Building the Reign together extends, moreover, to the different dimensions of the Reign of God, which can be called horizontal and vertical. Christians and others build together the Reign of God each time they commit themselves of common accord in the cause of human rights, each time they work for the integral liberation of each and every human person, but especially of the poor and the oppressed. They also build the Reign of God by promoting religious and spiritual values. In the building of the Kingdom the two dimensions, human and religious, are inseparable. In point of fact, the first is the sign of the second. There is, perhaps, nothing which provides interreligious dialogue with such a deep theological basis, and such true motivation, as the conviction that in spite of the differences by which they are distinguished, the members of different religious traditions, co-members of the Reign of God in history, are traveling together toward the fullness of the Reign, toward the new humanity willed by God for the end of time, of which they are called to be co-creators with God.

## II. The Church and the Religions in the Reign of God

### A. *The Necessity of the Church*

The necessity of the Church in the order of salvation is clearly affirmed by Vatican II. The constitution *Lumen Gentium* defines the Church as being "in Christ, in the nature of sacrament — a sign and instrument, that is, of communion with God and of unity among all human beings" (LG 1); or, again, as "universal sacrament of salvation" (LG 48). The same constitution insists that "the Church, a pilgrim now on earth, is necessary for salvation" (LG 14) and "the instrument for the salvation of all" (LG 9). The decree on ecumenism, *Unitatis Redintegratio,* while acknowledging that "the Spirit of Christ has not refrained from using [the separated churches and Christian communities] as means of salvation, affirms that the Catholic Church is 'the universal help (*auxilium*) towards salvation'" (UR 3).

The terms "universal sacrament," "sign and instrument," "general help," and "necessary" are in themselves sufficiently clear; the encyclical *Redemptoris Missio* recalls them when it speaks of the "specific and necessary role" of the Church in relation to the Reign of God (RM 18). However, the council does not explain the exact nature of the universal necessity of the Church; as for the encyclical, it seems somewhat embarrassed about determining the Church's "specific and necessary role." Hence, some questions arise. Has the universality of the Church in the order of salvation the same meaning, the same force, as is attributed by the Christian tradition to Jesus Christ, the Savior? Is the Church's necessity for salvation of the same order? How can we understand that the Church is not only a sign but also a universal means of salvation? Must a universal "mediation" be assigned to it — though one necessarily "participated" in relation to that of Jesus Christ, which is unique (1 Tim 2:5), and acquiring "meaning and value *only* from Christ's own mediation" (RM 5)?

Two extreme positions must be avoided here. The first would place the necessity and universality of the Church on one and the same level with that of Jesus Christ. This position would lead us back to an excessive interpretation of the ancient axiom *Extra ecclesiam nulla salus.*[20] The other would minimize the necessity and universality of the Church by simply reducing its function and operation to the salvation of its own members. This would amount to introducing two parallel ways of salvation without any mutual relationship — both derived from the unique mediation of Jesus Christ, yet one operative for the members of the Church while the other comes into play for people who are saved in Jesus Christ outside of it. Between these two extreme positions, equally unsustainable, is there a middle way? There exist, on this point, different opinions among theologians, among which one must choose. But two questions need to

---

20. See pp. 127–129, above, the letter of the Holy Office (1949) condemning the rigid interpretation of the axiom, proposed by L. Feeney.

be distinguished: (1) that of "belonging" to the Church; and (2) that of the Church's "mediation."

**1. Belonging to, or Orientation toward, the Church?**   We have recalled that a traditional, preconciliar ecclesiology identified the Reign of God, already present in history, with the Church. This theology considered the people saved by Christ outside the Church as belonging to it in some way. Distinctions were made: between actual members (*reapse*) and members in desire (*voto*); between belonging visibly and invisibly, explicitly and implicitly, to the soul and to the body of the Church; and so forth. The Council of Trent had recourse to this kind of distinction when it spoke of baptism *in voto* of people saved outside the Church.[21] It was further explained that the desire necessary for salvation outside the Church was not the explicit desire of catechumens but the implicit desire of those who, while finding themselves outside the Church, had the dispositions required for receiving salvation.[22]

Vatican II, as we have recalled, seems to have maintained the identification between the Reign of God present in history and the Church. It did not, however, repeat the current terminology. On the contrary, it has established precise distinctions concerning the relation to the Church of persons finding themselves in different situations. The term "members" is not used everywhere; that of *votum* is applied only to catechumens (LG 14). In general terms, it is said that "all are called to this catholic unity.... And in different ways belong to it (*pertinent*) or are ordained to it (*ordinantur*): the catholic faithful, others who believe in Christ, and finally all humankind, called by God's grace to salvation" (LG 13). This is, thereafter, explained and specified in detail: Catholics are fully incorporated (*plene incorporantur*) (LG 14) into the Church; the catechumens are united (*coniunguntur*) to the Church in virtue of their desire (*voto*) to join it (LG 14); non-Catholic Christians are "joined (*coniuncti*) for many reasons" to the Church (LG 15), while they are incorporated (*incorporantur*) into Christ. Finally, "those who have not yet received the Gospel are ordained (*ordinantur*), in various ways, to the People of God" (LG 16). This orientation toward the Church is realized under different forms, but in no case is mention made of a desire, explicit or implicit, of belonging (see Canobbio 1994a, 142–47).

The expression *ordinantur* is, in fact, taken from the encyclical *Mystici Corporis* (1943). The encyclical affirmed that all those who do not belong to the Catholic Church are "oriented toward [it] by a certain unconscious desire and wish" (*inscio quodam desiderio ac voto ad mysticum redemptoris corpus ordinari*),[23] while only Catholics are members of it actually (*reapse*). Karl Rahner notes that most likely this 1943 formulation had been intentionally substituted for the *voto essere in Ecclesia* of Bellarmine: "The encyclical did everything in

---

21. See Council of Trent, Decree on Justification, chap. 4. Text in DS 1524; ND 1928.
22. See the 1949 letter of the Holy Office mentioned above.
23. Text in AAS 35 (1943) 243.

its power to avoid giving the impression that the yearning for membership is already a 'being-in-the-Church' or a proper actual membership."[24]

However this may be, it is certain that Vatican II intentionally used, for persons outside the Church, the term of orientation (*ordinantur*) to the Church, while leaving out the language of a membership in desire or wish. According to the council, the members of the other religious traditions can be saved through Jesus Christ without belonging in whatever way to the Church; they are, however, "oriented" toward it, inasmuch as in it is found the fullness of the means of salvation. It would seem that the encyclical *Redemptoris Missio* continues and extends this view when it states, regarding those who do not have explicit faith in Jesus Christ and are not members of the Church: "For such people, salvation in Christ is accessible in virtue of a grace which, while having a mysterious relationship to the Church, does not make them formally part of the Church but enlightens them in a way which is accommodated to their spiritual and material situation" (10).

**2. Universal Mediation?** The encyclical *Redemptoris Missio* speaks of a "mysterious relationship to the Church" (RM 10) of persons saved in Jesus Christ but outside of it, and of a "specific and necessary role" of the Church (RM 18) in the order of salvation for all. These expressions, intentionally imprecise, raise further questions: How can we conceive, on the one hand, the "mysterious relationship" to the Church of the members of other religious traditions and, on the other hand, the "specific and necessary role" of the Church toward them? Can we, must we, speak of a universal "mediation" of the Church in the order of salvation, while considering it — as is required — as subordinated to the unique mediation of Jesus Christ?

It is, therefore, necessary to ask what the "mediation" of the Church, understood in the strict theological sense, consists of. The Church exercises its salvific mediation principally by announcing the word and through the sacramental economy, at the center of which is the eucharistic celebration ("the table of the word and of the body"). Thus says the constitution of Vatican II on the Sacred Liturgy:

> Christ is always present in his Church, especially in her liturgical celebrations. He is present in the sacrifice of the Mass, not only in the person of his minister..., but especially in the eucharistic species. By his power he is present in the sacraments so that when anyone baptizes it is really

---

24. Rahner 1963, 54. Rahner refers to the interpretation of Chavasse and Brinktrine. In an article entitled "Ordonnés au Corps Mystique" (1948), A. Chavasse wrote: "Pius XII speaks of an 'unconscious desire,' attempting to convey with one expression that the ontological situation of the separated person ordains one to the Church and that one remains unaware of it" (697). Congar 1963 writes in the same sense: "The encyclical would not favor the idea of invisible *belonging* to the visible Church; or even that they belong 'voto,' because, according to the encyclical, what the 'desire' brings about is merely an *orientation* to the mystical Body" (431). For other similar interpretations of the encyclical *Mystici Corporis,* see J. J. King 1960, 251–88. King, however, does not rally to such interpretations, which, he charges, undermine the doctrine of the necessity of the Church (288).

Christ himself who baptizes. He is present in his word since it is he himself who speaks when the Holy Scriptures are read in the Church. Lastly, he is present when the Church prays and sings. (SC 7)

The proclamation of the word and the celebration of the sacraments constitute a true mediation of the action of Jesus Christ in the ecclesial community. But, it is necessary to add, those factors do not — by definition — reach out to the members of the other religious traditions who receive salvation in Jesus Christ. It is true, indeed, that the Church fulfills in its eucharistic celebration all the ancient sacrifices. However, the *grace* of the Eucharist which it celebrates is not the salvation of people outside of it but the unity in the Spirit of its own members — as the eucharistic liturgy clearly indicates.[25] Is it possible, then, to speak, in the proper sense, of a mediation of grace on the part of the Church toward those who are not its members? A positive answer to this question has been sought by having recourse to the Church's intercession for the salvation of all (see, among others, Sullivan 1992).

The Church intercedes undoubtedly for the salvation of all, especially in the eucharistic celebration.[26] Yet it must be asked whether this intercession can be considered as 'mediation' in the proper theological sense. The universal mediation of Christ in the order of salvation concretely refers to the fact that his risen humanity is the obligatory channel, the instrumental cause, of grace for all people. Karl Rahner has stressed the perduring role of mediation by the humanity of Jesus Christ, even in the beatific vision (Rahner 1967). As for the Church, it exercises its derived mediation in the strict sense through the proclamation of the word and the sacramental economy celebrated in and by the Church communities. There is question here — to borrow the terminology of scholastic theology — of an instrumental efficient causality in the strict sense. Things are different where the Church's intercession is concerned; for the causality at work here seems to be of the moral rather than the efficient order. The Church prays and intercedes with God for all people that the grace of salvation in Jesus Christ may be granted to them. In this case, it would not seem legitimate to speak of "mediation" in the strict, theological sense. The causality involved is not of the order of efficiency but of the moral order and of finality.[27]

Some recent theologians did not fail to note this. Among these, Yves Congar may be mentioned in the first place. He wrote:

---

25. See the "epiclesis prayer" after the institution narrative: "May all of us who share in the body and blood of Christ be brought together in unity by the Holy Spirit" (Eucharistic Prayer II); "Grant that we who are nourished by his body and blood may be filled with his Holy Spirit and become one body, one spirit in Christ" (Eucharistic Prayer III).

26. See, for instance, in the "intercessory prayers" of Eucharistic Prayer III: "Lord, may this sacrifice, which has made our peace with you, advance the salvation of all the world."

27. A distinction could, perhaps, be made between two distinct aspects of the Church's "mediation": "descending" and "ascending." The "descending" aspect, implying an instrumental efficient causality, would then consist in the proclamation of the word and the sacramental economy; the Church's intercession, with the moral causality involved, would represent the "ascending" aspect. See, in a somewhat parallel way, the distinction between the descending and ascending aspects of Christ's mediation in Sesboüé 1988.

Every Catholic must admit and admits that there have existed and exist gifts of light and grace working for salvation outside the visible boundaries of the Church. We do not even deem it necessary to hold, as is nonetheless commonly done, that these graces are received *through* the Church; it is enough that they be received in view of the Church and that they orient people toward the Church.[28]

According to this text, the relationship between the Church and nonmembers is not of the order of efficiency but of finality: nonmembers are oriented toward (*ordinantur*) the Church. Congar concludes that the axiom *Extra Ecclesiam nulla salus* should be abandoned, for it can neither be taken in the literal sense nor be understood correctly without long explanations. This does not mean that it is altogether meaningless, for it contains, in effect, a biblical truth according to which the Church is the institution commissioned by God to bring to all people God's salvation in Jesus Christ.[29] If the formula is to be preserved, it must be given an "entirely positive" meaning:

There is, therefore, in the world *one* reality which represents the gift which God has destined for the world and which he has made to save it, that is, to make it reach to life and communion with God: this is Jesus Christ...dead and risen for us, Master of truth, who has entrusted to the Church, his Spouse and his Body, the deposit of the word and the sacraments that save. (Congar 1959, 131–32)

The traditional axiom thus takes on a positive meaning. The council affirms the necessity of the Church for salvation (LG 14), as the "universal sacrament of salvation" (LG 48). This necessity does not, however, imply a universal mediation in the strict sense, applicable to every person who is saved in Jesus Christ. On the contrary, it leaves room for "substitutive mediations" (*médiations de suppléance*) (Congar 1959, 133–47, see 144), among which will be found the religious traditions to which the "others" belong. From this one may infer that the causality of the Church in relation to the "others" is of the order not of efficiency but of finality. However, according to the recent magisterium, the Church remains the "ordinary way" for people's salvation (EN 80) inasmuch as it possesses the "ordinary means" of salvation (EN 80) or the "fullness of the means of salvation" (RM 55), even though the members of the other religious traditions can be saved in Jesus Christ "in ways known to God" (AG 7; see GS 22).[30] Saving grace must be called "Christic"; it may be called "ecclesial"

---

28. Congar 1965, 351; see Congar 1969. At the end of the text just quoted, Congar adds: "or that they incorporate them invisibly into it." This final recourse to a Church belonging, similar to Church membership *in voto*, seems to be what LG 16 deliberately chose not to resume in its own name.

29. Congar 1963 writes: "The Catholic Church remains the only institution (*sacramentum*) divinely instituted and commissioned for salvation, and whatever grace exists in the world is referred to it in finality, if not in efficiency" (431–32). See texts of Congar quoted on p. 101, above, and in n. 11 of chap. 3, above. See also Theisen 1976, 65–81.

30. EN 80 reads: "God can accomplish this salvation in whomsoever he wishes by ways which he knows. And yet, if his Son came, it was precisely in order to reveal to us, by his word and his life,

(*gratia ecclesialis*) insofar as it is tending toward the mystery of the Church, in virtue of the orientation toward it (*ordinati*) (LG 16) of people saved in Christ outside of it.

The thought of Karl Rahner seems more explicit here.[31] Rahner's "anonymous Christianity" — it is important to note it — stands for a relationship to Jesus Christ in the order of grace and salvation, not for a relationship directly to the Church. In principle, the entire human race is already saved in Jesus Christ; in virtue of this, the whole of humanity already constitutes the "people of God" (Rahner 1963, 82–88). People saved in Jesus Christ outside the Church are objectively oriented toward it (*ordinati*) *but* without being members of the Church. It is true that the Church is "the locus of the sending of the Spirit," in which the grace of salvation consists (Rahner 1956, 94–98). The Spirit is not, however, so bound to the Church, to its ministry and institutions, that its presence and work of salvation are impaired outside of it. Salvation outside the Church through the Spirit implies, nevertheless, an orientation, a reference, to the Church which, if it comes to full effect, emerges as belonging to the Church through membership. As locus of the Spirit, the Church must, therefore, be understood as the point toward which "nonecclesial" grace is tending, of which it is in the world the visible expression. Such orientation toward the Church exists wherever the Spirit is present and working. However, orientation does not imply universal mediation by way of efficient causality. For Rahner, especially in his later works — as we shall see in the next section — the necessity of the Church is to be viewed in the last analysis in terms of its function as sacramental sign of the presence of God's grace among people. Divine grace is operative where the Church is not present, but the Church is the sacramental sign of the presence of divine grace in the world.[32]

---

the ordinary paths of salvation." On the inversion in the order of ordinary and extraordinary means of salvation, proposed by H. Küng and H. R. Schlette, see pp. 154–155, above.

31. See Rahner 1963. On Rahner, see Theisen 1976, 81–103.

32. One may see, in this direction, Tononi 1994, 171–202. Tononi writes: "The Spirit is at work also outside of the Church and all human beings can experience [its] beneficial action.... But if the Spirit leads to adherence to Christ and his Paschal mystery, one may not forget that the place of full adhesion to Christ is the ecclesial communion, in such a way that by leading to Christ the Spirit cannot but also lead toward the Church" (191). See also G. Canobbio (1994a), who writes: "The necessity of the Church must therefore be understood in the sacramental line.... Compared to reflection in the past, something new is to be noted: the theme of the necessity of the Church frees itself at least in part from that of belonging to the Church, insofar as, in the last analysis, that which is absolutely necessary for salvation is faith.... The modalities in which the Church exercises her influence on those who do not yet know her, are not spelled out; the doctrine of implicit desire being dropped, recourse is had to the possibility of an encounter of people with the paschal mystery through the Spirit (GS 22).... [But], if the Church were not to exist in the world..., the plan of God would not be actualized, which consists in gathering all human persons 'in the unique people of God..., in the unique Body of Christ'" (155–56). And he adds later: "The problem of the necessity of the Church for salvation is founded on the nature of the Church and does not directly concern the problem of belonging to her.... That is to say: the problem must be seen not from the point of view of those who are saved, and hence of the conditions which must be verified to make salvation possible, but from the point of view of the Church, and therefore of the significance of the Church in the order of the salvation willed by God for humankind" (169; see also 179–83).

## B. The Church, Sacrament of the Kingdom

On the one hand, Vatican II defined the Church as the "universal sacrament of salvation" (LG 48). On the other hand, a certain theology has developed which considers the Church as the "sacrament of the Reign of God." We have recalled that, while Vatican II and the International Theological Commission seemed to still identify the Reign of God present in the world with the Church, the encyclical *Redemptoris Missio* (RM 20) and the document "Dialogue and Proclamation" (DP 35) have been the first official documents of the central magisterium to distinguish them clearly by affirming that the Reign of God is a wider reality than the Church, indeed a universal reality. The International Theological Commission has examined the meaning of the expression "the Church, sacrament of the Reign of God." However, its answer maintains the previous affirmation, according to which the Church represents the Reign of God already present in history. It is, therefore, the sacrament of the Reign of God in relation to the eschatological fulfillment of the Kingdom, insofar as the Church-Kingdom in history is marching toward the Church-eschatological Kingdom (see International Theological Commission 1989, 303–4).

Once the universality of the Reign of God is affirmed — as we have affirmed it here — the question of the sacramentality of the Church in relation to the Reign of God is necessarily asked in a different way. Between the Church and the Kingdom there is, according to the encyclical *Redemptoris Missio*, "a unique and special relationship which, while not excluding the action of Christ and the Spirit outside the Church's visible boundaries, confers upon her a specific and necessary role" (RM 18). How is this role to be understood? More specifically, how can it be understood that the Church is in history the sacrament of the Kingdom already present? The sacramental theory can be extremely helpful here. Rahner has applied it with great clarity to the relationship between the Church in the world and the Reign of God in history. He writes:

> The Church is not identical with the Kingdom of God. It is the sacrament of the Kingdom of God in the eschatological phase of sacred history which began with Christ, the phase which brings about the Kingdom of God. As long as history lasts, the Church will not be identical with the Kingdom of God, for the latter is only definitively present when history ends with the coming of Christ and the last judgment. Yet the Kingdom of God is not simply something due to come later, which later will replace the world, its history and the outcome of its history. The Kingdom of God itself is coming to be in the history of the world (not only in that of the Church) wherever obedience to God occurs in grace as the acceptance of God's self-communication.... For this Kingdom of God in the world, which of course can never simply be identified with any particular objective secular phenomenon, the Church is a part, because of course the Church itself is in the world and in its members makes world history. Above all, however, the Church is precisely its special fundamental

sacrament, i.e., the eschatological and efficacious manifestation (sign) in redemptive history that in the unity, activity, fraternity, etc., of the *world,* the Kingdom of God is at hand. Even here, therefore, as in the various individual sacraments, sign and thing signified can never be separated or identified. (Rahner 1968, 348)

The classical distinction made in sacramental theology between the sign and the thing signified — more exactly between the *sacramentum tantum,* the *res et sacramentum,* and the *res tantum* — is thus applied to the relationship in history between the Reign of God and the Church and to the role of the Church in relation to the Reign of God present in history. The Church, in its visible aspect, is the sacrament (*sacramentum tantum*); the reality signified (*res tantum*), which it both contains and confers, is the belonging to the Reign of God which is being conferred; the intermediate reality, the *res et sacramentum,* is the relationship to the Church which is realized in the members of the ecclesial community, by virtue of which they share in the reality of the Reign of God. Nevertheless, as the sacramental theory implies, God is not bound by the sacraments (*Deus non alligatur sacramentis*). That means that one can attain to the reality of the Reign of God without recourse being had to the sacrament of the Church and without belonging to the body of the Church. The "others" can thus be members of the Kingdom of God without being part of the Church and without recourse to its mediation. The Church remains, nevertheless, the efficacious sign, willed by God, of the presence in the world and in history of the reality of the Reign of God. It must bear witness to it and serve it.

It becomes possible, then, by considering the formulations provided by the council in a new light, to understand how the Church is the sacrament of the Kingdom in history. The council said that in the Church the Reign of God is "already present in mystery" (LG 3). According to the sacramental theory, this does not simply refer to the inchoate presence in the Church of the Reign of God ordered toward its final completion. Rather, what is implied is the mysteric or sacramental (*in mysterio*) presence of the reality of the Reign of God already present in the world and in history. The Church is "the sacrament of the Reign." This means — to adopt the formulation used in the final document of the episcopal conference at Puebla (1979) — that in it "we find the visible manifestation of the project that God is silently carrying out throughout the world. The Church is the place where we find the maximum concentration of the Father's activity" (227) (Eagleson and Scharper, eds., 1979, 152).

The presence of the Church-as-sign in the world bears witness, therefore, that God has established in this world his Reign in Jesus Christ. Furthermore, as efficacious sign, the Church contains and effects the reality which it signifies, giving access to the Reign of God through its word and action. Yet the Church still belongs to the sacramental realm, that is, to the realm of the relative. The necessity of the Church is not of such a nature that access to the Reign of God would be possible only through it. The "others" can be part of the Reign of

God and of Christ without being members of the Church and without recourse to its mediation. The sacramental presence of the Reign of God in the Church is, nevertheless, a privileged one, for it has received from Christ "the fullness of the benefits and means of salvation" (RM 18). It is the "universal sacrament" (LG 48) of this Reign. This is why those who have access to salvation and to the Reign through means other than the Church, though they are not incorporated into it as members, are nevertheless "oriented" (*ordinantur*) to it — as is noted in the constitution *Lumen Gentium* (16), which does not adopt the earlier teaching about "members of desire."

That the Church is sacrament of the Reign of God, universally present in history, does not necessarily imply on its part a universal mediatory activity of grace in favor of the members of other religious traditions who have entered the Reign of God by responding to God's invitation through faith and love. That is why, in the preceding chapter, we could uphold a "mediation" of their own religious tradition in their favor (see pp. 316–319, above). While not being in any way members of the Church or subject to its mediation, the "others" are, nevertheless, oriented toward it; its causality on their behalf is of the order not of efficiency but of finality.

Such is the meaning of the expression *sacramentum mundi,* from which the theological encyclopedia directed by Karl Rahner draws its title (see Rahner 1968). The concept of the Church-sacrament, which was developing before the council (Schillebeeckx 1963; Semmelroth 1953), led to the conciliar description of the Church as "sacrament of salvation" (LG 48). That of the Church as "sacrament of the world" (*sacramentum mundi*) has since then been repeatedly explained by Edward Schillebeeckx (Schillebeeckx 1965; 1968). What is its precise meaning? The Church is the sign willed by God to signify what his grace in Jesus Christ has accomplished and continues to accomplish in the world. Schillebeeckx specifies matters: "The Church is not the Kingdom of God, but it bears symbolic witness to the Kingdom through its word and sacrament, and in its praxis effectively anticipates the Kingdom" (Schillebeeckx 1990, 157). And Rahner explains equivalently: "That the Church is the sacrament of the world's salvation... means this: that the Church is the concrete historical *appearance* in the dimension of history become eschatological, in the dimension of society, for the unique salvation which occurs, through God's grace, across the length and breadth of humankind" (Rahner 1966c, 53–54).

In that sense one can transform the ancient controversial axiom and say: "No salvation outside the world" (*Extra mundum nulla salus*) (Schillebeeckx 1990, 5–15). J. P. Theisen sums up well this understanding of the Church-sacrament when he writes:

> The Church as sacrament may mean only that the Church exists in the world as the visible sign of the saving grace that God is effecting through Christ at a distance from the visible Church. The Church mirrors, articulates, and makes intelligible the process of salvation that is being

accomplished anywhere in the world.... In this sense the Church as sacrament exists to show forth the riches of God's mercy in Christ. It is a universal sacrament of salvation in that it becomes a sign of God's salvific activity in Christ wherever this occurs in the world. The thrust of the sacrament model of the Church leads to an understanding of the Church as visible event and concrete manifestation of God's grace effecting salvation of people anywhere in the world. (Theisen 1976, 134)

The sacrament of the Reign of God, the Church is also at the service of the Reign. As has been recalled earlier, the encyclical *Redemptoris Missio* distinguishes various ways in which the Church is at the service of the Reign of God. Among other ways, it affirms: "The Church serves the Kingdom by spreading through the world the 'Gospel values' which are an expression of the Kingdom and which help people to accept God's plan" (RM 20). The Church also contributes to the promotion of the Reign of God "through her witness and through such activities as dialogue, human promotion, commitment to justice and peace" (RM 20).

In a Christocentric and regnocentric perspective which overcomes a too narrow ecclesiocentric perspective, the mission of the Church will be seen under a new light. Its task will not be viewed in terms of a universal mediatory function; the term "mediation" will be used of Jesus Christ as it is in the New Testament (1 Tim 2:4–5). The task of the Church will be seen as witness, service, and announcing. The Church must show forth for all people the presence in the world of the Reign which God has inaugurated in Jesus Christ; it must serve the growth of the Reign and proclaim it. This supposes that the Church be entirely "decentered" from itself, to be entirely centered on Jesus Christ and the Reign of God (see Ellacuría 1984).

But the Church has no monopoly on the Reign of God. We have seen that the members of the other religious traditions, who perceive the call of God through their own tradition, share truly — even without being formally aware of it — in the Reign of God present in history, of which they are members in their own right. It must be added that the religious traditions contribute to the building up of the Reign of God not only among their followers but in the world at large. While the Church is in the world the "universal sacrament" of the Reign of God, the other traditions too exercise a certain mediation of the Reign, different, no doubt, but no less real.

### C. Reign of God and Eschatology

One further question remains: how to understand the relationship between the historical reality of the Reign of God and its eschatological fullness. Is the fullness of salvation to be understood in terms of the fulfillment of the Church at the end of time? Or will the Church in heaven be part of an eschatological Reign which extends beyond it? Or will the fulfillment of the eschatological

Kingdom bring the time of the Church to a close, its sacramental role now having been completed? Theologians are not unanimous on this point (see Mondin 1986, 389–98).

Following what Vatican II affirms about the "heavenly Church" (LG 49–53), Avery Dulles considers the fullness of the Kingdom as the fulfillment of the mystery of the Church (Dulles 1987, 103–22). Others, such as B. Mondin, see "the final reality in its perfect and definitive realization" as "embracing at the same time the Church and the world" (Mondin 1986, 395); this position can claim to be based on a combination of the statements on the "heavenly Church" in *Lumen Gentium* (LG 49–53) and those about the eschatological Reign in *Gaudium et Spes* (GS 39). Others, insisting on the Church's sacramental function in history, noted also by the council (LG 1, 48), come to the conclusion that it is provisional by nature and that it is due to disappear when the fullness of the Kingdom is achieved, since, as a sacramental reality, it was subordinated to the Kingdom.[33] When the perfect reality has been achieved, the sign loses its raison d'être. On this Karl Rahner writes:

> The Church, if only she be rightly understood, is living always on the proclamation of her own provisional status and of her historically advancing elimination in the coming Kingdom of God towards which she is expectantly travelling as a pilgrim, because God for his own part is coming to meet her in the Parousia and her own pilgrimage, too, is taking place in the power of Christ's coming. The essential nature of the Church consists in pilgrimage towards the promised future. (Rahner 1969b, 298; see also McBrien 1969, 98; Pannenberg 1989, 76–77)

In the context of the relationship between the Reign of God and the other religious traditions of the world, this last opinion is to be preferred. This is because it can show how the followers of other religious traditions, who have belonged to the Kingdom of God in history without being members of the Church, can at the end of time share in the fullness of the Kingdom without having to be linked at the last stage to an "eschatological Church." This is, moreover, in agreement with the statement of R. Schnackenburg, quoted above: "Christ's rule extends beyond the Church . . . , and one day the Church will have completed her earthly task and will be absorbed in the eschatological Kingdom of Christ and of God" (Schnackenburg 1968, 301). It is no doubt in this sense that Pierre Teilhard de Chardin understood the fullness at the end of time as the "universal Christification"; for him the Church represented on earth the "reflexively Christified portion of the world" (Teilhard de Chardin 1975, 191). The eschatological reality is the fullness of the Reign of God.

---

33. This should also follow from the analogy established by *Lumen Gentium* between the two natures of Christ and the Church's two aspects, divine and human, communion and institution: "The earthly Church and the Church endowed with heavenly riches are not to be thought of as two realities. On the contrary, they form one complex reality which comes together from a human and a divine element" (8). There are not two churches, one visible and the other invisible, one which is due to disappear while the other will remain.

## Fourteen

# Interfaith Dialogue — Praxis and Theology

WE NOTED in the preceding chapter that Christians and the members of other religious traditions share together in the reality of the Reign of God and are destined to build it together through history unto its eschatological fullness: they are co-members and co-builders with God of God's Reign on earth. We added that here, perhaps, is found what — in a Christian theological perspective — constitutes the deepest foundation for interfaith dialogue between Christians and the "others." Not surprisingly, then, a Christian theology of interreligious dialogue will adopt, preferentially, a regnocentric perspective.

Such a perspective coincides, moreover, with that of Jesus himself. We have recalled that the Reign of God was at the center of Jesus' life and mission, of his message and action; the Reign was for the historical Jesus the "truly ultimate objective" (see p. 345, above). So too ought it to be for the Church, if it is true that the Church is destined to prolong the mission of Jesus himself. The Gospel according to Mark shows this in a striking manner. At the beginning of his Gospel, Mark provides a programmatic summary of Jesus' mission: he went out "announcing the Good News," saying, "The Kingdom of God is at hand" (Mk 1:14–15). The same Mark has the risen Christ sending his disciples to the whole world to "announce the Good News" (Mk 16:15) of the Kingdom of God that has now come about through the mystery of his Passover.

The Church, we have shown in the previous chapter, is placed not at its own service but at the service of the Reign of God. The Reign of God is the horizon of its entire "missionary activity." This is well expressed by the "Theses on Interreligious Dialogue" (1987) of the Theological Advisory Commission of the Federation of Asian Bishops' Conferences, where we read: "The focus of the Church's mission of evangelization is building up the Kingdom of God and building up the Church to be at the service of the Kingdom. The Kingdom is, therefore, wider than the Church. The Church is the sacrament of the Kingdom, visibilizing it, ordained to it, promoting it, but not equating itself to it" (6, 3) (Theological Advisory Commission [FABC] 1987, 16).

What is to be shown now is that interfaith dialogue belongs to the Church's evangelizing mission. This has not always been perceived in mission theology, even in recent decades. In fact, it is a recent gain of post–Vatican II years, the background of which must be briefly recalled.[1]

The term "evangelization" had tended to replace that of "mission" in mission theology before the council years; the council used both terms, often combining them. However, "evangelization" in the council documents remains a narrow concept, practically identified with the "proclamation" of the Gospel, referring to inviting the "others" to join the Church community. The council—prompted by Paul VI's encyclical letter *Ecclesiam Suam* (1964)—made a vibrant appeal in favor of dialogue with the members of other religious traditions (NA 4; GS 92); but nowhere is it said that the council considers interfaith dialogue as a dimension of the Church's evangelizing mission. Whatever importance or merit may be attributed to dialogue, in terms of its relation to evangelization, it represents but a first approach to the others, to which the preconciliar theological term of "preevangelization" could still be applied.

This goes to show that viewing dialogue as an integral element of "evangelization" marks a significant qualitative change in postconciliar mission theology. It forms part of the development in post–Vatican II years of a broad and comprehensive notion of evangelization, of which dialogue—together with other elements—is an integral dimension. The change did not, however, come about without hesitation and setbacks. Witness the fact that the apostolic exhortation *Evangelii Nuntiandi* (1975) of Paul VI—the "pope of dialogue"—remained entirely silent on the subject. In this papal exhortation the "others" were viewed only as the "beneficiaries" of the Church's evangelizing mission—still mostly conceived in terms of the "proclamation" of the Gospel and the Church activities connected with it. The breakthrough, as will be seen hereafter, came with documents belonging to the 1980s and the 1990s.

However, before proceeding further, some clarifications regarding the terms are again in order. We will consider mainly "evangelization," "dialogue," and "proclamation." The definitions of those terms, as proposed here, are mostly borrowed from the document "Dialogue and Proclamation" (DP) (1991), to which reference has already been made.[2]

*Evangelization,* or the evangelizing mission of the Church, "refers to the mission of the Church in its totality" (DP 8), made up as it is of various elements. As regards *dialogue,* a distinction needs to be made between dialogue as an attitude or spirit and dialogue as a distinct element, in its own right, of the evangelizing mission of the Church. The "spirit of dialogue" refers to an "attitude of respect and friendship, which permeates or should permeate all [the] activities constituting the evangelizing mission of the Church" (DP 9). As a specific, integral element of evangelization, dialogue means "all positive and constructive interreligious relations with individuals and communities of other faiths which are directed at mutual understanding and enrichment (DM 3), in obedience to

---

1. I have expanded on this background and the subsequent developments in Dupuis 1991b, 207–29. Only the essential framework is recalled here. See also Sheard 1987.

2. Text in *Bulletin* (Pontifical Council for Interreligious Dialogue) 77/26/2 (1991) 210–50.

truth and respect for freedom. It includes both witness and the exploration of respective religious convictions" (DP 9).

*Proclamation,* or "announcing," in contrast, "is the communication of the Gospel message, the mystery of salvation realized by God for all in Jesus Christ by the power of the Spirit. It is an invitation to a commitment of faith in Jesus Christ and to entry through baptism in the community of believers which is the Church" (DP 10).

The importance of these notions, if we would avoid confusions and misunderstandings, will appear hereafter. For the time being, let it suffice to point out the following by way of further clarifications. The spirit of dialogue must inform every aspect or element of the evangelizing mission. Thus, the "proclamation" of the Gospel by which members of the other religious traditions are invited to become — freely — disciples of Jesus in the Church must be done in a "spirit of dialogue." Dialogue, however, as a specific element of evangelization, is distinct from proclamation; it does *not* — as we shall see clearly — aim at the "conversion" of others to Christianity, while, of course, it necessarily implies, on the part of the evangelizer, the witness of life — without which no evangelizing activity whatever can be either sincere or credible.

This chapter will be divided into two parts. The first part will show the place of interfaith dialogue in the evangelizing mission, as a distinct, integral element of that mission, in its own right. The second part will examine the challenges which interfaith encounter raises for the Church's evangelizing mission, as well as the fruits and benefits to be derived from dialogue for Christian faith and theology.

# I. Dialogue Is Evangelization

## A. *A Review of the Recent Magisterium*

The important contribution which the teaching of Pope John Paul II has made to a theology of religions consisted in his constant affirmation of the presence and action of the Spirit of God among the members of other religions (see pp. 173–177, above).[3] He thereby laid the theological basis for the significance of interreligious dialogue in the mission of the Church. Thus, addressing the peoples of Asia in 1981, the pope once more emphasized the theme of the Holy Spirit.[4] The Church today, he asserted, "feels a deep need to enter into contact and dialogue with all of these religions." What seems to gather and unite Christians and the believers of other religions in a special way is the recognition of a need for prayer. The pope expressed his conviction that the Spirit of God is

---

3. An extensive collection of documents by the pontifical magisterium on interreligious dialogue has been published by the Pontifical Council for Interreligious Dialogue. See Gioia, ed., 1997.

4. Address over Radio Veritas, Manila; the text is found in AAS 73 (1981) 391–98; ND 1040.

present in the prayer of every person who prays, Christian and otherwise (see text quoted on pp. 174–175, above). He concluded:

> All Christians must, therefore, be committed to dialogue with the believers of all religions, so that the mutual understanding and collaboration may grow; so that moral values be strengthened; so that God may be praised in all creation. Ways must be developed to make this dialogue become a reality everywhere, but especially in Asia, the continent that is the cradle of ancient cultures and religions. (5; ND 1040)

While the call to dialogue becomes more urgent here than in previous documents, the doctrine remains the same. An acknowledgment of the active presence of the Spirit among others transforms the interreligious dialogue into an important task and a need felt by the Church. But this doctrine is not yet explicitly propounded in terms of mission and evangelization.

The situation is the same if we consider the pope's speech to the Roman curia (22 December 1986) in which he saw, in the World Day of Prayer for Peace in Assisi (27 October 1986), a "visible illustration, a lesson in things," of the meaning of the Church's engagement in interreligious dialogue, recommended by the council (7).[5] Here, more clearly than ever before, the pope lays down the theological foundation for such dialogue, referring to the "mystery of unity" already existing between Christians and those who remain "oriented" toward the Church (8). The "universal oneness" is based on the common origin and destiny of all humanity in creation (3), on the oneness of the mystery of the redemption in Jesus Christ (4–7), and on the active presence of the Spirit of God in the sincere prayer of members of other religious traditions (11).

First, then, there is a "radical unity" proceeding from creation: "There is only one divine plan for every human being coming into this world (cf. Jn 1:9)" (3). "The differences are a less important element, when confronted with the unity, which is radical, fundamental, and decisive" (3). Next there is the fundamental unity based on the mystery of universal redemption in Christ (4). In the light of this twofold mystery of unity, "differences of every type, and first of all the religious differences, belong to another order to the extent that they are reductive of God's design.... [They] must be overcome, in progress towards the realization of the mighty plan of unity which dominates the creation" (5). Despite these differences, sometimes felt as insurmountable divisions, all men and women "are included in the great and unique design of God in Jesus Christ" (5). "The universal unity based on the event of creation and redemption cannot fail to leave a trace in the concrete life of human beings, even of those who belong to different religions" (7). These "seeds of the Word" sown among others constitute the concrete foundation of the interreligious dialogue encouraged by the council (7). Likewise belonging to the foundation is the influence of the Spirit on all authentic prayer, since "the Holy Spirit... is mysteriously present in the

---

5. Text in *Bulletin* (Secretariat for Non-Christians) 64/22/1 (1987) 54–62. See ND 1049–52.

heart of every person" (11). The Church, for its part, is "called to work with all her energies (in evangelization, prayer, and dialogue) so that the wounds and divisions — which separate people from their Origin and Goal, and make them hostile to one another — may be healed" (6).

The theological foundation for interfaith dialogue, as the pope sees it, is enunciated with great clarity in this text. Yet nowhere does the document state explicitly that interfaith dialogue belongs to the Church's evangelizing mission.[6] To find this clearly affirmed, we must turn to the document published by the Secretariat for Non-Christians entitled "Dialogue and Mission" (DM) (1984).[7]

The secretariat's document is especially interested in the relationship between dialogue and mission (5). It is to be noted — and regretted — that in the introduction to the document, the relationship is still conceived in terms of a dichotomy between evangelization and dialogue. Mention is made of "the simultaneous presence, in mission, of the demands of evangelization and dialogue" and of the difficulties that can arise from this (7). However, this impression of a dichotomy is quickly dissipated. In the first part, bearing on mission, the document explains that the Church's mission "is one, but comes to be exercised in different ways, according to the conditions in which mission unfolds" (11). The document intends to delineate "the different aspects and manners of mission" (12). It does so in a passage which, while not claiming to be exhaustive, lists five "principal elements" of the "single, but complex and articulated reality" of the evangelizing mission of the Church. The importance of this text calls for its extensive citation:

> Mission is already constituted by the simple presence and living witness of the Christian life [cf. EN 21], although it must be recognized that "we bear this treasure in earthen vessels" [2 Cor 4:7]. Thus, the difference between the way the Christian appears existentially and that which he/she declares himself/herself to be is never fully overcome.
>
> There is also the concrete commitment to the service of humankind and all forms of activity for social development and for the struggle against poverty and the structures which produce it.
>
> Also, there is liturgical life and that of prayer and contemplation, eloquent testimonies to a living and liberating relationship with the active and true God who calls us to his Kingdom and to his glory [cf. Acts 2:42].
>
> There is, as well, the dialogue in which Christians meet the followers of other religious traditions in order to walk together towards truth and to work together in projects of common concern.

---

6. In fact, the discourse seems, more than once, to distinguish interreligious dialogue from evangelization — which therefore is again surreptitiously conceived in terms of "proclamation" only. Thus, referring to the activities of the Church, the document enumerates "evangelization, prayer, and dialogue" (see no. 6, quoted here); see also no. 10.

7. Text in *Bulletin* (Secretariat for Non-Christians) 56/19/2 (1984) 126–41.

Finally, there is announcing and catechesis in which the Good News of the Gospel is proclaimed and its consequences for life and culture are analyzed.

The totality of Christian mission embraces all these elements. (13)

"The totality of Christian mission embraces all these elements," but the list is not complete. Let us make some observations. The proclamation of the Gospel by announcing and catechesis comes last, and rightly so, since mission or evangelization should be seen as a dynamic process.[8] This process indeed culminates in the proclamation of Jesus Christ by *kèrugma* (announcing) and *didachè* (catechesis). On the same principle, however, the phrase "liturgical life and that of prayer and contemplation" ought to have been inserted following the proclamation of Jesus Christ, to which they are directly bound—just as in Acts 2:42, to which the text refers—and of which they are the natural issue. Then the order would have been: presence, service, dialogue, proclamation, and sacramentalization—the last two corresponding to the ecclesial activities which in the narrower, but traditional, view constituted evangelization.

In the broader perspective, adopted by the document, the "single reality" of evangelization is presented as "complex and articulated" at the same time: it is a process. This means that, while all the elements of the process are aspects of evangelization, not all have the same place or meaning in the Church's mission. For example, interreligious dialogue normally precedes proclamation. The former may or may not be followed by the latter, but the evangelizing process is brought to its climax if proclamation follows: proclamation and sacramentalization represent the culmination of the evangelizing mission of the Church.

Having insisted once more on the "important place" (*l'importance*) of dialogue in mission (19), the document studies dialogue more closely in the second part. Dialogue is in itself a distinct expression of evangelization; it is also "an attitude and spirit" and thus "the norm and the indispensable style (*le style indispensable*) of every task of Christian mission, as well as of every aspect of it, whether it be a matter of simple presence and witness, service, or direct proclamation" (29). All the aspects of mission listed previously must be "permeated by...a dialogical spirit" (29). Dialogue as a distinct dimension of evangelization is thus clearly distinguished from the "spirit of dialogue" that must inform all the expressions of the Church's evangelizing mission.

The interreligious dialogue itself as a specific task of evangelization—"which finds its place in the great dynamism of the Church's mission" (30)—can take several forms. There is the dialogue of life, open and accessible to all (29–30). There is the dialogue of a common commitment to the works of justice and

---

8. The word "finally" does not occur in the original Italian text: "vi è l'annuncio e la catechesi...." However, as mission is first described as a "single, but complex and *articulated* reality," it seems clear that the document regards it as a dynamic reality and process. In the apostolic exhortation *Evangelii Nuntiandi*, Paul VI had likewise described evangelization as a "rich, complex, and dynamic reality" (17), but without mentioning interreligious dialogue among its components. See AAS 68 (1976) 17.

human liberation (31–32). There is the intellectual dialogue in which scholars engage in an exchange at the level of their respective religious legacies, with the goal of promoting communion and fellowship (33–34). Finally, on the most profound level, there is the sharing of religious experiences of prayer and contemplation, in a common search for the Absolute (35). All these forms of dialogue[9] are, for the Christian partner, so many ways of working for the "evangelical transformation of cultures" (34), so many opportunities of sharing with others the values of the Gospel in an existential way (35).

We must now turn first to the encyclical *Redemptoris Missio* (RM) and, thereafter, to the document "Dialogue and Proclamation" (DP), to ask how they conceive the place of interfaith dialogue in the Church's evangelizing mission and its rapport with the "proclamation" of the Gospel (see also Dupuis 1993a, 110–31).

Chapter 5 of *Redemptoris Missio* develops the diverse "paths of mission," which, it notes at the outset, is "a single but complex reality and...develops in a variety of ways" (41). The order in which the different ways of mission are mentioned and explained is of importance here. The first form of evangelization is witness: often it is the only way in which mission is possible (42). In the second place comes the proclamation of Jesus Christ which is "the permanent priority of mission"; all the forms of missionary activity tend toward it (44). In the complex reality of mission, initial proclamation has a central and irreplaceable role (44). The priority of proclamation in relation to other activities must, however, be understood not as being of a temporal order but as logical and ideal. The concrete way of proceeding will depend on circumstances; further on, *Redemptoris Missio* will note that dialogue may sometimes be the "only way of bearing sincere witness to Christ" (57). How all other forms of missionary activity "are directed to proclamation" (44) receives no further explanation.

In the third place are mentioned: conversion to Christianity, to which proclamation is directed, and baptism, which introduces believers in the Church (46). *Redemptoris Missio* insists that proclamation cannot be dispensed with under the false pretext of proselytism, for every person has a right to hear the Good News (46); nor can conversion to Christ be severed from baptism, for Christ has willed the Church as the "place" where people "would in fact find him" (47). Thus, the foundation of new communities and the development of new particular churches, which are connected with conversion-baptism, are recorded in the fourth place; this is "a central and determining goal of missionary activity" (48).

Thus far the following elements have been mentioned in organic succession: witness, proclamation, conversion and its sacramentalization in baptism, and the establishment and growth of the Church. At this point *Redemptoris Missio* treats rapidly the "basic ecclesial communities" as a force for evangelization and missionary outreach (51) and the inculturation of the Gospel message in the various cultures of the peoples (52–54). It is only after these — and be-

---

9. On the various forms of dialogue according to the document, see Dupuis 1985.

fore speaking of human development and promotion (58–59), which, it will be said, has a "close connection with the proclamation of the Gospel" (59) — that *Redemptoris Missio* deals explicitly with interreligious dialogue (55–57). The main points on this subject can be grouped under three headings: (1) dialogue and evangelization; (2) dialogue and proclamation; and (3) the aim of dialogue.

1. Interreligious dialogue, *Redemptoris Missio* states, "is a part of the Church's evangelizing mission" (55); it is "one of its expressions" (55) and, moreover, "a path towards the Kingdom" (57). These affirmations seem to imply a broad notion of evangelization. Interreligious dialogue and proclamation appear as "two elements" or distinct expressions of evangelization. There is no opposition between them; rather, there is both a close link and a distinction. This is spelled out as follows: "These two elements must maintain both their intimate connection and their distinctiveness; therefore, they should not be confused, manipulated (*nec immodice instrumentorum instar adhibenda*) or regarded as identical, as though they were interchangeable" (55).

On the one hand, that dialogue cannot be "manipulated" means, emphatically, that it cannot be reduced to a *means* for proclamation; on the other hand, it is said that "dialogue does not dispense from evangelization" — where, it may be observed in passing, *Redemptoris Missio* seems to fall back on a narrow view of evangelization which it now implicitly identifies with proclamation.

2. The intimate link between dialogue and proclamation notwithstanding (55), proclamation keeps the "permanent priority" in the Church's evangelizing mission (see 44). Dialogue does not dispense from it (55). On this point *Redemptoris Missio* recalls a letter which the pope wrote to the bishops of Asia: "The fact that the followers of other religions can receive God's grace and be saved by Christ apart from the ordinary means which he has established does not thereby cancel the call to faith and baptism which God wills for all people" (55).[10] The reason is that "the Church is the ordinary means of salvation and that she alone possesses the fullness of the means of salvation" (55).

3. Dialogue is understood as "a method and means of mutual knowledge and enrichment" (55). God "does not fail to make himself present in many ways, not only to individuals but also to entire peoples through their spiritual riches, of which their religions are the main and essential expression" (55). In interreligious dialogue the Church seeks to discover the "seeds of the Word" and the "rays of the Truth" which are found in the persons and in the religious traditions of humankind (56). It is stimulated "both to discover and acknowledge the signs of Christ's presence and of the working of the Spirit, as well as to examine more deeply her own identity and to bear witness to the fullness of revelation which she has received for the good of all" (56). Dialogue, finally, "leads to inner purification and conversion" (56). There is question here, not of

---

10. Letter to the Fifth Plenary Assembly of the FABC (23 June 1990), 4; text in *Osservatore Romano* (18 July 1990).

the conversion of the others to Christianity, but of the conversion toward God of both partners of dialogue, the Christian and the other.

Turning to "Dialogue and Proclamation" (DP),[11] the directly relevant material can be grouped under four headings: (1) theological foundation of dialogue; (2) dialogue in the evangelizing mission of the Church; (3) the aim of dialogue; and (4) dialogue and proclamation.

1. The document recalls the "mystery of unity," based on the common origin and destiny of humankind in God, on universal salvation in Jesus Christ, and on the active presence of the Spirit in all (28), of which John Paul II had spoken in his 1986 discourse to the Roman curia. "From the mystery of unity," "Dialogue and Proclamation" affirms, "it follows that all men and women who are saved share, though differently, in the same mystery of salvation in Jesus Christ through his Spirit. Christians know this through their faith, while others remain unaware that Jesus Christ is the source of their salvation. The mystery of salvation reaches out to them, in a way known to God, through the invisible action of the Spirit of Christ" (29). There follows an important text, already quoted (see p. 314, above), in which "Dialogue and Proclamation" assigns a positive role to the traditions themselves in the salvation of their members: it is "in the sincere practice of what is good in their own religious traditions" that they respond positively to God's offer of grace (29).

The members of other religions, then, are saved by Christ not in spite of, or beside, their own tradition but in it and in some mysterious way through it. This does not, however, mean that everything in the other traditions can be conducive to the salvation of their members. In fact, to identify in them "elements of grace capable of sustaining the positive response of their members to God's invitation" is a difficult task, requiring discernment (30). Not everything in them is the result of grace, nor do they contain only positive values; for sin has been at work in the world, and the traditions "reflect the limitations of the human spirit, sometimes inclined to choose evil" (31).

2. To show the place of interreligious dialogue in the mission of the Church, "Dialogue and Proclamation" first recalls the teaching of Vatican II on the Church as universal sacrament, that is, as sign and instrument of salvation (LG 1, 48) (33). Regarding the "mysterious and complex" relationship between the Church and the Kingdom, it quotes John Paul II to the effect that "the Kingdom is inseparable from the Church, because both are inseparable from the person and work of Jesus himself" (34). The members of other religious traditions are oriented (*ordinantur*) (see LG 16) to the Church, as to the sacrament in which the Kingdom is present "in mystery"; but they "already share in some way in the reality which is signified by the Kingdom" (35).

In fact, "Dialogue and Proclamation" goes on to say, in another important text already quoted (see p. 340, n. 15, above), that the Kingdom of God is in history a wider reality than the Church, even though the historical reality of the

---

11. Text in *Bulletin* (Pontifical Council for Interreligious Dialogue) 77/26/2 (1991) 210–50.

Kingdom outside the Church "needs to find completion" in it and in the world to come (35). On the other hand, the Church on earth is always on pilgrimage (36); therefore, notwithstanding its holiness "by divine institution," it is ever in need of renewal and reform, not only in its members but as an institution (36). As for divine truth, while the fullness of revelation of God in Jesus Christ has been entrusted to it (DV 2), yet, as Vatican II remarked (see DV 8), the Church "is always advancing toward the fullness of divine truth, until eventually the words of God are fulfilled in her" (37).

This situation of the Church makes it easier to see "why and in what sense interreligious dialogue is an integral element of the Church's evangelizing mission" (38). The foundation of the Church's commitment to dialogue "is not merely anthropological but primarily theological" (38). As is taught by Paul VI and John Paul II, the Church must enter into a dialogue of salvation with all men and women, even as God has entered into an age-old dialogue of salvation with humankind which is continued even today (38). "In this dialogue of salvation Christians and others are called to collaborate with the Spirit of the Risen Lord who is universally present and active" (40).

3. Regarding the aim of interreligious dialogue, the document has the following to say: interreligious dialogue does not merely aim at mutual understanding and friendly relations; in it Christians and others are invited to "deepen their religious commitment, to respond with increasing sincerity to God's personal call and gracious self-gift which, as our faith tells us, always passes through the mediation of Jesus Christ and the work of his Spirit" (40). Thus, the aim of interreligious dialogue is "a deeper conversion of all towards God"; as such it possesses "its own validity" (41). "Sincere dialogue implies, on the one hand, mutual acceptance of differences, or even of contradictions, and on the other, respect for the free decision of persons taken according to the dictate of their conscience" (41).

4. On the relationship between interreligious dialogue and proclamation, the document has the following important affirmation:

> Interreligious dialogue and proclamation, though not on the same level, are both authentic elements of the Church's evangelizing mission. Both are legitimate and necessary. They are intimately related, but not interchangeable.... The two activities remain distinct[,] but ... one and the same local Church, one and the same person, can be diversely engaged in both. (77)

Concretely and in actual fact, the way of fulfilling the Church's mission depends on the particular circumstances; it requires sensitivity to the situation, attentiveness to the "signs of the times through which the Spirit of God is speaking," and discernment (78). But in all situations the Church's mission extends to all persons. Indeed, the Church in dialogue "can be seen to have a prophetic role" toward the religions themselves as its witness to the Gospel raises questions to them; but it may find itself challenged in turn. So "the members of the Church and the followers of other religions find themselves to be companions on the common path which humanity is called to tread" (79). Moreover, "the Church encourages and fosters interreligious dialogue not only between herself and the other religious traditions, but even among these religious traditions themselves" (80). This is one way in which it fulfills its role as "sacrament, that is, a sign and instrument of communion with God and of unity among all people" (LG 1). Thus, on the one hand, interreligious dialogue is truly part of the dialogue of salvation initiated by God (80).

Proclamation, on the other hand, "aims at guiding people to explicit knowledge of what God has done for all men and women in Jesus Christ through becoming members of the Church" (81). Attentiveness to the promptings of the Spirit and discernment are required as to when the Church must fulfill this task. Proclamation must, moreover, be done in a progressive manner, keeping pace with the growth of the hearers in the obedience of faith (81).

Proclamation and dialogue are "two ways of carrying out the one mission of the Church" (82). The concrete way in which to fulfill the mission will depend on circumstances. But it must be remembered that "dialogue...does not constitute the whole mission of the Church, that it cannot simply replace proclamation, but remains oriented towards proclamation, in so far as the dynamic process of the Church's evangelizing mission reaches in it its climax and its fullness" (82).

Through the various stages of dialogue, in fact, "the partners will feel a great need both to impart and to receive information, to give and receive explanations, to ask questions of each other. Christians in dialogue have the duty of responding to their partner's expectation regarding the contents of the Christian faith, of bearing witness to this faith, when this is called for, of giving an account of the hope that is in them (cf. 1 Pet 3:15)" (82). In this dialogical situation they will hope and desire to share with others their joy in knowing and following Jesus Christ, Lord and Savior — a desire which, insofar as they have a deep love for the Lord Jesus, will be motivated not merely by obedience to the Lord's command but by their love for him (83). But it should be found normal that the followers of other religions are animated by a similar desire to share their own faith; "all dialogue implies reciprocity and aims at banishing fear and aggressiveness" (83). In all this Christians must "be prepared to follow wherever in God's providence and design the Spirit is leading them." "It is the Spirit who is guiding the evangelizing mission of the Church"; to us it belongs to be attentive to its promptings. But "whether proclamation be possible or not, the Church pursues her mission...through interreligious dialogue, witnessing to and sharing Gospel values" (84).

If a rapid comparison is established between *Redemptoris Missio* and "Dialogue and Proclamation" on interreligious dialogue and its relation to proclamation, the following main differences emerge, besides the points of contact.

1. A first significant difference consists in the distinct emphasis given in the two documents to interreligious dialogue. In *Redemptoris Missio*, dialogue (and human promotion) is mentioned in the chapter on "paths of mission" (or

"forms of evangelization"), after such items as basic ecclesial communities and inculturation. The emphasis remains overwhelmingly on proclamation, which is what missionary activity proper, that is, mission to the nations, is understood to be about (RM 34); proclamation has the "permanent priority" (RM 44). In comparison, "Dialogue and Proclamation" places more emphasis on interreligious dialogue. Where *Redemptoris Missio*'s main intention is to reaffirm strongly the relevance and urgency of proclamation, the primary concern of "Dialogue and Proclamation" is that the significance of dialogue be not undervalued.

2. Moreover, the perspective of *Redemptoris Missio* appears more ecclesiocentric in comparison with that of "Dialogue and Proclamation," which is more Christocentric and regnocentric. According to *Redemptoris Missio,* "missionary activity proper... can be characterized as the work of proclaiming Christ and his Gospel, building up the local Church and promoting the values of the Kingdom" (34); "the mission *ad gentes* has this objective: to found Christian communities and develop Churches to their full maturity" (48). Emphasis is thus placed, in a clearly ecclesiocentric perspective, on the building up of the Church. By contrast, the perspective of "Dialogue and Proclamation" is more Christocentric and regnocentric: linking with its predecessor of 1984 (DM 13), it defines mission simply in terms of evangelization, and the complex reality of evangelization as comprising, among other elements, interreligious dialogue and proclamation (see DP 8, 82, referred to above).

3. Let us come to the relationship between dialogue and proclamation. It has been seen that both *Redemptoris Missio* and "Dialogue and Proclamation" state clearly that in the evangelizing mission of the Church, dialogue and proclamation constitute distinct elements, not to be confused nor separated (see RM 55 and DP 77, quoted above). *Redemptoris Missio* states that they cannot be "manipulated," by which is meant that dialogue cannot be reduced to a "means" for proclamation. "Dialogue and Proclamation" affirms equivalently that dialogue "possesses its own validity" (DP 41). As for their interrelationship in the Church's mission, *Redemptoris Missio* states the "permanent priority" of proclamation, in virtue of which "all forms of missionary activity are directed to this proclamation" (RM 44). As noted above, this priority must not be understood as temporal, as if proclamation had in all circumstances to precede other forms of evangelization; for it will be said thereafter that interreligious dialogue is often the "only way of bearing sincere witness to Christ and offering generous service to others" (RM 57). The "permanent priority" is of a logical and ideal order of importance: proclamation has a "central and irreplaceable role" (RM 44). "Dialogue and Proclamation," for its part, affirms unambiguously that "interreligious dialogue and proclamation... [are] not on the same level" (DP 77), but their relationship is explained more theologically, saying that dialogue "remains oriented toward proclamation insofar as the dynamic process of the Church's evangelizing mission reaches in it its climax and its fullness" (DP 82).

4. Finally, the question may be asked whether and to what extent *Redemptoris Missio* and "Dialogue and Proclamation" have gone beyond what was previously affirmed by the central teaching authority with regard to the topics under consideration. The following may be said: Vatican II recommended dialogue with the other religious traditions (NA 2; GS 92), but without stating that it is an integral part of the evangelizing mission of the Church. This is clearly affirmed both by *Redemptoris Missio* and by "Dialogue and Proclamation," following the lead of "Dialogue and Mission." Furthermore, some ambiguity in *Redemptoris Missio*'s terminology notwithstanding, both *Redemptoris Missio* and "Dialogue and Proclamation" develop a broad concept of evangelization, which was not yet found in Vatican II; both assert, though in different ways, that dialogue cannot be reduced to a "means" for proclamation but has value in itself. In these and other ways *Redemptoris Missio* and "Dialogue and Proclamation," with their distinct emphases and nuances, constitute a step forward in the Church's doctrine on evangelization, dialogue, and proclamation.

## B. *"Mission Is Dialogue"?*

In the previous section, I intentionally allowed *Redemptoris Missio* and "Dialogue and Proclamation" to speak for themselves as they stand, without entering into a critical study of the mutual relationship between the two documents and of the influences and counterinfluences to which "Dialogue and Proclamation" has been subject down to the last stage of drafting. I have offered elsewhere such a critical study, in which I show how and why some of the most open and forward-looking assertions of the document have been toned down (by way of omission or addition), losing thereby a good deal of their cutting force (see Dupuis 1993b). Examples where such loss is noted are: the statements on the universal reality of the Reign of God (DP 35) and on the role of the other religious traditions as paths to salvation for their followers (DP 29). I indicated clearly that, as a result of some more unfortunate amendments, the text reflects a regrettable tension between divergent views, not without introducing some ambiguity (Dupuis 1993b, 154). I pointed, in particular, to the ambiguity resulting from the way in which the relationship between dialogue and proclamation is conceived in some parts of the document — an ambiguity which, I noted, has not escaped the attention of some reviewers. I wrote:

> While, on the one hand, interreligious dialogue is said to be in itself an authentic form of evangelization (DP 77), even, if circumstances are such, in the absence of proclamation (DP 76), on the other hand, following EN 27 and 22, evangelization is said "always to entail as simultaneous foundation" a clear proclamation of Jesus Christ (DP 75), which is the "central element" without which the others, "though in themselves genuine forms of the Church's mission, would lose their cohesion and vitality" (DP 76). If proclamation needs to be present always, is dialogue *in itself*

a genuine form of evangelization? And can it be maintained that both are "absolutely necessary" (DP 89)? (Dupuis 1993b, 154)

On the one hand, the shortcomings of the two documents — and, in particular, the narrow ecclesiocentric perspective of *Redemptoris Missio* — must be regretted, no doubt. So too must be the unnecessary ambiguities which "Dialogue and Proclamation" has not been able to withstand. On the other hand, as I pointed out at the end of my commentary on "Dialogue and Proclamation," "apart from some ambiguity that the document does not succeed in avoiding, it must be recognized that a certain tension remains and *must remain*, in the reality of the Church's evangelizing mission, between dialogue and proclamation."[12] The tension "is between the 'not yet' of the Church who, together with the 'others' is in history a pilgrim toward the fullness of the Kingdom, and the 'already' of the Church who is in time and in the world the sacrament of the Kingdom" (Dupuis 1993b, 155).

> The tension between the "already" and the "not yet" is reflected in the Church's evangelizing mission and, markedly so, in the relationship within it between interreligious dialogue and proclamation: Insofar as the Church remains on her pilgrimage, together with the "others," towards the fullness of the Kingdom, she engages with them in dialogue; insofar as she is the sacrament of the reality of the Kingdom already present and operative in history, she proclaims to them Jesus Christ in whom the Kingdom of God has been established by God. (Dupuis 1993b, 155)

In a somewhat similar fashion, the "Theses on Interreligious Dialogue" of the FABC Theological Advisory Commission — mentioned above — bases the bipolarity of dialogue and proclamation in the Church's evangelizing mission on the universal presence in the world of God's work of salvation (the Reign of God), of which the Church is the sacrament. There we read:[13]

> The one divine plan of salvation for all peoples embraces the whole universe. The mission of the Church has to be understood within the context of this plan. The Church does not monopolize God's action in the universe. While it is aware of a special mission of God in the world, it has to be attentive to God's action in the world, as manifested also in other religions. This twofold awareness constitutes the two poles of the Church's evangelizing action in relation to other religions. While proclamation is the expression of its awareness of being in mission, dialogue is the expression of its awareness of God's presence and action outside its boundaries. The action of the Church finds itself in a field of forces controlled by these two poles of divine activity. Proclamation is the affirmation of and witness to God's action in oneself. Dialogue is the openness and attention to the

---

12. Dupuis 1993b, 155. See, in the same direction, Bosch (1992, 483–89), who speaks of "creative tension."

13. Text in *FABC Papers*, no. 48 (Hong Kong, 1987), 16.

mystery of God's action in the other believer. It is a perspective of faith that we cannot speak of the one without the other.

The Spirit calls all peoples to conversion which is primarily a free turning of the heart to God and his Kingdom in obedience to this word. Dialogue as a mutual challenge to growth toward fullness involves such a call to conversion. Dialogue, however, does not aim at conversion, understood as a change of religion. But proclamation includes a further call to discipleship to Jesus Christ in the Church. It is not proselytism but a mystery of the call of the Spirit and the free response of the person. Because of this double movement of freedom in the Spirit, proclamation itself is dialogical. (6, 5, 6)

It is not possible, therefore, to agree on this question with Paul F. Knitter's book *Jesus and the Other Names* (Knitter 1996, 125–64). After having charged "Dialogue and Proclamation" with self-contradiction, Knitter himself proposes simply to identify mission with dialogue, from which proclamation must not be distinguished as a further element of mission. The received opinion according to which "dialogue *is* mission" — insofar as in itself it constitutes an intrinsic dimension, a genuine expression, of evangelization — is being turned around to become: "mission *is* dialogue," whereby evangelization is simply reduced to dialogue and the witness to one's faith dialogue implies (Knitter 1996, 142–47). Proclamation as a distinct expression of evangelization is thereby done away with. Several rectifications seem in order here.

First, concerning the alleged "contradictions" of "Dialogue and Proclamation," Knitter seems to forget the clear distinction made by DP 9 between the "spirit of dialogue," which must inform all dimensions of the evangelizing mission, and dialogue as a specific expression of that mission (Knitter 1996, 143). Witness must accompany dialogue — without it, dialogue is neither sincere nor credible. But witnessing — which is often done silently — is not by itself necessarily "announcing" or "proclamation," as Knitter seems to believe.[14]

Second, Knitter sees a contradiction between holding, on the one hand, that dialogue remains "oriented" toward proclamation (DP 82) and, on the other, that it may not be viewed as a means for proclamation but must be conceived as having "its own validity" (DP 41), that is, as an end in itself (Knitter 1996, 140–42). "Dialogue and Proclamation" shows clearly that the aims of dialogue and proclamation differ vastly: dialogue aims at a "deeper conversion" of the partners — Christians and others — toward God (DP 41, 80); announcing, on the contrary, is an invitation extended to the others to become disciples of Jesus in the Church (DP 81). The common conversion of the partners of dialogue toward God in mutual witness and under the impulse of the Spirit of God, present in all, is no covert means, on the part of one, to "convert" the other to one's own "way." Ends in themselves can, however, be diversified as

---

14. See Knitter 1996, 176, n. 3, where the question is asked: "What is the difference between witness and proclamation?"

stages of a process. Surely, God's covenant with Moses was an end in itself; this did not prevent it from being oriented to God's covenant in Jesus Christ, in which it finds its full realization. Similarly, the Kingdom of God already present in history is an end in itself; nevertheless, it remains oriented toward the eschatological fullness of the Kingdom of God.

In the last resort, Knitter's reduction of mission to dialogue is the natural outcome of his position in Christology and ecclesiology, dissent with which has been expressed in previous chapters. If Jesus Christ, no matter how "indispensable," is not "constitutive" of salvation for humankind (Knitter 1996, 134), the Church's mission, no matter how "necessary" its contribution for the promotion of the Reign of God (Knitter 1996, 122–23), has no irreplaceable role to play as "*the* sacrament of the Kingdom of God," everywhere present and operative in history. This is why a contradiction is alleged in "Dialogue and Proclamation" where, while affirming that the Kingdom is broader than the Church (DP 35), the document also claims that "the Kingdom is inseparable from the Church" (DP 34). "Inseparability" is unduly construed to mean "identification" (Knitter 1996, 128). The further statement according to which the Kingdom is "inseparable from the Church because both are inseparable from the person and work of Jesus himself" (DP 34), besides implying the same contradiction, is said to betray the "constitutive-exclusive Christology that the Vatican holds" (Knitter 1996, 134–35). But, it must be asked, is a "constitutive" Christology necessarily "exclusive"? Hopefully, an answer has already been given here to this question. For Knitter, however, constitutive and inclusivist Christology makes the practice of interfaith dialogue impossible (Knitter 1996, 134); it belies efforts at building a Kingdom-oriented ecclesiology and theology of mission (Knitter 1996, 135). It can neither honestly visualize mission *as* dialogue nor foster readiness to learn anything genuinely new (Knitter 1996, 146). Knitter writes: "Simply stated, it is impossible to develop a Kingdom-centered understanding of the Church that will coherently and persuasively present the Church as the Servant of the Kingdom on the basis of a Christology that insists that Jesus is the only cause of and the unsurpassable criterion for the salvation to be realized in the Kingdom" (Knitter 1996, 135).

What, however, if, while Jesus Christ is "constitutive" of the world's salvation, his universal impact of salvation leaves room, as has been proposed in chapters 11 and 12, above, for other "saving figures" and religious traditions in which God is also present and active through his Word and his Spirit? The answer seems clear: the Reign of God is then truly broader than the Church and destined to be built by Christians and the others alike; dialogue — which implies learning new truth — is an authentic expression of the evangelizing mission. It does not, however, exhaust it, for there remains room — if God so wishes — for inviting others to become disciples of Jesus in the Church. Everything hangs together and must be taken as a whole: with Christology — constitutive or not — the rest stands or falls!

Perhaps the best way to conclude these clarifications is to quote "Dialogue and Proclamation" where it explains what, in the last analysis, constitutes the deepest motivation of the Church's thrust to announce Jesus Christ:

> In [a] dialogical approach, how could [Christians] not hope and desire to share with others their joy of knowing and following Jesus Christ, Lord and Saviour? We are here at the heart of the mystery of love. Insofar as the Church and Christians have a deep love for the Lord Jesus, the desire to share him with others is motivated not merely by obedience to the Lord's command, but by this love itself. It should not be surprising, but quite normal, that the followers of other religions should also desire sincerely to share their faith. All dialogue implies reciprocity and aims at banishing fear and aggressiveness. (83)

## C. Interfaith Dialogue and Liberation Practice

Official Church documents distinguished four forms of interreligious dialogue: dialogue of life, of action, of theological exchange, of religious experience (DM 29–35; DP 42). "Dialogue and Mission" described the dialogue of action in a liberation perspective as "the concrete commitment to the service of humankind and all forms of activity for social development and for the struggle against poverty and the structures which produce it" (DM 13). "Dialogue and Proclamation," for its part, urged the importance today of this form of dialogue:

> The importance of dialogue for integral development, social justice and human liberation needs to be stressed.... There is need to stand up for human rights, proclaim the demands of justice, and denounce injustice ..., independently of the religious allegiance of the victims. There is need also to join together in trying to solve the great problems facing society and the world, as well as in education for justice and peace. (44)

It has been the merit of Aloysius Pieris, in the context of the Third World, and especially of Asia, to stress the need to unite into one combined concern a human liberation praxis with a praxis of interreligious dialogue.[15] Only from such a symbiosis of a twofold praxis can a Church *of* Asia be born and an Asian theology of liberation develop. Pieris defines what he calls "Thirdworldness" and the "Asianness" of Asia in the following terms:

> The common denominator between Asia and the rest of the Third World is its overwhelming poverty; the specific character which defines Asia within the other poor countries is its multifaceted religiosity. These are two inseparable realities which in their interpenetration constitute what might be designated as the Asian context which is the matrix of any theology that is truly Asian....

---

15. See Pieris 1980a, 1983. Both essays are reprinted in Pieris 1988a.

The *theological* attempts to encounter Asian religions with no radical concern for Asia's poor and the *ideological* programs that would eradicate Asia's poverty with naive disregard for its religiosity, have both proved to be a misdirected zeal. (Pieris 1980a, 75–76)

And he notes:

The irruption of the Third World is also the irruption of the non-Christian world. The vast majority of God's poor perceive their ultimate concern and symbolize their struggle for liberation in the idiom of non-Christian religions and cultures. Therefore, a theology that does not speak to or speak through this non-Christian peoplehood is an esoteric luxury of a Christian minority. Hence we need a theology that will expand the existing boundaries of orthodoxy as we enter into the liberative streams of other religions and cultures. (Pieris 1983, 113–14)

In such a context, Pieris warns, the Church in Asia cannot hope to become the Church *of* Asia unless, after Jesus' example, it first immerses itself in the twofold reality of Asian poverty and religiosity. To the local churches in Asia he makes this "final appeal": "Enter into the stream at the point where the religiousness of the Asian poor . . . and the poverty of the religious Asians . . . meet to form the ideal community of total sharing" (Pieris 1988a, 50). The true local churches *of* Asia are those prophetic basic human communities (made up of Christians and others) which "have been baptized in the Jordan of Asian religion and on the calvary of Asian poverty" (Pieris 1988a, 50).

The call to unite the praxis of human liberation and interreligious dialogue into one concern has had a deep echo in the Asian churches. Asian theologians have been quick to show that members of the different religious traditions must engage together in the struggle for human liberation; that they can so unite in action on behalf of human rights and justice for all, out of a common religious conviction and notwithstanding the differences between their respective religious faiths; that such common involvement will call for a critical discernment between what in the respective religious traditions constitutes true potential for liberation and what, on the contrary, has been a cause of discrimination and a factor of oppression; that, in a word, a combined interfaith liberative praxis is an urgent task of evangelization — and a *locus theologicus* for a theology of religious pluralism.

Thus the Thirteenth Annual Meeting of the Indian Theological Association (1989) wrote, under the heading "Liberative Praxis and Theology of Religious Pluralism":

In a situation of imposed poverty of the masses and of pluralism of religions and humanist ideologies, the combined struggles of the peoples of different faiths and ideologies for liberation, especially those of the awakened poor and marginalized, become the significant *locus theologicus* and term of reference for a theology of religions from a liberative perspective....Underlying [the] pluralism of liberation experiences, there is an implicit transformative understanding of religions. Such an understanding seems to be operative in all critical inter-human and inter-religious action and struggles for liberation....

The primacy of orthopraxis over orthodoxy brings sensitivity and attunement to the recovery of the liberative core of religions manifesting itself as a liberation-salvation process. We are, thereby, called to a re-reading and a re-articulating of the fundamental faith-affirmations for a liberating inter-human and inter-religious fellowship of peoples. In this hermeneutic, liberation is understood in terms of a wholeness of humans, nature, cosmos and the Ultimate. In a world divided between the powerful and the powerless, wholeness of liberation always includes a preferential option for the powerless and marginalized. (12, 14)[16]

The interreligious engagement for justice and peace has, in fact, become a universal concern. Hans Küng has given forceful expression to it when he declared:

There can be no peace among the nations without peace among the religions.

There can be no peace among the religions without dialogue between the religions.

There can be no dialogue between the religions without research into theological foundations. (Küng 1991, 105; see also Küng 1988)

Küng calls for a "world ethic" engaging the "global responsibility" of all peoples. He labors to show how, in spite of doctrinal and ethical differences between the religious traditions of the world, a basic ethic can be shared by all, on which justice and peace can be established. Such an ethic can only be based on a religious persuasion and the recognition of fundamental values. The criterion for establishing such values is the *humanum.* Küng asks: "Should it not be possible to formulate, with reference to the common humanity of all men and women, a universally ethical, truly ecumenical basic criterion which is based on the *humanum,* that which is truly human, and specifically on human dignity and the basic values which are subordinate to it?" (Küng 1991, 90). And he answers: "That would be morally good which allows human life to succeed and prosper in the long term in its individual and social dimension: what enables the best development of men and women at all levels...and in all their dimensions" (Küng 1991, 90).

A move in the direction of such a global ethic has been made, even if in very generic terms, by the declaration of the World Conference on Religion and Peace in Kyoto, Japan (1970), which—says Küng—"expresses in an admirable

---

16. Indian Theological Association 1991, 342–43. The same perspective is developed by various authors. The following can be mentioned: Wilfred 1991; Wilfred, ed., 1992; Arokiasamy and Gispert-Sauch, eds., 1987; John, ed., 1991; Irudayaraj, ed., 1989. See also Cohn-Sherbok 1992.

way what could be a concrete universal basic ethic, a world ethic of the world religions in the service of world society."[17] Another attempt has been made more recently — with limited success — at the Second Parliament of World Religions (1993) (see Küng and Kuschel 1993; see also Teasdale and Cairns, eds., 1996; Braybrooke 1992).

We have made reference earlier to the "soteriocentric" or "liberation-centered" model of a theology of religions proposed by Paul F. Knitter in continuity with, and partial replacement of, his previous theocentric paradigm (see p. 194, above). The same new model is further developed in Knitter's book *One Earth Many Religions*.[18] Partly resuming Küng's terminology, Knitter advocates a "globally responsible" dialogue between the various religious traditions for a universal "eco-human well-being." Human liberation as well as the well-being of creation require today the shared commitment of members of all the religious traditions. Social injustice and ecological abuse are intertwined; both must be overcome together. They can be overcome only through a "globally responsible, correlational dialogue of religions," capable of transcending differences in a common cause. For Knitter too — who is much inspired here by the Asian experience — interfaith dialogue and liberation praxis are inseparable.

# II. Theology of Dialogue

## A. *The Challenges of Dialogue*

We have shown earlier that the conditions for the possibility of interreligious dialogue have occupied an important place in the debate on the theology of religions. It was in order that dialogue be practicable that Paul F. Knitter advocated the paradigm shift from Christocentrism to theocentrism (Knitter 1985, 170–231). Notwithstanding the avowed changes which his position has undergone more recently (Knitter 1996, 77 and n. 13), he continues to believe that a "constitutive" and "inclusivist" Christology leaves no room for genuine dialogue (Knitter 1996, 146). The Christological problem is thus at the center of the theology of dialogue, much as it is and remains at the center of the theology of religions. Dialogue, it is observed, can only be sincere if it takes place on an equal footing between partners. Can, then, the Church and Christians be sincere in their professed will to enter into dialogue if they are not prepared to revoke the traditional claims about Jesus as "constitutive" Savior of humankind? The problem of religious identity in general, and of the Christian identity in particu-

---

17. Küng 1991, 63. On the WCRP, see Jack 1993; the declaration is found on pp. 437–40.

18. Knitter 1995a. This work was closely followed by Knitter 1996, conceived as a companion volume in which the "theological challenges" raised by the first volume are met. We have made reference to the second volume here above and in a previous chapter. See p. 284 and n. 7.

lar, is involved in this question, together with that of the openness to the others that dialogue requires.[19] Different aspects must, however, be distinguished.

**1. Commitment and Openness.**   First of all, one must not, on the pretext of honesty in the dialogue, bracket one's faith (practicing an *epochè*), even temporarily, against the expectation, as has been suggested (Knitter 1985, 205–31), of eventually rediscovering the truth of that faith through the dialogue itself. On the contrary, honesty and sincerity in the dialogue specifically require the various partners to enter upon it and commit themselves to it in the integrity of their faith. Any methodological doubt, any mental reservation, is out of place here. Were it otherwise, one could no longer speak of interreligious or interfaith dialogue. After all, at the basis of an authentic religious life is a faith that endows that life with its specific character and proper identity. This religious faith is no more negotiable in the interreligious dialogue than it is in one's personal life. It is not a commodity to be parceled out or exchanged; it is a gift received from God, of which one may not lightly dispose.

By the same token, just as sincerity in the dialogue authorizes no bracketing of faith, even a provisional one, so its integrity in turn forbids any compromise or reduction of the same. Authentic dialogue does not accommodate such expedients. It admits neither the "syncretism" that, in the quest for a common ground, attempts to surmount opposition and contradictions among the faiths of different religious traditions through some reduction of the content of faith[20] nor the eclecticism that, in the search for a common denominator among the various traditions, chooses scattered elements among them and combines these into a shapeless, inconsistent amalgam. If it is to be true, the dialogue may not seek facility, which is illusory in any case. Rather, without wishing to dissimulate any contradictions among religious faiths, it must admit them where they exist and face them with patience and in a responsible way. To dissimulate differences and possible contradictions would amount to cheating and would actually end by depriving the dialogue of its object. After all, dialogue seeks understanding in difference, in a sincere esteem for convictions other than one's own. Thus it leads both partners to question themselves on the implications for their own faith of the personal convictions of the other (see Taylor 1981).

It is self-evident that in the practice of the interreligious dialogue, Christians may not dissimulate their own faith in Jesus Christ. In turn, they acknowledge in their partners who do not share their faith the inalienable right and duty to engage in dialogue while maintaining their own personal convictions — even

---

19. On the theology of interreligious dialogue, besides those mentioned in the chapter reference can be made to the following works: Lochhead 1988; P. J. Griffiths 1991; Tracy 1990; Amaladoss 1990, 1992; Wiles 1992; Bernhardt 1994; *Interfaith Dialogue* 1994; Swidler 1990; Stubenrauch 1995; Basset 1996; Mouttapa 1996.

20. "Syncretism" is, however, a polyvalent concept. It can have a positive meaning, referring, for instance, to the process of "interculturation" of the Christian faith with other cultures. This is not the meaning intended here. See Gort et al., eds., 1989.

claims to universality that may be part of their faith.[21] It is in this fidelity to personal, non-negotiable convictions, honestly accepted on both sides, that the interreligious dialogue takes place "between equals" — in their difference. "All religions have their own jealousies," J. V. Taylor wrote. He went on to say:

> Seen from outside a particular household of faith, such claims are bound to seem narrowly possessive; but within the household they reflect an experience which cannot be gainsaid. Every profoundly convincing encounter with God is with a jealous God. This simply means that having experienced God in this way, no other God will do. It is totally unhelpful to condemn such responses as arrogant. The meaning of things conveyed by such an experience is of such moment that it must be seen to have universal relevance, and to deny this is to be false to the experience itself. (Taylor 1981, 104)

As the seriousness of the dialogue forbids the toning down of deep convictions on either side, so its openness demands that what is relative be not absolutized, whether by incomprehension or intransigence. In every religious faith and conviction there is the danger, and a real one, of absolutizing the relative. We have seen a concrete example of this in Christianity, apropos of the "fullness" of revelation in Jesus Christ. This plenitude, we pointed out, is not quantitative but qualitative: one not of extension and all-comprehensive, but of intensity. It is in no way opposed to the limited nature of Jesus' human awareness, much less therefore to that of the Christian revelation expressed in a particular, relative culture (see p. 249, above). It does not — it cannot — exhaust the mystery of the Divine; nor does it gainsay true divine revelation through the prophetic figures of other religious traditions.

Commitment to one's own faith and openness to the "other" must, therefore, be combined. A "constitutive" Christology seems to allow for both. Christian identity, as it has been understood through the centuries, is linked to faith in the "constitutive" mediation and "fullness" of divine revelation in Jesus Christ. But, as Claude Geffré observes pointedly, such a Christology leaves room — as we ourselves have shown in preceding chapters — for other mediations and divine revelations. He writes:

> Why should it be thought that only a radical theocentrism can meet the demands of interreligious dialogue? It seems that a deepened Christology can open more fruitful avenues, capable of doing justice at once to the demands of a true pluralism and to the Christian identity. Without bringing about a ruinous dissociation between the eternal Word and the incarnate Word, it is legitimate...to consider the economy of the incarnate Word as the sacrament of a vaster economy, that of the eternal Word, which coincides with the religious history of humankind. (Geffré 1991, 72; see 1993c)

---

21. We have pointed out such claims to universality in the other traditions. See pp. 289–292, above.

**2. Personal Faith and the Experience of the Other.**   If dialogue supposes the integrity of personal faith, it also requires openness to the faith of the other in its difference. Each partner in the dialogue must enter in the experience of the other, in an effort to grasp that experience from within. In order to do this, he or she must rise above the level of the concepts in which this experience is imperfectly expressed, to attain, insofar as possible, through and beyond the concepts, the experience itself. It is this effort of "com-prehension" and interior "sym-pathy" — or "em-pathy" — that Raimon Panikkar terms the "intra-religious" dialogue, an indispensable condition for true interreligious dialogue (Panikkar 1978). This has been described as a spiritual technique consisting of "passing over and returning." "Passing over" means encountering both the other and the religious experience which that other bears within, together with his or her worldview or *Weltanschauung*:

> To know the religion of another is more than being cognisant of the facts of the other's religious tradition. It involves getting inside the skin of the other, it involves walking in the other's shoes, it involves seeing the world in some sense as the other sees it, it involves asking the other's questions, it involves getting inside the other's sense of "being a Hindu, Muslim, Jew, Buddhist, or whatever." (Whaling 1986, 130–31; see Gort 1992)

Under these premises, we must ask ourselves whether it is possible, and up to what point, to share two different religious faiths, making each of them one's own and living both at once in one's own religious life. From an absolute view-point, this seems impossible. Even apart from any interior conflict that might arise in an individual, every religious faith constitutes an indivisible whole and calls for a total commitment of the person. It seems a priori impossible that such an absolute engagement might be divided, as it were, between two objects. To be a Christian is not only to find in Jesus values to be promoted or even a meaning for one's life; it is to be given over to his person, to find in him one's way to God.

Does this mean, however, that the concept of the hyphenated Christian is self-contradictory — that one cannot be Hindu-Christian or Buddhist-Christian or the like? To assert this would contradict experience, as such cases are not rare or unknown.[22] Account must, however, be taken of the various possible acceptations of a concept that it would be a mistake to label "hybrid" (see Amaladoss 1975b; Cobb 1980).

To be a Hindu-Christian can mean joining in oneself the Hindu culture and the Christian faith. Hinduism would then not be a religious faith, strictly speaking, but a philosophy and a culture, which, with the necessary corrections, could serve as a vehicle for Christian faith. Then the problem of the Hindu-Christian would be that of the inculturation of Christian faith and doctrine. Here, obviously, the concept of a Hindu-Christian will offer no difficulty in principle.[23]

---

22. See, for instance, Dupuis 1991b, 67–90, on the experience of H. Le Saux (Abhishiktananda).
23. This was the explanation proposed by H. Staffner (see Staffner 1978).

But does this explanation fully correspond to reality? Hinduism, while it is not primarily and uniformly doctrinal, nevertheless involves, in the concrete lives of men and women, a genuine religious faith. For that matter, the distinction between religion and culture is difficult to manage. Representing as it does the transcendent element in culture, religion is scarcely separable from culture.

Can one nevertheless hold in conjunction, and make one's own, Hindu faith and Christian faith? We must exercise discernment here. Surely there are elements of other faiths that are in harmony with Christian faith and can be combined and integrated with it. These will serve to enrich it[24] if it is true, as we have affirmed, that other faiths contain divine truth and revelation. There may be other elements, however, that formally contradict the Christian faith and are not assimilable.

In all events, with the cautions that we have indicated, it is sure that, in order to be true, the interreligious dialogue requires that both partners make a positive effort to enter into each other's religious experience and overall vision, insofar as possible. We are dealing with the encounter, in one and the same person, of two ways of being, seeing, and thinking. This "intrareligious dialogue" is an indispensable preparation for an exchange between persons in the interreligious dialogue.

## B. The Fruits of Dialogue

The interaction between Christianity and the Asian religions, Hinduism and Buddhism in particular, has been conceived differently by various promoters of interreligious dialogue (see, e.g., Swidler et al. 1990). Aloysius Pieris sees the Christian tradition, on one side, and the Buddhist tradition, on the other, as "two religious models which, far from being contradictory, are in fact, incomplete each in itself and, therefore, complementary and mutually corrective." They represent "poles of a tension, not so much geographical as psychological. They are two instincts emerging dialectically from within the deepest zone of each individual, be he Christian or not. Our religious encounter with God and human beings would be incomplete without this interaction" (Pieris 1980b, 64; 1988b). Pieris calls these two complementary poles the agapeic (Christianity) and the gnostic (Buddhism) (see pp. 326–328, above).

In a somewhat similar manner, John A. T. Robinson speaks of two "eyes" of truth and reality: Western Christianity represents one eye, Hinduism the other; more generally, the West stands for the first, the East for the second. Robinson sees the polarity of the two "centers" as that between the male and female principles. He too calls for a mutual complementarity between the two centers (Robinson 1979; see also B. Griffiths 1982).

John B. Cobb, for his part, advocates a "mutual transformation," beyond dialogue, between Christianity and Buddhism; such a mutual transformation

---

24. This solution is proposed more recently by H. Staffner (see Staffner 1985).

will result from the osmosis between the complementary approaches to reality, that is, between the worldviews characteristic of both traditions (Cobb 1982; Cobb and Ives, eds., 1990).

Raimon Panikkar's focus is somewhat different. He insists that the various religious traditions differ and must keep their distinct identity. He rejects a facile "eclecticism" which would destroy the respective identities; faith cannot be "bracketed" (*epochè*) to ease the dialogue. But, while the "cosmotheandric mystery," the object of faith, is common to all religious traditions, "beliefs" differ in each. Between these "beliefs" Panikkar advocates a "cross-fertilization" — which he terms "syncretism" — in view of a mutual enrichment.[25]

Panikkar has returned to this topic more than once. Recently he has described what he regards as the profile and the horizon of interreligious dialogue for the future. Going now beyond the problematic of "cross-fertilization," he calls for a further stage in which, transcending the static doctrinal identity of their respective traditions, the partners of dialogue will be able to contribute mutually to a deeper self-understanding (Panikkar 1990; see Prabhu, ed., 1996).

In this variety of opinions, what can be concluded regarding the fruits of dialogue, if we base ourselves on the principles enunciated above? We must first remember that the principal agent of interreligious dialogue is the Spirit of God who animates the partners. The Spirit is at work on both sides, the Christian and the other; thus the dialogue cannot be a monologue. The Christian partners not only will give but will receive as well. The "fullness" of revelation in Jesus Christ does not dispense them from listening. They do not possess a monopoly on truth. They must rather allow themselves to be possessed by it. Indeed, their interlocutors in the dialogue, even without having heard God's revelation in Jesus Christ, may be more deeply submitted to this truth that they yet seek and to the Spirit of Christ that spreads rays of that truth in them (cf. NA 2). One can in all certainty say that, by the dialogue, Christians and others "walk together towards truth" (DM 13).

Christians have something to gain from the dialogue. They will derive a twofold, combined advantage. On the one hand, they will win an enrichment of their own faith. Through the experience and testimony of the other, they will be able to discover at greater depth certain aspects, certain dimensions, of the Divine Mystery that they had perceived less clearly and that have been communicated less clearly by Christian tradition. At the same time they will gain a purification of their faith. The shock of the encounter will often raise questions, force Christians to revise gratuitous assumptions, and destroy deep-rooted prejudices or overthrow certain overly narrow conceptions or outlooks. Thus the benefits of the dialogue constitute a challenge to the Christian partner at the same time (see P. J. Griffiths 1991; Vroom 1996).

The fruits and challenges of the dialogue go hand in hand, then. However, above and beyond these sure benefits, we must say that the encounter and ex-

---

25. See Panikkar 1978; see the discussion in Dupuis 1991b, 184–90; see also pp. 149–153, above.

change have value in themselves. They are an end in themselves. While, to begin with, they presupposed openness to the other and to God, they also effect a deeper openness to God of each through the other.

Thus the dialogue does not serve as a means to a further end. Neither on one side nor on the other does it tend to the "conversion" of one partner to the religious tradition of the other. Rather it tends to a more profound conversion of each to God. The same God speaks in the heart of both partners; the same Spirit is at work in all. By way of their reciprocal witness, it is this same God who calls and challenges the partners through each other. Thus they become, as it were, for each other and reciprocally, a sign leading to God. The proper end of the interreligious dialogue is, in the last analysis, the common conversion of Christians and the members of other religious traditions to the same God — the God of Jesus Christ — who calls them together by challenging the ones through the others. This reciprocal call, a sign of the call of God, is surely mutual evangelization. It builds up, between members of various religious traditions, the universal communion which marks the advent of the Reign of God (see Dupuis 1995a; see also Sreenivasa Rao, ed., 1991).

A word may be added regarding the benefit which will accrue to Christian theology from the praxis of interreligious dialogue. We have stressed, from the beginning of this work, that, while being necessarily "confessional," Christian theology must adopt a "global" vision (see introduction, 5–6, above). It must be "dialogical theology" (Knitter 1996, 154–61): that is, built on the praxis of interreligious dialogue. The enrichment which such a Christian theology — as distinct from W. Cantwell Smith's "universal theology" — can derive, within its own global approach, from dialogue with world religions and theologies is the subject matter of F. Whaling's book, mentioned earlier.[26] Whaling notes the need to recognize that the great religious traditions, which respective theologies articulate, evolved distinctly and creatively. Far from being the same, it is not even the case that they were giving different answers to the same questions; they were asking different questions because they were perceiving the world through different lenses. "To understand others it is necessary in some degree to see the world through *their* eyes, in the light of *their* questions as they emerged in their history" (Whaling 1986, 29). The conclusion is that the opportunity lies open for Christian theology to renew itself through its encounter with the other religions (Whaling 1986, 65). He writes:

> Just as the dialogue with the rediscovered Aristotle enabled Aquinas to deepen his theological understanding and to recast Christian theology in the medieval situation, so too can the dialogue with Hindus, Buddhists, Muslims, Jews, and so on, in different parts of the world, enable us to deepen our theological understanding and to recast some of our theological ideas in the modern situation. (Whaling 1986, 94)

---

26. Whaling 1986. For a concrete application to the Hindu context, see Clooney 1993.

The question of what basic elements and religious insights can be shared by Christian theology and other religious traditions, as they come in contact with each other, is, however, a difficult one which admits of no easy solution. For each religious tradition constitutes a whole from which the various elements cannot be easily isolated. We are faced in fact with distinct, global worldviews within which, as within living organisms, each part plays its specific function, with the result that a "dynamic equivalence" between the components on either side is not easily available (see Frank 1979).

Granted that among symbols there exist universally valid archetypes, is there strict equivalence in the various religious traditions between such basic theological concepts as God, creation, world, grace, freedom, salvation-liberation, and so forth? We know that such is not the case. The experience of the Ultimate Reality as the Christian Father/Mother, the Jewish Yahweh, the Muslim Allah, the Hindu Brahman, the Buddhist Nirvana, the Taoist Tao, and so on, is not the same (see chap. 10, above). Is then every religious faith, and consequently every theology, so bound to a particular worldview that it can hardly express itself in, and be transposed to, another? Dialogical theology cannot ignore the problems.

Does not, for instance, the Christian experience of faith presuppose a density of the historical, not found as such in other traditions, without which it cannot be fully understood? The question has been raised earlier (see pp. 212–215). What, however, is certain and needs to be fully recognized is that history and interiority are two equally valid channels for a true experience of the Divine: he who acts in history according to the Judeo-Christian tradition is he who is experienced in the "cave of the heart" according to the Hindu. The God of history is also the "ground of being."

Whatever questions remain, however, as to the limits of mutual assimilation and "cross-fertilization" between religious and theological traditions, one thing seems clear, and it is this: harmony between religious communities will not be served by a "universal theology" which would claim to bypass differences and contradictions; it will be served by the development in the various traditions of theologies which, taking religious pluralism seriously, will assume their mutual differences and resolve to interact in dialogue and cooperation.

*Fifteen*

# Conclusion

THE INTRODUCTION to this work stated its aim to contribute to a Christian theology of religious pluralism for our time. By "Christian theology" was meant one that would reflect on the plurality of religions in our present world from within the vantage point of Christian faith, while at the same time adopting a global outlook that takes account of the complex religious reality as it is lived today. The method of such a theology would have to be inductive, which meant dialogical and comparative, in keeping with the hermeneutical circle from context to text and vice versa.

In the process of building up (in the second part) a synthetic, topic-wise presentation of such a theology, some basic principles and keys of interpretation have emerged which it may be useful to recall once more at the end. One is the mutual relationship and reciprocal implication, in a Christian theology of religions, of various models — often wrongly viewed as mutually exclusive paradigms — such as: Christocentrism, theocentrism, regnocentrism, soteriocentrism, and others. To separate these various aspects from each other is to fall short of the complexity and richness of the Christian experience.

Another is a Trinitarian and Spirit-Christology, which allowed a deeper appreciation and more positive evaluation of religious founders and traditions outside Christianity. The Trinitarian Christological key of interpretation made it possible to lay stress on the universal active presence of the Word of God and his Spirit, as a source of enlightenment and inspiration of religious founders and the traditions which have sprung from their experience. That key of interpretation has been put to use at various stages of the inquiry, including the treatment of divine revelation and God's self-gift in salvation, the diverse faces of the Divine Mystery, and the saving figures and paths to salvation proposed by the various traditions. This has led to viewing the mystery of God's self-disclosure in Jesus Christ as essentially relational to what God has done and continues to do to humankind through history, from beginning to end.

A third key of interpretation has been the Kingdom-centered model — transcending a narrow Church-centered perspective — which in turn made it possible to visualize how Christianity and the other religious traditions share together in the universal reality of God's Reign, which they are called upon to build together unto its eschatological fullness. The same model led to a truer view of the Church as "sacrament of the Kingdom," and of its mission at the service of the Kingdom, as including interfaith dialogue.

There is no need, as we come to the end of the journey, to summarize the results of the inquiry. It seems more useful to suggest, by way of conclusion, what answer can be given to three questions which have emerged repeatedly along the way. The questions have to do with the following matters: (1) the sense of religious pluralism; (2) the meaning of the relational uniqueness and universality of Jesus Christ; and (3) the way of understanding the mutual complementarity and convergence between Christianity and the other religious traditions of the world.

## I. Religious Pluralism

The question asked is whether religious pluralism is merely to be accepted or tolerated as a reality *de facto* in our present world. Or can it, on the contrary, be viewed theologically as existing de jure? In the first case, the plurality of religions, characteristic of the landscape of today's world — which, according to all human predictions, will abide in the future as well — is seen as a factor to be reckoned with, rather than welcomed. The reasons for its persistence are many — one of which is the partial failure of the Christian mission, especially in the vast majority of Asian countries. In the other case, the same plurality is welcomed as a positive factor which witnesses at once to the superabundant generosity with which God has manifested himself to humankind in manifold ways and to the pluriform response which in diverse cultures human beings have given to the divine self-disclosure. Seen from God's side, the question is whether religious pluralism is only permitted by God or, on the contrary, positively willed by him. Or else — if one prefers to avoid both these terms — whether theology is able to assign to the plurality of religious traditions a positive meaning in God's overall design for humankind.

It would be presumptuous to claim to be able to fathom God's plan for humanity; no human knowledge can ever claim a divine view of things. This being admitted, there is no dearth of theologians today who attribute to religious pluralism a positive role and value in God's sight. Affirmations to this effect have been repeatedly met through our inquiry. A clear witness may be recorded here. Edward Schillebeeckx formulates the question clearly: "In my view the question for us is whether the pluralism of religions is a matter of fact or a matter of principle" (Schillebeeckx 1990, 164). Without claiming to give a complete answer, he nevertheless affirms, apropos of the relationship between Christianity and the other religions, that

> (even in the Christian self-understanding) the multiplicity of religions is not an evil which needs to be removed, but rather a wealth which is to be welcomed and enjoyed by all....
>
> The unity, identity and uniqueness of Christianity over against [the] other religions ... lies in the fact that Christianity is a religion which as-

sociates relationship to God with a historical and thus a very specific and therefore limited particularity: Jesus of Nazareth. This is the uniqueness and identity of Christianity, but at the same time its unavoidable historical limitation. It becomes clear here that…the God of Jesus is a symbol of openness, not of closedness. Here Christianity has a positive relationship to other religions, but at the same time its uniqueness is nevertheless maintained, and ultimately at the same time the loyal Christian affirmation of the positive nature of other world religions is honoured.[1]

On what foundation, then, can the affirmation of a religious pluralism "of principle," or de jure, be made to rest? Here we may recall some of the conclusions arrived at in this book. I did affirm that the faith in a plurality of persons in the one God is *in itself* no sufficient foundation for religious pluralism; much less would a simple appeal to the "plural" character of all reality suffice: the plurality of the elements of nature, of seasons, of dimensions in space and time, and so forth. Nor will it do merely to refer to the inborn, unavoidable limitations of every human apprehension of the Divine Mystery. To stop there would amount to seeking to establish a plurality of principle on a truncated view of religion as representing but a human quest for the Divine.

If, however, religion has its original source in a divine self-manifestation to human beings, as we have shown, the principle of plurality will be made to rest primarily on the superabundant richness and diversity of God's self-manifestations to humankind. The divine plan for humanity, as we have explained, is one, but multifaceted. It belongs to the nature of the overflowing communication of the Triune God to humankind to prolong outside the divine life the plural communication intrinsic to that life itself. That God spoke "in many and various ways" before speaking through his Son (Heb 1:1) is not incidental; nor is the plural character of God's self-manifestation merely a thing of the past. For the decisiveness of the Son's advent in the flesh in Jesus Christ does not cancel the universal presence and action of the Word and the Spirit. Religious pluralism in principle rests on the immensity of a God who is love.

## II. Relational Unity

In agreement with the uninterrupted, mainline Christian tradition we have maintained the constitutive uniqueness and universality of Jesus Christ. This means that the person of Jesus Christ and the Christ-event are "constitutive" of salvation for the whole of humankind; in particular, the event of his death-resurrection opens access to God for all human beings, independently of their historical situation. Put in other words, the humanity of Jesus Christ, God's Son made flesh, is the sacrament of God's universal will to save. Such uniqueness

---

1. Schillebeeckx 1990, 167. See, in the same direction, Geffré 1993b, 353–54; 1995, 84.

must not, however, be construed as absolute: what is absolute is God's saving will. Neither absolute nor relative, Jesus' uniqueness is "constitutive"; in
addition, we called it "relational." In what sense?

The historical event of God's becoming flesh marks the deepest and most
decisive engagement of God with humankind; it establishes with it a bond
of union that can never be severed. But this event is, of necessity and irremediably, marked by the particularity of every historical happening. The
"transhistorical" character of the risen humanity of Jesus Christ notwithstanding, the event is limited by its insertion in history, without which its singular
significance and density would vanish. It is, then, at once particular in time
and universal in meaning, and, as such, "singularly unique," yet related to all
other divine manifestations to humankind in one history of salvation — that
is, relational.

In this way, not only the exclusivist paradigm but the inclusivist as well
can be gone beyond, without, however, recourse being had to the "pluralistic"
paradigm based on the negation of constitutive salvation in Jesus Christ. The
Trinitarian Christology model, the universal enlightenment of the Word of God,
and the enlivening by his Spirit make it possible to discover, in other saving figures and traditions, truth and grace not brought out with the same vigor and
clarity in God's revelation and manifestation in Jesus Christ. Truth and grace
found elsewhere must not be reduced to "seeds" or "stepping-stones" simply
to be nurtured or used and then superseded in Christian revelation. They represent additional and autonomous benefits. More divine truth and grace are
found operative in the entire history of God's dealings with humankind than
are available simply in the Christian tradition. As the "human face" or "icon"
of God, Jesus Christ gives to Christianity its specific and singular character.
But, while he is constitutive of salvation for all, he neither excludes nor includes other saving figures or traditions. If he brings salvation history to a
climax, it is by way not of substitution or supersession but of confirmation
and accomplishment.

The relational nature of the uniqueness of Jesus Christ has been brought
out by recent authors sensitive to the demands of an open-ended theology of
religious pluralism. Thus Claude Geffré writes: "Without compromising the absolute commitment inherent to faith, Christianity can be considered as a *relative*
reality; not, however, in the sense in which "relative" is opposed to "absolute,"
but in the sense of "relational." The truth to which Christianity witnesses is
neither exclusive nor inclusive of all other truth; it is related to all that is true
in other religions."[2]

---

2. Geffré 1993b, 358. See also O'Leary (1994), who writes: "If Jesus Christ is the incarnate Logos,
does it follow that the religious traditions of humankind can add nothing to what has been revealed in
Jesus? No; for the distance between the ideal dimensions of the incarnate Logos and the actual realization
of the truth in contingent history through Israel, the life of Jesus and Western culture, imposes limitations
to any claim of Christianity to exhaustive fullness" (279–80).

# III. Convergence — Historical and Eschatological

Complementarity and convergence have been repeatedly mentioned in the course of our exposé. A case in point is where it was shown that a convergence may exist between "faces of the Divine Mystery" proposed by other religious traditions and the mystery of the divine Trinity revealed in Jesus Christ. Another instance is where values were discovered in other "paths to salvation," complementary to those proposed by the Christian "way," thus justifying the affirmation of a complementarity between the various traditions.

Complementarity must, once again, be understood correctly here. It is not intended unilaterally, as though values found outside were one-sidedly "fulfilled" by Christian values and destined to be merely "integrated" into Christianity. It is a question of mutual complementarity, in which a dynamic interaction between two traditions results in mutual enrichment. The following have been singled out as examples: the symbiosis between the "nonduality" (*advaita*) of Hindu mystical experience and the mystery of interpersonal communion in the Triune God of the Christian tradition (see pp. 278–279); and the "agapeic gnosis" of Christians and the "gnostic *agapè*" of Buddhists (see pp. 326–329).

Mutual complementarity makes a reciprocal convergence possible. It is the task of interreligious dialogue to turn the potential convergence inherent in the religious traditions into a concrete reality. We have exposed — without complacency — the demands which interfaith dialogue, especially at the level of religious experience and theological discourse, makes on the partners if it is to be fruitful. We have also made reference to the mystery of communion in the Spirit existing between the partners of dialogue, which flows from their common sharing in the universal reality of the Reign of God. This anticipated communion guarantees that actual convergence through dialogue is possible — in full respect of the differences between faith-commitments.

Interfaith dialogue thus contributes to building up the Reign of God in history. But, as we know, the Reign of God in history remains directed toward its eschatological fullness at the end of time. It is permitted to think that convergence between the religious traditions will also attain its goal in the fullness of the Reign of God. An eschatological "reheading" (*anakephalaiòsis*) (Eph 1:10) in Christ of the religious traditions of the world will take place at the eschaton, and it will respect and preserve the irreducible character which God's self-manifestation through his Word and his Spirit has impressed upon each tradition. This eschatological reheading will coincide with the last "perfection" (*teleiòsis*) of the Son of God, as "source of eternal salvation" (Heb 5:9) whose influence remains, until this final achievement, subject to an "eschatological remainder." Thus the Reign of God being accomplished, the end will come, "when [Christ] delivers the Kingdom to God the Father," and, the Son himself being "subject to him who put all things under him," God will be "everything to everyone" (1 Cor 15:24–28).

It seems possible, then, to speak, after Pierre Teilhard de Chardin, of a "marvelous convergence," to take place in the eschaton, of all things and all religious traditions in the Reign of God and in the Christ-omega; of a "mystic of unification" toward which Christianity and the religious traditions of the East tend together.[3] Such eschatological convergence does not in any way overshadow the historical event of Jesus Christ: he is the end (omega) because he is the beginning (alpha), the "central axis." It is in this eschatological sense that Teilhard looks toward a "convergence of religions" in the "universal Christ": "A general convergence of religions upon a universal Christ who fundamentally satisfies them all: that seems to me the only possible conversion of the world, and the only form in which a religion of the future can be conceived."[4] The eschatological fullness of the Reign of God is the common final achievement of Christianity and the other religions.

---

3. See U. King 1980, 159–62. On the eschatological convergence of religions, see also Thils 1966, 161; O'Leary 1994, 283–84.

4. Teilhard de Chardin 1971, 130; see the whole section entitled "The Universal Christ and the Convergence of Religions" (126–30).

# Bibliography

Aagaard, A. M. 1974. "The Holy Spirit in the Word." *Studia Theologica* 28:53–171.

*L'abbé Jules Monchanin.* 1960. Tournai: Casterman.

Abel, K. 1969–70. "Non-biblical Readings in the Church's Worship." *Bijdragen* 30:350–80; 31:137–71.

———. 1974. "Non-Christian Revelation and Christian Worship." In *God's Word among Men,* ed. G. Gispert-Sauch, 257–303. Delhi: Vidyajyoti Institute of Religious Studies.

Abeyasingha, N. 1984. *A Theological Evaluation of Non-Christian Rites.* Bangalore: Theological Publications in India.

Acharuparambil, D. 1994. "Mistero trinitario e Induismo." In *Trinità in contesto,* ed. A. Amato, 199–211. Rome: LAS.

Adinolfi, M. 1991. *Ellenismo e Bibbia: Saggi storici ed esegetici.* Rome: Dehoniane.

Amaladoss, M. 1970. "Textes hindous dans la prière chrétienne." *Christus* 17:424–32.

———. 1975a. "Non-biblical Scriptures in Christian Life and Worship." *Vidyajyoti* 39:194–209.

———. 1975b. "Qui suis-je? Un catholique hindou." *Christus* 86/22:159–71.

———. 1985. "Other Scriptures and the Christian." *East Asian Pastoral Review* 22:104–15.

———. 1990. *Making All Things New.* Anand: Gujarat Sahitya Prakash.

———. 1992. *Walking Together.* Anand: Gujarat Sahitya Prakash.

———. 1994. "Being a Christian Community among Other Believing Communities: Theological and Pastoral Reflections and Questions." *Current Dialogue* 26/2:23–33.

Amaladoss, M., T. K. John, and G. Gispert-Sauch, eds. 1981. *Theologizing in India.* Bangalore: Theological Publications in India.

Amalorpavadass, D. S., ed. 1975a. *Evangelization in the Modern World.* Bangalore: NBCLC.

———. 1975b. *Research Seminar on Non-biblical Scriptures.* Bangalore: NBCLC.

Amato, A. 1992. "Gesù e le religioni non cristiane: Una sfida all'assolutezza salvifica del Cristianesimo." In *Gesù è il Signore: La specificità di Gesù Cristo in un tempo di pluralismo religioso,* ed. M. Farina and M. L. Mazzarella, 46–79. Rome: LAS.

———. 1994. "The Unique Mediation of Christ as Lord and Saviour." *Pro Dialogo, Bulletin* 85–86/1:15–39.

———, ed. 1994. *Trinita in contesto.* Rome: LAS.

Anderson, Gerald H. 1990. "Christian Mission and Religious Pluralism: A Selected Bibliography of 175 Books in English, 1970–1990." *International Bulletin of Missionary Research* 14:172–76.

Anderson, Gerald H., and Thomas F. Stransky, eds. 1974. *Critical Issues in Mission Theology.* New York: Paulist Press.

———. 1981a. *Christ's Lordship and Religious Pluralism.* Maryknoll, N.Y.: Orbis Books.

———. 1981b. *Faith Meets Faith.* New York: Paulist Press.

Antes, P., ed. 1996. *I fondatori delle grandi religioni.* Cinisello Balsamo: San Paolo.

Ariarajah, Wesley. 1985. *The Bible and People of Other Faiths.* Geneva: World Council of Churches.

Arnaldez, R. 1980. *Jésus, fils de Marie, prophète de l'Islam.* Paris: Desclée.

———. 1983. *Trois messagers pour un seul Dieu.* Paris: Albin Michel.

———. 1988. *Jésus dans la pensée musulmane.* Paris: Desclée.

———. 1993. *A la croisée des trois monothéismes: Une communauté de pensée au Moyen-Age.* Paris: Albin Michel.

Arokiasamy, S., and G. Gispert-Sauch, eds. 1987. *Liberation in Asia: Theological Perspectives.* Anand: Gujarat Sahitya Prakash.

Artigas, L. 1981. "Teologia della religione." In *Le scienze della religione oggi,* ed. C. Cantone, 233–306. Rome: LAS.

Aurobindo, Sri. 1959. *Essays on the Gita.* Pondicherry: Sri Aurobindo Ashram.

———. 1970. *The Life Divine.* Pondicherry: Sri Aurobindo Ashram.

Baillie, D. 1963. *God Was in Christ.* London: Faber and Faber.

Balasuriya, Tissa. 1984. *Planetary Theology.* London: SCM Press.

Balchand, A. 1973. *The Salvific Value of Non-Christian Religions according to Asian Christian Theologians Writing in Asian-Published Journals 1965–1970.* Manila: East Asian Pastoral Institute.

Balthasar, Hans Urs von. 1959. *Das betrachtende Gebet.* Einsiedeln: Johannes Verlag. Eng. trans. = Balthasar 1967b.

———. 1963. *Das Ganze im Fragment: Aspekte der Geschichtstheologie.* Einsiedeln: Benziger.

———. 1964. *A Theology of History.* London: Sheed and Ward.

———. 1966. *Dieu et l'homme d'aujourd'hui.* Paris: Desclée de Brouwer. Eng. trans. = Balthasar 1967a.

———. 1967a. *The God Question and Modern Man.* New York: Seabury.

———. 1967b. *Prayer.* New York: Paulist Press.

———. 1968a. *Cordula ou l'épreuve décisive.* 2d ed. Paris: Beauchesne. Eng. trans. = Balthasar 1969.

———. 1968b. *Love Alone: The Way of Revelation.* London: Burns.

———. 1969. *The Moment of Christian Witness.* New York: Newman Press.

———. 1976. *Theodramatik.* II, 2. Einsiedeln: Johannes Verlag.

———. 1978. "Catholicism and the Religions." *Communio* 5:6–14.

———. 1979a. *Das Christentum and die Weltreligionen.* Freiburg: Informationszentrum Berufe der Kirche.

———. 1979b. *Neue Klarstellingen.* Einsiedeln: Johannes Verlag.

———. 1983. *Christen sind einfältig.* Einsiedeln: Johannes Verlag.

———. 1986. *Homo Creatus Est: Skizzen zur Theologie.* Vol. 5. Einsiedeln: Johannes Verlag.

———. 1988. *Dare We Hope "That All Men Be Saved"?* San Francisco: Ignatius Press.

———. 1995. *Spirit and Institution*. Explorations in Theology 4. San Francisco: Ignatius Press.

Balthasar, Hans Urs von, et al. 1983. *Des bords du Gange aux rives du Jourdain*. Paris: Saint-Paul.

Barnes, M. 1989. *Christian Identity and Religious Pluralism*. Nashville: Abingdon Press.

———. 1991. *God East and West*. London: SPCK.

———. 1994. "Theology of Religions in a Post-modern World." *The Month* 28:270–74, 325–30.

Barth, K. 1970. *Church Dogmatics*. Vol. I, 2. Edinburgh: T. and T. Clark.

———. 1976. *Church Dogmatics*. Vol. IV, 3. Edinburgh: T. and T. Clark.

Barzel, B. 1982. *Mystique de l'ineffable dans l'hindouisme et le christianisme: Çankara et Eckhart*. Paris: Cerf.

Basset, J.-C. 1996. *Le dialogue interreligieux*. Paris: Cerf.

Baum, Gregory. 1974. "Is There a Missionary Message?" In *Critical Issues in Mission Today*, ed. G. H. Anderson and T. F. Stransky, 75–86. New York: Paulist Press.

Beasley-Murray, G. R. 1986. *Jesus and the Kingdom of God*. Exeter: Paternoster Press.

Behm. 1966. "Diathèkè." In *Theological Dictionary of the New Testament*, ed. G. Kittel, ed., 2:106–34. Grand Rapids, Mich.: W. B. Eerdmans.

Bermejo, L. 1990. *Church Conciliarity and Communion*. Anand: Gujarat Sahitya Prakash.

Bernhardt, R. 1993. "Deabsolutierung der Christologie." In *Der einzige Weg zum Heil?* ed. M. von Brück and J. Werbick, 144–208. Freiburg: Herder.

———. 1994. *Christianity without Absolutes*. London: SCM Press.

Bevans, Stephen B. 1992. *Models of Contextual Theology*. Maryknoll, N.Y.: Orbis Books.

Billot, L. 1919–23. "La providence de Dieu et le nombre infini d'hommes hors de la voie normale du salut." *Etudes:* 161–76.

Boismard, M.-E. 1953. *Le prologue de Saint Jean*. Paris: Cerf.

———. 1958. *L'évangile de Jean*. Bruges: Desclée de Brouwer.

Bonner, A., ed. 1985. *Selected Works of Ramon Llull*. Vol. 1. Princeton, N.J.: Princeton University Press.

Bordoni, M. 1995. *La cristologia nell'orizzonte dello Spirito*. Brescia: Queriniana.

Boros, Ladislas. 1973. *The Moment of Truth: The Mystery of Death*. New York: Crossroad.

Borrmans, M. 1990. *Guidelines for Dialogue between Christians and Muslims*. New York: Paulist Press.

———. 1996. *Jésus et les musulmans d'aujourd'hui*. Paris: Desclée.

Bosch, David J. 1992. *Transforming Mission: Paradigm Shifts in Theology of Mission*. Maryknoll, N.Y.: Orbis Books.

Bossuyt, P., and J. Radermakers. 1995. "Rencontre de l'incroyant et inculturation: Paul à Athènes (Actes 17:16–32)." *Nouvelle revue théologique* 117:19–43.

Boublik, V. 1973. *Teologia delle religioni*. Rome: Studium.

Braaten, Carl E. 1992. *No Other Gospel! Christianity among the World's Religions*. Minneapolis: Fortress Press.

Bracken, Joseph A. 1995. *The Divine Matrix.* Maryknoll, N.Y.: Orbis Books.

Braybrooke, M. 1990. *Time to Meet: Towards a Deeper Relationship between Jews and Christians.* London: SCM Press.

———. 1992. *Pilgrimage of Hope: A Hundred Years of Global Interfaith Dialogue.* London: SCM Press.

Breton, S. 1981. *Unicité et monothéisme.* Paris: Cerf.

Brown, Raymond E. 1960. *The Gospel of John and the Johannine Epistles.* Collegeville, Minn.: Liturgical Press.

———. 1966–70. *The Gospel according to John.* 2 vols. Garden City, N.Y.: Doubleday.

———. 1994. *An Introduction to New Testament Christology.* New York: Paulist Press.

Brück, Michael von. 1991. *The Unity of Reality: God, God-Experience, and Meditation in the Hindu-Christian Dialogue.* New York: Paulist Press.

Brück, Michael von, and J. Werbick, eds. 1993. *Der einzige Weg zum Heil?* Freiburg: Herder.

Brunner, Emil. 1947. *Revelation and Reason.* London: SCM Press.

Bühlmann, Walbert. 1976. *The Coming of the Third Church.* Maryknoll, N.Y.: Orbis Books.

———. 1982a. *All Have the Same God.* Slough, Eng.: St. Paul Publications.

———. 1982b. *God's Chosen Peoples.* Maryknoll, N.Y.: Orbis Books.

———. 1986. *The Church of the Future.* Maryknoll, N.Y.: Orbis Books.

Burghardt, Walter J., and William M. Thompson, eds. 1977. *Why the Church?* New York: Paulist Press.

Bürkle, H. 1977. *Einführung in die Theologie der Religionen.* Darmstadt: Wissenschaftliche Buchgesellschaft.

Burrows, William R., ed. 1993. *Redemption and Dialogue.* Maryknoll, N.Y.: Orbis Books.

Burtt, E. A. 1955. *The Teaching of the Compassionate Buddha.* New York: New American Library.

Camps, A. 1983. *Partners in Dialogue: Christianity and Other World Religions.* Maryknoll, N.Y.: Orbis Books.

Canobbio, G. 1994a. *Chiesa perché: Salvezza dell'umanità e mediazione ecclesiale.* Cinisello Balsamo: San Paolo.

———. 1994b. "Gesù Cristo nella recente teologia delle religioni." In *Cristianesimo e religioni in dialogo,* 79–110. Brescia: Morcelliana.

Cantone, C., ed. 1981. *Le scienze della religione oggi.* Rome: LAS.

Capéran, L. 1934. *Le problème du salut des infidèles: 1. Essai historique; 2. Essai théologique.* Toulouse: Grand Séminaire.

Caprile, G. 1975. *Sinodo dei vescovi, 1974: Terza assemblea generale (27 settembre — 26 ottobre).* Rome: Civiltà Cattolica.

Carpenter, David. 1995. *Revelation, History, and the Dialogue of Religions.* Maryknoll, N.Y.: Orbis Books.

Carruthers, G. H. 1990. *The Uniqueness of Jesus Christ in the Theocentric Model of the Christian Theology of Religions: An Elaboration and Evaluation of the Position of John Hick.* Lanham, Md.: University Press of America.

Caspar, R. 1983. "La rencontre des théologies." *Lumière et vie* 32:63–80.

———. 1987. *Traité de théologie musulmane*. Vol. 1: *Histoire de la pensée religieuse musulmane*. Rome: PISAI.

Cassirer, H. 1946. *Language and Myth*. New York: Dover.

———. 1979. *Symbol, Myth, and Culture*. New Haven: Yale University Press.

Castellanelli, G. 1994. "Il cristianesimo e le altre religioni nel 'De pace fidei' di Nicolò Cusano e nel 'De Christiana religione' di Marsilio Finico." In *Cristianesimo e religioni in dialogo*, 45–77. Brescia: Morcelliana.

Cazelles, H. 1981. "Quelques dettes de l'Ancient Testament envers les cultures ambiantes." In Commission Biblique Pontificale, *Foi et culture à la lumière de la Bible*, 17–27. Leumann (Torino): Elle Di Ci.

Cerfaux, Lucien. 1954. "L'Eglise et le Règne de Dieu d'après Saint Paul." *Receuil Lucien Cerfaux*, 2:365–87. Gembloux: Duculot.

Chavasse, A. 1948. "Ordonnés au Corps Mystique." *Nouvelle revue théologique*. 70:690–702.

Choy, Wai-Man. 1983. *For a Christology in Dialogue: A Critical Examination of Stanley J. Samartha's Attempt at a Christology in a Religiously Plural World*. Rome: Pontificia Università Gregoriana.

"Christian Existence in a World of Interreligious Dialogue." 1983. *Jeevadhara* 77/13:309–66.

*Christianity among World Religions*. 1986. *Concilium* 183/1.

Christiansen, E. J. 1995. *The Covenant in Judaism and Paul: A Study of Ritual Boundaries and Identity Markers*. Leiden: E. J. Brill.

Clarke, A. D., and B. M. Winter, eds. 1992. *One God, One Lord: Christianity in a World of Religious Pluralism*. Grand Rapids, Mich.: Baker.

Clooney, Francis X. 1993. *Theology after Vedanta: An Experiment in Comparative Theology*. Albany: State University of New York Press.

———. 1995. "Current Theology: Comparative Theology: A Review of Recent Books (1989–1995)." *Theological Studies* 56:521–50.

Coakley, Sarah. 1988. *Christ without Absolutes: A Study of the Christology of Ernst Troeltsch*. Oxford: Clarendon Press.

Cobb, John B., Jr. 1975. *Christ in a Pluralistic Age*. Philadelphia: Westminster.

———. 1980. "Can a Buddhist Be a Christian Too?" *Japanese Journal of Religious Studies:* 35–55.

———. 1982. *Beyond Dialogue: Toward a Mutual Transformation of Christianity and Buddhism*. Philadelphia: Fortress Press.

———. 1995. "The Christian Reason for Being Progressive." *Theology Today* 51/4:548–62.

Cobb, J. B., and C. Ives, eds. 1990. *The Emptying God: A Buddhist-Jewish-Christian Conversation*. Maryknoll, N.Y.: Orbis Books.

Cohn-Sherbok, D. 1992. *World Religions and Human Liberation*. Maryknoll, N.Y.: Orbis Books.

Colle, R. del. 1994. *Christ and the Spirit: Spirit-Christology in Trinitarian Perspective*. Oxford: Oxford University Press.

Commission Biblique Pontificale. 1981. *Foi et culture à la lumière de la Bible*. Leumann (Torino): Elle Di Ci.

Commission for Dialogue and Ecumenism. 1989. *Guidelines for Inter-religious Dialogue*. New Delhi: CBCI Centre.

Commission Pontificale "Justitia et Pax." 1987. *Assise: Journée mondiale de prière pour la paix*. Typographie Polyglote Vaticane.

Congar, Yves. 1952. "Ecclesia ab Abel." In *Abhandlungen über Theologie und Kirche: Festschrift für Karl Adam*, ed. M. Reding, 79–108. Düsseldorf: Patmos.

———. 1959. *Vaste monde ma paroisse*. Paris: Témoignage chrétien. Eng. trans. = Congar 1961.

———. 1961. *The Wide World My Parish: Salvation and Its Problems*. London: Darton, Longman and Todd.

———. 1963. *Sainte Eglise: Etudes et approches ecclésiologiques*. Paris: Cerf.

———. 1965. "L'Eglise, sacrement universel du salut." *Eglise vivante* 17:339–55. Trans. in Congar 1969.

———. 1969. *This Church That I Love*. Denville, N.J.: Dimension Books.

———. 1972. "Non-Christian Religions and Christianity." In *Evangelization, Dialogue and Development*, ed. M. Dhavamony, 133–45. Rome: Università Gregoriana Editrice.

———. 1983. *I Believe in the Holy Spirit*. 3 vols. London: G. Chapman.

———. 1984a. *Essais oecuméniques*. Paris: Centurion.

———. 1984b. *La parole et le souffle*. Paris: Desclée. Eng. trans. = Congar 1986.

———. 1986. *The Word and the Spirit*. London: G. Chapman.

Corless, Roger, and Paul F. Knitter, eds. 1990. *Buddhist Emptiness and Christian Trinity: Essays and Explorations*. New York: Paulist Press.

Cornelis, E. 1965. *Valeurs chrétiennes des religions non chrétiennes*. Paris: Cerf.

Cornille, C., and V. Neckebrouck, eds. 1992. *A Universal Faith? Peoples, Cultures, Religions, and the Church*. Louvain: Peeters Press.

Cottier, G. M.-M. 1966. "L'historique de la déclaration." In *Les relations de l'Eglise avec les religions non chrétiennes: Déclaration Nostra Aetate*, ed. A.-M. Henry, 37–78. Paris: Cerf.

Covell, Ralph R. 1986. *Confucius, the Buddha, and the Christ*. Maryknoll, N.Y.: Orbis Books.

Coward, Harold. 1985. *Pluralism: Challenge to World Religions*. Maryknoll, N.Y.: Orbis Books.

———. 1988. *Sacred Word and Sacred Text*. Maryknoll, N.Y.: Orbis Books.

———, ed. 1990. *Hindu-Christian Dialogue: Perspectives and Encounters*. Maryknoll, N.Y.: Orbis Books.

Cracknell, Kenneth. 1986. *Towards a New Relationship: Christians and People of Other Faiths*. London: Epworth Press.

Cragg, Kenneth. 1977. *The Christian and the Other Religions*. London: Mowbray.

———. 1984. *Muhammad and the Christian: A Question of Response*. London: Darton, Longman and Todd.

———. 1985. *Jesus and the Muslim: An Exploration*. London: George Allen and Unwin.

———. 1986. *The Christ and the Faiths: Theology in Cross Reference*. London: SPCK.

*Cristianesimo e religioni in dialogo*. 1994. Quaderni teologici del Seminario di Brescia, Morcelliana.

Croatto, J. 1981. *Exodus: A Hermeneutics of Freedom*. Maryknoll, N.Y.: Orbis Books.

———. 1983. "Biblical Hermeneutics in the Theologies of Liberation." In *Irruption of the Third World: Challenge to Theology,* ed. V. Fabella and S. Torres, 140–68. Maryknoll, N.Y.: Orbis Books.

———. 1984. *Biblical Hermeneutics: Towards a Theory of Reading as the Production of Meaning.* Maryknoll, N.Y.: Orbis Books.

Crouzel, H. 1956. *Théologie de l'image de Dieu chez Origène.* Paris: Aubier.

———. 1960. "Origène devant l'incarnation et l'histoire." *Bulletin de littérature ecclésiastique* 61:81–110.

———. 1962. *Origène et la philosophie.* Paris: Aubier.

———. 1985. *Origène.* Paris: Letthielleux.

Cullmann, Oscar. 1952. *Christ and Time: The Christian Conception of Time and History.* London: SCM Press.

———. 1967. *Salvation in History.* London: SCM Press.

Cupitt, Don. 1975. "The Finality of Christ." *Theology* 78:618–32.

Cuttat, J.-A. 1960. *The Encounter of Religions.* New York: Desclée.

———. 1964. *Le dialogue spirituel Orient-Occident.* Louvain: Eglise vivante.

———. 1965. "Expérience chrétienne et spiritualité orientale." In *La mystique et les mystiques,* ed. A. Ravier, 825–1095. Paris: Desclée de Brouwer.

———. 1967. *Expérience chrétienne et spiritualité orientale.* Paris: Desclée de Brouwer.

d'Alès, A. 1928. "Salut des infidèles." *Dictionnaire apologétique de la foi catholique.* Vol. 4, cols. 1157–82. Paris: Beauchesne.

Dalton, W. J. 1989. *Christ's Proclamation to the Spirits: A Study of 1 Peter 3:18–4:6.* 2d ed. Rome: Pontifical Biblical Institute.

Damboriena, P. 1973. *La salvación en las religiones non cristianas.* Madrid: BAC.

Daniélou, Jean. 1956. *Les saints "païens" de l'Ancien Testament.* Paris: Seuil. Eng. trans. = Daniélou 1957.

———. 1957. *Holy Pagans in the Old Testament.* London: Longmans, Green and Co.

———. 1958. *The Lord of History: Reflections on the Inner Meaning of History.* London: Longmans, Green and Co.

———. 1962a. *The Advent of Salvation.* New York: Paulist Press.

———. 1962b. *The Salvation of the Nations.* South Bend, Ind.: University of Notre Dame Press.

———. 1966a. "Christianity and Non-Christian Religions." In *The Word in History,* ed. P. Burke, 86–101. New York: Sheed and Ward.

———. 1966b. *Mythes païens, mystère chrétien.* Paris: Fayard.

———. 1970. *The Faith Eternal and the Man of Today.* Chicago: Franciscan Herald.

———. 1973. *Gospel Message and Hellenistic Culture.* Philadelphia: Westminster Press.

Darlap, A. 1965a. "Fundamentale Theologie der Heilsgeschichte." In *Mysterium Salutis: Grundriss Heilsgeschichtlicher Dogmatik,* ed. J. Feiner and M. Löhrer, 1:3–156. Einsiedeln: Benziger Verlag.

———. 1965b. "Histoire du salut." In *Encyclopédie de la foi,* ed. H. Fries, 2:219–25. Paris: Cerf.

———. 1970. "Salvation." In *Sacramentum Mundi,* ed. K. Rahner, 5:416–19. New York: Herder and Herder.

Davy, M. M. 1981. *Henri le Saux, Swami Abhishiktananda: Le passeur entre deux rives.* Paris: Cerf.

Dawe, D. G., and J. B. Carman, eds. 1978. *Christian Faith in a Religiously Plural World.* Maryknoll, N.Y.: Orbis Books.

D'Costa, Gavin. 1985. "Karl Rahner's Anonymous Christian — A Reappraisal." *Modern Theology* 1/2:131–48.

———. 1986. *Theology and Religious Pluralism: The Challenge of Other Religions.* Oxford: Basil Blackwell.

———. 1987. *John Hick's Theology of Religions: A Critical Evaluation.* New York: University Press of America.

———. 1990a. "Christ, the Trinity, and Religious Plurality." In *Christian Uniqueness Reconsidered: The Myth of a Pluralistic Theology of Religions,* ed. Gavin D'Costa, 16–29. Maryknoll, N.Y.: Orbis Books.

———. 1990b. "One Covenant or Many Covenants? Toward a Theology of Christian-Jewish Relations." *Journal of Ecumenical Studies* 27/3:441–52.

———. 1990c. "Taking Other Religions Seriously: Some Ironies in the Current Debate on the Theology of Religions." *Thomist* 54:519–29.

———. 1990d. "'Extra Ecclesiam Nulla Salus' Revisited." In *Religious Pluralism and Unbelief,* ed. I. Hamnett, 130–47. London: Routledge.

———. 1992. "Toward a Trinitarian Theology of Religions." In *A Universal Faith? Peoples, Cultures, Religions, and the Christ,* ed. C. Cornille and V. Neckebrouck, 139–54. Louvain: Peeters Press.

———, ed. 1990. *Christian Uniqueness Reconsidered: The Myth of a Pluralistic Theology of Religions.* Maryknoll, N.Y.: Orbis Books.

Denzinger, H. and A. Schönmetzer, eds. 1976. *Enchiridion Symbolorum, Definitionum et Declarationum de Rebus Fidei et Morum.* Ed. 36. Freiburg: Herder.

Dhavamony, M., ed. 1972. *Evangelization, Dialogue and Development.* Documenta Missionalia 5. Rome: Università Gregoriana Editrice.

———. 1982. *Prospettive di missiologia, oggi.* Rome: Università Gregoriana Editrice.

"Diathèkè." 1966. In *Theological Dictionary of the New Testament,* ed. G. Kittel, 2:106–34. Grand Rapids, Mich.: Eerdmans.

DiNoia, Joseph A. 1992. *The Diversity of Religions: A Christian Perspective.* Washington, D.C.: Catholic University of America Press.

Dodd, C. H. 1963. *The Interpretation of the Fourth Gospel.* Cambridge: Cambridge University Press.

Dournes, J. 1963. *Dieu aime les païens.* Paris: Aubier.

———. 1967. *L'offrande des peuples.* Paris: Cerf.

Driver, Tom F. 1981. *Christ in a Changing World.* New York: Crossroad.

Drummond, Richard H. 1985. *Toward a New Age in Christian Theology.* Maryknoll, N.Y.: Orbis Books.

Dulles, Avery. 1970. *Revelation Theology.* London: Burns and Oates.

———. 1987. *Models of the Church.* New York: Doubleday.

———. 1992. *Models of Revelation.* 2d ed. Maryknoll, N.Y.: Orbis Books.

Dumoulin, H. 1974. *Christianity Meets Buddhism*. La Salle, Ill.: Open Court Publishing.

Duperray, E. 1965. *J. Monchanin: Ecrits spirituels*. Paris: Centurion.

Dupont, J. 1967. *Etudes sur les Actes des Apôtres*. Paris: Cerf.

————. 1979. *The Salvation of the Gentiles*. New York: Paulist Press.

————. 1981. "La rencontre entre Christianisme et Hellénisme dans le discours à l'Aréopage." In Commission Biblique Pontificale, *Foi et culture à la lumière de la Bible*, 261–86. Leumann (Torino): Elle Di Ci.

————. 1984. *Nouvelles études sur les Actes des Apôtres*. Paris: Cerf.

————. 1989. "Note sur le 'Peuple de Dieu' dans les Actes des Apôtres." In Commission Biblique Pontificale, *Unité et diversité dans l'Eglise*, 209–22. Rome: Libreria Editrice Vaticana.

Dupuis, Jacques. 1966. "The Cosmic Christ in the Early Fathers." *Indian Journal of Theology* 15:106–20.

————. 1967. *"L'esprit de l'homme": Etude sur l'anthropologie religieuse d'Origène*. Tournai: Desclée de Brouwer.

————. 1971. "Trinity and World Religions." *Clergy Monthly* 35:77–81.

————. 1974. "The Use of Non-Christian Scriptures in Christian Worship in India." In *Worship and Ritual in Christianity and Other Religions*. Vol. 23 of *Studia Missionalia*: 127–43.

————. 1975. "Synod of Bishops 1974." *Doctrine and Life* 25/5:323–48.

————. 1976. "Apostolic Exhortation Evangelii Nuntiandi." *Vidyajyoti* 40:218–30.

————. 1977. *Jesus Christ and His Spirit*. Bangalore: Theological Publications in India.

————. 1985. "Forms of Interreligious Dialogue." *Bulletin* (Secretariat for Non-Christians) 59/20/2:164–71.

————. 1987a. "The Kingdom of God and World Religions." *Vidyajyoti* 51:530–40.

————. 1987b. "World Religions in God's Salvific Design in John Paul II's Discourse to the Roman Curia (22 December 1986)." *Seminarium* 27:29–41.

————. 1991a. "The Christological Debate in the Context of Religious Plurality." *Current Dialogue* 19:18–24.

————. 1991b. *Jesus Christ at the Encounter of World Religions*. Maryknoll, N.Y.: Orbis Books.

————. 1992a. "Evangelization and the Kingdom Values: The Church and the 'Others.' " *International Missiological Review* 14:4–21.

————. 1992b. "FABC Focus on the Church's Evangelizing Mission in Asia Today." *Vidyajyoti* 56/9:449–68.

————. 1992c. "Inculturation and Interreligious Dialogue in India Today." In *A Universal Faith? Peoples, Cultures, Religions, and the Christ*, ed. C. Cornille and V. Neckebrouck, 21–47. Louvain: Peeters Press.

————. 1992d. "Méthode théologique et théologies locales: Adaptation, inculturation, contextualisation." *Seminarium* 32/1:61–74.

————. 1992e. "Parole de Dieu et écritures sacrées." *Spiritus* 126/33:59–65.

————. 1993a. "Dialogue and Proclamation in Two Recent Roman Documents." In *Dialogical Dynamics of Religions,* ed. A. Thottakkara, 110–31. Rome: Centre for Indian and Interreligious Studies.

————. 1993b. "A Theological Commentary: Dialogue and Proclamation." In *Redemption and Dialogue,* ed. W. R. Burrows, 119–58. Maryknoll, N.Y.: Orbis Books.

————. 1994a. "Alleanza e salvezza." *Rassegna di teologia* 35/2:148–71.

————. 1994b. "The Church, the Reign of God and the 'Others.'" *Pro Dialogo* (Pontificium Consilium pro Dialogo inter Religiones) 85–86/1:107–30.

————. 1994c. *Who Do You Say I Am? Introduction to Christology.* Maryknoll, N.Y.: Orbis Books.

————. 1995a. "Communion universelle: Eglises chrétiennes et religions mondiales." *Cristianesimo nella storia* 16/2:361–81.

————. 1995b. "Les religions et la mission." *Gregorianum* 76/3:585–89.

————. 1995c. "Universalité du Christianisme: Jésus-Christ, le Règne de Dieu et l'Eglise." *Revue Africaine des sciences de la mission* 2:125–70.

Duquoc, Christian. 1977. *Dieu différent.* Paris: Cerf.

————. 1984. *Messianisme de Jésus et discrétion de Dieu.* Geneva: Labor et Fides.

————. 1988. "Per una cristologia." In AA.VV., *Il Gesù storico: Problemi della modernità,* 205–15. Casale Monferrato: Piemme.

Durrwell, F.-X. 1967. "Le salut par l'évangile." *Spiritus* 32/8:380–95.

————. 1972. *The Mystery of Christ and the Apostolate.* London: Sheed.

————. 1986. *Holy Spirit of God.* London: G. Chapman.

Eagleson, John, and Philip Scharper, eds. 1979. *Puebla and Beyond.* Maryknoll, N.Y.: Orbis Books.

Eliade, Mircea. 1959. *Cosmos and History: The Myth of Eternal Return.* New York: Harper and Row.

————. 1963. *Aspects du mythe.* Paris: Gallimard.

Ellacuría, I. 1984. *Conversión de la Iglesia al reino de Dios.* Santander: Sal Terrae.

Eminyan, M. 1960. *The Theology of Salvation.* Boston: Saint Paul.

Emprayil, T. 1980. *The Emergent Theology of Religions.* Padra: Vincentian Ashram.

Eterovic, N. 1981. *Cristianesimo e religioni secondo H. de Lubac.* Rome: Città Nuova.

"Evangelization in Asia." 1992. FABC Office of Evangelization, Theological Consultation (Hua Hin, Thailand, November 1991). *FABC Papers* 64:24–37. Hong Kong.

"Evangelization in Modern Day Asia (1974)." 1992. In *For All the Peoples of Asia: Federation of Asian Bishops' Conferences Documents from 1970 to 1991,* ed. G. Rosales and C. G. Arévalo, 11–25. Maryknoll, N.Y.: Orbis Books.

Fabella, V., ed. 1980. *Asia's Struggle for Full Humanity.* Maryknoll, N.Y.: Orbis Books.

Fabella, V., and S. Torres, eds. 1983. *Irruption of the Third World: Challenge to Theology.* Maryknoll, N.Y.: Orbis Books.

Falaturi, A., J. J. Petuchowski, and W. Strolz. 1987. *Three Ways to the One God: The Faith Experience in Judaism, Christianity, and Islam.* New York: Crossroad.

Fallon, P. 1964. "Image Worship." In *Religious Hinduism*, 168–78. Bombay: St. Paul Publications.

Farina, M., and M. L. Mazzarella, eds. 1992. *Gesù è il Signore: La specificità di Gesù Cristo in un tempo di pluralismo religioso*. Rome: LAS.

Farquhar, J. N. 1915. *The Crown of Hinduism*. London: Oxford University Press.

Fédou, M. 1988. *Christianisme et religions païennes dans le Contre Celse d'Origène*. Paris: Beauchesne.

———. 1992. "Les Pères de l'Eglise face aux religions de leur temps." *Bulletin* 80/27/2:173–85.

———. 1994. *La sagesse et le monde: Le Christ d'Origène*. Paris: Desclée.

———. 1996. *Les religions selon la foi chrétienne*. Paris: Cerf.

Feiner, J. 1968. "Particular and Universal Saving History." In *One, Holy, Catholic and Apostolic*, ed. H. Vorgrimler, 163–206. London: Sheed and Ward.

Feiner, J., and M. Löhrer, eds. 1965–76. *Mysterium Salutis: Heilsgeschichtlicher Dogmatik*. 5 vols. Einsiedeln: Benziger.

Feuillet, A. 1949a. "Isaïe." In *Dictionnaire de la Bible: Supplément*, ed. L. Pirot, vol. 4, cols. 647–730. Paris: Letouzey et Ané.

———. 1949b. "Jonas, Le livre de." In *Dictionnaire de la Bible: Supplément*, ed. L. Pirot, vol. 4, cols 1104–31. Paris: Letouzey et Ané.

———. 1966. *Le Christ Sagesse de Dieu d'après les épitres paulinennes*. Paris: Gabalda.

———. 1968. *Le prologue du quatrième évangile*. Paris: Desclée de Brouwer.

Fisher, N. F. 1990. *The Parables of Jesus: Glimpses of God's Reign*. New York: Crossroad.

Foster, D. 1990. "Christian Motives for Interreligious Dialogue." In *Christianity and the Wider Ecumenism*, ed. P. Phan, 21–33. New York: Paragon House.

*Founders of Religions*. 1984. *Studia Missionalia* 33.

*Francis and Clare: The Complete Works*. 1982. New York: Paulist Press.

Frank, H. 1979. *Christianity in Culture: A Study in Dynamic Biblical Theologizing in Cross-Cultural Perspective*. Maryknoll, N.Y.: Orbis Books.

Fries, Heinrich. 1965a. *Das Christentum und die Welt Religionen*. Würburg: St. Ottielien.

———. 1965b. "Die Offenbarung." In *Mysterium Salutis*, ed. J. Feiner and M. Löhrer, 1:159–238. Einsiedeln: Benziger. Eng. trans. = Fries 1970.

———. 1970. *Revelation*. London: Burns and Oates.

———. 1981. *Jesus in den Weltreligionen*. St. Ottielien: Eos Verlag.

Fries, Heinrich, et al. 1982. *Heil in den Religionen und im Christentum*. St. Ottielien: Eos Verlag.

Fuellenbach, John. 1993. *The Kingdom of God: The Central Message of Jesus' Teaching in the Light of the Modern World*. Manila: Logos Publications.

———. 1995. *The Kingdom of God: The Message of Jesus Today*. Maryknoll, N.Y.: Orbis Books.

Gaia, P. 1993. "L'ecumenismo religioso di Nicolò Cusano nel 'De pace fidei.'" In *Vangelo, religioni e cultura*, ed. R. Penna, 233–61. Cinisello Balsamo: San Paolo.

———, ed. 1971. *Nicolò Cusano: Opere religiose*. Torino: Unione Tipografica Editrice.

Gardet, L. 1953. *Expériences mystiques en terres non chrétiennes.* Paris: Alsatia.

———. 1986. *Regards chrétiens sur l'Islam.* Paris: Desclée de Brouwer.

Gardet, L., and O. Lacombe. 1981. *L'expérience du soi: Etude de mystique comparée.* Paris: Desclée de Brouwer.

Gasperis, F. Rossi de. 1993. "La permanenza di Israele: Meditazione tra Gerusalemme e Roma." In AA.VV., *Con tutte le tue forze. I nodi della fede cristiana oggi,* 223–68. Geneva: Marietti.

Gatti, V. 1982. *Il discorso di Paolo ad Atene.* Brescia: Paideia.

Gawronski, R. 1995. *Word and Silence: Hans Urs von Balthasar and the Spiritual Encounter between East and West.* Edinburgh: T. and T. Clark.

Geffré, Claude. 1983. "Le Coran, une parole de Dieu différente?" *Lumière et vie* 32:21–32.

———. 1985. "La théologie des religions non chrétiennes vingt ans après Vatican II." *Islamo-Christiana* 11:115–33.

———. 1987. *The Risk of Interpretation: On Being Faithful to the Christian Tradition in a Non-Christian Age.* New York: Paulist Press.

———. 1991. "Théologie chrétienne et dialogue interreligieux." *Revue de l'Institut Catholique de Paris* 38/2:63–82.

———. 1993a. "Paul Tillich et l'avenir de l'oecuménisme interreligieux." *Revue des sciences philosophique et théologique* 77:3–22.

———. 1993b. "La singularité du Christianisme à l'âge du pluralisme religieux." In *Penser la foi: Recherches en théologie aujourd'hui: Mélanges offerts à Joseph Moingt,* ed. J. Doré and C. Theobald, 351–69. Paris: Cerf — Assas.

———. 1993c. "Le fondement théologique du dialogue interreligieux." *Chemins du dialogue* 2:73–103.

———. 1995. "La place des religions dans le plan du salut." *Spiritus* 138/36:78–97.

Gibbs, P. 1996. *The Word in the Third World.* Rome: Università Gregoriana Editrice.

Gilbert, M. 1973. *La critique des dieux dans le livre de la Sagesse (Sg 13–15).* Rome: Biblical Institute Press.

Gillis, Chester. 1989. *A Question of Final Belief: J. Hick's Pluralistic Theology of Salvation.* London: Macmillan.

Gilson, Etienne. 1952. *Les métamorphoses de la cité de Dieu.* Louvain: Publications Universitaires de Louvain.

Gioia, F., ed. 1997. *Interreligious Dialogue: The Official Teaching of the Catholic Church (1963–1995).* Boston: Pauline Books and Media.

Gispert-Sauch, G., ed. 1974. *God's Word among Men.* Delhi: Vidyajyoti Institute of Religious Studies.

Goedt, M. de. 1992. "La véritable question juive pour les chrétiens: Une critique de la théologie de substitution." *Nouvelle revue théologique* 114:237–50.

Gort, J. D. 1992. *On Sharing Religious Experience: Possibilities of Interfaith Mutuality.* Grand Rapids, Mich.: Eerdmans.

Gort, J. D., et al. 1989. *Dialogue and Syncretism.* Grand Rapids, Mich.: Eerdmans.

Gozier, A. 1982. *Le Père Le Saux à la rencontre de l'Hindouisme.* Paris: Centurion.

GRIC (Muslim-Christian Research Group). 1989. *The Challenge of the Scriptures: The Bible and the Qur'an.* Maryknoll, N.Y.: Orbis Books.

————. 1993. *Foi et justice: Un défi pour le Christianisme et l'Islam.* Paris: Centurion.

Griffiths, Bede. 1976. *Return to the Centre.* London: Collins.

————. 1982. *The Marriage of East and West.* London: Collins.

————. 1985. *The Cosmic Revelation.* Bangalore: Asian Trading Corporation.

————, ed. 1994. *Universal Wisdom: A Journey through the Sacred Wisdom of the World.* London: HarperCollins.

Griffiths, Paul J. 1991. *An Apology for Apologetics: A Study of the Logic of Interreligious Dialogue.* Maryknoll, N.Y.: Orbis Books.

————, ed. 1990. *Christianity through Non-Christian Eyes.* Maryknoll, N.Y.: Orbis Books.

Grillmeier, A. 1975. *Christ in Christian Tradition: From the Apostolic Age to Chalcedon (451).* London: Mowbray.

Guerriero, E., and A. Tarzia, eds. 1992. *I volti di Dio: Il rivelato e le sue tradizioni.* Cinisello Balsamo: Paoline.

*Guidelines on Dialogue with People of Living Faiths and Ideologies.* 1979. Geneva: World Council of Churches.

Guillet, J. 1985. *Entre Jésus et l'Eglise.* Paris: Seuil.

Gutiérrez, Gustavo. 1973. *A Theology of Liberation.* Maryknoll, N.Y.: Orbis Books.

Hacker, P. 1980. *Theological Foundations of Evangelization.* St. Augustin: Steyler Verlag.

Haight, Roger. 1992. "The Case of Spirit-Christology." *Theological Studies* 53:257–87.

Hamnett, I., ed. 1990. *Religious Pluralism and Unbelief: Studies Critical and Comparative.* London: Routledge.

Harent, S. 1927. "Infidèles (salut des)." In *Dictionnaire de théologie catholique,* vol. VII, 2, cols. 1726–1930. Paris: Letouzey et Ané.

Harl, M. 1958. *Origène et la fonction révélatrice du Verbe Incarné.* Paris: Seuil.

Harris, M. J. 1992. *Jesus as God: The New Testament Use of Theos in Reference to Jesus.* Grand Rapids, Michigan: Baker Book House.

Hayek, M. 1959. *Le Christ et l'Islam.* Paris: Seuil.

Heim, S. Mark. 1989. *Is Christ the Only Way? Christian Faith in a Pluralistic World.* Philadelphia: Judson.

————. 1995. *Salvations: Truth and Difference in Religion.* Maryknoll, N.Y.: Orbis Books.

Henry, A.-M., ed. 1966. *Les relations de l'Eglise avec les religions non chrétiennes: Déclaration Nostra Aetate.* Paris: Cerf.

Hick, John. 1968. *Christianity at the Centre.* London: Macmillan.

————. 1973. *God and the Universe of Faiths: Essays in the Philosophy of Religion.* London: Macmillan.

————. 1977. *The Centre of Christianity.* London: SCM Press.

————. 1980. *God Has Many Names: Britain's New Religious Pluralism.* London: Macmillan.

————. 1983. *The Second Christianity.* London: SCM Press.

————. 1985. *Problems of Religious Pluralism.* London: Macmillan.

———. 1989. *An Interpretation of Religion: The Challenge of Other Religions.* Oxford: Basil Blackwell.

———. 1990. "Rethinking Christian Doctrine in the Light of Religious Pluralism." In *Christianity and the Wider Ecumenism,* ed. P. Phan, 89–102. New York: Paragon House.

———. 1993a. *Disputed Questions in Theology and Philosophy of Religion.* London: Macmillan.

———. 1993b. *The Metaphor of God Incarnate: Christology in a Pluralistic Age.* London: SCM Press.

———. 1995. *The Rainbow of Faiths.* London: SCM Press.

———, ed. 1975. *Truth and Dialogue: The Relationship between World Religions.* London: Sheldon Press.

———, ed. 1977. *The Myth of God Incarnate.* London: SCM Press.

Hick, John, and B. Hebblethwaite, eds. 1980. *Christianity and Other Religions.* London: Collins.

Hick, John, and H. Askari, eds. 1985. *The Experience of Religious Diversity.* Aldershot: Gower Publishers.

Hick, John, and Paul F. Knitter, eds. 1987. *The Myth of Christian Uniqueness: Toward a Pluralistic Theology of Religions.* Maryknoll, N.Y.: Orbis Books.

Hillmann, Eugene. 1968. *The Wider Ecumenism: Anonymous Christianity and the Church.* New York: Herder and Herder.

———. 1989. *Many Paths: A Catholic Approach to Religious Pluralism.* Maryknoll, N.Y.: Orbis Books.

Holwerla, D. E. 1995. *Jesus and Israel: One Covenant or Two?* Grand Rapids, Mich.: Eerdmans.

Holzer, V. 1995. *Le Dieu Trinité dans l'histoire: Le différend théologique Balthasar-Rahner.* Paris: Cerf.

Hospital, C. G. 1985. *Breakthrough: Insights of the Great Religious Discoverers.* Maryknoll, N.Y.: Orbis Books.

Houssiau, A. 1953. "L'exégèse de Matthieu 11:27b selon Saint Irénée." *Ephemerides Theologicae Lovanienses* 29:328–54.

———. 1955. *La christologie de Saint Irénée.* Gembloux: Duculot.

Iammarrone, G. 1995. *Redenzione: La liberazione dell'uomo nel cristianesimo e nelle religioni universali.* Rome: Paoline.

———. 1996. *Gesù di Nazareth Messia del Regno.* Padova: Messagero.

Indian Theological Association. 1991. "Towards an Indian Christian Theology of Religious Pluralism" (December 1989). In *Religious Pluralism: An Indian Christian Perspective,* ed. K. Pathil, 338–49. Delhi: ISPCK.

*Interfaith Dialogue.* 1994. *Studia Missionalia* 43.

International Theological Commission. 1989. *Texts and Documents 1969–1985,* ed. M. Sharkey. San Francisco: Ignatius Press.

———. 1997. "Il cristianesimo e le religioni." *Civiltà Cattolica* 3518/148/1:146:83.

"Interreligious Dialogue Today." 1981. *Jeevadhara* 65/11:317–94.

"Introduction to the Prophets." 1985. In *The New Jerusalem Bible.* London: Darton, Longman and Todd.

Irudayaraj, X., ed. 1989. *Liberation and Dialogue.* Bangalore: Claretian Publications.

Jack, H. A. 1993. *WCRP: A History of the World Conference on Religion and Peace*. New York: WCRP.

Jacquin, F. *Jules Monchanin, prêtre*. Paris: Cerf.

Jathana, O. V. 1981. *The Decisiveness of the Christ-Event and the Universality of Christianity in a World Religious Plurality*. Bern: Lang.

Jeremias, Joachim. 1958. *Jesus' Promise to the Nations*. London: SCM Press.

Johanns, P. 1932–33. *Vers le Christ par le Vedanta*. 2 vols. Louvain: Museum Lessianum. Eng. trans. = Johanns 1996.

———. 1938. *Introduction to the Vedanta*. Ranchi: Catholic Press.

———. 1946. "Pierres d'attente du Christianisme dans la philosophie indienne." *Lumen Vitae* 1:173–93.

———. 1952. *La pensée religieuse de l'Inde*. Namur: Facultés Universitaires.

———. 1996. *To Christ through the Vedanta*. 2 vols. Bangalore: United Theological College.

John, T. K., ed. 1991. *Bread and Breath*. Anand: Gujarat Sahitya Prakash.

Johnston, William. 1978. *The Inner Eye of Love: Mysticism and Religion*. New York: Harper and Row.

———. 1981. *The Mirror Mind*. New York: Harper and Row.

———. 1995. *Mystical Theology: The Science of Love*. London: HarperCollins.

Jüngel, E. 1983. *God as the Mystery of the World*. Edinburgh: T. and T. Clark.

Kalliath, A. 1996. *The Word in the Cave*. New Delhi: Intercultural Publications.

Kasper, Walter. 1972. "Are Non-Christian Religions Salvific?" In *Evangelization, Dialogue and Development*, ed. M. Dhavamony, 157–68. Documenta Missionalia 5. Rome: Università Gregoriana Editrice.

———. 1976. *Jesus the Christ*. London: Burns and Oates.

Kaufmann, Y. 1988. *Christianity and Judaism: Two Covenants*. Jerusalem: Hebrew University.

Keenan, John P. 1989. *The Meaning of Christ: A Mahayana Theology*. Maryknoll, N.Y.: Orbis Books.

———. 1995. *The Gospel of Mark: A Mahayana Reading*. Maryknoll, N.Y.: Orbis Books.

Kern, W. 1979. *Ausserhalb der Kirche kein Heil*. Freiburg: Herder.

Khodr, G. 1991. "An Orthodox Perspective on Interreligious Dialogue." *Current Dialogue* 19/1:25–27.

King, J. J. 1960. *The Necessity of the Church for Salvation in Selected Theological Writings of the Past Century*. Washington, D.C.: Catholic University of America Press.

King, Ursula. 1980. *Towards a New Mysticism: Teilhard de Chardin and Eastern Religions*. New York: Seabury Press.

Klootwijk, E. 1992. *Commitment and Openness: The Interreligious Dialogue and Theology of Religions in the Work of Stanley J. Samartha*. Zoetermeer: Boekencentrum.

Klostermaier, Klaus K. 1969. *Hindu and Christian in Vrindaban*. London: SCM Press.

Knitter, Paul F. 1974. *Towards a Protestant Theology of Religions*. Marburg: Elwert.

————. 1979. "Jesus — Buddha — Krishna: Still Present." *Journal of Ecumenical Studies* 16:651–71.

————. 1981. "Horizons on Christianity's New Dialogue with Buddhism." *Horizons* 8:40–46.

————. 1984. "Roman Catholic Approaches to Other Religions: Development and Tensions." *International Bulletin of Missionary Research* 8:50–54.

————. 1985. *No Other Name? A Critical Survey of Christian Attitudes to World Religions.* Maryknoll, N.Y.: Orbis Books.

————. 1986. "Catholic Theology of Religions at the Crossroads." In *Christianity among World Religions. Concilium* 183/1:99–107.

————. 1987. "Towards a Liberation Theology of Religions." In *The Myth of Christian Uniqueness: Towards a Pluralistic Theology of Religions,* ed. John Hick and Paul F. Knitter, 178–200. Maryknoll, N.Y.: Orbis Books.

————. 1990a. "Interreligious Dialogue: What? Why? How?" In L. Swidler et al., *Death or Dialogue? From the Age of Monologue to the Age of Dialogue,* 19–44. London: SCM Press.

————. 1990b. "Missionary Activity Revisited and Reaffirmed." In *Christian Mission and Interreligious Dialogue,* ed. P. Mojzes and L. Swidler, 77–92. Lewiston, N.Y.: Edwin Mellen Press.

————. 1991a. "A New Pentecost?" *Current Dialogue* 19:32–41.

————. 1991b. "S. Samartha's 'One Christ — Many Religions.'" *Current Dialogue* 21:24–37.

————. 1995a. *One Earth Many Religions: Multifaith Dialogue and Global Responsibility.* Maryknoll, N.Y.: Orbis Books.

————. 1995b. "Toward a Liberative Interreligious Dialogue." *Cross Currents* 45/4:451–68.

————. 1996. *Jesus and the Other Names: Christian Mission and Global Responsibility.* Maryknoll, N.Y.: Orbis Books.

Knox, J. 1967. *The Humanity and Divinity of Christ.* Cambridge: Cambridge University Press.

Kraemer, Hendrik. 1947. *The Christian Message in a Non-Christian World.* London: Edinburgh House.

————. 1957. *Religion and the Christian Faith.* London: Lutterworth.

————. 1960. *World Cultures and World Religions.* London: Lutterworth.

————. 1962. *Why Christianity of All Religions?* London: Lutterworth.

Kramer, Kenneth. 1986. *World Scriptures: An Introduction to Comparative Religions.* New York: Paulist Press.

Krieger, David J. 1991. *The New Universalism: Foundations for a Global Theology.* Maryknoll, N.Y.: Orbis Books.

Küng, Hans. 1967. "The World Religions in God's Plan of Salvation." In *Christian Revelation and World Religions,* ed. J. Neuner, 25–66. London: Burns and Oates.

————. 1968. *The Church.* London: Search Press.

————. 1977. *On Being a Christian.* New York: Doubleday.

————. 1987. "What Is True Religion? Toward an Ecumenical Criteriology." In *Toward a Universal Theology of Religion,* ed. L. Swidler, 231–50. Maryknoll, N.Y.: Orbis Books.

————. 1988. *Theology for the Third Millennium*. New York: Doubleday.

————. 1991. *Global Responsibility: In Search of a New World Ethic*. London: SCM Press.

Küng, Hans, and J. Ching. 1989. *Christianity and Chinese Religions*. New York: Doubleday.

Küng, Hans, and Karl-Josef Kushel. 1993. *A Global Ethic: The Declaration of the Parliament of the World's Religions*. New York: Continuum.

Küng, Hans, and P. Lapide. 1976. *Jesus im Widerstreit: Ein Jüdisch-christlicher Dialog*. Munich: Kösel.

Küng, Hans, et al. 1993. *Christianity and World Religions: Paths of Dialogue with Islam, Hinduism, and Buddhism*. Maryknoll, N.Y.: Orbis Books.

Kunnumpuram, K. 1971. *Ways of Salvation: The Salvific Meaning of Non-Christian Religions according to the Teaching of Vatican II*. Poona: Pontifical Atheneum.

Kuschel, Karl-Josef. 1992. *Born before All Time? The Dispute over Christ's Origin*. London: SCM Press.

————. 1995. *Abraham: A Symbol of Hope for Jews, Christians and Muslims*. London: SCM Press.

Kuttianimattathil, J. 1995. *Practice and Theology of Interreligious Dialogue: A Critical Study of the Indian Christian Attempts since Vatican II*. Bangalore: Kristu Jyoti College.

Lacombe, O. 1937. *L'absolu selon le Védanta*. Paris: Paul Geuthmer.

————. 1956. *Chemins de l'Inde et philosophie chrétienne*. Paris: Alsatia.

————. 1986. *L'élan spiritual de l'hindouisme*. Paris: OEIL.

Lai, Pan-Chiu. 1994. *Towards a Trinitarian Theology of Religions: A Study of Paul Tillich's Thought*. Kampen: Kok Pharos.

Lampe, G. 1977. *God as Spirit*. Oxford: Clarendon Press.

Lapide, P., and J. Moltmann, eds. 1979. *Jüdischer Monotheismus — Christliche Trinitätslehre: Ein Gespräch*. Munich: Kaiser.

Latourelle, René. 1987. *Theology of Revelation*. Staten Island, N.Y.: Alba House.

Latourelle, René, and R. Fisichella, eds. 1994. *Dictionary of Fundamental Theology*. Middlegreen, Slough: St. Pauls.

Lefebure, Leo D. 1993. *The Buddha and the Christ: Explorations in Buddhist and Christian Dialogue*. Maryknoll, N.Y.: Orbis Books.

Legrand, Lucien. 1974. "The Missionary Significance of the Areopagus Speech." In *God's Word among Men*, ed. G. Gispert-Sauch, 59–71. Delhi: Vidyajyoti Institute of Religious Studies.

————. 1981. "The Unknown God of Athens." *Vidyajyoti* 45:222–31.

————. 1987. "Aratos est-il aussi parmi les prophètes?" In *La vie de la parole: De l'Ancient au Nouveau Testament: Etudes d'exégèse et d'herméneutique bibliques offertes à Pierre Grelot*, 241–58. Paris: Desclée.

————. 1988. *Le Dieu qui vient*. Paris: Desclée. Eng. trans. = Legrand 1992.

————. 1992. *Mission in the Bible: Unity and Plurality*. Maryknoll, N.Y.: Orbis Books.

————. 1995. "Jésus et l'Eglise primitive: Un éclairage biblique." *Spiritus* 138/36:64–77.

Lelong, M. 1979. *J'ai rencontré l'Islam*. Paris: Cerf.

———. 1984. "Mohammed, prophète de l'Islam." In *Founders of Religions*. Vol. 33 of *Studia Missionalia*: 251–76.

Le Saux, H. (Abhishiktananda). 1973–74. "Hindu Scriptures and Christian Worship." *Word and Worship* 4:187–95; 5:245–53.

———. 1976. *Hindu-Christian Meeting-Point*. Delhi: ISPCK. Reprinted 1983.

———. 1981. "The Depth-Dimension of Dialogue." *Vidyajyoti* 45:202–21.

———. 1982. *Intériorité et révélation: Essais théologiques*. Sisteron: Editions Présence.

———. 1984a. *The Further Shore*. 2d ed. Delhi: ISPCK.

———. 1984b. *Saccidananda: A Christian Approach to Advaita Experience*. Rev. ed. Delhi: ISPCK.

———. 1986. *La montée au fond du coeur: Le journal intime du moine chrétien — sannyasi hindou*. Paris: OEIL.

Limet, H., and J. Ries, eds. 1980. *L'expérience de la prière dans les grandes religions*. Louvain-la-neuve: Centre d'histoire des religions.

Lipner, J. J. 1981. "Does Copernicus Help?" In *Inter-religious Dialogue: Facing the New Frontier*, ed. R. W. Rousseau, 154–74. Scranton, Pa.: Ridge Row Press.

Lochhead, David. 1988. *The Dialogical Imperative: A Christian Reflection on Interfaith Encounter*. Maryknoll, N.Y.: Orbis Books.

"Logos." 1967. In *Theological Dictionary of the New Testament*, ed. G. Kittel, 4:71–136. Grand Rapids, Mich.: Eerdmans.

Lohfink, Norbert. 1991. *The Covenant Never Revoked: Biblical Reflections on Christian-Jewish Dialogue*. New York: Paulist Press.

Lombardi, R. 1956. *The Salvation of the Unbeliever*. London: Burns and Oates.

Lonergan, B. 1967. *Verbum, Word and Idea in Aquinas*. South Bend, Ind.: University of Notre Dame Press.

Lubac, Henri de. 1946a. *Le fondement théologique des missions*. Paris: Seuil.

———. 1946b. *Surnaturel: Etudes historiques*. Paris: Aubier.

———. 1951–55. *Aspects du Bouddhisme*. 2 vols. Paris: Seuil.

———. 1952a. *Catholicisme: Les aspects sociaux du dogme*. Paris: Cerf.

———. 1952b. *La rencontre du Bouddhisme et de l'Occident*. Paris: Aubier.

———. 1965a. *The Faith of Teilhard de Chardin*. New York: Desclée.

———. 1965b. Preface to A. Ravier, ed., *La mystique et les mystiques*, 7–39. Paris: Desclée de Brouwer. Found in enlarged form in Lubac 1984.

———. 1967a. *Images de l'abbé Jules Monchanin*. Paris: Aubier.

———. 1967b. *The Mystery of the Supernatural*. London: G. Chapman.

———. 1967c. *Paradoxe et mystère de l'Eglise*. Paris: Aubier-Montaigne. Eng. trans. = Lubac 1969.

———. 1967d. *The Religion of Teilhard de Chardin*. New York: Desclée.

———. 1969. *The Church: Paradox and Mystery*. New York: Alba House.

———. 1974. *Pic de la Mirandole: Etudes et discussions*. Paris: Aubier-Montaigne.

———. 1984. "Mystique et mystère." In *Théologies d'occasion*. Paris: Desclée de Brouwer.

Luneau, A. 1964. *L'histoire du salut chez les Pères de l'Eglise: La doctrine des âges du monde*. Paris: Beauchesne.

———. 1967. "Pour aider au dialogue: Les Pères et les religions non chrétiennes." *Nouvelle revue théologique* 89:820–41, 914–39.

Macquarrie, John. 1992. *Jesus Christ in Modern Thought*. London: SCM Press.
———. 1995. *The Mediators*. London: SCM Press.

Magonet, J. 1992. "Jonah, Book of." In *The Anchor Bible Dictionary*, 3:936–42. New York: Doubleday.

Main, E. 1996. "Ancienne et nouvelle alliance dans le dessein de Dieu: A propos d'un article récent." *Nouvelle revue théologique* 118/1:34–58.

Mambrino, J. 1957. "Les deux mains de Dieu dans l'oeuvre de Saint Irénée." *Nouvelle revue théologique* 69:355–70.

*The Many Faces of the Divine*. 1995. Concilium: 2.

Marchesi, G. 1977. *La cristologia di Hans Urs von Balthasar: La figura di Gesè Cristo espressione visibile di Dio*. Rome: Pontificia Università Gregoriana.

Maréchal, J. 1964. *Studies in the Psychology of the Mystics*. Albany, N.Y.: Magi Books.

Masson, D. 1958. *Le Coran et la révélation Judéo-Chrétienne: Etudes comparées*. Paris: Adrien Maisonneuve.

———. 1976. *Monothéisme coranique et monothéisme biblique: Doctrines comparées*. Paris: Desclée de Brouwer.

Mattam, J. 1975. *Land of the Trinity: A Study of Modern Christian Approaches to Hinduism*. Bangalore: Theological Publications in India.

Maupilier, M. 1985. *Les mystiques hindous-chrétiens(1830–1967)*. Paris: OEIL.

Maurier, H. 1965. *Essai d'une théologie du paganisme*. Paris: L'Orante. Eng. trans. = Maurier 1968.

———. 1966. "Lecture de la Déclaration par un missionnaire d'Afrique." In *Les relations de l'Eglise avec les religions non chrétiennes*, A.-M. Henry, 119–60. Paris: Cerf.

———. 1968. *The Other Covenant: A Theology of Paganism*. New York.

———. 1976. "Théologie chrétienne des religions non chrétiennes." *Lumen Vitae* 31/1:89–104.

———. 1993. *Les missions: Religions et civilisations confrontées à l'universalisme*. Paris: Cerf.

McBrien, P. 1969. *Do We Need the Church?* New York: Harper and Harper.

McFadden, T., ed. 1974. *Does Christ Make a Difference?* New York: Seabury Press.

McKenzie, John L. 1963. *Myths and Realities*. Milwaukee: Bruce.

*Mediation in Christianity and Other Religions*. 1972. *Studia Missionalia* 21.

Menacherry, C. 1996. *Christ: The Mystery in History: A Critical Study on the Christology of Raymond Panikkar*. Frankfurt: Peter Lang.

Menard, C. 1990. "Jésus le Christ est-il l'unique sauveur? La salut chrétien confronté aux autres religions de salut." In *Jésus: Christ universel?* ed. J. C. Petit and J. C. Breton, 55–78. Montreal: Fides.

———. 1994. "L'universalité du salut en Jésus le Christ d'après E. Schillebeeckx." *Laval théologique et philosophique* 50/2:283–96.

Mendenhall, G. E., and G. A. Herion, eds. 1992. "Covenant." In *The Anchor Bible Dictionary*, ed. D. N. Freedman, 1:1179–1202. New York: Doubleday.

Menoud, P.-H. 1964. "Le peuple de Dieu dans le Christianisme primitif." *Foi et vie* 63:386–400.

Michel, T. 1985. "Islamo-Christian Dialogue: Reflections on the Recent Teaching of the Church." *Bulletin* (Secretariat for Non-Christians) 59/20/2:172–93.

Mojzes, Paul, and Leonard Swidler, eds. 1990. *Christian Mission and Interreligious Dialogue.* Lewiston, N.Y.: Edwin Mellen Press.

Molari, C. 1989. "Assolutezza e universalità del cristianesimo come problema teologico." *Credere oggi* 6:17–35.

———. 1994a. Introduction to *La teologia pluralista delle religioni: un mito? L'unicità cristiana riesaminata,* ed. G. D'Costa, 11–37. Assisi: Cittadella.

———. 1994b. Introduction to *L'unicità cristiana: Un mito? Per una teologia pluralista delle religioni,* ed. John Hick and Paul F. Knitter, 11–48. Assisi: Cittadella.

Moltmann, Jürgen. 1990. *The Way of Jesus Christ: Christology in Messianic Dimensions.* London: SCM Press.

Monchanin, J. 1953. "Le Saint-Esprit dans la Trinité." *Dieu Vivant* 23:71–76.

———. 1955. *De l'esthétique à la mystique.* Tournai: Casterman.

———. 1974. *Mystique de l'Inde, mystère chrétien.* Paris: Fayard.

———. 1985. *Théologie et spiritualité missionnaire.* Paris: Beauchesne.

Mondin, B. 1986. *La chiesa primizia del Regno.* Bologna: Edizioni Dehoniane.

Montcheuil, Y. de. 1949. *Aspects de l'Eglise.* Paris: Cerf.

Monti, J. E. 1984. *Who Do You Say That I Am? The Christian Understanding of Christ and Antisemitism.* Ramsey, N.J.: Paulist Press.

Moran, Gabriel. 1966. *Theology of Revelation.* New York: Herder and Herder.

———. 1972. *The Present Revelation.* New York: Herder and Herder.

———. 1992. *Uniqueness: Problem or Paradox in Jewish and Christian Traditions.* Maryknoll, N.Y.: Orbis Books.

Mouroux, J. 1962. *Le mystère du temps: Approche théologique.* Paris: Aubier.

Mouttapa, J. 1996. *Dieu et la révolution du dialogue.* Paris: Albin Michel.

Murray, R. 1992. *The Cosmic Covenant.* London: Sheed and Ward.

Mussner, F. 1984. *Tractate on the Jews: The Significance of Judaism for Christian Faith.* London: SPCK.

Neher, A. 1972. *L'essence du prophétisme.* Paris: Calmann-Lévy.

Netland, H. A. 1991. *Dissonant Voices: Religious Pluralism and the Question of Truth.* Grand Rapids, Mich.: Eerdmans.

Neudecker, L. 1960. *I vari volti di Dio: Cristiani e ebrei in dialogo.* Geneva: Marietti.

Neuner, J. 1954. "Das Christus-Mysterium und die indische Lehre von den Avataras." In *Das Konzil von Chalkedon: Geschichte und Gegenwart,* ed. A. Grillemeier and H. Bacht, 3:785–824. Würzburg: Echter Verlag.

———. 1964. "Missionstheologische Probleme in Indien." In *Gott in Welt: Festschrift für Karl Rahner,* ed. H. Vorgrimler, 2:397–426. Freiburg: Herder.

———, ed. 1967. *Christian Revelation and World Religions.* London: Burns and Oates.

Neuner, J., and J. Dupuis. 1996. *The Christian Faith in the Doctrinal Documents of the Catholic Church.* New York: Alba House.

Newbigin, L. 1990. *The Gospel in a Pluralistic Society.* Grand Rapids, Mich.: Eerdmans.

Newell, W. L. 1981. *Struggle and Submission: R. C. Zaehner on Mysticism.* Washington, D.C.: University Press of America.

Niebuhr, H. R. 1951. *Christ and Culture.* New York: Harper and Brothers.

Nissiotis, N. A. 1963. "Pneumatologie orthodoxe." In F. J. Leenhardt et al., *Le Saint-Esprit*, 85–106. Geneva: Labor et Fides.

———. 1967. "Pneumatological Christology as a Presupposition of Ecclesiology." *Oecumenica*: 235–52.

"Notes for a Correct Presentation of Jews and Judaism in the Preaching and Catechesis of the Catholic Church." 1985–86. Published by the Commission for Religious Relations with Judaism (14 June 1985). *Origins* 15:102–7.

Novak, P., ed. 1994. *The World's Wisdom: Sacred Texts of the World Religions*. San Francisco: HarperSanFrancisco.

Nys, H. 1966. *Le salut sans l'évangile*. Paris: Cerf.

Ochagavía, J. 1964. *Visibile Patris Filius: A Study of Irenaeus' Teaching on Revelation and Tradition*. Rome: Orientalia Christiana Analecta.

O'Collins, Gerald. 1968. *Theology and Revelation*. Cork, Ireland: Mercier.

———. 1993. *Retrieving Fundamental Theology*. New York: Paulist Press.

———. 1995a. *Christology*. Oxford: Oxford University Press.

———. 1995b. "The Incarnation under Fire." *Gregorianum* 76/2:263–80.

Oesterreicher, J. M. 1969. "Declaration on the Relation of the Church to Non-Christian Religions." In *Commentary on the Documents of Vatican II*, ed. H. Vorgrimler, 3:1–136. London: Burns and Oates.

Ogden, Schubert M. 1961. *Christ without Myth*. New York: Harper and Brothers.

———. 1963. *The Reality of God*. New York: Harper and Row.

———. 1992. *Is There Only One True Religion or Are There Many?* Dallas: Southern Methodist University Press.

O'Leary, J. S. 1994. *La vérité chrétienne à l'âge du pluralisme religieux*. Paris: Cerf.

"The One, the Christian and the Many." 1989. *Cross Currents* 38/3:268–351.

"On Interpreting the Bible." 1987. *Voices from the Third World* 10/2.

Orbe, A. 1958. *Hacia la primera teología de la procesión del Verbo*. Rome: Analecta Gregoriana.

———. 1966. "San Ireneo y el conosciemento natural de Dios." *Gregorianum* 47:441–77, 710–47.

"Orientations and Recommendations for the Application of the Conciliar Declaration *Nostra Aetate*, n. 4." 1974–75. Published by the Commission for Religious Relations with Judaism (4 January 1975). *Origins* 4:463–64.

"Orientations pastorales du comité épiscopal français pour les relations avec le Judaisme." 1973. *Documentation Catholique* 70:419–22.

Osborn, E. 1993. "Justin Martyr and the Logos Spermatikos." In *Theology of Religions*. Vol. 42 of *Studia Missionalia*: 143–59.

Oxtaby, Willard G. 1985. *The Meaning of Other Faiths*. Philadelphia: Westminster Press.

Paissac, H. 1951. *La théologie du Verbe: Saint Augustin et Saint Thomas*. Paris: Cerf.

Panikkar, Raimundo. 1964. *The Unknown Christ of Hinduism*. London: Darton, Longman and Todd.

———. 1972. *Salvation in Christ: Concreteness and Universality: The Supername*. Santa Barbara, Calif.

———. 1973. *The Trinity and the Religious Experience of Man*. Maryknoll, N.Y.: Orbis Books.

———. 1978. *The Intrareligious Dialogue.* New York: Paulist Press.

———. 1979a. *Myth, Faith, and Hermeneutics: Cross-Cultural Studies.* New York: Paulist Press.

———. 1979b. *The Vedic Experience: Mantramanjari.* London: Darton, Longman and Todd.

———. 1981. *The Unknown Christ of Hinduism: Towards an Ecumenical Christophany.* Rev. ed. London: Darton, Longman and Todd. Original edition, 1964.

———. 1984. "The Dialogical Dialogue." In *The World's Religious Traditions: Current Perspectives in Religious Studies,* ed. F. Whaling, 201–21. Edinburgh: T. and T. Clark.

———. 1987a. "The Invisible Harmony: A Universal Theory of Religion or a Cosmic Confidence in Reality?" In *Toward a Universal Theology of Religion,* ed. L. Swidler, 118–53. Maryknoll, N.Y.: Orbis Books.

———. 1987b. "The Jordan, the Tiber, and the Ganges: Three Kairological Moments of Christic Self-Consciousness." In *The Myth of Christian Uniqueness,* ed. John Hick and Paul F. Knitter, 89–116. Maryknoll, N.Y.: Orbis Books.

———. 1989. *The Silence of God: The Answer of the Buddha.* Maryknoll, N.Y.: Orbis Books.

———. 1990. "Foreword: The Ongoing Dialogue." In *Hindu-Christian Dialogue,* ed. H. Coward, ix–xviii. Maryknoll, N.Y.: Orbis Books.

———. 1992. "A Christophany for Our Times." *Theology Digest* 39/1:3–21.

———. 1993. *The Cosmotheandric Experience: Emerging Religious Consciousness.* Maryknoll, N.Y.: Orbis Books.

Pannenberg, Wolfhart. 1969. *Revelation as History.* London: Macmillan.

———. 1971. *Basic Questions in Theology: Collected Essays.* Vol. 2. London: SCM Press.

———. 1989. *Theology and the Kingdom of God.* Philadelphia: Westminster.

———. 1990. "Religious Pluralism and Conflicting Truth Claims." In *Christian Uniqueness Reconsidered,* ed. G. D'Costa, 96–116. Maryknoll, N.Y.: Orbis Books.

———. 1991. "Die Religionen als Thema der Theologie." *Stimmen der Zeit* 169:98–110.

———. 1991–94. *Systematic Theology.* 2 vols. Edinburgh: T. and T. Clark.

———. 1992. "Le religioni nella prospettiva della teologia cristiana e l'autocomprensione del cristianesimo nel suo rapporto con le religioni esterne alla chiesa." *Filosofia e teologia* 6/1:25–37.

Parrinder, Geoffrey. 1971a. *Avatar and Incarnation.* London: Faber and Faber.

———. 1971b. "Revelation in Other Scriptures." In *Revelation in Christianity and Other Religions.* Vol. 20 of *Studia Missionalia*: 101–13.

———. 1977. *Jesus and the Qur'an.* London: Shelton Press.

———. 1987. *Encountering World Religions: Questions of Religious Truth.* New York: Crossroad.

———. 1990. "Updating Within and Without." In *Christianity and the Wider Ecumenism,* ed. P. Phan, 47–58. New York: Paragon House.

———. 1995. "Only One Way? John 14:6." *Expository Times* 107/3:78–79.

Pascal, B. 1963. "Le mémorial." In *Oeuvres complètes,* ed. L. Lafuma. Paris: Cerf.

"Pastoral Orientations of the French Bishops' Commission for Relations with Judaism." 1970. *Documentation Catholique* 70:419–22.

Pathil, K., ed. 1991. *Religious Pluralism: An Indian Christian Perspective.* Delhi: ISPCK.

Pathrapankal, J., ed. 1973. *Service and Salvation.* Bangalore: Theological Publications in India.

Pawlikowski, John T. 1980. *What Are They Saying about Christian-Jewish Relations?* New York: Paulist Press.

——. 1982. *Christ in the Light of Jewish-Christian Dialogue.* New York: Paulist Press.

Penna, R., ed. 1993. *Vangelo, religioni e cultura: Miscellanea di studi in memoria de mons. Pietro Rossano.* Cinisello, Balsamo: San Paolo.

Perkinson, J. 1994. "Soteriological Humility: The Christological Significance of the Humanity of Jesus in the Encounter of Religions." *Journal of Ecumenical Studies* 31:1–26.

Perrin, Norman. 1963. *The Kingdom in the Teaching of Jesus.* London: SCM Press.

——. 1967. *Rediscovering the Teaching of Jesus.* London: SCM Press.

Petit, J.-C., and J. C. Breton, eds. 1990. *Jésus: Christ universel?* Montreal: Fides.

Phan, Peter, ed. 1990. *Christianity and the Wider Ecumenism.* New York: Paragon House.

Pieris, Aloysius. 1980a. "Towards an Asian Theology of Liberation: Some Religio-cultural Guidelines." In *Asia's Struggle for Full Humanity,* ed. V. Fabella, 75–95. Maryknoll, N.Y.: Orbis Books.

——. 1980b. "Western Christianity and Asian Buddhism: A Theological Reading of Historical Encounters." *Dialogue,* n.s., 7/2:49–85.

——. 1982. "Speaking of the Son of God." In *Jesus, Son of God. Concilium* 153/3:65–70.

——. 1983. "The Place of Non-Christian Religions and Cultures in the Evolution of Third World Theology." In *Irruption of the Third World: Challenge to Theology,* ed. V. Fabella and S. Torres, 113–39. Maryknoll, N.Y.: Orbis Books.

——. 1987. "The Buddha and the Christ: Mediators of Liberation." In *The Myth of Christian Uniqueness,* ed. J. Hick and P. F. Knitter, 162–77. Maryknoll, N.Y.: Orbis Books.

——. 1988a. *An Asian Theology of Liberation.* Maryknoll, N.Y.: Orbis Books.

——. 1988b. *Love Meets Wisdom: A Christian Experience of Buddhism.* Maryknoll, N.Y.: Orbis Books.

——. 1993a. "An Asian Paradigm: Interreligious Dialogue and Theology of Religions." *Month* 26:129–34.

——. 1993b. "Universality of Christianity?" *Vidyajyoti* 57:591–95.

——. 1994a. "Inculturation in Asia: A Theological Reflection on an Experience." In *Jahrbuch für kontextuelle Theologien,* 59–71. Frankfurt: Verlag für Interkulturelle Kommunikation.

——. 1994b. "The Problem of Universality and Inculturation with regard to Patterns of Theological Thinking." In *Why Theology? Concilium* 6:70–79.

——. 1996. *Basic Issues in Asian Buddhism and Christianity.* Maryknoll, N.Y.: Orbis Books.

Piret, P. 1991. *La destinée de l'homme: La cité de Dieu: Un commentaire du De Civitate Dei.* Brussels: Editions de l'Institut d'études théologiques.

Pittenger, Norman. 1970. *Christology Reconsidered.* London: SCM Press.

"Pneuma." 1968. In *Theological Dictionary of the New Testament,* ed. G. Kittel, 6:330–450. Grand Rapids, Mich.: Eerdmans.

Pontifical Council for Interreligious Dialogue. 1990. *Guidelines for Dialogue between Christians and Muslims.* 2d ed. New York: Paulist Press.

———. 1991. "Dialogue and Proclamation: Reflections and Orientations on Interreligious Dialogue and the Proclamation of the Gospel of Jesus Christ." *Bulletin* 77/26/2:210–50.

Potterie, I. de la. 1977. *La vérité chez Saint Jean.* 2 vols. Rome: Biblical Institute Press.

———. 1984. "Jésus-Christ, plénitude de la vérité, lumière du monde et sommet de la révélation d'après Saint Jean." In *Founders of Religions.* Vol. 33 of *Studia Missionalia:* 305–24.

Prabhu, J., ed. 1996. *The Intercultural Challenge of Raimon Panikkar.* Maryknoll, N.Y.: Orbis Books.

Puthanangady, P., ed. 1988. *Sharing Worship.* Bangalore: NBCLC.

Puthiadam, Ignatius. 1980. "Christian Faith and Life in a World of Religious Pluralism." In *True and False Universality of Christianity. Concilium* 135/5:90–112.

———. 1981. "Diversity of Religions in the Context of Pluralism and Indian Christian Life and Reflection." In *Theologizing in India,* ed. M. Amaladoss, T. K. John, and G. Gispert-Sauch, 383–438. Bangalore: Theological Publications in India.

Race, Alan. 1983. *Christians and Religious Pluralism: Patterns in the Christian Theology of Religions.* London: SCM Press.

Raguin, Yves. 1973. *Bouddhisme—Christianisme.* Paris: Epi.

———. 1975. *The Depth of God.* St. Meinrad: Abbey Press.

———. 1989. *La source.* Paris: Desclée.

Rahner, Karl. 1956. "Die Kirche als Ort der Geistsendung." *Geist und Leben* 29:94–98.

———. 1958. *Zur Theologie des Todes.* Freiburg: Herder.

———. 1961a. "Current Problems in Christology." In *Theological Investigations,* 1:149–200. London: Darton, Longman and Todd.

———. 1961b. *Inspiration in the Bible.* New York: Herder.

———. 1961c. "Theos in the New Testament." In *Theological Investigations,* 1:79–148. London: Darton, Longman and Todd.

———. 1963. "Membership of the Church according to the Teaching of Pius XII's Encyclical 'Mystici Corporis.'" In *Theological Investigations,* 2:1–88. London: Darton, Longman and Todd.

———. 1966a. "Christianity and the Non-Christian Religions." In *Theological Investigations,* 5:115–34. London: Darton, Longman and Todd.

———. 1966b. "Christology within an Evolutionary View of the World." In *Theological Investigations,* 5:157–92. London: Darton, Longman and Todd.

———. 1966c. *The Church after the Council.* New York: Herder and Herder.

———. 1966d. "History of the World and Salvation History." In *Theological Investigations,* 5:97–114. London: Darton, Longman and Todd.

———. 1966e. "On the Theology of the Incarnation." In *Theological Investigations,* 4:105–20. London: Darton, Longman and Todd.

———. 1966f. "Remarks on the Dogmatic Treatise 'De Trinitate.' " In *Theological Investigations,* 4:77–102. London: Darton, Longman and Todd.

———. 1967. "The Eternal Significance of the Humanity of Christ for Our Relation to God." In *Theological Investigations,* 3:35–46. London: Darton, Longman and Todd.

———. 1968. "Church and World." In *Sacramentum Mundi: An Encyclopedia of Theology,* 1:346–57. New York: Herder and Herder.

———. 1969a. "Anonymous Christians." In *Theological Investigations,* 6:390–98. London: Darton, Longman and Todd.

———. 1969b. "The Church and the Parousia of Christ." In *Theological Investigations,* 6:295–312. London: Darton, Longman and Todd.

———. 1970. *The Trinity.* New York: Herder and Herder.

———. 1973. "Church, Churches and Religions." In *Theological Investigations,* 10:30–49. London: Darton, Longman and Todd.

———. 1975. "Mysticism." In *Encyclopedia of Theology: The Concise 'Sacramentum Mundi.' "* New York: Seabury Press.

———. 1976. "Observations on the Problem of the 'Anonymous Christian.' " In *Theological Investigations,* 14:280–98. London: Darton, Longman and Todd.

———. 1978. *Foundations of Christian Faith: An Introduction to the Idea of Christianity.* London: Darton, Longman and Todd.

———. 1979. "The One Christ and the Universality of Salvation." In *Theological Investigations,* 16:199–224. London: Darton, Longman and Todd.

———. 1981a. "Basic Interpretation of the Second Vatican Council." In *Theological Investigations,* 20:77–89. London: Darton, Longman and Todd.

———. 1981b. "Jesus Christ in the Non-Christian Religions." In *Theological Investigations,* 17:39–50. London: Darton, Longman and Todd.

———. 1981c. "Mysterium Ecclesiae." In *Theological Investigations,* 17:139–55. London: Darton, Longman and Todd.

———. 1984a. "Oneness and Threefoldness of God in Discussion with Islam." In *Theological Investigations,* 18:105–21. London: Darton, Longman and Todd.

———. 1984b. "On the Importance of the Non-Christian Religions for Salvation." In *Theological Investigations,* 18:288–95. London: Darton, Longman and Todd.

———. 1988a. "Christianity's Absolute Claim." In *Theological Investigations,* 21:171–84. London: Darton, Longman and Todd.

———. 1988b. "Profane History and Salvation History." In *Theological Investigations,* 21:3–15. London: Darton, Longman and Todd.

Rahner, K., and J. Ratzinger. 1966. *Revelation and Tradition.* New York: Herder.

Ratschow, C. H. 1982. *Jesus Christus.* Gütterlosh: Gerd Mohn.

Ratzinger, Johannes. 1968. "Christianity and World Religions." In *One, Holy, Catholic and Apostolic,* ed. H. Vorgrimler, 207–36. London: Sheed and Ward.

———. 1970. *Das neue Volk Gottes.* Düsseldorf: Patmos.

Ravier, A., ed. 1965. *La mystique et les mystiques.* Paris: Desclée de Brouwer.

Rayan, S. 1983. "Models of History." *Jeevadhara* 13/1:5–26.

————. 1990. "Religions, Salvation, Mission." In *Christian Mission and Inter-religious Dialogue,* ed. P. Mojzes and L. Swidler, 126–39. Lewiston, N.Y.: Edwin Mellen Press.

Reid, J. B. 1990. *Jesus, God's Emptiness, God's Fullness: The Christology of St. Paul.* New York: Paulist Press.

"Religions." 1994. In *Dictionary of Fundamental Theology,* ed. R. Latourelle and R. Fisichella, cols. 819–86. Middlegreen, Slough: St. Paul.

"Religious Pluralism." 1978. *Jeevadhara* 47/8:353–408.

"Religious Plurality: Theological Perspectives and Affirmations." 1991. Statement of the Baar Consultation (January 1990). *Current Dialogue* 19: 47–51.

Remaud, M. 1983. *Chrétiens devant Israel serviteur de Dieu.* Paris: Cerf.

*Revelation in Christianity and Other Religions.* 1971. *Studia Missionalia* 20.

Richard, Lucien. 1981. *What Are They Saying about Christ and World Religions?* New York: Paulist Press.

Richards, G. 1989. *Towards a Theology of Religions.* London: Routledge.

Ries, J. 1985. *Les chemins du sacré dans l'histoire.* Paris: Aubier-Montaigne.

————. 1987. *Les chrétiens parmi les religions.* Paris: Desclée.

Rizzi, A. 1992. "Rapporto teologico tra alleanza ebraica e alleanza cristiana." Lecture given at the SIDIC Center of Rome (7 November 1992). From manuscript.

Robinson, John A. T. 1973. *The Human Face of God.* London: SCM Press.

————. 1979. *Truth Is Two-Eyed.* London: SCM Press.

Röper, A. 1966. *The Anonymous Christian.* New York: Sheed and Ward.

Rosales, G., and C. G. Arévalo, eds. 1992. *For All the Peoples of Asia: Federation of Asian Bishops' Conferences Documents from 1970 to 1991.* Maryknoll, N.Y.: Orbis Books.

Rossano, P. 1965. "Le religioni non cristiane nella storia della salvezza: Rasssegna delle proposizioni teologiche attuali." *La scuola cattolica: Supplemento* 2 93 (May–August): 131–40.

————. 1967a. "The Bible and Non-Christian Religions." *Bulletin* 4/2/1:18–28.

————. 1967b. "Le religioni non cristiane alla luce del Concilio e della Bibbia." *Rivista biblica* 15:123–30.

————. 1968. "Is There Authentic Revelation outside the Judeo-Christian Revelation?" *Bulletin* (Secretariat for Non-Christians) 8/3/2:84–87.

————. 1972. "La Bibbia e le religioni degli uomini." *Seminarium* 12:243–56.

————. 1975. *Il problema teologico delle religioni.* Catania: Paoline.

————. 1981. "Christ's Lordship and Religious Pluralism in Roman Catholic Perspective." In *Christ's Lordship and Religious Pluralism,* ed. G. H. Anderson and T. F. Stransky, 96–110. Maryknoll, N.Y.: Orbis Books.

————. 1982a. "Sulla presenza dello Spirito nelle religioni e nelle culture non cristiane." In *Prospettive di missiologia, oggi,* ed. M Dhavamony, 59–72. Università Gregoriana Editrice.

————. 1982b. "Theology and Religions: A Contemporary Problem." In *Problems and Perspectives of Fundamental Theology,* ed. R. Latourelle and G. O'Collins, 293–308. New York: Paulist Press.

————. 1993. *Dialogo e annuncio cristiano: L'incontro con le grandi religioni.* Cinisello, Balsamo: Paoline.

Rouner, L. S., ed. 1984. *Religious Pluralism.* South Bend, Ind.: University of Notre Dame Press.

Rousseau, A. 1982. "Notes justificatives." In *Irénée de Lyon, Contre les hérésies.* Book II. Sources Chrétiennes 293. Paris: Cerf.

Rousseau, R. W., ed. 1981. *Inter-religious Dialogue: Facing the New Frontier.* Scranton, Pa.: Ridge Row Press.

————. 1982. *Christianity and the Religions of the East: Models of a Dynamic Relationship.* Scranton, Pa.: Ridge Row Press.

Ruokanen, Mikka. 1992. *The Catholic Doctrine on Non-Christian Religions according to the Second Vatican Council.* Leiden: E. J. Brill.

*La Sagesse biblique: De l'Ancien au Nouveau Testament.* 1995. Paris: Cerf.

Saldanha, C. 1984. *Divine Pedagogy: A Patristic View of Non-Christian Religions.* Rome: Libreria Ateneo Salesiano.

*Salvation.* 1980. *Studia Missionalia* 29.

Samartha, Stanley J. 1959. *The Hindu View of History.* Bangalore: CISRS.

————. 1974. *The Hindu Response to the Unbound Christ.* Madras: Christian Literature Society.

————. 1975. *Living Faiths and Ultimate Goals: A Continuing Dialogue.* Maryknoll, N.Y.: Orbis Books.

————. 1982. *Courage for Dialogue: Ecumenical Issues in Inter-religious Relationships.* Maryknoll, N.Y.: Orbis Books.

————. 1991. *One Christ — Many Religions: Towards a Revised Christology.* Maryknoll, N.Y.: Orbis Books.

————. 1996. *Between Two Cultures: Ecumenical Ministry in a Pluralistic Age.* Geneva: World Council of Churches.

Sani, G. B. 1975. *L'Islam e Francesco d'Assisi: La missione profetica per il dialogo.* Firenze: La Nuova Italia.

Santinello, G. 1987. *Introduzione a Nicolò Cusano.* Bari: Laterza.

Schillebeeckx, Edward. 1963. *Christ the Sacrament of Encounter with God.* London: Sheed and Ward.

————. 1965. "The Church and Mankind." *Concilium* 1/1:34–50.

————. 1968. "De Ecclesia ut sacramentum mundi." In *Acta Congressus Internationalis de Theologia Concilii Vaticani II,* 48–53. Rome: Typis Polyglottis Vaticanis.

————. 1987. *Jesus in Our Western Culture: Mysticism, Ethics and Politics.* London: SCM Press.

————. 1990. *Church: The Human Story of God.* London: SCM Press.

————. 1994. "Universalité unique d'une figure religieuse historique nommée Jésus de Nazareth." *Laval théologique et philosophique* 50/2:265–81.

Schineller, J. P. 1976. "Christ and Church: A Spectrum of Views." *Theological Studies* 37:545–66. Reprinted in Burghardt and Thompson, eds., 1977.

Schlette, H. R. 1964. *Die Religionen als Thema der Theologie.* Freiburg: Herder. Eng. trans. = Schlette 1966.

————. 1966. *Towards a Theology of Religions.* New York: Herder and Herder.

————. 1967. "Religions." In *Encyclopédie de la foi,* ed. H. Fries, 4:59–68. Paris: Cerf.

————. 1969. *Epiphany as History.* New York: Herder and Herder.

Schlosser, J. 1980. *Le Règne de Dieu dans les dires de Jésus*. Paris: Gabalda.

Schnackenburg, Rudolph. 1968. *God's Rule and Kingdom*. London: Burns and Oates.

———. 1987. *The Gospel according to St. John*. 3 vols. New York: Crossroad.

Schwager, R., ed. 1996. *Christus allein? Der Streit um die pluralistische Religionstheologie*. Freiburg: Herder.

Schwöbel, C. 1990. "Particularity, Universality, and the Religions." In *Christian Uniqueness Reconsidered: The Myth of a Pluralistic Theology of Religions*, ed. G. D'Costa, 30–46. Maryknoll, N.Y.: Orbis Books.

Secretariat for Non-Christians. 1984. "The Attitude of the Church towards the Followers of Other Religions: Reflections and Orientations on Dialogue and Mission." *Bulletin* 56/19/2:126–41.

Semmelroth, Otto. 1953. *Die Kirche als Ursakrament*. Frankfurt: J. Knecht.

Senior, Donald, and Carroll Stuhlmueller. 1983. *The Biblical Foundations for Mission*. Maryknoll, N.Y.: Orbis Books.

Sertillanges, A. D. 1933. *Le miracle de l'Eglise*. Paris: Spes.

Sesboüé, B. 1984. "Karl Rahner et les 'chrétiens anonymes.'" *Etudes* 361:521–35.

———. 1988. *Jésus-Christ, l'unique médiateur: Essai sur la rédemption et le salut*. Vol. 1. Paris: Desclée.

Sharpe, Eric J. 1977. *Faith Meets Faith: Some Christian Attitudes to Hinduism in the 19th and 20th Centuries*. London: SCM Press.

Sheard, R. B. 1987. *Interreligious Dialogue in the Catholic Church since Vatican II: An Historical and Theological Study*. Lewiston, N.Y.: Edwin Mellen Press.

Sheth, N. 1984. *The Divinity of Krishna*. New Delhi: Munshiram Manaharlal.

Shorter, Aylward. 1983. *Revelation and Its Interpretation*. London: G. Chapman.

Sibony, D. 1992. *Le trois monothéismes: Juifs, chrétiens, musulmans entre leurs sources et leurs destins*. Paris: Seuil.

Smart, Ninian, and R. Hecht, eds. 1992. *Sacred Texts of the World: A Universal Anthology*. London: Macmillan.

Smet, R. 1981. *Essai sur la pensée de Raimundo Panikkar: Une contribution indienne à la théologie des religions et à la christologie*. Louvain-la-neuve: Centre d'histoire des religions.

———. 1983. *Le problème d'une théologie hindoue-chrétienne selon Raymond Panikkar*. Louvain-la-neuve: Centre d'histoire des religions.

Smith, W. C. 1967. *Questions of Religious Truth*. London: Gollanez.

———. 1979. *Faith and Belief*. Princeton, N.J.: Princeton University Press.

———. 1981. *Towards a World Theology*. London: Macmillan.

———. 1982. *Religious Diversity*. New York: Crossroad.

———. 1987. "Theology and the World's Religious History." In *Toward a Universal Theology of Religion*, ed. L. Swidler, 51–72. Maryknoll, N.Y.: Orbis Books.

———. 1993. *What Is Scripture? A Comparative Approach*. Minneapolis: Fortress Press.

Snyder, Howard A. 1991. *Models of the Kingdom*. Nashville: Abingdon Press.

Soares-Prabhu, G. 1976. "The New Testament as Model of Inculturation." *Jeevadhara* 6:268–82.

———. 1984. *Inculturation, Liberation, Dialogue*. Pune: Jnanadeepa.

Sobrino, Jon. 1987. *Jesus in Latin America.* Maryknoll, N.Y.: Orbis Books.

———. 1993. *Jesus the Liberator: A Historical-Theological Reading of Jesus of Nazareth.* Maryknoll, N.Y.: Orbis Books.

Song, C. S. 1985. *Christology and Other Faiths: Some Theological Reflections.* Toronto: Ecumenical Forum of Canada.

———. 1993. *Jesus and the Reign of God.* Minneapolis: Fortress Press.

———. 1994. *Jesus in the Power of the Spirit.* Minneapolis: Fortress Press.

"Sophia." 1971. In *Theological Dictionary of the New Testament,* ed. G. Kittel, 7:465–526. Grand Rapids, Mich.: Eerdmans.

Spae, J. J. 1980. *Buddhist-Christian Empathy.* Chicago: Chicago Institute of Theology and Culture.

Spanneut, M. 1957. *Le stoïcisme des Pères de l'Eglise de Clément de Rome à Clément d'Alexandrie.* Paris: Seuil.

Spink, K. 1989. *A Sense of the Sacred.* Maryknoll, N.Y.: Orbis Books.

Sreenivasa Rao, C. G. S. S., ed. 1991. *Inter-faith Dialogue and World Community.* Madras: Christian Literature Society.

Staffner, H. 1978. *The Open Door.* Bangalore: Asian Trading Corporation.

———. 1985. *The Significance of Jesus Christ in Asia.* Anand: Gujarat Sahitya Prakash.

Starkey, P. 1985. "Agapè: A Christian Criterion for Truth in the Other World Religions." *International Review of Mission* 74:425–63.

Stockwell, E. L. n.d. "One Perspective on Lausanne II in Manila, July 11–20, 1989." In manuscript.

Stoeckle, B. 1967. "Die ausserbiblische Menschheit und die Weltreligionen." In *Mysterium Salutis,* ed. J. Feiner and M. Löhrer, 2:1049–75. Einsiedeln: Benziger.

Stolz, A. 1937. *Théologie de la mystique.* Chevetogne, Abbaye de Chevetogne.

Straelen, H. van. 1965. *The Catholic Encounter with World Religions.* London: Burns and Oates.

———. 1982. *Ouverture à l'autre, laquelle?* Paris: Beauchesne.

———. 1994. *L'Eglise et les religions non chrétiennes au seuil du XXIe siècle.* Paris: Beauchesne.

Stuart, J. 1989. *Swami Abhishiktananda: His Life Told through His Letters.* Delhi: ISPCK. Revised edition 1996.

Stubenrauch, B. 1995. *Dialogische Dogma: Der christliche Auftrag zur interreligiösen Begegnung.* Freiburg: Herder.

Sugirtharajah, R. S., ed. 1991. *Voices from the Margin: Interpreting the Bible in the Third World.* Maryknoll, N.Y.: Orbis Books, 1991.

———. 1993. *Asian Faces of Jesus.* Maryknoll, N.Y.: Orbis Books.

Sullivan, Francis A. 1989. "The Significance of the Vatican II Declaration That the Church of Christ 'Subsists in' the Roman Catholic Church." In *Vatican II: Assessment and Perspectives Twenty-Five Years After (1962–87),* ed. R. Latourelle, 2:272–87. New York: Paulist Press.

———. 1992. *Salvation outside the Church? Tracing the History of the Catholic Response.* New York: Paulist Press.

Surgy, P. de. 1969. *Les grandes étapes du mystère du salut.* Paris: Editions ouvrières.

Swidler, Leonard. 1987. "Interreligious and Interideological Dialogue." In *Toward a Universal Theology of Religion*, ed. L. Swidler, 5–50. Maryknoll, N.Y.: Orbis Books.

———. 1989. "Jesus' Insurpassable Uniqueness: Two Responses." *Horizons* 16:117–20.

———. 1990. *After the Absolute: The Dialogical Future of Religious Reflection*. Minneapolis: Fortress Press.

Swidler, Leonard, et al. 1990. *Death or Dialogue? From the Age of Monologue to the Age of Dialogue*. London: SCM Press.

Swidler, Leonard, ed. 1987. *Toward a Universal Theology of Religion*. Maryknoll, N.Y.: Orbis Books.

Swidler, L., and P. Mojzes, eds. 1996. *The Uniqueness of Jesus: A Dialogue with P. Knitter*. Maryknoll, N.Y.: Orbis Books.

Swinburne, R. 1992. *Revelation: From Metaphor to Analogy*. Oxford: Clarendon Press.

Taylor, J. V. 1981. "The Theological Basis of Interfaith Dialogue." In *Faith Meets Faith*, ed. G. H. Anderson and T. F. Stransky, 93–110. New York: Paulist Press.

Teasdale, Wayne R. 1987. *Toward a Christian Vedanta: The Encounter of Hinduism and Christianity according to Bede Griffiths*. Bangalore: Asian Trading Corporation.

Teasdale, W., and G. Cairns, eds. 1996. *The Community of Religions: Voices and Images of the Parliament of the World's Religions*. New York: Continuum.

Teilhard de Chardin, Pierre. 1965. *Science and Christ*. New York: Harper and Row.

———. 1971. *Christianity and Evolution*. New York: Harcourt Brace Jovanovich.

———. 1975. *Toward the Future*. London: Collins.

TeSelle, Eugene. 1975. *Christ in Context*. Philadelphia: Fortress Press.

Theisen, J. P. 1976. *The Ultimate Church and the Promise of Salvation*. Collegeville, Minn.: St. John's University Press.

Theological Advisory Commission (FABC). 1987. "Theses on Interreligious Dialogue." *FABC Papers* 48. Hong Kong.

"Theological Colloquium, Pune, India, August 1993." 1994. *Pro Dialogo Bulletin* 85–86/1.

*Theology of Religions*. 1993. *Studia Missionalia* 42.

Thils, Gustave. 1966. *Propos et problèmes de la théologie des religions non chrétiennes*. Tournai: Casterman.

———. 1983. *Pour une théologie de structure planétaire*. Louvain-la-neuve: Faculté de théologie.

———. 1987. *Présence et salut de Dieu chez les 'non chrétiens.'* " Louvain-la-neuve: Faculté de théologie.

"Thinking about Theocentric Christology." 1987. *Journal of Ecumenical Studies* 24/1:1–52.

Thoma, C. 1980. *A Christian Theology of Judaism*. New York: Paulist Press.

Thomas, M. M. 1969. *The Acknowledged Christ of the Indian Renaissance*. London: SCM Press.

———. 1975. *Man and the Universe of Faiths*. Bangalore: Christian Literature Society.

———. 1987. *Risking Christ for Christ's Sake: Toward an Ecumenical Theology of Pluralism*. Geneva: World Council of Churches.

Thompson, William. 1985. *The Jesus Debate: A Survey and Synthesis*. New York: Paulist Press.

Tiessen, T. L. 1993. *Irenaeus on the Salvation of the Unevangelized*. Metuchen, N.J.: Scarecrow Press.

Tillich, Paul. 1957–63. *Systematic Theology*. Vols. 2–3. Chicago: University of Chicago Press.

———. 1963. *Christianity and the Encounter of World Religions*. New York: Columbia University Press.

———. 1983. *The Kingdom of God and History*. Chicago: University of Chicago Press.

Tononi, R. 1994. "Mistero pasquale e salvezza per tutti: Analisi storico-critica d'un testo della Gaudium et Spes." In *Cristianesimo e religioni in dialogo*, 171–202. Brescia: Morcelliana.

Tourenne, Y. 1995. *La théologie du dernier Rahner*. Paris: Cerf.

Toynbee, A. 1957. *Christianity among the Religions of the World*. New York: Scribner's.

Tracy, David. 1975. *Blessed Rage for Order: The New Pluralism in Theology*. New York: Seabury Press.

———. 1981. *The Analogical Imagination: Christian Theology and the Culture of Pluralism*. New York: Crossroad.

———. 1990. *Dialogue with the Other: The Interreligious Dialogue*. Louvain: Peeters Press.

Tracy, David, and John B. Cobb, eds. 1983. *Talking about God: Doing Theology in the Context of Modern Pluralism*. New York: Seabury Press.

Troeltsch, Ernst. 1971. *The Absoluteness of Christianity and the History of Religions*. Richmond: John Knox Press.

Troisfontaines, A. 1960. *Je ne meurs pas*. Paris: Editions universitaires.

*True and False Universality of Christianity*. 1980. *Concilium* 135/5.

"Universality and Uniqueness in the Context of Religious Pluralism." 1989. *Journal of Ecumenical Studies* 26/1:1–216.

*Utilisation des écritures hindoues, bouddhiques et islamiques dans le culte chrétien*. 1976. *Concilium* 112/2.

Vallet, O. 1996. *Jésus et le Bouddha*. Paris: Albin Michel.

Vanhoye, A. 1984. "Nuovo Testamento e inculturazione." *Civiltà Cattolica* 135/4:119–36.

———. 1994. "Salut universel par le Christ et validité de l'Alliance ancienne." *Nouvelle revue théologique* 116:815–35.

Veliath, D. 1988. *Theological Approaches and Understanding of Religions: Jean Daniélou et Raimundo Panikkar: A Study in Contrast*. Bangalore: Kristu Jyoti College.

Vempeny, I. 1973. *Inspiration in Non-biblical Scriptures*. Bangalore: Theological Publications in India.

———. 1988. *Krsna and Christ*. Anand: Gujarat Sahitya Prakash.

Verastegui, R. E. 1970. "Christianisme et religions non chrétiennes: Analyse de la 'tendance Daniélou.'" *Euntes Docete* 23:227–79.

Vroom, H. 1996. *No Other Gods: Christian Belief in Dialogue with Buddhism, Hinduism, and Islam.* Grand Rapids, Mich.: Eerdmans.

Waldenfels, Hans. 1980. *Absolute Nothingness: Foundations for a Buddhist-Christian Dialogue.* New York: Paulist Press.

————. 1985a. "Ist der christliche Glaube der einzig wahre? Christentum und nichtchristlichen Religionen." *Stimmen der Zeit* 112:463–75.

————. 1985b. *Kontextuelle Fundementaltheologie.* Paterborn: F. Schöning.

————. 1990. *Begegnung der Religionen.* Bonn: Borengässer.

————. 1994. *Phänomen Christentum: Eine Weltreligion in der Welt der Religionen.* Freiburg: Herder.

Ward, K. 1994. *Religion and Revelation.* Oxford: Clarendon Press.

Watt, William Montgomery. 1969. *Islamic Revelation in the Modern World.* Edinburgh: Edinburgh University Press.

————. 1983. *Islam and Christianity Today.* London: Routledge and Kegan Paul.

*Ways of Salvation.* 1981. *Studia Missionalia* 30.

Weinandy, T. 1995. "The Case for Spirit Christology: Some Reflections." *The Thomist* 59/2:173–88.

Westermann, C. 1982. *Dieu dans l'Ancient Testament.* Paris: Cerf.

Whaling, Frank. 1986. *Christian Theology and World Religions: A Global Approach.* London: Marshall Pickering.

————, ed. 1984. *The World's Religious Traditions: Current Perspectives in Religious Studies.* Edinburgh: T. and T. Clark.

Whitson, R. H. 1971. *The Coming Convergence of World Religions.* Westminster, Md.: Newman Press.

Wiles, Maurice. 1992. *Christian Theology and Interreligious Dialogue.* London: SCM Press.

Wilfred, Felix. 1984. "A Matter of Theological Education: Some Critical Reflections on the Suitability of 'Salvation History' as a Theological Model for India." *Vidyajyoti* 48:538–56.

————. 1991. *Sunset in the East: Asian Challenges and Christian Involvement.* Madras: University of Madras.

————. 1993. *Beyond Settled Foundations: The Journey of Indian Theology.* Madras: University of Madras.

————. 1994. "Some Tentative Reflections on the Language of Christian Uniqueness: An Indian Perspective." *Pro Dialogo Bulletin* 85–86/1:40–57.

————, ed. 1992. *Leave the Temple: Indian Paths to Human Liberation.* Maryknoll, N.Y.: Orbis Books.

Willet, M. E. 1992. *Wisdom Christology in the Fourth Gospel.* San Francisco: Edwin Mellen Press.

Williams, R. 1986. "Balthasar and Rahner." In *The Analogy of Beauty: The Theology of Hans Urs von Balthasar,* ed. J. Riches, 11–34. Edinburgh: T. and T. Clark.

————. 1990. "Trinity and Pluralism." In *Christian Uniqueness Reconsidered: The Myth of a Pluralistic Theology of Religions,* ed. G. D'Costa, 3–15. Maryknoll, N.Y.: Orbis Books.

Williams, T. S. M. 1995. Review of *Towards a Trinitarian Theology of Religions,* by Pan-Chiu Lai. *Theological Studies* 46:421–23.

Willis, W., ed. 1987. *The Kingdom of God in Twentieth Century Interpretation.* Peabody, Mass.: Hendrickson.

Wilson, A., ed. 1991. *World Scripture: A Comparative Anthology of Sacred Texts.* New York: Paragon House.

Wong, J. H. 1994. "Anonymous Christianity: Karl Rahner's Pneumato-Christocentrism and the East-West Dialogue." *Theological Studies* 55/4: 609–37.

"World Religions and the Economy of Salvation." 1981. *Indian Journal of Theology* 30/3–4:115–217.

*Worship and Ritual in Christianity and Other Religions.* 1974. *Studia Missionalia* 23.

Wright, G. E. 1960. *God Who Acts.* London: SCM Press.

Wright, J. H. 1992. "Roger Haight's Spirit Christology." *Theological Studies* 53:729–35.

Wright, N. T. 1992. *The New Testament and the People of God.* London: SPCK.

Zaehner, R. C. 1957. *Mysticism Sacred and Profane.* Oxford: Clarendon Press.

———. 1958. *At Sundry Times: An Essay in the Comparison of Religions.* London: Faber and Faber.

———. 1964. *The Catholic Church and World Religions.* London: Burns and Oates.

———. 1965. *Inde, Israel, Islam: Religions mystiques et révélations prophétiques.* Bruges: Desclée de Brouwer.

———. 1966. *Hindu Scriptures.* London: Dent.

———. 1970. *Concordant Discord.* Oxford: Clarendon Press.

Zago, Marcello. 1985. *Buddhismo e Cristianesimo in dialogo.* Rome: Città Nuova.

———. 1986. *Il dialogo inter-religioso a 20 anni dal Concilio.* Rome: Piemme.

Zapelena, T. 1955. *De Ecclesia Christi.* Pars apologetica, edition 6a. Rome: Pontificia Università Gregoriana.

Zizioulas, J. D. 1985. *Being as Communion: Studies in Personhood and the Church.* London: Darton, Longman and Todd.

## Supplementary Bibliography

Amell, K. *Contemplation et dialogue: Quelques exemples de dialogue entre spiritualités après le concile Vatican II.* Uppsala: The Swedish Institute of Missionary Research.

Arinze, F. 1997. *Meeting Other Believers.* Leominster: Fowler Wright.

Arregui, J. 1997. *Urs von Balthasar: dos propuestas de diálogo con las religiones.* Vitoria, Spain: Editorial ESET.

Bezançon, N. 1995. *Au carrfour des religions.* Paris: Beauchesne.

Boespflug, F., and Y. Labbé. 1996. *Assise, 10 ans après, 1986–1996.* Paris: Cerf.

Cantone, C., ed. 1992. *La svolta planetaria di Dio.* Rome: Borla.

Chenique, F. 1996. *Sagesse chrétienne et mystique orientale.* Paris: Ed. Dervy.

*Le Chiese cristiane e le altre religioni: Quale Dialogo?* 1998. Milan: Ancora.

Clooney, F. X. 1998. *Hindu Wisdom for all God's Children.* Maryknoll, N.Y.: Orbis Books.

Coda, P., ed. 1997. *L'unico e I molti: la salvezza in Gesù Cristo e la sfida del pluralismo.* Rome: Mursia.

Coward, H., ed. 1987. *Modern Indian Responses to Religious Pluralism.* Albany: State University of New York Press.

Cowdell, S. 1996. *Is Jesus Unique? A Study of Recent Christology.* Mahwah, N.J.: Paulist Press

Dalai Lama (His Holiness the). 1996. *The Good Heart.* London: Rider.

*Il Dialogo non finisce: Pietro Rossano e le relgioni non cristiane.* 1994. Brescia: Morcelliana.

Dhavamony, M. *Christian Theology of Religions.* Bern: Peter Lang.

*Dio l'unico: sulla nascita del monoteismo in Israele.* 1991. Brescia: Morcelliana.

Doré, J., ed. 1997. *Le Christianisme vis-à-vis des religions.* Namur: Artel.

Fabris, A., and M. Gronchi, eds. 1998. *Il Pluralismo religioso.* Cinisello Balsamo: San Paolo.

Fernandez, F. 1996. *In Ways Known to God: A Theological Investigation on the Ways of Salvation Spoken of in Vatican II.* Shillong, India: Vendrame Institute Publications.

Frenkemölle, H., ed. 1998. *Der ungekündigte Bund? Antworten des Neuen Testaments.* Freiburg: Herder.

Gillis, C. 1993. *Pluralism: A New Paradigm for Theology.* Louvain: Peeters.

Gnuse, R. K. 1997. *No Other Gods: Emergent Monotheism in Israel.* Sheffield: Sheffield Academic Press.

Imbach, J. 1992. *Three Faces of Jesus: How Jews, Christians, and Muslims See Him.* Springfield, Ill.: Templegate Publishers.

Ives, C., ed. 1995. *Divine Emptiness and Historical Fullness: A Buddhist-Jewish-Christian Conversation with Masao Abe.* Valley Forge, Pa.: Trinity Press International.

Lindbeck, G. 1984. *The Nature of Doctrine: Religion and Theology in a Postliberal Age.* Philadelphia: Westminster.

Lorizio, G., ed. 1998. *Religione e religioni: Metodologia e prospettive ermeneutiche.* Padova: Messaggero.

Merrigan, T. 1997. *Jews and Christians: Rivals or Partners for the Kingdom of God.* Louvain: Peeters.

Nicholls, B. J., ed. 1994. *The Unique Christ in our Pluralistic World.* Grand Rapids: Baker.

Odasso, G. 1998. *Bibbia e religione: Prospettive bibliche per la teologia delle religioni.* Rome: Urbaniana University Press.

Ogden, S. 1996. *Doing Theology Today.* Valley Forge, Pa.: Trinity Press International.

Raguin, Y. n.d. *Un message du salut pour tous.* Paris: Vie chrétienne.

Ratzinger, J. 1998. *Die Vielfalt der Religionen und der Eine Bund.* Hagen, Germany: Verlag Urfeld.

Rinaldi, G. 1998. *La bibbia dei pagani.* Vol. 1: *Quadro storico.* Vol. 2: *Testi e documenti.* Bologna: Dehoniane.

Rossi de Gasperis, F. 1997. *Comminciando da Gerusalemme: La sorgente della fede e dell'esistenza cristiana.* Rome: Piemme.

Russo, A. 1991. *Religioni e cristianesimo.* Naples: D'Auria.

Sanders, J. 1992. *No Other Name.* Grand Rapids: Eerdmans.

Senécal, B. 1998. *Jésus-Christ à l'incontre de Gautama le Bouddha.* Paris: Cerf.

Shink, C. E. 1997. *Who Do You Say That I Am? Christians Encounter Other Religions.* Scottdale, Pa.: Herald Press.

Smart, N., and S. Konstantine. 1991. *Christian Systematic Theology in a World Context.* Minneapolis: Fortress.

Stetson, B. 1994. *Pluralism and Particularity in Religious Belief.* Westport, Conn.: Praeger.

Thuruthiyil, S., ed. 1997. *La fede in un'epoca di pluralismo.* Rome: LAS.

Ucko, H. *People of God, Peoples of God: A Jewish-Christian Conversation in Asia.* Geneva: WCC.

Vanhoozer, K., ed. 1997. *The Trinity in a Pluralistic Age: Theological Essays on Culture and Religions.* Grand Rapids: Eerdmans.

Vidal, J. 1990. *L'église et les religions ou le désir réorienté.* Paris: Albin Michel.

# Index of Biblical Citations

## OLD TESTAMENT

# NEW TESTAMENT

# Index of Names

# Appendix 1

## Congregation for
## the Doctrine of the Faith

### NOTIFICATION

### on the Book

### *Toward a Christian Theology*
### *of Religious Pluralism*

### by Father Jacques Dupuis, S.J.

### Preface

After a preliminary study of the book *Toward a Christian Theology of Religious Pluralism* by Father Jacques Dupuis, S.J., the Congregation for the Doctrine of the Faith decided to proceed to a comprehensive examination of the text by means of its ordinary procedure, in accordance with Chapter 3 of the *Regulations for Doctrinal Examination.*\*

It must be emphasized that this text is an introductory reflection on a Christian theology of religious pluralism. It is not simply a theology of religions, but a theology of religious pluralism, which seeks to investigate, in the light of Christian faith, the significance of the plurality of religious traditions in God's plan for humanity. Aware of the potential problems in this approach, the author does not conceal the possibility that his hypothesis may raise as many questions as it seeks to answer.

Following the doctrinal examination of the book and the outcome of the dialogue with the author, the Bishop and Cardinal Members of the Congregation, in the Ordinary Session of June 30, 1999, evaluated the analysis and opinions of the Congregation's Consultors regarding the author's *Responses*. The Members of the Congregation recognized the author's attempt to remain within the limits of orthodoxy in his study of questions hitherto largely unexplored. At the same time, while noting the author's willingness to provide the necessary

---

\**Publisher's Note:* This document was issued by the Congregation for the Doctrine of the Faith on 24 January 2001. See http://www.vatican.va/roman_curia/congregations/cfaith/documents/rc_con _cfaith_doc_19970629_ratio-agendi_en.html. For the text of the *Notification,* see http://www.vatican.va/ roman_curia/congregations/cfaith/documents/rc_con_cfaith_doc_20010312_dupuis-2_en.html.

clarifications, as evident in his *Responses,* as well as his desire to remain faithful to the doctrine of the Church and the teaching of the Magisterium, they found that his book contained notable ambiguities and difficulties on important doctrinal points, which could lead a reader to erroneous or harmful opinions. These points concerned the interpretation of the sole and universal salvific mediation of Christ, the unicity and completeness of Christ's revelation, the universal salvific action of the Holy Spirit, the orientation of all people to the Church, and the value and significance of the salvific function of other religions.

At the conclusion of the ordinary procedure of examination, the Congregation for the Doctrine of the Faith decided to draft a *Notification,*[1] intended to safeguard the doctrine of the Catholic faith from errors, ambiguities, or harmful interpretations. This *Notification,* approved by the Holy Father in the Audience of November 24, 2000, was presented to Father Jacques Dupuis and was accepted by him. By signing the text, the author committed himself to assent to the stated theses and, in his future theological activity and publications, to hold the doctrinal contents indicated in the *Notification,* the text of which must be included in any reprinting or further editions of his book, as well as in all translations.*

The present *Notification* is not meant as a judgment on the author's subjective thought, but rather as a statement of the Church's teaching on certain aspects of the above-mentioned doctrinal truths, and as a refutation of erroneous or harmful opinions, which, prescinding from the author's intentions, could be derived from reading the ambiguous statements and insufficient explanations found in certain sections of the text. In this way, Catholic readers will be given solid criteria for judgment, consistent with the doctrine of the Church, in order to avoid the serious confusion and misunderstanding which could result from reading this book.

# I. On the Sole and Universal Salvific Mediation of Jesus Christ

1. It must be firmly believed that Jesus Christ, the Son of God made man, crucified and risen, is the sole and universal mediator of salvation for all humanity.[2]

2. It must also be firmly believed that Jesus of Nazareth, Son of Mary and only Saviour of the world, is the Son and Word of the Father.[3] For the unity of the divine plan of salvation centered in Jesus Christ, it must also be held that the salvific action of the Word is accomplished in and through Jesus Christ, the Incarnate Son of the Father, as mediator of salvation for all humanity.[4] It is therefore contrary to the Catholic faith not only to posit a separation between

---

*Publisher's Note:* The requirement to insert the *Notification* was not found in the draft of the *Notification* signed by the author in December 2000. It was added after the author signed it.

the Word and Jesus, or between the Word's salvific activity and that of Jesus, but also to maintain that there is a salvific activity of the Word as such in his divinity, independent of the humanity of the Incarnate Word.[5]

## II. On the Unicity and Completeness of Revelation of Jesus Christ

3. It must be firmly believed that Jesus Christ is the mediator, the fulfilment, and the completeness of revelation.[6] It is therefore contrary to the Catholic faith to maintain that revelation in Jesus Christ (or the revelation of Jesus Christ) is limited, incomplete or imperfect. Moreover, although full knowledge of divine revelation will be had only on the day of the Lord's coming in glory, the historical revelation of Jesus Christ offers everything necessary for man's salvation and has no need of completion by other religions.[7]

4. It is consistent with Catholic doctrine to hold that the seeds of truth and goodness that exist in other religions are a certain participation in truths contained in the revelation of or in Jesus Christ.[8] However, it is erroneous to hold that such elements of truth and goodness, or some of them, do not derive ultimately from the source-mediation of Jesus Christ.[9]

## III. On the Universal Salvific Action of the Holy Spirit

5. The Church's faith teaches that the Holy Spirit, working after the resurrection of Jesus Christ, is always the Spirit of Christ sent by the Father, who works in a salvific way in Christians as well as non-Christians.[10] It is therefore contrary to the Catholic faith to hold that the salvific action of the Holy Spirit extends beyond the one universal salvific economy of the Incarnate Word.[11]

## IV. On the Orientation of All Human Beings to the Church

6. It must be firmly believed that the Church is sign and instrument of salvation for all people.[12] It is contrary to the Catholic faith to consider the different religions of the world as ways of salvation complementary to the Church.[13]

7. According to Catholic doctrine, the followers of other religions are oriented to the Church and are all called to become part of her.[14]

## V. On the Value and Salvific Function of the Religious Traditions

8. In accordance with Catholic doctrine, it must be held that "whatever the Spirit brings about in human hearts and in the history of peoples, in cultures

and religions, serves as preparation for the Gospel" (Cf. Dogmatic Constitution *Lumen gentium*, 16).[15] It is therefore legitimate to maintain that the Holy Spirit accomplishes salvation in non-Christians also through those elements of truth and goodness present in the various religions; however, to hold that these religions, considered as such, are ways of salvation, has no foundation in Catholic theology, also because they contain omissions, insufficiencies, and errors[16] regarding fundamental truths about God, man, and the world.

Furthermore, the fact that the elements of truth and goodness present in the various world religions may prepare peoples and cultures to receive the salvific event of Jesus Christ does not imply that the sacred texts of these religions can be considered as complementary to the Old Testament, which is the immediate preparation for the Christ event.[17]

*The Sovereign Pontiff John Paul II, at the Audience of January 19, 2001, in the light of the further developments, confirmed the present Notification, which had been adopted in Ordinary Session of the Congregation, and ordered its publication.*

Rome, from the offices of the Congregation for the Doctrine of the Faith, January 24, 2001, the Memorial of St. Francis de Sales.

+ Joseph Cardinal RATZINGER
*Prefect*

+ Tarcisio BERTONE, S.D.B.
*Archbishop Emeritus of Vercelli*
*Secretary*

Congregation for the Doctrine of the Faith
Piazza del S. Uffizio, 11
00193 Rome, Italy

## References

1. Because of tendencies in some circles, which have become increasingly evident in the thinking of the Christian faithful, the Congregation for the Doctrine of the Faith [hereafter abbreviated "CDF" published the Declaration *"Dominus Iesus" on the Unicity and Salvific Universality of Jesus Christ and the Church, AAS* 92 (2000): 742–65, in order to protect essential truths of the Catholic faith. The *Notification* draws from the principles expressed in *Dominus Iesus* in its evaluation of Father Dupuis' book.

2. Cf. Council of Trent, Decree *De peccato originali*, DS [the standard abbreviation for Henricus Denzinger and Adolfus Schönmetzer, S.J., eds., *Enchiridion Symbolorum: Definitionum et Declarationum de Rebus Fidei et Morum*, 36th ed. (Fribourg: Herder, 1965) and subsequently] 1513; Decree *De iustificatione*, DS 1522–23, 1529–30; Second Vatican Council, Pastoral Constitution *Gaudium et spes*, 10; Dogmatic Constitution *Lumen gentium*, 8, 14, 28, 49, 60; John Paul II, Encyclical Letter *Redemptoris missio*, 5, *AAS* 83 (1991): 234–340; Apostolic Exhortation *Ecclesia in Asia*, 14, *AAS* 92 (2000): 449–528; CDF, *Dominus Iesus*, 13–15.

3. Cf. First Council of Nicaea, DS 125; Council of Chalcedon, DS 301.

4. Cf. Council of Trent, Decree *De iustificatione,* DS 1529–30; Second Vatican Council, Constitution on the Liturgy *Sacrosanctum concilium,* 5; *Gaudium et spes,* 22.

5. Cf. *Redemptoris missio,* 6; CDF, *Dominus Iesus,* 10.

6. Cf. Second Vatican Council, Dogmatic Constitution *Dei Verbum,* 2, 4; John Paul II, Encyclical Letter *Fides et ratio,* 14–15, 92, *AAS* 91 (1999): 5–88; CDF, *Dominus Iesus,* 5.

7. Cf. CDF, *Dominus Iesus,* 6; *Catechism of the Catholic Church,* 65–66.

8. Cf. *Lumen gentium,* 17; Second Vatican Council, Decree on Mission *Ad gentes,* 11; Second Vatican Council, Declaration on Relations with Non-Christian Religions *Nostra aetate,* 2.

9. Cf. *Lumen gentium,* 16; *Redemptoris missio,* 10.

10. Cf. *Gaudium et spes,* 22; *Redemptoris missio,* 28–29.

11. Cf. *Redemptoris missio,* 5; Apostolic Exhortation *Ecclesia in Asia,* 15–16; CDF, *Dominus Iesus,* 12.

12. Cf. *Lumen gentium,* 9, 14, 17, 48; *Redemptoris missio,* 11; CDF, *Dominus Iesus,* 16.

13. Cf. *Redemptoris missio,* 36; CDF, *Dominus Iesus,* 21–22.

14. Cf. *Lumen gentium,* 13, 16; *Ad gentes,* 7; Second Vatican Council, Declaration on Religious Liberty *Dignitatis humanae,* 1; *Redemptoris missio,* 10; CDF, *Dominus Iesus,* 20–22; *Catechism of the Catholic Church,* 845.

15. Cf. *Redemptoris missio,* 29.

16. Cf. *Lumen gentium,* 16; *Nostra aetate,* 2; *Ad gentes,* 9; Pope Paul VI, Apostolic Exhortation *Evangelii Nuntiandi,* 53, *AAS* 68 (1976): 5–76; *Redemptoris missio,* 55; CDF, *Dominus Iesus,* 8.

17. Cf. Council of Trent, Decree *De libris sacris et de traditionibus recipiendis,* DS 1501; First Vatican Council, Dogmatic Constitution *Dei Filius* 2, DS 3006; CDF, *Dominus Iesus,* 8.

# Appendix 2

### Statement of
### Peter-Hans Kolvenbach, S.J.,
### Superior General
### of the Society of Jesus

With the *Notification* just published by the Congregation for the Doctrine of the Faith, a long and important inquiry has ended. The book of Father Jacques Dupuis, professor emeritus at the Pontifical Gregorian University, which has been justly recognized for the seriousness of its methodological research, the richness of the scientific documentation, and the originality of its exploration, dares to venture into a dogmatically fundamental area for the future of interreligious dialogue. The *Notification* itself recognizes the intent and efforts of Father Jacques Dupuis to remain within the teaching of the Catholic Faith as enunciated by the Magisterium. In line with the orientations of the document *Dominus Iesus,* the *Notification* clearly establishes the limits of this teaching to which the author has tried to adhere even if he has not always succeeded. Thus the *Notification* helps the reader to interpret the book according to the doctrine of the Church. On this solidly established dogmatic basis we hope that Father Jacques Dupuis can continue his pioneer research in the field of interreligious dialogue which in his recent Apostolic Letter *Novo Millennio Ineunte,* John Paul II encourages as a challenge for the evangelization in the third millennium.

26 February 2001
Curia Generalizia della Compagnia di Gesú
Borgo Santo Spirito, 4
C. P. 6139
00195 Roma-Prati

# Appendix 3

### Foreword to the Indian Edition of
### *Toward a Christian Theology of Religious Pluralism*
### by the Most Reverend Henry D'Souza
### Archbishop of Calcutta

I am pleased to write a few lines as a foreword to the Indian edition of the book of Father Jacques Dupuis, *Toward a Christian Theology of Religious Pluralism.** I am particularly happy to do so after the notification of the Congregation for the Doctrine of Faith has cleared the book from the original concern that it contained "serious errors against essential elements of Divine and Catholic Faith." The final notification of 26 January 2001 states that "the members of the Congregation recognized the author's attempt to remain within the limits of orthodoxy in his study of questions hitherto unexplored."

At the same time the Congregation remains concerned about "notable ambiguities and difficulties on important doctrinal points which could lead a reader to erroneous or harmful opinions."

Interreligious dialogue is a new field of theological research. Given the reality that peoples of all faiths are to be found in most countries, even traditionally Christian ones, the topic assumes great importance for the church today. For us in India and in Asia the living religions are a reality which we have to address in our daily task of evangelization.

It is my belief that Father Dupuis has contributed very abundantly to further research, reflection, and understanding in the field of interreligious dialogue. His book is a pioneering effort in the new and complex issues of religious pluralism.

It is to be noted that *Dominus Iesus,* in number 14, states:

> Theology today in its reflection on the existence of other religious experiences and on their meaning in God's salvific plan, is invited to explore if and in what way the historical figures and positive elements of these religions may fall within the divine plan of salvation.

Father Dupuis has been striving to do just that.

---

*The Indian edition of *Toward a Christian Theology of Religious Pluralism* is published by Gujarat Sahitya Prakash, P B. 70, Annand (Gujarat) 3888 001, E-mail *gsp@satyan.net.in,* and is licensed for sale in Africa and Asia.

Part 1 of his book is an overview of Christian approaches to religions. This part is replete with material on how there has been a development in Christian thinking across the centuries.

Part 2 is entitled "One God — One Christ — Convergent Paths." In seven chapters Father Dupuis grapples with the various realities and possible understanding of the mystery. He has indeed courageously explored this new field of interreligious dialogue. In *Ecclesia in Asia*, the Holy Father has asked bishops to encourage theologians in this research. We are grateful to the Congregation for the Doctrine of the Faith for the guidelines within which we have to understand God's working in humankind's history.

I am sure that the Indian edition of the book *Toward a Christian Theology of Religious Pluralism* will help to prosper further research in the field of interreligious dialogue. It will also contribute toward a deeper appreciation of the singular privilege which we have received in coming to know and acknowledge Jesus Christ the one Lord and Saviour of all.

1 May 2001
Archbishop's House
32 Park Street
Calcutta 700 016 — India